EXCELLENCE IN ELECTRICAL
ADDISON-WESLEY ▲ THE SIGN
AND COMPUTER ENGINEERING
EXCELLENCE IN ELECTRICAL
ADDISON-WESLEY ▲ THE SIGN
AND COMPUTER ENGINEERING
EXCELLENCE IN ELECTRICAL
ADDISON-WESLEY ▲ THE SIGN
AND COMPUTER ENGINEERING
EXCELLENCE IN ELECTRICAL
ADDISON-WESLEY ▲ THE SIGN
AND COMPUTER ENGINEERING
EXCELLENCE IN ELECTRICAL
ADDISON-WESLEY ▲ THE SIGN
AND COMPUTER ENGINEERING
EXCELLENCE IN ELECTRICAL
ADDISON-WESLEY ▲ THE SIGN
AND COMPUTER ENGINEERING
EXCELLENCE IN ELECTRICAL
ADDISON-WESLEY ▲ THE SIGN
AND COMPUTER ENGINEERING
EXCELLENCE IN ELECTRICAL
ADDISON-WESLEY ▲ THE SIGN
AND COMPUTER ENGINEERING
EXCELLENCE IN ELECTRICAL
ADDISON-WESLEY ▲ THE SIGN
AND COMPUTER ENGINEERING

Second Edition

High-Performance
Computer Architecture

Second Edition

High-Performance Computer Architecture

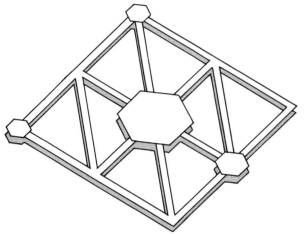

Harold S. Stone

IBM T.J. Watson Research Center
and
Courant Institute
New York University

◆▼ Addison-Wesley Publishing Company

Reading, Massachusetts
Menlo Park, California • New York
Don Mills, Ontario • Wokingham, England
Amsterdam • Bonn • Sydney • Singapore
Tokyo • Madrid • San Juan

This book is in the **Addison-Wesley Series in Electrical and Computer Engineering**

Sponsoring Editor • *Tom Robbins*
Production Supervisor • *Karen Myer*
Copy Editor • *Pat Steele*
Text Designer • *Herb Caswell*
Illustrator • *Hardlines* and *Textbook Art Associates, Inc.*
Technical Art Consultant • *Joseph Vetere*
Manufacturing Supervisor • *Hugh Crawford*
Cover Designer • *Gary Fujiwara*

Library of Congress Cataloging-in-Publication Data

Stone, Harold S., 1938–
    High-performance computer architecture / Harold S. Stone.—2nd
ed.
        p.   cm.
    Includes bibliographical references (p.   )
    ISBN 0-201-51377-3
    1. Computer architecture.   I. Title.
QA76.9.A73S76   1990   89-18262
004.2'2—dc20   CIP

BCDEFGHIJ-DO-93210

To Jan—colleague and companion

A precis from the pages of history

Chapter 1
Architecture is preeminently the art of significant forms in space—that is, forms signficant of their functions.
   — Claude Bragdon, 1931

Chapter 2
I know of no way of judging the future but by the past.
   — Patrick Henry, 1775

Chapter 3
Comparisons do ofttime great grievance.
   — John Lydgate, c. 1440

Chapter 4
The fickle multitude, which veers with every wind!
   — J. C. F. Schiller, 1800

Chapter 5
The tucked-up sempstress walks with hasty strides,
While streams run down her oil'd umbrella's sides.
   — Jonathan Swift, 1711

Chapter 6
Sat cit si sat bene. [It is done quickly enough if it is done well.]
   — Latin proverb

Chapter 7
Who depends upon another man's table often dines late.
   — John Ray, 1678

Preface

Teaching computer architecture is an interesting challenge for the instructor because the field is in constant flux. What the architect does depends strongly on the devices available, and the devices have been changing every two to three years, with major breakthroughs once or twice a decade. Within the brief life of the first edition of this textbook, a whole generation of processor and memory chips were first offered for sale, appeared in popular computers, and then gradually disappeared from the marketplace as their successors took their places. The particular features and strengths of those devices have given way to other features in various new combinations and new relative costs. Design practices are evolving to exploit the new devices for a new generation of machines. And they will evolve again as the next wave of devices appears in the coming years.

What then should be taught to prepare students for what lies ahead? What information will remain important over the technical career of a student, and what information will soon become obsolete, of historical interest only? This text stresses design ideas embodied in many machines and the techniques for evaluating those ideas. The ideas and the evaluation techniques are the principles that will survive. The specific implementations of machines that one might choose in 1990, 1995, or 2000 reflect the basic principles described here as applied to the device technology currently prevailing. Effective designs are those that use technology cleverly and achieve balanced, efficient structures matched well to the class of problems they attack. This text stresses the means to achieve balance and efficiency in the context of any device technology.

We use a multifaceted approach to teaching the reader how to prepare for the future. The major features are the following:

1. Each topic is a general architectural approach—memory designs, pipeline techniques, and a variety of parallel structures.

2. Within each topic the focus is on fundamental bottlenecks—memory bandwidth, processing bandwidth, communications, and synchronization—and how to overcome these bottlenecks for each topic area.

3. The material addresses evaluation techniques to help the reader isolate aspects that are highly efficient from those that are not.

4. A few machines whose structure is of historical interest are described to illustrate how the concepts can be implemented.

5. Where appropriate, the text draws on examples of real applications and their architectural requirements.

6. Exercises at the end of chapters give the reader an opportunity to sketch out designs and perform evaluation under a variety of technology-oriented constraints.

The exercises are particularly important. They help the reader master the material by integrating a number of different ideas, often by working through a paper design that must satisfy some unusual set of constraints. In several exercises, the student is asked to produce a series of designs, each reflecting a different set of underlying devices. This helps the student gain experience in adapting basic techniques to new situations.

The text is intended for the advanced undergraduate and first-year graduate students. It assumes the student has had a course in machine organization so that the basic operation of a processor is well understood. Some experience with assembly language is helpful, but not essential. Programming in a high-level language such as Pascal, however, is necessary to understand the applications used as examples. Mathematical background in probability is helpful for Chapter 2, linear systems or numerical methods for Chapters 4 and 5, and some exposure to operating systems will assist understanding of Chapter 7. In no case is the material absolutely required because the text contains sufficient discussion and references to source material to support the presentation.

The text purposely avoids detailed descriptions of popular machines because in time the machines so described will inevitably be obsolete. In future years, a reader of such material may be led to think that the specific details of a successful machine represent good design decisions for the future as well as for the period in which the design was actually done. A better approach is for the individual instructor to discuss one or two current machines while using the text, with the notion that current machines can change each year at the discretion of the instructor. It is also possible to use the text without such supplementary material because the design exercises provide challenges that represent technology through the 90s.

We jokingly tell students that the subject matter enjoys a positive benefit from the rapid change in technology. The instructor need not create new exercises and examinations for each new class. The questions may be the same each year, but the answers will be different.

A number of teaching aids are available with this edition. The exercises in Chapter 2 make use of traces of instruction execution for which a floppy disk with sample traces is available from the publisher for course adopters. The disk is in IBM-compatible format and can be accessed by programs written in a variety of programming languages.

Prior to the publication of this text, thorough studies of cache behavior required main-frame computers for analysis due to the massive amounts of data to process. The techniques described in Chapter 2 show how to reduce the processing by as much as two orders of magnitude and make possible the use of a personal computer as the primary analysis tool. The analysis techniques were first made widely available in the first edition of this text, and have now become standard among computer architects. The exercises for Chapter 2 give the student ample opportunity to practice cache analysis on the sample traces and to practice evaluating design alternatives.

An instructor's guide with solutions to selected exercises is also available from the publisher to course adopters. Among the solutions in the manual are sample solutions to some of the design exercises. The instructor should bear in mind that the design exercises can be satisfied by many different designs, and that the sample solutions are illustrative of good approaches, but are definitely not the only acceptable solutions. What is important is the reasoning used by the student to establish that a particular design meets the constraints imposed and is both efficient and effective in solving the given design problem.

Three sets of video-taped lectures provide instructional aid in a different form. A set of eight lectures that cover the highlights of the entire text can be ordered by writing to Addison-Wesley, Reading, MA 01867, Attn: Tom Robbins. A set of three lectures on the topics of multiprocessor cache coherence and synchronization is available from the IEEE Computer Society Press, 10662 Los Vaqueros Circle, Los Alamitos, CA 90720. Another set of three lectures on advanced topics in cache behavior and cache analysis is available from the National Technological University, 700 Centre Ave., Ft. Collins, CO 80526, Attn: Richard Soderberg. The videotapes focus on central issues, and describe these topics visually and orally in a way that cannot be done in writing. Students and instructors will find the video tapes very useful for intensive study in short courses or self-paced instruction. The video medium is an effective means for fast transfer of information, and it is a useful supplement to a slower paced program of classroom lecture and intensive reading that encourages deeper understanding.

Instructors familiar with the first edition will find new material on program behavior models, RISC architecture, and parallel synchronization. The material on program behavior has been introduced because machines have changed so quickly in recent years that designers are forced to produce new generations of processors without the benefit of traces of workloads for those processors. In such cases, the evaluation techniques described in Chapter 2 cannot be brought into play. The next best tool is to produce estimates of program behavior that can be used as input to design evaluations. We have incorporated some interesting new developments in program modeling that appeared after the publication of the first edition.

Similarly, RISC architecture and parallel synchronization have been developing very quickly in recent years and demanded additional space in the new edition. Beyond these topics, small incremental changes in the remaining topics have helped bring them up to date and streamlined their presentation.

The material in the text is structured in a modular fashion, with each chapter reasonably independent of every other chapter. The instructor can put together a course by selecting individual chapters and individual sections according to the background of the students, the prerequisites available, and the successor courses in the curriculum.

Chapters 2 and 3 form the core material. Cache memories and pipeline structures are widely used today, and they are likely to be effective in the technologies that will emerge in the next several years. These chapters should be taught in all course offerings.

For courses in which students have a good background in numerical methods, Chapters 4 and 5 show how parallel computer architectures are matched to problem domains. Students unfamiliar with the underlying mathematical applications will gain an understanding of computational methods in wide use from these chapters, and all readers will appreciate how data flow and synchronization of mathematical actions in an algorithm are directly supported by architectural features. The chapters are biased toward supercomputers and large-scale computations, but the material is useful as well for general purpose computers.

Chapters 6 and 7 treat multiprocessors, which are more general purpose than the machines of Chapters 4 and 5. Multiprocessors were almost exclusively research vehicles in the 1970s, and were in commercial use in niche areas in the 1980s. The 1990s will find a much broader use of multiprocessors as the speed of individual processors reaches the limit of metal interconnections. The highest sustainable clock rate for metal interconnections is roughly 200 to 250 MHz for a typical conductor geometry, although the clock rate can be boosted even higher at great expense by reducing the dimensions of all components and conductors. Computers in all classes from microprocessors to high-end machines started the 1990s within one to two generations of this clock limit. To sustain increases in performance through the decade, the industry must embrace multiprocessing in virtually all computers, or must abandon metal interconnection technology for another technology such as optical fiber or optical waveguide technology.

In this text, we explore the use of multiprocessors and leave the topic of optical interconnections for another time and another text. The multiprocessor discussion is oriented to where to seek performance improvement by using resources efficiently. The interplay of multiple disciplines is central to this discussion. Each specialist on a design team should have a broad shallow knowledge of the full scope of a design, including hardware, software, architecture, and applications, while enjoying a much deeper knowledge of a specialty area. Chapters 6 and 7 give a broad view of multiprocessors and delve deeply into particular topics such as algorithm design and performance models that are relevant to all specialties. These chapters are recommended especially for curricula that emphasize systems programming and computer engineering.

In one semester, it is reasonable to complete selected sections of all chapters, or to cover Chapters 2 and 3 and two other chapters in depth. Chapter 1, which has no exercises, is to be used as background reading to set the tone of the exposition. The text can easily satisfy the needs of a two-quarter or two-semester sequence if the instructor chooses to use the full material.

No matter which portion of the text is covered, working the exercises is critical for a thorough appreciation of the material. The design-oriented exercises can be rather frustrating at first because there is no clear indication of a correct answer. The reader wants to see exercises that can be answered quickly by jotting down a simple answer after a small amount of thought. What a pleasure to crank through a calculation and find the answer is 17.5. The design exercises are nothing like this. In a sense an answer is correct if it meets the constraints of the design. The reality is that the answer should be more than correct—it must be competitive.

The point of working such exercises is not the final design, but rather the process of arriving at the final design. What alternatives were considered? How does the final design overcome basic problems? Did the student consider a reasonable set of alternatives or was there a valid approach missed that should have been considered? Is the evaluation of the design reasonable? For what assumptions concerning technology factors and workload characteristics is the given design an efficient one?

After working through such problems the reader becomes familiar with the thought processes of the designer and gains both experience and insight into architectural design. Many exercises seem to capture real situations, and this is as intended. As in real situations, the reader may discover that there is no good solution, and a compromise has to be invented. Or there may be several reasonable solutions, and the reader has to pick one, possibly on the basis of characteristics that are secondary in importance because all solutions available have satisfactory primary characteristics. Many exercises have been drawn from design problems faced by the author, with constraints updated for the present and future.

The preparation of this text represents the fruits of labor of many parties. The author's students, Tom Puzak, Zarka Cvetanovic, Dominique Thiebaut, and John Turek contributed a number of ideas to the text and exercises. They also offered helpful comments and criticisms as the project progressed. Kevin Donovan and David Epstein produced high-quality solutions to the exercises that appear in the instructor's guide. Other reviewers whose comments are reflected in these pages are William F. Applebe, Georgia Institute of Technology; Richard A. Erdrich, Unisys Corporation; John L. Hennessy, Stanford University; K. C. Murphy, Advanced Micro Devices; Paul Pederson, New York University; Richard L. Sites, Digital Equipment Corporation; Henry Levy, University of Washington; Glen Langdon, University of California at Santa Cruz; Peter Hsu, Sun Microcomputers, and Phil Emma, Jeff Lee, K. S. Natarajan, Howard Sachar, and Marc Surette, all with IBM. Collectively and individually, their work has aided greatly the process of developing material to make it easily accessible to the intended audience. The publication crew at Addison-Wesley did a remarkable job in putting the project together. Bette Aaronson, Pat Steele, and Karen Myer demonstrated that they know pipelining in practice better than the author does in theory, smoothly flowing the chapters through the tedious process of markup, text editing, and page composition in a remarkable example of proficiency in high-performance publishing. To Tom Robbins, we offer gratitude for support and encouragement in the project from its inception to its completion.

Chappaqua, New York   H. S. S.

Contents

1 Introduction   **1**

  1.1 Technology and Architecture   1
  1.2 But Is It Art?   3
     1.2.1 The Cost Factor   4
     1.2.2 Hardware Considerations   7
  1.3 High-Performance Techniques   9
     1.3.1 Measuring Costs   10
     1.3.2 The Role of Applications   12
     1.3.3 The Impact of VLSI   13
     1.3.4 The Effect of Technological Change on Cost   14
     1.3.5 Algorithms and Architecture   17
  1.4 Historical References   19

2 Memory-System Design   **21**

  2.1 Exploiting Program Characteristics   23
  2.2 Cache Memory   29
     2.2.1 Basic Cache Structure   29
     2.2.2 Cache Design   32
     2.2.3 Cache Analysis: Trace Generation and Trace Length   39
     2.2.4 Cache Analysis: Trace Stripping   49
     2.2.5 Replacement Policies   59
     2.2.6 Footprints in the Cache   65
     2.2.7 Writing to the Cache   73
     2.2.8 Other Performance Metrics   76
     2.2.9 Modeling Cache Performance   79

2.3 Virtual Memory   87
      2.3.1 Virtual-Memory Structure   88
      2.3.2 Virtual-Memory Mapping   91
      2.3.3 Improving Program Locality   99
      2.3.4 Replacement Algorithms   102
      2.3.5 Buffering Effects in Virtual-Memory Systems   107
Exercises   112

3 Pipeline Design Techniques   122

3.1 Principles of Pipeline Design   123
3.2 Memory Structures in Pipeline Computers   135
3.3 Performance of Pipelined Computers   137
3.4 Control of Pipeline Stages   147
      3.4.1 Design of a Multi-Function Pipeline   147
      3.4.2 The Collision Vector and Pipeline Control   152
      3.4.3 Maximum Performance Pipelines   158
      3.4.4 Using Delays to Increase Performance   160
      3.4.5 Interlock Elimination   168
3.5 Exploiting Pipeline Techniques   170
      3.5.1 Conditional Branches   170
      3.5.2 Internal Forwarding and Deferred Instuctions   175
      3.5.3 Machines with Both Cache and Virtual Memory   184
      3.5.4 RISC Architectures   188
3.6 Historical References   196
Exercises   197

4 Characteristics of Numerical Applications   202

4.1 Classification of Large-Scale Numerical Problems   203
      4.1.1 Continuum Models   205
      4.1.2 Particle Models   207
4.2 Design Constraints for High-Performance Machines   209
4.3 Architectures for the Continuum Model   211
4.4 Algorithms for the Continuum Model   219
      4.4.1 The Cosmic Cube Versus the ILLIAC IV   219
      4.4.2 Data-Flow Requirements   221
      4.4.3 Parallel Solutions   226
      4.4.4 Recursive Doubling and Cyclic Reduction   232
4.5 The Perfect Shuffle   236
      4.5.1 The Perfect-Shuffle Interconnection Pattern   236
      4.5.2 Applications of the Perfect Shuffle   243
4.6 Architectures for the Continuum Model—Which Direction?   253
Exercises   255

5 Vector Computers   259

5.1 A Generic Vector Processor   260
    5.1.1 Multiple Memory Modules   262
    5.1.2 Intermediate Memories   270
5.2 Access Patterns for Numerical Algorithms   274
    5.2.1 Gaussian Elimination   275
5.3 Data-Structuring Techniques for Vector Machines   279
5.4 Attached Vector-Processors   287
5.5 Sparse-Matrix Techniques   292
5.6 The GF-11—A Very High-Speed Vector Processor   295
5.7 Final Comments on Vector Computers   297
Exercises   300

6 Multiprocessors   304

6.1 Background   305
6.2 Multiprocessor Performance   309
    6.2.1 The Basic Model—Two Processors with Unoverlapped
        Communications   311
    6.2.2 Extension to N Processors   312
    6.2.3 A Stochastic Model   316
    6.2.4 A Model with Linear Communication Costs   317
    6.2.5 An Optimistic Model—Fully Overlapped
        Communication   319
    6.2.6 A Model with Multiple Communication Links   321
    6.2.7 Multiprocessor Models   323
6.3 Multiprocessor Interconnections   325
    6.3.1 Bus Interconnections   326
    6.3.2 Ring Interconnections   331
    6.3.3 Crossbar Interconnections   333
    6.3.4 Two- and Three-Dimensional Meshes   338
    6.3.5 The Shuffle-Exchange Interconnection and the
        Combing Switch   339
    6.3.6 The Butterfly Operation and the Reverse-Binary
        Transformation   340
    6.3.7 The Combining Network and Fetch-and-Add   346
    6.3.8 Hypercube Interconnections   352
6.4 Cache Coherence in Multiprocessors   353
6.5 Summary   358
Exercises   359

7 Multiprocessor Algorithms   361

7.1 Easy Parallelism   362
    7.1.1 The **do par** and **do seq** Constructions   364
    7.1.2 Barrier Synchronization   365
    7.1.3 Performance Considerations   367
    7.1.4 Increasing Granularity   370
    7.1.5 Initiating Tasks   374
7.2 Synchronization Techniques   376
    7.2.1 Synchronization with Test-and-Set   377
    7.2.2 Synchronization with Increment and Decrement   381
    7.2.3 Synchronization with Compare-and-Swap   384
    7.2.4 Synchronization with Fetch-and-Add   392
    7.2.5 Other Architectural Support for Parallel
       Synchronization   395
    7.2.6 Cache Coherence Versus Synchronization   402
7.3 Parallel Search—How To Use and Not Use Parallelism   405
    7.3.1 Seaching for the Maximum of a Unimodal Function   406
    7.3.2 Parallel Branch-and-Bound—The Traveling-Salesman
       Problem   410
    7.3.3 Speed-Up and Parallel Complexity   415
7.4 Transforming Serial Algorithms into Parallel Algorithms   417
    7.4.1 Dependence Analysis   418
    7.4.2 Exploiting Parallelism Across Iterations   419
    7.4.3 The Effects of Scheduling on Parallelism   424
7.5 Final Comments on Multiprocessors   425
Exercises   428

References   433

Index and Glossary   443

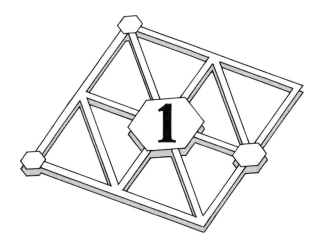

Introduction

1.1 Technology and Architecture
1.2 But Is It Art?
1.3 High-Performance Techniques
1.4 Historical References

This text is devoted to the study of the architecture of high-speed computer systems, with emphasis on design and analysis. We view a computer system as being constructed from a variety of functional modules such as processors, memories, input/output channels, and switching networks. By *architecture*, we mean the structure of the modules as they are organized in a computer system. The architectural design of a computer system involves selecting various functional modules such as processors and memories and organizing them into a system by designing the interconnections that tie them together. This is analogous to the architectural design of buildings, which involves selecting materials and fitting the pieces together to form a viable structure.

1.1 Technology and Architecture

Computer architecture is driven by technology. Every year brings new devices, new functions, and new possibilities. An imaginative and effective architecture for today could be a klunker for tomorrow, and likewise, a ridiculous proposal for today may be ideal for tomorrow. There are no absolute rules that say that one architecture is better than another.

The key to learning about computer architecture is learning how to evaluate architecture in the context of the technology available. It is as important to know if a computer system makes effective use of processor cycles, memory capacity, and input/output bandwidth as it is to know its raw computational speed. The objective is to look at both cost and performance, not performance alone, in evaluating architectures. Because of changes in technology, relative costs among modules as well as absolute costs change dramatically every few years, so the best proportion of different types of modules in a cost-effective design changes with technology.

This text takes the approach that it is methodology, not conclusions, that needs to be taught. We present a menu of possibilities, some reasonable today and some not. We show how to construct high-performance systems by making selections from the menus, and we evaluate the systems produced in terms of technology that exists at the start of the 1990s. The conclusions reached by these evaluations are probably reasonable through the middle of the decade, but in no way do we claim that the architectures that look strongest today will be the best as we turn to a new millenium.

The methodology, however, is timeless. From time to time the computer architect needs to construct a new menu of design choices. With that menu and the design and evaluation techniques described in this text, the architect should be able to produce high-quality systems in any decade for the technology at that time.

Performance analysis should be based on the architecture of the total system. Design and analysis of high-performance systems is very complex, however, and is best approached by breaking the large system into a hierarchy of functional blocks, each with an architecture that can be analyzed in isolation. If any single function is very complicated, it too can be further refined into a collection of more primitive functions. Processor architecture, for example, involves putting together registers, arithmetic units, and control logic to create processors—the computational elements of a computer system.

An important facet of processor architecture is the design of the instruction set for the processor, and we shall learn in the course of this text that there are controversies raging today concerning whether instruction sets should be very simple or very complex. We do not settle this controversy here; there cannot be a single answer. But we do illuminate the factors that determine the answer, and in any technology an architect can measure those factors in the course of a new design.

Computer architecture is sometimes confused with the design of computer hardware. Because computer architecture deals with modules at a functional level, not exclusively at a hardware level, computer architecture must encompass more than hardware. We can specify, for example, that a processor performs arithmetic and logic functions, and we can be reasonably sure that these functions will be built into the hardware and not require additional programming. If we specify memory management functions in the processor, the actual implementation of those functions may be some mix of hardware and software, with the exact mix depending on performance, availability of existing hardware or software components, and costs.

When very large scale integration (VLSI) was in its infancy, memory-management functions were implemented in software, and the processor architecture had to support such software by providing only a collection of registers for address mapping and protection. With VLSI it becomes possible to embed a greater portion of memory management in hardware. Many systems employ sophisticated algorithms in hardware for performing memory-management functions once exclusively implemented in software.

The line between hardware and software becomes somewhat fuzzy when last year's software is embedded directly in read-only memory on a memory-management chip where it is invisibly invoked by the programs being managed. Once such a chip is packaged and is then a "black box" that does memory management, the solution becomes a hardware solution. The architect who uses the chip need not provide additional software for memory management. If a chip does most, but not all, memory-management functions internally, then the architect must look into providing the missing features by incorporating software modules.

In retrospect, computer architecture makes systems from components, and the components can be hardware, software, or a mixture of both. The skill involved in architecture is to select a good collection of components and put them together so they work effectively as a total system. Later chapters show various examples of architectures, some proven successful and some proposals that might succeed.

1.2 But Is It Art?

An article in the *New York Times* in January 1985 described a discovery of an unsigned painting by de Kooning that raised a few eyebrows among art critics. Although it does not bear his signature, there was no doubt that it is his work, and it was hung in a gallery for public viewing. The piece is a bench from the outhouse of his summer beach house that de Kooning painted abstractly to give the appearance of marble. Is this piece a great work of art by a renowned master, or is it just a painted privy seat? The point is that art appreciation is based on aesthetics, for which we have no absolute measures. We have no absolute test to conclude whether the work is a masterpiece or a piece of junk. If the art world agrees that it is a masterpiece, then it is a masterpiece.

Computer architecture, too, has an aesthetic side, but it is quite different from the arts. We can evaluate the quality of an architecture in terms of maximum number of results per cycle, program and data capacity, and cost, as well as other measures that tend to be important in various contexts. We need never debate a question such as, "but is it fast?"

Architectures can be compared on critical measures when choices must be made. The challenge comes because technology gives us new choices each year, and the decisions from last year may not hold this year. Not only must the architect understand the best decision for today, but the architect must factor in the effects of expected changes in technology over the life of a design. Therefore, not only do evaluation techniques play a crucial role in individual decisions, but by using these techniques over a period of years, the architect gains experience in understanding the impact of technological developments on new architectures and is able to judge trends for several years in the future.

Here are the principal criteria for judging an architecture:

- Performance;
- Cost; and
- Maximum program and data size.

There are a dozen or more other criteria, such as weight, power consumption, volume, and ease of programming, that may have relatively high significance in particular cases, but the three listed here are important in all applications and critical in most of them.

1.2.1 The Cost Factor

The cost criterion deserves a bit more explanation because so many people are confused about what it means. The cost of a computer system to a user is the money that the user pays for the system, namely its price. To the designer, cost is not so clearly defined. In most cases, cost is the cost of manufacturing, including a fair amortization of the cost of development and capital tools for construction. All too often we see comparisons of architectures that compare the parts cost of System *A* with the purchase price of System *B*, where System *A* is a novel architecture that is being proposed as an innovation, and System *B* represents a model in commercial production.

Another fallacious comparison is often made when relating hardware to software. In the early years of computing, software was often bundled free of charge with hardware, but, as the industry matured, software itself became a commodity of value to be sold.

We now discover that what was once a free good now commands a significant portion of a computing budget. The trends that people quote are depicted in Fig. 1.1, where we see the cost of software steadily rising with inflation and complexity, and with apparently little relief from advances in software tools. Plotted on the same curve is the general trend for hardware in the same period of time. Hardware components appear to be diminishing in cost at an unbe-

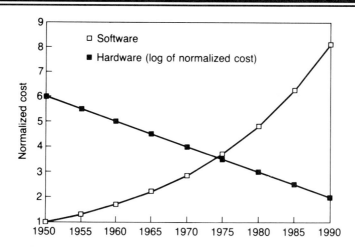

Fig. 1.1 A naive view of computer-cost trends.

lievable rate. If we project these trends forward ten to twenty years, we may believe that hardware might be bundled with software, given free with the purchase of the software that runs on it. But this view is rather naive.

Software and hardware costs each have two components:

1. A one-time development cost; and

2. A per-unit manufacturing cost.

The actual cost of a product, be it software or hardware, is shown in Fig. 1.2 as a function of the volume of production of a product. Note that the cost of the first unit is equal to the cost of the development. The cost curve moves upward with volume, but the slope tends to diminish with very high volumes because of manufacturing experience that tends to reduce per-unit costs over large volumes of production. The curve in Fig. 1.2 shows accumulated cost of the total volume of a product. The *price* of the product is the cost shown on the curve divided by the volume, plus a markup for profit. So price is very sensitive to volume when development costs are high.

When software was essentially free, the development costs were either bundled with the hardware development costs, borne by the users who developed the bulk of their own software, or simply not accounted or recovered by the software producers. Since hardware manufacturing costs were very high compared to today, software manufacturing costs were small relative to hardware manufacturing costs. As long as development costs did not have to be

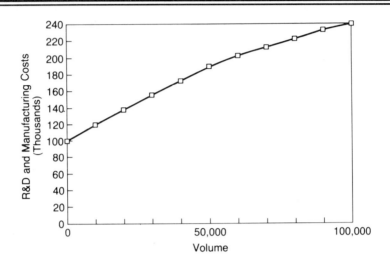

Fig. 1.2 Cumulative production costs versus volume.

covered through the direct sale of software, it was reasonable to give away the software.

Eventually, software development costs became significant and could no longer be ignored. But software replication is still essentially free. We can easily draw a parallel with some VLSI chips in mass production (for example, a complex microprocessor chip with a few hundred thousand transistors). The chip-development cost may be about the same order of magnitude as the cost of the development of the operating system or of a database-management applications package that run on the chip.

In very high volume, the manufacturing cost per chip is the same order of magnitude as the manufacturing cost of the software. Yet we see the chip sold at a price that may be as little as one-tenth the price of the software, and the computer system that contains the chip may be priced at ten times the cost of the software. The price of the chip, software, and computer system seem to be unrelated to manufacturing costs. In part, the price is determined by volume of sales, because the price must recover the development costs. Several million copies of the chip may be sold, but perhaps only a few hundred thousand copies of the database-management software may be sold. This alone can account for a factor-of-ten difference in price.

Our analysis also shows why in years to come hardware costs will still prove to be significant compared to software costs. At issue here is the cost of manufacturing. Software manufacturing costs are near zero today and can only go lower, so that software pricing in a competitive market mainly reflects the amortization of development costs.

Hardware manufacturing costs, while small on a per-chip basis, are many times more than software manufacturing costs. It is far less costly today to replicate accurate copies of software than it is to replicate hardware. Hardware requires assembly and testing to make sure that each copy is a faithful copy of the original design. This is far more complex today than the quality assurance on a software manufacturing line that simply has to compare each bit of information in software to see if it agrees with the original program.

We see that hardware pricing carries the burden of per-unit manufacturing costs together with development costs, whereas software pricing reflects development costs to a much greater extent. When computers fit on a single chip, their prices should bear some similarity with software prices. Indeed, we see hand calculators sold for roughly the same price as the most popular simple software tools. But computers that contain hundreds or thousands of individual components are far more complex to reproduce than any software package. At the very least, the hardware manufacturer has to test the chips and systems to reject the failures, and the corresponding process in software manufacturing is negligible because copying software is low cost, reliable, and inexpensively verified. In a competitive market, it is very unlikely that computers of moderate or high performance will be given away to purchasers of the accompanying software.

1.2.2 Hardware Considerations

Another fallacious argument about new designs for the future concerns the lavish use of hardware components in a system. The architects state convincingly that with current trends in force, the cost of hardware will be negligible, so that we can afford to build systems of much greater hardware complexity in the future than we can today. Clearly, there is truth in this argument to the extent that future systems will surely be more powerful and complex at equal cost to today's systems. But the argument must be used with care because it does not excuse gross waste of hardware.

In the future, given System A, with 100 times the logic as present systems, and System B, whose performance is essentially identical to A's but has only 10 or 20 times the logic as present systems, System A will be at a serious competitive disadvantage. For a few hundred or a few thousand copies of System A sold, System A may be priced competitively with System B. For higher volumes of production, however, the inefficiency of the architecture of System A will force its price higher than System B's for equal system value. Of course, this presumes that both System A and System B are built from components of the same generation of technology. If A's chips are 10 times as dense as B's chips and therefore 10 times less costly per device, then the argument changes, and device technology, not architecture is the determining factor in the price of the system.

Throughout this text we explore the study of architecture by considering innovations of the future that depend on low-cost components. But we shall always heed the efficiency of the architectures we examine to be sure that we are using our building blocks well.

Consider, for example, a multiprocessor system in which there exists no shared memory, and suppose that we want to run a parallel program in which each processor executes the same program. Obviously, we can load identical copies of the program in all processors. When the program is small or the number of processors is rather modest, the memory consumed by the multiple copies may be quite tolerable.

But what if the program is a megabyte in size, and what if we plan to use 1000 processors in our system? Then the copies of the program account for a gigabyte of storage, which need not be present if there were some way to share one copy of code across all processors.

If System *A* uses multiple copies of programs, and System *B* through a clever design, achieves nearly equal performance with a single copy, then the extra gigabyte of memory required by System *A* could well make System *A* totally uncompetitive with System *B*, unless the cost of storage becomes so insignificant that a gigabyte of memory accounts for a paltry fraction of the cost of a system. System *A*'s architect hopes that the cost per bit of memory will tumble in the future, but System *A* requires 10^{10} more bits, and this is an enormous multiplier. If current historical trends continue, a drop in cost per bit to offset an inefficiency of this magnitude would probably take 20 to 30 years.

In the example just presented, the architect of System *A* has to be aware of other approaches that could overcome a basic flaw in System *A* for the particular application. System *A* might be totally effective for other applications in which each processor requires a different program. But in the given context, System *B* has a tremendous, probably insurmountable advantage. The architect should measure the quality of the architecture across a number of applications that characterize how an architecture is to be used. The effectiveness may vary considerably from application to application, and such measurements should reveal where the architecture is truly beneficial to the user and where other approaches are superior.

A computer architecture might well have some minor but costly inherent flaws that escape the scrutiny of its designer. A different designer who can build essentially the same architecture with those flaws repaired can produce a more effective, and therefore more competitive, machine. Architects cannot hide inefficiency by arguing that hardware costs nothing.

As a simple example of this rule, consider an architecture with a rather large number of processors, such as 16,000, and assume that the processors are to be used in an application where the speedup attributed to N processors is proportional to $\log_2 N$. (As astonishing as this sounds, such proposals have been made.) The 16,000 processors yield only a speedup of $14x$ for some constant x. The architect argues cogently that the 16,000 processors are so inexpensive that we can ignore their cost. The important fact is that the application runs $14x$ times faster than it runs on a single processor, and the speed increase is worth the small extra cost for the processors.

In this competitive world, the gross inefficiency of the architecture cannot escape notice for long. Soon there appears a System B to compete with this System A. System B's architecture is identical to A's in this case, except that it is a rather scaled-down version. In fact, System B has only 128 processors, not 16,000, so it runs only $7x$ times faster than a single processor.

System A is over 100 times more complex than System B, and yet System A runs only twice as fast. The cost of hardware would have to be near zero for System B to fail to compete with System A. For the next decade at least, it appears to be unjustifiable on a cost basis to double performance by replicating hardware one-hundred-fold.

The arguments in this section have taught us:

- We can evaluate architectures by their cost and performance;
- The effectiveness of an architecture must be measured on workloads for which the architecture is intended; and
- An architecture that is inefficient because of wasted resources will compete poorly against a simpler but more efficient architecture.

If computer architecture were purely an art, and aesthetics alone determined the quality of an architectural design, we would not have a basis for technical advances. Computer architecture combines the art of design with insight derived from careful analysis to create new forms of computer systems that yield ever greater service to their users.

1.3 High-Performance Techniques

Of the criteria discussed in the preceding section, this text emphasizes high performance. Our objective is to describe many different ways to improve system performance and give some additional information for evaluating those techniques. The menu of available techniques is rather extensive today, and each new generation of technology brings new ideas to the fore.

This text covers the highlights of the existing menu of design choices, but is by no means complete as of its publication date. Therefore we explore the design methodology—identify the critical design problems, generate solutions to these problems, evaluate, and select the best or most reasonable solution.

Although we emphasize performance, a thorough evaluation should consider all the criteria for comparing architectures. We simply place a greater weight on performance. For the majority of the design space, cost and performance are treated together as a single parameter, the *cost-performance* ratio. The ratio is appropriate because it stays constant as you increase performance and cost by equal factors.

We would like to believe that users are willing to pay 10 percent more for a machine that is 10 percent faster, that is, a machine whose cost-performance ratio is equal to their current one. If a machine yields 20 percent higher performance for 10 percent higher cost, the users may see a genuine benefit in moving to the new machine, and indeed it has a lower cost-performance ratio reflecting a lower cost per computation. In most cases, users would not be interested in a machine that yields only 5 percent higher performance at 10 percent higher cost because their cost per computation goes up, not down, if they move to the new machine.

The exceptional cases occur when the present facilities are saturated, and the user absolutely must have greater capacity. Now the cost-performance ratio does not tell the whole story because the total benefit of greater capacity for the user may be much greater than the cost to achieve that capacity. The fact that the user is actually paying a higher cost per computation to obtain that capacity is incidental to the value in being able to do computations that could not be done before. However, if the user has a choice in how to obtain the necessary capacity, the user may still pick a solution based on the lowest cost-performance ratio, even though all possible solutions have higher ratios than the ratio for the user's current system.

1.3.1 Measuring Costs

We have been careful to give examples based on small changes in performance and cost. The cost-performance ratio is a good indicator of relative quality for small changes, but its usefulness breaks down when costs and performance vary by large factors.

It would be very deceptive, for example, to measure the cost-performance ratio of a small computer, such as an 8-bit video-game system, and to compare this to a much more powerful system, such as a workstation for computer-aided design. Although both systems are used to display images and interact with the images in real time, the video game probably has a much better cost-performance ratio than the workstation, assuming we can find some way of measuring relative performance. The problem is that the relative costs of the systems vary by a factor of up to 1000 to 1, and similarly, the relative performance factor is very large, although probably not as large as the relative cost.

The video game cannot do the same job as the workstation. Moreover, if you put enough copies of the video game together to have a performance equal to the workstation, the cost would be less than the workstation cost, but the collection of video games still could not do the same job. So just to be sure that comparisons based on cost-performance ratios are valid, one should be careful to make the comparisons between computers that are similar in function and relatively close in performance.

This discussion points to two important ways to make architectural advances:

1. Make small perturbations in cost and performance that yield lower cost-performance ratios; and

2. Boost absolute performance to make new computations feasible at reasonable cost.

By "small" changes, we mean roughly a factor of 10 or less. Changes larger than this are surely welcome, but the cost-performance ratio cannot be trusted as a measure to evaluate the change. For the second point, the cost-performance ratio can actually increase, provided that the additional cost can be absorbed by the user, because the benefit of the greater capacity exceeds the cost to attain the capacity. We use both of these criteria throughout the text as informal ways to evaluate ideas.

Because absolute cost measured in currency is changing every year, it is more useful to define cost in terms of other parameters that influence cost. These parameters include the physical parameters, such as pin count, chip area, chip count, board area, and power consumption, derived from an implementation of an architecture. The parameters also include factors associated with development, such as elapsed design time, amount of associated software to be written, and size of development team required.

This text cannot easily account for all the factors that affect cost, but it can isolate the most important ones, especially when comparing two closely related architectures whose differences are limited to a few critical design choices. The intent is to focus on the differences and discuss the ways they affect the cost factors. Each different approach has its own advantages and disadvantages, and they in turn affect the cost of the approach. We cannot give absolute costs, but we can show the influence of the design decision on the cost parameters. The reader can then apply the prevailing cost functions to complete the evaluation.

1.3.2 The Role of Applications

With dramatic changes in technology ahead, how do we approach the problem of high-performance architecture design? For example, the new technology makes feasible massive parallelism. How much additional effort should be invested in increasing the performance of a single processor before we seek higher levels of performance by replicating processors? There is no simple answer to these questions. We need a combination of solutions, and what we choose almost certainly will be application dependent.

The role of applications is critical in the high-performance arena because costs tend to be very high to wring the greatest possible throughput from an architecture. Inefficiency is especially costly in this context because inefficiency adds greatly to already high cost, while contributing less than its fair share to performance. If the application area is heavily biased to some well-identified workload, then it becomes possible to design the architecture for that type of workload. The result is that the architecture can be stripped clean of irrelevant functions that might otherwise be necessary for general purposes. It can then be heavily armed with functions pertinent to the particular workload.

The objective then is to reduce inefficiency by making sure that all the functional components of the architecture contribute effectively to achieving high performance. If it were possible to build a general-purpose machine that would be equally effective for all high-performance applications, the industry would do so. And we cannot rule out this possibility in years to come. However, for the next decade, specific problem areas are so demanding of computational cycles that it is fruitful to design architectures specialized for these problem areas.

Among the important problem areas that have evolved are:

- *Highly structured numeric computations*—weather modeling, fluid flows, finite-element analysis;
- *Unstructured numeric computations*—Monte Carlo simulations, sparse matrix problems;
- *Real-time multifaceted problems*—speech recognition, image processing, and computer vision;
- *Large-memory and input/output-intensive problems*—database systems, transaction systems;
- *Graphics and design systems*—computer-aided design; and
- *Artificial intelligence*—knowledge-base-oriented systems, inferencing systems.

Obviously, the numerical areas call for sophisticated floating-point processors in the architecture, and the more demanding applications may require hundreds of such processors. The graphics systems may be more strongly oriented to fixed-point computations to provide the mathematical support required for windowing and perspective viewing. Floating point, however, plays an important role in some graphics applications, such as those that require smooth-curve rendering and ray-tracing calculations. The artificial-intelligence systems may require very little arithmetic capability, but they are usually heavily endowed with memory.

A high-performance architecture that meets the needs of all the areas mentioned must carry a burden of inefficiency for each problem area because a substantial portion of its capability would not be useful for individual applications. If the inefficiency is high enough for any one application area, then an efficient specialized machine for that area is more attractive than a general-purpose machine because the specialized machine should cost less to manufacture.

The cost advantage depends on having a large enough market for the specialized machine so that the cost of development can be spread across many copies produced. The advantage is lost if only a few copies are sold. Consequently, even the specialized high-performance machines should be as general purpose as possible within their problem domains so that the fixed costs can be amortized over as large a base as possible.

As special-purpose architectures are extended to broaden their problem domains, their potential market increases, but at the same time they tend to make less efficient use of their hardware. So the architect faces a trade-off. The idea is to balance the efficiency of the special-purpose architecture against the broad market base of the general-purpose architecture.

The architect has to find a place in the spectrum between single-purpose and all-purpose architecture for which a new design yields high performance at competitive cost. Design decisions are changing in time because they depend both on development costs and per-unit production costs, both of which are changing dramatically as the underlying technology advances.

1.3.3 The Impact of VLSI

There have been dramatic changes in the cost structure of high-performance architecture because of the development of VLSI. In the 1950s, when hardware was so expensive that one user could not afford to purchase a 1 M-byte machine, users shared the costs of large-scale computers and ran their programs concurrently on a single machine, thereby reducing the time that the memory, processor, and peripherals were idle. There seemed to be some economy by going to increasingly larger machines. The number of users served tended to grow linearly with computational power, but the price of the machines tended to grow more slowly.

Grosch's law was a popularly believed rule-of-thumb that stated that the cost of computational power grows at the rate of the square root of computational power. Although a great deal of evidence supported Grosch's law through the early 1960s, it is not clear whether the law reflected a fundamental notion about cost/performance or merely the prices being charged for computers.

In the 1980s, VLSI changed the economics of computers dramatically. We no longer try to wring every last cycle from a 1M-byte machine, and it is common to find such machines lying idle for most of a 24-hour day. So, for the huge number of small computations, the user buys a machine big enough to get the job done, and maybe a little bigger than that to have some reserve capacity. It is not particularly economical to buy enormously big machines, then gain access to the machine cycles by sharing the cycles among many users.

Strictly from a performance point of view, we do not see an economy of scale that drives all users to larger machines regardless of their needs, as once appeared to be the case. Rather, to describe the situation in simplistic terms, we see small jobs run on small machines, and large jobs run on large machines. The "small" machine of today has about the same computational power as the "large" machine of 25 years ago, so the machine formerly shared by 100 users, is now owned outright by one user.

The need to access shared data complicates the arguments here somewhat. We discover that large machines or networks of smaller machines support many concurrent users today because the need to access shared data, as opposed to the need to share machine cycles, is the driving force. And we still see the supercomputers shared among many users because these machine cycles are very expensive for any single user.

1.3.4 The Effect of Technological Change on Cost

If we look at the underlying technology at any given time, we see curves that look something like the curve in Fig. 1.3. This figure shows performance measured in millions of instructions per second (MIPS). It shows a rough picture of relative cost per MIPS as a function of MIPS of performance. The figure is intentionally imprecise because the data on which it is based is highly volatile. The idea is that the curve consists of several plateaus. The lowest plateau represents the cost per MIPS for computers that use the dominant technology for that plateau.

In the 1980s, the dominant technology for low-performance machines was metal-oxide semiconductor (MOS), mostly NMOS (MOS devices with negatively doped channels) in the early 1980s with CMOS (complementary MOS, devices with both negatively and positively doped channels) becoming prevalent in the later 1980s. At any given time, the cost per MIPS is fairly constant for all machines made from this technology.

The next plateau is the next level of technology, presumably a bipolar technology such as emitter-coupled logic (ECL). The cost per MIPS is nearly constant for all machines of this technology as well.

The third plateau is a more exotic device technology fabricated especially for peak performance. Gallium-arsenide devices appear in this plateau. This technology has the highest cost because of cooling requirements, manufacturing difficulties, lower chip density, or other similar factors. This plateau too

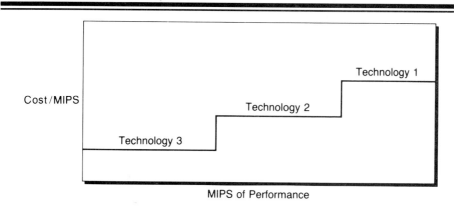

Fig. 1.3 Cost/performance as a function of performance.

has almost constant cost per MIPS for all machines produced from the technology.

Although the graph in Fig. 1.3 is imprecise, it is intended to show how a device technology influences the cost-performance relationship. The devices dictate the basic cycle time of the computer. A rough measure of processing power is the width of the address and data paths times the clock frequency; this is an upper bound on the information-transfer rate of a computer system.

For a given technology, most high-speed designs adopt a maximum or near-maximum clock frequency that is usually dependent on the technology and fairly consistent for all designs that use that technology. Consequently, the most appropriate way to improve performance is to move from 8-bit to 16-bit to 32-bit data paths, with a corresponding increase in memory capacity to support higher levels of performance. This produces a performance gain that grows linearly with the bus width, but the cost tends to grow linearly as well in bus width, so that as bus widths increase, the additional performance produced is achieved at a constant cost per MIPS.

The assumption that cost grows linearly in bus width is certainly true in regard to the cost of data paths, drivers, and physical wires on the data paths, but the cost of memory need not grow linearly with bus width. The critical assumption that produces the plateau-like curve in Fig. 1.3 is that memory size tends to increase linearly with performance. That is, a typical configuration for a system rated at 2 MIPS might be 4 M-bytes, and faster versions of the same system that run at 4 MIPS and 8 MIPS would be configured at 8 M- and 16 M-bytes, respectively. If indeed this growth rate is true, then Fig. 1.3 is quite reasonable.

The main conclusion to draw from Fig. 1.3 is that if the curves are truly flat, then within a device technology there is no particular economy of scale. Worse yet, if an architecture's performance exceeds the capabilities of one device technology, then the move to the next higher plateau of technology may result in a higher cost per MIPS. This is directly contrary to the principle of economy of scale. At the very highest levels of performance, the device technology may be quite exotic, raising the cost per MIPS well over the cost per MIPS of less powerful systems.

If Fig. 1.3 is accurate as drawn for the beginning of the 1990s, one would conclude that once a device technology for an architecture implementation is selected, the cost-performance ratio is not strongly influenced by the absolute performance of a system, so there is no particular bias to produce high- or low-performance machines for that technology. If Fig. 1.3 is not accurate, and there exists an economy of scale, then the cost-performance ratio improves as performance goes up, and there is a strong bias toward building the highest possible performance for each different device technology. No matter what is true at the time this text is written, a future version of Fig. 1.3 may be totally different, and the architect has to take the shape of the curve into account in machine design.

Now let us reflect on the variables that the architect can control in creating a high-performance machine. By measuring performance in MIPS, we can write

$$\text{MIPS} = (\text{instructions/cycle})(\text{cycles/second}) \cdot 10^{-6}$$

The first factor is a function of the architecture, which is controlled by the architect. The second factor is determined by the devices, which are controlled by the technology.

Actually, the dichotomy between architecture and device technology is not as sharp as we depict it because the second factor, the clock speed, is partially dependent on architectural factors such as the complexity of instruction decoding. Nevertheless, to a first approximation we can affect performance by concentrating on the first factor, the number of instructions executed per machine cycle. What are the alternatives available?

- *Reduce the number of instructions to execute.* By using better algorithms, it may be possible to do equal work with fewer instructions.
- *Build hardware assists into the architecture to improve the architecture's efficiency.* Advances in architecture such as cache memory can increase the number of instructions executed per cycle. Another possibility is to create higher-level instructions such as SORT and SEARCH that have been optimized for particular purposes.
- *Execute many instructions concurrently.* Use parallel hardware in some fashion to increase the number of instructions that can be executed in a single cycle.

It is strange to see the first item in this list in a text on architecture. One might assume that the computer architect does not dabble with algorithms. Quite to the contrary. Since the goal is high performance as measured on some set of applications, how that goal is achieved is important because of its impact on system cost, but there are no constraints that force the solution to be architectural only. In fact, algorithmic improvements may be the most cost effective of any of the approaches mentioned previously because copies of algorithms can be manufactured for essentially zero cost as compared to the cost of hardware-intensive solutions.

1.3.5 Algorithms and Architecture

The architect has to look carefully at algorithms to decide how to achieve high performance in an architecture. Applications that are limited by the speed of floating-point division, by internal sorting, or by the ability to interpret bit-mapped representations of visual data may require extensive study by the architect. Changes to the original algorithms, sometimes simple changes and sometimes totally new approaches, may transform an application from one for which high-performance architectures are poorly suited to one that can easily be enhanced by some inexpensive hardware assists.

An algorithmic breakthrough might even eliminate the need for high-performance architectures for a particular application. Floating-point division and sorting are each reasonably well understood areas for which major changes to existing algorithms are unlikely to be developed, but many new areas are emerging for which the current crop of algorithms represents the early, immature efforts to solve the problems. Additional study of the algorithms may well produce much greater performance.

Although we cannot expect a computer architect to step into an application area and produce a breakthrough in algorithms for that area, it is possible for an architect to recast basic algorithms into forms more suitable for processing. The architect may partition a problem in new ways to reduce the size of working memory or the number of high-speed registers required. Or the architect may find a way to structure the problem so that it fits well on a parallel architecture.

The architect actually has control of both the algorithm and the architecture. The objective is to manipulate both to create an algorithm and architecture that mutually constitute an effective solution. Usually a class of algorithms, rather than a single algorithm, must be considered, and the more difficult objective is to create a single architecture that is good for all the problems in the class.

The second solution technique involves changes to the basic architecture. In the past we have seen many different techniques used to improve performance. Such things as instruction buffers, cache memories, and pipelined execution have appeared in many commercial machine implementations. We have seen complex instructions installed in machines to reduce the number of instruction fetches, and we have seen complex instructions eliminated from instruction sets to reduce the basic instruction-cycle time for a machine.

The architect needs to know where bottlenecks may exist in a system, and then, if possible, take steps to remove those bottlenecks. At peak performance a well-designed system has many different components near saturation. A poorly designed system has some single bottleneck when running at maximum speed, and all other functional units are underutilized. By eliminating some excess capacity, this kind of system may be made less expensive at no loss of performance. Or by dealing with the bottleneck exclusively, it may be possible to improve performance relatively inexpensively.

The last choice on the list is parallelism. This is usually the most costly way to achieve high speed, but VLSI technology has changed the economics so dramatically that parallel hardware has become a viable alternative. Returning to Fig. 1.3, we see that there is some advantage in using inexpensive technology in seeking high performance. Figure 1.3 suggests that each device technology is most effective over some range of performance.

Parallel architectures, however, provide a way of using the inexpensive device technology at much higher performance ranges. An architect can attempt to exploit the plateau structure of Fig. 1.3 to create an efficient parallel machine out of low-cost devices. The objective is to increase MIPS by adding performance in a way that performance grows proportionally with cost. If this can be accomplished, the architect stays on the flat plateau of the low-cost technology while moving performance into the region dominated by high-cost technology. Certainly, this is one of the attractions of moving to parallel architectures, although the gains achieved through less-expensive device technology are negated in part by a lower efficiency in executing a program in parallel rather than on a serial machine. In fact, because of the inefficiency of parallelism the cost per MIPS grows with the number of processors in a complex of parallel processors. The challenge is to keep this growth small enough so that a parallel machine built with low-cost devices is less costly than a serial machine of equal speed built with high-cost devices.

These three techniques for making improvements are important, but not exhaustive. All opportunities are worth investigating. Because the real world does not follow the highly idealized world of design presumed in this text, pressures that exist in the real world might lead to unbalanced configurations that are difficult to justify on the merits of cost and performance.

Consider a situation in which System A has 256 K-bytes of a cache memory, and System B competes with System A by offering 512 K-bytes or 1 M-byte to gain a competitive edge through larger numbers, even when other factors cannot justify the larger cache memory. If not cache, then main memory size might be offered at 4 G-bytes instead of at 1 G-byte, or 32 processors in place of eight processors. Consequently, competitive pressures could easily cause an architect to configure poorly balanced systems.

Over a period of years, however, cost and performance measures prevail. If systems are unbalanced at first release, the cost to the user or to the system producer will be too high for the performance levels actually realized. Eventually configurations are altered to bring them back into a reasonable range of cost and performance. Designing for the shorter-term view by playing a numbers game may be a fact of life, but quality, efficiency, and effectiveness dictate that a sound architectural approach drives computer design over the long term.

In closing this section, we summarize by saying that all three of the approaches—algorithms, architectural assists, and parallel architectures—must be considered by the architect. High performance may require a combination of all three approaches in any given system.

In each new design lies a significant challenge for the architect because the rules of the game change continuously. The factors that influenced the design decisions last year may no longer hold this year. The architect has new devices to use as building blocks, and new organizations that are feasible to implement. And the applications have changed, too, with totally new problem areas becoming targets of computing technology. In addition, the older areas are increasing in scope and scale. The constant in architectural design is the methodology for putting together the various components available to create effective solutions for application areas.

1.4 Historical References

We use the term *computer architecture* in a broader sense than it was used when it was first introduced by Amdahl *et al.* [1964]. Their definition of computer architecture is the computer as seen by the programmer, which is essentially the instruction set plus a model of the execution of the instruction set. The importance of this notion is that a family of computers can have an identical architecture, yet span a large range of performance and capacity. Programs that execute on different models in one family give identical results. Different members of a family are different in implementation and may have varying degrees of hardware, microcode, and software embedded within them to support the execution of instructions defined for the family.

This narrow sense of computer architecture proved to be invaluable for defining the characteristics of a family without committing to particular implementations of architectural characteristics. The concept has been crucial in the development of the IBM 360 and 370 families, the PDP-11 and VAX families, and in recent microprocessor families such as the Motorola 680XX and the Intel 80X86 families.

Changes in technology have made the architectural definition offered by Amdahl *et al.* somewhat obsolete. The original reason for defining the architecture with the instruction-set definition was to ensure compatible execution of a program on any member of the family large enough to run the program.

Instruction-level compatibility is not sufficient in itself since program execution can depend on libraries, operating system facilities, local configuration, and other factors that are not part of this narrow sense of architecture. This has led to the standardization at other levels of interfaces, such as the operating system interface or the source language.

Meanwhile, the rapid development of VLSI and the changing cost structure of digital components forced some computer families to bring out new instruction sets. The 24-bit address of System 360 and 370 of 1964 vintage evolved to a 31-bit address in System 370 XA in 1982 and within a few years evolved again to a 44-bit address in the System 370 ESA architecture in 1988. The 16-bit address of the PDP-11 family (first offered in 1968) eventually became a 32-bit address in the VAX family in 1978.

With new devices to use in designs and the flexibility to change instruction sets, the computer designer of today faces a set of constraints somewhat different from those faced in decades past. Hence, we have enlarged the definition of computer architecture to include the design of a computer system from its instruction set and structure down to functional modules. Many topics treated in this text are issues of implementation that are not within the scope of the narrow definition of computer architecture as defined in Amdahl *et al.*

Readers interested in the historical development of computer architecture and in prerequisite material will find a wealth of information in Bell and Newell [1971] and Siewiorek, Bell, and Newell [1982]. Both books reprint a collection of historically important papers in computer architecture and include authors' commentary, which serves to organize the material and fill voids not covered in the literature.

Text books in the area appeared rather late in the development of computers, with Stone [1974] being among the early offerings. This is a collection of original contributions structured as a textbook. Hayes [1978] and Baer [1980] are both high-quality texts that brought updated material into the classroom. Tanenbaum [1976] covers an interesting combination of computer architecture and operating systems, an interface of two subject areas that has become increasingly important as the operating-system level has begun to displace the instruction-set level as the standard interface for applications. Stone's second edition [1980] includes material on operating systems as well as an evolution of the architecture-based material from the first edition.

Many texts covering both specialized and general aspects of computer architecture started appearing early in the 1980s. They are too numerous to include in this section, but books that are useful supplements for specific topic areas covered in this book are cited in the appropriate place in the text.

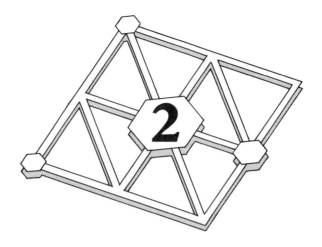

Memory-System Design

2.1 Exploiting Program Characteristics
2.2 Cache Memory
2.3 Virtual Memory

Some architecture researchers have called the memory system of a computer "the von Neumann bottleneck" because of the critical role it plays in affecting peak throughput. The design of the memory system is our starting point in this text, and it is frequently the starting point in machine designs. The central problem is to:

- Bring the input data from the outside world into memory;
- Buffer the data there until they can be passed to a processor;
- Compute the output data and buffer them in memory until they can be delivered outside the computer; and
- Transmit the output data from memory to the outside world.

The bandwidth between memory and the outside world limits how fast we can obtain input and deliver output. The memory system also limits how fast input data can be delivered to a processor and how fast the results can be received from the processor. Since instructions are also stored in memory, the architect must provide for concurrent demands on memory for data to process, instructions to execute, and input/output transfers between memory and the external world.

In this chapter we examine the use of *cache* and *virtual memory* to produce very efficient hierarchical memory systems. These systems are composed of a mix of memory devices that range in performance and cost. A well-designed memory system of this type tends to perform as if the entire memory were composed of the fastest devices in its structure, yet its cost tends to be dictated by slower, less expensive devices.

We explore the basic principles of the hierarchy here, but because the best possible memory design depends on workload and the available technology, we cannot give a concise formula for a good design. We do, however, present some powerful techniques for evaluating designs that will enable both the professional architect and the student to explore a range of memory designs with simple programs running on personal computers.

Why is memory so critical to performance? The major constraint imposed by high-speed memory in a von Neumann architecture is:

> A single memory module of conventional design can access no more than one word during each cycle of the memory clock.

The *bandwidth* of memory is the measure of the number of bits per second that can be accessed. If our memory system has a 100 ns cycle time and accesses 64 bits (8 bytes) per cycle, its bandwidth is 640 M-bits (80 M-bytes) per second.

If we absolutely must increase memory bandwidth to increase performance, then there are several choices available to the memory designer:

- Reduce the cycle time.
- Increase the word size of memory by accessing more bits per cycle.
- Replicate the memory modules and access two or more of them concurrently. (This is one way of increasing the word size of memory.)

The designer may also explore unconventional schemes, such as parallel-search memories, "intelligent" memories with internal sorting and searching capability, or hierarchical memories with a variety of speeds and functional capabilities. If an unconventional design proves to be an effective design, it will be incorporated in many computer systems, and eventually it will become conventional.

Advances in hardware technology have made available larger and faster memories at an almost unbelievable rate, and the trend is likely to continue through the 1990s. The designer can tap the new technology in a variety of ways, including brute-force techniques that have an inefficiency that would have been totally unacceptable in former years. For example, to increase memory bandwidth, a machine architect today can choose a very long word and wide bus, such as 256 bytes, even though there is a strong probability that many of the bytes accessed over the bus will never be used.

Inefficient techniques abound, and new technology may provide the means for using such techniques at acceptable cost. But efficient techniques are much more difficult to invent and analyze, and they will always have an advantage over the inefficient ones. Therefore, this chapter dwells on some efficient techniques that have proved to be useful in the last few years and presents new tools for evaluating these techniques.

2.1 Exploiting Program Characteristics

The basic building block of central memory is *random-access memory* (RAM). Figure 2.1 shows a diagram of the structure of a typical memory module. Note the two registers, ADDRESS and DATA. During a READ cycle, the memory accesses the item at the location given by the contents of ADDRESS and places a copy of the item in DATA. During a WRITE cycle, the memory also accesses the item as indicated by the contents of ADDRESS, but in this case the contents of DATA are copied to the location in memory.

The term *access* refers to the physical actions that occur in the memory module during a READ or WRITE cycle. What happens is that there is a logical path set-up between the selected location and DATA. The direction that data flows along this path depends on whether the operation is READ or WRITE, but in either case, to access a location the memory system uses the contents of the address register to enable or disable internal gates in such a way that for

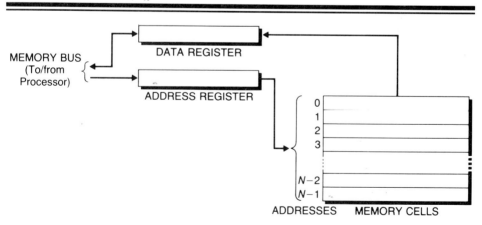

Fig. 2.1 The structure of a random-access memory (RAM).

each address value, exactly one location becomes logically connected to the DATA register.

The name *random access* conveys the idea that each access to any location in memory takes a fixed amount of time, independent of what sequence of accesses occur. Suppose, for example, a READ to Location 20 takes 10 ns, and the READ is followed by a WRITE to Location 347. For a random-access memory, the WRITE also takes 10 ns because all cycles are 10 ns, no matter what location is accessed.

Contrast this random-access behavior with *sequential access*. If a memory were organized as a shift-register or as a continuous magnetic tape, then access times would depend on the sequence of addresses issued to memory. An access to Location 11 immediately after an access to Location 10 would take, for example, 10 ns if this were the time required to access consecutive items. But, by this reasoning, an access to Location 17 that immediately follows an access to Location 10 would take 70 ns. To access Location 17 after accessing Location 10, the memory cycles through Locations 11 to 17, with each location requiring 10 ns to process. Access time is potentially very large in a sequential memory when items are far apart.

Obviously, there is a tremendous performance advantage for random-access memories over sequential-access memories, but the cost per bit of sequential-access memory is usually quite low compared to random-access memory.

The trade-off between cost and performance for these two types of memory is but one example of the design choices open to the computer architect. Suppose, for example, the architect can exploit the low cost of a sequential-access memory without necessarily incurring a performance penalty if the programs to be run on the computer system can be organized so that the bulk of their accesses is sequential. Then nonsequential accesses must be either negligible or executed inexpensively, perhaps by means of a small random-access memory.

If a particular site has a workload that does not directly use a sequential-access memory, then the users must convert their workload in order to capture the cost-performance benefit of the hypothetical sequential-access machine. The users may have to alter the applications programs by hand, or, better yet, they might produce a translator to alter the existing programs automatically.

A translator that minimizes access time may be quite feasible to write for this particular example, but in general there is no guarantee that program conversion will be successful, and the cost of conversion may be very high. Therefore, the decision to use a sequential memory in addition to random-access memory requires careful consideration of many related factors regarding how the software can make effective use of the new facilities. Consequently, the cost-benefits of the new architecture are less apparent to the user who must invest in a conversion with its cost, risk, and delay.

All advances, whether they are in device technology or architecture, result in the same considerations by the user community as the advances compete with existing technology for wide acceptance. If a new architecture is incompatible with existing technology, then its cost-performance benefits must be great enough and visible enough to motivate the users to convert to the new architecture. If a new architecture is compatible with existing technology to the extent that conversion can be done quickly and at low cost, it just has to be better than existing alternatives, not necessarily much better.

As we look at the history of virtual memory and cache memory, we can see how these concepts permitted systems to make use of rotating magnetic memory for bulk store while performing most execution from high-speed random-access memory. The success of the idea is due both to the cost-performance benefit and to the fact that it is immediately useful for all programs without forcing the programs to be rewritten.

The development of virtual memory and cache memory was stimulated by a need to use magnetic tape with purely sequential access as the storage medium for bulk data. In the 1950s, computers had small central memories (usually 128 K-bytes or less) and could not contain the larger programs and their associated data. So programmers were forced to partition their programs into separate overlays, each of which was small enough to fit into central memory. Program execution moved from overlay to overlay, with a memory load required each time one overlay reached a point at which it invoked a new overlay.

The partitioning process was tedious and error-prone, but necessary for programs that were otherwise too large to fit into memory. Loading overlays from magnetic tape was very time consuming, so programmers took extra care to assure that as few overlays as possible occurred during the execution of a program.

This crude way of managing large programs eventually revealed program characteristics that can easily be exploited to create very high-performance systems at relatively low cost. The cache memories and virtual-memory systems that are widely used today have been developed largely because of the observations of program behavior that revealed the strong tendency for memory accesses to be clustered in small regions of memory during any short period of time.

The historical development of this technique received a major boost at the University of Manchester in the course of the design of the Atlas computer [Kilburn *et al.* 1962] shown in Fig. 2.2. The approach used by this design team was called *one-level store* to indicate that programs viewed memory as made up of one level of homogenous devices, as if it were one large random-access memory. Actually, there were two levels in the memory hierarchy, a small random-access main memory with 16K words, and a much larger magnetic-drum memory, with 96K words, that held the bulk of the program and data.

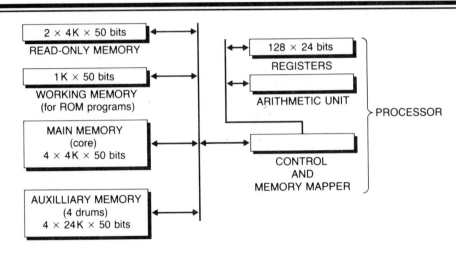

Fig. 2.2 The block diagram of the Atlas computer.

The user programmed the Atlas machine as if the size of memory were the size of drum memory. The Atlas had special hardware that treated memory as composed of individual pages of 512 words each and automatically loaded main memory with 32 pages of the program and data. If the Atlas requested an item from a page not resident in main memory, the requested page would be brought into main memory, and some other resident page would be written back to drum.

The Atlas used a "learning program" that attempted to retain the most useful pages in main memory. All of the swapping between drum and main memory was totally invisible to the user. The user did not have to specify when to bring data from drum to main memory or when to move it back again. The user had the convenience of programming with a large memory the size of the drum, whose apparent cycle time was closer to the cycle time of the central memory.

Because the Atlas made main memory appear to be much larger than it actually was, the name *virtual memory* was eventually applied to this general scheme, and the term *one-level store*, used by Kilburn *et al.*, is seldom used today. Drum memory on the Atlas had a long average latency of between 2 and 14 ms to obtain the first word of a page, and the sequential access to successive words in the page occurred at the rate of about 4 μs per word. The cycle time for a random access to main memory was about 2 μs per word.

As long as the required pages were resident in main memory, computations proceeded at maximum computation rate. A missing page caused a tremendous penalty in time, since access to an item in a missing page took about 500 times longer than access to the same item when it was resident in main memory.

In current terminology the attempt to access a missing page is called a *page fault*. It is clear that maintaining a very low rate of page faults is critical to the success of a virtual-memory system. As the page-fault rate increases, the apparent cycle time of memory grows much larger than the cycle time of the faster memory, and instead approaches the cycle time of the slower memory. Performance at high fault rates is disastrously low.

The characteristic that drove the invention of virtual memory on the Atlas machine is called *locality*. Program references tend to be locally clustered in time. That is, there is a strong tendency for future patterns of access to be similar to access patterns that occurred in the near past. If an instruction stream truly shows no sequential correlation so that the item accessed on any cycle is independent of the history of accesses, then for any given cycle, all items in the program are equally likely to be accessed. If this were the case, a small high-speed memory would be of marginal benefit. But if there is significant serial correlation, then the history of accesses can be used to predict the accesses that will occur in the future. With such predictions, the computer system can move pages between low- and high-speed memory in a way that tends to reduce faults.

There are really two questions here:

1. Is there a significant sequential correlation in typical streams of address references?

2. If there is a serial correlation, how can it be exploited?

The first question has been studied in depth. The answers obtained over a broad class of programs running on almost every possible machine consistently report a very strong sequential correlation. The findings suggest that at any given moment of time, the probability distribution for what might be referenced next looks something like the graph shown in Fig. 2.3. This figure shows the probability of access as a function of memory address (in virtual memory). Note that a few regions are highly probable, a few other regions have a low-to-moderate probability, and the remainder of the address space is very unlikely to be accessed in the near future. Note also that the regions with the highest probability of access are scattered throughout virtual memory.

One region that has a high probability is the one that contains the present program counter because it is likely to execute the next instruction in sequence. Other regions contain active data, the instructions for subroutines that might be entered, and the return point to a subroutine that called the presently executing subroutine. If the executing program were written in a block-structured language such as Pascal, then the present stack frame for

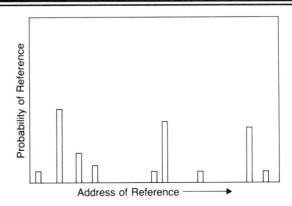

Fig. 2.3 The instantaneous value of the probability of a reference as a function of the address of the reference.

local variables and parameters is another area with a high probability of access.

Another possible model for the probability distribution is shown in Fig. 2.4. In this model, the probability of access falls off with the distance from the currently executing instruction, where distance is defined to be the absolute difference of two memory addresses. This model is not a good characterization of the characteristics of programs that execute on the machines most commonly used today, but it too displays sequential correlation.

This type of correlation is easily exploited because the computer system would attempt to retain in main memory those items whose addresses are closest to the address of the executing instruction. Moreover, this model suggests that it is a good idea to make pages fairly large because once an item on a page is referenced, the probability is very high that other items on the same page will be referenced.

Early designs of virtual-memory systems occasionally made the assumption that memory references were characterized better by Fig. 2.4 than by Fig. 2.3, with the result that these systems tended to use too large a page size and had more traffic between low- and high-speed memory than was necessary. The large page size resulted in many words being transferred to high-speed memory that were never accessed while resident in high-speed memory. That portion of high-speed memory would have been better used for other regions of memory, and a small page size would have made more high-speed memory available.

Although Fig. 2.3 is a more accurate characterization of streams of address

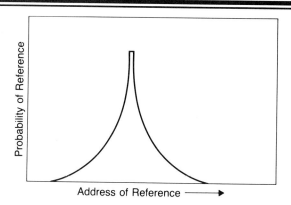

Fig. 2.4 A possible, but unrealistic, model of address-reference probability.

references than is Fig. 2.4, there is always the possibility that a designer can bias the statistics of accesses through some unusual characteristics of a design. For example, compilers and loaders may attempt to place subroutines together on the same page if there is evidence that the subroutines work together in some way. Or through a combination of instruction-set design and compiler design, it may be possible to reduce branches to far away regions.

Machines with vector instructions may behave more nearly like Fig. 2.4 than Fig. 2.3. Nevertheless, no matter what the details of the correlation are, there is overwhelming evidence that streams of address references exhibit strong sequential correlation. Hence there is an opportunity to exploit this correlation through schemes such as the one-level store of Atlas.

In the next two sections we examine cache memory and then virtual memory as we seek ways to reduce the memory bottleneck.

2.2 Cache Memory

2.2.1 Basic Cache Structure

Two years after the publication of the paper that described the Atlas one-level store, there appeared a brief article by Wilkes [1965] that describes an evolution of this idea to a different level of the memory hierarchy. Wilkes describes a system that contains two kinds of main memory. One kind is conventional; the other is a high-speed unconventional memory that Wilkes calls a *slave memory*. Present terminology calls such memories *cache memories*.

The idea of cache memories is similar to virtual memory in that some active portion of a low-speed memory is stored in duplicate in a higher-speed cache memory. When a memory request is generated, the request is first presented to the cache memory, and if the cache cannot respond, the request is then presented to main memory.

The difference between cache and virtual memory is a matter of implementation; the two notions are conceptually the same because they both rely on the correlation properties observed in sequences of address references.

Cache implementations are totally different from virtual memory implementations because of the speed requirements of cache. If we assume that cache memory has an access time of one machine cycle, then main memory typically has an access time anywhere from 4 to 20 times longer, not 500 times longer, which we cited previously for the delay due to page faults.

Earlier we defined a *page fault* to be a reference to a page in virtual memory that is not resident in main memory. The corresponding concept for cache memories is an access to an item that is not resident in cache, but is resident in main memory. This is called a *cache miss* to distinguish it from a page fault.

For cache misses, the fast memory is cache and the slow memory is main memory. For page faults the fast memory is main memory, and the slow memory is auxiliary memory, the next level of the memory hierarchy. In many virtual-memory systems of the 1980s and 1990s, auxiliary memory is high-speed disk, but in the higher performance systems, auxiliary memory is itself a buffer memory for disk memory at the next level of the memory hierarchy. Regardless of the implementation of auxiliary memory, its access time is longer, possibly much longer, than the access time to main memory. Although misses are still rather costly for cache-based systems, they are not nearly as costly as page faults are, and we can afford to sustain cache misses more frequently than we can sustain page faults.

The time available for updating the status of a cache during a cache miss is minuscule compared to the time available during a page fault. Consequently, caches are controlled by hardware algorithms that can process cache misses automatically within the constraints dictated by the time available during a cache miss.

In the following material we describe in detail the operation of a cache and then consider practical cache designs. Then we examine efficient ways to use traces of programs to evaluate different designs.

Figure 2.5 shows the structure of a typical cache memory. Each reference to a cell in memory is presented to the cache. The cache searches its directory of address tags shown in the figure to see if the item is in the cache. If the item is not in the cache, a miss occurs. In the figure, the reference to address 01173 matches the tag 0117X, where the X designates any octal digit from 0 to 7. Since there is a match, the item sought is in the cache. The data associated with tag 0117X have addresses 01170 through 01177, so the access must be made to the fourth item, whose address is 01173. This datum, which has the

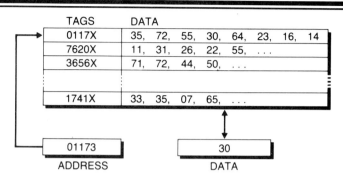

TAGS   DATA

TAGS	DATA
0117X	35, 72, 55, 30, 64, 23, 16, 14
7620X	11, 31, 26, 22, 55, . . .
3656X	71, 72, 44, 50, . . .
1741X	33, 35, 07, 65, . . .

01173	30
ADDRESS	DATA

Fig. 2.5 A cache-memory reference. The tag 0117X matches address 01173, so the cache returns the item in the position $X = 3$ of the matched line.

value 30, is copied to the data register of the cache. A reference to address 01163 produces a miss for the tags shown since no tag matches this address.

For READ operations that cause a cache miss, the item is retrieved from main memory and copied into the cache. During the short period available before the main-memory operation is complete, some other item in cache is removed from the cache to make room for the new item.

The cache-replacement decision is critical; a good replacement algorithm can yield somewhat higher performance than can a bad replacement algorithm. The effective cycle-time of a cache memory is the average of cache-memory cycle time and main-memory cycle time, where the probabilities in the averaging process are the probabilities of hits and misses.

If we consider only READ operations, then a formula for the average cycle-time is:

$$t_{\text{eff}} = t_{\text{cache}} + (1 - h)t_{\text{main}} \tag{2.1}$$

where h is the probability of a cache hit (sometimes called the *hit ratio*), and the time t_{cache} and t_{main} are the respective cycle times of cache and main memory. The quantity $(1 - h)$, which is the probability of a miss, is known as the *miss ratio*.

If main memory is 10 times slower than cache, then a decrease in the hit ratio from 0.99 to 0.98 (roughly 1 percent fewer hits) results in an increase in t_{eff} of roughly 10 percent. Thus small changes in hit ratio are amplified by the ratio of main-memory cycle time to cache-memory cycle time, and the resulting average cycle time is very sensitive to small changes in the hit ratio.

A 10-percent decrease in the hit ratio from 0.99 to 0.89 almost doubles the effective cycle time and halves net performance when the cycle-time ratio is

10. If the cycle-time ratio is 20, that same 10-percent decrease in hit ratio increases the effective cycle time by more than a factor of 2.5. It is clear that we must have as high a hit ratio as possible, and that under many circumstances techniques that result in marginal improvements of the hit ratio, such as just 1 or 2 percent, may yield substantial performance improvement.

In Fig. 2.5, we show an item in the cache surrounded by nearby items, all of which are moved into and out of the cache together. This group of cache data corresponds to the memory page for virtual-memory systems. For cache memories, we call such a group of data a *line* of the cache, although some papers refer to this group as a *block* of the cache. The smallest a line can possibly be is a single addressable item, which is anywhere from 1 byte to 4 bytes for the most popular computer systems. However, if items are as small as possible, then the cache directory becomes larger because there is a cache directory entry for each item in the cache. Doubling the size of a cache line while holding the number of bytes in the cache fixed reduces the size of the directory by a factor of 2 because two items in the same line share the same directory entry.

The cache in Fig. 2.5 requires the directory to behave *associatively*, that is, the cache directory retrieves information by key rather than by address. To determine if a candidate address is in the cache, the directory uses the tag bits from the candidate address as a key and compares this key to all tags now in the cache directory. To maintain high speed, this operation must be done as quickly as possible, which should be within one machine cycle.

A parallel memory that has the search capability just described is called an *associative memory*. An associative memory, however, has a longer cycle than a random-access memory built from identical technology. This is strictly a consequence of the need to propagate signals through a larger number of gates in the associative memory than in a random-access memory of equal size. If we attempt to speed up the associative memory by adding more gates, the effect generally is to introduce additional delays that partially offset the gains attributable to the additional hardware. So, for practical reasons, the associative memory is less attractive than is an implementation that uses ordinary random-access memory technology.

2.2.2 Cache Design

Figure 2.6 shows a typical implementation of a cache memory. This system is called *set associative* because the cache is partitioned into distinct sets of lines, and each set contains a small fixed number of lines. For machines built at the beginning of the 1990s, the number of lines per set is as few as one and as many as 16, with four lines per set shown in Fig. 2.6.

In this scheme, each address reference is mapped to a particular set by means of a simple operation on the address. If the address is in the cache, then it is stored as one of the lines in the set. Therefore, the cache need not be searched in its entirety. Only the set to which the address is mapped needs to

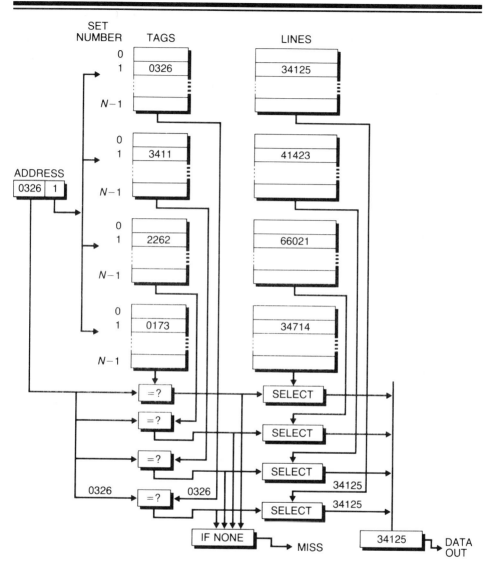

Fig. 2.6 The structure of a four-way set-associative cache with N sets.

be searched. Figure 2.6 shows an address mapped to Set 1. The cache access proceeds by reading simultaneously all four directory entries. Also, the data lines in the set are read concurrently so they will be available at the end of the READ cycle. If a cache line is larger in size than the size of the data bus to the processor, then only the portions of a cache line that will be sent to the processor are read from the cache.

At the end of the READ operation, all four directory entries are compared to the address reference. If a match is found, then the corresponding data line of the cache is gated to the cache output-data buffer, and from there it is transmitted to the processor.

The timing of the cache activity is such that all reads from the memory occur as early as possible to allow maximum time for the comparison to take place. At least three of the four items accessed, and possibly all four, are discarded at the end of the cycle. Which line to use, if any, is decided late in the cache cycle, but at that time the data required have reached high-speed registers, so the data can be gated to the processor very quickly after the cache comparison-logic discovers a match.

Now let us reexamine Fig. 2.6 to see which parameters describe the cache design. This cache has:

1. L bytes per line;
2. K lines per set; and
3. N sets.

The total number of bytes in the cache is the product LKN. A cache in which the directory search covers all lines in the cache is said to be *fully associative*. In this case, $N = 1$, and the number of bytes in the cache is the product LK. For reasons mentioned earlier, fully associative caches are less attractive to build than are set-associative caches. The logic to compare two, four, or eight directory entries concurrently can be made sufficiently fast that the comparison and subsequent line selection can be completed without a significant impact on the machine cycle-time. But as the number of entries to compare increases to 16, 32, and above, cycle time starts to climb and the advantage of the larger set associativity is negated by the longer cycle time.

At the other end of the spectrum is the case for which $K = 1$, that is, the case in which there is only one line per set. Here, for any given candidate address, there is only one line in the cache that may contain the address reference. The cache in this case consists of one ordinary random-access memory with a simple comparator for the directory check. This special case is called *direct mapping* because address references map directly to a unique place in the cache.

There are several questions regarding cache design that are suggested by Fig. 2.6. The figure shows a possible mechanism for mapping address references into cache references.

Figure 2.7 provides more detail on this mapping. The address shown in this figure is a physical address M bits long that will be sent to main memory if the item is not in the cache. In this case, we assume that each byte in memory has a unique address. Since all L bytes within one line are present or absent as a

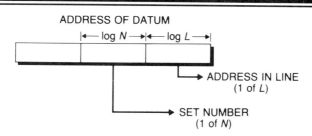

Fig. 2.7 Address partitioning for a cache search.

group, to determine if that line is present, we must strip off the least significant $\log_2 L$ bits of the address to prepare to interrogate the cache. The remaining address bits are common to all members of a single cache line, and these are the bits that we must check when looking for a hit.

The next facet of the mapping operation is to determine which of N sets to interrogate. We must find some way of mapping the remaining address bits into $\log_2 N$ bits, which are then used to select among N different sets in the cache directory. The method used most frequently is to use the least significant $\log_2 N$ bits of the remaining address bits, which has the effect of scattering lines with successive addresses to successive sets of the cache. This tends to randomize address references through the cache and reduce clustering by mapping contiguous active regions in main memory across many sets of the cache, thereby making for the best use of the cache.

Figure 2.7 shows the low-order $\log_2 L$ bits of the address reference being stripped away to account for the number of bytes per line, and then shows the next low-order $\log_2 N$ bits being used as the address for access to a conventional random-access memory. From this memory, we read all K tags simultaneously. Also, the required data from the lines in the cache are read from random-access memories that hold the cache data.

The latter memories use the $\log_2 N$ bits together with some of the $\log_2 L$ bits to access specific regions within a line in case the processor cannot accept the entire cache line. Portions of all K lines in a set are accessed, and the greater the number of bits from the L field used to address the lines, the smaller will be the size of the data fields read from memory.

In making the directory comparison, note that it is necessary to store only the leading bits of the address reference, $M - \log_2 N - \log_2 L$ bits in this case. All lines stored in a set have the same values for the set number, so it is not necessary to store the $\log_2 N$ bits that identify the set number.

In Fig. 2.6, the set number 1 is stripped from the address 03261 to create a

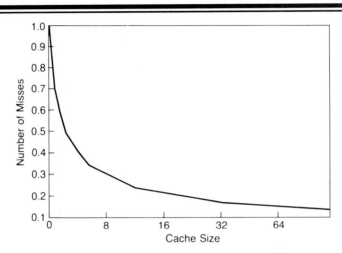

Fig. 2.8 Cache performance—the number of misses versus cache size.

tag of 0326 for comparisons. The first tag shown in the same set has a value 0173, so the corresponding memory address is 01731.

The parameters mentioned thus far give us at least three degrees of freedom in designing a cache, and there are more choices yet to be discussed. Let us reflect a moment on the choices at hand to see what trade-offs are available and what guidance we have to complete our design.

Figure 2.8 shows the general form of the curves that describe cache behavior as a function of some single parameter choice. The x-axis plots caches of increasing size, but the curve does not indicate the structure of the successively larger caches. For the moment it is not important which of the parameters L, K, or N increases in this figure. The y-axis plots the relative number of misses with the number of misses, for a cache of size 0 normalized to unity. Note that the curve drops sharply at first and then bends and drops less steeply as the cache size increases.

Most of the improvement in this graph is obtained by the initial small changes in X. As X increases beyond the knee of the curve, relatively little additional benefit is obtained. Hence, a good design point is a value of X around the knee of the curve.

One problem that cache designers face is that the data available are not nearly as clean as the data in Fig. 2.8. The data are often at best sketchy and are highly dependent on the method in which they were gathered. So the designer has to make critical choices using a combination of hunches, skill, and experience to supplement the meager information at hand.

Good engineering sometimes requires a small degree of overdesign and inefficiency to protect against unusual cases. For the data in Fig. 2.8, the smallest cache that operates well is a cache of size 8 (relative misses = 0.34) or possibly size 16 (relative misses = 0.24). A cache of size 32 (relative misses = 0.17) would be difficult to justify because the performance change is small considering that the cost of cache is doubled to obtain this change. Nevertheless, a reasonable cache design may well incorporate a cache of size 32 or even size 64 as an intentional strategy to assure a low number of misses over a wide range of workloads. In this case, the designer is protecting against workloads whose characteristics are quite different from those in Fig. 2.8.

How can we be sure that all workloads are accurately modeled by Fig. 2.8? In fact, we cannot. Some workloads might have a much shallower slope and exhibit a knee at larger values of cache size. If we design a cache that just barely runs a workload of the type characterized in Fig. 2.8 at an acceptable performance, that cache may deliver unacceptably poor performance for more stringent workloads. If we overdesign for the workload in Fig. 2.8, we can still run acceptably well on some workloads that demand larger caches.

The designer has to obtain the most useful performance data possible and then use good judgment to estimate the characteristics of other important types of workloads that are not reflected in the data available to decide how much the architecture should be overdesigned. The idea is to examine the cost of the excess capacity against the possibility that the capacity will be necessary and beneficial. Decisions of this type are usually driven by cost considerations because the cost has a major impact on the competitive marketing of the machine, whereas the value of the excess capacity is more difficult to assess if it does not contribute identifiably to higher performance on normal workloads.

Returning to the problem of cache design, how can we develop data that will enable us to select a cache size as well as the values of the cache-structure parameters K, L, and N? To answer this question, we need to develop data, as shown in Fig. 2.8, that plot cache misses against cache size.

Because a cache of a given size may be organized in various ways through different choices for K, L, and N, we suggest that K and L be fixed and N varied when this study is conducted. That is, the set associativity and the line size should be fixed while the number of sets is varied. What is typically observed is that the number of misses decreases, as shown in Fig. 2.8, and the knee of the curve will be at a point that is dependent on the particular processor and the workload.

Extensive data on the subject has appeared in the literature. Specifically, A. Smith [1982, 1985, 1987] has excellent collections of typical results. Empirical observations of typical programs turned up a simple rule of thumb: each doubling of the size of the cache reduces misses by roughly 30 percent. Figure 2.8 shows this characteristic and demonstrates what is often observed in real systems.

The 30-percent rule is useful for rough estimates, but should not be used when accurate data are needed. Specific programs and processors do not obey this rule. The reader should establish a similar formula when designing a cache for a particular architecture and workload and use the new formula to evaluate various cache designs.

Given a total size of cache, how should the cache be organized? We recommend choosing line size L next and then the set associativity factor K, although they could be chosen in the opposite order. To find the cache performance as a function of line size, fix the parameter K to a value that is likely to be its final value.

From experience with other cache designs, we intuitively know that the set associativity will be a small number, and it will probably not be 1. So we set $K = 2$ and examine cache behavior as a function of line size. Note that we have fixed the total size of cache, so that as line size doubles, we must reduce N, the number of sets, by a factor of 2 to keep the product LKN constant.

The best performance is obtained with $L = 1$ because each individual address is cached independently. But in this case, the directory may be enormous and rather costly. When L is maximum, $N = 1$, and there is but a single set in the cache. This has the worst performance, but it is the least expensive to build.

By plotting L along the x-axis in Fig. 2.8, with misses on the y-axis, we obtain the knee of the curve for some value of L. Note that to obtain the shape of the curve shown in the figure, fix N and let L increase. Then produce a family of curves, each for a different value of N.

Since the size of the directory depends on the value of L, the selected value of L may be very small and require too large a directory to be practical. Consequently, it may be necessary to increase L while reducing N to obtain a practical directory size. The cost of this change is greater bus traffic per miss.

The final step is to choose the set-associativity factor K. This too can be accomplished by plotting a curve similar to the one in Fig. 2.8. In this case we perform cache analyses that hold the line size L and number of sets N fixed while varying set associativity K. The resulting curve should have the shape of the curve in Fig. 2.8 when K is plotted along the x-axis, increasing to the right, and with misses plotted on the y-axis.

If the study suggests that a better choice for K is 8 instead of 2, then we should restudy the effect of line size on performance, but use the new value of K in place of $K = 2$.

Eventually we can find a collection of values for $K, L,$ and N that represent a satisfactory trade-off between cost and performance. Generally speaking, we obtain better performance as we increase the absolute size of cache. We estimate that performance by estimating the average memory-cycle time

$$t_{\text{eff}} = t_{\text{cache}} + (1 - h)t_{\text{main}} \qquad (2.2)$$

where h is the hit-ratio for the given cache. Then we factor in the effect of technology. How much does that extra performance cost? If we are willing to pay for the performance, then we use larger caches. If the cost is very high—too high for the performance gained—then we use a smaller cache.

The cache-parameter values used in commercial systems have tended to increase in time as technology has made it possible to build larger caches at reasonable expense. High-performance minicomputers were produced with caches as small as 2 K-bytes at the start of the 1970s and moved to larger caches that reached 8 K-bytes in one decade and 256 K-bytes in two decades. In that same timeframe, cache memories for high-end machines evolved from 16 K-bytes to 64 K-bytes to 1 M-bytes.

Although we expect the trend toward larger caches to continue, it is certainly not clear that they will increase in size in the future at the same rate as they have increased in the past. As main memory capacity increases from 10^7 bytes to 10^8 and 10^9 bytes, there is a strong possibility that cache memory need not grow linearly with main memory. Instead, it may grow as some slowly growing function that reflects the growth of the active areas of memory as a fraction of the total size of memory. In fact, several manufacturers such as Amdahl and Hitachi have produced machines with two levels of cache memory, with the first level very fast, very expensive, and relatively small, and the second-level cache much less expensive, but still costly compared to main memory.

The second-level cache may be the architectural feature that grows larger with new generations of device technology. The first-level cache captures most of the hits. As cache size grows and the performance curve bends around a knee, the additional hits obtained are rather infrequent. These should be fielded in the second-level cache, whose cost is relatively low compared to first-level cache, but whose performance is much better than main memory.

Two levels of cache further complicate the design picture. Now we have to consider three different memory costs and two different cache structures. The design possibilities are very rich, but rather overwhelming in their number, making thorough analysis of alternative designs very costly to perform. The next two sections treat the efficient use of address traces for exploring the design space.

2.2.3 Cache Analysis: Trace Generation and Trace Length

In the previous section we glibly assumed that the reader can construct curves such as those in Fig. 2.8 from data on hand. This is hardly the case. Cache-analysis input data usually consist of extremely lengthy address-reference sequences obtained through great effort. The fastest way to obtain such information is through special hardware attached to an operational machine. The special hardware monitors memory requests and logs each individual reference on a tape for later use by a cache-evaluation program.

Although this method is very fast, if the operational machine happens to be a very high-performance machine, then the specialized hardware must run several times faster than the high-performance machine to keep up with it. Such hardware monitors are costly, and are difficult or impossible to build for the very fastest machines. They are quite useful, however, for studies involving slower machines.

By far the most popular means for generating an address-reference stream for studying cache performance is the machine simulator. This is a program that simulates the instruction execution of a computer under study. The input to the simulator is a typical workload. As each instruction is executed by the simulator, the simulator writes to an external file the sequence of address references generated during the simulation.

Some processor architectures have the capability of trapping to the operating system after the execution of each instruction. On such architectures, simulation can be done very efficiently because each instruction is executed at full machine speed. Software in the operating system is required only to determine what addresses were generated by the instruction and to transmit these addresses to the output file.

Since we presume that cache design is to be done by examining the performance of various design alternatives on address traces, we have to be sure that the address trace is representative and does not have particular biases that could produce misleading evaluations. Actually there are three distinct problems.

1. The workload on the trace may not be representative of the actual workload for which the machine is to be used;
2. The initialization transient during which the cache is filled with relevant data may grossly affect the evaluation; and
3. The trace may be too short to obtain an accurate measure of the miss ratio.

The first problem is particularly nasty. Because simulations run 1000 to 100,000 times slower than real time, it is not feasible to create traces that cover long periods of real time. Typical simulations cover hundreds of milliseconds at most, which raises a question about the fidelity with which the simulation captures the characteristics of the workload.

High-performance machines specialized to particular applications typically spend the bulk of their time in predictable ways, which should account for the majority of an address trace for such machines. But a representative fraction of the address trace should also be devoted to other activities, such as input/output and loop initialization.

General-purpose machines present a much more difficult problem because their workloads are not easily characterized. Moreover, any user may choose to dedicate a computer to an unusual function whose characteristics are vastly different from normal uses of the same computer. So the cache designer can at best evaluate a cache for some good estimate of the workload. Individual users may experience performance that deviates from the expected performance if their workload has dramatically different characteristics from the workload used for cache design.

Various models of address references have been postulated with the idea that the models can be used in place of traces for cache evaluation. Trivedi [1982, pp. 305–308], for example, describes a statistical model that captures the notion of locality of references in a way that is useful for designing an operating system for a virtual-memory system. This model in turn is a refinement of the models of Coffman and Denning [1973, pp. 275–278]; Denning, Savage, and Spirn [1972]; Shemer and Gupta [1969]; and Shemer and Shippey [1966]. Later in this section we describe a useful model that captures the 30-percent rule depicted in Fig. 2.8, and is due to Thiebaut [1989] with refinements by Singh, Stone, and Thiebaut [1988].

Such models give insight into the characteristics of address-reference strings, but because cache design is so critical and so much is at stake, cache designs have to be validated by testing them on the address references produced by a real workload when this is possible. So the use of actual address traces for evaluating cache designs will continue to be the primary tool for cache analysis. For large caches, the length of traces required to yield accurate data becomes prohibitive, and models of program behavior become an acceptable alternative. When designing caches for machines with new instruction sets, workloads do not exist, so that a combination of analytical models and data from caches for similar architectures may be required.

Apart from the fidelity of a trace in capturing workload behavior there are two problems related to the accuracy of the results obtained for a particular trace. The first problem is that data are corrupted by an initialization transient, but fortunately the corrupted data can be removed as indicated below. The second problem is more serious. The trace has to be long enough to capture enough misses to produce an accurate measure of the miss ratio. Unfortunately, the trace length required grows roughly as the cache size raised to the 1.5 power. For each quadrupling of cache size, the trace length increases by roughly a factor of 8. For 2 M-byte caches, trace lengths required for moderate precision can exceed 100 million references.

When miss ratios are so small that extremely long traces are required to measure them, they are also relatively unimportant factors in the overall performance model of a machine, and other factors tend to be more important. The other factors may be cache related, and may include the bus traffic generated by processor WRITEs to the cache, as well as traffic to and from the cache due to input/output and interaction with other processors in a multiprocessor system. These other factors are often measured by trace simulation in much the same way that hit ratios are measured, but the traces need not be as long because the events of interest occur more frequently. In any case, the cache designer can rely heavily on detailed trace information in order to evaluate performance as a function of cache size and structure, but the designer should rely on the techniques below to remove bias in the data and to determine what confidence should be placed on the interpretation of the data.

The problem of cache initialization is that during a cache simulation, the first reference to each line in the cache will generate a miss, whereas in a real environment the corresponding reference may have been a hit because in the real environment the cache would have been holding a recently used item. The cache simulator cannot preload the environment so that it cannot generate a hit where the actual cache it simulates produces a hit.

One may argue that the beginning of a cache simulation is something like the behavior of the real computer at a context swap. In that situation a new process takes control and generates cache misses until it loads itself into the cache. In this way the cache simulator captures not only the steady-state effect but the cache-reload transient as well. The problem is that the two effects are combined in a fashion determined by the total length of the trace. This is rather arbitrary, and may not reflect the true ratio of transient reload effects to steady-state effects. Moreover, when caches of different sizes are simulated with a trace of fixed length, the larger caches use a larger portion of the trace to initialize the state of the cache, and thus the transient contributes a greater proportion of the simulated miss ratio for the larger caches than for the smaller caches. To the extent that the transient effect is a distortion of reality, the larger caches suffer a larger distortion in their simulated data. As we shall see in this section, the distortion is so bad on large caches that most published data on simulated miss ratios of large caches reports effects almost entirely due to the initialization transient and the steady-state miss ratio is totally lost in the transient.

We recommend an approach that measures the steady-state miss ratio in isolation, and then factors in the reload transient by a means described later in this chapter. To do so, it is essential to remove the bias introduced by misses attributed to the cache initialization. Such misses are quite easy to recognize and can be factored out with a minimum of effort.

The cache-simulator program can easily be modified to record which misses are true misses and which are artifacts of the initial state of the cache. Simply initialize the cache with address tags that are illegal. Since address tags of a physical cache are several bits shorter than a full address, and since a cache-simulator program can manipulate data as wide as a full address, we can write the cache simulator to store address tags that are wider than actual tags. Consequently, we can initialize the values of address tags to some illegal value, for example, by setting the sign bit, if we know that while simulating the cache no valid tag can be generated with a sign bit set.

The value of initializing tags in this way is that we can examine the address tag of each line that is removed from the cache. If the tag is invalid, then the line removed is one that was placed there during cache initialization, and in a real environment it might have produced a hit.

Now that we can recognize a miss due to cache initialization, what action should we take? Focus attention on any one of the N sets in the cache. The addresses that can be stored in this set are disjoint from the remainder of the addresses. In essence, this set is a small cache that operates on $1/N$th of the address space of the computer. If the cache is direct mapped ($K = 1$), the cache contains one entry. The first reference to this set produces a miss due to initialization. If we simply ignore the first reference, then this set is properly initialized for subsequent simulation. That is, we do not count the first reference, a miss, to a set. The trace length is effectively shortened by one address per set referenced. (If our intent is to measure the transient together with the steady-state miss ratio, then we should record both the reference and the miss.)

Thus when simulating a direct mapped cache with N sets, when the initialization transient is factored out, the trace length is reduced by N references, and N misses are removed (assuming that all N sets are touched during the trace). The impact on total trace length is negligible, but the miss ratio may be greatly affected, depending on how many additional misses are on the remainder of the trace.

As an example of how initialization misses can dominate steady-state misses, we draw data from a study by J. E. Smith and J. R. Goodman [1985]. Smith and Goodman study a model in which the cache-reload transient is present and can impact performance. Their goal is to measure the impact of that transient, and their experiment indeed produced a large reload transient. For example, their Table 1 gives a hit ratio of 0.994 for an 8 K-byte direct-mapped cache with a line size of 16. The trace length used for this simulation is 100,000. This cache has 512 lines and there are 600 misses recorded for this trace. Although we do not know how many of these 600 misses are due to cache-initialization misses, at one extreme all 512 lines in the cache could have suffered one initialization miss. In this extreme case, the miss ratio reported would be produced by 512 initialization misses and 88 steady-state misses. Their hit-ratio data for 2K-line cache structures with 4-byte line size approaches the asymptote of 0.985, which is about 1500 misses per 100,000 references or about 0.75 misses per line, which is not enough to initialize the full cache. If the cache simulations did not specifically remove the initialization misses, then the reported data on the large caches are due largely to the initialization of the cache rather than to the steady-state misses. For the smaller caches, the initialization effects are much less dominant in the data. It is clear that for their parameters the treatment of initialization data can make very large changes in the relative size of the measured miss ratio, and this is consistent with their conclusions regarding the effect of the cache-reload transient. Had their traces been longer, their miss ratios for the 8 K-byte caches would be lower to the extent that the initialization effect becomes small relative to the remainder of the trace.

We have argued that the initialization of direct-mapped caches can be treated very simply with minimal shortening of the trace lengths. Set-associative caches can be treated equally easily, but the effect is to shorten the trace length more dramatically than for direct-mapped caches. When creating traces, the shortening phenomenon caused by cache initialization has to be considered, and thus requires the trace lengths to be somewhat longer than the length estimates produced by statistical considerations. For set-associative caches, the rule is to treat each of the N sets independently. After K misses are recorded to one set of a K-way associative cache, the statistics for that set can be recorded. Until that point, no statistics on that set are kept. The reason for this rule is that until the set has been fully initialized, the set is acting as if were smaller than its true size. For example, after one miss is recorded in a four-way set, one line holds a valid datum and the other three hold uninitialized data. At this point in the simulation, the effect of having only one initialized entry in the set is the same as if the set were one-way associative. It experiences a miss somewhat sooner than expected for a four-way cache. If the references were recorded at this point for that cache, the next three misses to the set produce a higher than average miss ratio and influence the final data of the simulation. Consequently, all references to that set should be ignored until the set is fully initialized, and then the recording can begin for that set. This notion first appeared in Laha, Patel, and Iyer [1988] where they introduce the term *primed set* for a set that has its initial contents purged.

A variety of techniques for dealing with the initialization transient have been reported in the literature. Some researchers "warm" the cache by running a fixed number of references through it. This technique works to the extent that it removes the transient. However, it may not remove all of the transient, or even may remove very little, depending on the size and structure of the cache. Moreover, if the length of the trace for initialization is fixed for all caches rather than dependent on the cache structure, then as a variety of structures are simulated, the transient effects will contribute differently to different cache structures, and the data obtained will not be comparable across the various caches. To be absolutely certain that the transient is absent and to use the fewest possible references for initialization, we recommend beginning a simulation on each distinct set when the set is fully initialized.

The next question is how long should a trace be? We cannot give a precise answer because the statistical behavior of cache misses is not well understood. But we can model the cache misses by a different, but understood process that enables us to obtain a length estimate. This length estimate is a lower bound on what is required for the cache-miss process. At this writing, we do not know how much longer than the lower bound the traces should be. The lower bound is very long for large caches, which casts doubt on the practicality of producing statistically accurate measures of miss ratios of large caches.

To obtain a bound on trace length, we assume that the cache-miss process is a Bernoulli process. That is, each address reference has a probability h of being a hit and $m = 1 - h$ of being a miss. Each reference is generated independently in time. This is equivalent to flipping a coin whose probability of coming up tails is m. We know that the independence assumption is false for the process that produces cache misses. Misses tend to cluster in time and occur in bursts rather than as predicted by a Bernoulli process. To measure the average of clustered references over long periods of time requires more observations than the measurement of the average of statistically independent references. Below we use the independence assumption to produce trace lengths, but we recognize that the lengths produced are only lower bounds on the actual lengths required.

Let a trace contain T references. Then the mean number of misses, M, is mT and the variance in M is $mTh = Mh$. The estimate of the miss ratio is M/T and the variance in the estimate is $Mh/T^2 = mh/T$. This is true because given a random variable X with variance V, the variance of the random variable cX, for constant c is c^2V. The true miss ratio of the underlying process is not necessarily equal to the estimate, but it lies close to the estimate. In fact, the standard deviation, which is the square root of the variance, gives us an estimate of how far away the true mean lies from the observed mean. For Bernoulli processes, we know with over 95 percent confidence that the true mean lies within two standard deviations of the observed mean [cf., Brunk, 1960]. To obtain the 95 percent confidence interval for small miss ratios, we can safely approximate the hit ratio h by 1. This yields

$$\text{True mean miss-ratio} \cong m \pm 2\sqrt{\frac{m}{T}} \qquad (2.3)$$

As an example, let the miss ratio be on the order of 1 percent, and find the size of T that produces a confidence interval of 20 percent of the miss ratio. The standard deviation term is $2\sqrt{m/T}$ and we require this to be less than 0.002. Equivalently, we require T to be greater than 10,000 for $m = 0.01$. Note that we bound the relative size of the confidence interval about the mean by forcing the standard deviation to be a fixed percentage of the mean, say β times the mean. To achieve this bound we increase the length of the trace T until twice the standard deviation decreases to that percentage of the mean. For a specified β, the confidence interval is within two standard deviations of the measured mean when $2 \leq \beta \sqrt{(mT)}$. Since this inequality involves the product of m and T, for a fixed value of β, T grows inversely with m. As the hit ratio falls away from unity, the approximation used here for the variance becomes inaccurate, and it becomes necessary to use the factor h in the variance expression in order to improve accuracy. In terms of M, the number of misses observed, a little manipulation of the formulas shows that $M \geq 4/\beta^2$. To double the relative precision of an estimate by reducing β by a factor of 2, the number of misses observed must quadruple.

This calculation suggests that by observing as few as 10,000 references, the calculated values of miss ratios lie within 20 percent of the actual values. This assumes all of the references lie in a single set. What happens if those references are distributed across N sets? For the Bernoulli process, the variance per set increases by a factor of N when the number of observations per set is reduced by a factor of N, but the average of N independent observations across the N different sets decreases the variance by a factor of N, so that there is no net change in the size of the confidence interval.

Unfortunately, the cache-miss process has highly clustered references as reported by Voldman *et al.* [1983]. The activity across N sets has very high correlation, and thus the distribution of references across N sets does not reduce the variance in the estimated variance as predicted. When one set experiences misses, many sets experience misses. When a reference stream produces a relatively long miss-free period, all of the sets see a proportion of that long miss-free period. If the correlation across sets is near unity, then observations of the activity in N sets produces very little additional accuracy than the observation of a single set.

More specifically, assume that the variance in the number of misses per set is V, for each set, and that the correlation coefficient between any pair of sets is ρ. Then for N sets, the variance in the average number of misses per set is equal to $(V/N)(1 + (N - 1)\rho)$. When the correlation coefficient is zero, N observations reduce the variance by a factor of N and the standard deviation by a factor of $\sqrt{N}$. When the correlation coefficient is unity, the variance in the observed mean for N observations is the same as the variance in a single observation, so that the additional observations do not reduce the confidence interval.

Because of the potential for high correlation of activity among different sets, it is essential to record enough misses per set to obtain reasonably tight confidence intervals for one set rather than rely on the averaging of the misses across many sets to reduce the confidence interval to acceptable accuracy. Ultimately we are attempting to measure the average length of an interval between two events. We must record at least two events per set to obtain a rate of occurrence, and ideally we should have many events to obtain an accurate measure of that rate.

When caches are sufficiently large, the miss ratios may drop to a region where high relative accuracy is not important. At miss ratios of 0.005 or below, we may be satisfied with a relative accuracy of ± 100 percent. The Bernoulli bound requires only four misses per set in this case, or about a factor of 25 less than is required for a confidence interval five times tighter. Traces too short to produce at least four misses per set yield confidence intervals on a per set basis that are larger than the observed mean. Because of the clustering in the cache-miss process, we do not know what the overall confidence interval on the observed mean may actually be, but when the misses per set drop below four, there may be a problem in the precision of the answers obtained. The designer must be cautious in using the results of the trace data, and should seek independent means of estimating or measuring the miss ratios of a prospective design to confirm the results of trace simulation.

To give some idea of the potential lack of precision of cache measurements, recall the data reported by Smith and Goodman [1985] mentioned earlier. The number of misses observed for the cache with 512 lines is on the order of 600 misses, or just over 1 miss per set out of roughly 200 references per set. For one set, the Bernoulli bound on the 95 percent confidence interval is 0.006 ± 0.011. For the caches with 2K lines, the number of misses observed were fewer than 1500, or about 0.75 misses per set out of roughly 50 references per set. The Bernoulli bound on the confidence interval for a single set of this collection of caches is 0.015 ± 0.0346. For both the 512-line and 2K-line caches the uncertainty in the size of the mean in one direction is about twice the size of the mean. Also, the interval includes negative miss ratios, which is not meaningful. By taking the measurements over many sets, the confidence interval of the overall mean is smaller than that of a single set, but the true size of the interval is unknown because of the high correlation of the activity of the sets. For these caches, Smith and Goodman appear to have too few misses per set to produce trustworthy measures of miss ratios. To be sure of the data, it is necessary to repeat the experiments with longer traces to obtain tighter confidence intervals. The bounds on the confidence intervals for the smaller caches studied by Smith and Goodman are tighter and useful, so that the uncertainty in their data shows up mainly in the extreme points in their study.

Given this information we can develop some estimates for trace lengths required to evaluate caches. Let's start with a design point of a cache of size 32 K-bytes, with four-way set associativity, and 16-byte lines. This cache has 512 sets. Assuming a nominal miss ratio of 1 percent, to achieve 4 misses per set, we require 400 hits per set or about 200,000 references after initialization. For higher precision, a trace length of 5 million references produces 100 misses per set, which should yield satisfactory accuracy. A cache four times as big has roughly half the miss ratio and four times the number of sets. To achieve the same number of misses per set for this cache, the length of the trace must increase by a factor of 8, or, equivalently, the trace length grows roughly as the cache size raised to the 1.5 power under these assumptions. Hence, by this approximation, to obtain only 4 misses per set, we need a trace of 1.6 M references for a 128 K-byte cache, 12.8 M for a 512 K-byte cache, and 102 M for a 2 M-byte cache after initialization. If we insist on 100 misses per set, the trace for the 2 M-byte cache reaches a length of 2.5 billion, which is prohibitively large. These are all nominal estimates and must be calculated more carefully when doing cache designs by using miss-ratio data for the architecture or for related machines. What may be devastating is the effect of initialization misses. For four-way set associative caches we need 4 misses per set before we record data, and we need to simulate long enough to record at least another 4 misses per set. For direct mapped caches, the additional trace length required is negligible. For four-way set associative caches, the additional trace length for initialization is considerable and may be from 25 percent to 50 percent of the trace length needed for simulation. Note that in this case both the initialization and the simulation portions of the trace produce four misses per set, but the initialization trace is shorter because it has a higher miss ratio.

Laha, Patel, and Iyer [1988] report a successful technique for higher miss ratios in which they average 35 trace samples taken at different points in time. Each sample is large enough to initialize all sets, and still have a sufficient number of misses per set to obtain meaningful information. The effect of using 35 different samples is to obtain a better estimate of the overall miss ratio than can be obtained by a long continuous observation. Although this scheme is useful for larger miss ratios, at very low miss ratios the number of references used for initialization of the sets becomes excessive. The cost of 34 additional initializations negates some or all of the gain in shortening the trace by sampling in time. The only fool-proof way to obtain accurate estimates of the rate of rare events is to observe many of them.

The analysis above suggests that very long traces are required to analyze the behavior of large caches, and traces of such lengths are much larger than lengths actually used in the literature. Can we trust the data in the literature? An interesting study by Agarwal, Hennessy, and Horowitz [1989] produces a model of cache behavior that matches closely with cache simulation data. The largest caches studied in this paper are of size 256 K-bytes. These are large enough to require longer traces than used by Agarwal *et al.* in their study, and thus the question of the accuracy of the measurements arises.

Figure 2.9 illustrates the approximate shape of the simulated data and the predicted data produced by the model. Note how the model tracks the simulated data reasonably closely. Both curves flatten out horizontally at an asymptote that is equal to the initialization transient for the trace. This is equal to the number of distinct lines in the trace divided by the length of the trace. So their model explicitly incorporates the initialization transient and the cache simulation captures the same transient. The trend line in the figure shows an extrapolation of the straight portion of the data. The extrapolation follows the rule that each doubling of cache size reduces the miss ratio by a constant percentage, and is essentially the 30-percent rule for a different percentage. The curve that veers downward vertically at 64K shows what we expect to be the case for a workload that fits entirely within a 64 K-byte cache.

In analyzing the data in the figure, note that at 64K the miss ratio is close to 1 percent. This 64K cache has 4K lines, and at that miss ratio requires roughly 400K references to produce enough misses to fill the cache. Although they used many traces for their analysis, the longest trace was only 500K. Hence the longest of their traces barely filled the 64K cache in the initialization period before it ended and other traces may not have filled the cache completely prior to completion. For the 256K cache, at most 25 percent of the cache

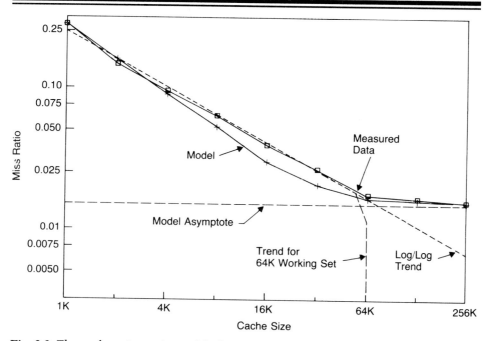

Fig. 2.9 The cache-miss ratio model of Agarwal, Hennessy, and Horowitz.

was initialized by any one trace. Because the miss-ratio during initialization is higher than the steady-state miss ratio, the data give us very little indication of what the steady-state miss ratio might be for a 256K cache.

Because their model specifically estimates the initialization misses, Agarwal *et al.* correctly conclude in their paper that the observed miss ratios for the caches larger than 64K are almost totally due to the initialization transient. Many other studies similar to the one conducted by Agarwal *et al.* produce curves with the same flattening of the miss ratio for large caches, but Agarwal *et al.* produce along with the data a correct explanation of the phenomenon. It is interesting that the vertical trend is what we expect to see when caches are sufficiently large, but published data tends to show a horizontal trend rather than a vertical trend because the traces are generally too short to eliminate the initialization effects.

2.2.4 Cache Analysis: Trace Stripping

At this point we presume that the cache designer has a collection of traces available for cache studies. Our earlier remarks suggest that the designer will try to evaluate many different caches, and therefore may have to use one address trace several different times. This could be extremely time consuming and costly. A trace with 5 million references may contain 4 bytes per reference, for a total of 20 million bytes. Processing this trace may require an hour of computer time on a high-speed computer. To evaluate 100 variations of cache designs on separate passes of the trace would be an enormous computational burden for an analysis that is conceptually very simple. The remainder of this section treats a set of techniques that together reduce processing requirements by as much as a factor of 1000.

We use three different techniques to reduce processing requirements:

1. Multiple analyses per run;

2. Elimination of hits to the most recently used line; and

3. Set sampling.

The first technique is due originally to Mattson *et al.* [1970]. The idea is that a single simulation run for one pass of a trace can produce data for several cache evaluations. However, this result depends on the replacement policy that specifies what line to remove when a new line enters the cache. We describe the work of Mattson *et al.* by example in the context of cache analysis, and explore more fully the impact of replacement policies later in this section.

Figure 2.10 illustrates a situation in which an eight-way set-associative cache is being analyzed. We shall see that we can obtain analyses for K-way set-associative caches for each K less than eight while performing the analysis for the eight-way cache. Figure 2.10 shows the directory for one of N sets in a cache. Note that this directory has eight positions because the cache is eight-way set associative.

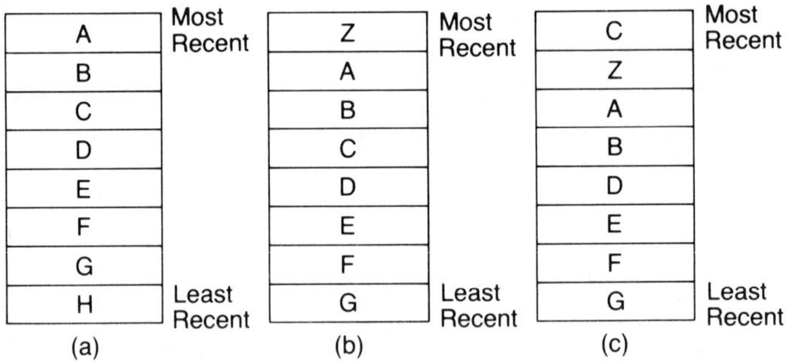

Fig. 2.10 An eight-way cache directory maintained with an LRU policy:
(a) Initial state;
(b) After reference to Line Z; and
(c) After reference to Line C.

Let us examine a typical sequence of address references to this set and observe the effects of a particular replacement policy. Suppose the set initially contains the addresses A through H as shown in Fig. 2.10(a). If the next address reference to this set is a miss, the new item is brought into the cache and entered into the set. But which item is displaced to make room for the new item? A policy that is implemented almost universally is the least-recently used (LRU) policy, which says that the item displaced is the least-recently used item in the set.

If the addresses in Fig. 2.10(a) are arranged in order of their last reference so that A is the most-recently used item and H is the least-recently used item, then the new state of the set will be as shown in Fig. 2.10(b), which shows the new reference Z at the top of the set, references A through G moved down one cell in the set, and reference H discarded from the bottom. Suppose in this state that the next reference is to address C, a hit in the set. Then the next state should be as shown in Fig. 2.10(c), which places C at the top of the set, pushes down Z, A, and B, and leaves other items unchanged. Even though no item is removed from the set when a hit occurs, the contents of the set should be reordered because we must be able to locate the least-recently used item at any given time. The reordering maintains the set in the order from most- to least-recently used item.

The key idea contributed by Mattson *et al.* is that for the LRU replacement policy the contents of a set for a K-way set-associative cache contains the contents of sets for all K'-way set-associative caches for each K' less than K. In Fig. 2.10, the eight-way set contains the contents of one-way, two-way, and so on up to seven-way set-associative caches whose number of sets and line size are equal to the number of sets and line size for the eight-way cache. In fact, if we look at the behavior of a seven-way set-associative cache, we discover that the items held in that cache occupy the first seven positions of the sets for an eight-way cache.

To keep track of the performance of stacks with one-way to eight-way set associativity, we simply have to note the position of each hit in the stack. For example, the reference to item C in Fig. 2.10(b) touches C lying in position 4. This is a hit in a four-way cache, but a miss in a three-way cache. In fact, this is a hit in a K-way cache if and only if $K > 3$.

Let us keep track of the position of a cache hit in a vector of counts that we call HIT(I), where I runs from 1 to 8. The HIT vector is initialized to 0. If a hit occurs at position I, then we increment HIT(I). At the end of the cache evaluation, if we want to know how many hits there will be for an eight-way cache, we simply sum HIT(I) for $I = 1$ to 8.

To find the hits for a four-way cache, we compute the sum of HIT(I) for $I = 1$ to 4. Since HIT(5) counts the number of hits at Position 5 in the set, none of those hits are hits in a set with four or fewer lines. Hence, the contents of HIT(5) must be excluded from the hit count for a four-way set-associative cache. Similarly, we can reason that the count for HIT(3) must be included in the hit count for a four-element set because hits in a three-way cache are also hits in a four-way cache under the LRU-replacement policy. That is why the number of hits for a K-way cache can be found by summing HIT(I) for $I = 1$ to K.

Mattson *et al.* [1970] treat other replacement algorithms in addition to LRU replacement. Some of the replacement strategies have the same property that LRU has, that is, as you increase the size of a set, all of the hits of a K'-way set-associative cache are hits in a K-way set-associative cache for all $K' < K$. But some of the replacement strategies do not have this property. In particular, if you select the item to be replaced at random, then it is perfectly possible, for example, for a hit in a three-way cache to miss in a two-way cache.

A replacement policy that has the containment property is called a *stack-replacement policy* because the candidates to be replaced can be placed in a push-down stack as shown in Fig. 2.10. The stacks for K-way set-associative caches nest one inside the other as K increases. As a general rule, when evaluating stack-replacement policies, one can simulate many different caches during one pass of the trace. This technique could reduce evaluation effort by as much as a factor of 10 over the process of performing separate passes of the input data for each set size evaluated.

The other two techniques are trace-reduction techniques attributable to Puzak [1985], who discovered that the two techniques together can reduce effort by two orders of magnitude. A trace with 5 million references can be reduced by stripping out selected addresses to a trace length of only 50,000 references, yet the reduced trace can give extremely accurate estimates of the miss and hit ratios of the cache.

A short trace permits extensive cache analysis to be done with microcomputers, whereas an analysis of the full trace would be far too large a task to be done in reasonable time on a microcomputer. Both of Puzak's techniques rely on stripping from the address trace a large number of references that do not affect the final results. The first stripping technique is the following:

> Assume that a set of analyses is to be done for caches with a fixed line size L and at least N sets. Then prepare a reduced address trace by simulating a one-way associative cache with N sets and line size L operating on the full trace. Output a reduced trace that contains only the addresses that produce misses in the N-set, one-way set-associative cache.

The trace produced by this simulation process throws away all hits to a one-way associative cache with N sets. That is, it throws away all address references to a line in a set that was the most recently referenced line in that set. What remains on the reduced trace are just the misses experienced by the N-set, one-way set-associative cache. Typically, a cache of reasonable size with this structure should have a miss ratio of 10 percent or less, so that the trace reduction should produce a new trace that is about 10 percent of the original length.

When the reduced trace is used to evaluate the same cache that produced the reduced trace, the number of misses will be identical to the number obtained from the unreduced trace. Of course, the number of hits will be different, so the observed hit and miss ratios will also be different for the reduced trace. If we know the original length of the address trace, however, then from the absolute number of misses observed we can compute the number of hits and the hit and miss ratios. So all information relevant for a cache analysis is still available on the reduced trace, provided that we know the length of the original trace.

What makes this technique more interesting is that we can use the reduced trace to evaluate many different cache structures in a single pass and still obtain exact or near-exact values of the hit and miss ratios. Puzak proved the following result:

> Create a reduced trace by simulating a one-way cache with N sets and line size L, retaining on the reduced trace only the addresses that produce cache misses. Simulate a K-way set-associative cache with N sets and line size L on the original trace and the reduced trace. The two simulations produce the same number of cache misses.

Puzak's proof of this statement is a modification of the argument of Mattson *et al.*, which says that as you increase the stack depth (in this case K), the contents of stacks for smaller K are subsets of the contents of the stack for larger K. The key idea in the proof is that each miss on the reduced trace is a miss on the full trace, and conversely, each miss on the full trace is a miss on the reduced trace.

The process of producing a reduced trace by discarding cache hits for the one-way cache discards no misses for the K-way cache. Because of the stack-algorithm property developed by Mattson *et al.*, no misses for the K-way cache are discarded either. The misses for the K-way cache are a subset of the misses of the one-way cache and will appear in the reduced trace. Moreover, the references discarded from the full trace to produce the reduced trace are hits to the most-recently used set in a one-way cache, but each of these is a hit to the most-recently used set of a K-way cache, and each such hit does not result in a reordering of the K lines within a K-way set. When such references are removed from a trace, the number of misses observed does not change. From this argument we conclude that the reduced trace and the full trace yield an identical number of misses for any K-way cache with N sets and line size L.

Not only can you vary set associativity on a reduced trace, but you can also study the effects of varying N. Puzak showed that the following result is true:

> Let N be a power of 2. Prepare a reduced trace by simulating an N-set, one-way set associative cache with a line size L, and retain on the reduced trace only those address references that produce cache misses. Simulate a one-way set associative cache with $2N$ sets and line size L on the full trace and on the reduced trace. The two simulations produce the same number of misses.

To prove this statement it is sufficient to show that any cache miss on the full trace is a miss on the reduced trace, and conversely, any miss on the reduced trace is a miss on the full trace.

To illustrate the proof, consider Fig. 2.7, which shows how addresses are mapped to sets. When we double the number of sets from N to $2N$, we do so by increasing the set field by one bit. The effect is to split into two groups the addresses that map into one set of an N-set cache. Each group maps into distinct sets of the $2N$-set cache.

For example, consider an address for a cache with $2N$ sets and line size L. Let us break up the left-most field of the address shown in Fig. 2.7 into two fields, one of which contains only the right-most bit of the field, and the other of which contains the remaining bits on the left.

This produces a total of four fields in the address, which we denote as (T, B, S, L) for tag, bit, set, and line. The L field gives an address within line and is ignored by the cache when matching addresses. The S field gives a set number for an N-way cache and is $\log_2 N$ bits long. The B field has a length of 1, and the B field concatenated with the S field gives the set number for a cache with $2N$ sets. The T field is the tag field for a cache with $2N$ sets, and the T field concatenated with the B field is the tag field for a cache with N sets.

When a cache lookup is in progress, a K-way cache uses the set number to initiate a read in each of K memories and compares the tag stored there to the tag derived from the address. Hence, when an address (T, B, S, L) is used by an N-set cache, the tag is (T, B), and the set number is S. When that same address is used by a $2N$-set cache, the tag is T, and the set number is (B, S). Since B is a single bit, the set number is either $(0, S)$ or $(1, S)$. Consequently, any address that is in Set S of an N-set cache falls in either Set $(0, S)$ or $(1, S)$ of a $2N$-set cache.

We will simulate a $2N$-set one-way cache to show why each miss on the full trace appears as an address on the reduced trace and yields a miss there as well. Without loss of generality, let us focus on a particular set, Set $(0, S)$, of the $2N$-set cache and observe an address sequence that produces a miss. Suppose that the address $(T_1, 0, S, L)$ produces a miss on the full trace. The prior reference to Set $(0, S)$ in the $2N$-set cache must have a different tag in order for the present reference to be a miss. Consequently, the prior reference must be an address of the form $(T_0, 0, S, L)$ where tags T_0 and T_1 are not equal, and the values of the L field for the two addresses do not matter. Is $(T_1, 0, S, L)$ on the reduced trace? Yes it is, because this reference produces a miss in an N-set cache.

On the full trace, the prior reference to the Set (S) of an N-set cache is either the reference $(T_0, 0, S, L)$ or a reference of the form $(T, 1, S, L)$ for some tag field T. If the prior reference were $(T, 1, S, L)$, this reference would appear between $(T_0, 0, S, L)$ and $(T_1, 0, S, L)$, and it would be treated as a reference to Set $(1, S)$, not $(0, S)$, when simulating the $2N$-set cache.

Since the prior reference to Set S for the N-set simulation has either tag $(T_0, 0)$ or tag $(T, 1)$, neither of which is equal to tag $(T_1, 0)$, the reference to $(T_1, 0, S, L)$ is a miss on the full trace and does appear on the reduced trace. This reference is a miss on the reduced trace because of the rule used in discarding addresses to produce a reduced trace. We can discard address reference $(T_1, 0, S, L)$ from the full trace only if the prior reference on the full tape to Set S in an N-set cache has tag $(T_1, 0)$. But this was not the case, since the preceding discussion indicates that the prior reference to Set $(0, S)$ in a $2N$-set cache must have a tag different from T_1.

To prove that during the simulation of a $2N$-set cache every miss observed on the reduced trace is a miss on the full trace, we use a similar argument. Now we assume that the address reference $(T_1, 0, S, L)$ on the reduced trace produces a miss when simulating a cache with $2N$ sets. On the reduced trace the prior reference to Set $(0, S)$ must have a different tag, so it must be an address of the form $(T_0, 0, S, L)$ where T_0 and T_1 are unequal, and the values of the L fields are immaterial. Both of these references must occur in sequence on the full trace. Between these references there may be other references to Set $(0, S)$ that do not appear on the reduced trace, but all such references are eliminated from the full trace only if they are hits to Set S of a one-way N-set cache. They must be address references of the form $(T_0, 0, S, L)$ because the tag must be of the form $(T, 0)$, and the latest reference to Set S with a tag of this form is the reference to $(T_0, 0, S, L)$.

We have now shown that when we simulate a one-way $2N$-set cache on the full and reduced traces we obtain the same number of misses. Puzak actually used the proof technique given here to prove the following statement:

Let N be a power of 2, and let M be a power of 2 no less than N. Create a reduced trace by simulating a one-way N-set associative cache with line size L. Retain on the reduced trace only those addresses that produce misses. Now simulate a K-way M-set cache for any $K > 0$ on both the full and reduced traces. The number of misses observed during the two simulations will be equal.

This statement says that a reduced trace can be used to simulate caches with any combination of set associativity and number of sets, provided that

- The line size L for the simulated cache is equal to the line size of the cache used for the trace reduction;
- The simulated cache uses at least as many bits in the set-number field as the cache uses for the trace reduction; and
- The set associativity is arbitrary.

Given that trace reduction is useful for studying caches with increased values of set associativity and number of sets, is it also useful for studying caches with increased values of line size? The answer is a qualified yes. When a trace reduced by simulating a cache with line size L is used to evaluate a cache with line size $2L$, we quickly discover that the sets for the cache with line size L do not have a direct relation to the sets for the cache with line size $2L$.

Wang and Baer [1989] made an interesting discovery that permits a single trace to be used to simulate caches with different line sizes at perfect fidelity. The idea is based on the observation that a reference that is a hit to a cache with a certain line size is probably also a hit to a cache of equal or larger size whose line size is different. Where Puzak recommends producing a stripped trace for each different line size, Wang and Baer produce a single stripped trace that contains the union of the references of Puzak's stripped traces. To create such a trace from a full trace, use the full trace as input to a set of cache simulators. Simultaneously simulate the smallest one-way set associative cache of each line size of interest. Record on the stripped trace a reference if it is a miss in any simulated cache. In other words, cast out hits only if they hit in every simulated cache. Because so many references hit in all the caches, the trace reduction is effective. Wang and Baer report that it increases the length of a single trace by a percentage that was observed as high as 40 percent, but it removes the necessity for creating a single trace for each different line size, and thereby substantially reduces the volume of data saved.

Mattson's techniques for simulating caches that cover a range of set-associativities in a single pass have been extended by Hill and Smith [1989] to the simulation of caches whose structures differ both in set associativities and in number of sets. That this is possible follows from the inclusion property that, for a given line size, a hit in a one-way N-set cache is a hit for a cache with any greater associativity and number of sets. The exploitation of the inclusion property complicates the cache simulator slightly but it reduces the number of passes of the reduced trace to one pass per line size rather than one pass for each distinct value of N per line size. The details of their method are not reproduced here.

Having reduced the original trace by roughly 90 percent, let's explore how to make a second reduction that again reduces the reduced trace by 90 percent. The trick here is to observe that each of the N sets behaves statistically like any other set, so that the performance of the full cache can be estimated by observing only one set. In fact, as we observed earlier, the references across sets are highly correlated. The measurement of miss ratios by using all sets does not increase the accuracy of the estimate of the miss ratio by as much as it would if the references were independent. Hence some effort can be saved without a severe loss of accuracy by restricting attention to only a fraction of all the sets in the cache.

In most designs, N is fairly large, usually 64 to 1024, so the opportunity for reducing effort by a factor of N has a high payoff. There is some danger in selecting a single set, however, because it might just happen to be an unusual set whose statistics are not representative. To be safe, the designer can use two, three, or more sets, with accuracy increasing as the number of sets increases, but at the cost of additional processing time. The idea is to select a few sets and examine their behavior characteristics.

Using standard statistical techniques, one can obtain confidence intervals on the evaluation measures produced from a few sets, where the confidence intervals give an estimate of the error introduced by sampling a few sets instead of using all of them. Similar techniques are used for quality control and for predicting the outcome of elections. In both of these instances, the sampling process is used on a small population to determine the characteristics of a much larger population.

Puzak discovered that selecting 6 of 64 sets was sufficient to reduce the 95-percent confidence interval to less than 1 percent of the measured data. That is, the data obtained from 6 sets would be within 1 percent of the data values for the full trace in 95 percent of the experiments that sample random populations with similar statistical distributions. Hence, the reduced trace can be stripped again to retain the references from some small number of sets. The number of sets to use does depend on the variance in the observed data, so we cannot give a specific number that holds for all cases. Puzak's experience indicates that for reasonable data, retaining only 10 percent of the sets is sufficient.

To summarize how the various techniques described in this section can be put to use, consider the design of a cache that nominally has from 8 K-bytes to 32 K-bytes. The designer has to determine how this cache can be organized. Here is one typical sequence of steps that might be followed:

1. Pick a candidate line size for the 8K cache. This is usually determined by the width of the path between main memory and the processor. The line size can be a multiple of this width, but should not be smaller than the width. In the running example, we assume that the path width is 8 bytes, but we choose to have a line size of at least 16 bytes to reduce the number of directory entries in the cache.

2. Determine what cache structures are to be studied. In our case we want to examine caches with at least two-way set associativity. Hence, the 8K caches of interest are 2 by 256, 4 by 128, and so on, and larger caches are obtained by doubling and quadrupling the number of sets. If we choose to examine larger line sizes, we halve the number of sets for each doubling of the line size.

3. The largest number of lines among the caches under consideration occurs for the 32K cache with 16-byte lines. The number is 2048. Assuming a miss ratio during initialization of about 1 percent, it takes about 200K references to fill this cache initially. To produce accurate estimates of hit ratios, we must find the trace length required for measuring misses after cache initialization. A direct mapped implementation of this cache has 2K sets. With 16 misses per set and and a steady-state miss ratio of 0.5 percent, we

require more than 6.4 million references to produce a confidence interval of no less than 50 percent of the miss ratio. If either the initialization miss ratio or steady-state miss ratio are lower than estimated, the trace has to be longer. To give some additional margin of safety, we choose to make the traces 10 million references in length.

4. Prepare a collection of programs that comprises a representative work-load. Prepare an address trace from these programs of a length of at least 10 million addresses. The proportion of the trace devoted to each type of program should reflect the anticipated workload, and the transients caused by changing from one program to another should also reflect the expected frequency of such transients.

5. Prepare a reduced trace by stripping from the full trace all hits to a cache with line size 16, set associativity 1, and 128 sets. Also, select some fraction of the sets at random, for example, 10 percent, and strip out all references in the trace to sets other than the selected sets. During the stripping process, observe the total miss ratio, the miss ratio on each of selected sets, and the composite miss ratio for the collection of selected sets. If the composite miss ratio differs significantly from the actual miss ratio, use the data obtained from the individual sets to find a sample variance for the observed miss ratio. From this, estimate how many sets are actually required to reduce the sampling error to a tolerable amount. If more sets are needed, obtain them from the original trace by repeating the process given here.

6. Using the reduced trace, simulate caches with 256 sets and two-, four-, and eight-way set associativity in one pass of the trace. (These are 8K, 16K and 32K caches.)

7. Again using the reduced trace, simulate caches with 512 sets and two-, four-, and eight-way set associativity.

8. Repeat the simulation process for a cache with 1024 sets and two-, four-, and eight-way set associativity. These three passes of the trace can be done as separate passes, or by using the method of Hill and Smith [1989], they can be done in a single pass.

9. Plot the data and determine the most reasonable trade-off of performance and cost.

Note that some of the data collected is for caches larger than the design point. This gives additional information on the merits of moving to a larger cache in the future and should be useful if there is some need to plan for the larger cache in present designs. Note also that the line size has been fixed to 16 bytes throughout the study.

If other line sizes are to be considered, the designer can use Wang and Baer's method to prepare a slightly longer stripped trace during the stripping process by simulating caches with other line sizes of interest. Using the one stripped trace, we can repeat the simulation steps above for caches with different line sizes.

Together the methods described in this section should make cache-memory analysis accessible to all designers. It becomes feasible to use personal workstations to conduct such studies that formerly taxed the facilities of the largest computers. In closing, we make one additional observation that greatly simplifies the collection of the data. It is quite feasible to strip the trace while collecting address references. Simply record only those addresses that are misses to a few selected sets of an N-set one-way set associative cache. If we randomly select three bits from the set field and record only the misses to the sets for which these bits have a specific value, for example, $(0, 0, 0)$, then we will be recording references to 12.5 percent (one-eighth) of the sets, and only the misses to those sets.

Because this scheme selects only one address in a hundred for output, the address references can easily be gathered in real-time, even for very fast machines. However, it is necessary to have a buffer that can accept references at very high instantaneous data rates because the cache misses that are captured do not necessarily occur uniformly through a simulation, but rather may bunch together in small regions of the simulation.

Nevertheless, the almost 100-to-1 reduction in the volume and data rate of the data to capture makes this technique very attractive. It may well be more effective to produce traces for different line sizes by capturing a new address-reference stream for each different line size than it is to produce a single full trace to be used as raw data for all simulation runs in a line-size study. A full trace is far more difficult to obtain than is a reduced trace, so a designer may prefer to produce as many as a half-dozen different reduced traces than a single full trace.

2.2.5 Replacement Policies

In this section we look into the replacement policies and their impact on cache performance. Nearly all caches in commercial production use least-recently used (LRU) policies to manage the lines in a set. Recent work by Puzak [1985] points out ways to obtain improvements over LRU replacement at reasonable cost. This section explores the characteristics of LRU and compares them with an optimal (but nonrealizable) replacement policy to conjecture how one might design a realizable, near-optimal replacement policy for a cache.

The main objective of a replacement policy is to retain the lines likely to be referenced in the near future and discard lines that are no longer useful or whose next access is in the more distant future. We can easily evaluate any replacement policy by comparing it to an optimum policy that has perfect knowledge of the future. Belady [1966] described such a policy in the context of virtual-memory systems. The same algorithm holds for cache memories. The characterization of this algorithm described here first appeared in Mattson *et al.* [1970].

Assume that a cache has perfect knowledge of the future: What should its replacement policy be? In fact, the optimal replacement policy (OPT) is identical to an LRU replacement policy that operates on the reference stream reversed in time. More specifically:

> The optimal replacement policy (OPT) discards the line of a set whose next reference is furthest in the future of any other line in the same set.

Figure 2.11 shows the OPT policy in action. Figure 2.11(a) shows a set of lines ordered so that the line at the top is the next of the set to be referenced, and the remaining lines appear in the order in which their next reference appears in the address-reference stream. We assume that the future reference stream is $A, Z, B, Z, C, A, D, E, F, G, H$. In this case, Line A is the next of the lines in the set to be referenced. To maintain the order of the lines in the set, it has to be reordered after each reference, just as LRU has to reorganize the set after each reference.

Figure 2.11(b) shows the state of the set after a reference to Line A. At this point, Line A is not necessarily the next line to be referenced. In fact Lines B and C are touched before A is touched again, so Lines B and C move up in the set, and Line A is inserted after Line C.

Figure 2.11(c) shows the state of the cache after a miss. Line Z has caused a miss and might be brought into the cache. In this case Line Z will be inserted into the set at a position corresponding to its next reference relative to the next reference to any other item in the cache. If Z is touched before H, H will be

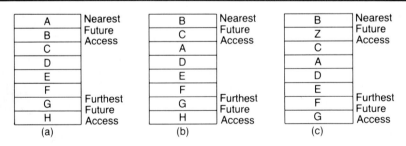

Fig. 2.11 An eight-way cache directory maintained with OPT policy:
(a) Initial state for future reference-string *AZBZCADEFGH*;
(b) After the cache hit to Line *A*; and
(c) After the cache miss to line *Z*.

discarded, some lines will be moved down in the set, and Z will enter the vacant position. If Z is touched after H, then Z is discarded, and the set is left unchanged. Figure 2.11(c) shows Line Z inserted after Line B, and line H being discarded.

Why is OPT optimal? Suppose it were not. Then some other optimal policy would make a decision different from OPT at some point. Consider the first point in time at which the better policy has a hit and OPT has a miss.

Suppose that the hit is to Line A and that OPT has discarded Line A and retained Line B because Line B was referenced before Line A. Then the other policy must have missed on Line B when B was referenced. If OPT had a hit at Line B, at that point we have a hit for OPT and a miss for the other policy. If OPT actually discarded Line B before that reference to B, then OPT did so in favor of some other line, which we can easily show directly or indirectly produces a hit for OPT that the other policy does not produce.

In any case, we have shown that if the other policy produces a hit when OPT has a miss, OPT must at some earlier time produce a hit when the other policy produces a miss. In fact, OPT has at least one hit for every hit of the other policy, and it may have more.

It is rather interesting that LRU, which looks only backward, works well compared to OPT, which looks only forward. The recent past appears to be a good estimate of the near future. Perhaps this is due to the nested structure of programs, which leads to the characteristic that the recent past is a reversal of the near future. Consider, for example, a series of nested loops.

```
for i = 1 to N do
    for j = 1 to M do
        for k = 1 to L do
        (body of inner loop)
        end; {* k loop *}
    end; {* j loop *}
end; {* i loop *}
```

In this nesting the indices are incremented and tested on a last-in, first-out basis. In the loop body the index that is next to be touched is the last to have been touched, and similarly, the index to be touched furthest in the future is the index touched furthest in the past. The last-in, first-out data access characteristic associated with nested loops, nested subroutine calls, and nested interrupts accounts for the future being similar to the past.

If this were the only characteristic of programs, then LRU would almost always closely mimic OPT. But other characteristics of programs strongly interfere with cache management. One problem with the LRU replacement policy is that it does not anticipate the future well when sequential or cyclical activity is in progress. In either of these cases, once an item has been processed, it can be removed from the cache. If it is to be used again, the next access occurs further in the future than the access to other items available in the same cycle.

Consider, for example, the difference between LRU and OPT when each processes a cycle of references of length 6. Let the reference string be $A, B, C, D,$ $E, F, A, B, C, \ldots, F, A, \ldots, F, \ldots,$ and observe how LRU manages this cycle in a set of size 2. LRU retains the last two references and misses on each new reference. OPT retains A and B while accessing C through F, so that the next references to A and B are hits. OPT thus obtains two hits out of six per cycle, but LRU obtains no hits per cycle. Therefore, a long cycle whose length exceeds the set-associativity factor can be devastating for LRU. Similarly, sequential access to any data structure tends to clog up the LRU cache, while such data are immediately discarded by OPT.

Therefore, to create a replacement policy that performs nearly as well as OPT we must do some replacements that are not LRU replacements, and we should try to do these when references are sequential or cyclical or in some other pattern that is poorly handled by LRU. From the preceding description of the characteristics of OPT, we discover the following interesting fact about OPT:

> For any set-associativity size K, OPT considers only one of two lines for replacement. One candidate is the line *most* recently used, the other is the line referenced furthest in the future.

LRU has only one possible candidate for replacement, the line least recently used. It never replaces the line most recently used unless the set-associativity factor K is 1. Presumably, LRU does as well as it does because the least-recently used line is frequently the line to be referenced furthest in the future.

Puzak's analysis [1985] of OPT and LRU policies turned up another interesting characteristic of LRU replacements. Consider a situation in which a set managed by an LRU policy happens to contain exactly the same lines that OPT would retain. Now assume that LRU elects to replace a line of the cache that OPT elects to keep, and conversely, OPT replaces a line, Line A, that LRU elects to retain.

Puzak notes that Line A is a *dead line* in the LRU cache and that it must leave the cache before it is touched again. If this were not the case, then OPT would have retained Line A and cast out some other line. Since Line A is dead, the set associativity is effectively reduced by one until Line A is swept from the cache by an LRU replacement decision. If Line A happens to be the most-recently referenced item when OPT disposes of it, then in a K-way set-associative cache managed with LRU, $K - 1$ misses must occur before Line A is replaced. As each miss occurs, Line A moves down one position in the set, until at last it reaches the least-recently used position from where it is removed from the cache. Here is an opportunity for a better policy!

For example, if a cache-management algorithm were clever enough to prefetch data in anticipation of future references, the obvious place to store the new data is in place of dead lines because these lines will not be referenced again. If we replace lines that are not dead, then each such replacement might change a future hit to a future miss. Therefore, there is some risk in replacing live lines, and no risk in replacing in dead lines.

Quite apart from prefetching, there is a great deal that can be done just to improve LRU replacement. For the cache parameters he studied, Puzak found that OPT's performance for a cache with M lines is approximately the same as LRU's performance for a cache with $2M$ lines. The actual performance difference is not a factor of two. Although the cache sizes differ by a factor of 2, OPT replacement produces only about 30 percent fewer misses than does LRU replacement.

These data are strictly empirical and depend on the architecture, the workload, and the ranges of cache parameters. There is no reason to believe that his observations hold in general. Cache designers should make their own observations based on their specific context and then compare their results with Puzak's.

In any case, by comparing LRU with OPT we can obtain an estimate of the improvement available. Although we can try to improve the cache as much as possible, in reality, we are likely to gain only from 10 to 30 percent of the available improvement because the hardware cannot have perfect knowledge of the future.

Here is a description of one scheme for improving LRU that is based on work by Pomerene et al. [1984]. The objective is to distinguish between transient lines that must be flushed from cache quickly and lines that become active after long periods of inactivity.

Pomerene et al. propose to use a *shadow directory*, as shown in Fig. 2.12. On the left side of Fig. 2.12 is an ordinary cache divided into a directory and data area. Let us presume that this is a K-way associative cache. To the right in the figure is a duplicate of the cache, except that the duplicate contains only the directory and no data area. This part of the cache is the shadow directory. The cache is generally managed as if it were a $2K$-way set associative cache, except that a directory hit in the right half of the cache produces no data, just directory information.

When a new item is brought into the main cache, one of K items in the same set is discarded from that cache. The discarded item is entered in the shadow directory, displacing one of K items from the corresponding set in that directory. If in each case, the item removed is the least recently used item of the K in its set in the respective directories, the effect of this strategy is to create a cache that is $2K$-way set associative, managed by LRU replacement. There is usually plenty of time available to update the cache and both directories because the update occurs during a cache miss, when cache activity essentially comes to a standstill.

The key to the cache's operation is that there are two kinds of misses:

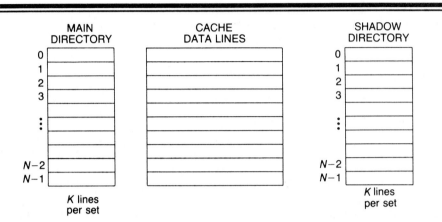

Fig. 2.12 The organization of a cache with a shadow directory. The main cache has N sets, K lines per set. The shadow directory has only the directory entries for an additional K lines per set.

- A *transient miss*, in which the datum is not in the cache, and there is no entry in the shadow directory; and
- A *shadow miss*, in which the datum is not in the cache, but there is an entry for the datum in the shadow directory.

A shadow miss is a miss to line that was used in the distant past and is being used again. There is some likelihood that it will repeat the same behavior in the future by having a lengthy period between two successive accesses.

As each new item is loaded into the cache, a bit is set to indicate whether the item was a transient miss or a shadow miss. That information is used to control replacement. When a replacement decision occurs, the cache manager can examine how lines entered the cache. It can tend to retain the lines that were in the shadow in favor of the lines that were transient misses, and in this way it will tend to flush transients from the cache more quickly than an LRU algorithm will flush them.

As the replacement algorithm chooses lines closer and closer to the most-recently used line, however, the risk becomes greater that the replacement algorithm will make a mistake and cast out a line that should be retained for a future hit. Puzak discovered that it is effective to place a limit on the region of the cache over which the cache manager can give preference to shadow misses over transient misses. For a four-way cache, a reasonable policy is to limit non-LRU decisions to the bottom two cells, that is, the LRU and next-to-LRU entries.

In terms of cost, the shadow directory is surprisingly inexpensive. Most of the cost of a cache is in the data memory. For example, for a line size of 16 bytes and an address-tag size of 4 bytes, a data memory will have four times the number of bytes as has a cache directory. For larger line sizes, such as 64 bytes, the shadow directory will have less than 10 percent of the storage capacity of the data memory.

Since the directory also has comparators, the costs are not in storage alone, but the storage ratio of data memory to directory does give some idea of relative costs. Consequently, it is conceivable to put 10-percent additional cost into a shadow directory to obtain 5- to 10-percent performance improvement. From a cost-performance view, such improvement could be better than doubling the size of the cache. Note that the improvement range for performance corresponds to a very small absolute change in the miss ratio, roughly 0.5 to 1 percent. The percentage reduction in the number of misses is somewhat larger, possibly 10 to 30 percent. The point is that the shadow directory does not have to be extremely accurate to achieve the improvement we seek.

The shadow directory also avoids a serious problem that develops as caches become larger. Generally, the larger a cache, the slower the cache cycle becomes. Since the shadow directory is not accompanied by a data memory, the volume and power consumed by the data memory is avoided, which is a tremendous advantage for high-speed systems.

Moreover, the shadow directory need not increase the cache-cycle time since the shadow does not have to be consulted on every memory access. The only time it needs to be consulted is on a cache miss, and at this point there are many cycles available to handle updating and replacement. To conserve on power and cooling, it is feasible to build the shadow directory with logic slower than that used in the main cache. The shadow can be included fairly inexpensively to obtain a small, but worthwhile, increase in performance.

2.2.6 Footprints in the Cache

In this section, we expand upon some of the ideas of the shadow directory to derive a simple and useful model of transient misses in a cache. Voldman and Hoevel [1981] and Voldman et al. [1983] conducted empirical studies of misses in caches. Their data show that cache misses are not distributed uniformly through an address trace, but instead tend to be clustered into clumps. Between the clumps are relatively long periods of time during which cache misses are rare.

Attempts to model this behavior statistically have not been very successful because the distributions that best characterize the behavior do not have finite variance. Voldman et al. [1983] showed a characterization based on fractals, which is helpful for explaining an empirically observed sequence of misses, but is not directly useful in predicting the effects of cache parameters on miss ratios.

The importance of the transient effect on cache performance led Strecker [1983] to develop a model of miss ratios for the case when two or more processes compete alternately for a cache. Strecker observed that as each process takes control, it expends its initial references reloading the cache. As the cache becomes partially loaded, the misses decline, and eventually the miss ratio reaches the long-term steady-state miss ratio. Strecker's model estimates the average miss ratio for a process over an interval of time that includes the transient period when the process is reloading the cache. Although the model is fairly complex, Strecker showed that it gives reasonably accurate results for the specific processes he modeled. The value of the method is limited because it relies on fitting a curve at two points to calculate the values of two parameters that define the curve. If you have the data to fit the two points, you probably have the data for the remainder of the points. The objective is to determine the transient using as little additional information as possible. Another interesting study of note is by Laha, Patel, and Iyer [1988] who show that reasonable estimates of the reload transient can be obtained by piecing together many different small segments of a larger trace.

Both of the studies cited here attempt to explore the reload transient in conjunction with the steady-state miss process. The material in this section shows how to calculate the reload transient in isolation. This permits the transient to be combined with the steady-state miss ratio in various ways to reflect the true cache reload transients that take place in a computer system. The trick is to count the number of lines that have to be reloaded without attempting to measure instantaneous miss rates. Since each cache miss carries a penalty, and for many architectures the penalty is a fixed cost, the model can give the total cost penalty of a reload transient. The penalty drops off for larger caches in a predictable way, and the predictions have been confirmed by experiment. The work described here is by Thiebaut and Stone [1987].

The model for determining how different processes compete for the cache is illustrated in Fig. 2.13. Figure 2.13(a) shows Process A and Process B running alternately in time. These two processes may be quite independent, as is the case if Process A is an interrupt-driven program servicing some input/output device, and Process B is a compute-bound main program. Or the processes could be quite dependent on each other, as is the case if Process A invokes Process B repeatedly because of a call on B placed within a loop in A.

In a cache-based architecture, what actually happens is shown in Fig. 2.13(b), where we see a reload transient at the beginning of the second iteration of Process A. Before calling Process B, Process A fills the cache with various instructions and data that were referenced frequently and will be referenced frequently again. When Process B runs, it displaces many of A's data and instructions in the cache with data and instructions that belong to B. When Process A reinitiates, it spends some time reloading the cache while displacing B's lines. The shaded area shown in the figure represents this transient.

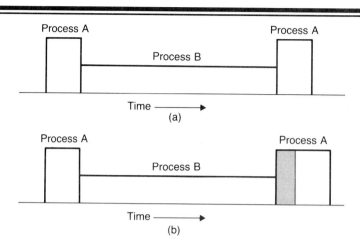

Fig. 2.13 Execution profile of two processes that share one processor:
(a) Ideal execution profile; and
(b) Actual execution profile of Process *A* when it contends for the cache with Process *B*.
The shaded area denotes lost time from a cache reload when lines of *A* are displaced
by *B*.

We show the transient occurring at the beginning of *A*'s second cycle.
Actually it occurs throughout the cycle, with the initial miss-ratio quite heavy
but gradually diminishing until the transient is over, or until Process *B* is
reinvoked, whichever occurs first. The miss-ratio may be as high as 40 or 50
percent at the beginning of the transient and eventually falls off to a steady
state of 1 or 2 percent.

The average miss-ratio over the period of Process *A*'s activity depends on
the relative size of the transient as compared to the length of the reference
string for Process *A*. A similar transient not shown in Fig. 2.13 occurs for
Process *B*. In fact, the lines belonging to *A* discarded by *B* are those that are
reloaded by *A* when *A* takes control, so that the number of misses in *B*'s
transient due to Process *A* is equal to the number of misses in *A*'s transient due
to Process *B*.

The key to measuring the size of a transient is the notion of a *footprint*, as
illustrated in Fig. 2.14. Figure 2.14 shows an *N*-set cache with potentially
infinite associativity. The lines in the cache marked with an *A* are the lines that
Process *A* touches when it runs in isolation. We call this set of lines the *footprint*
of Process *A*, and the number of such lines is the *footprint size*. For fixed line size
L, footprint size is fixed. That is, we can double or halve the value of *N* in Fig.

	Set Associativity								
	0	1	2	3					
Set 0	A	A	A						– – –
Set 1	A	A	A	A					– – –
Set 2	A	A	A	A	A				– – –
Set 3	A	A							– – –
Set 4	A	A	A	A	A	A			– – –
Set 5	A								– – –
Set 6	A	A	A						– – –
Set 7	A	A							– – –

Fig. 2.14 The footprint of Process A in an eight-set potentially infinite set-associative cache. Three lines fall outside a four-way set-associative cache and produce steady-state cache misses.

2.14, and the lines marked A will redistribute in the infinite cache accordingly, but no lines will disappear. The footprint shape changes with cache structure, but the footprint size is independent of N.

The double vertical lines in Fig. 2.14 isolate the four left-hand columns from the remainder of the cache, and show Process A's footprint in a finite cache with set associativity 4. Note that some sets (rows) of the footprint contain more than four entries, and therefore these sets do not fit into the finite cache. When A runs by itself, these sets cause cache misses at a rate that depends on the frequency and exact sequence of references to those sets.

The model of cache behavior is very simple to state. We assume that Process A runs first and firmly implants its footprint in the cache. Then Process B runs. If Process B is agile enough to step around Process A's footprint, then many lines of Process A will be resident when A restarts after B finishes. If Process B steps on part or all of Process A's footprint, those lines from Process A will be displaced from the cache and will have to be reloaded when A restarts. How many lines will have to be reloaded? The relevant parameters are the footprint sizes of A and B and the cache size and structure. We show here how to estimate the number of lines to reload using statistical assumptions that turn out to be very good.

If the cache is very large compared to the footprint sizes of A and B, then with very high probability Processes A and B can run together without interference, just as two mice can ramble in a football stadium without bumping into each other. But if the cache is small relative to the footprint sizes, B's footprint will land directly on A's, and most or all of Process A will have to be reloaded.

The size of the footprint that Process A actually occupies in the finite cache is equal to the number of entries posted in the first four columns on the cache shown in the figure. How big is this footprint? We can estimate its size rather easily for a K-way cache by considering the probability of having more than K lines per set in Process A's footprint for an infinite cache.

If we assume that the lines are distributed uniformly to the sets of the cache so that each set is equally likely to be the target of any line in the footprint, then the probability that the first line referenced by Process A falls into a set, such as Set 1, is $p = 1/N$, since there are N sets, each equally likely to receive this line. The probability of not falling into this set is $q = 1 - p = 1 - 1/N$. Let the size of Process A's footprint in an infinite cache be S_A.

The model developed here is a binomial probability model in which we toss a coin with a probability $p = 1/N$ of landing head's up, which represents a line falling into Set 1. We flip the coin S_A times, once for each line in the footprint, and count the number of heads. The probability distribution of heads tells us the probability distribution of lines to Set 1. In an infinite cache, the distribution is given by the formula

$$Pr[i \text{ lines of Process } A \text{ in a set}] = \binom{S_A}{i} p^i (1-p)^{S_A - i} \qquad (2.4)$$

If the cache is finite, with only K-way set associativity, then Eq. (2.4) holds for $i < K$, and the probability of having K entries in a set is obtained by summing the probabilities in the tail of the binomial distribution. Thus we have,

$$Pr[i \text{ lines of Process } A \text{ in a set}] = \binom{S_A}{i} p^i (1-p)^{S_A - i} \qquad \text{for } i < K$$

$$(2.5)$$

$$= \sum_{j=K}^{S_A} \binom{S_A}{j} p^j (1-p)^{S_A - j} \qquad \text{for } i = K$$

This is the probability distribution that we use in the remainder of the derivation.

Process B is governed by a similar probability distribution, except that its footprint size is S_B. For example, the equation corresponding to Eq. (2.5) for $i = K$ is

$$Pr[i \text{ lines of Process } B \text{ in a set}] = \sum_{j=K}^{S_B} \binom{S_B}{j} p^j (1-p)^{S_B - j} \qquad \text{for } i = K \quad (2.6)$$

Now we can estimate the cache reload transient. Figure 2.15 shows two possible states of the cache with both footprints resident. Figure 2.15(a) shows the cache in the state that exists when Process A runs first, then Process B, and we are about to reload Process A. The entries within a set (shown as a row in the figure) are ordered so that the most-recently used items appear on the left, and

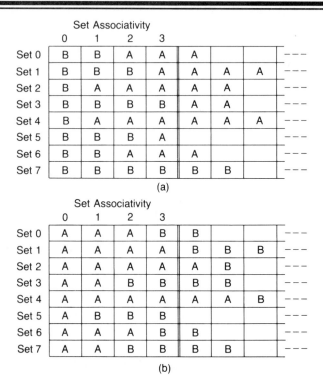

Fig. 2.15 The footprints of two processes that compete for the cache:
(a) An eight-set, four-way set-associative cache in a state obtained by running Process A, then Process B (the A's to the right of Column 3 are the lines that form the reload transient);
(b) The same cache in a state obtained by running Process B, then Process A.

the least-recently used items appear on the right. All B's in this cache are to the left of all A's because Process B's references are more recent than Process A's.

Figure 2.15(b) shows the same cache in a state in which Process B runs first, then Process A, and we are about to reload Process B. In Fig. 2.15(a) the A's that appear in Columns 0–3 are lines that do not have to be reloaded when A is restarted. The A's in the other columns represent lines that are reloaded during the reload transient, and the number of such A's is the size of the transient. In Fig. 2.15(b), the reload transient for Process B is equal to the number of B's that appear outside of Columns 0–3.

The binomial probability model makes the computation of the size of the transient quite straightforward. Let us focus attention on Set 1, since all sets are assumed to behave the same. There are three related random variables of interest to us for this set:

- X is the number of lines of Process A's full footprint in this set;
- Y is the number of lines from Process B's full footprint in this set; and
- $Z = X + Y$ is the total number of lines in this set.

If Z does not exceed K, then Set 1 contributes nothing to the reload transient. The probability of this event is the probability

$$Pr[Z \le K] = \sum_{i=0}^{K} \left(Pr[X = i] \sum_{j=0}^{K-i} Pr[Y = j] \right) \tag{2.7}$$

If X and Y are binomially distributed, both with probability $p = 1/N$, then Z is also binomially distributed. That is, Eq. (2.7) is the probability of having K or fewer heads among $S_A + S_B$ coin flips. Hence, Eq. (2.7) is the area under the tail of a binomial density. For values of p near 0.5, Eq. (2.7) is closely approximated by a normal distribution. For the values of p of interest to us, however, Eq. (2.7) is only crudely approximated by a normal distribution, although the general shape of the curve is the same.

The interesting situation occurs when Z exceeds K. Let W be the number of lines of Process A that are overwritten by B in Fig. 2.15(a). Then the probability that exactly i lines of Process A are overwritten is given by

$$Pr[W = i] = \sum_{j=i}^{K} Pr[X = j]Pr[Y = K + i - j] \qquad \text{for } 1 \le i \le K \tag{2.8}$$

Each term in the summation of Eq. (2.8) accounts for a case in which precisely i lines of Process B fall on i lines of Process A in a K-way cache. Note that the first and last terms of the summation involve summations from Eqs. (2.2) and (2.3).

To compute the cache-reload transient from Eq. (2.8), we note that the transient to reload Process A is S_A minus the number of lines of Process A left in the cache when A resumes. This number is given by

$$\text{Cache-reload transient} = S_A - N(E[X] - E[W]) \tag{2.9}$$

The term in parentheses is the expected number of lines from Process A remaining in each set of the cache. The term is equal to the number of lines in the full footprint reduced by the number of lines overlaid by Process B.

Figure 2.16 shows an example of the cache-reload transient for caches of various sizes and structures. This figure is based on actual data, and the curves produced by the model have been confirmed in practice up to the ability to determine which misses are part of the reload transient and which are not.

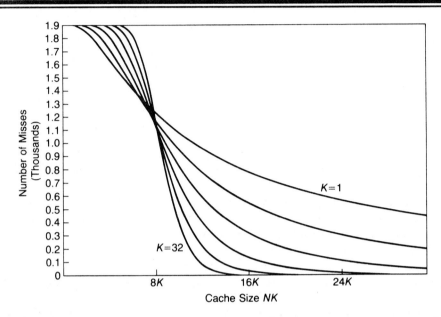

Fig. 2.16 The cache-reload transient (Program *A* footprint = 1900; Program *B* footprint = 7900).

The shape of the curve is rather interesting because it is similar to the appearance of the area under the tail of a normal density function. We would obtain that curve exactly if the binomial parameter $p = 1/N$ were not so small, and if the only lines in Fig. 2.15(a) that lie outside the first K columns belonged to Process *A*.

Note that, for a fixed cache size, the curve becomes steeper as set associativity increases. There is a threshold phenomenon displayed here. If the cache is sufficiently large to hold Process *A* and *B* concurrently, the reload transient is very small. If the cache cannot hold both processes comfortably, they conflict with each other. When a cache is smaller than the footprint of Process *B*, when Process *B* reloads the cache it tends to displace Process *A* almost completely, and the displacement is greater as the associativity becomes greater.

This particular model has been successfully used to select a cache size for a computer system in which an interrupt-driven process had to remain cache resident between interrupts. The interrupt-driven process had to execute its task in real time, and could not pay a large cache-reload penalty. The objective was satisfied by making the cache large enough to hold both the interrupt-driver and the background process so that both could run with the full benefit of cache.

The probabilistic model gives better answers than does a deterministic model because the probabilistic model shows the effects of different background processes on the reload transient. With this model we can obtain fairly accurate estimates of the reload transient under the most adverse conditions likely to be encountered, as well as for typical conditions, and thereby have a very good estimate of the real-time performance of the interrupt-driver.

The model is also useful for explaining cache behavior in ordinary programs. Processes A and B in Fig. 2.15 might well be two processes within one program that are executed alternately. Figure 2.16 shows that the benefit of a large cache falls off fairly rapidly when the cache is big enough to hold contending processes.

The cache-design question centers on how large to make the cache so that contending processes do not step on each other. Since the footprint size is the critical parameter, the distribution of footprint sizes of processes within programs gives valuable information regarding how large to make caches. The architect should measure footprints for a variety of subroutines, inner loops, and other identifiable processes, especially processes that are invoked frequently.

We also need to know the cumulative sum of the footprint sizes of processes invoked between successive runs of a given process. With such information the architect can develop a model for cache transients that gives an estimate of total performance as a function of cache size. This can be used for gross estimates before detailed estimates are produced from simulation experiments on long traces.

2.2.7 Writing to the Cache

The discussion up to this point has not mentioned any special actions to take for WRITE operations, whether they hit or miss in the cache. Handling the WRITE operations is somewhat tricky because of the interaction of the cache with the input/output system. Figure 2.17 shows typical organizations of processor, cache, and input/output processor.

Figure 2.17(a) shows an organization in which all references, whether from the input/output processor or the central processor, go through the cache. This scheme is seriously flawed because there is too much activity in the cache. The two ports to the cache require interlocks and arbitration, which tend to affect performance adversely.

The scheme shown in Fig. 2.17(b) is definitely preferable to that of Fig. 2.17(a) because the central processor and the input/output processor do not conflict with each other on the majority of the accesses. The central processor operates mostly with the cache memory, and independently, the input/output processor operates mostly with main memory.

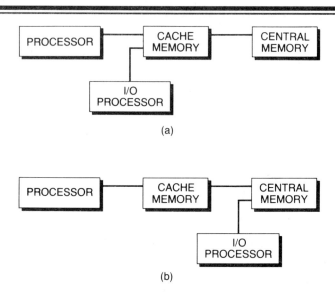

Fig. 2.17 Two possible ways of organizing a cache memory with respect to an I/O system:
(a) The cache multiplexes requests from the I/O processor and central processor; and
(b) The I/O processor has a direct path to memory. This scheme requires interlocks between the cache and the I/O system.

Although the latter scheme is good from a performance view, it is not good from the view of logical consistency unless we embellish the scheme in some way. The problem is that each item has two places where it may be resident—main memory or cache memory. If the item is in both places, the two values must be identical. If ever the values are not identical, then we can have a situation in which the processor accesses the cache to find one value for the item, while the input/output processor accesses main memory and discovers a totally different value. We must forbid this situation from happening, and, in so doing, some designers have opted to implement the organization of Fig. 2.17(a), which solves the problem directly.

Figure 2.18 shows one way to approach the problem. The idea is to have two copies of the cache directory, one read by the central processor and the other read by the input/output processor. With two separate copies, each processor can read the directory without interfering with the other processor.

Figure 2.18 shows the directories resident in two physically separate regions of the computer system, but they obviously can both be resident in the cache. The cache directory is read for every READ or WRITE operation, but the

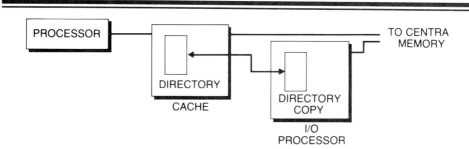

Fig. 2.18 A system organized with a direct route to memory for the I/O processor. All changes to the cache directory are maintained in a copy in the I/O processor. The I/O processor invalidates entries in the cache directory when the entries are updated by an I/O operation to central memory.

directory is changed only when a miss occurs. Since this happens rather rarely, roughly every 25 to 100 memory operations, there is very little overhead from contention between the central processor and the input/output processor. The key idea is to make sure that the input/output processor always reads the correct datum, and that every datum written by the input/output processor to main memory is made available to the central processor.

Let's consider the details of operation of Fig. 2.18. WRITE operations are tricky to handle in this structure; READ operations depend on how WRITEs are implemented. If the input/output processor writes an item to main memory, it must also check to see if the item is also in the cache. If so, the input/output processor should invalidate the cache entry to be sure that the central processor will access main memory when that item is next requested. Otherwise, the central processor might discover an out-of-date value for the item if the processor happens to find the item in the cache. Thus the input/output processor invalidates the cache entry for each cache hit it observes while writing new data in main memory.

Another possible strategy is to rewrite the new data to the cache instead of invalidating the data. For most systems, however, the probability of that update leading to a cache hit for the processor is rather low and does not justify the extra traffic to the cache.

The central processor actually has two different ways of handling WRITE operations, both of which have been implemented in commercial machines. One method is called *write-through*, in which every WRITE operation to the cache is accompanied by a write of the same data to main memory. If this is implemented, then the input/output processor need not consult the cache directory when it reads memory, since the state of main memory is an accurate reflection of the state of the cache as updated by the central processor. Although this scheme simplifies the accesses for the input/output processor, it does result in fairly high traffic between central processor and memory, and the high traffic tends to degrade input/output performance.

A different scheme is sometimes called *write-back* or *write-in cache*. In this scheme the central processor updates the cache during a write, but the actual updating of memory is deferred until the line that has been changed is discarded from the cache. At that point the changed data are *written back* to main memory.

Because the input/output processor must be informed of WRITEs to the cache, just in case an input/output operation has to move such data from the computer system to an external device, the input/output processor must consult a cache-directory copy when it reads an item from main memory. If there is a hit, the input/output processor requests the item from the cache. Note that it is not necessary to update the cache directory read by the input/output processor on every WRITE by the central processor; it is sufficient to change this directory only when the main cache directory changes, which occurs on every miss, not on every WRITE.

2.2.8 Other Performance Metrics

The connection between main memory and processor is by means of a high speed bus. Because the bandwidth is finite and because it may at any given time have to respond to competing requests, there is a possible performance degradation due to contention on this bus. For example, in the previous section we learned that WRITEs to caches can be treated in different ways. In this section we examine schemes for evaluating performance degradation due to bus traffic caused by WRITEs and by multiple bus cycles when line size is a multiple of bus width.

The possible ways to treat WRITEs in cache raise a question of evaluating the impact of these alternatives on system performance, and the main difference is attributed to the difference in bus traffic produced by the two schemes. The finite bandwidth of the bus also produces degradation on READ misses because the various components of a long cache line arrive at cache from main memory in a sequence of cycles. It is possible to generate a series of misses to the same cache line in such circumstances when our model to this point predicts that after the first miss the subsequent references to the same line will generate hits. This section considers the mechanisms that impact performance, and indicates how the cache simulation techniques can be extended to measure their effects.

The effect of the WRITE policy is the starting point of this discussion. What is the difference in the WRITE traffic generated by a write-through policy as compared to that generated by a write-in cache policy? Every item in cache that has been altered while resident there must be rewritten to main memory before the item is removed from cache. The write-through policy copies the item to main memory as early as possible and the write-in cache copies the item as late as possible. The latter policy avoids some traffic when it modifies items in cache multiple times before they leave cache. The earlier modifications need not be reported to main memory. The difference in the traffic produced by the two policies can be computed by answering the following questions:

1. What is the WRITE rate of the workload, measured in the number of bus cycles per instruction devoted to modifying data?
2. What is the rate at which WRITEs hit modified data in the cache, measured in the number of bus cycles per instruction required to rewrite modified data hits.

The first measure is the bus traffic generated by writes in a write-through cache policy. The second measure counts the reduction in the number of bus cycles of write traffic that are available from a write-in cache policy. To capture the first set of performance data, a simulator counts bus cycles of write traffic for each instruction simulated. If a reduced trace is used for input to the simulator, then as part of the trace reduction process when a sequence of references is removed from the full trace, a special record that contains the sum of the write bus-cycles produced by the discarded references is written in its place. Since these are hits in a one-way set-associative cache, the sums of such records contribute to the measures for both the cycles expended for write-through policy and the cycles deducted from that measure for the write-in policy.

To capture the second set of performance data, it is not immediately clear that one-way, two-way, and four-way caches can be simulated on one pass of the trace as suggested by the method of Mattson *et al.* [1970]. A little reflection shows that the basic algorithm of Mattson *et al.* is not sufficient. Suppose, for example, that a modified item is read and a hit is recorded in a four-way cache, but not in a cache with less associativity. The one-way and two-way caches will not contain the item so that they will retrieve a clean copy of it and put it in the most recently used position of the cache. But the four-way cache produces a hit and moves the modified item to the most-recently used position of the cache. A subsequent write to the item that produces hit cannot tell if the item is modified (moved from the four-way cache on a hit) or unmodified (copied from main memory on a miss in a one-way or two-way cache). Thus it is not clear how to account for bus cycles saved by writing to a modified item.

The problem was neatly solved by Thompson and Smith [1989] who show that it is sufficient to keep track of the stack depth at which an item is written. In the example above, if a modified item is the target of a read hit for a stack depth of 4 (four-way cache), place the number 4 with the item as a reminder of where it came from. Then when the subsequent write-hit occurs, we know that bus cycles are saved for four-way caches but not for caches with less associativity. To treat all cases correctly, the tag stored with a modified item is set to 1 when the item is written. (Caches with associativity of 1 or more see a modified version of this item on a cache hit.) Otherwise the tag is made equal to the stack depth at which the item is hit by a read hit if the stack depth of the hit is greater than the current tag stored with the item. (Caches with an associativity as large as the tag see a modified version of the item on a cache hit; otherwise a cache sees an unmodified version of the item because it has been reloaded from memory.) When a write hit finds an item, assume that the value of tag it contains is k before the tag is updated. Then the bus cycles caused by a write modification are avoided by a write-in policy for a k-way cache and all larger caches. The simulation maintains a vector of running sums and updates the item at position k in this vector. At the close of the simulation, the number of cycles saved in a k-way cache is the sum of the components with indices k or larger.

Apart from the rate at which bus requests are issued, there is an additional performance concern regarding the time required to reload a cache line from main memory. The line size of a cache line need not be identical to the bus width between main memory and cache. It is usually a multiple of the bus width, and varies from one to eight times the bus width in practice, but could be larger in principle. Consider an extreme example in which the factor is eight so that at least seven additional bus cycles elapse after the first part of the line reaches cache, and before the last part of the line reaches cache. Assuming that instruction execution suspends momentarily on a cache miss and restarts when the first part of a cache line reaches cache, during the next seven cycles it is quite likely for another reference to the same line to occur, possibly to a part of the line that has not yet reached the cache. Such a reference also causes a processor idle period, but the idle period lasts only until the missing line elements reach the cache. Since the access to those elements is in progress, the wait is not as long as the wait for the first part of line. We distinguish the performance degradation due to the two kinds of misses by calling the wait associated with a normal miss the *leading-edge effect* and the wait due to line transfers in progress the *trailing-edge effect*.

With very little additional work we can compute the additional degradation due to the trailing edge effect, which we have ignored up until now, while computing the leading edge effect, which has been the primary subject of the discussion. The trick here is to produce a stripped trace with sufficient additional information to compute the trailing edge effect for a variety of bus widths. We record on the stripped trace, not just the misses to a one-way set-associative cache, but we also record summary information for the references that have been stripped from the trace. For each miss, the cache simulator stores with the miss the simulated time of the miss. Any subsequent hit to that line that occurs within a fixed period of time might result in a delay that contributes to the trailing edge fact. So when such a hit is detected the simulator writes summary information to the stripped trace. When the stripped trace is used as an input trace for cache evaluation, the summary information should be detailed enough to compute the additional performance degradation due to the trailing edge effect.

The trailing-edge effect and the bus traffic for the write-in cache policy are just two of several fine details of processor performance that merit attention. From the discussions in this chapter regarding techniques for measuring performance, the reader should have no difficulty adapting these techniques or developing similar new techniques to other aspects of performance not covered in this text.

The common thread to performance evaluation so far has been the use of traces of real workloads. The next section addresses what to do in the absence of such traces.

2.2.9 Modeling Cache Performance

One important trend produced by the development of VLSI technology is the reduction in the number of different processors in wide use. When a single chip contained only a few logic gates or registers, designers put them together in a variety of ways to form different kinds of processors with different instruction sets. VLSI changed the design rules somewhat by offering computer architects entire processors on a single chip to use as building blocks in their designs. Moreover, the cost of those processors drops very low when the volume of production is very high, so that there is an incentive to incorporate widely used processors in a design. Another advantage is that a widely used processor usually has a large base of applications and systems software already in place. Hence, the cost-performance and marketplace trends are driving toward a state in which relatively few different processor types are used in the majority of computers sold.

In spite of this trend, there is also an incentive to produce novel machines that incorporate advances in some form or other. The appearance of reduced instruction-set computer (RISC) architecture with its potential reduction in cycle time resulted in the development of very high speed processor chips from each of several manufacturers. Meanwhile, more conventional processors evolved in an orderly fashion that brought along enormous changes in the typical workload on such processors. The greatest impact in workload change has been caused by the increase in address space and basic processor speed. For example, in the Intel family of microprocessors, the 2 MHz 8080 became the 5 MHz 8086, the 10 MHz 80286, the 20 MHz 80386, and the 40 MHz 80486 in successive generations. A significant change between the 8080 and the 8086 was the increase of the memory address from 16 bits to 20 bits, and an even more dramatic change was the increase to the 32-bit address of the 80286 and 80386. Even though the 8080 ancestry is quite evident in an 80486, there is very little in common in the typical workloads of an 8080 and 80486. The differences between two successive generations may be very large, as indicated in this example by the differences between an 8086 and an 80286. When such differences exist, workloads for the present generation are not likely to capture the features of workloads likely for the next generation, and thus cache designs based on present workloads may not perform as predicted on the workloads of the next generation.

Most RISC processors and the later chips in the 80X86 family are designed to work with caches. Many RISC processors and the 80486 processor have caches on-chip, and provide for larger second-level caches off-chip. No real workloads existed for these chips during their design. How were the caches for these processors designed? They were not designed by the trace-driven techniques presented earlier in this chapter. They had to be designed by estimating the performance of various cache structures on the projected workload. What can you do to estimate performance when you cannot perform detailed simulation?

We would like to have in hand a general method for estimating miss ratios as a function of cache size and structure on which we can rely for crude but close estimates of performance in the absence of precise data. Figure 2.19 illustrates a model due to Thiebaut [1989] that can answer many of the questions posed. Recall that the footprint of a process is the number of unique cache lines touched by the process. The function plotted in Fig. 2.19(a) is the footprint function for a workload as a function of time. The first time that each line is accessed, it increases the footprint function by one. The function is essentially the number of misses in an infinite cache as a function of time.

Fig. 2.19(a) is plotted on a log/log scale. Notice that it is composed of two straight lines—an initial line with a steep slope and a steady-state line with a gentler slope. Thiebaut observed this behavior when analyzing a number of different processes on a number of different machines. Independently the same observation was made by Kobayashi and MacDougall [1989] for seven different workloads on a 370 architecture. The dotted line at the right end of the curve shows a trend in the data of Kobayashi and MacDougall where the footprint function tapers off. Their data may cover just the initialization part of the curve plotted by Thiebaut, and it may be possible that the dotted line shown in Fig. 2.19(a) itself has a long-term straight trend, but the paper does not give sufficient information to determine if this is the case.

In Fig. 2.19(a) in the regions where the footprint function is approximated by straight lines the footprint function $u(t)$ (for *unique* references) obeys the power law

$$u(t) = At^B \tag{2.10}$$

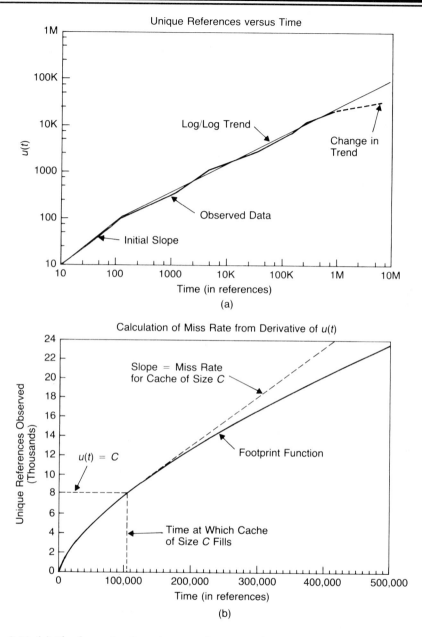

Fig. 2.19 (a) The footprint function as a function of time plotted on a log/log scale. (b) The same footprint function plotted on linear axes to illustrate its relation to miss ratio.

for some constants A and B. B determines the slope of the curve and A determines the y-intercept. Thiebaut's model indicates that the footprint function can be used to predict miss ratios of fully associative caches.

The idea behind the model is illustrated in Fig. 2.19(b) where the same function is plotted on linear axes to show the curve of the power-law function. Thiebaut claims that the miss rate of a fully associative cache of size C lines is the derivative of the footprint function (measured in lines) evaluated where the footprint function takes on the value C. The reason as shown in the figure is that at this point in time a fully associative cache with C lines has just filled. When the next unique reference appears, this cache will experience a miss. Hence, the instantaneous miss rate at this point in time is the slope of the footprint function.

Now consider the future. At any time in the future, the fully associative cache with C lines produces a hit if a new reference is among the lines in the cache and otherwise produces a miss. The miss rate in the future is assumed to be a function only of the size of the cache. Consequently, the future miss rate of the cache is equal on the average to the instantaneous miss rate at the point it first fills since it depends only on the fact that C lines are in the cache memory. When you work through the calculus, you discover that the miss rate of a cache of size C is:

$$\text{Miss rate}(C) = BA^{1/B}C^{1-1/B} \qquad (2.11)$$

for a footprint function given by Eq. (2.10). The power law in Eq. (2.11) is the general form of the 30-percent rule we have informally used throughout this chapter. Specifically, the 30-percent rule holds when B has the value 0.6603, at which the exponent of C in Eq. (2.11) has the value -0.5146. When cache size C doubles to $2C$ the number of misses is multiplied by $2^{-0.5146} = 0.700$, for a 30 percent reduction in miss rate. Thiebaut reports values of B (the reciprocal of his coefficient θ) that range from 0.484 to 0.544, and produce, respectively, a 52 percent and 44 percent reduction in cache misses for each doubling of cache size for his sample workloads. Although Thiebaut's workloads show greater locality than indicated by the 30-percent rule, Kobayashi and MacDougall's values of B range from 0.43 for scientific workloads to 0.75 for supervisor workloads, which is a somewhat larger variation than observed by Thiebaut. These exponents produce, respectively, 60 percent and 21 percent reduction in miss ratios for each doubling of cache size. This range of reductions brackets the 30-percent rule and the observations of Thiebaut.

In essence, the slope of the curve of the footprint function is a measure of the locality of references of the workload. If the slope is steep, the workload touches many new items per unit time. If the slope is shallow, the workload tends to touch a greater proportion of items seen in the past. The coefficient of 0.43 for scientific workloads is very shallow and indicates that cache is very effective for such applications.

Since Fig. 2.19(a) shows the footprint curve to be composed of two different straight lines, the derivative of the footprint curve plotted on log/log axes also consists of two straight lines as indicated in Fig. 2.20. For small caches, the process has a high miss rate that is not strongly affected by cache size. As the cache becomes large, the slope steepens, and the miss rate changes more rapidly with cache size. This exemplifies the *working-set* model described later in this chapter, and is originally due to Denning [1968b]. The working set of a process is some minimal set of lines that have to be resident in fast memory in order for the process to execute mostly out of fast memory. Until the full working set is resident in fast memory, the process experiences a high miss rate. The miss rate drops quickly when the full working set resides in cache. If this is the case, then the intersection point in Fig. 2.19(a) of the straight lines occurs when the number of unique lines in the footprint function approximates the working set size.

Singh, Stone, and Thiebaut [1988] refined the model further to show how miss rate depends on line size as well as cache size. Figure 2.21 shows the general form of the curves they derived. The footprint functions plotted in Fig. 2.21(a) show the footprint functions for different line sizes plotted as function of time. Note that each footprint function has a straight-line trend on the log/log scale. The slopes of the footprint functions as a function of line size are

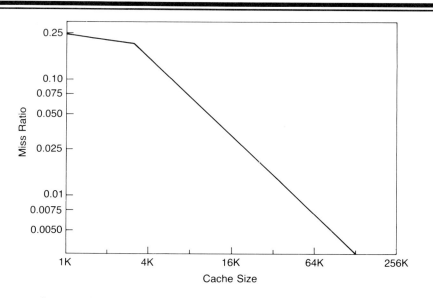

Fig. 2.20 The time derivative of a footprint function plotted on a log/log scale.

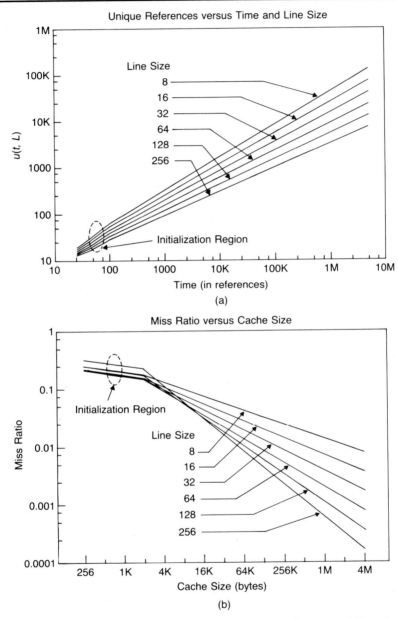

Fig. 2.21 (a) The footprint-function model as a function of time and line-size, plotted on a log/log scale; and
(b) The miss-rate function model as a function of line size and cache size.

related in a way that makes the footprint function a power function of both time and line size. That is, in addition to satisfying Eq. (2.10), the footprint function satisfies an equation of the form

$$u(L) = DL^E \tag{2.12}$$

for line size L and constants D and E. Putting Eq. (2.10) and Eq. (2.12) together yields the most general composite function of this type which is:

$$u(t,L) = WL^a t^b d^{\log L \log t} \tag{2.13}$$

where W is a measure of working-set size, a is a measure of spatial locality, b is a measure of temporal locality, and d is a measure of the interaction between spatial and temporal locality. *Temporal locality* is the tendency for references to cluster together in time and reflects the probability of referencing something that has recently been referenced. *Spatial locality* is a measure of the probability of referencing something located near to an item recently referenced. The two locality measures are not independent, and their interaction is reflected in the coefficient d. The derivative of this function gives an estimate of the miss ratio of a fully associative cache. It is plotted in Fig. 2.21(b) for a variety of line and cache sizes. Still unknown at this writing is how to change this to the miss ratio of a set-associative cache. Although fully associative caches have better miss ratios than four-way set associative caches of equal size, the miss ratios are fairly close, and the fully associative cache can serve as an approximate model to the four-way set-associative cache in the absence of other information.

There are a number of concepts from this model that are useful to the cache designer. Here are the major ones:

1. The power-law function indicates that there is a law of diminishing returns. Each successive doubling of cache size to exploit temporal locality gives less absolute improvement in miss ratio for double the expenditure of hardware. Each doubling of line size gives less absolute improvement in miss ratio for double the expenditure in bus traffic per miss. Very large caches can cost more than their performance justifies.

2. No cache size and structure is characterized by one miss ratio. The cache performance depends strongly on the workload. Miss rates are low if the working set of the workload fits in cache, and they are high otherwise.

3. The size of a cache should be large enough to contain the full working set of the majority of the workloads to be run on the cache. Although, in general, performance improves with increasing cache size, the most performance gain per change in cache size is in the region where the cache reaches and exceeds the working set of most typical workloads. If the cache is too small, the performance of larger workloads is compromised. If the cache is too large, the machine will be priced higher than its performance justifies. It is

probably best to produce too large a cache than too small a cache because the working-set size of applications tends to increase in time as new applications with large working-sets are released. Consequently, excess cache size will be put to use eventually.

4. To estimate the cache size needed for a new processor design, estimate the working-set size of typical programs. This tends to be much larger in large address spaces than in small address spaces.

5. Steady-state miss-rate functions depend on the nature of the workload but all workloads are likely to have exponents in Eq. (2.10) that lie between 0.400 and 0.700. Pick sample exponents in this interval, and model cache behavior for such exponents. The smaller exponents tend to be associated with scientific or numerically intensive applications and the larger ones tend to be associated with less structured applications such as operating systems, database management, and artificial intelligence.

6. The line-size effects are also workload dependent. Kobayashi and Mac-Dougall [1989] have a limited amount of data on line-size effects as a function of workload type, and A. Smith [1987] has extensive data on line-size effects independent of workload. Both of these studies provide typical data that are useful in the absence of simulation data.

The cache designer can explore the impact of workload parameters through Eq. (2.13). Singh *et al.* [1988] give values to a, b, and d in Eq. (2.13) of 0.0333, 0.827, and 0.740, respectively, for a general workload that includes operating system functions and user applications. Scientific applications can be expected to have greater spatial locality than the workload used in the study, which can be modeled by decreasing the coefficients a and d in combination.

Cache design is considered again later in this text when we discuss cache design for multiprocessor systems. The important principles of cache design are:

1. Cache memories retain needed information physically close to the central processor where the information is quickly accessible. As a general rule for high-performance systems, the data most frequently accessed should be physically close to where it is used.

2. The traffic density between the central processor and main memory is anywhere from 10 to 30 times lower than the traffic density between central processor and cache. An important goal in high-performance systems is to keep traffic density low on long interconnections and on shared interconnections.

3. The cache mechanism works only because programs exhibit particular behavior that can be exploited by the cache. If programs behaved differently, caches as we know them could fail badly. Programs are not forced to work the way they do; they just happen to do so. Other facets of programs might be exploitable to attain high performance, especially if processors are designed for particular applications.

4. The cache mechanism adapts to execution streams by learning what items have been used and favoring recently used items over items that have not been used recently. It is possible to incorporate other kinds of hardware into a system that help the system adapt to observed behavior in an execution stream. The question is open as to where and what kind of hardware to use, and whether or not the cost of the extra hardware is justified by the performance gained.

2.3 Virtual Memory

The designers of the Atlas computer gambled heavily on program characteristics that tend to keep the active pages in high-speed memory. The cache memories described in the previous section are successful because address references show strong sequential locality, and cache management easily exploits such characteristics.

Virtual-memory systems, as they exist today, fulfill a role similar to cache memories, except that virtual-memory systems manage a different portion of the memory hierarchy. Cache-management algorithms attempt to make optimum use of a high-speed memory for which main memory serves as a backup buffer. Active items tend to move from main memory to cache, and inactive items tend to migrate back to main memory.

Virtual-memory systems attempt to make optimum use of main memory, while using an auxiliary memory, usually a rotating magnetic disk memory, for backup. Therefore, to the first order of approximation, the high-speed buffer memory of a cache system corresponds to main memory of a virtual-memory system, and the main memory of a cache system corresponds to an auxiliary memory of a virtual-memory system. The principles that govern the behavior of cache and virtual-memory systems are largely the same. Namely,

1. Keep active items in the memory that has the higher speed;
2. As items become inactive, migrate them back to the lower-speed memory; and
3. If the management algorithms are successful, the performance will tend to be close to the performance of the higher-speed memory, and the cost will tend to be close to the cost per bit of the lower-speed memory.

We have learned some implementation techniques for cache memories in the previous section, so one might believe that those implementation techniques carry over to virtual-memory systems. Unfortunately, they do not carry over directly because the details of costs and timing are dramatically different when you move from cache memories to virtual memories.

Effective designs are driven by details of performance and costs. Because cache and virtual memory are dramatically different in such details, implementations of the two memory-management schemes may be quite different. In this section we examine a very simple virtual-memory system to identify the design parameters. Then we look more closely at available implementation techniques to satisfy the needs of the design.

2.3.1 Virtual-Memory Structure

A simplified view of virtual memory is illustrated in Fig. 2.22. In this figure the address produced by the processor, which is called a *virtual address*, is mapped by hardware to a physical location in central memory if the item is located in main memory. If not, the result is a page fault that moves the page containing the item being moved to main memory. The size of the virtual address-space that contains the addresses produced by the processor need not bear any relation to the size of the physical address-space that contains the addresses in central memory produced by the mapper shown in the figure.

We tend to view virtual memory as the Atlas designers originally viewed it. That is, virtual memory is much larger than physical memory, and the objective of the virtual-memory system is to produce a large memory with high performance and low cost per byte. But the mapping scheme has been used successfully in situations in which virtual memory is much smaller than

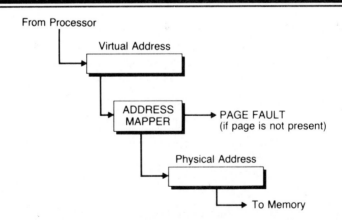

Fig. 2.22 The structure of a virtual-memory mapper.

physical memory, although such uses are becoming rarer. The applications in question arose because of technological changes that led to large, central memories whose costs were dramatically lower than the costs of prior generations.

Some computer families had been designed with relatively small address spaces, which cannot be changed because of compatibility requirements. Designers can create a machine whose physical memory is many times larger than the addressable memory available in the family, and then use virtual-memory mapping to permit software to run unchanged in the large physical memory. To make effective use of the large physical memory, the systems run several independent applications concurrently in a time-shared mode of operation frequently called *multiprogramming*.

In the early 1970s, for example, a limitation of 16 bits for addresses was natural, and, therefore, the typical virtual-memory space in minicomputers was 64K. When a memory of size 1M became available, then approximately 16 independent programs, each of maximum size 64K, could be run concurrently in the one physical memory of size 1M. Moreover, if the memory manager were successful in retaining the active pages in main memory and returning inactive pages to auxiliary memory, perhaps the main memory used per program could drop from 64K to something less, such as 32K. Then the number of independent programs that can run concurrently increases to about 32 programs, which makes the system reasonably cost-effective per user program.

The use of virtual memory in this example remains attractive only as long as it is necessary to run the software developed for the 16-bit address space. New programs should be written to take full advantage of the larger address space when the extra memory can be put to good use.

In the late 1970s the first machines with 32-bit addresses appeared, and by the mid-1980s, the multigigabyte virtual-address space was firmly entrenched in machines that ranged in size from engineering workstation to the high-end mainframe computer. Even with this large virtual address, it is just a matter of time before it becomes economical to deliver physical memories larger than four gigabytes. In recognition of this possibility, some architectures evolved to 48-bit virtual addresses by the start of the 1990s. Nevertheless, for any 32-bit architecture that does not evolve to a larger virtual address, in the present and immediate future the virtual-memory system maps a large address space into a smaller one. When technology can provide gigabyte memories at an economical price for the prevailing 32-bit environment, these same systems are likely to be redesigned to map the virtual space into larger physical spaces.

A significant difference between virtual-memory and cache-memory systems lies in the relative penalty of a page fault and a cache miss. In present technology, a cache miss is 4 to 20 times as costly as a cache hit, but a page fault is 1000 to 10,000 times as costly as a page hit. Rotating memory has a latency time fixed by mechanical limitations. Although electronic random-access memory has had speed improvements on the order of 1000 to 1 over the last two decades, the latency of mechanical memories has not improved by more than a factor of 10. Moreover, the mechanical limitations inherent in the design of rotating memories suggest that disks will not spin 1000 times faster, nor are they likely to have 1000 heads, which exhaust the two obvious ways to reduce latency.

For the near future, we are more likely to see the relative cost of a page fault increase as semiconductor memories continue to improve performance, while no significant improvements reduce disk latency. Over a longer period, we may see a new memory technology filling the gap between semiconductors and rotating mechanical memories. Such a technology would have a profound impact on virtual-memory implementation as we know it today.

The huge cost of page faults results in very different strategies for cache and virtual-memory management. During a cache miss, the processor becomes idle while waiting for data to arrive from main memory. Some activity pertaining to table maintenance may take place during the miss, but there is insufficient time available for other processes to do useful work on the processor. Hence, a cache miss is not accompanied by a change in task for the duration of the cache miss.

In a virtual-memory system, relatively large amounts of unused time are available while awaiting a page transfer from auxiliary memory. This time is so long that it is reasonable to put the processor to work on other tasks during the latency period attributed to a page fault. In typical systems, the latency experienced is from 1 to 100 ms, and a 10-MIPS processor can execute somewhere between 10,000 and 1,000,000 instructions of other programs during this period.

The earliest commercial implementations of virtual memory attempted to improve efficiency by turning the processor over to other pending tasks. The processor costs made the processor cycles a precious resource that should be conserved, if possible. Consequently, virtual memory was implemented in several different multiprogramming systems and in remote-access time-sharing systems. The idea was to create queues of pending tasks by amalgamating many users on a single system. When one user was delayed by a page fault, the processor could be dispatched with a second user's task in the interim.

The sharing of the processor is a natural solution when processor cycles are expensive. But sharing has its own negative factors. As processor utilization goes up and approaches 100 percent, each user sees a longer response time because the time to process a job depends on how long the job takes when running without contention and how long it spends in queues waiting for other users to terminate. Increased efficiency in the use of a processor generally is accompanied by increased waiting time for each job because of contention with other jobs for access to the processor.

As the cost per machine cycle has become very small, a new alternative has become possible. Instead of turning over control to a different job while

waiting for a page from auxiliary memory, it is reasonable in some circumstances to retain the processor and simply wait for the new page to arrive. In
such cases, the performance gain due to lack of contention for the processor is
more valuable than the loss due to cycles lost by the processor during page
faults.

There is another major negative impact on system design if a virtual-
memory manager forces an application to relinquish the processor on a page
fault. The policy interferes greatly with the ability to evaluate designs by using
address traces. Each page fault is accompanied by the execution of 1000 to
100,000 new instructions that would not be executed if the processor were not
reassigned during a page fault. If a simulation run is used to evaluate the
effects of a new control strategy, then what should be simulated during page
faults?

In essence, the attempt to evaluate new policies inevitably increases or
decreases the page faults observed. But there is no convenient mechanism for
modifying a trace dynamically to obtain an accurate description of the execution that actually takes place during page faults.

We have no difficulty evaluating cache designs from trace tapes, but we
have a great difficulty evaluating virtual-memory designs the same way.
Moreover, we can simulate a few seconds of processor time to obtain thousands
of cache misses, but the same simulation produces only tens or hundreds of
page faults, so trace data are subject to large statistical errors.

Consequently, virtual-memory evaluation is best performed in real time
with hardware or software measurements of activity. To obtain repeatability
and to evaluate different strategies on a common workload, the architect must
rely at least in part on a synthetic workload.

There are three major design considerations described in the next sections:

1. The mapping mechanism;
2. Partitioning for locality; and
3. The replacement strategy.

As these topics are presented, bear in mind how different the approaches
are from approaches that address similar functions for cache memories. The
differences are all attributable to the difference in the values of performance
and cost figures. This clearly shows the impact of specific values of design
parameters on architectural decisions and suggests how major technological
advances that alter these values will affect designs.

2.3.2 Virtual-Memory Mapping

The mapping device shown in Fig. 2.22 is grossly simplified for purposes of
exposition. Let us consider the requirements for a mapper and then discover
what additional complexity is required to make an effective mapper.

The basic function is to map a large address space into a much smaller one, so that we may view the virtual-memory mapper as performing the function shown in Fig. 2.23, where some large field of bits in a virtual address is replaced by a smaller field of bits to create a physical address. In Fig. 2.23, the displacement field describes the offset from the base of a page. The displacement is not changed by the mapper because the offset within a page is the same for a virtual address as it is for a physical address. We need to know only where the page begins in physical memory, and by adding the offset to this address, we can find the physical address of any item. Hence, the mapper uses the virtual-address bits other than the offset bits as it transforms addresses.

What makes the problem challenging is the very large number of pages in the virtual address. Consider the difference in the mapping problem for a virtual memory with 64K addresses (16 bits) as compared to a virtual memory with 4G addresses (32 bits). For purposes of comparison, in both cases we assume that the page size is 1K (10 bits).

In the smaller memory, there are only 6 bits, or 64 pages permitted in a program of maximum size. It is perfectly reasonable to store the translation table in a set of 64 registers and consult the translation table on each reference.

The larger memory system permits programs to grow to as large as 4M pages. A translation table with 4M entries is far too large to place in a set of dedicated registers, and it is costly by present standards to store in memory, although this is a possible solution in the future.

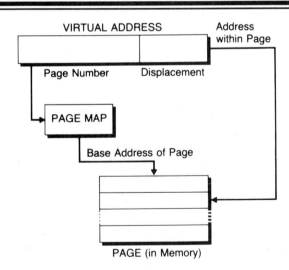

Fig. 2.23 A typical virtual-address translation.

How do you deal with such a large translation table? To reduce the memory demands for storing the translation table, most solutions in use today break up the one-level translation into two translations. The effect of having two levels could be disastrous on performance because each access then becomes three accesses, and worse yet, each of the two accesses into the translation table could generate its own page faults before the access to the requested page has occurred. So performance could be dramatically poorer just because of the overhead of the mapping process.

The overhead of mapping is reduced by means of an artifice called a *translation-lookaside buffer* (TLB), which is a cache for holding recently used mappings. Figure 2.24 gives the general structure of a virtual-memory mapper. We examine the details of the pieces in the following discussion.

In Fig. 2.24, a virtual address is broken into two fields, one for the offset and one that identifies a virtual page. The virtual-page field is presented to the translation-lookaside buffer, which checks its cache-like memory to see if a recent translation for that page took place. If so, the translation-lookaside

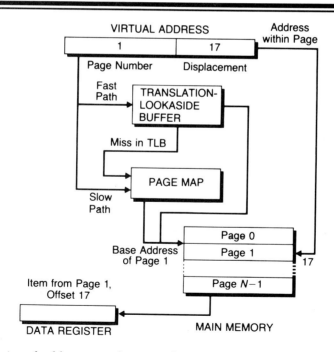

Fig. 2.24 A virtual-address translation with a translation-lookaside buffer (TLB) for fast operation.

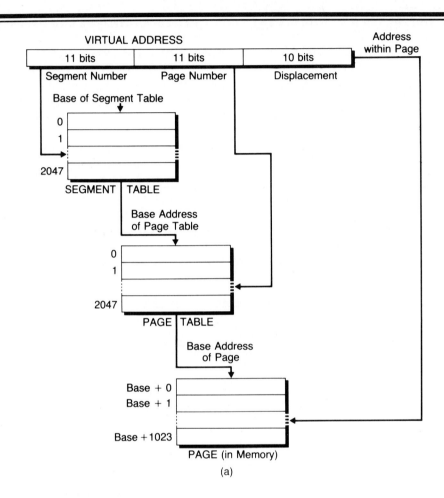

Fig. 2.25 Two-level mappings:
(a) A typical two-level mapping; and

buffer returns the base address of the page, and the mapping is completed. Just from our knowledge of cache behavior, we would expect almost all references to be satisfied by the lookaside buffer.

If an address misses in the lookaside buffer, the two-level mapping is performed. We describe the details later in this section. A miss in the two-level mapping is a page fault, and the virtual-memory manager must intervene to correct it. Otherwise, the mapping produces the base address of a physical page that can be added to the offset to obtain the full physical address.

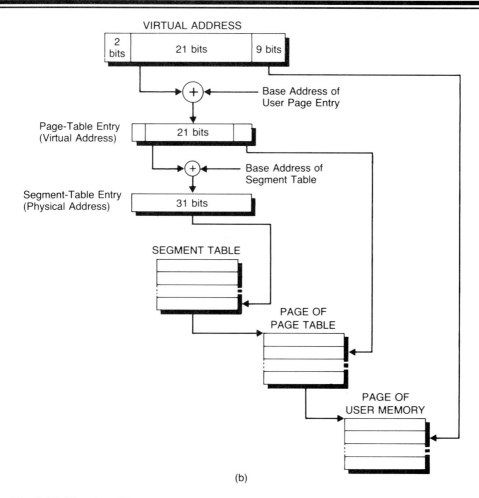

Fig. 2.25 (Continued)
(b) A two-level mapping used in the VAX architecture.

In the last operation, if we force pages to begin on addresses that are multiples of the page size, then we can save an addition operation in the mapping transformation. In this case, since the low-order bits of the full base address are known to be zero, the page offset can be concatenated to a shortened base address rather than be added to the full base address.

One possible two-level mapping is shown in Fig. 2.25(a). The idea is to break up the large field into two smaller fields. Common terminology is to designate the high-order field as a *segment number* and the next field as a *page number*, although the term *segment* is used to denote other concepts related to virtual memory.

In this example, the 22 bits remaining after stripping off the 10-bit offset are broken into an 11-bit segment number and 11-bit page number. The segment number is used in the first level of the transformation as the index to a Segment Table. From the Segment Table we obtain the base address of a page table. The page number is combined with this base address to consult a page-table entry that has the base address of the page itself.

The effect of using two levels is to reduce the page-table number from 22 bits to two indices, each of which is no more than 11 bits, so that no single table needs to be larger than 2048 entries. What has happened in the two-level mapping is that a very large page table has been broken into many pieces, each of which is no larger than 2048 entries. The smaller tables need not reside in main memory if they are not in active use. Hence, we need have in memory only the portions of the page table that are active.

The penalty for the two-level mapping is the second level of lookup. Moreover, both levels can have page faults during a lookup, although the Segment Table rarely faults because it is accessed relatively frequently. If we had a choice, we would prefer not to pay the penalty for the second access, but the enormous size of the resulting page table makes the alternative one-level mapping impractical under most cost measures. The scheme becomes practical only when the cost of tables of size 4M can be ignored.

There is a problem with the scheme in Fig. 2.25(a), resolved by the scheme shown in Fig. 2.25(b). The problem pertains to shared pages that are accessed by independent programs. Each program in a shared page produces virtual addresses that must be mapped to physical addresses. The virtual addresses produced by shared code may conflict with the virtual addresses selected by users or by other shared programs that are linked to run as part of the same job. It is necessary to ensure that shared programs generate virtual addresses that do not conflict with each other or with user addresses.

The scheme shown in Fig. 2.25(b) models the address-transformation mechanism used on the VAX architecture. In this scheme, virtual memory is divided into two regions, each with 2G bytes (31-bit addresses). The scheme uses two levels of mapping for addresses that lie in user virtual memory, but only one level of mapping for virtual addresses that lie in system virtual memory. The leading 2 bits of a 32-bit address uniquely identifies the virtual address as belonging to one of two user regions or to one of two system regions. Shared system programs reside in one of the system regions. The leading 2 bits of a virtual address thus determine which of four possible tables are to be used during the address mapping.

The VAX implementation treats the entire 21-bit field of an address with the leading 2 bits and 9-bit offset removed as a page number to be used in an address transformation. A page number is converted into an address by adding to it the contents of a base register identified as the User Page Table base address in Fig. 2.25(b). (The page number is multiplied by four before doing the addition to account for the length of each entry in the VAX-11 page tables, but this is not shown explicitly in the figure.)

The address produced by this transformation is a virtual address, not a physical address, which is one key difference between Fig. 2.25(a) and (b). This virtual address lies in system space, so that only one level of access is required to change it into a physical address of a page-table entry. After that transformation is completed, the physical address of the page-table entry goes through one additional level of access to produce the final physical address that corresponds to the original user virtual address.

To map the virtual address of the page-table entry, the processor extracts a 21-bit page number from the page-table entry address, and adds this to the base address of a table in system space to produce a true physical address. The system table in this case is identified in the figure as the Segment Table to be consistent with Fig. 2.25(a), but the VAX architecture documentation uses the name System Page Table for this table [Eckhouse and Levy 1980]. The physical address obtained from this mapping is an address in the Segment Table. The first memory access in the mapping process occurs at that address.

The Segment Table lookup produces the higher-order bits of the base address of a page in the user page table. These bits, when concatenated with the 9-bit displacement field of the virtual address of the page-table entry produce a physical address of a single page-table entry, and the next access occurs at this location. From the page-table entry, the process finds the higher order bits of the base address of the user page. To these bits the processor concatenates the 9-bit displacement field of the original virtual address and produces the physical address of the item sought.

The two base addresses, User Page Table and Segment Table, both reside in processor registers. No memory access is required to obtain these base addresses, so the first access to physical memory is the access to the Segment Table.

References to shared pages of system programs are handled by placing the shared pages in system space, not in user space. System-space addresses are transformed to physical addresses by just a single level of mapping, as shown in the figure, and only the Segment Table is used for this mapping.

Hence the page table used to access shared pages is the Segment Table, which is shared among all processes, whereas the page table used to access unshared user-pages resides in user memory and is private to each process. In this way, user addresses are distinct from addresses produced by shared programs, and shared programs can produce addresses without contention provided that they occupy disjoint regions of the system virtual memory.

Obviously, the system virtual memory must be large enough to accommodate all shared pages in distinct areas, which is possible only for large virtual memories. Although 2G bytes available for the VAX is very large by some standards, even this may not be enough for all possible shared programs. In actual practice, VAX uses both the scheme described here for sharing system functions, and conventional schemes for sharing other items in user memory by pointing to the shared items through user page tables. Thus, the commonly shared items are handled efficiently through a one-level mapping while the less commonly shared items require two levels of mapping.

Let us return momentarily to the translation-lookaside buffer that appears in Fig. 2.24. We described it as functionally similar to a cache memory, and indeed its design is very close to that of a cache. Clark and Emer [1985] describe the analysis of a translation-lookaside buffer for the VAX-11/780 architecture, and their paper is a model of the classic design and analysis techniques for cache. They use a trace-driven approach to simulate a variety of structures varying from 64 to 512 sets and with both one-way and two-way set associativity. Some aspects of their paper are different from cache studies and are worth commenting on here.

The Clark-Emer data suggest that misses occur in the translation-lookaside buffer at the rate of between 0.5 to 3.0 per 100 instructions. This is not the same as the miss and hit ratios described earlier because the ratios for cache references are developed on a *per-reference* basis, whereas the Clark-Emer data are on a *per-instruction* basis. Since one instruction produces several references, including instruction fetch, indirect address fetch, operand fetch, and operand store, the equivalent miss ratio for translation look aside buffers is probably a factor of 3 or 4 smaller than the misses per 100 instructions. So, indeed, misses in the translation-lookaside buffer are rather rare.

The penalty for a miss in the buffer is also quite different from the penalty for a cache miss. The cache miss is followed by an access to main memory, which is perhaps ten times slower than is the cache. But the cost of a buffer miss is an access to the cache, which is somewhat faster than an access to main memory.

Clark and Emer report a surprisingly small hit rate to the cache to retrieve items that miss in the lookaside buffer. The hit rate is only about 40 percent. Perhaps this is the case because the lookaside buffer may be very successful in handling most references to page table entries—so successful in fact that such references are quickly purged from cache once they are placed there.

If eventually a miss occurs in the lookaside buffer, then the likelihood of finding that reference in the cache apparently is very low, only 40 percent as opposed to over 90 percent for other references. Another possible explanation for the high miss rate is that a miss in the lookaside buffer occurs most frequently when a program changes its activity or a total change of process takes place. But these times are precisely the same times when a cache produces the bulk of its misses.

Another aspect of the lookaside buffer that is different from the cache is that the translation mapping is dependent on the process running. The look-aside buffer sees virtual addresses, not physical addresses. These addresses are not unique, so there must be some mechanism for identifying which virtual addresses go with which process in the lookaside buffer. This mechanism does not need to exist for a cache memory that stores physical addresses in its directory because physical addresses are unique.

One way to handle the problem of associating the correct mapping with an address reference is to place a process tag in the lookaside buffer with each entry. Then a match occurs only if the process tag in the buffer matches the process tag of the running process.

The approach used in the VAX-11/780 lookaside buffer is to flush the lookaside buffer of entries for private (per-process) mappings when a context switch occurs. This could be a fairly expensive process depending on the size of the lookaside buffer, the time it takes to purge the entries, and the frequency of context switches. Instead of selectively purging just the entries for private mappings, it may be faster to purge the entire buffer, and thereby purge the entries for shared as well as private mappings. In this case there is a penalty paid later for reloading the shared mappings.

We do not have specific advice on which approach is better because there is no absolute answer. Here is a case in which the designer should perform a thorough analysis following the model of Clark and Emer to determine which approach yields both the best cost/performance for the technology to be used and the presumed workload for the architecture.

2.3.3 Improving Program Locality

The mapping transformations described thus far have presumed that large programs are broken into equal-sized pages, and the pages are managed by a virtual-memory operating system. The pages are arbitrary and need not have any relation to the logical structure of the program. Since the page is the atom to be used by the virtual-memory manager, a reference to any single item on a page results in the entire page being present in main memory.

If the contents of a single page are logically related, then bringing in a page when any item on that page is accessed makes available inexpensive accesses to the other related items. If the items on a page are unrelated, the page fetch may bring in unwanted items, resulting in poor use of both available memory bandwidth and resident memory.

Structuring programs so that related items are packed together on rela-tively few pages is definitely advantageous. In essence, this postulates a new structure in which programs and data are grouped together according to their logical relations rather than because of arbitrary factors. Virtual-memory systems that attempt to account for logical relationships within programs are sometimes called *segmented-memory systems*, as opposed to paged-memory systems. A *segment* is a collection of related programs and data that forms a subprogram unit. Segments can invoke other segments, and some commonly used segments can be shared among many users.

What makes segments different from pages is that segments are not fixed in size. They can be as large or small as the programmer chooses to make them. Because segments are not uniform in size, memory management is far more complex than for pages of a fixed, uniform size.

Although various techniques have been developed for memory allocation of variable-length structures, it is also possible to combine paging and segmentation in a single virtual-memory system. The idea here is to use segmentation to produce logical structures of program and data, and then move portions of segments in and out of memory by breaking segments into pages of fixed size. Techniques for paged virtual memories carry over directly to this scheme, and no significant added difficulty for handling variable-sized segments is imposed.

There are a few differences between segmented and paged systems, however, that should be brought to light. One difference is in the structures of a segmented-address space and a paged-address space. A paged-address space is a one-dimensional space in which all addresses lie in one contiguous region in virtual memory. Given any address (except possibly the last address) in this memory, you obtain the address of the next item by increasing the current address by one.

A segmented memory is a two-dimensional space. Each address consists of two fields, a segment number and an offset within the segment. All addresses within a segment lie in one contiguous area of virtual memory. However, segments are not contiguous to each other; they are distinct.

When you increment the highest possible address of a segment, you do not obtain the address of an element in a new segment. You create a condition that is recognized as an attempt to access an out-of-bounds address.

For example, consider a virtual memory system with 48-bit addresses, of which 24 bits indicate an offset within a segment, and 24 bits indicate a segment number. In this system, a program can create references to up to 16M different segments, each of which has up to 16M addressable locations. If a program attempts to reference an item in Segment i and calculates an address whose offset exceeds 16M, the virtual address produced will not increment the segment portion of the address field when the offset overflows. Hence, the reference continues to be to Segment i, except that the overflow from the offset field is detected and produces a program exception.

Given this structure, we have an interesting problem in handling shared memory. Suppose a segment is shared by two programs, Program A and Program B. Shall we impose the restriction that both programs designate this segment as Segment 10? Or will we permit Program A to designate the segment as Segment 2, while Program B designates it as Segment 11? To restrict all shared segments to unique numbers is similar in spirit to the handling of shared segments in the VAX virtual memory, as we discussed earlier. This method makes sense for sharing system programs that are available essentially at all times.

In a more general context, however, we may want all segments to be shareable, or we may have a huge collection of shared segments that exceeds the number of unique segment numbers available. So for one reason or another, we want to let Program A and Program B refer to a shared segment by their own respective indices for this segment.

One possible way to provide access to the shared data under this stipulation is to provide a segment table with each process. The segment table provides the information to translate a segment reference from Process A or from Process B into the correct physical reference to a shared segment. Figure 2.26 shows this scheme. Note that the shared segment is Segment 1 for A but is Segment 2 for B.

In this scheme, the virtual addresses for referring to the shared segment depend on which segment has issued the address. Then each process has a private segment table for accessing shared segments, as opposed to the common table used for the VAX architecture.

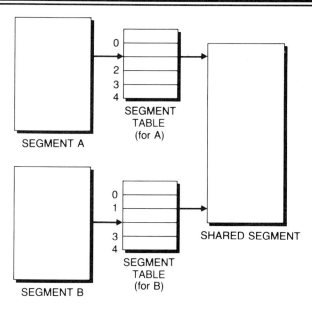

Fig. 2.26 Access to a shared segment through private segment tables.

Moreover, the addresses produced by the shared segments have to be mapped correctly for each context in which they operate. Thus, it may be necessary to force a shared segment to access a variable in Process *A* at Segment 10, but when running in a different context, that same access is made to a shared variable in Process *B* at Segment 15.

The segment number of a reference produced by a shared program in general is dependent on the context in which it runs, and the ability to produce segment numbers that depend on the context may have to be incorporated into the architecture. The VAX solution to sharing avoids the complication of the general solution and is satisfactory for shared system programs.

To eliminate the burden of consulting the segment table on each reference to an external segment, designers usually incorporate a translation-lookaside buffer or the equivalent to catch the majority of references without accessing the segment table. As control passes from one segment to another, it is rather important to purge the lookaside buffer so that its translation is correct for each context.

2.3.4 Replacement Algorithms

The obvious way to manage virtual memory is to manage it in the same way that cache is managed. In fact, Belady's work [1966] on optimal replacement strategies (cited in our cache discussion) was done in the context of virtual-memory systems. But, in general, virtual-memory systems are sufficiently different from cache memories as to require dramatically different techniques for management. The principal differences between virtual memory and cache memory are:

1. Page faults are very costly. There is a greater relative savings in reducing page faults than there is in cache misses.

2. While responding to a page fault, there is substantial time available for memory-management functions that might reduce future faults.

3. Virtual-memory systems may run competing programs when a program reaches a page fault. The competing programs may interfere with memory management and could grossly impair performance. No competing programs are run during the processing of cache misses.

Early implementations of virtual-memory systems examined various replacement policies, and soon the strengths of least-recently used replacement in predicting the future were recognized. However, when LRU replacement and other similar policies were implemented in early commercial virtual-memory systems, the systems occasionally entered periods of instability during which almost all machine cycles were devoted to handling page traffic and essentially no useful work could be accomplished. The problem was not the fault of the replacement policy *per se*, but rather a lack of understanding of the dynamics of a virtual-memory system. Detailed studies revealed that some critical factors had been overlooked.

One problem stemmed from trying to accomplish too much in a single virtual-memory system. The instabilities occurred at high loads; otherwise performance was acceptable.

Denning [1968a] termed the instability *thrashing* because the prime characteristic was a very high traffic between main memory and auxiliary memory of frequently used pages. A page might be brought to main memory, used a few times, then returned to auxiliary memory, only to be recalled to main memory.

Another related mode of instability occurred when a process lost some critical pages from main memory, but eventually recovered those pages, only to have lost other critical pages in the interim. Every program enters phases during which some subset of pages is used frequently. Denning [1968b] called this subset the *working set* of pages.

The working set is in essence the footprint of a program execution over a short period of time. If a program has its entire working set in main memory, it will have a very low page-fault rate as computation progresses. Page faults increase dramatically when portions of the working set are not available. So one key principle is to run programs by striving to have the full working set in memory at the time the program is run.

A corollary of this principle recognizes that it is unrealistic to move an entire working set from memory to disk and back again between successive time slots allocated for program execution in a multiprogrammed, virtual-memory system. In fact, it is unrealistic to move any significant portion of a working set out of main memory and back in again under the same conditions.

In essence, if a program is to run effectively, its working set must be resident and must stay resident in main memory until the program terminates. This rule can be relaxed somewhat for programs that interact with humans because some displacement of the working set can be tolerated during the time that the human is thinking and reacting to prior output. Otherwise, as a general rule, main memory must hold the working sets of the active programs.

If the working sets exceed in total size the area reserved for them, then the system is likely to become unstable. Figure 2.16 tends to confirm the need to hold working sets in main memory. Virtual memories tend to behave like caches with large K (set-associativity) values. The figure shows a sharp drop in the reload transient as cache size increases. This drop occurs at the point where the cache is big enough to hold both footprints. If the cache is smaller than this critical size, the reload transient is very large, which means that one program completely overlays the other as they successively take control of the processor and cache.

Therefore, to eliminate thrashing, a reasonable approach is to estimate the size and content of working sets, and to load into main memory a collection of complete working sets whose total size does not exceed the memory available. Any additional requests for machine cycles should be deferred until some process or processes terminate and make sufficient memory available to hold the working set of the new process.

If this principle is to be used to manage memory, then we need some way to calculate the working set dynamically during program execution. Denning [1968b] provides some guidance by describing a mechanism for discovering the working set. He defines the function $W(t, w)$, the working set at time t for window w. This is the set of pages referenced in the last w seconds at time t.

A memory manager based on the notion of the working set attempts to hold in memory only those pages that belong to the working set because references are most likely to be made to the working set and are very unlikely to be made to pages outside the working set, except during periods when the working set is changing because the program is moving into a new phase. Therefore the memory manager brings in a new page when a page fault occurs and adds the new page to the working set. The memory manager deletes from the working set those pages that have not been referenced within the last w seconds.

Here is one possible memory-management policy that takes advantage of the properties of the working set.

1. When a page fault occurs, add the new page to working set.
2. From the set of pages not referenced within a window of w seconds immediately prior to the page fault, select the least-recently used page, and discard it. If all pages have been referenced within the working-set window, then discard no page, and let the working set grow.
3. If two or more pages have not been referenced within the working-set window, then discard the two least-recently used pages.

Note that there must be some rule that diminishes the number of pages allocated; otherwise the size of memory allocated to a process grows until no free memory is available for references to new pages. That is the purpose of the third rule. This set of rules is slightly different but similar in intent to the rules proposed by Coffman and Denning [1973, p. 299].

It is very important that the working-set window be measured in *virtual* time, by counting clock ticks only while the process is executing. No clock ticks are counted during page faults or during other periods when the given process is inactive.

The size of the window can be determined experimentally. If it is too large, some pages will tend to be retained too long. If the window is too small, it may not span the times of references to the actual working set. The optimum window size is just large enough to cover the working sets of all programs. It is better to err by using too large a window than too small a window because the consequences of using the wrong window size are less severe when the window is too large.

The working-set concept is an intuitively appealing way of handling page replacement, but measuring the working set is somewhat difficult, even with special hardware. One possible way to approximate the working set is to identify which pages are accessed during the brief execution of a program in a system that grants the processor in round-robin fashion to a collection of programs.

We assume that each program is granted some fixed quantum of time during which the processor executes that program. Before the quantum begins, access tables are initialized to show that no page has been touched. These tables are best kept in hardware such as a translation-lookaside buffer or a special memory devoted to tracking page accesses. As each page is touched, the hardware automatically sets an activity bit in the access table to record this occurrence. At the completion of the quantum, the working set is deemed to be the pages whose activity bits have been set, and the remaining pages may be removed from main memory.

This form of the memory-management algorithm is quite workable if supported by hardware that can turn off all activity bits for a process and can turn them on selectively on access. Other solutions are possible as well, and the architect has a great deal of freedom in trading off the cost of implementation against approximations to the working set. The working set itself is an approximation to a perfect predictor of the future.

Chu and Opderbeck [1976] proposed an alternative approach to the working-set approach that has the advantage of using directly measurable variables for guiding the replacement decision. The method is called the *page-fault-frequency method*. It exhibits different policies when the frequency of page faults is above or below a fixed threshold. The reasoning behind this method is that programs tend to operate in phases, accessing one working set consistently while in one phase, and then moving to a new working set in the next phase. The page faults tend to occur during a change of phase.

Our earlier discussion of the cache-reload transient examines the corresponding phenomenon for cache memories. A high frequency of page faults is a signal that the program is entering a new phase and that the current working set may have to be replaced. It is clear that as new pages are touched, they should enter the new working set. All pages in the former working set are candidates for replacement.

One way of implementing a replacement policy based on the notion of page-fault frequency is the following, which is similar to the method proposed by Chu and Opderbeck.

1. Assume a threshold θ for page-fault frequencies.
2. When a page fault occurs, estimate the page-fault frequency for the given

program. A crude estimate is $1/(t_1 - t_0)$, where t_1 is the virtual time of the present fault, and t_0 is the virtual time of the last fault. A better estimate is an average taken over the last few faults.

3. If the estimated frequency exceeds θ, then assume that the program has entered a transient phase or that there is presently insufficient memory allocated to the process to hold its full working set. Add the newly referenced page to the working set and increase the amount of memory allocated to the program by one page.

4. If the estimated frequency does not exceed θ, then assume that the program is in a stable pattern of memory references. Add the new page to the working set and remove some page not referenced since the last page fault, preferably the least-recently used page.

5. If the estimated frequency does not exceed θ over some fixed time period, then assume that the program has entered a stable phase and that it may have some dead pages within its present allocation. If there are pages that are currently allocated to the program and that have not been referenced recently, then decrease the number of pages allocated to the program and discard a corresponding number of unreferenced pages. We presume that the pages are discarded in the order of least-recently used, if this is possible.

The role of the last rule is to provide a means for decreasing the allocation of pages to a process. Without this rule, the number of pages allocated would grow until no memory remained for allocation to new pages. Another way to implement this rule is to establish a different lower threshold on page-fault frequency, below which a process has pages removed from its working set.

One can easily measure the frequency of page faults by means of a process timer that is normally present in an architecture. The memory manager takes note of the length of execution time between faults each time a page fault occurs. This is easy for the memory manager to do because it is invoked when a fault occurs and has access to the process timer.

If recent history for a process shows that faults are occurring at a rate that exceeds a system threshold, the memory manager increases the allocation of pages for the program, using a decision criterion similar to the working-set criterion. If the fault rate is below the threshold, the memory manager either performs a one-for-one replacement or reduces the allocation by discarding one or more pages that have not been referenced recently, in addition to performing one-for-one replacement. The latter strategy may occasionally produce costly page faults if too much is discarded, but it may be useful to invoke when the pages used to hold active working sets occupy nearly all available memory. Also, by attempting to replace pages when page faults are low, the probability of finding a dead page is somewhat higher than when page faults are high.

The working-set and page-fault frequency algorithms ultimately retain only the pages in the working set while programs are executing continuously in one phase of computation. There is a difference in the behavior of these algorithms during transients. The page-fault frequency algorithm anchors its observation point at a page fault, and by doing so, the memory manager can fix its observation at a time when a transient appears to have begun. Then the manager can observe all of the pages touched since that fixed time.

In a sense, this is a working-set algorithm in which the window size varies dynamically, depending on the observed fault rate. It provides for narrowing that window during transients and widening the window when transients have ended. This will tend to discard old pages when they are no longer needed. A pure working-set algorithm has a fixed window size, but this is very difficult to implement. In reality, the working-set window used by typical memory managers begins each time the memory manager takes control.

We have purposely avoided a detailed specification of the page-fault-frequency and working-set-replacement algorithms because an implementer is free to adjust and modify a replacement algorithm to fit the characteristics of the architecture and the workload. There is no single implementation of either algorithm that is preferred or standard. The general idea behind the algorithms is what is important.

The working-set concept is based on the assumption that the immediate future will be something like the recent past. The page-fault-frequency algorithm is based on the notion that a transient between two program phases is signaled by a higher-than-normal page-fault rate.

The working-set algorithm in its purest form is difficult to implement because a sliding window of fixed size is not easily incorporated into hardware or software. The page-fault-frequency algorithm provides for policies that depend on more readily observable quantities and on hardware logging of accesses, which is easier to implement than is a working-set window.

In spite of these apparent differences, the practical implementations of working-set-replacement policies use the same hardware and the same observations as the page-fault-frequency algorithms, and the actual replacement policy for a working-set algorithm may be implemented almost identically to a page-fault-frequency algorithm. In fact, Coffman and Denning [1973, p. 289] describe a working-set-replacement policy that is essentially a page-fault-frequency model as we have described previously.

2.3.5 Buffering Effects in Virtual-Memory Systems

The preceding section describes how to exploit the characteristic reference patterns of almost all programs to hold the frequently used data in the fastest memory. This section describes another characteristic of virtual-memory systems that is not widely recognized. The characteristic is that a certain amount of space must be allocated permanently to buffering disk operations, and the amount of space to use grows proportionally with the access delay to disk data. We examine the implications of this characteristic and suggest that the amount of buffer space in future systems is likely to grow because access delays are likely to be relatively longer.

We indicated earlier that accesses to data on rotating memories suffer a delay anywhere from 10 to 100 ms or more. If we break this access delay into components, part is due to the time required for a read/write head to position itself over the track that contains the data requested. An additional delay stems from the rotational delay while waiting for an item to reach the read/write head. Yet another delay is the time required to transmit data from the auxiliary memory through an input/output port to main memory. The rotational delay averages a half revolution when access requests are honored in a first-come, first-serve order and the requests are randomly generated. By batching requests and carefully reordering them to reduce waiting time, the average delay due to rotational latency can be reduced, but this is partially offset by an increase in the average time due to time lost by reordering or other aspects of contention for disk resources.

Obviously, mechanical limitations prevent the rotational speed of disk drives to be so fast that the average rotational latency is comparable to the time needed to access random-access memory. Moreover, very large memories will inevitably suffer from access delays to individual data, regardless of the storage technology, simply because an effective means to reduce the cost per bit of large memories is to share access circuitry over many bits.

In present technology, the single read/write mechanism of a disk drive is shared by all bits on the disk, and it takes mechanical motion to position the read/write mechanism over any designated position on the disk. In future technologies, the motion might be nonmechanical by, for example, deflecting a laser beam to a particular physical position on a storage surface. Nevertheless, the time required to redirect a laser beam may be long compared to the cycle times of very high speed memory devices, even though the time is much shorter than the time would be if mechanical motion were required.

Now consider how a long latency time affects a computer system. In virtual-memory systems, the long latency experienced after a page fault requires that the system be used for other purposes. There is typically a queue of processes ready to use the machine when a running process faults. Let us assume momentarily that we have as much capacity as required in available memory and input/output bandwidth to ensure a large queue of ready processes. Under these conditions disk latency does not necessarily lead to idle processor time, although in actual practice these ideal conditions are not realized, and latency could lead to substantial idle time.

Consider what happens when a program experiences a page fault. The portion of the program resident in main memory remains inactive in main memory while the missing page is retrieved. The longer the access time to the missing page, the longer that the resident program occupies main memory without doing useful work. The effect of latency is to create certain regions in memory that are inactive. In a sense, they have become buffer regions awaiting pages arriving from the disk and holding pages awaiting transfer back to the disk.

If latency is truly very large, then it may be reasonable to remove inactive data from main memory when a page fault occurs and reload them at a later time. Even so, some physical pages of main memory are still being used as buffer memory. These pages buffer the data moving out of main memory immediately after a page fault. They also buffer the data of a new process being moved into main memory. Once a new process becomes resident, it can become active, and the physical pages are again activated after being used solely for buffering.

To give some idea how much memory has to be dedicated to buffering in a steady state, consider a simple model of a program that experiences page faults. Suppose that on the average a program with a working-set size of W pages can execute for N seconds between faults. Let the delay due to disk latency be D seconds. Then for D seconds out of every $N + D$ seconds, the working set is idle, and we have in a sense a buffer of an average size $WD/(N + D)$ if the program executes without any other programs in memory.

Since we assume that the processor is to be fully utilized by other programs waiting to run, we need to determine how many such programs should be available. The given program has to wait D seconds when it faults, and during this time we can run roughly D/N other programs, each faulting after N seconds, to use up a total of D seconds. At the end of D seconds, the original page fault should be cleared, and the initial program can be restarted. Since this ideal system has $(N + D)/N$ programs running concurrently, each of which is acting like a buffer with an effective size of $WD/(N + D)$, the total buffer storage is something on the order of WD/N. Hence, the amount of main memory dedicated to buffering page faults increases linearly with D.

In this analysis we have been counting the space occupied by programs as buffer space, but the space is quite distinct from the regions that are set aside as disk buffers. These regions, too, must grow in size in proportion to latency.

When a record or a page is transmitted to a buffer to await transfer to a disk, the relative time spent in that buffer is a function of the latency. Together, the memory requirements for input/output buffers and programs delayed by page faults must grow proportionately to disk latency. Since the timing factors are relative, we discover that the growth must take place if we hold disk latency fixed and double processor performance. This particular event happens to be a likely one in an era when advances in semiconductors improve processor performance by larger factors than advances in mechanical technology can reduce access delays in auxiliary memories.

There are several implications of this observation. Suppose, for example, that we have a high-performance virtual-memory system with 100 M-bytes of main memory, and the system is very efficient in its current implementation. Now suppose that we obtain a new disk with double the capacity of the present disk, but with twice the average access time. When the new disk replaces the old disk, we should also increase the size of main memory to compensate for longer access time or reduce the number of concurrently running processes by a factor of 2. If we do not compensate for the longer access times, the longer latency will degrade performance.

A second implication is that the page-replacement algorithms are somewhat sensitive to the physical characteristics of the rotating memory. As the amount of memory dedicated to buffering disk operations increases, the amount of memory left available to hold working sets decreases. In other words, the page-replacement algorithm must relate disk latency to the amount of memory that can be allocated among requesting programs. If new disks replace old ones, the page-replacement policy has to alter its estimate of memory available for user programs.

A third implication is that it becomes reasonable to consider where that buffer should be located. In fact, the buffer might well be located in the auxiliary memory rather than in the main processor. Such a scheme is shown in Fig. 2.27. The disk buffers (sometimes called *disk caches*) first appeared in volume in the mid-1970s as the costs of memory diminished.

When memory is very expensive, one can argue that the wisest way to design a memory system is to place all the memory in one unit, the central processor, so that it can be allocated freely as necessary. As memory costs decrease, the need to conserve memory by using a single pool is diminished. Other factors dictate that there are benefits to breaking memory into two or more pools that are preallocated to specific purposes.

Figure 2.27 shows a system with a disk buffer contained within the disk system that is distinct from the memory associated within the central processor. The disk buffer is dedicated to disk operations and cannot be used as executable memory.

The purpose of the disk buffer is, in effect, to create one more level in the memory hierarchy. The disk buffer acts as an auxiliary memory with a very short latency, thereby reducing the buffer requirements in main memory.

In essence, the buffers that we have observed earlier have been moved out of main memory and now reside at the other end of the input/output channel. There will still be some buffering of pages in main memory because latency is small but nonzero because of transmission delays in the input/output channel and page faults in the disk buffer. If the system of Fig. 2.27 is well designed, the page faults will occur mostly in the disk buffer and seldom in main memory.

There are several performance gains that can be achieved by moving the buffer to the disk. One advantage is that the data-management algorithms for the buffer can be optimized to the specific characteristics of the disk system.

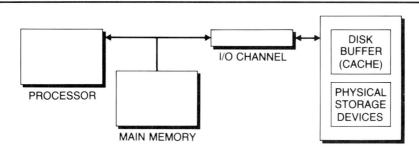

Fig. 2.27 A storage system with a disk buffer.

Thus, when a disk system is replaced with a new system, the memory-management algorithms in the central processor need not be altered because the device-dependent characteristics are being treated within the disk system. The disk buffer creates an auxiliary memory whose performance characteristics as seen by the central processor tend to be independent of the true physical characteristics of the disk.

Earlier we discussed how changes in latency result in changes in the amount of memory serving as a buffer for pages. In the configuration of Fig. 2.27, almost all effects of latency can be absorbed within the disk-system buffer, making such changes completely invisible to the central processor memory-management algorithm. Thus, when new equipment imposes a need for additional buffer capacity, that buffer capacity can be added in the disk subsystem where it is of direct use.

To obtain full benefit of the disk buffer, the buffer controller must have information regarding the requests for data because various types of requests have different management algorithms that work best. We have been discussing page traffic, and for such requests a memory-management algorithm should attempt to identify current working sets.

The disk system also receives requests for data files, and for such requests the type of access is a major consideration. For example, the manager should prefetch records associated with sequential files and deallocate space for sequential records immediately after their first use. Database management treats indices differently from data records, so a disk-buffer manager should manage indices differently than records. Therefore, the disk buffer in Fig. 2.27 is ideally implemented as an "intelligent" disk buffer that can manage the buffer memory in a manner that takes best advantage of each identifiable type of access.

There is a performance benefit in Fig. 2.27 over a system that has no disk buffer. The performance enhancement is due to the ability to hold data in fast memory without burdening the input/output channel. The disk buffer may actually access and hold many records that are never requested if the buffer-management algorithms attempt to bring data that are likely to be accessed into the buffer memory. This incurs the costs of wasted accesses and additional hardware for the buffer memory to hold the unused requests, but it does not load the input/output channel.

There are situations in which the input/output channel is the primary bottleneck, and the disk system has spare capacity to read data into the buffer. Under these conditions, the ability to have new data in the buffer can reduce average access time without contributing to the channel overload.

Exercises

2.1 The object of this exercise is to work through the design of a cache.

a) The instruction set for your architecture has 44-bit addresses, with each addressable item being a byte. You elect to design a four-way set associative cache with each of the four lines in a set containing 64 bytes. Assume that you have 256 sets in the cache. Show how the 44-bit physical address is treated in performing a cache reference.

b) Consider the following sequence of addresses. (All are hex numbers)

0E1B01AA050 0E1B01AA073 0E1B2FE3057 0E1B4FFD85F 0E1B01AA04E

In your cache, what will be the tags in the set(s) that contain these references at the end of the sequence? Assume some initial state. Show the initial and final states.

c) The cost of your cache is roughly proportional to the number of bits of storage required. The purpose of this question is to determine how many bits are used for each function.

How many bits are required to hold the cache data? How did you get this number?

How many bits are required to store address tags? How did you get this number?

The cache is four-way set associative. What is the fewest number of bits required to keep track of which line to replace when replacement is LRU? How did you get this number?

d) We can construct a cache with the identical number of data bytes by doubling the line size and by reducing set associativity to 2. How does this change the cost of the cache as measured in total bits?

2.2 This problem asks you to consider the performance effects of doubling the line size of a cache as compared to doubling the number of sets in a cache.

Suppose you have a basic cache design such as that given in the first problem. You wish to increase the size of the cache because memory prices have dropped since the last design was completed. You have two options—double the line size of the cache or double the number of sets. You want to estimate the performance difference of the two designs. Make any assumptions that you wish about the basic design.

a) Find a sequence of address references that produces more misses in the cache with longer line size than in the cache with more sets.

b) Find a sequence of address references that produces more misses in the cache with more sets than in the cache with longer line size.

c) Given these two sequences, describe qualitatively the characteristics of an address trace that determine which of the two ways to double cache size will perform better.

2.3 After some careful experimentation, you discover that each time you double the size of a cache, you reduce the absolute number of cache misses by a factor of $1 - k$ where $k < 1$. That is,

$$Misses(2N) = k \; Misses(N)$$

Find a general solution to this recurrence equation in the form

$$Misses(N) = A \; N^B$$

where A and B are constants.

2.4 The object of this exercise is to work through the design of a cache together with a virtual memory mapping.

a) The instruction set for your architecture has a virtual address 32 bits long, and the virtual address is mapped into a physical address that is 28 bits long. Suppose pages have P bytes, and suppose p is the base 2 logarithm of P. Then the page mapping is done by stripping the page displacement (the least-significant p bits of the address) from the full virtual address, using the remaining bits as the index of a very large page table. The page table produces $28 - p$ bits, which are concatenated with the p-bit page displacement to form a physical address of 28 bits. This is used for the cache reference.

Suppose that $p = 11$. Work out a scheme that permits you to overlap in time as much as possible the virtual-memory function and the cache look-up. Explain your scheme and show the relative timing of the operations. Explain how you selected the number of sets in the cache to enable the overlapping of operations.

b) Suppose that $p = 10$. Explain how you can modify the scheme for $p = 11$ to continue to permit the maximum amount of overlapping of cache lookup and virtual-address mapping in this case.

c) Now let $p = 12$. Indicate how you can modify the cache scheme for $p = 11$ for this case.

d) What can you say is the general rule that you should use for the relationship of page size and the cache design parameters?

2.5 The object of this exercise is to practice cache analysis. This exercise and the ones that follow refer to the trace files on the disk available from the publisher as supplementary material for adopters of the text. If you do not have access to these files, you are invited to obtain traces from any source available to you, and to repeat the experiments on those traces.

- a) Simulate a cache with 32 sets, one-way set associativity, and 8-byte line size on TRACE1, and verify that there are no hits on the trace. This is the size of the cache on which the original trace was stripped.

- b) Write your cache simulator so that you can detect the first miss of each line of the cache that you simulate. Let the first miss for each line be called a "simulation transient-miss." Simulate the following caches, and record the total number of misses observed (including simulation transient-misses), the number of misses if all simulation transient-misses are treated as hits, and the estimate for the number of misses if the simulation transient accesses had the same hit ratio as the other accesses on the trace. Also record at the end of the simulation the number of sets that are fully initialized.
  Simulate using both TRACE1 and TRACE2 the following cache structures:
  - i) one-way associative: 32, 64, 128, 256, and 512 sets.
  - ii) two-way associative: 32, 64, 128, 256, and 512 sets.
  - iii) four-way associative: 32, 64, 128, 256, and 512 sets.

- c) Plot the log (base 2) of the estimated number of misses as a function of the log (base 2) of the cache size in bytes. Plot three different curves on the same graph, one each for one-way, two-way, and four-way associativity. Do you see any regularity in this graph? Comment on what you see.

- d) You can double the size of the cache by doubling the number of sets, doubling the set associativity, or doubling the line size. Your data does not give you information on the effect of doubling the line size. However, for this trace, it gives a great deal of information on the relative performance attained from doubling the number of sets versus doubling set associativity. What do you observe?

2.6 The purpose of this question is to explore cost-performance trade-offs in regard to the structure of caches.

- a) The stripped trace TRACE1 on the floppy disk containing trace information is assumed to be exactly 10 percent of the length of the original trace for the purposes of this question. Cache access time is one cycle. Main memory access time is four cycles. Each instruction causes exactly one instruction fetch and one operand fetch or store. Compute the cost-performance ratio for each of the 15 caches studied in Exercise 2.5, using the best estimate for your hit ratios and your cost estimates from Exercise 2.1 for costs.

- b) Which cache structure (or structures) are most reasonable to build, according to your interpretation of the cost-performance data?

2.7 The purpose of this exercise is to explore how to do set sampling and to examine its accuracy. For this exercise use the traces supplied on the floppy disk, or use a source of traces available to you. Also use your simulation program that was created in Exercise 2.5.

a) Alter your cache simulator to examine only the addresses whose set number ends with the 3-bit pattern (0 1 0). This should cause your simulator to sample exactly 12.5 percent of the sets. Then with sampling in place, simulate the caches that you simulated in Exercise 2.5 on TRACE1 and TRACE2 data.

b) From your data, estimate as closely as you can how many misses would be observed on the full trace. Compare your estimates with the answers in Exercise 2.5. Calculate the relative error in the estimate of performance produced by set sampling as compared to performance as calculated in Exercise 2.5. The relative error is defined to be

Rel error = abs(sampling answer − true answer)/sampling answer

Plot the relative error in percent as a function of cache size, using 3 curves, one each for set associativity of 1, 2, and 4.

c) From the plots of relative error, comment on the ranges of cache parameters for which the sampling technique is accurate enough to be useful.

2.8 This problem concerns the theory behind trace stripping.

a) Suppose you produce an address trace for a computer system, and you process that trace in the following way. You simulate the behavior of a cache with 64 sets, one-way set associativity (direct mapping), and lines of size 32 bytes. Addresses are byte addresses. As you process the trace, you produce an output trace that contains just the addresses of the cache misses.

Now suppose that you use the output trace as the input trace to a cache simulator. Assume that the cache you simulate has 64 sets, one-way set associativity, and 64-byte lines. Will this trace generate more, equal, or fewer cache misses than the original trace? Prove that your answer is correct.

b) Assume that you use the same reduced trace and use it as input for the simulation of a cache with 32 sets, one-way set associativity, and 32-byte lines. Will this trace generate more, equal, or fewer cache misses than the original trace? Prove that your answer is correct.

2.9 The object of this exercise is to explore trace stripping more deeply.

a) The chapter states that if a trace is stripped by simulating an N-set, one-way set-associative cache, the stripped trace can be used for any cache with a multiple of N sets and K-way set associativity for any K greater than or equal to 1. Consider such a trace and prove that it can be used to evaluate a $2N$-set four-way cache. Specifically, prove that every miss on the full trace is a miss on the reduced trace for the new cache, and conversely, every miss on the reduced trace is a miss on the full trace for the new cache.

b) Suppose that a trace is stripped by simulating an N-set four-way cache. The reduced trace contains just the misses produced by this cache. Prove or disprove the following statement:
If a $2N$-set cache is simulated on the full trace and on the reduced trace, the number of misses observed in both cases is equal.

2.10 The object of this exercise is to work through the design of a virtual-memory system.

a) Consider the design of a mapping device that maps virtual-memory addresses into physical addresses. The size of physical memory is 64K bytes, virtual addresses are 24 bits, and by experimentation you learn that page faults are reduced by 20 percent for each doubling of page size for the range of page sizes that are reasonable for your design. Work out the design parameters for a virtual-memory mapper, including a translation-lookaside buffer. Discuss your reasoning in selecting the parameters you choose.

b) Repeat *a* for a physical memory of size 64 M-bytes and a virtual address of 36 bits.

c) Repeat *a* for a physical memory of size 1 M-bytes and a virtual address of 22 bits.

d) Repeat *a* for a physical memory of size 512 M-bytes and a virtual address of 48 bits.

2.11 This problem concerns replacement algorithms for virtual-memory systems.

a) Page-fault-frequency (PFF) and working-set-replacement algorithms have similar behavior except during the transient as a program changes from one phase to another and thereby changes its working set. Assume that if a working set is entirely resident within main memory, the expected fault rate is about one fault per 1000 instructions, and the number of instructions between faults increases by ten percent for each additional page in main memory over and above the pages that hold the working set.

If the working set is not contained in memory, the fault rate is one fault per 25 instructions, and this improves by 25 instructions between faults for every page of the working set that is added, up to the point that the working set of 20 pages is resident in main memory. Given this information, what is the threshold that you would set for PFF, how many faults would occur, and what would be the maximum number of pages resident as you change from one phase of the program to another program with identical page-fault characteristics? Discuss how you selected the threshold and show how arrived at your answers.

b) Repeat the first part of this exercise for the case in which the replacement algorithm is working set, but in this case indicate how you selected the working-set window instead of explaining the choice of a threshold.

c) Describe a practical mechanism for determining whether or not a page is in a working set for a program. Your mechanism does not have to use Denning's definition exactly as stated in the text, but it should yield a reasonable approximation to the working set. What aspect of your solution, if any, is the most costly in time expended? What aspect is likely to be the most costly to implement assuming current cost conditions?

2.12 The object of this exercise is to examine performance characteristics of virtual memory.

a) Consider a physical disk system that is capable of performing an average of 50 accesses per second. Assume that an average working set is 50 K-bytes, that the mean number of instructions between page faults is 100 when less than the full working set is present in memory and is 5000 when the 50K working set is wholly contained in memory, and the page-fault rate drops off by 30 percent for each doubling of the number of pages in memory in excess of 50K. Assume that each instruction takes 1 ms on the average to execute. Plot the throughput (completed instructions per second) as a function of memory size for a single program being executed.

b) Repeat the first part of this exercise for the case in which two programs share memory equally.

c) How should you partition memory to obtain maximum throughput for the statistics given when memory contains 100 K-bytes? 250 K-bytes? An arbitrarily large number of bytes? Describe how you obtained these answers.

2.13 Modern disks incorporate disk cache, which is a high-speed semiconductor memory that buffers disk accesses. Assume that the disk controller understands how data are being requested from disk and that it has the ability to treat executable programs, sequential files, and pages of virtual memory that have been swapped out of main memory. Describe how you would manage the memory in the disk cache to do a reasonable job of avoiding accesses to the rotating physical disk. Make reasonable assumptions concerning the frequency of accesses, the size of disk cache, and the fault rate as a function of data size.

2.14 This problem concerns buffer requirements for virtual-memory systems. Assume the performance data for programs given in Exercise 2.12. For the 250K memory example at maximum performance, how much of the memory system for your answer to Exercise 2.12 is serving as buffer memory on the average? Show how you obtained this answer. Assume that the disk-access time increases by a factor of 2, and you want to obtain equal throughput as for a system with the faster disk-access time. Determine how to obtain increased throughput by adding additional memory, using as little extra memory as possible. How will you allocate memory in the new system to achieve the necessary throughput? How much of the memory on the average is serving as buffer?

2.15 This problem addresses the design of a disk cache.

a) Assume that a program has to access a sequential file. What should the disk cache do in managing the records in this file? Describe the commands and replies that would pass back and forth between the processor and disk system that enables the disk system to implement the managing strategy that you outline. In your explanation describe each command by listing its name and operands, followed by a description of what the command does.

Example: READ RECORD <track number> <sector number>. This command tells the disk system to obtain the specified record and transmit the record to the processor.

b) Assume that the processor that uses the disk system as a paging system for virtual memory must read pages during page faults and must write back pages that have been altered. What should the disk system do to manage this type of access? To implement this management policy, what should be the commands and replies between processor and disk system?

c) Assume that the processor is using the disk system to store the database for a banking center that serves customers and tellers through on-line queries. How might this database be managed by the disk cache? What should the command and reply interface be for this type of access to implement your suggested management algorithm?

2.16 The object of this exercise is to confirm the footprint model.

a) Measure the footprints for Trace 1 and Trace 2. The footprint is the number of distinct lines touched.

b) Now measure the cache-reload transient under two different conditions. Run Trace 2, then Trace 1, then Trace 2. The reload transient for the second running of Trace 2 is equal to the size of its footprint minus the number of lines of Trace 2 that are resident in the cache when Trace 2 begins to run the second time. Measure the reload transient for one-way and two-way set associative caches of size 32, 64, and 128. (Six different caches.)

c) Calculate the reload transient by using the size of the footprints and the cache structures in the mathematical model for the reload transient as described in the textbook.

d) Compare your answers.

e) Repeat the three parts of this question assuming that you run Trace 1, then Trace 2, then Trace 1. Measure and calculate the reload transient for the second running of Trace 1.

2.17 This problem concerns footprints in caches and in virtual memories.

a) The footprint model developed in the text appears for caches. What are the appropriate values for the cache-footprint model that describe a virtual-memory system in which two programs, A and B, execute alternately? Define the parameters you need to make the virtual-memory problem correspond to the cache-footprint model.

b) Now consider a collection of programs to execute concurrently in a virtual-memory system. How can the cache-footprint model help you determine which subset of programs to run together?

2.18 The purpose of this question is to analyze the relative advantages and disadvantages of two cache designs. In a computer system that uses both virtual memory and a high-speed cache, a cache tag can be either a virtual address or a physical address. If the tag is a virtual address, it is compared to the virtual address produced by a program before the virtual address is mapped to a real address by a segment and page transformation. If the tag is a real address, it is compared to the virtual address of a reference after that virtual address has been mapped to a real address.

These are the basic cache schemes mentioned in the following parts of this exercise. In response to the questions, you are asked to add more capability or other functions to one or both caches to gain higher performance.

a) Consider the relative performance of the two basic approaches. Which of the two, if any, is the faster? Explain your answer.

b) Consider the problem of handling references to main memory by an input/output processor while maintaining the cache to reflect changes made by the input/output operations. Also, consider how changes made by the central processor to data in the cache can be made available to the input/output processor so that the input/output processor always accesses fresh data when it reads from memory. Which of the two basic schemes, if any, leads to higher performance? Explain your answer. If you have found one scheme to be slower than the other, find a way to improve the performance of the slower scheme to bring it as close to the performance of the faster scheme by augmenting the cache structure, the control of the cache, or its implementation.

c) A cache flush is a purging process that is performed in some virtual-memory systems. When a process in a virtual-memory system relinquishes the processor, and a new process takes its place, the second process may generate the same virtual addresses as the former process, but the second process refers to totally different items. We assume that when a process relinquishes the processor, all of its data held in the cache that might be accessed by another process are purged from the cache. With regard to the cache flush to purge these data, which of the two schemes—real or virtual address tags—leads to higher performance, or are they about equal in performance? Explain your answer. How can the slower of the two schemes be augmented to improve its performance in handling the cache flush? In answering these questions, assume that the caches are four-way set associative.

d) It may be possible to reduce the overhead of cache flushes. Consider how you might augment both of the cache designs (real-address tags and virtual-address tags) so that data resident in the cache for a process need not be purged each time the process relinquishes the processor. Discuss how both cache schemes can be modified to support this behavior.

2.19 Having studied the design of cache-memory systems, consider the parts from which caches are made. Each memory chip in a cache is a standard random-access memory (RAM) chip that contains M bits of information, where M is a power of 2. The memory chip can be designed to have any one of several different organizations. It can, for example, have 1 bit at each of M different addresses, or with a slightly different design, have 2 bits at each of $M/2$ different addresses, or 4 bits at each of $M/4$ addresses, and so forth. A single cache line made up of, for example, 16 bytes (128 bits) can be built from $128\ M \times 1$ chips or from $64\ M/2 \times 2$ chips, and so forth. If $M \times 1$ chips are used, the chips create not just one cache line, but a total of M sets of cache lines.

a) Show a scheme for organizing $M \times 1$ chips to form a memory with 1024 sets, four-way set associativity, and 16 bytes per cache line. For what value or values of M do you achieve the minimum number of chips in the memory? For this scheme how many address and data bits have to be supplied to a memory chip for each access?

b) Show a scheme for organizing $M/4 \times 4$ chips to form the memory described in the previous part of this exercise. How many address and data bits have to be supplied to each chip?

c) Suppose that $M = 1024K\ (= 2^{20})$. What size cache would you design, and how would you organize the memory chips to achieve this size?

2.20 We want to explore the behavior of a multilevel memory hierarchy. Let Level 1 be small and very fast, Level 2 be much larger than Level 1 and somewhat slower, and

Level 3 be a very large and very slow memory. The objective is to retain information in Level 2 that will be needed in the near future. All transfers occur on demand, and no prefetching is used.

Assume that both Level 1 and Level 2 are maintained as LRU caches. When a miss occurs, an item is moved immediately to Level 1 from main memory or from Level 2, wherever it is found. If an item is moved from Level 2 to Level 1, no copy of the item remains in Level 2. When an item ages out of Level 2, it is discarded, and future accesses for the item are made to main memory.

a) Assume that Level 1 is organized as N sets and is K-way set associative. Assume that Level 2 is organized as N sets and is J-way set associative. Consider a situation in which a Process A runs, then Process B runs, and then A is to be resumed. Find expressions that show the expected number of lines of A in Level 1, in Level 2, and in main memory at the time that A is resumed.

b) Repeat the previous part of this exercise under the assumption that Level 2 is organized as a $2N$-set cache, J-way set associative.

c) Repeat the first part of this exercise assuming that Level 2 is an RN-set cache, J-way set associative where R is some power of 2.

2.21 This problem examines models for preallocating cache to different functions.

a) Assume that a particular computer architecture produces one instruction reference followed by one data reference for each instruction executed. The stream of instruction references has a miss rate $M_I(x)$ in a cache of size x. Similarly, the stream of data references has a miss-rate function $M_D(x)$ for a cache of size x. (Ignore the exact structure of the cache, and just assume that the miss rate depends on the total number of bytes available.) Assume that both of these functions are known to you. Given C bytes to use for a cache, how should it be partitioned into a data cache and an instruction cache in a way that minimizes the overall miss rate. (Assume that the partitioning can be of any size, not necessarily into pieces that are good for cache structures.)

b) Now assume that r data references occur on the average for each instruction reference, for some real number r. What partitioning of cache produces the least miss ratio in this case?

c) Now assume that the program in the first part is running without having instructions and data prepartitioned. Assume that the cache allocation between data and instructions varies randomly as misses occur and cache replacements change the allocation between data and instructions. Show that when the cache reaches a state in which the number of bytes holding data is equal to the optimum number of bytes to assign to data in a partition, then the cache is in equilibrium. That is, the rate at which bytes change from holding instructions to holding data is equal to the rate at which bytes change from holding data to holding instructions.

d) Assume that the unpartitioned cache in the previous part is in equilibrium. Assume that the program changes so that its M_I and M_D functions change as well. Construct a mathematical model whose solution describes the number of data lines and instruction lines in cache as a function of time. (This model could be very complex, so simply construct the model, but make no attempt to solve it.)

2.22 For this part of the problem assume that two different programs are sharing a computer. Each program takes over the processor, runs for a fixed quantum time Q, and then relinquishes control while the other program takes over. The programs have identical cache footprints. Their streams of address references produce miss rates at the rate of $M_1(x)$ and $M_2(x)$, respectively, in caches of size x. As above, assume that you know both of these functions. Compare two different ways of using C bytes of cache storage for this situation.

The first method is to use cache in a conventional way so that each program runs, uses all cache available as best it can, and then yields the processor to the other program. The second method preallocates a fixed amount of cache storage to each program. The cache storage allocated to a program is private to that program, and is inaccessible to the other program. All storage is allocated to one program or the other.

To answer the following questions, develop the mathematical models required for the comparisons assuming that the miss-rate functions and footprint functions have been given to you.

a) For the scheme that uses a fixed cache allocation, what fixed allocation of cache produces the lowest composite miss rate? (The answer to this question is an allocation of cache bytes to each process that depends on the problem parameters. What is that dependence?) Consider three cases: Neither footprint fits fully in cache, both footprints fit fully in cache, and one footprint fits in cache together with a fraction α of the second footprint.

b) Which of the two schemes produces the lower miss rate in each of the three cases? Show how to compute the difference in the miss rates if the mathematical behavior of the programs were given to you. Indicate for which of the three cases, one scheme is clearly better than another and in which cases you cannot tell.

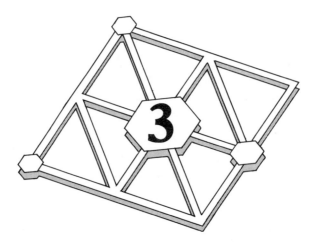

Pipeline Design Techniques

3.1 Principles of Pipeline Design
3.2 Memory Structures in Pipeline Computers
3.3 Performance of Pipelined Computers
3.4 Control of Pipeline Stages
3.5 Exploiting Pipeline Techniques
3.6 Historical References

We learn in Chapter 2 that memory is a major bottleneck in high-speed computers, and that the bottleneck can be relieved somewhat by taking advantage of the characteristics of typical programs. The objective has been to store the most-frequently referenced items in fast memory and less-frequently referenced items in slower memory. It is not necessary to make all memory equally fast; we need use only as much fast memory as necessary to hold the active regions of a program and data.

This chapter concerns a different approach to relieving bottlenecks. The idea is to use parallelism at the point of the bottleneck to improve performance globally. If the design techniques are successful, then the extra hardware devoted to performance enhancement is present in only a small portion of a computer system, yet its effect is to increase performance as if the full computer system were replicated.

To contrast the approaches of the last chapter and the present one, in one case the speed differential is due to faster hardware whereas in the second case the speed increase is obtained by replicating slower hardware. In both cases, clever architecture is required to create efficient computer systems in which enhancements of a relatively small cost have a global impact on performance.

Pipeline computer techniques described in this chapter are by far the most popular means for enhancing performance through parallel hardware. The basic ideas from which pipeline techniques developed are apparent in von Neumann's proposal to build the first stored-program computer. In Burks *et al.* [1946], a discussion on input/output techniques describes a buffer arrangement that would permit computation to be overlapped with input/output operations and thereby provide a crude form of pipeline processing that is used widely in today's machines.

Although von Neumann did not build the input/output capability into his first machine, the basic ideas for pipelined computer design evolved rapidly after the first appearance of magnetic-core memory as the primary storage medium for main memory. This storage was roughly a factor of 10 or more slower per cycle than the transistor technology used in high-speed registers and control logic. Designers quickly conceived of a variety of techniques to initiate one or more concurrent accesses to memory while executing instructions in the central processor. This body of techniques eventually evolved and is exemplified in the pipeline-processing structures described in this chapter.

In the 1960s, when hardware costs were relatively high, pipelined computers were the supercomputers. IBM's STRETCH and CDC's 6600 were two such designs from the early 1960s that made extensive use of pipelining, and these designs strongly influenced the structure of supercomputers that followed. By the 1980s, hardware costs had diminished to the extent that pipeline techniques could be implemented across the entire range of performance, and indeed, even the Intel 8086 microprocessor that costs just a few dollars uses pipeline accesses to memory while performing on-chip computation.

Our approach is to develop a basic understanding of the principles of pipeline design in the next section. In subsequent sections we observe where it can be used and how to design effective pipelines.

3.1 Principles of Pipeline Design

The basic idea behind pipeline design is quite natural; it is not specific to computer technology. In fact the name *pipeline* stems from the analogy with petroleum pipelines in which a sequence of hydrocarbon products is pumped through a pipeline. The last product might well be entering the pipeline before the first product has been removed from the terminus. In the remainder of this section we treat pipeline design first in abstract terms, and then follow with concrete examples.

The key contribution of pipelining is that it provides a way to start a new task before an old one has been completed. Hence the completion rate is not a

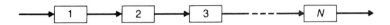

Fig. 3.1 An N-step sequential process.

function of the total processing time, but rather of how soon a new process can be introduced.

Consider Fig. 3.1, which shows a sequential process being done step-by-step over a period of time. The total time required to complete this process is N units, assuming that each step takes one time unit. In the figure, each box denotes the execution of a single step, and the label in the box gives the number of the step being executed.

To perform this same process using pipeline techniques, consider Fig. 3.2, which shows a continuous stream of jobs going through the N sequential steps of the process. In this case each horizontal row of boxes represents the time history of one job. Each vertical column of boxes represents the activity at a specific time. Note that up to N different jobs may be active at any time in this example, assuming that we have N independent stations to perform the sequence of steps in the process.

The pipeline timing of Fig. 3.2 is characteristic of assembly lines and maintenance depots as well as oil pipelines. The total time to perform one process does not change between Fig. 3.1 and Fig. 3.2, and it may actually be longer in Fig. 3.2 if the pipeline structure forces some processing overhead in

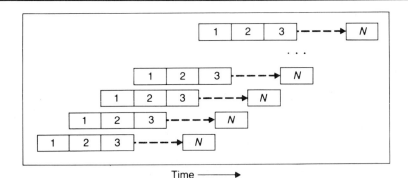

Time ⟶

Fig. 3.2 Pipelined execution of an N-step process.

moving from station to station. But the completion rate of tasks in Fig. 3.2 is one per cycle as opposed to one task every N cycles in Fig. 3.1.

Figure 3.3(a) shows a box that represents a server that can perform any of the N processing steps in a single unit of time. If the job stream is processed by this one server, then the rate of completion is one job every N steps, and the time behavior of the job stream is as described in Fig. 3.1.

Compare Fig. 3.3(a) with Fig. 3.3(b), which shows N servers concatenated in a sequence. A task flows through the collection of servers by visiting Server 1, then Server 2, and so on, and finally emerging from Server N after N steps. The time behavior of this system is described by Fig. 3.2. Figure 3.3(b) is an ideal model of a constant-speed assembly line, such as an automobile assembly plant.

Now let's relate the general ideas presented in Figs. 3.1–3.3 to computer design. Where can we find an N-step task that can conveniently be broken up, as shown in Fig. 3.2? Consider the steps required to execute a single instruction. This sequence has traditionally been implemented using pipeline design. A typical instruction-execution sequence might be:

1. *Instruction fetch*: obtain a copy of the instruction from memory.

2. *Instruction decode*: examine the instruction and prepare to initialize the control signals required to execute the instruction in subsequent steps.

3. *Address generation*: compute the effective address of the operands by performing indexing or indirection as specified by the instruction.

4. *Operand fetch*: for READ operations, obtain the operand from central memory.

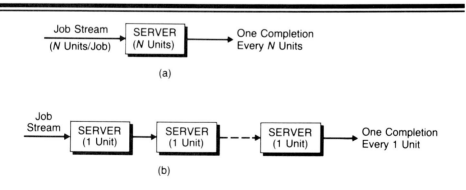

Fig. 3.3 Two ways to execute N-unit jobs in a stream;
(a) Sequential execution with an N-unit server; and
(b) Pipelined execution with 1-unit servers.

5. *Instruction execution*: execute the instruction in the processor.
6. *Operand store*: for WRITE operations, return the resulting data to central memory.
7. *Update program counter*: generate the address of the next instruction.

If we simply map these steps onto the model of Fig. 3.3(b), we obtain a block diagram of a pipeline computer as shown in Fig. 3.4. For reasons discussed later this structure might have to be tuned somewhat to obtain a good balance between cost and performance. More important, the structure has to be designed to work correctly and efficiently in the face of difficulties caused by interactions between events at different stages in the pipeline.

In the normal mode of operation, the first stage of the pipeline in Fig. 3.4 continuously fetches instructions, even though the address of a fetch has not been produced by the last stage of the pipeline, the stage that updates the program counter. Thus, the first stage is operating with a program counter value, several cycles before the counter value is produced in the last stage. Since most changes to the program counter are increments, the first stage estimates the future value of the program counter quite easily by successive increments of the program counter. The interaction between the first and last stages occurs when a branch alters the program counter nonsequentially.

The address of the instruction that follows a conditional branch might not be known until the branch instruction reaches the last stage of the pipeline, but Fig. 3.4 suggests that subsequent instructions have followed the conditional branch down the pipeline and may have altered the state of one or more machine registers even before the outcome of the conditional branch is known. The danger is that we cannot be sure what to execute until the condition has been evaluated.

One way to assure correct execution of conditional branches is to interlock the instruction-fetch stage with the program-counter update stage. Immediately after a conditional branch is fetched by the first stage, no further fetches take place until the branch reaches the last stage. At this point the last stage produces the correct target address and removes the interlock, allowing the first stage to continue instruction fetches at the new address.

The problem with this solution is the lost performance caused by the inactive pipeline during the period a conditional branch is pending. Conditional branches occur quite frequently in most conventional computers, possibly once every five to ten cycles on the average. If a pipeline were idled when each such branch is encountered, then every five to ten instructions a few cycles would potentially be lost waiting for branches. This is a fairly hefty penalty for the inefficiency of a pipeline implementation.

There are other interactions of concern as well, all of which tend to force the designer to add complexity to ensure correct pipeline operation. These interactions could severely impede performance if the resulting implementa-

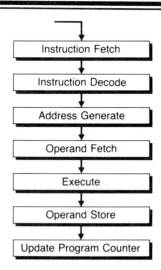

Fig. 3.4 Pipelined execution of a single instruction.

tion is idle a significant fraction of time because of the stage-to-stage interlocks. Consequently, the designer is concerned with building a pipeline that is
simultaneously correct, efficient, and fast. How this is done is the subject of the
material that follows.

If we assume that each of the steps in the execution sequence is a single
cycle, then a typical instruction takes seven cycles to execute. In several
computer systems the pipeline takes advantage of the fact that the majority of
instructions do not perform both a READ and a WRITE operation, and the
number of stages is shortened to six. For our discussion we use the simpler, but
possibly less realistic, pipeline shown in Fig. 3.4.

The structure of Fig. 3.4 produces one instruction completed during each
machine cycle, for an improvement in performance of a factor of 7 over a purely
sequential implementation (or a factor of 6 faster than a sequential implementation that provides for only a READ or a WRITE cycle, but not both for each
instruction). In actual practice the performance improvement depends on the
ability to split the processes into steps of equal duration. Suppose, for example, that a memory access takes four machine cycles, not just one, as we have
presumed thus far. Then the three different steps in Fig. 3.4 that refer to
memory accesses take four cycles each, whereas all other steps take just one
cycle. Now the average rate of instruction completion depends on the slowest
process in the sequence, which in this case is a memory operation that

produces one result every four cycles. No matter how fast the other processes are, they cannot produce results any faster on the average than the slowest processor in the chain.

In effect, we can run all processes in Fig. 3.4 at a rate that produces one result every 4 cycles at the output of each process. The original instruction execution requires three memory accesses—an instruction fetch, a READ, and a WRITE—and four single-cycle steps for a total of 16 cycles. The structure in the figure produces one result every 4 cycles, for a speedup of 4. This is somewhat lower than our original estimate of a speedup of 7.

By adding some delays to the pipeline of Fig. 3.4, we can create a longer pipeline that produces one result every cycle. In Fig. 3.5 we have added three stages of delay to every memory operation, making the pipeline a total of 16 units long. But in this pipeline new instructions can be initiated every cycle rather than every four cycles, so that it produces results at a rate about 16 times faster than a purely sequential implementation of a processing unit.

Although Fig. 3.5 seems to make the speedup deceptively simple to obtain, actually the memory system must be able to support the processing rate, and this may be quite a feat to accomplish. For the structure shown running at its full processing rate, there are 12 active stages with different memory operations at any given time. So the memory system must be able to support 12 independent concurrent accesses in a nonconflicting way.

In this case, a pipelined structure in one subsystem shifts the processing bottleneck to a different subsystem. Obviously, to make the best use of pipelining for a processor structured in a pipeline fashion as shown in Fig. 3.5, the architect should extend pipeline techniques or other high-speed techniques to the memory system as well so that the maximum processing capacities of various subsystems are matched to each other.

Up to this point the design principles have been very simple. We identify a task that performs a sequence of operations. Then we build a chain of processors and perform one step of the sequence on each processor in the chain. We have just observed that we may have to break some of the steps into smaller steps to create a pipeline in which all stages produce results at the same rate. Lengthy steps may have to be broken into two or more smaller steps to meet this requirement.

The design would be satisfactory at this point if there were no interactions among two or more tasks that were at different stages of the pipe. If such interactions are present, then the pipeline must account for these in some way, which considerably increases the difficulty of producing an efficient design and adds to the complexity of the final result.

For the moment, however, let us explore a practical application of the structure we have outlined. One way to guarantee that there are no interactions among tasks in a pipeline is to make sure that any two or more tasks concurrently in the pipeline are totally independent and have no conflicts. The

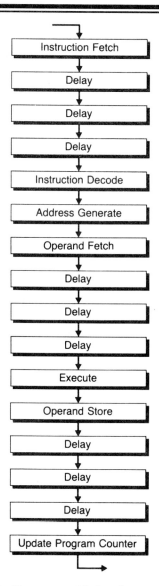

Fig. 3.5 Modification of a pipeline to provide for slow memories. Three units of delay have been inserted after each memory operation. (Note that the program counter can be updated during a delay period, reducing total delay by 1 unit.)

16 cycles allocated in Fig. 3.5 could be allocated to 16 different processors on a round-robin basis. And this is the thinking that guided the design of the CDC 6600 peripheral controllers.

Figure 3.6(a) shows the pipeline structure of the peripheral controller "barrel" for the CDC 6600. Each stage takes one cycle, and ten cycles are required to execute one instruction, including a fetch or store to local memory. In this particular design all events take place at one of the ten steps in the process cycle. The other nine steps are simple delays that hold the machine state while awaiting a memory access. The state of each task held in a CDC 6600 peripheral processor is very small, only 51 bits, and consists of:

- The accumulator (18 bits);
- The program counter (12 bits);
- The operand address or other instruction-specific data (12 bits); and
- The instruction code and trip counter (9 bits).

During one traversal of ten stages, a peripheral processor performs one READ or WRITE to local memory, together with related actions. If more machine traversals are required, the instruction traverses the stages multiple times. The trip counter indicates which traversal is currently in progress, and it thereby controls how each instruction is executed as a function of its trip number through the barrel.

All processor activity occurs between Stages 9 and 10 shown in Fig. 3.6(a). In one trip through the ten stages, the processor can do an instruction fetch, an operand fetch together with an instruction execution, or one fetch of an indirect address. (The processor can also fetch long operands from the main memory. This takes five trips through the pipeline since the operand width of the pipeline is only 12 bits, but operands in main memory contain 60 bits.)

In this architecture, the first trip through the ten-stage pipeline is an instruction fetch, which starts at the clock that latches a processor state in Stage 10. At this time the program counter is sent to memory to initiate a READ cycle to obtain the next instruction. That instruction reaches the processor at the clock time that latches the corresponding processor state into Stage 9, and is ready to join that processor state as the state moves from Stage 9 to Stage 10 at the end of the next trip through the pipeline.

Since each instruction in this processor contains two fields, one each for the instruction code and operand address, the instruction fetch concludes by loading the instruction code and address registers with the instruction obtained by the memory fetch. The trip counter is also initialized and the instruction decode takes place at this point, so the processor is prepared for the next cycle to read or write an operand or to read an indirect address as required by the instruction.

Assume that the instruction is a LOAD or an ADD and that the addressing mode is direct. Execution of this instruction is completed during the second

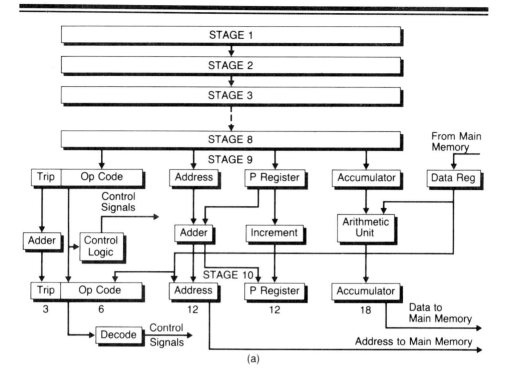

(a)

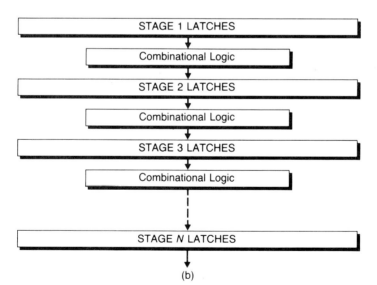

(b)

Fig. 3.6 Two pipeline structures:
(a) The pipeline for the 10 CDC-6600 peripheral processors; and
(b) An ideal pipelined implementation of a processor.

trip through the pipeline. In that trip, the operand from memory is fetched, and it arrives at the processor just as the corresponding processor state reaches Stage 9 and is ready to move to Stage 10.

Note that Fig. 3.6(a) shows a data path for the accumulator that passes through an adder/shifter at the execution stage. As the accumulator data propagate on this path, the operand data join it. The instruction sets the adder/shifter to add, subtract, logical AND, or logical OR its two operands, or shift or copy one of the two operands into the accumulator in Stage 10. Hence, the logic to perform the full repertoire of instructions is in the path between Stages 9 and 10. At the same stage, the program counter is adjusted by incrementing it (for sequential execution) or by loading it from the address register (for branches).

It is clear from Fig. 3.6 why this design is both fast and efficient. The basic logic for one processor is placed only in the execution stage of the pipeline. All other stages of the pipeline contain state storage only. Consequently, this implementation of ten processors contains one execution unit (but ten full register sets and ten memory systems), so the cost is less than the cost of ten individual machines. Yet the performance capacity is equal to the capacity of ten machines, provided that the ten machines operate independently and do not contend for shared data, nor interfere mutually in other ways. The cost benefit of this approach was very high in the mid-1960s when the cost of the logic saved was quite substantial. The reader should consult Thornton [1970] for a detailed description of the implementation.

Figure 3.6(a) illustrates an actual implementation of the idealized pipeline design for the processor shown in Fig. 3.6(b). Each stage in this design consists of a set of latches (data registers) that hold data in transit through the pipeline.

Between stages is combinational logic through which data propagates. The idea is that all activity occurs at successive clock times. At a clock tick, each bank of latches reads its input data and captures that data in its internal storage. After a short propagation delay, the data appear at the latch outputs and begin propagating to the next stage in the pipeline.

The logic between stages transforms the data, for example, by shifting or adding, or by some other elementary operation that implements one stage of the pipeline function. Eventually the transformed data reach the input pins of the next rank of latches. The next clock tick is delayed long enough with respect to the preceding clock tick to ensure that all data in the pipeline have propagated to the input pins of the next stage. Only then are the stage outputs allowed to change.

The purpose of the clock is to synchronize the data at the input to each stage. The clock is set as fast as possible within the normal constraints of reliability, power consumption, and engineering tolerances. It must be slow enough to accommodate the slowest propagation path.

The simplicity of the design in Fig. 3.6(a) is somewhat deceptive. Because the ten processors are totally separate, there are no interactions in the pipeline, and no extra hardware is required to deal with unusual conditions. If we consider the design of a processing unit for a single stream of instructions, the situation is complicated by several factors. The ones that normally require attention are:

- Conditional branches must complete their execution before the address of the next instruction is known. Therefore, when a conditional branch is encountered at Stage 1 of a pipeline, subsequent data that reaches Stage 1 must be treated tentatively until the target of the conditional branch is known.

- An instruction in the pipeline might produce a result that is used by a later instruction in the pipeline. The second instruction must be delayed somehow until the result is available.

- An instruction in the pipeline might produce a result for a register whose previous contents must be read by an earlier instruction in the pipeline. The second operation must not destroy the current contents of that register until that register is free to be rewritten.

- Two different instructions in the pipeline may write data into a common location, but the pipeline may reverse the order in which the location is updated.

We have already mentioned the problem concerning conditional branches. The other three points are instances of a more general problem of concurrent operations on shared resources. In the specific cases here, the shared resources are registers or data in main memory.

If the basic operations are READ and WRITE, we have four ways that two processes can interact, namely READ/READ, READ/WRITE, WRITE/READ, and WRITE/WRITE, where the first label indicates the earlier operation and the second label indicates the second operation. The idea is that a program is written for correct execution under the assumption that instructions are executed sequentially, with one instruction fully completed before the next is started. The pipeline implementation violates this assumption, but it must give the appearance that the assumption holds.

For READ/READ interactions, we have a situation in which a datum is to be read first by Instruction 1 and then by Instruction 2. Can we permit these operations to be done out of order? The answer is yes, so this conflict is not of concern. However, if done out of order, WRITE/WRITE interactions leave the shared cell in the wrong state, and subsequent READs to the shared item will obtain the wrong value. Similarly, if the order of WRITE/READ is reversed, the READ obtains old data, not new data as intended. And if READ/WRITE is reversed, the READ obtains new data, not the old data as intended. Each of these three operation pairs needs to be detected and interlocked when they occur on shared data.

The WRITE/WRITE conflict appears to be unusual because it requires a program to write a datum to memory and then immediately overwrite that datum. Such sequences could happen, however, if a WRITE is followed by a conditional branch, one of whose outcomes immediately performs the second WRITE.

A common WRITE/WRITE conflict on a shared variable is updating of a processor's state bits (often called the *condition codes*) that are written as a consequence of instruction execution. The need to avoid WRITE/WRITE conflicts on these variables requires that they be updated in the order that they are written on a purely sequential processor without pipeline execution. If a processor can detect that no intervening READ occurs between two WRITEs to a shared variable, the processor can execute the second WRITE first, then abort the first WRITE when its point of execution occurs.

READ/WRITE and WRITE/READ conflicts are a fact of life and the bane of pipeline designs. The CDC 6600 design faces this problem in a central processor that had ten independent functional units dedicated to such functions as add, multiply, divide, shift, normalize, branch, increment, and logic (Boolean). The divide is rather lengthy compared to the shift and Boolean functions. Consequently, it is quite possible to encounter pipeline conflicts resulting from instructions completing execution out of order.

The approach used in the CDC 6600 is to implement instructions with three addresses to support overlapped execution and use a hardware structure that the designers called a *scoreboard* to search for conflicts. The three-address format of instructions takes the general form:

$$R_1 := R_2 \, OP \, R_3$$

where *OP* designates one of the functional units. In this fashion it becomes possible to take advantage of pipeline execution when evaluating such functions as $(A \times B) + (C \times D)$, which can be encoded as:

$$R_3 := R_1 \times R_3$$

$$R_6 := R_4 \times R_5$$

$$R_1 := R_3 + R_6$$

The second instruction uses a distinct set of registers from the first instruction so that it can be executed in a pipelined fashion, provided that two distinct multipliers are available. The third instruction is interlocked with the first two instructions, and must be delayed for their completion. Note the WRITE/READ conflicts for Registers 3 and 6 and a READ/WRITE conflict for Register 1, any of which would result in deferring the execution of the addition instruction.

The scoreboard keeps track of conflicts and defers instructions for any of the following conditions:

- WRITE/WRITE conflict;
- WRITE/READ conflict;

- READ/WRITE conflict; and
- Function unit conflict.

In the case of WRITE/READ and READ/WRITE conflicts, the conflicting instructions are passed through the early stages of the pipeline, in spite of the conflicts, so that they can be decoded and their operands can be requested. They are moved to their respective function units and deferred at those places to wait until the conflicting conditions are cleared. In so doing, the early stages of the pipeline are cleared and made available for new instructions. The WRITE/WRITE and function unit conflicts are deferred before being issued to the function units, which causes the pipeline to freeze until the conflicting condition is cleared.

3.2 Memory Structures in Pipeline Computers

The previous section indicates a general structure for pipeline computers and illustrates how pipeline execution has been implemented in an early supercomputer. The major innovation of pipeline design is the ability to complete instructions at a rate much faster than that achievable by executing instructions without overlapping. We have learned that one major obstacle to continuous execution at the maximum pipeline rate is the requirement that pipeline execution must behave exactly as if the same instructions were executed without overlap. This gives rise to conflicts that are detectable by hardware and results in freezing of some operations pending the completion of others.

Let us reconsider how pipelined processors work in the context of memory systems. In the previous section, an ideal pipelined processor decodes one instruction in each machine cycle. To maintain that rate, we clearly need to supply instructions and data to the processor at a rate consistent with the needs of the pipeline. No single large physical memory available today can meet such demand because, at best, a memory cycle usually runs from 4 to 20 processor cycles. Moreover, the ratios are not likely to change in the future. However, cache memory can be implemented to deliver one result per cycle, and therefore cache memory can potentially supply the demands of a pipelined processor.

The actual requirements for a pipelined processor depend specifically on the structure of the instruction set. The CDC 6600 instruction set provides for fetching at most one operand from memory. A CDC-6600 instruction can be as short as 15 bits of a 60-bit physical word. The requirements imposed by this processor can be almost fully satisfied by a one-cycle cache memory, provided that once an instruction is read from cache, its entire 60-bit word is held in the processor in order to obtain other instructions from that same word without returning to cache for additional fetches.

The number of instruction and data accesses required on the average per instruction is strongly dependent on the nature of the instruction set. As a norm, let us consider an instruction set that accesses one word of instruction and one word of data per instruction executed. This structure requires a cache that can deliver two words per machine cycle for a pipelined processor.

One obvious way to meet this requirement is to have independent instruction and data caches. Instruction fetches are directed to the instruction cache, and operand fetches (produced concurrently from a later stage of a pipeline) are directed to the data caches. This structure works very well in most cases, but it could be a problem in systems where instructions are treated as data, modified, and immediately executed. If this were the case, then references to the data cache would have to be checked against the presence of the same data in the instruction cache, which severely reduces available bandwidth to the instruction cache. However, current software-engineering practice advises strongly against programs that modify themselves as we have described, and there is nothing more forceful than erroneously executing programs to convince programmers to refrain from writing such code.

We cannot expect caches to be the universal answer for pipeline computers because there are special situations in which vast amounts of data are touched for the first time in some single phase of processing. Each datum in such a situation produces a cache miss, and the large number of cache misses occurring close together severely reduces processor performance. For this case there is often an opportunity to pipeline the memory itself by partitioning memory into independent banks, as shown in Fig. 3.7.

The timing for accessing the banks is shown in Fig. 3.8. Note that the banks are active in an overlapped fashion, with the second bank starting its access one machine cycle behind the previous bank. So even though cycle times are large, the processor can request a vector of data and will receive one datum per cycle after a startup transient. The key to this technique is that successive elements of the vector of data must lie in successive memory banks.

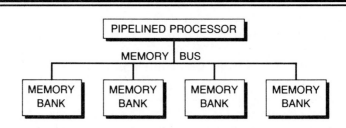

Fig. 3.7 Multiple memory banks in a pipelined computer system.

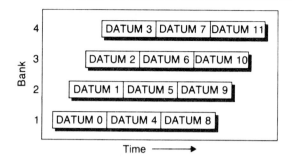

Fig. 3.8 Timing for pipelined fetches for the memory shown in Fig. 3.7.

3.3 Performance of Pipelined Computers

The major performance characteristic of pipelined computers is that the *rate* of computation can be very high even though the elapsed time of individual operations might be very long. Since performance is the number of completed operations, pipeline-design techniques produce high performance in spite of long delays associated with specific operations.

To the extent that a high rate of completion can be maintained, pipeline design is an effective method for increasing performance. But when the rate of completion drops off, possibly because of the inability to keep data flowing through a pipeline on a continuous basis, the pipeline becomes rather costly and may outweigh the benefits from using this design technique.

A very interesting way to view the efficiency of pipelined computers is to compare them to highly parallel array (vector) computers. The analysis for the array computer is very easy to derive and understand, and it corresponds directly to the analysis for pipelined computers. This discussion is originally due to observations by T. C. Chen [1980].

Consider a computation that is natural to execute on a parallel computer because of its highly repetitive structure. A typical computation of this type is a calculation to be made concurrently (in the time domain of the program) at every point in a mesh of points. This structure is typical of partial differential equations that solve such problems as heat transfer, the strength of mechanical structures, turbulent air flow across aircraft and spacecraft wings, and weather models. A reasonable means for solving such problems is to build a computer composed of many processors and assign the computations at each node in the mesh to individual processors.

The timing diagram for such a processor is shown in Fig. 3.9, where time appears on the horizontal axis, and the processors are plotted on the vertical axis. For a short period of time, only one processor is busy. During this period, the processor initializes variables for the computation, parcels out the work to be done, and performs other similar overhead computations that are serial in nature and not replicated at other processors in the system. Following the initialization, all processors perform the computation in parallel. The process repeats as shown in the figure, with a new parallel operation being preceded by a serial initialization section.

The diagram in Fig. 3.9 shows both the advantage of parallelism and the degradation in performance due to serial computations embedded in the program. The use of many processors provides a potential for high performance, but the serial operations reduce the actual effective parallelism below the maximum attainable. To obtain a reasonable measure of performance for the situation depicted in Fig. 3.9, one interesting parameter to study is the *efficiency* of a computation. This is a measure of the proportion of time that the processors are busy. Therefore it measures the degradation in peak performance due to serial operations and other effects.

In Fig. 3.9, let the fraction of time spent in serial code be α and the fraction spent in parallel code be $1 - \alpha$. With N processors available, the fraction of time that processors are busy is given by:

$$\text{Efficiency} = \frac{\alpha}{N} + 1 - \alpha \tag{3.1}$$

$$= 1 - \alpha(1 - 1/N)$$

As the number of processors increases, the limiting efficiency is $1 - \alpha$. Compare Fig. 3.9 with Fig. 3.10, which shows the timing diagram for the same problem with twice as many processors used. The serial code is the same

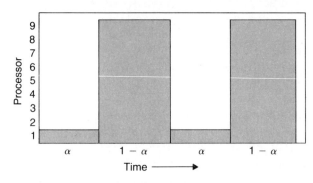

Fig. 3.9 The timing history of a computation for an array processor.

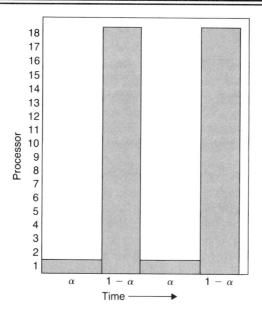

Fig. 3.10 The timing diagram for a highly parallel computation for an array processor.

length, but the time devoted to parallel code has been shortened, and the fraction α has increased.

In fact, α for any specific problem is a function of N, the number of processors used to solve that problem in parallel. To show this relation, let us normalize the computation times so that the serial execution time takes one unit, and the code that can be run in parallel takes time p on a single processor. The parallel time shrinks to p/N when run on N processors. The fraction α is the ratio of serial time to total execution time, and is therefore given by

$$\alpha = \frac{1}{1 + p/N} = \frac{N}{N + p} \tag{3.2}$$

The bad news is that for very large N, α approaches 1, so efficiency approaches 0. What is happening is that the parallelizable portions of code take a vanishingly small fraction of time, and what remains is serial, occupying one processor while the remaining processors are idle.

Figure 3.11 shows plots of the efficiency function

$$\text{Efficiency} = 1 - \frac{N(1 - 1/N)}{N + p} = 1 - \frac{N - 1}{N + p} \tag{3.3}$$

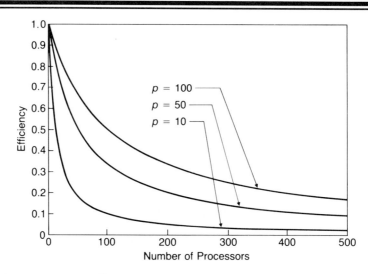

Fig. 3.11 Array-processor efficiency.

for various values of N and p. Consider, for example, the curve for $p = 10$, which shows the efficiency for programs for which serial code accounts for only one-tenth as much time as the parallel code when executed on a serial processor. At $N = 10$ the efficiency is only 0.55 and at $N = 100$ the efficiency drops to roughly 0.10.

The situation is somewhat better for programs that have an inherently larger potential for parallelism. Consider the curve for $p = 100$, for example. At $N = 10$, the efficiency is quite high, approximately 0.92, but it drops to 0.505 at $N = 100$, and to 0.168 at $N = 500$.

Another way of looking at the curves is to measure the *speedup* of parallel execution. We define speedup by the formula

$$\text{Speedup} = \frac{\text{Time for serial execution}}{\text{Time for parallel execution}} \tag{3.4}$$

This formula is somewhat ambiguous because there are many different algorithms that solve particular problems. If we were to take a grossly inefficient algorithm and make it run faster by using massive parallelism, the speedup defined previously may look very good, but in reality the performance may be quite bad just because the algorithm is inherently bad.

To eliminate ambiguity and give a realistic appraisal of performance, we define speedup more precisely by the formula

$$\text{Speedup} = \frac{\text{Best serial time}}{\text{Parallel-program time}} \qquad (3.5)$$

The numerator is the running time of the most efficient serial program, and the denominator is the running time of the parallel program under study. By comparing a parallel program with the most efficient serial program, we avoid misleading answers that stem from using an inefficient program to execute in parallel.

We assume in this discussion that the parallel program under analysis is also an efficient program when executed serially. If not, the data presented is overly optimistic. Figure 3.12 shows a plot of the speedup obtained from this model for various values of N and p. Note how the speedup initially grows linearly with increases in N, and then drops away from the linear growth to become almost horizontal. Large values of p (the amount of parallelizable code) yield higher speedups, but eventually the speedup falls away from linear growth for high enough N.

Figure 3.9 is particularly easy to analyze because of the rectangular shape of the regions of interest, and its analysis has led us through the discussion up to this point. Let us use similar techniques to analyze the efficiency of pipelined computers.

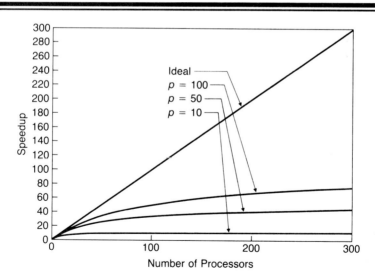

Fig. 3.12 Array-processor speedup.

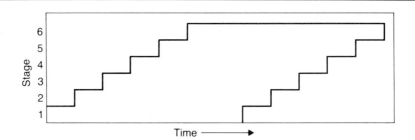

Fig. 3.13 The timing history of a computation for a pipelined processor.

A timing diagram equivalent to Fig. 3.9 for pipelined computers appears in Fig. 3.13. The horizontal axis shows time, and the vertical axis represents the individual stages of a pipeline. The familiar stair-step diagram shows how stages are busy as a function of time. The diagram is redrawn in Fig. 3.14, but with a region of activity shaded. Chen [1980] observed that this region is identical in shape to the idle region that develops as the pipeline empties.

In fact, for purposes of analysis we can move the busy region to the idle region, creating the diagram shown in Fig. 3.15, which shows a period during which a single stage is busy, followed by a period during which all stages are busy. This diagram has the same general shape as Fig. 3.9 for the processor array, and we can therefore apply the same analysis.

The serial time for a pipelined computer represents the time during which the pipeline is filling. The parallel time represents the time during which the

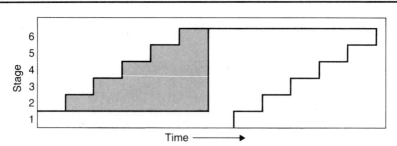

Fig. 3.14 The timing history of a computation before the shaded region is moved to the idle region.

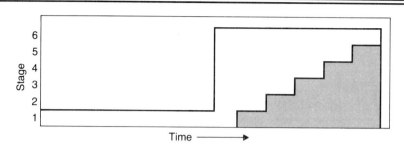

Fig. 3.15 The timing history of a computation after the shaded region is moved to the idle region.

pipeline is completely filled, and all stages are busy. Efficiency and speedup are high when time for filling the pipeline is low compared to the time during which the pipeline is busy. Efficiency drops off dramatically for pipeline designs just as for processor arrays when the time devoted to initialization becomes large compared to the time for actual use. It is crucial, therefore, to keep a pipeline filled with activity and prevent the pipeline from emptying for significant periods of time.

The discussion thus far seems to be pessimistic from the point of view of being able to apply massive amounts of hardware to speed up individual programs. It seems to say that just a small fraction of serial code for the processor array or an equally small fraction of idle time in a pipeline could dramatically reduce efficiency as the amount of parallelism becomes large, and therefore the use of large amounts of parallelism is not attractive. But while the arguments hold for the models presented, these are certainly not the only ways to build parallel machines. Some ways of structuring machines can violate assumptions made in this analysis, and the analysis presented will not hold for those machines.

One tacit assumption made in Fig. 3.9 is that the machine either does serial overhead or parallel execution, and that there is no way to do both concurrently. Such an assumption leads to a drastic impact on efficiency. The impact was well known to the designers of the ILLIAC IV, a computer with 64 identical processing elements. To cushion the impact, the designers built in the ability to overlap serial execution with parallel execution by using a 65th processor to perform control and overhead functions while mesh calculations were performed in the processor array.

The timing diagram for ILLIAC IV is more nearly like Fig. 3.16. Here, the serial code for Loop 2 is executed while the parallel code for Loop 1 is in progress. In ideal circumstances, the serial code can be completed while Loop

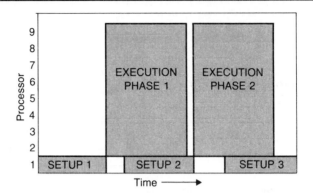

Fig. 3.16 Overlapping of a computation of one phase with the initialization of another on an ILLIAC IV-type array processor.

1 is in progress, and no time will be devoted exclusively to serial execution of the overhead between the execution of Loops 1 and 2.

In less ideal circumstances, only some of the serial code can be overlapped with the parallel code of the previous loop, so that there remains some residual time dedicated to overhead that cannot be overlapped, although such overhead time may be greatly diminished by overlapping execution. Figure 3.16 shows that the ILLIAC IV combined pipeline execution with parallel execution. The serial initialization code of the second loop is pipelined with the parallel execution of the body of a loop.

The corresponding idea for pipelined computers appears in Fig. 3.17. Figure 3.17(a) shows one pipeline operation closely following another in a single pipeline. The initiation of the second operation occurs shortly after the first operation leaves the first stage of the pipeline. The stages of the pipeline are almost fully utilized, and efficiency is high.

Contrast this behavior with the behavior shown in Fig. 3.17(b), in which a pipeline must first empty before a new operation can be initiated. In this case the startup transient is very costly and leads to a severe performance degradation as the number of stages in the pipeline becomes large.

The two different behaviors shown in Fig. 3.17 are characteristics of specific designs, and not inherent characteristics of pipeline designs. For example, the CDC STAR is a high-speed pipelined processor that operates on vectors. It behaves like the diagram in Fig. 3.17(b) in that one vector operation must terminate before the next can begin. However, the fraction of time during which a pipeline is empty depends on the length of a vector, and for very long vectors this fraction can be negligible. For short vectors, the overhead of

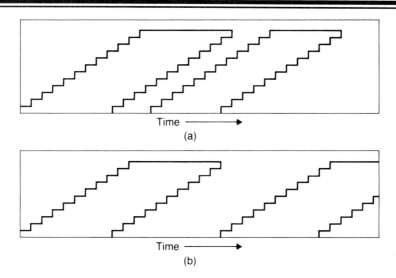

Fig. 3.17 Two possible ways of controlling a pipelined processor:
(a) Overlap permitted between successive initiations; and
(b) No overlap permitted between successive initiations.

operation initiation can be rather severe, so the machine architecture is rather biased towards processing long vectors.

The Cray I architecture is a pipelined machine whose behavior is more like Fig. 3.17(a) in that two and sometimes three different vector operations can be overlapped. For example, when computing expressions of the form

$$A := B \times C$$

$$D := E + A$$

where all variables are vector quantities, the output of the multiply pipeline is routed directly to the addition pipeline, and the addition operation is overlapped partially with the multiplication operation, thereby eliminating idle time due to initiation of the addition operation.

Although the ability to chain computations in this fashion depends to a great extent on the nature of the computation, the Cray I architecture is somewhat more efficient for computations where chaining is possible than for those where chaining is not possible.

The introduction of the Cray II, with different relative timings, leads to different conclusions with regard to chaining. Vector lengths cannot exceed 64 on the Cray II, so long vectors have to be treated as a sequence of short vectors. So the vector equations

$$A := B \times C$$
$$D := E + A$$

actually can be implemented as a sequence of vector operations of the form

$$A_0 := B_0 \times C_0$$
$$D_0 := E_0 + A_0$$
$$A_1 := B_1 \times C_1$$
$$D_1 := E_1 + A_1$$

$$\ldots$$

where each subscripted variable denotes a vector of length 64.

Potential overlap is available by overlapping either the add and multiply operating on the same set of data, or by overlapping an add with an add or a multiply with a multiply where the operations are applied to different sets of data. The overlap of addition with multiplication involves chaining the output of one computation to the input of the next. But the overlap of two vector addition or two vector multiplication operations on independent data requires no chaining of this type.

The architecture of the Cray II is such that both ways of obtaining overlap yield roughly equal speed. Hence, some programs that might require chaining on other architectures receive relatively less benefit from chaining on the Cray II when there are other viable alternatives for overlapping computations.

In actual practice, pipelines rarely exceed 10 to 20 stages, and systems with hundreds of stages are rather unrealistic. The corresponding model for array processors is a system with 10 to 20 processors, not one with hundreds of processors. There is a noticeable inefficiency when pipelines empty for short periods of time, but at low levels of parallelism, the inefficiency may be tolerable compared to the cost of extra hardware required to keep the pipeline full. At higher levels of parallelism, the inefficiency due to an empty pipeline would be much more pronounced, and almost surely should be eliminated if possible.

Consequently, for the pipelines with 10 to 20 stages, designers choose between the cost of extra hardware to maintain a full pipeline and the inefficiency produced by allowing a pipeline to empty partially or completely between operations. The best choice is quite dependent on the available technology as well as on the cleverness of the designer to find inexpensive ways to maintain maximum use of a pipeline. Some very effective techniques for designing pipelined computers with maximum throughput appear in the next section.

3.4 Control of Pipeline Stages

The key idea of the last section is the importance of overlapping pipeline operations as much as possible. In this section we look at a technique originated by Davidson [1971] and subsequently refined by Shar and Davidson [1974], Patel and Davidson [1976], and Kogge [1981]. Kogge's work is particularly illuminating because of the breadth of the information covered and the detail presented.

The idea is to build a very simple controller that gates operations at the entry to a complex pipeline. The controller admits new operations to the pipeline in a manner that can sustain the maximum throughput of the pipeline, while guaranteeing that two or more operations do not collide at a stage within the pipeline even when different operations may take different routes through the system.

The approach we take is to develop a running example of a floating-point arithmetic unit to show basic design techniques and then discuss the control techniques required to maximize throughput of the arithmetic unit.

3.4.1 Design of a Multi-Function Pipeline

We first briefly examine floating-point multiplication and addition to construct a reasonable approximation to a pipelined arithmetic unit for these operations. The simpler of the two operations to describe is multiplication.

Floating-Point Multiplication

1. The input values are assumed to be two normalized floating-point numbers represented by the tuples ($Mantissa_1$, $Exponent_1$) and ($Mantissa_2$, $Exponent_2$), respectively. The first step is to add the exponents to form $Exponent_{out}$.

2. Multiply the two mantissas to form a double-length mantissa. This step may be overlapped with the addition of exponents, and the step may take several time units if the design breaks up the multiplication into chunks that use a common multiplier unit in successive periods of time.

3. Examine the product mantissa, and if it is not normalized, normalize it and adjust the exponent accordingly. (To renormalize the product, the mantissa may have to be adjusted by as much as one digit position.)

4. Round the product mantissa to a single-length mantissa, and, if the rounding should cause the mantissa to overflow, adjust the exponent.

This description maps into a linear pipeline something like the one shown in Fig. 3.18. The number of stages for the multiplication operation is left unspecified in this figure. Actually a multiplication operation can be broken into two components, done sequentially:

1. Produce a collection of partial products; and
2. Add the partial products.

This creates two stages for the multiplier if we can produce all partial products at once. One stage produces the partial products, and the next stage sums them and propagates carries. In practice, this form of a multiplier is extremely hardware intensive and is somewhat reduced in complexity by breaking down the multiplication into more pieces.

For example, simply by breaking the operands into high and low halves, we can form four products by forming all combinations of high and low halves of two operands. These four products can be combined to form the overall product. This breaks the multiplication into four pieces, each of which involves generating a collection of partial products and adding their results to a running sum. The time is longer by a factor of 4, but the hardware is reduced by roughly a factor of 4. Obviously, there is a trade-off between hardware and time for this problem.

Figure 3.19 shows how the design might look if we pass through the two mantissa-multiply stages several times. The design provides a feedback path around the partial product stage so that on subsequent cycles different collec-

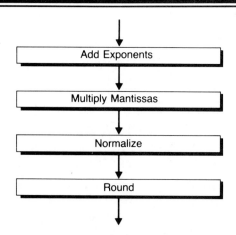

Fig. 3.18 A linear pipeline for floating-point multiplication.

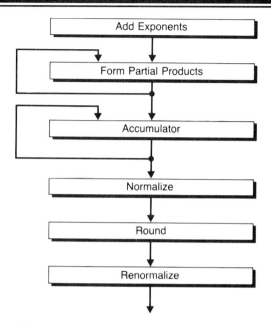

Fig. 3.19 A pipelined floating-point multiplier with feedback loops.

tions of partial products can be produced. Similarly, there is also a feedback path around the partial-product accumulator, which provides a means for summing partial products into the current one.

The feedback path breaks up the pipeline into a structure that is somewhat more complex than the regular structure of a linear pipeline. In the new structure, we have to be careful when we launch a new operation into the beginning of the pipeline. It is possible to launch a new operation too early, in which case it may collide with an operation in progress.

Now let us consider floating-point addition. This process can be described as follows:

Floating-Point Addition

1. The input values are assumed to be two normalized floating-point numbers represented by the tuples (Mantissa$_1$, Exponent$_1$) and (Mantissa$_2$, Exponent$_2$), exactly as for floating-point multiplication. Subtract exponents to find the difference Exp$_{diff}$ and to determine which exponent is larger. If Exponent$_2$ is smaller than Exponent$_1$, swap the operands.

2. Shift Mantissa$_2$ to the right the number of digit positions given by Exp$_{diff}$.

3. Add the mantissas and initialize the exponent of the sum to be $Exponent_1$.

4. Renormalize the sum mantissa, adjusting $Exponent_{sum}$ to reflect the number of digit positions of adjustment required.

5. Round the sum to a single-length mantissa and, if the rounding causes the mantissa to overflow, renormalize and adjust the exponent.

If this operation were implemented in a pipeline structure, the pipeline might look like the one in Fig. 3.20. This pipeline has the simple structure of a linear pipeline, but it might well be more complex. The shifting operation, for example, is very costly to implement in a single cycle, and a designer may choose to implement only a few shift paths in a shifter.

Suppose, for example, that a single stage has shift paths of 1 digit, 4 digits, or 16 digits so that it can shift by amounts such as 0, 1, 5, 16, or 21, which use

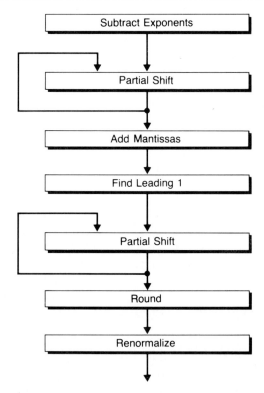

Fig. 3.20 A pipelined floating-point adder with feedback loops.

each of the existing paths in combinations of zero or one time per path. Suppose too that this stage cannot shift by amounts, such as 3 or 8 positions, that require an existing path to be used more than once in a single cycle. In multiple cycles this shifter can shift any amount between 0 and 63 positions if data are circulated through it up to four times. Consequently, the designer can trade-off hardware complexity of the shifter for additional time in the pipeline. The shifter can be installed much like the multiplication unit in the floating-point multiplier of Fig. 3.19.

In comparing Figs. 3.19 and 3.20, we see several common operations. Both units require an adder/subtracter/incrementer for exponents. The normalizer of the floating-point multiplier is less complex than the normalizer of the floating-point adder, but a floating-point multiplication could certainly use the normalizer of a floating-point adder if one were available. Finally, the accumulator for partial products can easily be used to add the operands in the floating-point adder if it were available to the floating-point adder.

The point is that we can combine the two structures of Figs. 3.19 and 3.20 into a single structure that can serve both purposes. One possible way to do this appears in Fig. 3.21. There are two possible paths through this floating-point unit, depending on the nature of the operation. The control of this unit appears to be very complex because the danger of a future collision exists if a new operation is admitted to the arithmetic unit while one or more operations are in progress within the unit.

To anticipate future collisions, we need to develop a timing diagram that shows the flow of data through the arithmetic unit. Davidson [1971] developed the notion of a *reservation table*, shown in Fig. 3.22, that gives the timing information we need. In Fig. 3.22(a) we show the floating-point multiplication operation. Each row of the table represents a physical stage within the arithmetic unit. Each column of the table represents a time step.

In Fig. 3.22(a) we assume that an operation passes through the first two steps in successive time steps and then reaches the stages that perform the mantissa multiplication. For sake of discussion, assume that mantissa multiplication takes two time steps to form all partial products and two time steps (shifted one step later in time) to add the partial products. The last three steps normalize the product, round to single length, then renormalize again if the mantissa overflows.

The reservation table for floating-point addition in the unit appears in Fig. 3.22(b). Note how the flow is quite different from the flow for multiplication. Also note that the tables have their rows labeled by the same stages in the same order, which is very important for the analysis to come. Our problem then becomes one of determining how to control a pipeline with the given reservation tables. At this point, the reservation tables contain all the pertinent information needed to develop a control methodology. Note how the reservation table is derived directly from the pipeline design, but some information is

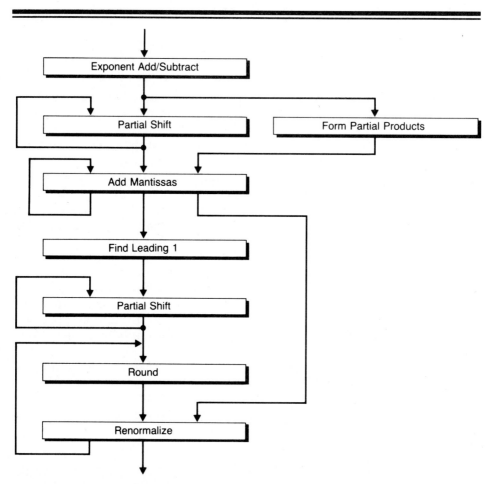

Fig. 3.21 A combined floating-point adder and multiplier.

lost in the construction of the table. It is not possible to recover the data flow of the pipeline from the information in the table, in general, and two quite different pipelines might have identical reservation tables.

3.4.2 The Collision Vector and Pipeline Control

We will simplify the problem initially to consider how to control a pipeline unit that performs a single function. To derive the control algorithm we need to construct a reservation table such as the one given in Fig. 3.22(a). If we launch

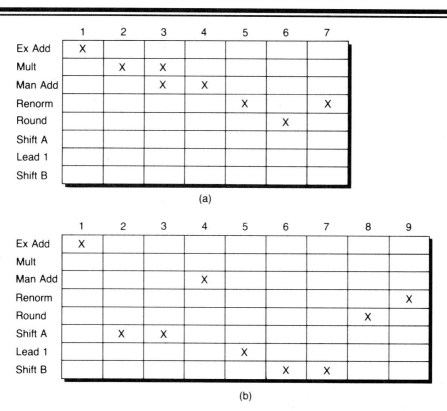

Fig. 3.22 Reservation tables for the floating-point arithmetic unit:
(a) Multiplication; and
(b) Addition.

an operation into the pipeline, at what future times can we launch another identical operation? The solution is very simple. We use the reservation table as a template and overlay one copy of the template on the table, shifted to represent an initiation later in time.

Figure 3.23(a) shows what this might look like when we shift one template by one time unit with respect to the other one. The Xs show the template of Fig. 3.22(a), and the Ys are the same template shifted to the right one time unit. Note how the two templates together show the total activity in the pipeline for two multiplies, delayed with respect to each other by one time unit. A nonempty cell denotes that the corresponding function unit will be busy at the corresponding time, and the entry in the cell indicates which operation has

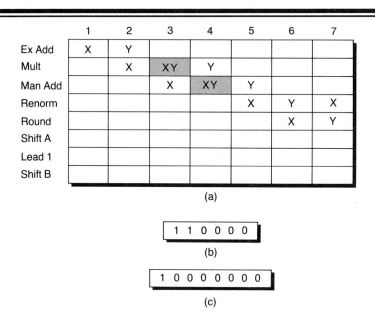

	1	2	3	4	5	6	7
Ex Add	X	Y					
Mult		X	XY	Y			
Man Add			X	XY	Y		
Renorm					X	Y	X
Round						X	Y
Shift A							
Lead 1							
Shift B							

(a)

1 1 0 0 0 0

(b)

1 0 0 0 0 0 0 0

(c)

Fig. 3.23 Derivation of collision vectors for addition:
(a) Collisions of operation X with operation Y, launched one cycle before X;
(b) Collision vector for a multiplication reservation-table; and
(c) Collision vector for an addition reservation-table.

reserved the function unit. If a cell contains both an X and a Y, then both operations require the same unit at the same time. In this case we say that a *collision* exists.

In Fig. 3.23(a) there is a collision at the multiply unit at the third clock, so we conclude that it is not possible to launch a new multiply one time unit after launching the first multiply. We represent the collision information in a binary vector that we call a *collision vector*, as shown in Fig. 3.23(b). Position i contains a bit that indicates whether or not a new operation can be launched i units after a multiplication has been initiated, with a 1 indicating that a collision will occur and a 0 indicating that no collision will occur. The 1 in Position 1 in the figure indicates that we cannot initiate a new multiplication one time unit after initiating a multiplication.

The full collision vector is 110000, indicating that a collision occurs if we attempt to enter a new multiplication at either of the two clock cycles immediately after initiating a multiplication, but any time thereafter we can initiate a new one. The reader can verify this by shifting a transparency containing a copy of the reservation table over the same table and observing the set of delays that produce collisions.

The collision vector for additions appears in Fig. 3.23(c). It has the value 10000000 because the cycle immediately after an addition operation is unavailable for a new addition, but any of the subsequent seven cycles can begin new addition operations. Again, the reader should verify this result by using Fig. 3.22(b) as a template on a transparency and shifting the template over the same table. The two shifters in this pipeline tend to eliminate collisions with the adder. If a single shifter is shared for the two functions, the collision vector tends to become more heavily populated, thereby limiting the frequency of initiation of new operations at some savings in hardware because of the shared logic.

We can also determine if an addition will collide with a multiplication in progress, and conversely, if a multiplication will collide with an addition in progress. Simply place the reservation table from Fig. 3.22(a) on top of the table from Fig. 3.22(b) and shift the two relative to each other. In positions where an X from one table collides with an X from the other, no initiation of the second operation is permitted at that particular value of delay with respect to the first operation.

The problem of major interest here is how to control a pipeline dynamically. We cannot afford a complex control scheme, not because hardware is particularly expensive, but because the control information must be computable within a single clock cycle to keep up with the requests for entry to the pipeline. A complex algorithm might not be able to meet the performance requirements of a high-speed pipeline.

Davidson [1971] produced a very clever control element from the collision vector. For a single-function pipeline, the pipeline controller is simply a shift register that shifts its contents to the left during each clock cycle. The collision vector can be ORed with the contents of the shift register at any clock cycle. The controller operation is basically the following:

1. Grant a request for access to the pipeline during a clock cycle for which the bit emerging from the shift register is a 0. Deny access in the current cycle if the bit is a 1 and hold the request for the next cycle.

2. If a request is granted, when the shift register is updated at the end of the current cycle, its new contents will be the shifted value of its former contents ORed with the collision vector.

3. If no request is granted during a clock cycle, update the register by shifting its contents to the left, as shown in the figure. At the right-hand end, 0s are shifted into the register. If any operation has to wait, the operation is guaranteed to gain access to the pipeline within a time no longer than the length of the collision vector. By waiting for this period of time, we are guaranteed to clear the contents of the shift register. Hence, a 0 must

appear at the shift-register output by then, thereby permitting a new initiation.

If only one operation is in progress when a request occurs, the shifted version of the collision vector in the shift register indicates those relative delays between initiations that will produce a collision in the pipeline. This follows because the 1s in the collision vector show the relative delays that produce collisions. If two or more operations are in progress, then a new operation cannot be started if it collides with any of the ones in progress. The INCLUSIVE OR operation produces a vector whose 1s show relative delays for which at least one of the operations currently in progress will collide with a new operation if the new operation is initiated on the present cycle.

This argument shows that the basic idea of collision vector and shift-register controller is quite workable for a single-function pipeline.

The calculations become somewhat trickier when a pipeline supports multiple functions, as we show in the present example. There are now four collision vectors:

1. Multiply following multiply;

2. Add following add;

3. Add following multiply; and

4. Multiply following add.

The first two collision vectors show the delays at which a new operation collides with the same type of operation started earlier in the pipeline. These are the vectors computed in Fig. 3.23(b) and (c). The last two vectors show the delays at which an addition collides with an earlier multiply, or a multiply collides with an earlier addition. These are computed by overlaying the table in Fig. 3.22(a) on Fig. 3.22(b) and observing at what delays there is a collision. The vectors produced by this process are shown in the controller in Fig. 3.24. The reader should verify how these vectors have been produced.

The controller in Fig. 3.24 admits either an addition or a multiplication to the pipeline, and it guarantees that no collisions occur after an operation is admitted, no matter what the current state of the pipeline is. Here we use two shift registers, one that keeps track of when adds can be initiated and one that keeps track of when multiplies can be initiated.

Suppose the controller receives a request to perform an addition. The controller consults the bit emerging from the ADD shift register. If the bit is a 1, the request is deferred; otherwise the request is granted. Once the request is granted, a new operation (an addition) enters the pipeline and becomes an operation that can conflict with future requests. In this case, the MULTIPLY shift register is updated by ORing in the multiply-following-add collision vector, and the ADD shift register is updated by ORing in the add-following-add collision vector. The new vectors contain 1s in positions that lead to

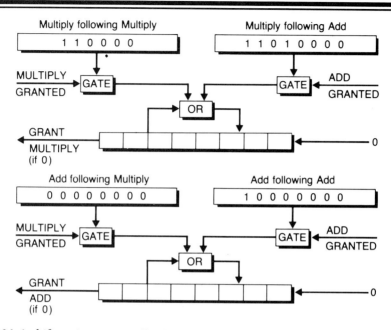

Fig. 3.24 A shift-register controller for a dual-function pipeline. The collision vector "multiply following add" shows what will occur when a multiplication enters while an addition is in progress.

collisions if a subsequent addition or multiplication is initiated at the corresponding time.

The treatment of multiplication requests is completely symmetric with addition requests. The multiplication requests inspect the MULTIPLY shift register for the bit that grants or denies access, and if access is available, the MULTIPLY shift register is updated by ORing it with the multiply-following-multiply collision vector, and the ADD shift register is updated by ORing in the add-following-multiply collision vector.

As the number of different paths through the pipeline increases, the number of shift registers required in the controller increases in proportion, one shift register for each possible path. The computation required per cycle is at worst the selection of one collision vector from a collection of such vectors and the ORing of the selected vector to the shift register during the register's normal update cycle.

This concludes the discussion of how to control a pipeline correctly at very high rates of computation, but we shall continue to develop this idea to determine how to achieve maximum throughput.

3.4.3 Maximum Performance Pipelines

The control strategy to which we alluded in the previous section suggests that a new computation should be started at the first clock cycle for which the computation is guaranteed not to collide with computations now in progress. This is sometimes called a *greedy* strategy because the controller tries to initiate new operations as quickly as possible. The strategy is not necessarily the best, but it is certainly the easiest to implement.

When the greedy control strategy is an optimum strategy, we have a welcome situation because the least-costly control strategy yields highest performance. By looking more closely at the reservation table and collision vector concepts, we can bias designs so that they yield a combination of high performance and simple control.

To understand more thoroughly the principles that govern collision vectors, consider all of the possible states of a shift-register controller. Figure 3.25 shows a collision vector derived from a reservation table and the various states derivable from this collision vector by initiating new operations at all possible combinations of times.

The diagram in the figure, called a *reduced state-diagram*, shows each state of a shift register just after a new operation has been initiated. The labels on the arrows between states indicate the number of clock cycles that intervene as the shift register moves from an initial state to a final state. Since the initial vector is 1001011, we know that at least one clock must occur after initiating an operation, and a new operation can be initiated at the second clock.

Immediately after initiating the first operation, the shift register contains 1001011, the collision vector. Immediately after initiating another operation two clocks later, the new contents of the shift register are 0101100 OR 1001011 = 1101111. Consequently, Fig. 3.25 contains an arrow starting at state 1001011 that ends at state 1101111 with the label 2 to indicate that the state is entered two cycles after a new operation is initiated from the initial state. By proceeding in this manner, all new states and transition times between states can be enumerated, and we obtain the figure shown.

Specifically, we build the reduced state-diagram by the following algorithm:

1. Create a set of states to examine by placing an initial state into this set. That initial state is labeled with the collision vector. Initialize the state diagram to a single node bearing the label of the collision vector. (This represents the state of the controller when one operation has just been launched down the pipeline.)

2. Remove a state from the set of states to examine. For each 0 in the label of this state, find the state of the controller shift-register that would be obtained if a new operation were launched just when the corresponding 0 emerges from the shift register. The label of the successor state corre-

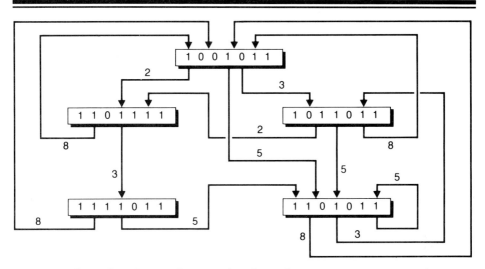

Fig. 3.25 The reduced state-diagram for the collision vector 1001011. The states shown are all possible states at which a new operation has just been initiated. The numbers on the arcs show the delay between successive states.

sponding to the ith 0 is obtained by shifting the present label i positions to the left, appending i 0's on the right, and ORing in the collision vector to the resulting label.

3. If a successor state is new, add it to the state diagram and place the successor state in the list of states to be examined.

4. In any case draw an arc from the present state to the successor state in the state diagram and label the arc with the value i to indicate the number of cycles of delay that occur between the present state and the entry to the successor state.

5. Add an arc to the initial state of the diagram with the label N, where N is one more than the length of the shift register.

6. When the successors of a state have been exhausted, return to the set of states to be examined for a new state to process. If there are no more states to be examined, terminate the construction of the reduced state-diagram.

We can find the maximum rate that can be sustained for the pipeline by examining the cycles in the reduced state-diagram. There are cycles of various lengths, including 5 and 8. Each cycle in this diagram corresponds to some way of repeatedly initiating operations. The cycle of length 5 that touches state 1101011 is a cycle with one initiation every five cycles, for a rate of completion of 0.2 operations per cycle. The cycle of length 8 that visits states 1011011 and 1101011 has two completions every eight states, for a rate of 0.25 operations per cycle.

Note the arcs of length 8 from each state to the initial state. They appear because, after seven shifts, the shift register is empty, and the next initiation brings us to the initial state of the reduced state-diagram.

The greedy strategy starts with a delay of 2 and then falls into a pattern of 3, 5, 3, 2, which is a stable cycle with 4 completions every 13 clock cycles, for a rate of roughly 0.31 completions per cycle. This particular cycle leads to the highest rate of use of the pipeline. In this example, the greedy strategy happens to give the best performance.

Designers of pipeline systems should perform the analysis given here to derive the highest rate cycles and determine a strategy for the controller to follow to achieve the highest rate. As a measure of the effectiveness of the control strategy, we can easily obtain a bound on the highest possible rate as determined from the reservation table. Simply examine the reservation table, such as the table in Fig. 3.22(a), and find the row with the greatest number of entries.

In Fig. 3.22(a), both the second and third rows have two entries. These rows are bottlenecks and limit maximum throughput. In fact, because the corresponding physical stages are used in two of the seven clock times represented by the table, they saturate when the controller initiates $7/2$ operations per seven clocks, or equivalently when the average delay per initiation is two clock periods. In general, if there are D marks in a row of a reservation table, the average delay between initiations must be D or greater, and the maximum attainable rate of execution is N/D, where N is the number of stages in the pipeline.

3.4.4 Using Delays to Increase Performance

If a pipeline cannot sustain initiations at the maximum possible rate, the cause is collisions within the pipeline that prevent new operations from being initiated at certain crucial instants of time. By adding delays within the pipeline, it is always possible to attain maximum performance. Although the delays lengthen the total transit time through the pipeline, they increase the rate at which operations terminate if they remove collisions that restrict the initiation rate.

In this section we explore the design process for inserting delays into a pipeline to attain maximum performance. The original research on which the material is based was done by Patel and Davidson [1976] and is developed at some length in Kogge [1981].

Figure 3.26 shows a typical reservation table and its corresponding collision vector and reduced state-diagram. The maximum rate for new initiations

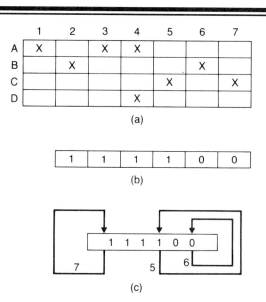

Fig. 3.26 Components of a reservation table:
(a) The reservation table;
(b) Its collision vector; and
(c) Its redued state-diagram.

as indicated by the table is $1/3$ because Row A has three entries. But the cycle with the least average latency is the cycle with initiation rate $1/5$, which is substantially slower than the minimum latency. We presume that it is possible to achieve an initiation rate of $1/3$ and set out to modify the reservation table to achieve this rate.

There are various ways to initiate on one out of three cycles on the average, and we are guaranteed to find at least one way that supports maximum throughput. For example, we can initiate exactly every three cycles, or we can initiate by delaying just two cycles between the first and second initiation, followed by four cycles between the second and third initiation. In the course of this analysis, we will discover that it is impossible to modify the table to initiate every six cycles with a delay of 2 followed by a delay of 4, and it is illuminating to discover why this is so.

Let us assume that we will examine the context in which the pipeline is used to select the cycle with the best behavior. For example, in this case we might discover that there is a high probability of a pair of requests for the pipeline spaced only two cycles apart, in which case a fixed delay of 3 between requests would cause buffering to occur outside the pipeline. Hence, the cycle with delays of 2 and 4 between successive initiations may lead to somewhat better overall performance than would the cycle with a fixed delay of 3 between initiations.

To modify the table for a cycle with successive delays of 2 and 4, we examine the first row in the table; it is the critical row since it has the maximum number of Xs. To achieve the desired cycle, we need to make sure that we can initiate nonconflicting operations two and six time units after starting an operation.

The important observation is that conflicts are caused solely among Xs in each row. Their relative positions in a row totally determine at what delays conflicts will occur. To remove conflicts for particular amounts of delay, we can move any given X to the right in a row. Physically speaking, this is the same as delaying that reservation by one or more time units, and it requires the insertion of an equivalent number of stages of delay.

To create a table from the one in Fig. 3.26(a) that permits initiation to occur at two and six units of delay relative to the start of an operation, we have to spread the Xs apart in Row A in such a way that no conflicts occur at delays of 2 and 6. We attempt to construct a suitable new row in a modified table as shown in Fig. 3.27(a), where we have inserted the X from Column 1 and marked an F in "forbidden" cells.

A cell is forbidden if, by placing an X in the cell, a collision will occur when any pair of operations launched at times $0, 2, 6, 8, 12, 14, \ldots$ collide at that cell. The F in Column 3 is placed there because this is a delay of 2 relative to the X in Column 1. Hence, if there is an X in this cell and an operation is started at a delay of 2, a collision will occur because an X in this cell will collide with the X in Column 1. Similarly, the F in Column 5 is delayed by 4 with respect to the X in Column 1. This is forbidden because an operation initiated at a delay of 4 will cause an X in this cell to collide with the X in Column 1.

Consequently, we must place Fs in the row at delays of 2 and 4 with respect to the initial X. The remaining Fs account for delays of one full cycle or more. A delay of 2 or 4 is forbidden within one cycle, and from cycle to cycle we must also forbid $2 + 6 = 8, 2 + 2 \times 6 = 14, 2 + 3 \times 6 = 20, \ldots$, and $4 + 6 = 10$, and $4 + 2 \times 6 = 16. \ldots$ Note too that delays of $0, 0 + 6 = 6, 0 + 2 \times 6 = 12, \ldots$, are forbidden. Therefore, placing the first X in Column 1 has resulted in eliminating all odd-numbered columns from further consideration.

We can place a second X in an even-numbered column. The original table has an X in Column 3, which is forbidden, so instead we insert a delay in Column 3 and reserve Row A at Column 4, as shown in Fig. 3.27(b). The D corresponds to a new stage in the pipeline that has been added as a buffer to prevent a collision. In this case the new D stage holds an operand intended for Unit A so that the operand can enter Unit A one clock time later than it otherwise would.

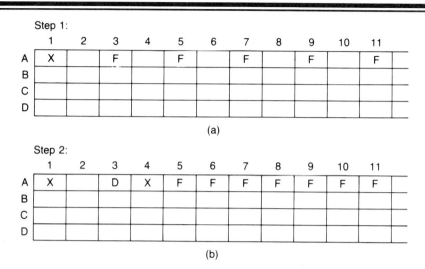

Fig. 3.27 Steps in modifying a reservation table to add delays.
(a) Place first *X* and mark forbidden cells; and
(b) Place next *X* after adding delay *D* and mark additional forbidden cells.

The new reservation in Column 4 forces us to place *F*s in all the even-numbered columns after Column 4 to prevent collisions with this *X*. And the result is that the entire row after Column 4 is filled with *F*s, thereby preventing us from adding the third *X* to Row *A*. Hence, for this table, it is impossible to construct a cycle of length 6 whose two delays are 2 and 4.

Figure 3.28 shows that it is possible to construct a cycle that lets us initiate one new operation every three cycles. The idea is very simple. In Fig. 3.28 we march from left to right, column by column, placing the *X*s from Fig. 3.26. First we put an *X* in Row *A*, Column 1, and place *F*s in Columns 4, 7, 10, . . . , because these positions are forbidden in order to prevent collisions at a delay of 3.

We attempt to place *X*s in successive columns, as shown in Fig. 3.28(b). The next *X* is placed in Row *B*, Column 2, and it too results in a series of *F*s being placed in the table at positions 5, 8, 11, . . . , of the same row. The next *X* is placed as shown in Fig. 3.28(c) in Row *A*, Column 3, where we show its *F*s marked in Columns 6, 9, 12, . . . , leaving Column 5 for the third *X*. But this *X* was originally in Column 4, so it must be delayed by one additional delay time. We place a *D* in Column 4 in Fig. 3.28(d) to signify that one stage of pure delay must be inserted into the pipeline at this time, and the operation can be initiated one unit time later, as signified by the *X* in Column 5.

Now we have to modify other *X*s in the table. The new table produces the

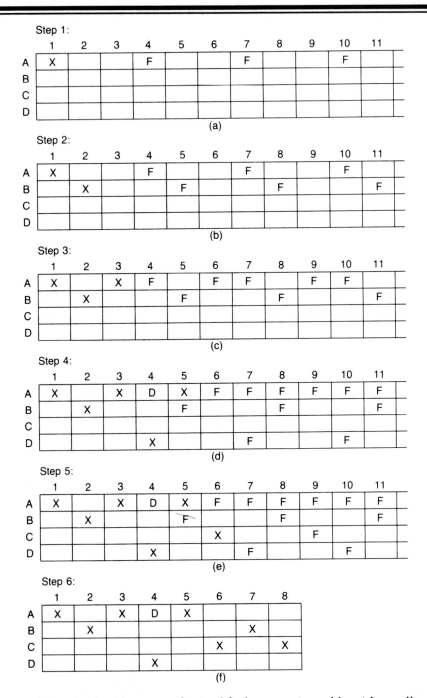

Fig. 3.28 Steps in the derivation of a modified reservation table with an allowable initiation cycle of one operation every three time units.

Row B result one time unit later than the original table. All other stages that depend on this result to appear at Time 4 have to be delayed by 1 or more clock times because the D inserted in Column 4 forces the result to appear at Time 5, not Time 4. Moreover, if other stages are delayed because of this change, then their results will be delayed as well, and the stages that depend on those results will have to be delayed. The remainder of the description shows to ensure that all delays are handled properly.

The reservation table does not give us the dependency information we need to complete this process, and in practice it is necessary to go back to the original pipeline to determine the stage-to-stage dependence. For the current discussion, we assume that all Xs in the original reservation table in Columns 5 through 7 are forced to be delayed by 1 cell because of the new delay in Column 4.

The X in Row C, Column 5, of Fig. 3.26 can be placed in Column 6, as shown in Fig. 3.28(e), which forces the second X in Row B to start no earlier than Column 7. Column 7 is satisfactory for the X in Row B, and this in turn delays the second X in Row C to start in Column 8. The complete reservation table with the Fs removed is shown in Fig. 3.28(f).

Figure 3.29(a) shows a possible structure for a pipeline unit described by the original reservation table, and Fig. 3.29(b) shows the modified pipeline with the delay added. In the original reservation table, Stage A at Time 3 is followed by Stage A at Time 4, which is made possible in Fig. 3.29(a) by the feedback path from Stage A to Stage A. In Fig. 3.29(b) that feedback path is lengthened by a unit delay.

Although we have represented delays by the letter D in the modified reservation table, a physical delay corresponds to a new pipeline stage, and thus it can be represented by an additional row in the reservation table. When represented in this fashion, each distinct delay corresponds to a distinct row.

It is possible to combine rows that do not conflict and thereby share a delay stage for two or more purposes. To decide if it is possible to combine such rows, one simply introduces Fs in forbidden cells. Then it is relatively simple to determine which rows can be combined by noting where, after combining two rows, the Xs do not fall into forbidden cells.

In attempting to build an initiation cycle with relative delays of 2 and 4, we discovered that no such cycle could exist for the original table, but that we could build an initiation cycle with a single fixed delay of 3. Both cycles that we have examined yield an average initiation rate of one initiation every three clock times, but only one of the two is realizable.

The figures show graphically that, because we can move Xs around freely to avoid forbidden cells, the realizability of an initiation cycle depends only on the relative delays in the cycle and not on the initial placement of Xs in a reservation table. Consequently, we can analyze an initiation cycle as specified by its delays, and we can determine which tables can be modified to satisfy the cycle without having to know the particular details of the reservation tables.

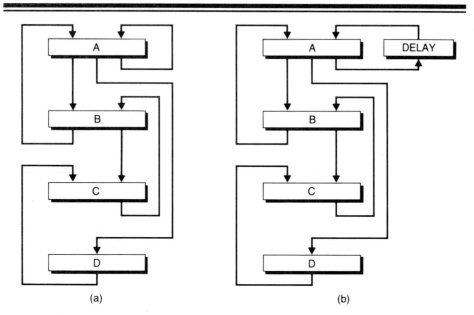

Fig. 3.29 Two pipeline versions:
(a) The original pipeline; and
(b) The pipeline modified for maximum throughput.

Figure 3.27 illustrates the key idea in the analysis of an initiation cycle by showing the role of the forbidden cell. Let $(d_1, d_2, \ldots, d_k)$ represent an initiation cycle for which Operation 2 is launched d_1 cycles after Operation 1, Operation 3 is launched d_2 cycles after Operation 2, and so on. Let L be the sum of the delays, which is also the length of the cycle. From the example, we know that at a delay d_1 after an X in a row, there is a forbidden cell, and in fact there are such cells at all delay positions p relative to X that satisfy the congruence

$$p = d_1 \bmod L \qquad\qquad (3.6)$$

In Fig. 3.27, for a delay of 2, this formula describes the cells at delays 2, 8, 14, ..., relative to the first X. Also, there are forbidden cells at delay positions p that satisfy

$$p = d_i \bmod L \qquad\qquad (3.7)$$

for each distinct delay d_i since two successive operations are launched d_i units apart. But we may still have missed some forbidden cells. In fact, there is a forbidden cell for each distinct value of the sum:

$$d_i + d_{i+1} + \cdots + d_{i+k-1} \qquad (3.8)$$

where the sum is taken over k successive delays in the cycle, beginning at delay i.

We need only consider those sums whose value does not exceed L, since we can construct the forbidden values of size greater than L by adding arbitrary multiples of L to forbidden values of size L or less. In Fig. 3.27, the forbidden delay values are those congruent to 0, 2, and 4 mod 6, and are thus represented as the set {0,2,4} for a cycle length of 6. For Fig. 3.28, the forbidden values are those congruent to 0 mod 3, and are represented as the set {0} for a cycle length of 3.

From the forbidden values we can obtain the permissible values. The permissible values dictate where to place Xs in a modified table. Obviously, any nonforbidden value is permissible, but not all *sets* of nonforbidden values are permissible. In Fig. 3.27, {0,2,4} are forbidden delays, so 1, 3, and 5 are permissible. But if we choose to use both 1 and 3 as relative delays for new Xs from a given X, the difference between a delay of 1 and a delay of 3 is 2, which is a forbidden value. Hence we cannot use both relative delays 1 and 3 when placing Xs in a modified table. Likewise, we cannot use both 3 and 5, nor can we use 1 and 5. In the latter case the relative delay between delays 1 and 5 is a relative delay of 4, which is a forbidden value.

We have discovered that for a cycle of length 6 composed of the delays 2 and 4, the forbidden cells are at relative positions 0 mod 6, 2 mod 6, and 4 mod 6. We can construct a new table by placing new Xs at either 1 mod L, 3 mod L, or 5 mod L from an X, but we cannot place new Xs at any two of the permissible positions. Hence we cannot have more than two Xs in any row of a table for the cycle composed of delays 2 and 4.

In Fig. 3.28, the forbidden delay set is {0} mod 3, and the permissible cells are 1 mod 3 and 2 mod 3 away from an X. In this case we can place two new Xs— one at a delay of 1 mod 3 and the other at a delay of 2 mod 3 from an initial X. The new Xs do not conflict with each other, nor do they conflict with the initial X. We represent the set of permissible delays as the set {1,2}. We call the set {1,2} a *maximal compatible set* of delays because it satisfies the following conditions:

- *Permissibility:* each member of the set is permissible;
- *Compatibility:* the difference between any two distinct members is not congruent to a forbidden value modulo L; and
- *Maximal size:* it is not possible to add another permissible delay value to the set and still satisfy the compatibility criterion.

To give some examples of maximal compatible sets, consider a cycle of length 8 composed of the delays 3 and 5. The set of forbidden delays is represented by the set {0,3,5}, with the delays representing their congruence classes modulo 8. Permissible delays are 1, 2, 4, 6, and 7. The maximal compatible sets are $\{1,2\}, \{1,7\}, \{2,4,6\},$ and $\{6,7\}$. In this case, if a set contains a 1, it cannot contain a 4 or 6, and if it contains a 2, it cannot contain a 7. Hence, the first two sets show every possible way of constructing a set containing a 1.

The remaining sets show every possible way of building a set without a 1. Note also that if a set contains a 7, it cannot contain a 2 or 4. The maximal compatible set $\{2,4,6\}$, which has the most members, indicates that we can safely assign four Xs in a single row at an arbitrary initial position and at distinct delays of 2, 4, and 6 modulo 8 relative to this position. This assignment satisfies the constraint that no two Xs collide on a cycle of length 8 composed of delays 3 and 5.

The computation of maximal-compatible classes can be done algorithmically through a backtrack process, but in practical cases it can usually be done by hand. The preceding analysis guarantees that it is always possible to modify a reservation table to initiate a new operation every L cycles if the maximum number of Xs in a row is L or less.

In this case the forbidden set is the set $\{0\}$, and the maximum compatible set is $\{1,2,3, \ldots, L - 1\}$. This means that we can safely assign the initial X arbitrarily, and up to $L - 1$ Xs at distinct relative delays selected from $\{1,2,3, \ldots, L - 1\}$ modulo L.

The modification of a reservation table reduces to a process of placing Xs in cells that satisfy the stage-to-stage precedence constraints and that are at relative delays dictated by some maximal-compatible class. The procedure is guaranteed to succeed if the size of the maximal-compatible class is at least $L - 1$.

3.4.5 Interlock Elimination

The general characteristic of pipeline units is that the rate of completion is related to the clock time of a single stage and may be quite different from the total time required to traverse a pipeline. When this characteristic holds, we are willing to insert delays into a pipeline if the completion rate increases. But some computations are sensitive to the total delay in a pipeline. In this section we examine how to reduce the sensitivity to total delay in certain selected, but important, cases.

When a pipeline performs a succession of steps of the form

$$SUM := SUM + A_i \times B_i \tag{3.9}$$

which is the main loop of an inner-product computation, the delay of the pipeline has a serious impact on throughput. If the computation is executed as written, a new product can be added to SUM only after SUM has completed the previous addition. If addition takes, for example, four cycles, then a new term can be added to SUM only every four cycles. This is the case even when the addition is pipelined to be able to produce one result per cycle. The problem is that there are conflicts due to the common access of SUM.

Kogge [1981] describes a technique for avoiding this particular bottleneck in some common situations. In the case at hand the problem becomes one of producing a useful result every cycle in spite of the conflict for access to *SUM*. To derive Kogge's method, rewrite the main loop of the original formula in the form:

$$SUM_i := SUM_{i-1} + A_i \times B_i \qquad (3.10)$$

where the index on *SUM* denotes the value of *SUM* at the end of the corresponding iteration. The problem as written is that SUM_{i-1} is not available immediately for the calculation of SUM_i when the product term has emerged from the multiplier in the pipeline. An earlier value of *SUM* is available, however, so we can change the equation to become

$$SUM_i := SUM_{i-4} + A_i \times B_i \qquad (3.11)$$

for a pipeline with a delay of 4 through the adder.

More generally, if the adder has a delay d, the index of *SUM* used as input to the adder is $i - d$. The advantage here is that the input value of *SUM* required for an addition is the value that emerged as the output of the last cycle of the adder. Hence, the output of the adder can be latched and fed back to the input as one operand for the next cycle. This produces the results quickly, but the results are not quite what we need.

In fact, in this example we obtain four different independent sums, with each sum involving approximately one quarter of the terms. The final answer is obtained by adding the four independent sums together. The final summation requires just a small overhead compared to the time required to obtain the four sums as the number of elements in the inner product grows large. During the main computation, the rate of completion is equal to the delay of a single stage of the pipeline. The rate has been decoupled from the total delay of the adder, which limited the speed of the original computation.

This technique is limited to operations that can be executed in an order different from the original specification. Addition and multiplication are both associative and commutative operations, so as idealized mathematical operations, there is some flexibility in scheduling a sequence of additions or multiplications. But computer arithmetic is arithmetic on a finite, rather than an infinite, set of numbers, and the precision of the numbers is finite, not infinite. Consequently, sequences of arithmetic operations on computers can display unexpected answers in the face of round-off errors.

Many numerical algorithms have been cast in a form that leaves them less sensitive to round-off errors. When the order of operations is changed, there is some danger that the work of the numerical analyst has been undone. For example, when forming large sums of numbers, round-off error can be significant if small addends are added to large intermediate sums.

To be sure that small addends are added to small intermediate sums to limit the accumulation of round-off errors, analysts suggest that the terms be ordered so that they increase in magnitude. However, the suggestion given previously reorders the sequence of additions and may well produce a different, possibly less accurate, final result than the answer produced with the original computation.

We suspect that in the majority of situations the reordering of operations for high performance does not introduce unacceptable numerical errors, and the performance attainable is dramatic. For the infrequent situation in which the order of evaluation is important, there should be an override or some other mechanism to ensure that a computation is evaluated in precisely the order stated by the instructions.

3.5 Exploiting Pipeline Techniques

We have examined the general principles of pipeline computers and looked at their control in great detail. In this section we examine ways to structure systems for pipeline execution.

3.5.1 Conditional Branches

The performance analysis earlier in this chapter describes the importance of keeping the pipeline full. If an input stage lies idle on a particular cycle, and the idleness is due to lack of available input data rather than to a potential future collision, the idleness eventually propagates through the entire pipeline and detracts materially from the pipeline efficiency.

Conditional branches have long been a source of difficulty for pipeline computers because they can halt a pipeline momentarily until the branch target can be determined. Designers have used a number of different techniques for reducing the effects of conditional branches on performance. This section treats the most important ones used in practice:

1. Delayed branching;
2. Branch prediction; and
3. Branch history.

One widely used technique has found its way into the design of microprogrammed processors. Microcode executes at the rate of one microstep per cycle, but the actual time required to execute a microinstruction is two cycles—one cycle to fetch the instruction and one to execute it. Hence, many machines use a two-cycle pipeline for microcode execution and achieve the rate of one completion per cycle.

Conditional branches in microcode could be rather devastating if the pipeline had to wait because of indecision regarding branch targets. In fact, when a conditional branch is executed, many machines defer the effect of that

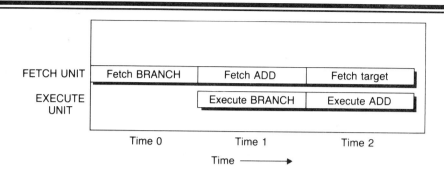

Fig. 3.30 Timing for the execution of a conditional branch in a microprogrammed control unit. The instruction ADD follows immediately after the BRANCH and is executed before control passes to the target of the BRANCH.

branch by one cycle in order to execute the next instruction in the pipeline. That instruction is the one fetched from memory during the execution of the conditional branch; it is fetched before the branch target is known.

Figure 3.30 shows the timing for the execution just described. At Time 0, the conditional-branch instruction is fetched from memory, and at Time 1 it is executed, resulting in a new value of the microprogram-counter register. Also at Time 1, the ADD instruction that immediately follows the BRANCH is fetched. At Time 2 the address of the target of the conditional branch is used to fetch the next microinstruction, but that microinstruction is not available for execution until Time 3. So during Time 2 the ADD microinstruction is executed, since it is available immediately for execution. In a sense, the BRANCH microinstruction has the meaning, "Execute the next microinstruction and then branch conditionally."

This basic idea has been adapted to the instruction sets of a class of processors called reduced-instruction-set computers (RISC). Like microprogrammed controllers, RISC computers attempt to complete the execution of one instruction per cycle, and because the delay in the execution pipeline is normally two or more stages, the delayed-branch technique becomes quite attractive in order to sustain high performance.

Delayed branching makes very good sense for RISC machines because the delay required for determining the branch outcome is just a single cycle. If the delay needs to be much longer because of complexities within the conditional-branch instruction, the idea is more difficult to use.

While it is conceivable to delay a branch until after the next instruction, it becomes somewhat more difficult to make use of branches that delay their execution until after the execution of the next N instructions where N is a small integer greater than 1. This type of delayed branching has not been widely used in the industry, primarily because it is difficult for programmers to use effectively, and there is a certain danger in the use of such instructions when assembly code is written and maintained by humans. But the delayed branch is used almost universally in microcode, and, in recent years, in RISC architectures. RISC instructions are very much analogous to microinstructions since they execute in a single cycle. The effective use of the delayed branch in these computers depends very strongly on generating executable code by means of optimizing compilers for high-level languages. This puts the difficulty of dealing with delayed branches in the hands of the compiler writers, who have to solve this problem only once. All users benefit from that solution. Moreover, maintenance difficulties due to delayed branching vanish because it is not the machine-language translation, but the high-level language version of a program that is maintained.

The second idea is the most popular one for high-performance pipelined processors. The idea is to guess the branch target and proceed on that path in the pipeline. Any results produced in the pipeline are marked tentative, and they cannot overwrite user-accessible registers or memory locations while so marked. Eventually the outcome of the branch is decided, and if the guess is correct, the special tags on tentative results are removed. If not, the tentative results are purged, and any tentative operations in progress are cancelled.

When guesses are correct most of the time, branch prediction is very effective. The benefit diminishes as guesses become less accurate, and if guesses are rather poor, the cost of implementation of branch prediction exceeds the value of the idea. Making good predictions is not particularly difficult if characteristics of the software are known.

A FORTRAN end-of-loop test, for example, takes the conditional branch back to the beginning of the loop on all but the last iteration. Similarly, searches fail on all iterations, except possibly the last one. So there are reasonable ways of discovering situations in which the overwhelming majority of conditional branches selects a particular target.

The problem becomes quite challenging when branch instructions are used totally differently by different software, particularly when generated automatically by different compilers. For example, the branch address of a JUMP IF POSITIVE instruction might be the normal-case branch produced by one compiler and might be the exceptional case in the code produced by another compiler. What should the hardware do? Should it guess that the positive case is normal and assume the branch is taken? Or should it assume that the negative case is normal and assume the branch is not taken?

In some architectures, the hardware can quickly tell if the branch is backward or forward because a relative offset appears in the instruction. It may be prudent to assume the branch is taken if the offset is negative, under the assumption that backward branches are loops. If the offset is positive, it is not clear what to do.

The type of instruction and the size and direction of the offset are all factors in the branch decision, and the designer must weigh their effects carefully in making a choice of a branch-prediction strategy. Designers usually validate their strategies against traces of program execution in much the same way that caches are evaluated.

With sufficient information available, the designer ought to be able to do better than a random choice. Even a random choice with equal probabilities is correct half of the time, which might lead to better performance than using no branch prediction at all if this results in making the wrong choice almost always. So branch prediction is a reasonable and effective method for dealing with conditional branches, but it does have the flaw that some programs may use their branches precisely opposite the way that prediction is built into the hardware. No fixed strategy can avoid this pitfall.

To improve performance beyond that achievable by branch prediction requires the ability to adapt to a program's execution behavior. Caches are superb at adapting. They quickly identify the frequently used items and manage memory to retain those items in high-speed storage. Can the idea of a cache be used for branch prediction? Indeed it can. Figure 3.31 illustrates a device called a *branch-history table* [Sussenguth 1971]. The idea of the branch-history table is to store information regarding a branch so that fairly accurate predictions of the branch outcome are available. An easy strategy is to predict that the branch will do what it did last time.

Figure 3.31 illustrates one way to implement a branch-history table. The table is essentially a cache memory accessed concurrently with each instruction fetch to a cache. If a match is found, the table produces the address of the next instruction, which will be used on the next cycle of the pipeline. The execution from this point forward proceeds in a manner identical to branch prediction, with all results marked as tentative until the true outcome of the branch is known.

The branch-history table is updated each time the execution of a branch is completed. An update writes into the table the instruction address of the branch just executed and the target address to which it branched. Old history is purged from the table using algorithms similar to cache-management algorithms. Figure 3.31 illustrates the instruction execution pipeline and shows the branch-history table accessed by both the instruction-fetch unit and the execution unit.

The disadvantage of the structure shown in Fig. 3.31 is that it has to sustain somewhat more than one access per cycle if instructions are fetched at the rate of one per cycle. The table can be designed for much less frequent access if it is accessed only after instruction decoding when the instruction is known to be a branch instruction. This form of the table is known as a *decode-history table* [Losq, Rao, and Sachar 1984].

Because the target address of a branch instruction is usually available when the instruction is decoded, the decode-history table need contain only

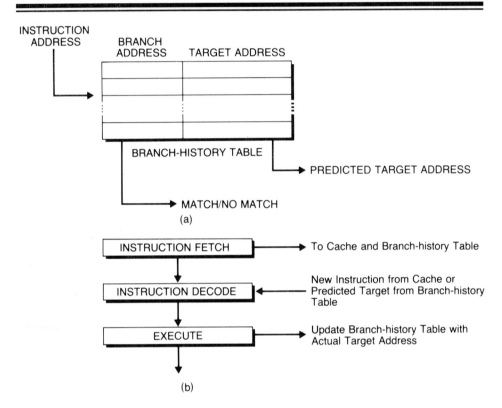

Fig. 3.31 A branch-history table:
(a) The structure, whose function is similar to a cache uses the address of the instruction as a key and reads out the predicted target address if there is a match. Only conditional branches are held in this table.
(b) Timing for access and use of the branch-history table.

one bit to indicate if a branch is taken or not taken, and therefore it is much smaller than a branch-history table. Moreover, it is accessed only when conditional branches are decoded, so it sustains a much lower bandwidth than does the branch-history table. By waiting until decode time to find the branch target, however, the instruction for the branch-not-taken condition has already been fetched into the pipeline and will be decoded next. If the prediction is to take the branch, we would like to have the instruction after the branch ready to enter the decoder. Clearly, a better approach for a decode-history table is to hold a copy of the target instruction rather than, or in addition to, the decision to branch or not, so that the target instruction is ready for decoding on the next machine cycle.

Many variations of the idea behind the branch-history and decode-history tables are possible, especially regarding the strategy of what prediction to store in the table. For example, if it is common to end a loop with a DECRE-MENT AND BRANCH instruction, it may be possible to detect a situation in which the current iteration branches, but the next iteration will not. Obviously, if the decrement is 1 and the branch condition is BRANCH IF ZERO, then when the register reaches the value 1 after executing the instruction, the next time the instruction is reached there is a very high probability that the branch will not be taken. So the hardware may look for a value of 0 in a register to decide if the current iteration will branch, and it may look for a 1 in the register to decide if the next iteration will branch. For other branch instructions, the simplest strategy is to store in the table what happened the last time that same instruction was executed. This should yield correct outcomes substantially more frequently than does random guessing.

Neither the branch-history table nor the decode-history table has been widely used in practice, but current trends for high performance and the ability to add small amounts of hardware to achieve that performance make both ideas very attractive. A decode-history table has been incorporated into the IBM 3090 model 400, a machine first delivered in 1986, which may signal a trend in computer architectures for the 1990s.

3.5.2 Internal Forwarding and Deferred Instructions

The objective of a pipelined functional unit is to execute instructions at a fixed maximum rate, usually one instruction per cycle. The instructions themselves take as few as 1 cycle and occasionally as many as 20 cycles to complete, with additional time lost to cache misses and contention for memory or other resources.

The discussion in this chapter has so far revealed several potential problem areas that tend to degrade performance:

- Interlocks because of READ/WRITE, WRITE/READ, and WRITE/WRITE conflicts for data;
- Conflicts within a pipeline caused by the structure of the reservation table; and
- The inability to predict accurately the outcome of conditional branch instructions.

An easy way to handle these problems is to identify them at the entrance to the pipeline and restrict entrance unless the conditions for use of the pipeline are satisfied. We have seen that this is the way collision vectors are used to control execution. We have also learned that the branch-history table provides a means for continuing at full speed at the entrance to a pipeline, while the problem is resolved elsewhere in the pipeline at a later time.

The latter form of solution is preferable from a performance viewpoint because it maintains activity in the pipeline rather than halts further activity. We want to explore techniques that allow the pipeline to continue activity when a problem is encountered rather than force the pipeline to halt until the problem is resolved.

A technique called *internal forwarding* is one way of dealing with interlocks. Consider, for example, the inner loop of a linear programming code in which we might see the following sequence of operations:

$$REG[1] := A;$$

$$REG[2] := REG[1] \times B;$$

$$REG[3] := REG[2]/C;$$

$$REG[4] := REG[4] + REG[3];$$

Each instruction depends on the completion of the previous instruction through register dependencies. If we halt at the beginning of a pipeline because of an interlock, then the pipeline would drain between each instruction in the sequence, and the net performance would be related to the delay required to execute each instruction in isolation. To bring performance much closer to one instruction completed per clock cycle, it is essential that instructions be launched into a pipeline in spite of interlocks, and that the interlocks be detected at a later point.

Let us view internal forwarding in the context of a pipeline machine that consists of the six basic stages shown in Fig. 3.32.

1. Instruction Fetch;
2. Instruction Decode;
3. Generate Operand Address;
4. Fetch Operand;
5. Execute; and
6. Save Result.

In the absence of problems, an instruction proceeds from stage to stage, one clock cycle per stage. An interlock or cache miss may result in one or more operands failing to be ready at the Execute stage.

Figure 3.33 shows a magnified view of an Execute stage that handles missing operands, interlocks, and other related problems. This idealized model of the Execute stage shows a set of registers, called *forwarding registers,* that are stand-ins for the actual complement of registers visible to the instruction set. Machine instructions refer to these registers, but the registers in the

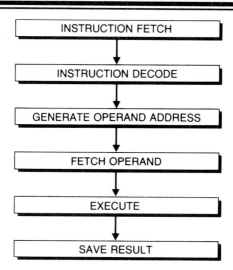

Fig. 3.32 The six-stage pipeline model for an Execute stage that uses internal forwarding.

figure do not hold operands; rather they hold pointers to the machine registers that actually hold operands. The figure shows four forwarding registers and eight operand registers. The contents of the forwarding registers point to four of the eight operand registers.

By having more physical registers than the registers visible to the instructions, it becomes possible for one instruction to read or write an operand in a register, such as REG[1], while another instruction concurrently reads or writes a totally different operand in that same register. In physical terms, the operations manipulate different operand registers, and the operations are directed to different registers by the contents of the forwarding registers.

The basic idea of internal forwarding is to initiate immediately an instruction that has its operands available and a free function unit on which to execute. Other instructions must be deferred because:

- One or both operands are missing;
- A destination register cannot be modified immediately; or
- The required function unit is busy.

These instructions are passed to reservation stations associated with LOAD, STORE, and each of the functional units in the Execute stage. Having scheduled a deferred instruction for execution at some time in the future, the

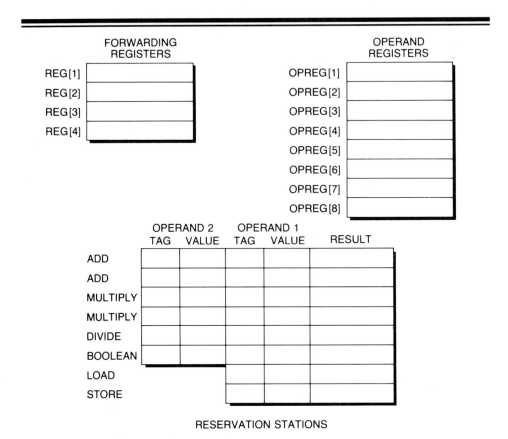

Fig. 3.33 The registers and tables required for internal forwarding.

Execute stage is free to examine the next instruction in the pipeline. Consequently, the Execute stage need not suspend operation when it encounters an instruction that has to be deferred.

Figure 3.33 shows that the Execute stage in our example contains a collection of *reservation stations*, where instructions are held pending execution. Each station contains a field for each operand and for a result. Each operand field contains the operand value (if the value is available), a tag indicating whether or not the operand is present, and an identifier that tells which OPREG is to hold the operand value if the value is not concurrently available. The result field contains the index of the OPREG that is to receive the function result. Each station is associated with one specific function such as ADD, MULTIPLY, DIVIDE, LOAD, STORE, and BOOLEAN.

To see how internal forwarding works, let us consider the preceding example and observe its behavior, as illustrated in Fig. 3.34.

1. **REG[1] : = A.** Assume that the operand is not available because of a cache miss. The Execute stage obtains the index of a free operand register from a pool of free registers. Assume this is OPREG[4]. The instruction with the

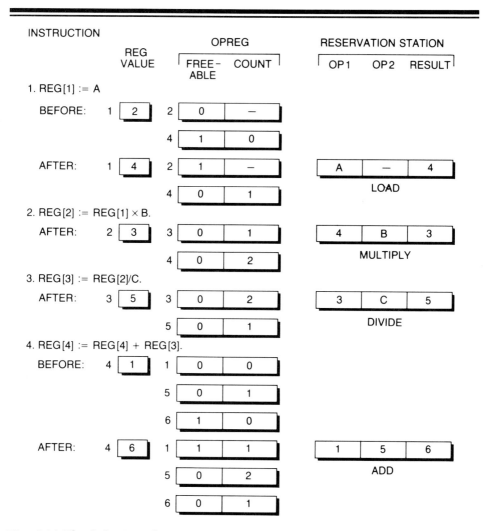

Fig. 3.34 The behavior of an Execute stage with internal forwarding on a short sequence of instructions.

destination field set to the value 4 (for OPREG[4]) is transmitted to a reservation station for LOAD. When operand A eventually arrives from memory, its address will be compared to the address stored in the reservation station at the LOAD reservation station, and the match there will cause the operand to be transmitted to OPREG[4], not to REG[1].

Meanwhile, the Execute stage continues the scheduling process by reading the present contents of REG[1]. Suppose that this is the number 2, designating OPREG[2] as currently holding the contents of REG[1]. Since REG[1] is to be overwritten, OPREG[2], which currently holds the contents of REG[1], is marked "freeable" when all pending operations on OPREG[2] have completed. When OPREG[2] has actually been freed, its index will be returned to the pool of free registers.

One way to keep track of operations waiting for a register is to use a counter. In this case, there is a pending operation on OPREG[4], the LOAD operation, so that the counter for OPREG[4] is initialized to 1.

2. **REG[2] := REG[1] × B.** For this instruction, assume that operand B arrives with the instruction. The Execute stage learns from REG[1] that OPREG[4] contains the current value of REG[1]. It transmits a reservation to the multiplier for OPREG[4] together with the value of B. The destination register for the multiply is OPREG[3] in this case because OPREG[3] was available from the free pool for reassignment. The count for OPREG[4] is increased by 1 because this instruction references REG[1], whose contents are held in OPREG[4].

3. **REG[3] := REG[2] / C.** This instruction posts a reservation at the division unit with a reference to OPREG[5], which holds the current contents of REG[3]. The count for OPREG[3] is increased.

4. **REG[4] := REG[4] + REG[3].** This instruction posts a reservation at the adder using OPREG[1] (for REG[4]) and OPREG[5] (for REG[3]). The output of the adder is directed to OPREG[6], which will hold the new value of REG[4] after the operation. The counts for OPREG[1] and OPREG[5] are increased.

During execution of the reservations, as a function completes its operation and writes a result to an OPREG, the OPREG count is decremented by 1, and the value of the function to be stored in the OPREG is passed to all reservation stations awaiting that value. For each value accepted, the count is decremented.

If an OPREG is marked as being freeable, then when its count reaches zero, the index of the OPREG is placed on the free list. The OPREG becomes freeable when its corresponding machine register has been reassigned a value by an instruction and is now being held in a different OPREG. If an OPREG has a count of 0, and the register is not freeable, the register holds the actual contents that are supposed to be held in the corresponding visible register. References to an OPREG in this state result in a copy of its contents being placed in a reservation station together with a tag indicating that no waiting for this operand is required.

Reservations are placed sequentially in the order shown in Fig. 3.34. Although our example forces the instructions to execute in the same order as the reservations are placed, one can easily construct examples in which the order of actual execution is different from the order in which reservations are placed.

The example illustrates two key elements present in the Execute stage— interlocks and concurrency. Interlocks (WRITE/READ interlocks in this example) force each instruction that reads a register to wait until the register has been written. READ/WRITE conflicts are handled by permitting concurrency instead of by interlocking. That is, if one instruction reads REG[1] and a later one writes REG[1], internal forwarding will create two different OPREGs, one to be read and the other to be written. Reservations and instruction execution on both OPREGs can proceed concurrently and will generate correct results. Similarly, WRITE/WRITE conflicts lead to concurrent operation.

The description of internal forwarding as presented here is rather idealized to show the processes of forwarding, placing reservations, and function-unit completion. There are endless variations of this basic idea, and many different ones have actually been implemented in practice.

Two early examples described in the literature are the CDC-6600 [Thornton 1970] and the IBM 360 Model 91 [Tomasulo 1967]. Neither of these machines had cache memories, so LOAD commands in both machines involved access delays and required substantial hardware support in the Execution Stage to sustain pipeline activity when LOADs were encountered. The two machines used quite different techniques for interlocks and control of execution. Let us consider some of the details of both machines to compare their implementations.

CDC-6600 Scoreboard. [Thornton 1970]

The physical machine registers contain both the current value of the operand (if the current value has been computed) and a tag that indicates which function unit will produce that value in the future if the value has not yet been computed.

1. Each instruction that reaches the Execute stage consults the register set to learn if the register value is immediately available or will be produced in the future. If the result is immediately available, the instruction is so marked with a register identifier, and, if not, the instruction is marked with the function-unit identifier that will produce the result.

2. The instruction, together with its register and function-unit identifiers, is sent to a reservation station for the function unit specified by the instruction. If the function unit is free and all operands are available, the function

initiates immediately. Otherwise, the instruction is deferred at the reservation station.

3. A central scoreboard receives information from each function unit as the function unit completes an operation. The function unit passes result data back to the physical register that holds the result and concurrently notifies all active reservations that the result is available. Because the notification is done in broadcast mode, only one function-unit completion can be treated at a time, and arbitration by priority is required to resolve conflicts when two or more units complete in one cycle. All instructions that are awaiting the completion of the corresponding function update their reservations. Those that can execute immediately proceed to do so by requesting their operands from the machine registers.

4. In case an instruction at the Execute stage cannot be executed immediately or deferred because a reservation station is already occupied, the Execute stage freezes and issues no more instructions until the pending instruction can be initiated or moved to a reservation station.

The CDC-6600 had multiple buses for accessing physical registers, which permitted some simultaneity in initiating new operations. However, not all function units had independent access to the registers, and those that shared buses had to arbitrate for register access if they required access to different registers simultaneously. A key characteristic of this architecture is that data had to flow from function unit to a register and then back to a function unit because there were no direct paths from function unit to function unit.

IBM 360/91 Common Data-Bus [Tomasulo 1967].

1. In this design, there are multiple reservation stations per function unit and many more operand registers than are visible to the instruction set. As is characteristic of internal forwarding, the design provides for a set of forwarding registers whose contents indicate for each visible machine register which reservation station has an instruction to produce a future value for that register. A tag on each forwarding register indicates whether the value concurrently in the register is the true value of the register or identifies a reservation station that will produce the future value.

2. Operands become available when LOAD operations complete or when arithmetic functions terminate. A Common Data-Bus is tied to all units that either produce new results or require results. Producers arbitrate for the bus, and the winner of an arbitration cycle places its identifier, together with the operand value, on the bus. Reservation stations and physical registers that are awaiting operands match their local identifiers with the broadcast identifiers, and if the two are equal, the operand value broadcast on the bus is copied into the station or register, and a corresponding tag is set to indicate that the contents are valid. When all

operands become available at a reservation station, the reservation initiates execution of the associated function unit at the next available cycle.

In this scheme, data can be forwarded directly from one function unit to another and may never need to be stored in a register visible to the instruction set.

An obvious difference in the two schemes is due to the ability of the IBM 360/91 to move data directly from function unit to function unit over the Common Data-Bus. The CDC-6600 has to move data from function unit to register to function unit, which incurs additional overhead. The reasons for these design differences relate to differences in the instruction sets of the two machines.

Because the IBM/360 family uses only four floating-point registers, for a high-performance machine in the family there was a pressing need to create additional registers to be used during execution. The instruction set is a two-address format of the type $R_1 := R_1$ op R_2, which tends to reuse registers. The CDC-6600 design uses a three-address format of the type $R_1 := R_2$ op R_3, which provides the freedom to use more registers. The CDC-6600 instruction set was designed from the start for high-speed execution and contained as many visible registers as reasonable to incorporate in a high-performance design of that period. Consequently, the CDC-6600 had less need to create additional high-speed registers to enhance concurrent execution.

To increase the number of high-speed registers, the IBM 360/91 design places these registers in reservation stations in a way that allows visible machine registers to have multiple identities. Any particular register might be represented in two or more reservation stations concurrently, with each instance of the visible register stemming from independent instructions decoded at different points in time. This structure creates a need to move data between reservation stations instead of or in addition to moving data to and from a visible forwarding register, since each forwarding register potentially may represent several different reservation-station registers.

The CDC-6600 design does not have direct connections between function units. The visible registers hold data; the reservation stations hold control information only. So the high-speed data storage is in the visible registers, rather than the reservation stations. There is a need for high bandwidth between function units and result registers, and the design uses multiple buses for this purpose.

With two decades of machine design passing since the design of the CDC-6600 and IBM 360/91, the principles of pipelining, internal forwarding, and other design techniques from that era have remained the same, but new ideas have been added and VLSI has provided a far greater capability for hardware sophistication than was available in the 1960s. The major impact has been from cache memory, which has led to a much simpler way of treating

LOADs and STOREs in pipeline computers since both of these operations now execute in one or two machine cycles instead of ten to 20.

The number of machine registers has increased to the extent that 128 registers is easily possible, and the number could conceivably increase to 1024 or more. When the number of registers becomes this large, the WRITE/WRITE and READ/WRITE interlocks mostly disappear because a potentially conflicting instruction can usually be assigned a free register to be the target of the WRITE, and thereby remove the conflict. To achieve the effective use of a large number of registers, however, requires a sophisticated optimizing compiler that can perform register allocation globally over a large program, or over large segments of a program. With such use of registers, the main source of conflicts that impedes execution stems from WRITE/READ conflicts and conflicting requests for particular functions.

To summarize the most important characteristics of pipelined execution examined in this section, we note the following observations:

- Instructions execute when ready to execute, not necessarily when they first reach the Execute stage. Thus, some instructions execute out of sequence.
- Interlocks are treated at the Execute stage to ensure that the behavior of an execution is identical to the behavior of a purely sequential execution of the same sequence.
- The performance depends on the number of reservation stations, arithmetic units, and other related facilities at the Execute stage. Because of internal forwarding these numbers can be increased or decreased to achieve a desired level of performance. The changes are independent of the instruction set. The instruction set refers to a fixed repertoire of operations and uses a fixed number of registers, regardless of the facilities actually available at the Execute stage.

These points show the advantages and flexibility of building the Execute stage to defer instructions, rather than defer instructions earlier in the pipeline. The biggest gain in performance is due to the ability to execute instructions out of sequence. If an instruction must be delayed because of an interlock, the instructions that follow need not be delayed as well.

3.5.3 Machines with Both Cache and Virtual Memory

In Chapter 2 we learned that cache memory speed has a critical impact on performance, and that designers try to keep the cache cycle as short as possible. When cache is coupled with virtual memory, there is an additional complication that might lead to a lengthening of the basic cache cycle to accommodate the virtual-memory translation. We show in this section how the cache lookup and the virtual-memory translation can be pipelined so as to eliminate the potential extra cycle for address translation.

Figure 3.35 shows two possible arrangements for the address mapper that produces real addresses from virtual addresses. Figure 3.35(a) shows a cache in which virtual, not real, addresses are stored in the tag area. If a cache miss occurs, the virtual address is then translated to a real address, and the request is sent to main memory.

The advantage of this scheme is that the address translation is not part of the cache cycle, so the cache lookup is potentially faster than a cache cycle for a cache that stores real addresses in the address tags. This latter cache appears in Fig. 3.35(b). In this cache, a virtual address is first translated to a real address and is then presented to the cache. If a cache miss occurs, the real address is then sent to main memory.

The second cache is the poorer performer of the two, but the first cache has two serious flaws that greatly reduce its attractiveness. The first flaw concerns the ability to invalidate items in the cache that are altered by I/O operations. If an item in main memory is overwritten by the I/O system, and a copy of the old value of that item happens to be in cache, then the copy in cache must be invalidated. Otherwise, the processor will find the stale item in cache when it next attempts to access it and will fail to load the new value resident in main memory.

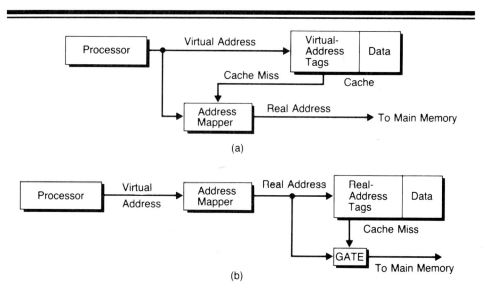

Fig. 3.35 Two possible cache structures in computer systems with virtual addresses: (a) Virtual addresses in a cache, with mapping occurring after a cache miss; and (b) Real addresses in a cache, with mapping occurring before each cache lookup.

Therefore, when the I/O system alters main memory, the address where this occurs must be sent to the cache, where it can be used to invalidate copies that happen to be in the cache. If the cache holds tags in virtual-address form, then the real address available to the I/O system must first be translated back to a virtual address and then be presented to the cache. The inverse translation is shown in Fig. 3.36. If a cache holds real addresses, an inverse translation is not required for this particular purpose, although there may be other problems whose solution makes use of an inverse translation.

The second flaw with the idea of holding virtual addresses in cache concerns the problem of synonyms. Each cell in main memory has a unique real address, but it may have many different virtual memory-addresses, and several can be active concurrently. This is particularly true of items that are shared among several processes. If a cache holds virtual addresses, how do we know if it holds the item with virtual address V? That the cache lookup fails to find a tag with the value V is not conclusive. The item may be held under the name W, where W is the virtual address at which that item is accessed by a different process that has shared access to the item. This is a serious flaw with the use of virtual addresses in the cache, and overcoming the flaw leads to complexities in the cache design.

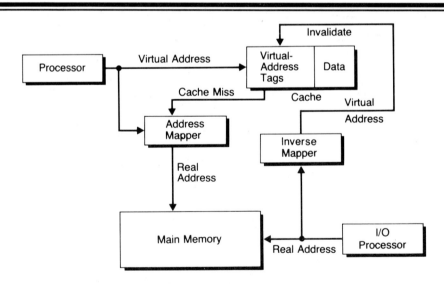

Fig. 3.36 A cache memory that uses virtual-address tags. Each change in main memory is mapped back to a virtual address and used to invalidate a corresponding entry in the cache.

The pipeline shown in Fig. 3.37 is a nice solution to the problem because it combines the speed advantage of virtual addresses in cache with the simpler implementation of real addresses in cache. The idea is to pipeline a cache lookup into two steps. The first step causes an access to the set of lines to be accessed for the real address of the datum sought. This access occurs before we actually know the full real address.

If the virtual-to-real address transformation does not alter the least significant b bits of a virtual address, then any subset of these b bits can be used as the set index for the cache in Fig. 3.37. The mapping from virtual address to real address is performed simultaneously with cache access. In the second cycle, the real address is compared to the tags returned by the cache memory, and the processor determines if there is a cache hit or cache miss.

Although this operation takes two cycles, because the steps can be pipelined, we can access the cache every cycle and achieve a throughput that is potentially as high as for the one-cycle cache shown in Fig. 3.35(a). Pipelining of the cache accesses as described in Fig. 3.37 has been implemented on many large-scale computers, including those produced by Amdahl, Fujitsu, and

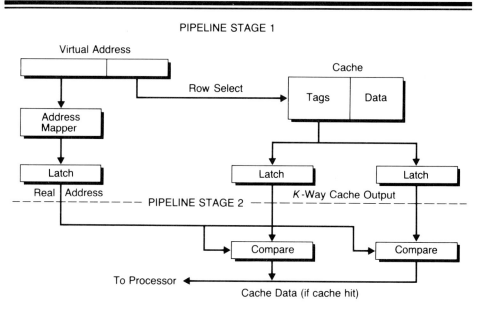

Fig. 3.37 A two-stage pipeline for performing virtual-memory mapping and cache lookup. Real addresses are held in the cache. The system can sustain one cache lookup per cycle.

IBM. Although this solution is both fast and efficient, a designer may want to explore the one-cycle cache with virtual-address tags because its performance is higher than is a two-cycle cache in an environment where it is difficult to keep the pipeline full.

3.5.4 RISC Architectures

Earlier in this chapter we describe delayed branching and mention that it has been used in RISC architectures. Because such architectures make extensive use of pipeline techniques, this section describes RISC architectures in somewhat more detail.

The term *RISC* (reduced instruction-set computers) is somewhat misleading in the context of the technology of the 1990s. The original notion of RISC is to create a machine with a very fast clock cycle that can execute instructions at the rate of one per cycle. RISC machines are often associated with pipeline implementation because pipeline techniques are natural ones to achieve the goal of one instruction executed per machine cycle.

The implementation of this idea began at IBM in the mid-1970s under the guidance of John Cocke and eventually led to the development of an internal machine called the 801 computer [see Radin 1982]. To achieve the fastest possible cycle rate, this type of architecture reduces decoding delays by requiring that all instructions conform to a simple format.

The original development explored a format in which all memory operations are LOAD and STORE operations, and all other operations such as ADD and COMPARE operated exclusively on registers. All instructions are of one length, and the instructions fit a scheme compatible with a pipeline implementation in which each stage of the pipeline performs roughly the same type of operation as each instruction passes that stage. (For some instructions, a pipeline stage may do nothing.)

As a concrete example of RISC machines, consider the structure of a typical RISC process in Fig. 3.38. This example is drawn from an unpublished report by Agerwala and Cocke [1987]. The central part of the figure is a cyclical 3-stage pipeline. It starts at the bank of general registers whose outputs are latched in one clock cycle in the *A*, *B* and *D* registers. The *A* and *B* registers drive an arithmetic/logic unit (ALU) to an output register, *F*. The *F* register, in turn, stores back into the general registers.

The interface to the data cache is through two paths, one for data to cache and one for the cache address. The cache address is developed at the output of ALU and is clocked into the *D*-cache address register. Data to the cache passes from the general registers to the *D*-register, and from there through a shift/logic unit to the *D*-cache data out register. Data from the cache to the processor is latched into the *D*-cache data in register, and from there it is stored into the general registers.

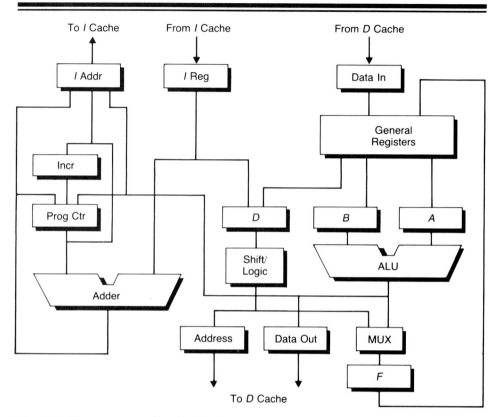

Fig. 3.38 The structure of a pipelined RISC processor.

At the left of the figure is the program counter, a 1-cycle increment path, and a separate adder for updating the program counter from the instruction stream. The interface with the instruction cache is similar to the interface with the data cache, except that there is no provision for writing into the instruction stream.

One feature of this structure that differentiates it from pipelines described earlier is that the pipeline does not contain a separate stage for address generation. Address generation is done in the ALU for LOADs and STOREs. For STOREs, the address generation in the ALU is done concurrently with the flow of data to cache through the D-register path. But the arithmetic and logic instructions use the ALU for execution, and thus these instructions do not both generate addresses and perform arithmetic manipulations. The advantage of removing the address generation stage is that the pipeline is shorter, and the penalty is less when interlocks or conditional execution cause the pipeline to empty. The offsetting disadvantage is that since arithmetic instructions cannot also load data from memory, this architecture requires more LOADs than one that has an address-generation stage.

Since the primary goal of the architect is to produce a machine that keeps the pipeline filled at all times, this machine has three Read and two Write ports to the general registers array. All five ports can be active concurrently without conflict. This is an unusual design in the light of our assumption that conventional memory can support one access per cycle. Multiple ports can be built economically for small amounts of memory such as for the general registers. But there is a definite cost in chip area for this capability. Because the function is not free, the function has to pay its way by adding dramatically to performance. And this is the case in the example.

With the potential for performing two writes and three reads concurrently on any cycle, the processor can execute a sequence of register instructions at the rate of one per cycle, provided the register instructions are nonconflicting. That is, the input register for any instruction is not altered by its immediately preceding instructions.

The three-cycle pipeline can easily be reduced to a pipeline with an effective length of two for many cases. The idea is that when a specific general register is written and read in the same cycle, the data reported out by the READ should be the new data written into the register, not its former contents. Consequently, when data from the F register is written to some general register, that data can flow through the general register array and be written into the A, B, or D registers in the same cycle.

From this structure we can see roughly how the pipeline works. A sequence of general register instructions moves data from the general registers, through the ALU to the F register and back to the general registers in three cycles. If the input register of an instruction is the output register of an instruction currently in the pipeline, an interlock prevents the new instruction from proceeding. Because the effective length of this pipeline is only 2 cycles, the register interlock adds at most one cycle of delay. (The new instruction can initiate on the cycle immediately after the cycle that brings the datum it needs to the F-register.)

LOAD instructions and cache misses also force the pipeline to empty occasionally. The address of a LOAD instruction is generated and latched in the D-cache address register as a normal pipelined computation. At a later time, the data from the cache are latched in the D-cache data-in register. Until the data appear there, an interlock prevents any instruction from using the destination register of the input data. The interlock is essentially a register interlock, except that it can be active for many cycles if a cache miss occurs.

The instruction decode pipeline is independent of the execution pipeline except that conditional branches have to be interlocked to the results of data registers. We can conceive of the instruction pipeline working in lock step with the execution pipeline, performing in one cycle each of the operations: generate instruction address, accept instruction from cache, and decode instruction. This will operate in synchrony with the execution unit as long as interlocks or conditional branches do not break the synchrony. If the execution pipeline unit stalls for some reason, the instruction pipeline can continue if there is work to be done. In fact, unconditional branches can be performed in the instruction pipeline free of interaction with the execution pipeline unless the target address has to be computed from register contents that are currently locked from access. Ditzel and McLellan [1987] describe a scheme of this type that treats branches in a separate portion of the pipeline so that they can be fully overlapped with normal operations in the arithmetic and instruction-decode pipelines.

Performance analysis of pipelined processors such as the RISC machine in this example is normally done by calculating the average number of cycles per instruction executed. The goal is to bring this down to 1, which is its minimum value for a machine that executes at most one instruction per cycle. As a simple example of this analysis, assume that conditional branches occur once every four instructions, and that the processor logic is clever enough to guess the outcome of the conditional branch correctly 80 percent of the time. A correct guess produces no penalty, and the penalty for an incorrect guess we assume to be 2 cycles (1 cycle to calculate the condition, and 1 cycle to fetch the instruction for the other branch). Then on 25 percent of the instructions, there is a 20 percent penalty of 2 cycles, or an average penalty of 0.1 cycles per instruction. Hence the conditional-branch effect raises the number of cycles per instruction from 1.0 to 1.1. If the data cache misses 2 percent of the time, and each miss produces 10 cycles of empty output from the pipeline, then data cache misses add 0.2 cycles per instruction. The effect increases the number of cycles per instruction to 1.3.

The finite-cache effect may occur jointly with a conditional-branch effect, in which case one delay is overlapped with another. Adding delays of the two effects individually produces a number that is higher than what is actually observed. If the error introduced by simple addition of delays is sufficiently large, the performance estimate may require a more detailed model or may have to be done through simulation. In most cases, it is possible to add the delays of the individual effects to obtain a rough estimate of performance and with such rough estimates it becomes possible to isolate the best candidate designs from a collection of possible candidates. When choices have been restricted to a small number, more detailed models can be brought into play.

Figure 3.38 also illustrates the potential of RISC architectures for attaining higher speed by simplifying the work done per stage. Consider, for example, the function of the A, B, and D registers in the figure. They serve as staging registers for data from the general registers. This machine takes two clock cycles to move data from the general registers through the ALU to the F register. The first clock cycle is associated with the time required to decode the register fields of an instruction, send these fields to the register array, and retrieve the data. The cycle ends by latching the data into the A, B, and D registers. The next cycle carries the data through the ALU to the F register. We could combine the two cycles into one longer cycle and move data from the general registers through the ALU to the F register in one clock. The A, B, and D registers would be absent from such a design.

Although the pipeline is shorter, the performance is not necessarily better. The maximum rate of completion in either design is one instruction per clock time. The shorter pipeline has a longer clock cycle, so its maximum rate of computation is lower than for the original design shown in Fig. 3.38. This is a major advantage of RISC architecture. But the advantage is partially offset by paying a potentially greater penalty for an empty pipeline in the original design. Register and conditional-branch interlocks potentially can leave the pipeline empty for a greater proportion of time. For example, in the second design, it is possible to design the timing in a way that a result produced in the F register on one cycle can participate in the next cycle and influence the result to be stored in the F register on that cycle. No register interlocks are required for such a design. But the original design has to be capable of deferring the execution of an instruction when one of its operands is in the process of being computed and has not yet reached the F register.

When comparing the RISC design to more conventional designs, it is clear that the cycle time of a RISC computer can be made somewhat smaller than the cycle time of computers with richer and more complex instructions. If we view the latter class of computers as *CISC* (complex instruction-set computer) machines, then we have a taxonomy that tends to group instruction sets such as those of the Motorola 680XX, VAX, and those of the IBM 370 into the CISC category and the IBM 801, Berkeley RISC machine [Patterson and Sequin 1982], and HP Spectrum into the RISC category. The ideas and technology of the 1970s, however, have evolved to the extent that the basic notion of RISC architecture is different today, and the name RISC is rather misleading because it is no longer an accurate description of the new generation of so-called RISC machines.

Although the obvious advantage of a pure RISC architecture is fast cycle time, the RISC architecture could easily be a poor performer if the reduced instruction set were its only characteristic. At least two problems are evident:

- RISC architectures lack the more powerful instructions of CISC architectures, and therefore they must execute more instructions to do the work of a CISC architecture.
- In executing more instructions to do equal work, at best data traffic may be the same for CISC and pure RISC machines, but instruction traffic must be

higher, so RISC machines require higher instruction bandwidth to do equal work of a CISC architecture.

Because of these problems, the benefits of the fast cycle of a RISC machine are partially offset. If a RISC machine lacks crucial complex instructions, such as integer divide and multiply and the full spectrum of floating-point instructions, then a RISC machine performance would almost surely fall below that of a CISC machine on workloads with a hefty percentage of numerical operations.

There is then very little point in building a pure RISC machine with only a fast clock cycle. It is necessary to address the negatives of the pure architecture and embellish the RISC architecture so that it has higher performance than a pure RISC machine, with as little compromise on the cycle time as possible.

To address the two criticisms raised, note that it is not necessary to ignore complex instructions entirely. If floating-point arithmetic is important, then floating-point operations should be a part of the architecture. If they cannot be done in the normal pipeline, then they should be done in a separate pipeline either within the RISC processor or in a separate coprocessor. Similarly, to improve throughput, other complex operations that take lengthy instruction sequences should be considered as candidates for special implementation techniques.

To explore the arithmetic issue, consider a very basic RISC architecture without integer division. An architect may choose to omit this instruction in a basic RISC architecture because it cannot be executed in a single cycle, and thus it does not fit well with the remainder of the instructions in the RISC architecture. Instead of a division operation, the architect provides a single step of a division. To do a 32-bit integer division, a programmer initializes the divisor, dividend, and quotient registers, and then executes 32 consecutive divide steps. Because there is no loop and no conditional branch, the 32 instructions execute at the ideal speed of one cycle per instruction. This appears to be a reasonable alternative. But is it?

This solution lengthens a divide from a few cycles to 32 cycles. It impacts total performance, but the impact will not be revealed by an analysis based solely on cycles per instruction. Because an integer divide instruction will almost surely cause the pipeline to empty for a few cycles, if it is included in the architecture, the cycles per instruction will be higher, but absolute performance may be better.

The integer divide is one of many complex instructions that are not directly compatible with the RISC philosophy. An architect must investigate how to add such instructions to a RISC architecture in a way that will improve net performance at low cost. A missed opportunity for one design is an opportunity that can be exploited by a competitor.

The Intel i860 microprocessor illustrates a viable approach to incorporating complex instructions into a RISC architecture. It has two independent pipelines, one for floating-point arithmetic and one for fixed-point and logical operations. Each pipeline has the capability of generating output at the rate of one clock cycle per output under ideal conditions. So a program can have a long sequence of floating-point instructions, or a long sequence of fixed-point instructions, and in either case it can generate results at the rate of one clock per output. Although this rate appears to be good, the processor is actually running at half of its potential throughput in this mode because one pipeline is idle while the other is active.

To permit both pipelines to be run concurrently the i860 provides a mode in which the machine decodes and executes two instructions per clock cycle. The instruction stream has to have alternating fixed-point and floating-point instructions in this case. When the machine is placed in the dual-decode mode, it fetches two instructions per cycle and sends one to each pipeline. This illustrates how creative approaches can capture the advantages of RISC architecture while overcoming some of the limitations of a pure-RISC approach.

The second problem mentioned above, high instruction-fetch traffic, can easily be resolved by incorporating an instruction cache into the VLSI implementation of a RISC machine where a CISC machine might not have such a cache. The point here is that RISC design has eliminated the logic for decoding complex instructions; that logic can be utilized instead in an instruction cache.

In current technology it is more appropriate to count chip area, instead of logic gates, as a precious resource, so RISC architecture provides a way of saying that chip area formerly used for decoding and executing complex instructions can be used instead for caching instructions. Whether a chip is a CISC architecture without an on-chip instruction-cache or a RISC architecture with an on-chip instruction cache, the net effect of the use of chip area is to reduce instruction traffic between the processor and main memory.

Chip area made available with the RISC approach can also be used to reduce data traffic. The Berkeley RISC project [Patterson and Sequin 1982] created a machine with 128 registers that strongly influenced a commercial version known as the SPARC processor. The registers of this architecture are cleverly allocated to subroutines by means of a concept known as *register windows*. Each procedure sees a region of registers, and that region overlaps partially with the window seen by the calling procedure and by procedures that it calls. The windows automatically change dynamically as procedures are entered and exited.

The windows provide a means for passing parameters and receiving results in the registers without having to save and reload registers to provide the necessary register space. The net result is a reduction in data traffic between processor and memory. This embellishment of the basic RISC philosophy suggests that there is much to be gained by taking advantage of what new technology has to offer, and there is no need to stick to a pure RISC architecture.

Because pure RISC machines have obvious deficiencies that are easily corrected, the directions taken in recent years have been to use a variety of techniques, both standard and nonstandard, to correct the problems. The design changes have resulted in machine architectures that bear little resemblance to the original RISC concept, except that RISC is the starting point before the enhancements have been added.

An interesting study of the evolution of the Berkeley RISC machine appears in Hill *et al.* [1986]. This particular implementation of RISC architecture is a multiprocessor with virtual-memory support and cache-coherency control. The architecture supports complex operations in a variety of ways. Floating-point operations are performed in a separate coprocessor. List-oriented operations that depend on tagged data to interpret the meaning of bit patterns include instructions that treat tags distinctly from the remainder of an operand. In fact, the instruction set is rather rich, and the architecture has a remarkably larger set of facilities available than do earlier RISC designs. We expect the evolution of RISC architecture to continue as VLSI advances make it possible for new generations to be enhancements of their predecessors.

One thing is clear from this discussion. Good ideas from CISC machines can show up in RISC machines, and conversely, good ideas developed for RISC machines can be used in CISC machines. There is no particular reason to be a purist and stick entirely to one class of architectures. If an idea is good, and by using it performance improves, then the architect should use the idea. This means that the delayed-branch instructions, originally proposed for microcode and then used in RISC machines, can easily find their way to CISC machines, just as floating-point instructions have moved from CISC machines to RISC machines.

To investigate this last point, Colwell *et al.* [1985] studied the effect of register windows on RISC and CISC machines. The idea here is to view register windows as an independent feature of an instruction set and determine its net benefit in performance. Colwell *et al.* studied a RISC architecture with and without register windows and two CISC architectures with and without register windows.

The technique used for the study was to run a common set of benchmarks on the architectures and evaluate performance in terms of relative traffic between processor and memory. The benchmarks chosen were rather unusual because they use procedure calls intensively and are probably not representative of most workloads. The reason for this selection of benchmarks is that differences attributable to register windows are most likely to be visible in such benchmarks, so they represent an upper bound on the effect of register windows. Register windows are likely to affect performance much less when realistic workloads are used.

Colwell *et al.* created the candidate machines by treating a Berkeley RISC machine as designed with register windows and in a hypothetical implementation without windows. Similarly, they created CISC machines from real ones by extending VAX and Motorola 680XX architectures from the real versions without register windows to hypothetical versions with register windows.

The findings of these studies were rather interesting because the net decrease in memory traffic when register windows were added is about a factor that ranges from 2 to 4 depending on the specific benchmark. But for each individual benchmark, the factor was remarkably similar for all architectures. Consequently, the benefit of register windows is likely to be quite similar for both CISC and RISC machines, and the idea is not exclusively limited to one class of architectures.

3.6 Historical References

Several techniques for implementing high-speed arithmetic worthy of further study are beyond the scope of this text. In the area of multiplication, Wallace's work on multiplier trees [1964] has shaped the structure of VLSI multipliers for the past decade. Booth's algorithm [1951] for multiplication has also played a major role in fast implementations.

The basic idea of Booth's algorithm is to skip over individual iterations in an iterative shift-and-add implementation of multiplication. The algorithm skips over 0 bits in the multiplier, which is a fairly obvious optimization, but it also skips over a sequence of 1 bits. The idea is that a sequence of N 1s in the multiplier is numerically equal to $2^N - 1$, so the effect of multiplying by this group of 1s is the same as a subtraction in the least-significant position, followed by an addition N positions to the left. This reduces multiplication to an addition and subtraction for each consecutive string of 1s in the multiplier.

A variety of texts on computer arithmetic covers details of major interest to implementers. Sterbenz [1974] examines implementation of floating-point operations from the point of view of the requirements of the number system. This is a classic view of floating-point operations; it has evolved somewhat in recent years because of the development of the IEEE Standard on Floating-Point Arithmetic [IEEE 1985].

The IEEE Standard incorporates a data structure richer than conventional floating-point arithmetic and includes representation of infinity and numbers that lie below the underflow threshold. It also requires unbiased rounding in a manner consistent with the requirements posed by Sterbenz. Coonen [1980] covers some techniques for implementing the IEEE Standard that are not elicited in the standard itself.

Widely used techniques for hardware implementation of arithmetic receive thorough coverage in Hwang [1978]. For very high speed operation, because of the availability of large fast read-only memory, a new means of computation becomes possible. Instead of calculating the result of an arithmetic operation, it is possible to use a memory for table lookup to produce all or part of an answer. Waser and Flynn [1982] investigate some possible memory-intensive approaches to arithmetic that formerly were too costly to implement.

One of the disappointing aspects of the existing literature in high-performance systems is that relatively few machines have been thoroughly documented in the published literature. Thornton's [1970] analysis of the CDC-6600 is one notable exception, and there are a few others, such as Organick [1972] on the MIT Multics system and Organick [1973] on the Burroughs' B5700 and B6700 machines.

High-speed implementations have grown far more complex since these books appeared, and there are many opportunities to increase that complexity to achieve greater performance by steadily increasing the average number of instructions completed per clock cycle. The literature of the 1970s and 1980s does not adequately reflect the actual state of the art in machine design, because in this field many advances are realized in physical machines and in the hands of users well before the research and academic community have the opportunity to study them.

Exercises

3.1 The object of this exercise is to write programs for a high-speed computer architecture and determine the performance of the architecture.

a) Consider the program below (taken from Forsythe and Moler [1967, p. 69]).

```
for i := 1 to N − 1 do
    ips[i] := i;
for k := 1 to N − 1 do
begin
    big := 0;
    for i := k to N do
    begin
        size := abs(ul[ips[i],k]);
        if big < size then
        begin
            big := size;
            idxpiv := i;
        end; {* if test *}
    end; {* i loop *}
    if big = 0 then
        go to singular_exit;
    if idxpiv <> k then
    begin
        j := ips[k];
        ips[k] := ips[idxpiv];
        ips[idxpiv] := j;
```

```
        end; {* if test *}
        kp := ips[k];
        pivot := ul [kp,k];
        for i := k+1 to N do
        begin
            ip := ips[i];
            em := - ul[ip,j]/pivot;
            for j := k+1 to N do
                ul[ip,j] := ul[ip,j] + em × ul[kp,j];
        end; {* i loop *}
    end; {* k loop *}
```

Analyze this program and determine how many times each statement is executed as a function of N. Assume that all input data are nonsingular matrices.

b) Encode the entire most-frequently executed loop in the instruction format of a two-address assembly language. Show the execution of this loop on a machine with internal forwarding of the type described in the class notes. Make reasonable assumptions on the number of function units available and the number of cycles that each unit takes to complete. Be sure that your code is optimized to reduce the inner loop to as few operations as possible.

c) Determine the performance of your code on a pipelined computer that has no internal forwarding. This machine uses pipelining as much as possible, but lets the pipeline drain when it encounters an instruction that cannot execute immediately.

3.2 For each of the collision vectors shown, construct a reduced state-table and find a maximum-rate cycle. The last of these is fairly complex. You may wish to write a computer program to produce the answer rather than do the work by hand.

a) 01101101

b) 0110010101

c) 1100100100001

3.3 For the reservation table shown, add delays to achieve a maximum rate of operation. Because the table does not show dependence of one entry on other entries, assume that each entry depends directly on all entries in the immediately preceding column.

	0	1	2	3	4	5	6	7
A	X	0	X	X	0	0	X	0
B	0	X	0	0	X	0	0	0
C	0	0	X	0	0	0	0	X
D	0	0	0	X	X	X	0	0
E	0	0	X	0	0	X	0	0

3.4 The object of this exercise is to explore design techniques for pipeline controllers.

Consider the design of a pipelined multiplier unit that performs the following operations:

- Exponent add.
- Mantissa multiply.
- Sum partial products.
- Post normalize.
- Exponent adjust.

Assume that mantissa multiply produces half the partial products required in one cycle, and the remaining half in the next cycle. Assume that the stage that sums partial products can add the partial products produced by the mantissa multiplier to an accumulator with an initialized value, and that all of this can be accomplished in one cycle.

a) Draw a block diagram of a pipelined implementation of the multipler unit.

b) Construct the collision table for the multiplier unit.

c) Construct the collision vector.

d) Construct the reduced state-diagram.

e) Find a maximum-rate cycle.

f) Determine a bound on the upper rate of execution.

g) If the cycle that you find does not meet the bound, alter the reservation table by inserting delays to create a different table that meets the maximum rate.

3.5 This is a second exercise on the design techniques for pipeline controllers. Consider the design of a pipelined division unit that performs the following operations:

- Exponent subtract;
- Guess inverse of divisor;
- Improve guess;
- Multiply dividend by inverse;
- Postnormalize; and
- Exponent adjust.

Assume that the inverse guess is done by table lookup that takes two clock cycles for a single function unit. Also assume that the improvement of the guess involves a two-stage iteration unit (Stages A and B) that requires one clock cycle to pass through each stage. The improvement process passes through these two stages twice, in the order A, B, A, and B, occupying a total of four cycles. The inverse produced is a normalized mantissa that is used to produce the quotient through a multiplication operation essentially the same as the floating-point multiplication described in this chapter.

a) Draw a diagram of a pipelined implementation of the divider.

b) Construct the collision table for the divider.

c) Construct the collision vector.

d) Construct the reduced state-diagram.

e) Find a maximum-rate cycle.

f) Determine a bound on the upper rate of execution.

g) If the cycle that you find does not meet the bound, alter the reservation table by inserting delays to create a different table that meets the maximum rate.

3.6 The inner loop of a linear-equation solver does the following operation:

$$sum := sum + b \times c(i)/d$$

Assume that b, $c(i)$, and d are variables that can be streamed into a pipeline from memory, with one cycle delay between accesses to each variable, so that memory is not a bottleneck for computation. The objective is to perform the operation given to produce the final sum in minimum time.

a) Design the block diagram and functional behavior of a three-function pipeline whose operations are multiply, add, and divide. Find the collision vectors for controlling the system and find the fastest possible cycle for the sequence of operations $\times$, $/$, and $+$, when operating on independent operands. (This does not account for the interlocking necessary to make sure that the value of sum used as an input is derived from the most recent value of sum used as an output).

b) Now consider the maximum speed attainable when the input to the adder is interlocked to the output of the adder. What is this maximum speed in your design?

c) If we want to produce one update of sum per cycle on the average, how can we structure a pipeline to achieve this rate? Show a structure that achieves this rate and describe how you propose to control the pipeline. A satisfactory answer is one that achieves a rate a little lower than one result per cycle on the average when vectors are very long. The performance for short vectors is permitted to be substantially lower than one result per cycle on the average.

3.7 Consider the following recurrence relation:

$$X_i = (A_i \times X_{i-1} + B_i)/(C_i \times X_{i-1} + D_i)$$

The initial value X_0 is 0. Assume that the constant vectors A, B, C, and D are variables that can be streamed into a pipeline from memory, with one cycle delay between accesses to each variable, so that memory is not a bottleneck for computation. The objective is to perform the operation given to produce the final sum in minimum time.

a) We want to design a pipelined arithmetic unit that computes one cycle of the recurrence equation. Each block in the pipeline takes one clock period. The divide operation produces a quotient mantissa by repeating a basic operation for four clocks. All operations are floating point. (To compute the full recurrence requires an interlock from output to input. Ignore the interlock for this part of the question.)

Draw a pipelined unit that implements the right-hand side of the recurrence. Discuss briefly the function of each block in the pipeline. Design the pipeline for minimum delay and minimum conflicts, replicating logic freely. Produce the collision table for the pipeline and the collision vector for controlling it. Ignore interlocks.

b) Redesign the pipeline to use minimal hardware by reusing blocks when possible. Show the block diagram and discuss the flow of results through the pipeline for one cycle of the recurrence. Produce the collision table and collision vector for the pipeline. Ignore interlocks.

3.8 The purpose of this problem is to examine the loss in efficiency due to conditional branches.

a) Consider the innermost loop of the program in Exercise 3.1. Write this loop in assembly language for an architecture that has a sufficiently large number of registers to allow the variables for up to three successive loops to be saved in the registers. Unroll the loop by three iterations to make use of these registers.

b) Construct the block diagram of a pipelined processor that executes your program efficiently, assuming that all operands require two cycles for READ and WRITE from a local cache and that the arithmetic unit is a pipelined unit that can produce a new product every cycle and accumulate successive products at the same rate. It is not necessary to design the arithmetic pipeline. Assume that it is collision free. Design your system to match available memory bandwidth and processing bandwidth so that the processor produces one result per cycle for the inner iteration, when operating at its peak rate.

c) How many cycles are lost if the pipeline has to drain completely when a conditional branch is reached? How efficient is this design when executing the given iteration? (This is the ratio of results produced to total cycles between conditional branches.) How does the efficiency change if six, not three, loops can be unrolled?

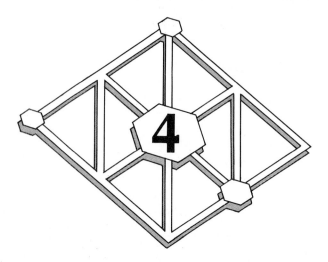

Characteristics of Numerical Applications

4.1 Classification of Large-Scale Numerical Problems
4.2 Design Constraints for High-Performance Machines
4.3 Architectures for the Continuum Model
4.4 Algorithms for the Continuum Model
4.5 The Perfect Shuffle
4.6 Architecture for the Continuum Model—
Which Direction?

Large-scale numerical applications typically are highly structured computations. Some very large programs require 10^{12} to 10^{15} floating-point operations to achieve solutions at the desired level of accuracy. Since there are approximately $3.15 \cdot 10^{13}$ microseconds per year, and a conventional high-performance machine can complete roughly one floating-point operation per microsecond, it is clear that these problems can occupy conventional machines for several years.

To solve the largest problems an architecture almost certainly must have a large amount of parallelism, and it must exploit the particular characteristics of the problem. This tends to force the large numerical machines to become more special purpose and more oriented to specific applications than the architectures described thus far. When a computer program can occupy every available cycle of an architecture for months or years at a time, changes that bring down computation time dramatically are quite beneficial, even if they bias the architectural structure toward particular purposes.

The computer architect has to understand the special needs of large-scale problems to produce designs that can meet the extremely taxing requirements of such problems. Even then, the architect has to be aware of the needs of a broad class of problem areas because, when a choice of approaches is possible, the architect should know which approaches can satisfy the needs of several areas. If one architecture can serve several different areas, then the design effort, software development, and other development costs can be shared by a larger community of users, thereby greatly reducing the cost of the machine per user.

The architect has to weigh carefully those design decisions that enlarge the community of users if they might compromise maximum performance for some subset of users. For example, if a machine attains its highest performance when processing vectors, how useful will the machine be to a community that requires scalar processing exclusively? In this case the architect has to decide the level of performance for scalar mode, and this decision may greatly affect both the users who operate exclusively in scalar mode and those who operate almost exclusively in vector mode. There is some risk that both communities may be burdened with design capability that cannot be utilized fully.

For the example of scalar performance in a vector machine, there happens to be a body of evidence that shows that high-speed scalar performance is important for all high performance programs, including those that appear to be mostly vector operations. An effective design achieves high-performance on scalar operations, even for applications where there is a large fraction of vector operations. Other aspects of architectural design are not so clear cut. These include the handling of input/output, internal interconnections and data paths, and algorithm support within the architecture.

How can these areas be developed to support the most stringent computational demands and still be of benefit to the bulk of the user community? The approach in this chapter is to explore the applications themselves in a general way to identify problem characteristics that strongly influence computer architectures for these problems. The discussion has been modeled after Hoshino [1986, 1989].

4.1 Classification of Large-Scale Numerical Problems

The large-scale computations described in this section are numerical techniques that model physical processes. The common features of the problems are:

- There is a heavy dependence on floating-point arithmetic because of a potentially large dynamic range of values.

- The calculation model uses discrete points in space and time to model what physically might be a continuous function of space and time.
- The algorithm designer has some flexibility in determining the size of the problem by choosing the discrete representation of the model. Hence the designer selects the number of physical points in a mesh, the size of a time step, and the number of particles to track in a Monte Carlo simulation. These values can generally be chosen to meet architectural constraints.
- The algorithm designer can trade-off the precision of the result against the time to compute the result. Generally, the more precision obtained in an answer, the greater the number of points that will be needed to compute it to that precision, and the greater the number of machine cycles that will be expended while performing the calculations.

All of these characteristics suggest that the algorithm designer has the freedom to adapt the algorithm to particular architectures where constraints are strongly felt in the architecture. For example, the ILLIAC IV is an array-processor design containing 64 processors. In 1972, one was built and installed at NASA Ames Research Center, where it performed very large computations for about ten years before it was decommissioned.

On the ILLIAC IV architecture, calculations involving 64, 128, 256, . . . , grid points are easily spread among the processors so that all processors can process grid points concurrently. For calculations involving 65 grid points, however, the ILLIAC IV architecture has a serious problem. The first 64 out of 65 points are assigned to the 64 processors, 1 processor per point. When these have completed their work, the remaining point is assigned to 1 of the 64 processors, leaving 63 processors idle. So, in a very real sense, the use of 65 grid points leads to gross inefficiency as compared to using just 64 points.

Rarely if ever was the ILLIAC IV programmed to deal with problem models for which the number of data points was poorly suited to its architecture. Since efficiency depended so strongly on the number of data points, the models developed for the ILLIAC IV invariably used a number of points that was an exact multiple of 64 or was a number that allowed most of the processors to be utilized throughout a computation.

The number of points within a typical problem was selected by the algorithm designer; it was not a number inherently fixed by the nature of the problem. With the flexibility to choose the size of the problem within certain bounds, the algorithm designers were able to adjust their problem sizes to sizes that were efficient for the structure of the ILLIAC IV.

It is an unfortunate fact of life that the algorithms for high-performance machines are dependent on the architecture. The algorithm designer who makes certain that the number of data points is well suited to an ILLIAC IV may have to redesign the algorithm if it is moved to a different machine.

The present state of the art of high-level languages and optimizing compilers for high-performance machines is only now reaching the point where it has become feasible to submit a program written in FORTRAN for a conventional computer to an optimizing compiler for a highly parallel machine, and thereby produce a machine-language program that makes effective use of the facilities contained within the parallel machine. The best of such compilers outperform the capabilities of programmers with a moderate amount of experience writing programs for parallel computers. Very experienced programmers usually do better than the compilers.

This situation is not very different from the one that exists for compilers for conventional machines, except that optimizing compilers for conventional machines may well outperform a larger segment of the programming population than do the compilers for parallel machines. The human work involved in producing better code than what an optimizing compiler produces is often so large that it is rarely done for conventional machines except in special cases when the payoff in high performance is worth the effort required to produce fast code.

Unfortunately, in the realm of high-performance machines, the majority of programs make heavy use of processor resources, and therefore a large percentage of these programs fall in the class of programs for which special effort in improving efficiency is worth while. A factor of 2 improvement in overall speed, which is often attainable through hand coding instead of automatic compilation, may reduce computation time by several hours or days, and it may make the difference between being able to run the code or not run the code at reasonable cost.

In the near term, we expect the algorithm designer to be responsible for building algorithms to tap the resources of the architecture. This places an extra burden on software development because algorithm design is likely to be dependent on the architectural structure. In the long term, compiler technology may carry the burden of restructuring an algorithm written for conventional architectures into a form suitable for a high-performance, specialized architecture.

Given this background discussion, it is clear that computer architects need to understand the general characteristics of the workload for which they are designing machines. This holds for all problem areas, be they scientific and numerical, business and data processing, or nonnumerical combinatorial workloads. The remainder of this section treats large-scale, scientific problems.

4.1.1 Continuum Models

Hoshino [1986, 1989] finds that physical computational models fall mostly into two categories:

1. Continuum models; and
2. Particle (discrete) models.

The continuum model accounts for calculations in which time and space are considered to vary continuously, and typical parameters are charge density, temperature, and pressure. These are physical measures averaged over regions. The particle model views the universe as composed of discrete particles. The parameters in this model are physical variables such as velocity, force, and momentum, where the variables measure the current state of individual particles.

The notion of temperature of a plasma, for example, views the plasma as a continuous entity with an internal temperature that varies continuously through the plasma according to physical laws. The discrete view of the plasma treats each particle within the plasma as a distinct entity and does not directly contain the notion of temperature. However, the temperature of a plasma is a direct function of the velocity and density of the particles within the plasma, and it can be calculated by taking averages over many particles.

The digital computer is a discrete device, and therefore all digital computations have to be cast in a discrete form, regardless of whether or not they were continuous initially. Analog computers can model continuous problems without requiring a conversion first to discrete form. A wind tunnel, for example, is an analog computer for calculating fluid flows. In this case, the real physical variable is modeled by an identical physical variable scaled appropriately for the dimensions of the wind tunnel.

The very large numerical problems addressed by parallel machines generally do not lend themselves to fast computation on inexpensive analog computers, and therefore the use of digital computers has become an attractive alternative. The cost of a wind tunnel, for example, that can simulate the range of velocities and effects of interest today may well exceed the cost of ten digital supercomputers. (Although the factor of 10 is speculative, it is of the right order of magnitude.)

The major difference between continuum models and particle models is the following:

> A continuum model obeys partial differential equations. When cast in discrete form, it produces equations in which all changes to variables are functions of nearby variables. Remote variables do not have a direct effect. They act indirectly through the medium by actions on their neighbors, which act on their neighbors, and so forth, and thereby propagate an action through the entire medium through local interactions.

> A particle model permits particles to be affected by distant particles. Any single particle may depend directly on all other particles in the model at each instant of time.

The nice property of the continuum model is that each point within the continuum acts like an independent autonomous computer. Each point examines its near neighbors to determine their states. Then based only on its current state and the states of its near neighbors, each point applies the equation that governs the behavior of the continuum and updates its state.

The computations made at each point are made independently and proceed in parallel. So when you visualize convective heat flow, fluid flow, or other continuous physical processes, view the dynamics of the process as if each point in the continuum were performing a small computation on local and neighboring data. If this model correctly characterizes the process, it becomes quite clear what the characteristics should be for a highly parallel computer that performs calculations with this model.

4.1.2 Particle Models

If the continuum model is well suited to parallel computation, then the particle model may be considered to be poorly suited. Because of the property of action at a distance, each particle must examine all other particles to determine how its state will change. As the number of particles in a model increases, the work per particle increases, and the total computation increases faster than linearly in the number of particles. This finding is at odds with the continuum model in which the computation at each point is fixed regardless of the size of the model. We have to reconcile the two models because both models can be used to describe a single physical process.

For example, gravitation is an excellent example of a physical phenomenon of action at a distance. As matter is created and destroyed in far reaches of the universe through massive nuclear interactions, the change in the amount of matter changes the gravitational force on objects here on earth.

When Newton's apple fell from the tree, how did the apple know to fall to earth? Because of action at a distance, the apple was accelerated by gravitational interactions with all other matter in the universe. A discrete model of the forces on the apple may well examine all other matter in the universe, sum up the effects, and then accelerate the apple according to the resultant effect.

In actual practice, action at a distance is too strong a notion for gravitational interactions. Since gravitational forces are proportional to mass and fall off with the inverse square of distance, faraway objects can be ignored unless they are very large. For most objects on earth, the planet earth itself is the only object of consequence. In exceptional cases, such as tidal movements, the sun and the moon have to be considered. For trajectories of spacecraft, it is sufficient to treat planets, major satellites, and the sun, and ignore objects outside the solar system and small objects within it.

The same notion holds in particle physics, except that a greater fraction of the particles have to be considered. Again, in models in which forces fall off with the inverse square of distance, particles sufficiently far away need not be examined unless they are very large individually or of a sufficiently high concentration that their total effect is large. To determine the effects of remote particles, note that the volume of a sphere around a discrete particle grows proportionally to the square of the radius of the sphere for small changes in radius. That is,

$$dV = 4\pi r^2 \, dr$$

If particle density is uniform in space, and if forces drop off as the square of the radius, then the sum of the magnitudes of the forces experienced at the center of the sphere is a constant independent of the radius of the sphere of influence. The actual force experienced at the center of the sphere of influence may fall as the radius grows when the forces tend to cancel.

If particle density falls off as the volume increases, then the total forces felt by a particle will also fall off with the distance to the remote particles. So the first principle we have learned here is that there are practical limits to action at a distance, and therefore we may be able to limit attention to a small portion of the particles at hand, depending on the nature of the model.

The second principle concerns remote effects in a continuum model. Even though all computations in the continuum model are local, it is clear that remote conditions eventually affect each point. In a heat-transfer model, for example, when some boundary face of a solid metallic object is raised to a high temperature, that temperature eventually propagates through the metal and raises the temperature of the entire object, unless the heat can be dissipated through other surfaces. The near-neighbor computation in the continuum model forces that heat propagation to move from point to point in the physical model, until every point has been affected indirectly.

If we modeled the same process through a corresponding particle model, each particle within the object would directly examine all others, including those particles associated with the heated surface. Each particle could change its internal state immediately if it were to compute the effect of the heated surface on itself, properly taking into account heat dissipation within the solid object. (This is not a simple calculation.)

The continuum view produces a simple calculation model that is inherently highly parallel and local, but the model has some delay associated with the propagation of effects through the continuum. The particle view produces a model that handles propagation quickly by making all interactions direct interactions, but the computations may be more complex, and the number of pairwise interactions to examine may be very large.

The continuum model may actually have fewer elementary arithmetic operations than the discrete model in certain circumstances. Specifically, the effect of propagating the influence of several active particles within the continuum model is to propagate each of the particles through near-neighbors. As the effects of distinct particles reach common intermediate points, the effects combine and propagate as a combined effect instead of as multiple individual effects. That is why an individual point within the continuum need look only at its near-neighbors instead of at every other point in the continuum. All effects combine eventually and affect each point only through its near-neighbors. So instead of examining all pair-wise interactions, which can be a very large number, the continuum model combines effects to reduce the number of pair-wise computations to make at each node.

When the number of individual particles is very large, the pairs grow as the square of the number of particles. On the other hand, the continuum model requires at least a number of computations proportional to the product of the number of points in the continuum, the number of neighbors, and the length of the longest propagation path. Since path length grows only as the square root or cube root of the number of points, the number of operations for the continuum model may be smaller than the number of operations for the discrete model. Usually the number of points in the continuum is independent of the number of particles in the discrete model, so the two models cannot be compared directly.

4.2 Design Constraints for High-Performance Machines

Our objective in the text as a whole is to show the major trends for future developments in high-performance architecture. In the numerical algorithm area, the ability to formulate and attack very large problems has grown much faster than the ability of industry to supply single processors whose performance is high enough to solve the problems posed. The clearest trend for the very large problems is to use parallelism in some fashion, either through extensive use of pipeline design or through replication of individual processors into arrays of processors.

Early formulations of parallel programs for numerical calculations occasionally lacked a realistic view of the architecture of parallel machines. Most of the weaknesses in the models of machines that were studied lay in the fact that the machine models had capabilities that are difficult or impossible to build from the devices with the functional characteristics of those in use today.

To give accurate insight into future trends, we must first identify the major constraints on designs. These constraints make designs difficult and challenging. Breakthroughs occur when some mixture of designer cleverness, new devices, and sophisticated software can live within the physical constraints and still achieve major performance improvements.

Let us first examine the principal constraints and then consider how various designs have dealt with them. The most constraining technology factors are:

- *Memory bandwidth*: each physical memory of conventional design can support at most one READ or one WRITE per cycle.

- *Processor bandwidth*: a conventional processor can execute only one instruction at a time.
- *Input/output bandwidth*: a conventional bus that connects a computer's input/output port with the external world can carry no more than one datum per cycle.

To achieve high performance without parallelism using conventional architectures, the only reasonable approach is to have more machine cycles per second, that is, to use inherently faster devices.

Parallel architectures provide a way of increasing performance without relying on a new generation of high-speed devices. For example, parallel-computer memories may provide the ability to support multiple independent concurrent READs or the ability for one READ operation to examine the contents of several memory locations during one memory cycle.

To design an effective parallel computer, the architect must find solutions to each of the following problems:

- *Processor bandwidth*: find a way to partition individual computations among many processors so that each computation can be executed concurrently on those processors.
- *Memory bandwidth*: design a memory system and find a way to store data in that system so that the data required to be accessed during any cycle can be accessed in parallel.
- *Input/output bandwidth*: design an input/output system that can move data into and out of a parallel machine at a rate that can sustain the full computational power of the machine.
- *Communication bandwidth*: design a means for interprocessor communication that can move data from where it resides to where it is needed.
- *Synchronization*: design a mechanism for coordinating the activity of the processors.
- *Multiple purposes*: incorporate sufficient flexibility in the design to support several different kinds of computations.

The first three problems to be attacked are the constraints inherent in conventional architecture:

1. Executing more than one instruction per cycle;
2. Accessing more than one datum per cycle; and
3. Boosting input/output capacity to support a data rate required for very high speed computations.

As a consequence of using a parallel approach, the other three problems that are not usually present in serial architectures appear in parallel architectures. With many processors, it becomes necessary to exchange information so some type of communication network among the processors is required. Because the processors must work together on a computation, they must synchronize to coordinate such things as data transfers among processors, access to shared data, and the initiation of tasks that depend on the completion of other tasks.

The last problem area reflects the economics of computer design as discussed in the first chapter. Development costs for hardware and software have to be amortized over the number of copies of a machine that can be installed. A very high speed, single-purpose machine can be very costly if all development expenses are amortized over a few copies and the ratio of cost to performance that each user sees grows very large.

By incorporating sufficient flexibility to cover several purposes into a design, the ratio of cost to performance to each user may be significantly lower, and thereby the design produces a greater benefit to each user. Moreover, there is very great risk in designing an architecture for a single purpose because the architecture may be too wedded to a particular algorithm.

Scientific advances often produce alternative computational techniques, and thus there is some possibility that what was once thought to be an efficient algorithm can be supplanted by a more efficient algorithm. Hence a high-speed architecture built around one algorithm may deliver somewhat less performance than can a lower-speed architecture that is based on a better algorithm. And the lower-speed architecture is likely to be less costly than the high-speed architecture.

These problems represent the challenge to the computer architect. In the light of this discussion let us return to the problem of designing high-speed computers for numerical algorithms and illustrate various choices available to the architect.

4.3 Architectures for the Continuum Model

The continuum model of computation is especially attractive for parallel computation because it provides relatively simple solutions to the major design problems. The earliest proposals for parallel machines focused on this type of computation, partly because of the natural parallelism inherent in this model, and partly because several important large-scale problems can be solved within a continuum framework.

In this section we pursue the reasoning that leads to the design of an array processor architecture and describe how this architecture is an effective solution to each of the design problems, except for the multi-purpose objective. The very special structure of this type of architecture limits its use mainly to the continuum model of problems, and even within this model there are problems whose demands cannot be met by the basic architecture.

As a paradigm for the continuum model, let us choose Poisson's equation for the potential in a region as a function of charge density in that region. The equation in two dimensions can be written as:

$$\frac{\partial^2 V(x,y)}{\partial x^2} + \frac{\partial^2 V(x,y)}{\partial y^2} = -C(x,y) \qquad (4.1)$$

where $V(x, y)$ is the voltage potential at the point (x, y), and $C(x, y)$ is the charge at point (x,y). A solution to this equation in a region depends on boundary conditions, which can be expressed in a variety of ways. For this example, we assume we are to solve the equations in a region $0 \le x \le 1, 0 \le y \le 1$, and that we are given the values of $V(x, y)$ on the boundaries of this region.

The continuous equations do not lend themselves to direct solution on a digital computer. We must first transform them into a discrete form that can be treated numerically. To do so, we can represent a continuous region by discrete points, as represented by the mesh shown in Fig. 4.1. At the intersection (i, j) in this mesh is a point at which we store the values $V(i, j)$ and $C(i, j)$. The indices on i and j run from 0 to $N - 1$, so the corresponding values of x and y are given by $x = i/N$ and $y = j/N$.

If the points in the region are sufficiently close together, we obtain a good approximation of the potential in a continuous region. The fidelity of the discrete version of the problem depends entirely on the mesh spacing. Of course, the number of points grows quadratically with the spacing, so computation time can become very large as spacing diminishes. The user must strike a balance between the resolution of the model and the cost of computation. As computation speeds become greater, the user can explore problems with much greater resolution by refining the meshes used in discrete approximations.

Having transformed continuous physical space into discrete space, we can transform the continuous equations into their discrete analog. Equation (4.1) relies on second derivatives, which we explore by finding the discrete approximation to first derivatives. Consider, momentarily, a continuous first derivative for a one-dimensional problem. The equation of interest is Eq. (4.2):

$$\frac{dV(x)}{dx} = -C(x) \qquad (4.2)$$

Using the classical definition of a derivative, we are tempted to use a discrete analog of the derivative that has the form:

$$\frac{dV(x)}{dx} = \frac{V_{i+1} - V_i}{\left(\frac{1}{N}\right)} \qquad (4.3)$$

The denominator is the mesh spacing, which is $1/N$ when there are $N + 1$ uniformly spaced points starting at 0 and ending at 1. Equation (4.3) expresses

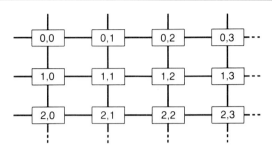

Fig. 4.1 A mesh representation of continuous space. Each box represents one node in the mesh. The integers within a box represent its spatial coordinates.

the derivative at a region of space about halfway between the points located at i and $i + 1$ on the x-axis. The value of the derivative at point i is more appropriately given by this equation:

$$\frac{dV\left(\frac{i}{N}\right)}{dx} = \frac{V_{i+1/2} - V_{i-1/2}}{\left(\frac{1}{N}\right)} \tag{4.4}$$

where the grid points $i + 1/2$ and $i - 1/2$ are fictitious. If we needed to use real grid points, we could use $i + 1$ and $i - 1$ in Eq. (4.4), and adjust the denominator to twice the mesh spacing. This is not necessary, however, because the fictitious grid points cancel out when we take the second derivative.

Let us calculate the discrete approximation to the second derivative in one dimension:

$$\frac{d^2V(x)}{dx^2} = \frac{d}{dx}\left(\frac{dV(x)}{dx}\right)$$

$$= \frac{(V_{i+1} - V_i) - (V_i - V_{i-1})}{\left(\frac{1}{N}\right)^2} \tag{4.5}$$

$$= \frac{V_{i+1} + V_{i-1} - 2V_i}{\left(\frac{1}{N}\right)^2}$$

When we use Eq. (4.5) in Eq. (4.1), the resulting discrete equation becomes:

$$\frac{V_{i+1,j} + V_{i-1,j} + V_{i,j+1} + V_{i,j-1}}{4} = V_{i,j} - C_{i,j}/4N^2, \qquad \text{for } 0 < i < N, 0 < j < N \quad (4.6)$$

In other words, the potential at each point in the mesh is the average of the points at its four neighbors plus a term that reflects the charge located at that point.

Equation (4.6) is a linear system of equations involving the $(N - 1)^2$ unknown values of $V(x, y)$ on the interior of the mesh. By solving this linear system we can obtain a close approximation to the solution of the original continuous system.

How can we solve Eq. (4.6)? Standard algorithms for solving linear systems will work, but this system is very special because it is sparse and highly structured. To achieve greater efficiency, we should take advantage of the specific form of the system. Of the many possible approaches, one in particular has great appeal for parallel architectures. This approach solves the equations implicitly rather than by direct solution. Varga [1962] describes the methodology in great detail. The essential idea is to use an iteration of the form:

$$V_{i,j}^{(t+1)} = \frac{V_{i+1,j}^{(t)} + V_{i-1,j}^{(t)} + V_{i,j+1}^{(t)} + V_{i,j-1}^{(t)}}{4} + C_{i,j} \qquad (4.7)$$

The superscript indicates the iteration number. In this case each point is updated with a value equal to the average of the four neighboring points, plus a value due to the charge at the point. A solution is obtained when no point changes value as a result of performing the iteration.

A computer architecture for solving the equations in the form given by Eq. (4.7) is shown in Fig. 4.2. Each mesh point has a processor associated with it. Each processor is connected to its four immediate neighbors, and along this connection the processors obtain the values required for Eq. (4.7). Since all processors execute the same iteration, we need only one instruction stream for all processors. Instructions are broadcast by a single control processor, and they are received and obeyed by the processors performing computations at the nodes of the mesh. In this form, the architecture is essentially that proposed by Slotnick et al. [1962]. Eventually this proposal led to the development of the ILLIAC IV.

Program 4.1 is a program for this architecture that computes the solution to Poisson's equation. We assume that each processor has a memory, a collection of general registers, and a routing register that is connected to the north, east, south, and west neighbors.

The instruction format in Program 4.1 has the form OPCODE DEST,SOURCE, where OPCODE specifies the operation to be done, DEST is the destination of the result, and SOURCE is the location of one of the

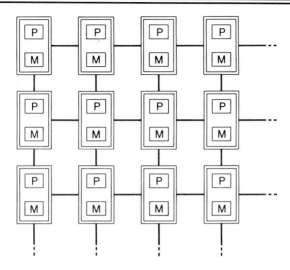

Fig. 4.2 An array of processors for continuum-model calculations. The *P* and *M* designate the processor and memory at each node. Instructions are broadcast to all processors from a control unit not shown in the figure.

Program 4.1 Main iteration for Poisson solver on array processor.

```
LOOP:
        LOAD    REG[1], V           Local value of potential to REG[1]
        MOVE    ROUTE,REG[1]        Prepare to route the value
        ROUTE   NORTH               Send it north
        MOVE    REG[2],ROUTE        Save value from the south
        ROUTE   EAST                Send it east
        ADD     REG[2],ROUTE        Add in the value from the west
        MOVE    ROUTE,REG[1]
        ROUTE   SOUTH               Send it south
        ADD     REG[2],ROUTE        Add in the value from the north
        MOVE    ROUTE,REG[1]
        ROUTE   WEST                Send it west
        ADD     REG[2],ROUTE        Add in the value from the east
        DIV     REG[2]/4            Form the average of the neighbors
        ADD     REG[2],MEM[C]       Add in the local charge
        MOVE    MEM[V],REG[2]       REG[2] has the new value of V
        . . .   . . .               REG[1] has old value of V
                                    Add code here to detect convergence
```

operands. If the instruction has two operands, as do ADD and MULTIPLY, the second operand is found in location DEST. With this convention, the instruction MOVE REG[1],MEM[V] copies the contents of local memory, cell V, into Register 1; conversely, the instruction MOVE MEM[V],REG[1] copies the register back into memory.

To transfer data among processors, each datum is first loaded into the routing register with an instruction of the form MOVE ROUTE,MEM[V] for a transfer from memory to the routing register, or of the form MOVE ROUTE,REG[1] to transfer from a general register into the routing register. The transmission of data across processors is done by the ROUTE instruction, such as ROUTE NORTH, which has the effect of moving data from each routing register to the routing register of its northern neighbor. Immediately after a ROUTE NORTH instruction, the routing register contains the value transmitted by the southern neighbor. ROUTE NORTH is both a SEND TO NORTH and RECEIVE FROM SOUTH instruction.

With this convention, the program for Eq. (4.6) becomes the program shown in Program 4.1. Note that no subscripts are required here because the mesh point (i, j) is held in processor (i, j). If the number of mesh points exceeds the number of physical processors, then it is possible to process a large mesh by breaking it into small regions, each containing a number of nodes equal to the number of processors. In this case, the calculation for each region is performed in turn in the processor array, and each processor has to calculate the equations for one point in each of several different regions. To differentiate one region from another the program may have to resort to indexing, so MEM[V] becomes MEM[V[K]] to access the potential for Region K.

Let us return to the problems posed in the previous section and consider how the architecture in Fig. 4.2 solves each problem.

- *Processor bandwidth*: the problem is inherently parallel, and it partitions easily by assigning each processor the work of one node in the mesh.

- *Memory bandwidth*: the memories at each node are conventional random-access memories. Because they are independent, an independent access can be made to each memory in the system in the course of a single cycle.

- *Input/output bandwidth*: each processor in the system can have its own input/output channel to the external world.

- *Communication bandwidth*: all communication between processors is done between neighboring processors. There is no contention for communication paths. Communication bandwidth does not limit computation speed in this architecture for the class of problems that require only near-neighbor connections.

- *Synchronization*: the processors operate in lock-step fashion. All processors execute the same program and are locked together during execution. The processors are synchronized at the individual cycle level and do not have to be synchronized at a higher level.

- *Multiple purposes*: the basic architecture depicted in Fig. 4.2 is best suited to mesh calculations that have specific characteristics, such as calculations with uniform grid spacing, with a nontime-varying mesh, and with a mesh geometry that matches the interconnection geometry. Relative performance is much poorer for other kinds of problems.

For all but the last point, this architecture has very positive answers. For synchronization specifically, the ROUTE instruction shows the effectiveness of the architecture. All processes transmit data concurrently, so no processor has to wait to receive data from a neighbor.

In spite of the positive qualities of the architecture, no machine with this architecture has been successful commercially, although the ILLIAC IV produced useful output for about ten years. It is clear that the architecture is extremely effective for some problems. Why then has the architecture not been widely exploited? The answer is probably because the architecture is too narrowly focused on a single solution methodology.

The architecture is ideal for the continuum model, but the architecture as presented here lacks facilities for handling requirements that exist in other models and that appear in many computations that use the continuum model. For example, mesh size might need to be varied dynamically when the resolution required is a function of spatial coordinates or time. The architecture as presented appears to be best suited to a uniform rectangular mesh.

Some computations break up into two or more regions, within each of which a different computation must be performed. The basic architecture as presented cannot perform two or more different computations in parallel, so each different computation would have to be done serially on some subset of processors.

In essence, the architecture in Fig. 4.2 has a narrow area of application. Because the potential user community is small, the cost per user is likely to be high. Moreover, the effort required by the user to write working programs on a new architecture might also be excessive.

Whether an architecture is an ILLIAC IV, a PAX, or yet another form of highly parallel computer, raw speed by itself does not solve real problems. New architectures require new tools such as compilers, debuggers, and operating systems. The development of such tools takes considerable time. Without such tools, the user is forced to program in a low-productivity environment until good software-development tools begin to appear. Hence, high performance by itself must be coupled with reasonable cost and good software tools to make an architecture attractive for a community of users.

The ILLIAC IV architecture is an outgrowth of the SOLOMON architecture, which is essentially the architecture described in Fig. 4.2. ILLIAC IV provides more generality than SOLOMON, and it proved to be adaptable to a larger class of problems than was foreseen in the SOLOMON proposal.

In spite of its broader applicability, the ILLIAC IV was a one-of-a-kind machine. Delays in development of supporting hardware and software took its toll on the ILLIAC IV user community. But the necessary support did develop, although somewhat more slowly than envisioned, and the ILLIAC IV proved to be effective for the class of problems for which it was designed. Its 64 processors led to achievable speedups in the neighborhood of 10 to 50 over the speed of a single ILLIAC IV processor. Faster devices eventually led to faster competitive machines, and 64 ILLIAC IV processors became less attractive than other alternatives with lesser parallelism. When the ILLIAC IV was decommissioned, the users turned to other machines that were not one-of-a-kind machines. The software available on these machines, together with the later, faster devices, yielded at least equal performance to the ILLIAC IV for many programs.

There are several important points in this section that capture the lessons of history in the development of machines for the continuum model.

- A SOLOMON or ILLIAC-IV architecture is very efficient for this model. This general architecture should influence the architects of commercial high-speed machines for the continuum model.

- An architecture that solves only the continuum model well and is poorly suited to other problems may have a greatly limited user community, which tends to increase the cost to the user and places a greater software burden on the user than do architectures that are attractive to larger communities.

- The speed of high-performance serial processors doubles every three to four years. A speedup of 10 can be obtained by serial machines over a period of ten years. Therefore a parallel architecture that produces a speedup of 10 has a window of effectiveness of about ten years.

- If software support tools for an architecture are delayed, the window during which that architecture can return the highest possible value is shortened. If some crucial tools such as optimizing compilers are never developed, the architecture's value to the user may be severely diminished.

- Building the best possible architecture for a particular purpose is not necessarily in the best interest of the user. The architecture must also appeal to a community of reasonable size.

In later sections we shall explore in more depth various techniques for enhancing architectures to be more general in purpose.

4.4 Algorithms for the Continuum Model

Thus far in this chapter we have learned that the continuum model leads naturally to computations that use highly parallel near-neighbor communication. Moreover, the computations that take place concurrently over large regions can be synchronized to execute in lock step at all sites simultaneously. To exploit these characteristics, designers have proposed and built machines whose interconnections reflect the near-neighbor structure of the continuum model. We have discussed briefly the ILLIAC IV computer whose two-dimensional grid structure seems to be well suited to calculations on mathematical meshes. That machine interconnects each point to its four nearest neighbors in the plane.

4.4.1 The Cosmic Cube Versus the ILLIAC IV

Seitz [1985] developed an architecture called the Cosmic Cube in which 64 processors are arranged in the logical structure of a six-dimensional binary cube. Each processor is directly connected to each of six neighbors in each of the six directions on the cube. The Cosmic Cube is the first embodiment of an architecture known as a hypercube architecture.

To be more specific, let each processor be given a unique 6-bit label, and consider, for example, Processor $(0,0,0,0,0,0)$. Each bit gives the coordinate of that processor in six-dimensional space. Then the neighbors of Processor $(0,0,0,0,0,0)$ are those processors whose coordinates differ by exactly one bit position. In this case the neighbors are $(1,0,0,0,0,0)$, $(0,1,0,0,0,0)$, $(0,0,1,0,0,0)$, ..., and $(0,0,0,0,0,1)$. The more general N-dimensional hypercube has 2^N processors and direct connections for N near neighbors.

It is curious that this architecture is six-dimensional, but physical space has only three geometrical dimensions and is only four-dimensional when time is treated as an additional dimension. The dimensions in the Cosmic Cube reflect interconnections that are useful for algorithmic purposes and do not correspond directly to physical dimensions in space and time. Nor is the Cosmic Cube specifically oriented to the continuum model of calculations, although the continuum model is a major class of algorithms that run efficiently on the Cosmic Cube.

The processors in the Cosmic Cube are independent processors, capable of executing their own local programs. In the original working model, each processor was, in fact, a microcomputer that uses an 8086 processor chip with an 8087 floating-point of chip. The Cosmic Cube is not required to perform the same instruction concurrently at all nodes. Rather, execution is independent at the various nodes, and neighboring processors communicate through messages when routing data though the computer system.

The Cosmic Cube differs from the architecture of the ILLIAC IV and other continuum architectures in two fundamental ways:

1. The interconnections of the Cosmic Cube reflect the needs of a variety of algorithms. The interconnections of the ILLIAC IV reflect specific mesh geometries.

2. The independence of the processors of the Cosmic Cube permits the system of processors to perform different computations simultaneously. Processors within the ILLIAC IV must execute the same instruction concurrently (or can remain idle).

The Cosmic Cube architecture is quite well-suited for implementation by means of independent microprocessors. Intel released several commercial versions of this architecture under the name Intel Hypercube, and this was followed by several other commercial releases of machines with a similar architecture. As the 1990s began, hypercube-based architectures led the number of offerings in highly parallel computers.

The 64-processor ILLIAC IV was successful in its time in attaining extremely high performance, but on a rather limited class of problems. Researchers explored many different problem types on the ILLIAC IV and achieved blinding speed if they were able to cast the problem into a structure that fit the ILLIAC IV constraints. They learned new techniques for solving problems and discovered that the near-neighbor geometry of ILLIAC IV is not usually the best interconnection structure, although it is very good.

For 64 processors, inefficiencies in execution due to near-neighbor connections are not terribly large. In reality, the ILLIAC IV connections are richer than the connections proposed by Slotnick *et al.* [1962], with the enhancements providing additional facilities that are useful in parallel programs. We describe some of the differences in more detail later in this chapter.

The most serious flaw of an ILLIAC IV architecture is the inability to run different programs concurrently. There is a trade-off here, however, because independence of operation brings with it additional overhead for synchronization of activity plus some performance degradation due to contention for shared resources.

Hoshino [1989] describes a variant of the ILLIAC-IV type of architecture that overcomes a number of the problems raised here. Specifically, his **PAX** computer has

1. An independent instruction stream in each processor rather than a single instruction stream for all processors,

2. A fast global synchronization bus that provides extremely efficient synchronization of the processors, and

3. A limited means for broadcasting from any selected processor to a selected set of receiving processors.

The independent processors overcome the deficiency of the ILLIAC IV's single instruction stream and make the PAX more like the Cosmic Cube. The high-speed global synchronization enables PAX processors to synchronize in a very few machine cycles, which is a capability that is not shared by the Cosmic Cube. The additional features of PAX give the machine sufficient generality to be useful both for the continuum model and the particle model, which makes the architecture more nearly general purpose, although it is clearly best suited for highly structured scientific applications.

4.4.2 Data-Flow Requirements

In this section, we explore some examples of parallel algorithms whose characteristics illustrate the types of data flow that are inherent in large-scale numerical computations. Although the algorithms are only examples, we argue that the data-flow requirements are representative, and high-performance machines must provide for this type of data flow if they are to be efficient. The requirements are compatible with the Cosmic Cube and in part explain why it has its particular set of interconnections.

To illustrate the basic information flow that some problems exhibit, consider Fig. 4.3, which shows a computing device that produces N outputs from N inputs. We presume that the timing is synchronized so that all inputs are presented concurrently, and sometime later, all outputs are produced concurrently. Of special interest to us is a class of functions that impose the most stringent requirements for internal data flow within the computing device.

This class of functions is the class for which each input influences every output, and in turn, each output is influenced by every input. We call functions in this class *full-information* functions. Any computing device that computes a full-information function must provide interconnection paths internally from every input to every output. We can measure the shortest path between each input and each output, and the longest such connection gives a bound on the

Fig. 4.3 A full-information function in which each output depends on all inputs.

worst-case computation time. At least one set of inputs transmits data along that path (or on a longer path), and at least one output depends on the value of that data.

Computations that fit the particle model tend to be full-information functions. In examining particle motion in particle-interaction models, for example, each particle experiences a force from every other particle in the system, and in turn, each particle imparts a force on every other particle in the system. The position and velocity of each particle as a function of time is calculated by propagating information about each particle to every other particle in the system. The idea of "action at a distance" is reflected in the computing device by requiring each input to "act" on each output.

Figure 4.4 demonstrates that sorting is a full-information problem. The functional module in Fig. 4.4 is a device that produces at its output a copy of the input data sorted into ascending order. The input data in Fig. 4.4(a) happen to be presented in sorted order, and they appear at the output unchanged in order. For this one particular input set, the internal structure required to put the set into sorted order might well be very simple.

In Fig. 4.4(b), however, we make one change on the first input, and discover that every output has changed. Hence the first input must be connected to every output. It is very easy to extend this example to show that every input influences the outputs in the same way. Simply change the two input patterns in Fig. 4.4 so that each distinct input plays the role played by the first input in

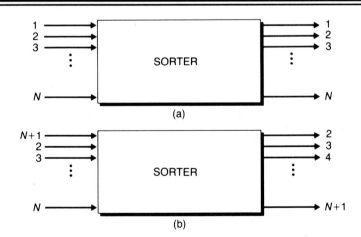

(a)

(b)

Fig. 4.4 A demonstration that sorting is a full-information function. Changing the value of the first input causes all outputs in (a) to change in (b). A similar argument shows that every input affects every output.

the figure. Then a single change of value on each input can cause all outputs to change their values, and it becomes clear that sorting is a full-information function.

Readers familiar with signal analysis techniques may recognize that the Fourier transform is also a full-information function. Let the input data to a computing device be N time samples of a time-varying signal and assume that the device computes the Fourier transform of that signal. The output of the computing device is the frequency spectrum of the signal, in the sense that the ith output value is the amplitude of the ith harmonic of the fundamental frequency. The frequency spectrum depends on all time samples. If a single change is made to any time sample, then possibly every frequency amplitude can change.

What is sometimes overlooked is that computations done within the continuum model can also be full-information functions. This is rather surprising because the continuum model seems to be so well suited to near-neighbor connections. But for those computations that require full information interchange, the near-neighbor connections are simply the highways along which the information travels. Remote pairs of points must still influence each other.

Consider, for example, the classical paradigm of the continuum model, Poisson's equation. Figure 4.5 shows a mesh imposed on physical space and some charge located at a few points in the mesh. The potential at each mesh point depends on the charge placed at all other points in the mesh. The parallel algorithm proposed earlier for calculating the potential uses only near-neighbor information, but the calculation must be repeated until the answers converge.

What is actually happening is that the influence of the charge at each node

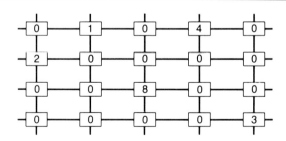

Fig. 4.5 A mesh of points for the solution of Poisson's equation in the continuum model. Each node in the mesh contains the value of the charge at the corresponding point in space.

spreads further through the mesh with each iteration. If the mesh has N nodes in each dimension, then at least N iterations are required for each node to influence every other node. If we choose to solve a continuum problem with a computing device such as the one shown in Fig. 4.3, we need not limit the interconnections to near-neighbor interconnections, and therefore the calculations might complete faster than a time that grows linearly with the dimension of the mesh.

The idea of information flow is a powerful one in the design of a parallel computer. The model of a sorting network in Fig. 4.4 characterizes all sorting networks. Suppose we use as basic building blocks in our sorting network a logic device whose fan-in and fan-out are limited to a small constant, such as 2. Then it is easy to see from the tree-like construction in Fig. 4.6 that each device can influence at most 2^k devices k levels away. By this argument, a sorting network for N items must have at least $\log_2 N$ logic levels.

If the fan-in and fan-out is greater than 2, but still bounded by some constant, then the number of levels still grows as $\log N$, but the base of the logarithm is equal to the fan-in and fan-out constraint. The only way to remove the logarithm from the lower bound is to have unbounded fan-in and fan-out.

In Program 4.1, we have simply ignored the data-flow requirements and concentrated on the near-neighbor data flow. The program excerpt is not a complete iteration because it shows the iteration only up to the point where the average of the neighboring values has been calculated. The iteration actually ends with a convergence test to determine if the iteration should be repeated. An exit is taken only if all nodes in the mesh have converged—otherwise the iteration is repeated. But the convergence test requires information from all nodes in the mesh, and there is no direct way to make this test when the only interconnections are near-neighbor interconnections.

Figure 4.7 shows a more complete view of the ILLIAC IV to indicate that

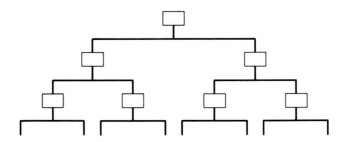

Fig. 4.6 A logic network with a fan-out of 2. The device at the top of the network can influence a number of gates that grows exponentially in the depth of the network.

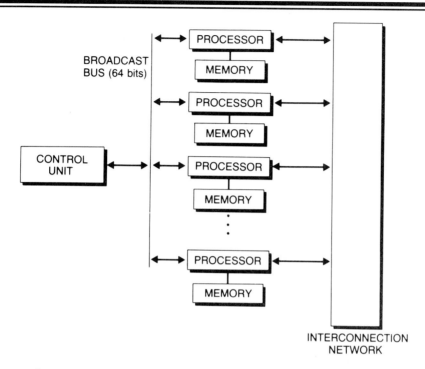

Fig. 4.7 The ILLIAC IV architecture, showing the bidirectional broadcast bus. Each of the 64 processors can return 1 bit on the broadcast bus.

other interconnections exist in that architecture to support the fast interchange of data from remote points in the mesh. This figure shows the 65th processor, the control unit, and its broadcast bus, which presents a single instruction stream to all processors in the mesh. The figure shows the broadcast bus to be bidirectional. The bus provides a return path from the processor array to the control unit.

The bus width of the ILLIAC IV architecture is 64 bits. ILLIAC IV instructions are 64 bits in length, and operands are 32 or 64 bits in length. In broadcast mode, the control unit can supply one instruction, one long operand, or two short operands per cycle. The bus provides a 64-bit return path to the control unit, through which each processor can supply one bit of information per cycle, or a selected processor can supply 64 bits.

When all processors respond in the same cycle, the ith processor sets or resets the ith bit of the operand returned to the control unit. If the processors are performing an iteration of the Poisson calculation, then at the end of the loop the following actions could take place:

1. Each processor compares the magnitude of the change in the potential function to a fixed small constant EPSILON.

2. The control unit requests a response to the comparison.

3. The ith processor places a 1 in the ith bit of the response vector if the change exceeds EPSILON, otherwise the processor places a 0 in that position.

4. The response vector is transmitted over the bus to the control unit.

5. The control unit examines the response locally, and if any bits are nonzero, the control unit initiates a new iteration; otherwise, the control unit continues to a new phase of computation that takes place after the calculation has converged.

It is the control unit that has the ability to gather information globally across the entire grid of processors and make decisions based on global information. The restricted communication within the grid greatly increases the cost of global decisions such as the determination of convergence. The ILLIAC IV architecture is richer than a pure continuum-problem architecture because of the additional capability for the global flow of information.

The implementation of this data path usually has a lower bandwidth than a bus for near-neighbor connections because the length of a global communication path is much longer than the length of a near-neighbor path. The ILLIAC IV cycle time for the global data path for return information is several times the cycle time for near-neighbor paths, and even at this clock rate, each processor returns only a single bit per cycle.

4.4.3 Parallel Solutions

Given the general constraints that dictate how information must flow, let us now consider some techniques that put this knowledge to use in practical parallel solutions of numerical problems. Let us begin with a simple calculation stated as a serial computation and demonstrate a technique for performing the calculation in parallel. Consider the recurrence:

$$x_i = a_i + x_{i-1}, \qquad i > 0$$
$$x_0 = a_0$$

(4.8)

In this case, the unknowns are the parameters x_i, and the variables a_i are constants given in advance. To obtain the value of x_i as quickly as possible in a parallel machine, we can easily use a tree-like combining scheme shown in Fig. 4.8(a). The processors in this diagram are shown in a row, numbered from left

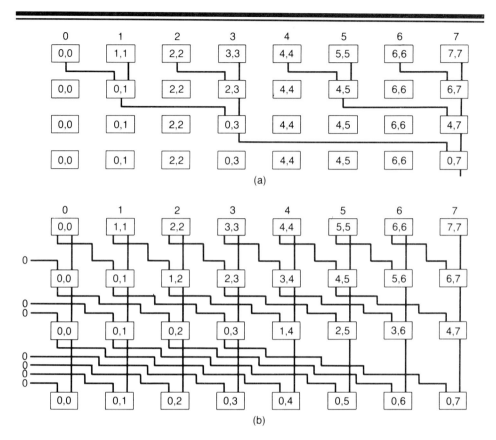

Fig. 4.8 Two Parallel Methods:
(a) A parallel method for forming the sum of eight variables; and
(b) A parallel method that yields the sum of the first i variables simultaneously for all
i. Each node sums its input variables. The pair of digits in each node indicate the lower
and upper indices for variables summed at each node.

to right starting at 0. Each successive row shows the activity one time unit
later.

During the first iteration, the odd-numbered processors reach across to the
neighbor one lower in number and add the values obtained to the internal
value. This leaves partial sums of pairs of numbers in the odd-numbered
processors.

In the next iteration, the processors whose numbers are congruent to 3 modulo 4 reach two processors away for a partial sum and add that value to their internal value. This produces partial sums of four numbers.

At the jth iteration, partial sums of 2^j numbers have been formed, and if i has the form $i = 2^j - 1$, at the end of j iterations, we will have computed the value of x_i. Since the depth of the tree represents time, and the breadth of the tree represents the length of the recurrence, we can compute a recurrence of length N in time proportional to $\log N$ because the depth of a tree with N leaves is proportional to $\log N$.

Figure 4.8(a) yields only a single answer after $\log N$ steps, and it makes very poor use of processors since most of them are idle most of the time. Figure 4.8(b) shows how the values of all x_i can be computed concurrently in the same time that one value can be computed. In the first step, each processor retrieves the value of the item from the processor whose index is one lower. In the second step, the data comes from the processor with an index two lower, and in the jth step the data comes from the processor whose index is 2^j lower. If the request for data is made to a nonexistent processor, the value 0 is substituted instead of a retrieved value.

Within each cell in the figure is a pair of integers, such as "2,3", that indicates the range of subscripts added together in that cell at that point in the algorithm. Note that all partial sums are produced concurrently.

The algorithm suggests that an important interconnection pattern is one that connects processors whose indices differ by $1, 2, 4, 8, \ldots$, and we begin to see why the near-neighbors in the Cosmic Cube have the geometry of a six-dimensional cube. If we treat the 6-bit label of each processor of the Cosmic Cube as an integer, then each processor is connected to processors whose integer labels differ by 1, 2, 4, 8, 16, and 32.

This statement is correct in terms of the absolute value of the difference, but the signs of the differences vary from processor to processor. If a processor label has a 0 bit in a particular position, such as in the position of weight 4, then its neighbor has a 1 bit in that position and therefore has a label whose integer representation is 4 higher. Conversely, if a processor's label has a 1 in the position of weight 4, then the neighbor has a 0 in that position, and the neighbor's label has an integer representation 4 lower than the integer interpretation of the processor's label.

For the operation depicted in Fig. 4.8(b), every processor has to reach a neighbor whose index is 4 less, but only half of Cosmic Cube processors have this property. Nevertheless, the Cosmic Cube can form tree-like sums as shown in Fig. 4.8(b) by doing the communication indirectly, at a small additional cost in communication overhead.

It is no great surprise that the tree in Fig. 4.6, and the interconnections in Fig. 4.8 have a use beyond the simple linear recurrence that yields the partial sums. Consider the multiplicative recurrence:

$$x_i = a_i x_{i-1}, \qquad i > 0$$
$$x_0 = a_0 \qquad\qquad\qquad\qquad (4.9)$$

Again we assume that the x_i are unknown variables and that the coefficients a_i are given constants. The solution to this recurrence involves partial products, whereas the solution to Eq. (4.8) involves partial sums. In fact we can compute all variables concurrently using a computation structure shown in Fig. 4.8, with the addition operation replaced by multiplication.

Why do Eqs. (4.8) and (4.9) yield such similar results? The answer is that the operations of addition and multiplication are both associative, so the manner in which a string of additions or a string of multiplications is evaluated is independent of the order of evaluation. More specifically, the recurrence relation of Eq. (4.8) specifies that the values of the unknowns are calculated serially as if the expression for x_3 were written:

$$x_3 = ((a_0 + a_1) + a_2) + a_3$$

The method for computing the values shown in Fig. 4.8 computes x_3 as if the expression were parenthesized as:

$$x_3 = (a_0 + a_1) + (a_2 + a_3)$$

If the operation on the values is associative, then by definition of associativity, the regrouping of parentheses is permitted. The associative rule is very powerful. It enables us to solve immediately a number of frequently encountered recurrences. Among the more useful ones are:

- $MAX(a, b)$ = maximum of a and b;
- $MIN(a, b)$ = minimum of a and b;
- $XOR(a, b)$ = exclusive OR of a and b if a and b are boolean;
- $OR(a, b)$ = logical OR of a and b if a and b are boolean; and
- $AND(a, b)$ = logical AND of a and b if a and b are boolean.

Now let's see how far this idea can be developed. Consider the following recurrence:

$$x_i = a_i x_{i-1} + b_i \qquad\qquad\qquad\qquad (4.10)$$

This recurrence does not have an associative operation, so the observations made above for associative operations do not appear to be helpful. But we can remap Eq. (4.10) into a different form that does have an associative operator. Let us define $\mathbf{X}_i$ to be the column matrix

$$\mathbf{X}_i = [x_i \ 1]^t$$

where the superscript t denotes matrix transpose. We capture Eq. (4.10) in matrix form by defining the matrix $\mathbf{A}_i$ to be

$$\mathbf{A}_i = \begin{bmatrix} a_i & b_i \\ 0 & 1 \end{bmatrix}$$

Using these two definitions in Eq. (4.10) produces a new equation that has a familiar form.

$$\mathbf{X}_i = \mathbf{A}_i \mathbf{X}_{i-1} \qquad\qquad (4.11)$$

Note that the first row of $\mathbf{A}_i$ represents Eq. (4.10), and the second row is the trivial equation $1 = 1$. The important characteristic of Eq. (4.11) is that matrix multiplication is associative, so the recurrence in that equation can be evaluated by the same scheme used to evaluate Eq. (4.9), except that the operation performed at each node for Eq. (4.11) is a 2×2 matrix multiplication.

The full matrix multiplication is a little more than what needs to be done, and it is possible to reduce the operation count a little bit. The matrix-multiplication framework of this discussion introduces a small inefficiency that should be eliminated in practice, but the framework makes quite clear the role of the associative operator.

The recurrence techniques described here extend to more general recurrences, as indicated in Kogge and Stone [1973]. The order of the recurrence can be increased, for example, to 2, in which case Eq. (4.10) becomes:

$$x_i = a_i x_{i-1} + b_i x_{i-2} \qquad\qquad (4.12)$$

To solve this recurrence in parallel we use new definitions for $\mathbf{X}_i$ and $\mathbf{A}_i$.

$$\mathbf{X}_i = [x_i \quad x_{i-1}]^t$$

$$\mathbf{A}_i = \begin{bmatrix} a_i & b_i \\ 1 & 0 \end{bmatrix}$$

When the substitution of these definitions is made into Eq. (4.12), we obtain Eq. (4.11) again. More generally, a linear recurrence of order d, that is, a linear recurrence that depends on the d prior values of the recurrence variable, can be solved by substituting $d \times d$ matrix multiplication into the evaluation scheme for Eq. (4.9).

Unfortunately, inefficiencies creep into the algorithm and it becomes unattractive for large values of d. For $d = 1$, the parallel algorithm for evaluating N terms takes time proportional to $\log_2 N$, whereas the serial algorithm takes time proportional to N so that the speedup is proportional to $N/\log_2 N$. This is actually quite good, although not as good as linear speedup.

The function $\log_2 N$ grows very slowly with N, and it acts almost like a constant factor. We would prefer to have linear speedup and not suffer the degradation from the $\log_2 N$ factor, but if we can live with this factor for small N, we are likely to be able to live with it for large N because it changes so slowly with N.

For higher-order recurrences, such as recurrences of order d, $d \times d$ matrix multiplication takes time proportional to d^3, so the time for parallel calculation of the first N terms of the recurrence is proportional to $d^3 \log_2 N$. The time for serial evaluation is proportional to $d N$, so the speedup is proportional to only $N/(d^2 \log_2 N)$. Now we have to contend with an additional factor of d^2 of inefficiency. Hence the attractiveness of parallel evaluation of recurrences tends to be limited to recurrences of small order.

The technique explored thus far generalizes to recurrences of the form:

$$x_i = \frac{a_i x_{i-1} + b_i}{c_i x_{i-1} + d_i}, \qquad i > 0$$

$$x_0 = a_0 \tag{4.13}$$

To solve this recurrence, find x_i as a function of x_{i-2} and observe that the relation has the same structure as Eq. (4.13), but with coefficients that depend only on the eight coefficients that define x_i and x_{i-1}. This functional relation shows how to perform a set of operations that collapse eight coefficients into four coefficients and produce an equation for x_i as a function of x_{i-2}. Hence, we have taken an equation in which each x depends on the previous x to an equation in which each x depends on the x two steps earlier in the recurrence.

The scheme for collapsing the eight coefficients into four coefficients is the node operation that replaces the associative operator in the scheme that solves Eq. (4.9). We can repeat this iteration, and we discover how to produce a new x from the x four steps earlier. The next repetition of the same iteration produces an equation in which each x depends on only the x eight steps earlier in the recurrence. Each iteration doubles the distance to the earlier x in the recurrence equation. $\log_2 N$ iterations of the reduction step moves the dependence of x to an x that occurs N steps earlier in the recurrence. Therefore we can achieve a speedup on the order of $N/\log_2 N$.

In the ideal case, we want to achieve a speedup of N with N processors. For recurrence equations, we can obtain this speedup trivially if we evaluate N or more recurrences in parallel, each on a different processor, with each done serially. However, we cannot assume that we will always be so fortunate to have N independent recurrences. When we need to solve one recurrence as fast as we can, the theory here indicates that we can do so with a speedup proportional to $N/\log_2 N$. Because of the factor of $\log_2 N$ in the denominator, the parallel scheme described here should be used only if the program is forced to evaluate a single recurrence as fast as possible.

Now we can put the recurrence theory to work by reconsidering equations for the continuum model. In one dimension, the Poisson equation has the form:

$$x_{i-1} - 2x_i + x_{i+1} = -b_i \qquad (4.14)$$

for points interior to a mesh on a line, with special equations for the end points. The right-hand side is proportional to the charge density at mesh point i, and the left-hand side expresses the notion that the potential at a point is equal to the average of its neighboring potentials (in the absence of charge), and when charge is present, the effects of the charge are added to the influence of the neighboring points.

In an earlier section we learned that Eq. (4.14) and its two-dimensional counterpart can be solved iteratively. But here we shall show how fast recurrence solutions allow us to solve Eq. (4.14) in parallel directly. When we use Eq. (4.14) for $i = 1$ to $N - 2$, together with boundary equations for $i = 0$ and $i = N - 1$, a system of N equations is formed. This system is known as a *tridiagonal* system of equations. The name suggests that all of the nonzero terms of the matrix form of this equation lie on three diagonals. This equation is in matrix form

$$\mathbf{Ax = b}$$

where the main diagonal of A contains only the value of -2, and the major subdiagonal and superdiagonal have the constant value of 1. The right-hand side is a vector $\mathbf{b}$ that reflects the charge density on the line, and the unknown potential is the vector $\mathbf{x}$ that we can obtain by solving the system of equations.

4.4.4 Recursive Doubling and Cyclic Reduction

In this section, we examine two solution methods for tridiagonal systems:

1. Recursive doubling (parallel solution of recurrences); and

2. Cyclic reduction.

Recursive doubling is the natural extension of the results presented previously, but it is not recommended in practice because of numerical stability problems. Cyclic reduction is also unstable numerically in the form presented here, but it can easily be altered into stable form. Interested readers should consult Stone [1973] for background in recursive doubling and Buzbee, Golub, and Nielson [1970] for an analysis of cyclic reduction. The stable form of cyclic reduction is attributed to Buneman.

Three simple steps form the basis of the recursive doubling approach to tridiagonal equations. The first step is to factor the matrix $\mathbf{A}$ into the form $\mathbf{LU = A}$, where $\mathbf{L}$ and $\mathbf{U}$ are bidiagonal matrices whose names stand for *lower* and *upper*. Of the many possible ways to factor $\mathbf{A}$ into the product of bidiagonal

L and **U**, we choose the factorization: **L** is lower bidiagonal—all nonzero entries are on the major diagonal and the diagonal immediately below—with 1s on its major diagonal; and **U** is upper bidiagonal—all nonzero entries are on the major diagonal and the diagonal immediately above.

With the constraints as given, the factorization is unique when it exists. We have a total of four diagonals, and one diagonal is all 1s. That leaves three diagonals to find:

1. The lower diagonal of **L**, whose entries are denoted as m_i for $i = 1$ to $N - 1$;
2. The major diagonal of **U**, whose entries are denoted by u_i for $i = 0$ to $N - 1$; and
3. The upper diagonal of **U**, whose entries are denoted by f_i for $i = 0$ to $N - 2$.

By factoring **A** into the product of **L** and **U**, we can write:

$$\mathbf{Ax} = \mathbf{LUx} = \mathbf{Ly} = \mathbf{b}$$

where we define **y** by the equation **Ux** = **y**.

The next two steps involve the solution to bidiagonal systems.

Given **L** and **b**, solve **Ly** = **b** for **y**.

Given **U** and **y**, solve **Ux** = **y** for **x**.

These two steps are extremely simple to evaluate in parallel because they take the respective forms:

$$m_i y_{i-1} + y_i = b_i$$

$$u_i x_i + f_i x_{i+1} = y_i$$

with boundary conditions specified for y_0 and x_{N-1}. Each y_i satisfies an equation similar to Eq. (4.10), and each such equation is solved by the same parallel scheme used to solve Eq. (4.10). The x_i unknowns are found in the same way except that, instead of going forward, the recurrence works backward from x_{N-1} towards x_0.

The most difficult part of the computation is solving for the diagonal elements of **L** and **U**. The trickiest diagonal to compute is the major diagonal of **U**, whose terms satisfy the following recurrence

$$u_i = a_{i,i} - \frac{a_{i,i-1}a_{i-1,i}}{u_{i-1}}, \qquad 1 < i < N$$

$$(4.15)$$

$$u_0 = a_{0,0}$$

This is a special case of Eq. (4.13), so all of the u_i elements can be computed by the parallel evaluation of the recurrence. The other two diagonals can be computed easily because of the relations

$$m_i = \frac{a_{i,i}}{u_{i-1}}, \qquad 0 \le i \le N - 2$$

$$f_i = a_{i,i+1}, \qquad 1 \le i \le N - 1$$

The lower diagonal of **L** (the m_i terms) can be computed by a single vector division of the major diagonal of **A** by the major diagonal of **U**. The upper diagonal of **U** is exactly equal to the upper diagonal of **A**.

This brief discussion establishes that the full solution of the tridiagonal system can be done with N processors in parallel to achieve a speedup proportional to $N/\log_2 N$. The connection pattern for a parallel processor for this purpose is not like the near-neighbor pattern we have been using for the continuum problems. It is a pattern derived from Fig. 4.8. That is, processors must be directly or indirectly connected to processors that are from one away, two away, four away, . . . , up to $N/2$ away for N processors.

If you visualize the data flow in Fig. 4.8 in terms of processors influencing other processors, then each step of a calculation doubles the number of processors influenced by each processor. In $\log_2 N$ steps, one processor can influence all N processors in a system. The factor of $\log_2 N$ that we observed in the denominator of the speedup expression is a factor of inefficiency that reflects the cost of communication, because $\log_2 N$ steps are required for parallel communication that are not required for serial communication.

The second method for solving tridiagonal equations is called *cyclic reduction*. It works extremely well for the Poisson matrix whose diagonals contain only 1s and -2s. The cyclic-reduction method can be generalized to other matrices as well. The idea behind cyclic reduction is to sum three consecutive equations as indicated here:

$$
\begin{aligned}
x_{i-2} - 2x_{i-1} + x_i \qquad &= -b_{i-1} \\
x_{i-1} - 2x_i \quad + x_{i+1} &= -b_i \\
x_i \quad - 2x_{i+1} + x_{i+2} &= -b_{i+1}
\end{aligned}
\qquad (4.16)
$$

We combine twice the middle equation of Eq. (4.16) with the other two equations to obtain:

$$x_{i-2} - 2x_i + x_{i+2} = -(b_{i-1} + 2b_i + b_{i+1}) \qquad (4.17)$$

If we start with a number of equations that is one less than a power of two and apply this technique to the odd-numbered equations (with special treatment for the end points), we produce a set of equations that depend only on the odd-numbered unknowns. In fact, that set of equations is identical in form to the original set, except that there are only roughly half as many equations.

We can renumber the variables in Eq. (4.17) so that their indices are contiguous. When we do so we have placed the reduced set of equations into the form of Eq. (4.16). So we can repeat the process, each time removing roughly half of the equations in the system, until finally there remains a single equation that can be solved directly.

To solve the full system of equations, we substitute the one known answer in the equations produced at the last step, and solve for two more unknowns. With three quantities known, these can be substituted into equations produced at the second-to-last step to obtain the values of seven variables.

The back-substitution process repeats cyclically, roughly doubling the known variables at each step until all variables have been completed. Both the reduction and back-substitution steps can be done in parallel. The speedup for cyclic reduction is of the same order of magnitude as for recursive doubling, but it is preferred because it can be stabilized.

It is interesting to compare the communication requirements for cyclic reduction with those for recursive doubling. The subscripts that participate in computation differ by 1 at the first iteration, then by 2, 4, ..., up to $N/2$ at successive iterations. Again we see the influence of a variable doubling at every step so that in $\log_2 N$ steps the influence has propagated through the entire system.

The algorithms we have studied earlier for the continuum model use near-neighbor connections that propagate information a fixed limited distance at every step. Both recursive doubling and cyclic reduction move information twice as far at every successive step. From a communication point of view, the direct methods appear to be more powerful and efficient than do the iterative methods. But iteration itself is powerful, and in a practical sense, it becomes possible to iterate quickly to a solution when the forces that count are nearby, and the influence of faraway items is negligible.

Heller [1976] has shown, however, that the direct methods can be used essentially iteratively and converge faster than do the iterative methods. His idea is to use a cyclic-reduction scheme, but terminate early and initiate the back-substitution process before going the full $\log_2 N$ steps. In our description of cyclic reduction, this would occur if the new values of the right-hand sides produced by a reduction step were perturbed only minimally from their values before the reduction. If this case, further reduction steps will produce only a negligible change in the right-hand sides, so that the right-hand sides are available immediately for back substitution.

The key ideas to remember from the discussion in this section are:

1. Some serial computations that look sequential can be solved with reasonable speedup using parallel algorithms.

2. Good parallel algorithms for full-information problems appear to double the sphere of influence of each variable after each iteration.

3. A natural communication pattern that supports the doubling sphere of influence is one in which items communicate with items that are 1 away, 2 away, 4 away, ..., on successive iterations.

In the next section we shall propose an interconnection pattern called the *perfect shuffle* to support such communication.

4.5 The Perfect Shuffle

What we have learned thus far about the continuum model is that near-neighbor interconnections provide a natural mechanism for mimicking physical interactions. But we have learned in the preceding section that near-neighbor operations in some cases are less effective than are operations that treat pairs of nodes progressively twice as far apart at each successive iteration. In this section we examine the perfect-shuffle interconnection pattern, which has a remarkable property that supports this pattern of doubling.

We propose that the perfect shuffle be used in addition to or in place of near-neighbor connections to exploit the doubling property for parallel implementations of cyclic reduction and recursive doubling. The Cosmic Cube described earlier in this chapter has in fact an interconnection pattern that is related to the perfect shuffle, and thus has the ability to double the range of influence on successive operations.

4.5.1 The Perfect-Shuffle Interconnection Pattern

The interconnection pattern of interest to us appears in Fig. 4.9 for a vector of length 8. It is called the *perfect shuffle* because the elements of a vector undergo a reordering analogous to the shuffling of a deck of cards in which the interlacing of cards is ideal. In this case the deck has eight cards. The deck is cut, leaving cards 0 through 3 on top, and 4 through 7 on the bottom. Then the deck is shuffled, with 0 emerging on top, followed by 4 from the top of the lower cut, then 1, then 5, . . . , with one card picked alternately from each cut.

Figure 4.9 shows the deck before and after the shuffle. Note that the basic property we seek is exhibited by the shuffle, in that cards that are adjacent before the shuffle are two apart after the shuffle. For decks with 2^N cards, cards that are adjacent before a sequence of i shuffles are moved to positions that are 2^i cards apart after the shuffles.

We show this more rigorously later in this section, but for the moment the general property of the shuffle suggests that with each shuffle the breadth of a neighborhood of cards is doubled, and this is the property that we need in several algorithms of interest.

Figure 4.10 shows what happens when we repeat a shuffle of eight cards three times. The cards return to their original order after three shuffles. Adjacent pairs of cards are grouped together in the diagram to illustrate how the shuffle operation matches different items in a vector.

After one shuffle, the pairs matched are 0-4, 1-5, 2-6, and 3-7. Note

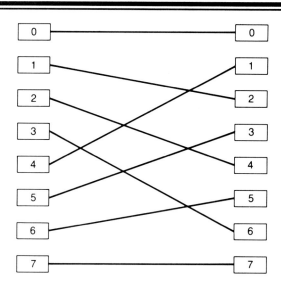

Fig. 4.9 The perfect-shuffle interconnection pattern.

that these items are four apart in the original vector. After two shuffles, the paired items are 0–2, 1–3, 4–6, and 5–7. These items are two apart in the original vector. After the third shuffle, the pairs are 0–1, 2–3, 4–5, and 6–7, items that are adjacent in the original vector. If we measure the distance between two items in the original vector, then after the first shuffle, the distance between items brought together is halved at each step.

On the other hand, with bidirectional interconnections in place, we are free to run data in either direction. With data moving from right to left in Fig. 4.10, the data that are paired initially are 0–1, 2–3, . . . , at a distance of one apart. At subsequent stages the pairs are 0–2, 1–3, . . . (distance two apart) and 0–4, 1–5, . . . (distance four apart). Data moving from right to left tends to double the distance between paired items at each step, and data moving from left to right tends to halve the distance between paired items at each step.

Compare this characteristic to cyclic reduction and note that cyclic reduction has two phases. In the first phase, the difference between subscripts doubles at each step, and in the second phase the difference between subscripts halves at each step. This suggests that cyclic reduction can be done by moving first from right to left and then from left to right in a network such as that shown in Fig. 4.10.

In fact the processors might be arranged in the structure shown in Fig.

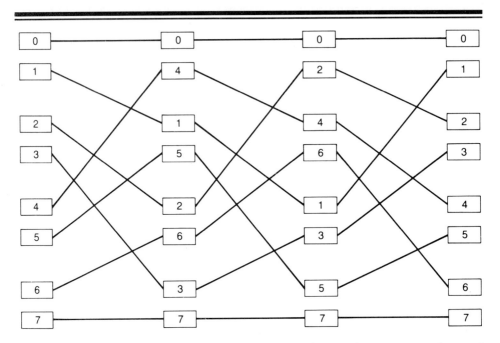

Fig. 4.10 The perfect shuffle repeated three times. Observe the items paired at each step. Their indices differ by a power of 2.

4.11, where we see four processors operating on adjacent pairs of data. When the algorithm requires subscript differences to halve, the data emerge from the processors on the left-hand ports and reenter the right-hand ports after a perfect shuffle. When the algorithm requires subscript differences to double, the data exit from the right-hand ports of each processor and reenter the destination processors at the left ports after an inverse perfect shuffle.

Figure 4.12(a) shows a possible architecture for a processor shown in Fig. 4.11. The processor in this figure accepts data from its left-hand ports, combines the data internally, then produces output data on its right-hand ports. If we label the two inputs x_0 and x_1 as shown in Fig. 4.12(a), then the outputs y_0 and y_1 are equal respectively to $F(x_0, x_1)$ and $G(x_0, x_1)$. A straight connection shown in Fig. 4.12(b) is obtained by choosing $F(x_0, x_1) = x_0$, and $G(x_0, x_1) = x_1$. The exchange interconnection shown in Fig. 4.12(c) is obtained by making $F(x_0, x_1) = x_1$, and $G(x_0, x_1) = x_0$.

A reasonable model for the architecture of a processor is for there to be several built-in functions for F and G, possibly including the straight

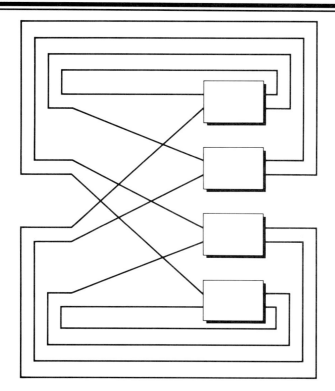

Fig. 4.11 A bidirectional parallel computer for iterating perfect shuffles and inverse perfect shuffles.

connection and the exchange connection show in Fig. 4.12, and possibly including other functions. Programming the processors involves selecting particular built-in functions or constructing complex functions as sequences of simple functions, so that the output of a processor is a pair of data that depends in some complex way on the pair of input data, and perhaps on other factors, including the current iteration count or the location of the processor within a collection of processors.

The perfect-shuffle structure shown in Fig. 4.11 was conceived independently by Batcher [1968] for a sorting network and by both Singleton [1967] and Pease [1968] for Fourier transforms. Singleton produced a program for fast Fourier transforms whose internal data flow is described by a sequence of shuffles. Pease developed a similar idea into the structure of a parallel processor for Fourier transforms that is much like the system shown in Fig. 4.11.

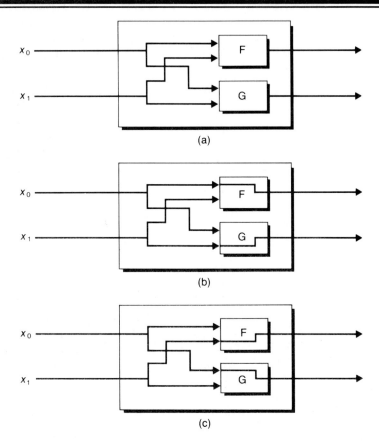

Fig. 4.12 Elements of the perfect-shuffle system in Fig. 4.11:
(a) A processor structure;
(b) Pass-through functions for F and G; and
(c) Swap functions for F and G.

Although these results point to the use of the perfect shuffle in specific contexts, the following discussion shows that the perfect shuffle is useful in a broad sense for parallel computation because it has crucial characteristics required by many parallel algorithms. Our discussion of the perfect shuffle follows the development of Stone [1971].

Although the discussion gives the general idea of what happens to data after one or more shuffles, clearly we need to be more specific and verify that the pairs of data brought together at each processor are indeed the pairs that we intend to bring together. We need a way to track each datum as it is shuffled by the network.

A very simple means for calculating the trajectory of a datum while undergoing a sequence of shuffles is illustrated in Fig. 4.13. This figure depicts a cyclic shift register with three stages, and the discussion that follows is for an n-stage shift register. The operation of the shift register is very simple. Each cell holds a single bit. During each clock period the bits shift to the left in the register, with the leading bit moving cyclically back to the low-order position, as shown in the figure. The purpose of the shift register is to model the movement of data in a system that treats $N = 2^n$ operands concurrently, such as the system shown in Fig. 4.10 for $N = 8$.

In any column of registers, number the input values from top to bottom with the integers 0 through $N - 1$. If we pass the data through the shuffle interconnection once, twice, or more, can we predict the destination of each datum? The obvious way to find the destination of each datum is to trace the path through the network. But the shift register in Fig. 4.13 gives us a much easier way to find the destination when N is a power of 2.

The following observation dates from Stone [1971].

> Consider a datum on the ith input line of a rank of registers in a perfect-shuffle network of the type shown in Fig. 4.10. To find the destination of that item after k shuffles, place the binary representation of i in the shift register shown in Fig. 4.13. Then shift the register cyclically to the left k times. The destination of the datum is input line j, where j is the number whose binary representation appears in the shift register after k left cyclic shifts.

For example, consider the datum on Line 5. After one shuffle, that datum moves to Line 3, and we note that the left cyclic shift of (1,0,1), which is the binary representation of 5, is (0,1,1), which is the binary representation of 3. Similarly, after a second shift, the item moves to input Line 6, as shown in Fig.

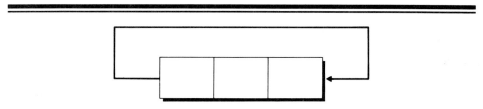

Fig. 4.13 A three-stage shift register that shows the trajectory of items permuted by a perfect shuffle for $N = 8$. Put the index of an item in the register. A shuffle of the item moves the item to the index obtained by a left cyclic shift of the register.

4.10. But this is predicted by the shift register in Fig. 4.13 because, after two cyclic shifts to the left, (1,0,1) becomes (1,1,0), the binary representation of 6.

Why is this property true? Consider any item with an index less than $N/2$ in the vector just prior to a shuffle. The index position must have the binary representation $(0, \ldots)$. The shuffle operation separates adjacent items so that they reach destinations that lie two apart after the shuffle. Therefore the shuffle operation applied to elements with an index less than $N/2$ moves the element in Position i to Position $2i + C$ for some constant C. By inspection, Position 0 is shuffled to Position 0, and Position 1 is shuffled to Position 2. Hence, constant C must be 0 for the items with an index less than $N/2$.

Similarly, consider any item whose index is at least $N/2$. The shuffle moves elements in this half of the vector from Position i to Position $2i + C$, where C is a constant that is not necessarily equal to the constant C that holds for the other half of the vector. In this case, Positions $N - 2$ and $N - 1$ are moved, respectively, to Positions $N - 3$ and $N - 1$, so we conclude that $C = - N + 1$ for elements in this half of the vector.

To summarize the effect of a shuffle, we have:

$$\text{Shuffle } (i) = 2i, \quad \text{if } i < \frac{N}{2}$$

$$\text{Shuffle } (i) = 2i - N + 1, \quad \text{if } i \geq \frac{N}{2}$$

Now consider what happens in the shift register when its initial state is $(0, \ldots)$ and the register is shifted cyclically to the left. The resulting state is $(\ldots , 0)$. But this is identical to doubling the representation of the initial state. Hence, for any item whose index is less than $N/2$, the shift register correctly predicts the destination of the item after a shuffle.

For the remaining case, since $N = 2^n$, each binary representation of the indices in the shuffle vector has n bits. If an item has an index at least as large as $N/2$, then the binary representation of the index is $(1, b_{n-2}, \ldots , b_0)$, and the left cyclic shift produces the representation $(b_{n-2}, \ldots , b_0, 1)$. This is almost double the index.

In fact, doubling the index produces the binary representation of length $n + 1$ of the form $(1, b_{n-2}, \ldots , b_0, 0)$, which differs in value from the left cyclic shift by the leading bit and the least-significant bit. Therefore, if we double the index, drop the leading bit, and change the least-significant bit from 0 to 1, we create the left cyclic shift. This is equivalent to doubling index i, subtracting $2^n = N$, and adding 1, which is precisely the destination index for those items whose indices are at least as large as $N/2$.

This discussion has defined the perfect shuffle and the shift-register property, but the value of the shuffle is not clear until we see how the shuffle fits the needs of applications. That is the subject of the next section.

4.5.2 Applications of the Perfect Shuffle

The following discussion shows that the perfect shuffle is ideally suited to the communication needs of several parallel algorithms. In fact, the perfect shuffle is a "neighborhood" interconnection pattern in which the neighborhood halves after a shuffle and doubles after an inverse shuffle.

To understand the utility of the perfect shuffle, we examine how a sequence of shuffles brings together different pairs of data. The ability to track items with the cyclic shift-register representation is extremely useful for observing how a sequence of shuffles permutes the elements of a vector.

Consider, for example, a parallel processor of the form shown in Fig. 4.12(a). Initially, two items whose indices differ only in the least-significant bit lie within each computation unit. Now consider an algorithm that must first bring together those items whose positions differ by their leading bit, then those items whose positions differ in their next leading bit, and so forth, with the last iteration bringing together those items whose positions differ in their least-significant bit. For a vector of length of 8, this algorithm pairs 0–4, 1–5, 2–6, and 3–7 in the first iteration, then pairs 0–2, 1–3, 4–6, and 5–7, and then pairs 0–1, 2–3, 4–5, and 6–7.

Using the shift-register analysis, we can easily see that if the vector initially is in the state 0, 1, 2, ... , 7, then after one shuffle the items paired differ in the leading bit of the representations of their initial indices. Consider, for example, the items at index positions 0 and 4 before a shuffle. The indices differ only in the leading bit of the binary representation, assuming that $N = 8$.

After the shuffle, the shift-register analogy indicates that the item at Position 0 remains in place, and the item at Position 4 is moved to Position 1. Note that the destination indices 0 and 1 differ only in their least-significant bits. Consequently, two items in positions whose indices differ only in the leading bit will be brought together at some processor after one shuffle. Similarly, after two shuffles, the items paired at a processor differ only in the second-most-significant bit of their initial index representations.

The fast Fourier transform can be implemented efficiently on a parallel computer that has the perfect shuffle [Singleton 1967; Pease 1968]. For this application, the F and G functions in Fig. 4.12(a) produce a weighted sum and difference of the inputs. In fact, $F = x_0 + w \times x_1$ and $G = x_0 - w \times x_1$, where all operations are on complex numbers, and the weighting factor w is a function of the iteration number and the processor position in the parallel computer.

For $N = 2^n$, the transform is complete after n iterations through the processor shown in Fig. 4.12(a). However, the items in the output vector are not arranged in ascending order by index in the processor at the conclusion of the n iterations. They have to be permuted to bring them into index order, and the perfect shuffle is very poorly suited for the final permutation. In processors specialized for Fourier transforms, it may be necessary to add a set of interconnections to facilitate the final permutation required for the algorithm.

Both recursive doubling and cyclic reduction seem to require a flow of data opposite from the one just described for the fast Fourier transform. These algorithms need to combine data whose indices differ in the least significant bit, then data whose indices differ in the two least-significant bits, and so forth.

Indeed data does flow in the opposite direction in these algorithms, and we make use of the *inverse perfect shuffle*, which is obtained by moving data from right to left in the network shown in Fig. 4.10. For example, to form the sum of N items, at each iteration we let the F and G functions in Fig. 4.12(a) form the sum of their inputs. But instead of using the perfect-shuffle connections after a summation step, we reverse the data flow and use the inverse perfect-shuffle connections. After n steps, we have the sum of $N = 2^n$ items in each element of the vector.

A very simple modification of this basic idea produces not only the sum of N items, but the sum of the first i items for each i less than N. The modification is shown in Fig. 4.14. There are eight processors in this system, and they are interconnected both cyclically and with an inverse perfect shuffle. Because of the cyclic connection, each processor can accept as an operand the contents of the accumulator from the processor whose index is one less or one greater. The inverse shuffle connection permutes the data among processors.

Figure 4.15 shows a computation unrolled in time, with inverse shuffles occurring between addition operations. Each addition adds the contents of the accumulator from one processor to the accumulator in the processor immediately below. The shaded processors leave their contents unchanged. For $N = 8$, there are three iterations, each consisting of an addition and an inverse shuffle.

The notation (i, j) shown at the processor inputs and outputs indicates that the corresponding wire carries the sum of positions i through j. The fact that this structure can produce all partial sums follows because the items combined at the first stage have indices that differ by 1, and at the ith stage the indices differ by 2^i. So, except for the shaded processors, each processor at Stage i produces the sum of 2^i consecutive positions. The shaded processors take into account the boundary conditions, and they do no summing.

Compare Fig. 4.15 with Fig. 4.8(b). The computations are the same but the difference in the two figures is due to the interconnections. The interconnections in Fig. 4.8(b) differ from stage to stage, but Fig. 4.15 uses identical interconnections at every stage. Hence, one stage of interconnections used repeatedly is sufficient to implement Fig. 4.15, but Fig. 4.8(b) must have O(log N) stages of interconnections. Note also that the shaded processors in Fig. 4.15 correspond to those processors in Fig. 4.8(b) whose inputs have a 0 forced on them.

The perfect shuffle combined with a cyclic shift or a pair-wise exchange operation provides full communication among processors in the following sense.

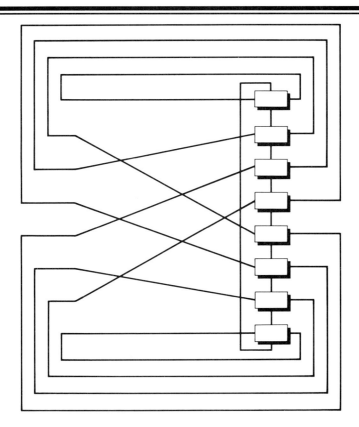

Fig. 4.14 A parallel computer for computing partial sums. The connections are the inverse perfect shuffle and cyclic shift.

Every processor in an N-processor system can reach every other processor by means of a path of a length no longer than $\log_2 N$.

Consider Fig. 4.16, which shows an eight-processor pattern unrolled in time for three time units. The interconnection pattern shown is a perfect shuffle, followed by a module that can either do a pair-wise exchange or pass the two inputs straight through to the outputs. At the left side of the diagram, Processor 3 is shown shaded, and moving from left-to-right, each processor accessible from Processor 3 at that particular time is shown shaded.

Note that Processor 3 can reach all other processors in 3 time steps. In fact, every processor on the left can reach any other processor on the right in three time steps because each processor is the root of a binary tree that at successive

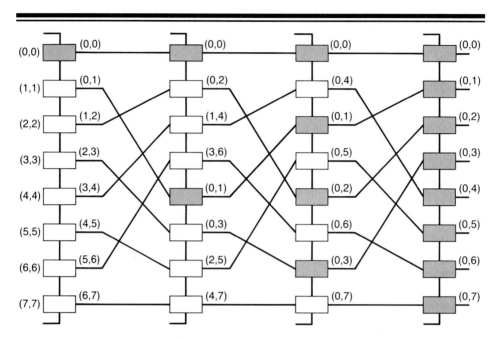

Fig. 4.15 A computation performed by the computer depicted in Fig. 4.14. Shaded modules do not use the cyclic shift connection.

stages in the network touches two, then four, then finally all eight processors. The depth of such a tree in an N-processor network is $\log_2 N$.

This particular property of the shuffle-exchange network follows from the shift-register description of the trajectories within a perfect-shuffle network. Figure 4.17 shows a three-stage register that contains the binary representation of the number 3. A left cyclic shift of this register corresponds to a perfect shuffle, and the complement of the rightmost bit of the register corresponds to a pair-wise exchange.

To track any datum from Processor 3 through the network in Fig. 4.16 after any shuffle or exchange, we simply apply the corresponding left cyclic shift or bit complement to the register in Fig. 4.17, and the resulting register contents will be the binary representation of the new position of the datum.

To move a datum from Processor 3 to an arbitrary processor in the system, we force the binary representation of the destination processor into the register in Fig. 4.17. To do so, we force the register to agree with the destination index one bit at a time, starting with the most-significant bit position.

For example, to find a path from Processor 3 to Processor 4, shift the

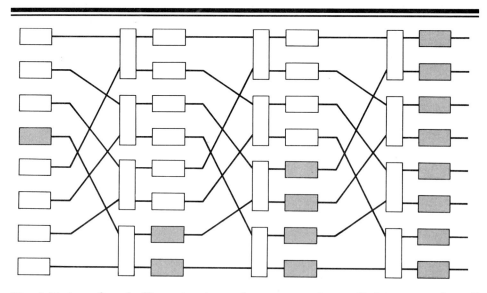

Fig. 4.16 A perfect-shuffle, pair-wise-exchange network unrolled in time. The tall rectangles depict modules that can exchange their inputs. Shaded modules are reachable from Processor 3 via some sequence of shuffles and exchanges.

register whose initial contents are (0,1,1) and obtain the new value of (1,1,0). This shift corresponds to an initial shuffle applied to the data in the processors. The final bit position of the shift register is to be forced to agree with the leading bit position of the destination index. The destination index is 4, and its binary representation is (1,0,0). The leading bit is a 1, which differs from the current least-significant bit in the shift register. Consequently, we apply a pair-wise exchange, which is represented as a complement of the final bit. The shift register now contains (1,1,1), and the last bit of the shift register is the first bit of the destination index.

For the next iteration, we cycle the register again and compare the final bit in the shift register to the next bit of the destination. If the bits agree, no bit complement is done. If the bits differ, we complement the bit in the register to force it to agree with the corresponding bit in the destination index. In this example, the left shift of (1,1,1) produces (1,1,1). The least-significant bit is 1, but the next bit of the destination index 4 is a 0.

As in the previous iteration, we apply a pair-wise exchange and represent this operation by complementing the last bit of the shift register. The shift register now contains (1,1,0), and the datum has been moved to index position 6. The reader can verify that the next shuffle changes the shift register to

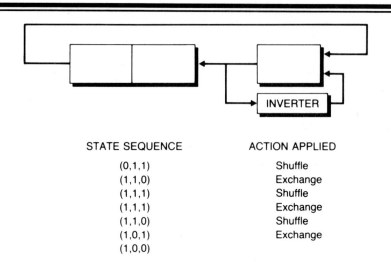

STATE SEQUENCE	ACTION APPLIED
(0,1,1)	Shuffle
(1,1,0)	Exchange
(1,1,1)	Shuffle
(1,1,1)	Exchange
(1,1,0)	Shuffle
(1,0,1)	Exchange
(1,0,0)	

Fig. 4.17 A shift register for analyzing the perfect shuffle and pair-wise exchange. A left cyclic shift corresponds to a shuffle. Inverting the right-most bit corresponds to a pair-wise exchange. The state sequence shows an initial state, and the subsequent states obtained after a shuffle or exchange. The final state is the index of the item in the shuffle-exchange network after the item has undergone the corresponding sequence of shuffles and exchanges.

(1,0,1), and that a pair-wise exchange changes the register to (1,0,0), which is the binary representation of the desired final destination.

Observe that each left cyclic shift corresponds to a shuffle, and each bit complement corresponds to a pair-wise exchange. After at most $\log_2 N$ shuffles and exchanges, the contents of the shift register can be placed into an arbitrary state. Consequently, the datum initially located in Processor 3 can be moved to an arbitrary processor.

In fact, the datum in any processor can be moved to any other processor in at most $\log_2 N$ shuffles and exchanges. However, in general, we may not be able to move any two or more items to arbitrary positions in $\log_2 N$ steps because the trajectories required might collide at some common point within the network.

Figure 4.17 shows the successive steps required to move a datum from Processor 3 to Processor 4. Compare the shift-register model in Fig. 4.17 with the actual flow of data in Fig. 4.16 and note the exact correspondence of the two models.

Recall from our earlier discussion that some computations, such as the fast

Fourier transform, the solution to Poisson's equation, and sorting have the full communication property, which causes each output to depend on all inputs. Note that the perfect shuffle provides a means for supporting this communication, and it does so at a much lower cost than the cost of a network that connects all processors directly to each other.

As a final example of an application of the perfect shuffle, we show a scheme due to Batcher [1968] for sorting. Obviously, sorting can be done in a processor that uses near-neighbor connections exclusively, but the worst-case time to sort in such a processor is proportional to the length of the longest path. Near-neighbor connections tend to produce long paths, although two- and three-dimensional connections decrease this length over one-dimensional connections. But the perfect shuffle can be used to decrease the worst-case time below that of near-neighbor connections.

Figure 4.18 shows a structure for sorting a vector of data that is constrained in a special way. A vector of data is called *bitonic* if

- The elements of the vector increase monotonically, then decrease monotonically (either the increasing or decreasing portions may be empty); or

- The elements of the vector are a cyclic shift of a vector that satisfies Property 1.

The structure in Fig. 4.18 is a called a *bitonic sorter* because it produces a fully sorted output when the input vector is bitonic. The initial operation in the bitonic sorter is a shuffle. This aligns the second half of the vector with the first half. The pairs are compared, and the smaller item of each pair is transmitted to the upper output. The larger item of each pair is transmitted to the lower

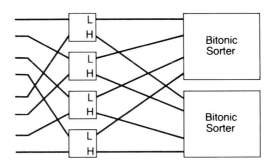

Fig. 4.18 The structure of a bitonic sorter. The comparators route the low value to the upper output and the high value to the lower output.

output. Then the data are passed through an inverse shuffle and enter two bitonic sorters, each capable of sorting half as many data as the full structure.

Figure 4.18 is recursive in the sense that the structure of the bitonic sorter for $N/2$ items has the same structure as the original sorter. The smallest bitonic sorter is the bitonic sorter for a single pair of data. It is a single comparator that places the smaller of a pair on the upper output and the larger of a pair on the lower output.

To prove that the bitonic sorter is indeed able to sort bitonic sequences, it is necessary to show that after the comparison and inverse shuffle, each of the vectors input to the smaller bitonic sorters are bitonic. Moreover, every element of the upper bitonic vector does not exceed any element of the lower bitonic vector, so if the upper and lower vectors are each sorted independently, and if the resulting sorted vectors are concatenated, then the final vector will be fully sorted. This proof is one of the problems at the end of this chapter; we omit the discussion in the body of the text.

To create a full sorter from a bitonic sorter, you can build up bitonic sequences from smaller ones. Figure 4.19 shows how to build a bitonic sequence of length 4 from two sorted sequences of length 2. The trick is to sort one sequence into ascending order and one into descending order, then concatenate the sequences. The shaded pattern designates a comparator that places its larger input value at the top output, which is exactly the opposite of the behavior of the unshaded comparators.

Figure 4.20 shows how to construct an eight-sorter with perfect-shuffle interconnections. The computation is unrolled in time. It actually is done with a single vector of $N/2$ comparators with the vector of N outputs fed back to the N inputs through a perfect-shuffle interconnection pattern.

The first comparison produces two bitonic sequences of length 4 by sorting pairs of inputs into ascending and descending sequences, with the shaded modules producing descending sequences. The next three comparisons produce a bitonic sequence of length 8, by sorting the two bitonic sequences of length 4 in ascending and descending order, respectively. The last three stages

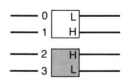

Fig. 4.19 A method for building a bitonic sequence of length 4 by sorting two sequences of length 2 in opposite ways, then concatenating the results.

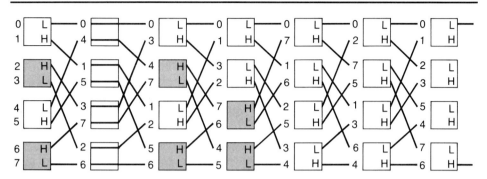

Fig. 4.20 A bitonic sorter unrolled in time. The second stage performs no comparisons.

sort the bitonic sequence of length 8 into a single sequence sorted in ascending order.

In general, a set of $\log_2 N$ stages accepts bitonic sequences at the input of the set and produces half as many bitonic sequences, each double the length of the input bitonic sequences. The last set of stages is a bitonic sorter for sequences of length N. Since there are $O(\log N)$ sets of stages required to increase bitonic sequences from length 2 to length N, and since each set contains $O(\log N)$ stages, the total number of stages through which data pass is $O((\log N)^2)$. Compare this with the sorting time of $O(N)$ for a one-dimensional near-neighbor connection, and it becomes clear that the perfect shuffle has a great advantage for large N, although for small N, the near-neighbor connection may be quite competitive.

The thrust of our discussion is that the perfect-shuffle interconnection pattern is potentially useful to incorporate in a system. Variations of this particular pattern may be equally useful, but may have other more attractive properties in terms of implementation.

Preparata and Vuillemin [1981] describe a scheme called *cube-connected cycles*, which is an interconnection scheme that provides the interconnectivity of the perfect shuffle, but uses area more efficiently when implemented in VLSI.

The perfect shuffle interconnection has been used in various computers for research projects and in a few commercial releases. The Butterfly processor [Crowther *et al.* 1985] from Bolt, Beranek, and Newman connects up to 128 processors with an interconnection scheme equivalent to the shuffle exchange. The RP3 at IBM [Pfister *et al.* 1985] planned to use the perfect shuffle embellished with other processing capabilities, described later in this text. The actual implementation connects 64 processors by means of a perfect-shuffle interconnection network but some of the additional features were dropped from the implementation.

Although our discussion suggests that the perfect shuffle has good qualities for parallel processing, the good qualities come at some expense. Physical packaging is very important and can have a major impact on the practical implementation of the perfect shuffle. Because the distance between two points connected by a perfect shuffle is potentially very long, propagation effects are potentially disruptive for a perfect shuffle, whereas the near-neighbor two-dimensional mesh connection is much less susceptible to this problem because all interconnection lengths are held to small values.

Another problem for the perfect shuffle is that cable density can be very high, forcing the designer to provide cabling paths that tend to increase the physical volume of a system and thereby contribute to longer propagation delays for interprocessor communication. When the perfect shuffle is implemented in VLSI, the equivalent problem is one of interconnection density, and indeed the interconnection area in a two-dimensional layout of the perfect shuffle may well be much larger than the area devoted to the active nodes connected by the shuffle.

The relative attractiveness of a perfect-shuffle connection when compared to a two-dimensional mesh or other similar near-neighbor connection is highly dependent on the implementation technology. The perfect shuffle has an advantage over near-neighbor mesh connections when propagation delays on long cables are small compared to node-to-node delays experienced when sending data between two remote points via a sequence of near-neighbor moves. With new developments coming at a rapid rate, at any given time the current technology could favor either near-neighbor connections or perfect-shuffle connections.

As an example of the effective use of mesh connections, Kung and Leiserson [1978] proposed a highly efficient VLSI implementation of parallel processing that they call *systolic arrays*. These are near-neighbor connected arrays of very simple processors. The geometry is typically a rectangular or hexagonal geometry, but could be any repetitive geometry in two dimensions. The data flows through the array of processors in a pipeline mode.

The high efficiency of this type of implementation increases the attractiveness of near-neighbor connections, but the utility of such devices is limited to the calculations that fit the specific array geometries. Nevertheless, such devices could be put in high production and swing the cost-performance pendulum to favor near-neighbor communication. On the other hand, breakthroughs in optical transmission and optical switching may swing the balance towards the perfect-shuffle. Such advances would make communication faster over the longer interconnections, and reduce the cost of sending data much further than the nearest neighbor.

Consequently, new advances in architectures for the continuum model are driven by the advances yet to come in devices and communications.

4.6 Architectures for the Continuum Model—Which Direction?

The continuum model is a natural model for parallelism. Near-neighbor interactions can be modeled by networks of processors connected together as near-neighbors. The advantage of the near-neighbor structure is very strong for those problems that are ideally matched to such a structure.

In a broad spectrum of problems, as the fit becomes less ideal, the performance of near-neighbor connections becomes poorer and poorer, to the extent that gains due to parallel execution are offset by the inefficient use of hardware. Here are the basic choices available to the architect:

1. Build a highly specialized, near-neighbor architecture that is very fast and effective for some class of problems within the continuum model.
2. Build a somewhat more general machine, but maintain high speed for the continuum model. Provide extra capability through richer interconnections, such as the perfect shuffle, and through other mechanisms that provide speed enhancement for problems that fall outside the continuum model.
3. Build a very general parallel machine that has broad applicability, including the continuum model, although its speed for continuum calculations may not be as high as for an architecture specialized for the class of problems.

The potential size of the user community increases by one to two orders of magnitude as you move from the first to the second choice, and again as you move from the second to the third choice. A large user base tends to provide cost reductions to each user because they have to support a much smaller share of the hardware and software development costs.

A large demand also provides greater profit motivation, but if a designer chooses to serve the large community and produces a fairly general architecture, the users who absolutely need a machine for the continuum model will be unsatisfied if the general architecture is significantly slower than an architecture specialized for the continuum model. Moreover, this same user group will question the value to themselves of the hardware and software that support the more general classes of problems, since this group of users may be paying for these aspects of the computer system and yet derive no discernible benefit from them.

Which community should the architect serve? There is no obvious answer to this question. The architect should be prepared to build any of the possible machines, from the most specialized to the most general, each optimized for the best possible cost and performance for that architecture.

Market forces and other priorities will dictate which machine actually gets built. Some developers will choose the most general approach, and hope to install many copies of a machine. Some developers will choose to a carve a niche for their ideas by producing a relatively small number of copies of a highly specialized machine. Yet other developers may choose a design that falls in between.

Whichever choice is made, the architecture has to be cost-effective for the user community. For the smaller markets, a significant portion of the challenge is to keep hardware and software development costs low, so that these costs when amortized over copies actually sold are still within reasonable bounds. Thus, not only must the architect produce a cost-effective design, but the design process itself must be done efficiently.

One important observation from this chapter is that what appears to be an ideal architecture for a class of problems may not be ideal at all. An architect who produces a machine that executes a particular code very efficiently may be somewhat disappointed when research advances in basic algorithms produce a new, efficient solution technique not at all suited to the specific architecture. In such a case the very specialized machine may have difficulty competing with a less specialized machine that happens to be able to run the more efficient algorithm.

Breakthroughs do occur from time to time, such as with the formulation of the fast Fourier transform [Cooley and Tukey 1965]. The more specialized the architecture, the more susceptible it is to competitive methods when breakthroughs do occur. The architect of the specialized machine has to assess the risk of a breakthrough. For the continuum model, the risks are high enough to merit attention.

In recent years, algorithm improvements have changed the basic flow of data in various solution techniques, have altered the grid structure that models the continuum, and have even provided for multiple grid spacing. A machine built specifically for algorithms of 20 years ago would do relatively poorly when executing some of the new algorithms for the same problems.

As an example of the evolution of parallel algorithms, the fast algorithms for the continuum model described earlier in this chapter may make better use of connection patterns like the perfect shuffle than of connection patterns that are near-neighbor mesh connections, but the near-neighbor connections were the backbone for the first large-scale computers for the continuum. Another step in the evolution is represented by the Cosmic Cube described earlier in this chapter, which in a sense combines the near-neighbor interconnections and the perfect shuffle. It uses near-neighbor connections in six dimensions, but at best only three of those dimensions lead to short interconnections in a three-dimensional packaging world. The other three dimensions force interconnections to have relatively long physical lengths.

The six-dimensional connection structure of the Cosmic Cube gives the same adjacency pattern achieved by the perfect shuffle. The difference is that all dimensions are adjacent at all times in a Cosmic Cube, whereas the adjacency changes in time in a perfect shuffle structure. Because processors that are directly connected within a Cosmic Cube have indices that differ by a single power of 2, this structure is well suited for recursive doubling, cyclic reduction, Fourier transforms, and other applications mentioned in this section.

Hoshino [1989], on the other hand, has shown that for the general class of scientific calculations the overwhelming majority of processor-to-processor interactions occur across near-neighbor links on a two-dimensional mesh. The additional connectivity provided by a hypercube and the greater distances spanned by the perfect shuffle rarely come into play, and provide only a marginal decrease in the number of operations while contributing greatly to cost. He provides a strong case for two-dimensional mesh connections based on extensive experience in implementing scientific applications. Even though his applications occasionally force some processors to communicate over long distances, this happens sufficiently infrequently that it degrades performance only slightly. Hence, Hoshino's case rests on the fact that the communication constraints imposed by a two-dimensional mesh do not degrade performance of actual programs. Indeed, his PAX architecture is a compromise between the ILLIAC IV and Cosmic Cube architectures, incorporating some good features of each together with some features unique to PAX.

Nevertheless, experience with parallel applications is still rather limited but growing every year. New techniques and new algorithms are still appearing in abundance. As these appear, they force us to rethink our conclusions on what combination of algorithms, architecture, applications produce an efficient way to solve problems.

In summary, there is no obvious best design for parallel processors for the continuum model. The available approaches depend on how specialized the processing system can be. A processor for the continuum model undoubtedly will be somewhat specialized—it will probably have an interconnection system to speed up typical programs for this model. Which approach, if any, becomes dominant is most likely to depend on the directions of device technology in the coming years, with near-neighbor structures dependent on VLSI advances and perfect-shuffle structures dependent on advances in interconnections technology.

Exercises

4.1 The object of this exercise is explore calculations for the continuum model. Assume that you have a square array of points, 9 × 9, and that the value of the potential function on the boundary is 0 on the top row, and is 10 along all other boundary points.

   a) Initialize the potential function to 0 on all interior points. Calculate the Poisson solution for the values of all interior points by replacing each interior point with the average value of each of its neighboring points. Compute the new values for all interior points before updating any interior points. Run this simulation for five iterations and show the answers you obtain at the end. Note: The values on the boundary are fixed and do not change during the computation.

b) Repeat the process in the previous problem, except update a point as soon as you have computed the new value and use the new value when you reach a neighboring point. You should scan the interior points row by row from top to bottom and from left to right within rows.

c) The second process seems to converge faster. Give an intuitive explanation of why this might be the case.

d) How do your findings relate to the interconnection structure of a processor for solving this problem?

4.2 The purpose of this exercise is to show the effect of information propagation within a calculation. Use the Poisson problem of Exercise 4.1 and write a computer program that iterates until no point value changes by more than 0.1 percent. Let this be the initial state of the problem for the following exercises.

a) Increase the boundary point at the upper left corner to a new value of 20. Perform five iterations of the Poisson solver and observe the values obtained.

b) Now restore the mesh to the initial state for a. Change the program so that, in effect, the upper left corner is rotated to the bottom right corner. To do this, scan the rows from right to left instead of left to right and scan from bottom to top instead of top to bottom. Perform five iterations of the Poisson solver and observe the values obtained.

c) Both a and b eventually converge to the same solution because the initial data are the same and the physical process modeled is the same. However, the results obtained from a and b are different after five iterations. Explain why they are different. Which of the two problems has faster convergence? Why?

4.3 The purpose of this exercise is to examine the cyclic-reduction algorithm. Explore the solution of a one-dimensional Poisson problem by treating 15 points on a line. Let the left boundary point have the value 10 and the right boundary have the value 0. Each intermediate point has a value that is the average of its immediate neighbors.

a) Write a matrix equation of the form $\mathbf{Ax} = \mathbf{b}$ that describes this problem.

b) Simulate an iterative process that updates each interior point with the average of its neighboring points. Obtain the interior values of points for the first three iterations of the technique previously used, in which each interior point is updated by the average of its neighbors.

c) Now apply the cyclic reduction algorithm in the text for three iterations to find one equation for the point in the middle. Solve this equation and use three iterations of back substitution to find the remainder of the points. Show your solution and the equations you obtain after one iteration. (Hint: The first iteration should produce new equations for points 2, 4, 6, 8, 10, 12, and 14. The second iteration produces new equations for 4, 8, and 12.)

d) Compare the results produced in b and c with respect to the precision obtained. Count and compare the total number of additions, multiplications, and divisions for each algorithm after three iterations.

e) Explain from an intuitive point of view why cyclic reduction yields high speed and high precision as compared to the near-neighbor iteration. What implications can you draw with regard to interconnections for processors for solving the Poisson problem?

4.4 The purpose of this exercise is to investigate how to implement conditional branches in an array computer. Program 4.1 does not show instructions that determine if convergence has been reached. The instructions should determine if every processor has obtained a satisfactory solution, and, if not, the program should branch back to the top of the loop.

a) Write the instructions that do this job, inventing the instructions as you need them. Describe the operation of each instruction that you invent.

b) Redraw the block diagram of the ILLIAC IV computer and describe the data flow on the block diagram necessary to support the test for termination.

c) Assume that the control processor of the ILLIAC IV can execute its instructions in parallel with instructions that are broadcast to the 64 numerical processors. Can any or all instructions of the termination test be overlapped with the calculation of a loop iteration? If so, describe how to implement the instructions in your program and in Program 4.1 to facilitate this overlapped execution.

4.5 The purpose of this exercise is to explore the interconnection structure of a hypercube computer such as the Cosmic Cube. Assume that you are to calculate all partial sums of i items up to the sum of 64 items.

a) Construct a program for a Cosmic Cube computer system that performs this operation in a time that grows as $O(\log N)$ if the number of processors is N. Assume that every node in the computer executes the same program, although the program can be slightly different from node to node since the processors in a Cosmic Cube are independent. Show explicitly the instructions that send and receive data between processors. Invent instructions as you need them and describe what the instructions do. Include some type of instruction for synchronization that forces a processor to be idle until a neighboring processor sends a message or a datum that enables computation to continue.

b) Which communication steps if any in your answer require communications with processors that are not among the six processors directly connected to a given processor? How do you propose to implement such communication in software (assuming that the hardware itself does not provide remote communication as a basic instruction)?

4.6 The purpose of this exercise is to examine the recursive doubling solution to a linear tridiagonal system of equations. Consider the solution of the equation $\mathbf{Ax} = \mathbf{b}$, where $\mathbf{A}$ is a tridiagonal equation.

a) Prove that the recurrence in Eq. (4.15) is a correct expression for the major diagonal of matrix $\mathbf{U}$ in an **LU** decomposition of $\mathbf{A}$.

b) Using recursive doubling, show all of the steps required to factor **A** into **LU** and to solve the equations **Ly** = **b** and **Ux** = **y**. For each major step of the algorithm, show the basic recurrence solution. Show the mathematical formulation of your solution and indicate the basic operation in the recursive-doubling iteration.

4.7 Find a recursive-doubling technique for solving Eq. (4.13).

4.8 The purpose of this exercise is to explore some of the properties of the perfect-shuffle interconnection scheme.

a) Consider a processor that has the perfect shuffle and pair-wise exchange connections shown in Fig. 4.16. For an eight-processor system, show that the permutation that cyclically shifts the input vector by three positions is realizable by some setting of the exchange modules. Draw the network unrolled in time to show the setting that realizes this permutation.

b) Repeat *a* to show that a cyclical shift of two positions is realizable.

c) Prove that a shuffle-exchange network can realize any cyclical shift in $\log_2 N$ iterations for an N-processor system when N is a power of 2.

4.9 Find a means for evaluating a polynomial of degree $N - 1$ in the variable x in parallel on an N-processor computer that uses the shuffle-exchange interconnection pattern. Assume that N is a power of 2.

4.10 Prove that the scheme shown in Fig. 4.18 produces a sorted sequence of length N from a bitonic sequence of length N. Specifically, prove that after the comparison and exchange is performed, each sequence of length $N/2$ is bitonic and all elements of one sequence do not exceed the value of any element of the other sequence.

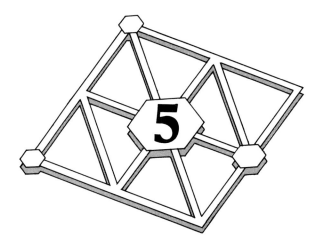

Vector Computers

5.1 A Generic Vector Process

5.2 Access Patterns for Numerical Algorithms

5.3 Data-Structuring Techniques for Vector Machines

5.4 Attached Vector-Processors

5.5 Sparse-Matrix Techniques

5.6 The GF-11—A Very High Speed Vector Processor

5.7 Final Comments on Vector Computers

The last chapter introduces the idea of building a parallel architecture matched to a specific class of problems. The discussion there mentions that there are two major models of numerical processes—a continuum model based on near-neighbor interactions and a particle model based on discrete point-to-point interactions. The major emphasis of Chapter 4 is the continuum model, together with the architectures that support processing of near-neighbor interactions for that model.

This chapter extends the discussion of numerical architectures to vector computers with the idea that these computers can be used for the majority of continuum-model problems, as well as for many particle-model problems. The vector computer has emerged as the most important high-performance architecture for numerical problems. It has the two key qualities of efficiency and wide applicability.

Most vector computers have a pipelined structure. When one pipeline is not sufficient to achieve desired performance, designers have occasionally provided multiple pipelines. Such processors not only support a streaming mode of data flow through a single pipeline, they also support fully parallel operation by allowing multiple pipelines to execute concurrently on independent streams of data.

By the mid-1980s, more than twenty manufacturers offered vector processors based on pipeline arithmetic units. They ranged from relatively inexpensive auxiliary processors attached to microcomputers to high-speed supercomputers with computation rates from 100 Mflops to rates in excess of 1000 Mflops. (One *Mflops* is 10^6 floating-point operations per second.)

The price-performance ratio of these vector processors is rather remarkable because they yield one to two orders of magnitude increased throughput for vector computations when compared to serial processors of equal cost. But this throughput increase is limited to the problems that fit the architecture— that is, to problems that can be structured as a sequence of vector operations whose characteristics make efficient use of the facilities available.

Many of the supercomputers are also high-performance serial processors for general-purpose problems, but the throughput of these supercomputers on nonvector problems is only a few times greater than the throughput of more conventional high-speed serial processors. In fact, although throughput might be high because of fast device technology, if a vector-structured supercomputer is used exclusively on nonvector problems, the computational cost may be excessive because this cost includes the cost of the vector facilities, which presumably are left idle by scalar computations.

The purpose of this chapter is to describe the general architecture of vector machines and then describe how algorithms and architecture can be matched to each other to obtain efficient processing over large classes of computations.

5.1 A Generic Vector Processor

The basic idea of a vector processor is to combine two vectors, element by element, to produce an output vector. Thus, if **A, B,** and **C** are vectors, each with N elements, a vector processor can perform the operation

$$\mathbf{C} := \mathbf{A} + \mathbf{B}$$

which is interpreted to mean

$$c_i := a_i + b_i, \qquad 0 \le i \le N - 1$$

where the vector **C** can be written in component form as $(c_0, c_1, \ldots, c_{N-1})$. The form is similar for vectors **A** and **B**.

A very simplified way to implement this operation with a pipelined arithmetic unit is shown in Fig. 5.1. The two streams of data supplied to the

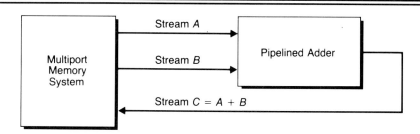

Fig. 5.1 A processor that is capable of adding two vectors by streaming the two vectors through a pipelined adder.

arithmetic unit carry the streams for **A** and **B,** respectively. The memory system supplies one element of **A** and **B** on every clock cycle, one element to each input stream. The arithmetic unit produces one output value during each clock cycle. (Actually, the input data rate need be only as fast as the output data rate. If the arithmetic unit can produce results at a rate of one output value every d cycles, then the input data rate need be only one input value on each stream every d cycles.)

Figure 5.1 shows only the barest details of the vector processor to indicate the general flow of data through the pipelines. The pipelined arithmetic unit is discussed in Section 3.4 and that unit is the core of the architecture in Fig. 5.1.

The difficulty, however, is the design of the memory system to sustain a continuous flow of data from memory to the arithmetic unit and the return flow of results from the arithmetic unit to memory. The majority of the architectural tricks used in vector processors are devoted to sustaining that flow of data and to scheduling sequences of operations to reduce the flow requirements.

In this example we assume a basic one-cycle rate for the delivery of operands, production of results, and restoring of the result data into memory. This calls for a memory system that can read two operands and write one operand in a single cycle.

Conventional random-access memories can perform at most one READ or one WRITE per cycle, so the memory system in Fig. 5.1 has at least three times the bandwidth of a conventional memory system. Of course this ignores any additional requirement for bandwidth for input/output operations. Also, we have ignored the bandwidth for instruction fetches, but a major advantage of a vector architecture is that a single instruction fetch can initiate a very long vector operation. Consequently, the bandwidth required to fetch instructions for a vector architecture is negligible as compared to the 20 to 50 percent of the bandwidth used for instruction fetches in conventional architectures.

The major problem facing the architect is to design a memory system that can meet the bandwidth requirements imposed by the arithmetic unit. Two major approaches have emerged in commercial vector machines.

1. Build the necessary bandwidth in main memory by using several independent memory modules to support concurrent access to independent data; or

2. Build an intermediate high-speed memory with the necessary bandwidth and provide a means for high-speed transfers between high-speed memory and main memory.

The first approach acknowledges that if one memory module can access at most one datum per access cycle, then to access N independent data in one access cycle requires N independent memory modules. The second approach produces higher bandwidth by shortening the access cycle in a small memory. But the small memory is loaded from a large memory, and the large memory can still be the ultimate bottleneck in the system in spite of the high bandwidth of the small memory.

To make best use of the small high-speed memory, we should make multiple use of operands transferred to this memory. In this way the net demand by the processor on the large memory is reduced, and bandwidth of the large memory need not be as large as the peak bandwidth required by the processor.

In the latter part of this chapter we see that another use of the high-speed memory is to provide for access patterns not available in main memory. Thus, we can move a data structure such as a matrix from main memory to intermediate memory by using the access patterns supported by main memory.

When the matrix is stored in intermediate memory, we can provide for efficient access to rows, columns, diagonals, or subarrays of the matrix, not all of which can be done efficiently when the matrix is stored in main memory. The second approach has been embellished in some cases by providing more than one level of intermediate memory, with the size, cost, and performance of each level selected to give a good cost-performance ratio of the total memory system.

5.1.1 Multiple Memory Modules

The first approach is illustrated in Fig. 5.2. In this figure main memory is composed of multiple modules. Eight modules are shown; they comprise a system with eight times the bandwidth of a single module. Each of the three data streams associated with the arithmetic pipeline has an independent path to the memory system so that each stream can be active simultaneously, provided that each individual module serves only one path at a time.

Consider how this system can be used to implement vector arithmetic. We assume that a basic memory cycle takes two processor cycles, so the

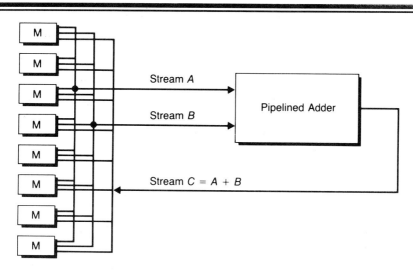

Fig. 5.2 A vector processor with a memory system composed of eight 3-port memory modules.

bandwidth required to service the pipeline in Fig. 5.2 is at least six times the bandwidth of a single memory module. Figure 5.3 illustrates an ideal solution to our vector arithmetic example. The vectors **A**, **B**, and **C** are laid out in memory so that they start respectively in Modules 0, 2, and 4, and their successive elements lie in successive memories at addresses that are easily calculated.

The timing for the activity in this architecture is shown in Fig. 5.4. Time is shown on the horizontal axis, and the activity of the memory modules and pipeline unit is shown on the vertical axis. Note that the arithmetic pipeline has four stages, thereby producing each output value four units after the corresponding input data arrive at the pipeline. The pipeline is busy continuously after it fills with data.

A busy pipeline stage is indicated by the integer within the cell, which gives the subscript of the vector element that is being processed at the given time. A busy memory module is indicated by an R followed by a letter and a digit. The symbol $RA0$ indicates that the module is reading the element of vector **A** with subscript 0. The letter W indicates a WRITE operation in progress to the element of **C** whose subscript follows the W.

For this example, we have purposely allocated the vectors to modules so that no conflicts occur. To simplify this discussion we ignore the addressing of items within modules and focus only on which modules are active. At Clock 0,

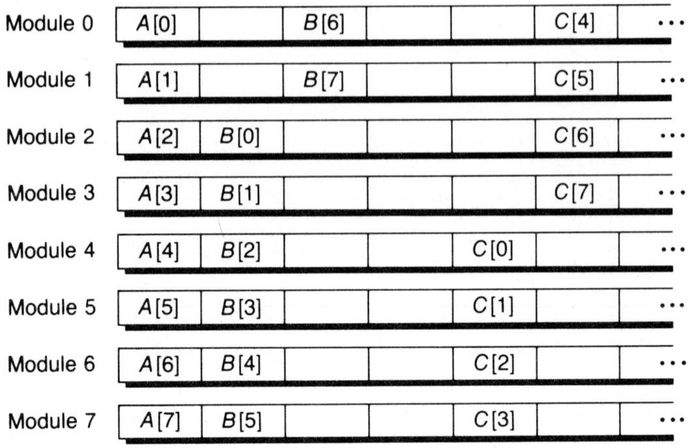

Module 0	A[0]		B[6]			C[4]	...
Module 1	A[1]		B[7]			C[5]	...
Module 2	A[2]	B[0]				C[6]	...
Module 3	A[3]	B[1]				C[7]	...
Module 4	A[4]	B[2]			C[0]		...
Module 5	A[5]	B[3]			C[1]		...
Module 6	A[6]	B[4]			C[2]		...
Module 7	A[7]	B[5]			C[3]		...

Fig. 5.3 The physical layout of three vectors in the modular memory of the pipelined vector processor of Fig. 5.2.

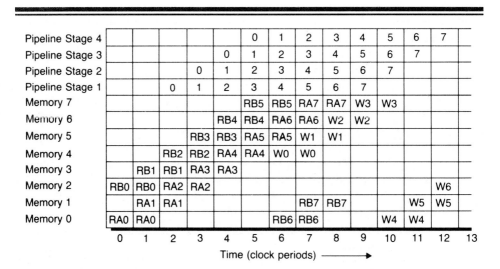

Fig. 5.4 A timing diagram for the addition of two vectors, component by component, in pipeline mode.

Modules 0 and 2 initiate READs to the first elements of vectors **A** and **B**. These elements appear at the pipeline inputs at Clock 2, and the corresponding output appears at the end of Clock 5.

Meanwhile at Clock 1, Modules 1 and 3 initiate READs to the second elements of the input vectors, and at each subsequent clock cycle, successive modules initiate READs to the next elements of the input vectors. At the end of Clock 5 the first output value emerges from the arithmetic pipeline.

During the next clock period, Clock 6, Modules 5 and 6 are busy reading the next elements of the vector **A**. Module 5 delivers a_5 at the beginning of Clock 7, and Module 6 delivers a_6 at the beginning of Clock 8. Similarly, Modules 7 and 0 are busy reading b_5 and b_6, respectively, during Clock 6. Modules 1, 2, and 3 are unoccupied. Module 4 initiates a WRITE to put away c_0 during Clock 6, and during the next clock cycle, Module 5 initiates a WRITE to put away c_1.

Note how well the arithmetic and memory operations dovetail in the timing diagram in Fig. 5.4 so that all operations proceed without a collision. That is the beauty of pipelined data flow when data flows can be made collision free. But reality is never as well behaved as ideal examples are.

What happens when we cannot arrange the vectors to begin in the modules where we want them to begin? For example, the structure of the vector add prevents the vector **C** from beginning in Modules 0, 5, 6, or 7 when the input data are arranged as shown in Fig. 5.3. If **C** is computed somewhere else in the program as the sum of **D** and **E**, the vectors **D** and **E** might well be stored in memory in a way that prevents **C** from beginning in Modules 1 through 4. Hence, we might discover that **C** is too constrained and cannot be stored in any manner to support conflict-free memory operations.

Figure 5.5 shows how buffers at the input and output of the arithmetic

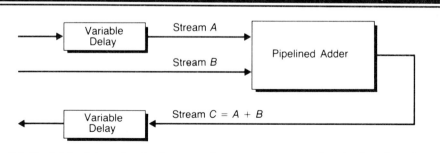

Fig. 5.5 Variable delays in the input and output streams of a pipelined arithmetic unit.

pipeline can eliminate contention at the memory. Suppose, for example that all vectors start in Memory 0. The timing diagram in Fig. 5.6 shows how the vector operation proceeds without conflict. The input buffer on the **A** input is set to a delay of two clocks, and the output is set to a delay of four clocks.

In Fig. 5.6 note that **A** is read before **B,** so that each element of **B** reaches the pipeline exactly two clocks after the corresponding element of **A** emerges from the memory. By buffering **A** for two clock cycles, we provide for corresponding elements of **A** and **B** to reach the arithmetic pipeline concurrently. When the first result appears at the output of the pipeline at the end of Clock 7, it arrives just when Module 0 is busy for four clock cycles fetching a_8 and b_8.

Hence, the output buffer holds each output for four clock cycles and then passes the output to the memory system. Thus the first result is stored during Clock 12, and the total duration of the vector operation is lengthened by six clock cycles over the timing shown in Fig. 5.4. After the initial delay, however, results are produced and stored at the rate one result per clock cycle, which is the same rate as in Fig. 5.4. The technique of adding buffers to the inputs and outputs of an arithmetic unit to eliminate memory conflicts is similar in spirit to the idea of adding buffering in the interior of a pipeline to eliminate internal conflicts, which has been explored earlier in Section 3.4.4.

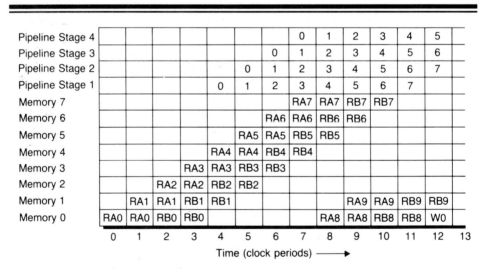

Fig. 5.6 A timing diagram for the addition of two vectors when storage conflicts arise. After reading, Vector **A** is delayed by two clocks, and, before writing, Vector **C** is delayed by four clocks. The first WRITE takes place at Clock 12.

One implementation of this idea is shown in block diagram form in Fig. 5.7, which is intended to represent the structure of the CDC STAR Computer, a supercomputer produced in the mid-1970s. This diagram shows a variable delay inserted into one of the operand streams and the result stream. The delays are set to specific values depending on the location of the first elements of each of the operands and the result vector. This ensures that the pipeline can run at full speed after an initialization period during which the operand and result streams fill their respective buffers. Unfortunately, if vectors are short, a relatively long buffering delay can have a strongly negative influence on performance.

Figure 5.7 shows that several functions can be selected within the arithmetic subsystem. The CDC STAR has no capability to overlap two or more vector operations with each other, so it is reasonable in this architecture to share common arithmetic functions among different vector operations. Thus the floating-point addition and multiplication operations use the same hardware for exponent add, shift, and mantissa add, which are common to the two functions. The CDC STAR actually provides for two single-precision operations or one double-precision operation within one pipeline, where the flexibility is

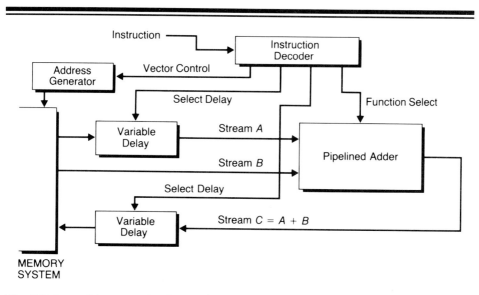

Fig. 5.7 An architecture similar to the CDC STAR. The instruction decoder sets the variable delays as a function of the starting addresses of the vectors and the throughput rate of the arithmetic pipeline for the specied operation. The address generator produces the load and store addresses during the execution of the instruction.

obtained by special logic inserted in the arithmetic stages that lie in the boundary region between the two single-precision halves of a double-precision operand. This logic disables the carries between halves in 32-bit mode and enables the carries between halves in 64-bit mode. This permits the result rate for single precision to be double the result rate for double precision, when you measure the result rate in terms of result operands produced per unit time. However, the number of physical bits produced per unit time is the same for single and double precision.

The variable delays in Fig. 5.7 are rather interesting entities in themselves because they can be costly both in dollars and setup time. Even if the dollars are unimportant, setup time is very important, and we require the delay to be set quickly to a particular value.

One possibility is to use a tapped delay line wherein the data stream enters a series of delay stages at a specific input, but a tap control selects a specific output to serve as the output of the delay line. This is shown in Fig. 5.8. Each of the N stages in this delay line is a potential network output, but the actual network output is determined by the output control.

This line can yield any delay from 0 to $N - 1$, provided that data can be clocked in and out of the delay line within a single clock cycle. In some technologies, the logic required to implement the variable delay results in relatively long access paths that may be too long for the clock cycle of the full system. This is technology dependent, however, but it must be considered by the architect.

An alternative way to achieve the variable delay is shown in Fig. 5.9. This requires N cells of a special memory. This particular memory can simul-

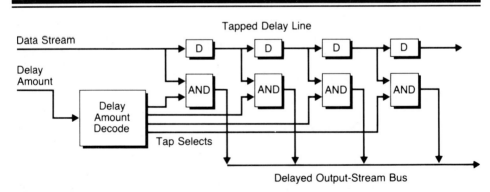

Fig. 5.8 A variable delay built from a tapped delay line. The D modules are unit delays. One tap is gated to the output bus by a tap-select control line produced by decoding the delay amount.

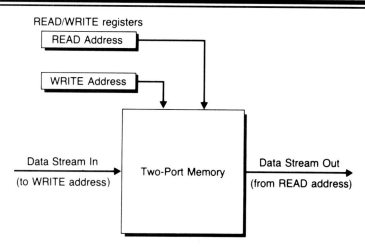

Fig. 5.9 A variable delay implemented with a two-port memory. The delay is the difference between the READ and WRITE addresses. For 0 delay, the input stream is shunted directly to the output by means of bypass logic not shown in the figure.

taneously read any cell in the system and write any other. There are two address registers, one for READ and one for WRITE. The initial value of the WRITE register is 0, and as each datum arrives at the memory and is written, the WRITE address increments by 1.

To achieve a delay of an arbitrary amount up to N, the initial address of the READ register is $-d$, the selected delay. This register is incremented at the rate of operand arrivals, but no data are read until the READ address is 0. At this point the READs occur at the same rate as the WRITEs, and thus the output stream is the same as the input stream shifted d units in time.

The memory in Fig. 5.9 has exactly N locations, numbered 0 to $N - 1$. As READ and WRITE addresses to memory increment beyond $N - 1$, they reset to 0 and continue incrementing, so the memory operates as a circular queue. The value of N need only be large enough to provide for the longest delay required for synchronization. Vector operands can be much longer than N because the delay memory does not have to store an entire vector at any given instant of time.

The delay 0 case is a special situation that can easily be detected because the READ and WRITE addresses are identical in this case. In this situation the input data stream must be shunted directly to the output without being stored in the buffer. Interested readers will find more discussion on variable delays in Kogge [1981].

The variable delay memory in Fig. 5.9 is capable of delaying a stream any amount from 0 to N clock cycles. It has several advantages over the tapped delay-line because no more than two addresses in Fig. 5.9 change state each cycle, as compared to changes in potentially all stages of a tapped delay-line. Each time a cell changes state, there is a change in a physical parameter such as voltage or current. Each such change usually requires power, and with power is produced heat and electrical noise. The fewer changes in the memory system of Fig. 5.9, as compared to the delay memory of Fig. 5.8 in which many cells change on each clock cycle, lead to potentially fewer transient effects and noise problems.

5.1.2 Intermediate Memories

We indicate earlier that an alternative to providing high bandwidth in main memory is to provide one or more intermediate levels of memory to form a hierarchy of memories, with the highest bandwidth memory placed closest to the processor. In this architecture, vectors migrate from main memory to the fastest memory in the hierarchy as they are needed by the processor. Other memory levels, if they exist, provide intermediate storage points to hold vectors in transit just before or just after their use in the fastest portion of the hierarchy.

The Cray I, a landmark high-speed architecture, bases its high-speed operations on a hierarchical memory structure. A simplified diagram of the Cray I appears in Fig. 5.10. Its main memory (8 M-bytes) is separated from the processing units by one or two levels of intermediate memories. For vector operations, the intermediate memory is a set of eight vector registers (the V registers), each capable of holding a 64-element vector of double-precision numbers. The vector pipelines obtain data from the vector registers, not from main memory. Similarly, the result vectors from the pipelines are returned to the vector registers.

Scalar operands have two levels of intermediate memory, much like conventional cache-based high-performance systems. The fastest level contains eight 64-bit scalar registers (the S registers), which communicate directly with the pipeline units for scalar arithmetic.

A slower, but still very high speed, level of intermediate memory is composed of 64 scalar registers (the T Registers), each 64 bits in length. The T-register scalar memory has the same purpose as a cache memory in that it is intended to hold those data that overflow from the high-speed scalar registers. Such data may become idle temporarily, but should be held close to the processor in anticipation of future need rather than moved to the more remote main memory between periods of use. Also, new data can be prefetched to the intermediate scalar memory from main memory just prior to use in the arithmetic unit.

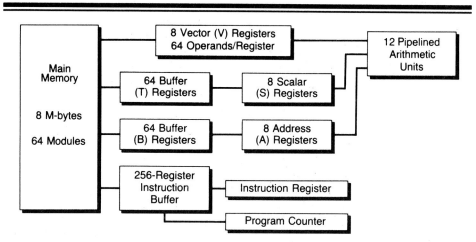

Fig. 5.10 The Cray I—an architecture based on hierarchical memories. One to two levels of high-speed intermediate memories isolate the arithmetic and instruction logic from main memory.

Unlike a cache memory, this intermediate memory is not managed automatically. Data must be transferred explicitly to and from the intermediate memory by means of ordinary program instructions. The disadvantage of this scheme over cache memory is that the Cray I intermediate memory has to be managed by the programmer or the compiler. The big advantage of this type of memory over cache memory is speed—intermediate memory is accessed by means of physical register addresses, not by a cache lookup. The cache lookup tends to take longer because a cycle must be long enough to support both the normal read operation plus an address comparison, whereas the Cray I intermediate memory does not require the time to compare address tags in a cache.

Cray designs usually provide for short high-speed registers to hold addresses, and the Cray I follows this general philosophy. It has eight address registers (the A registers), each 24 bits in length. These are backed up by an intermediate level of memory in the form of 64 registers (the B registers), each 24 bits in length. Thus the B registers function as a cache for the A registers, except that all operations on the B registers are explicitly controlled by program instructions rather than automatically controlled, as are the registers of a cache memory.

One more intermediate-level memory appears in the diagram. This is an instruction buffer that holds portions of the instruction stream that are fetched just prior to the execution of those instructions. Tight inner loops tend to lie completely within the instruction buffer and can execute repeatedly without requiring fetches to main memory. Because many applications written for the Cray tend to spend the great majority of time in tight loops, instruction fetches tend be rather rare events.

Note in Figure 5.10 that every functional portion of the processor has a high-speed memory attached to it. No function is directly attached to main memory, as is the case for the processor structure shown in Fig. 5.7. Moreover, some of the high-speed memories are backed up by memory buffers that lie between main memory and high-speed memory.

The structure of the design clearly shows the major idea of the architecture—keep the processing units busy by keeping their operands close at hand. The intermediate memories represent a compromise in the sense that they provide a pool of data readily accessible to the processing units at lower cost than the cost of storage in the fastest levels of the memory hierarchy.

The performance of the intermediate memories is, however, below the performance of the highest-speed memories. To design such a hierarchy involves comparing the performance trade-offs, with and without intermediate memory, and the savings attributed to using intermediate memory in place of high-speed registers. Note that the savings is partly due to cost and partly due to decreased volume and power consumption, which may be the deciding factors in supercomputer design.

An intermediate memory can also provide a buffer for reformatting data structures for efficient processing. The idea is that the pipeline is optimized for access to successive elements from a vector register, but the items to be processed need not lie in consecutive cells of memory. The operands can be fetched into an intermediate memory and from there sent to the vector registers. In so doing, the operands can be reorganized so that the items to be processed next are moved to contiguous cells of a vector register. Methods for making this transformation are covered in more detail in the next section.

The most distinguishing feature of the two architectures described in this section is in regard to coupling operand memory to the pipeline. The first architecture relies on main memory to hold pipeline operands, so main memory must have a bandwidth at least as large as is required by the arithmetic unit. This forces all of main memory to either be fast or partitioned into many independent memory modules, or both, because the peak bandwidth requirement of the arithmetic unit is very high.

The second design provides for the very high bandwidth to be supplied by a register memory much smaller than main memory, and thus, the slower speed of main memory need not handicap the arithmetic pipeline. Another facet of the second design is that it provides for the possibility of overlapping pipeline operations because the gross bandwidth of the high-speed registers can be made high enough to meet peak processing requirements of several pipelined arithmetic units combined.

The cost of providing extra bandwidth for the registers is the cost of providing extra ports for reading and writing the registers. While this cost can be relatively high per bit of storage, the high-speed registers have only 10^4 to 10^5 bits, as compared to the 10^8 to 10^{10} bits of main memory. Thus, it is feasible to supply extra ports to the registers but impractical to do so for main memory.

The Cray I does provide for overlapping pipelined arithmetic operations so that as many as three independent vector operations can be done concurrently. A vector operation produced on one output stream can be routed directly to the input of the next operation. The first architecture has no provision for additional data streams, so the result stream has to be stored in memory before it can be rerouted to an arithmetic pipeline for additional processing.

Because the variable delay is shared by all vector operations, the buffer in the variable delay has to empty before the delay can be reset for the next pipelined operation. Hence the pipeline must drain between operations, and no overlap is possible. The Cray I's ability to overlap pipelined operations is strictly due to its intermediate buffers and high-speed registers.

In our discussion of cache memory, our assumption is that cache memory is an extremely important architectural feature of high-speed computers. Yet the Cray I has no cache-organized memory, although it does have several memories that occupy a place in a memory hierarchy similar to the place of cache memory. The absence of cache is due partially to design decisions and partially to characteristics of vector programs that may differ from the characteristics of scalar programs.

The design decision for this class of machine has to weigh the cost and difficulty of programming an intermediate memory that is not cache organized against the performance penalty for a cache access as compared to a register access. The Cray I is built for performance. Its users are rather sophisticated and are willing to expend extra effort in software to obtain a performance boost. This biases design decisions against the use of cache and toward the use of programmable registers.

Moreover, a cache may not work as well for vector operations as it does for scalar operations, although currently there is very little experience on which to make a judgment. The designer has to consider these questions:

- How large should a cache be on a vector machine?
- Should it be large enough to hold a few full-length vectors?
- Or should it be smaller and instead hold fragments of many different vectors?

These questions are largely unanswered today, but we can expect them to be explored in the next few years as vector technology becomes more mature and implementers seek methods for boosting performance of machines built today without caches.

Serial access to vectors dictates against a cache that uses LRU replacement because one vector load may flush an entire cache and leave only dead data in the cache. Perhaps a cache organized to manage vectors may be useful, but this is still a matter of conjecture and needs further study. Therefore, vector registers should be organized as program-accessible registers rather than as a cache until performance studies show how to improve throughput with a vector-organized cache.

The various intermediate registers, including the T (scalar) registers, the B (address) registers, and the instruction buffer, are the most obvious candidates for cache organization. The hit ratio should be comparable to the hit ratio for conventional serial machines if these registers were cache organized, but interlocks across the caches to maintain consistent data would be a serious problem.

Several units in the Cray I can modify data. Any such modification has to be reflected in a cache that holds copies of such data. Some cache-consistency protocols require that each time a new item is placed in cache, a cross check is made at all other caches to see if the same item is contained there. This could hurt performance by causing conflicts for cache access.

Although this implementation is not the only way to interlock cache access, interlocking is almost always accompanied by a reduction in performance and possibly by a modest increase in cost. So cache may well be unattractive for a Cray-type environment.

Future designs, however, need not follow the directions of the Cray I. Device technology can change dramatically, resulting in different available densities, speeds, and costs of memory. Major changes in any or all of these factors could produce vastly different architectures. As memory becomes smaller, faster, and less expensive, there is a potential for intermediate memories of much greater capacity. Higher power densities, however, may require that volumes be held small to enable the computer systems to be cooled and may force the designer to resort to small intermediate memories or elect not to use them in some areas of the design. A reasonable rule of thumb in the supercomputer area is to build as much capacity and performance capability as possible, and then look for ways to reduce volume, power consumption, and total cost without drastically hurting performance.

5.2 Access Patterns for Numerical Algorithms

High performance requires that the architecture fit the workload. A high-speed machine must do the job for which it is intended. Although the discussion in the previous chapter cautioned against structures that are too special purpose, we must at least understand the requirements for a large class of problems to make sure that we can solve those problems effectively.

If design compromises are necessary, then we should understand a pure design with no compromises and then evaluate the compromises separately. In this section we examine some numerical problems and learn that access patterns play a critical role in determining the execution speed of the algorithms. We show how to build machines that support the special access patterns frequently encountered in large numerical calculations.

Heller's excellent review of parallel algorithms for numerical methods [1978] focuses on linear algebra because most large-scale practical applications of numerical methods are expressed in terms of matrices and vectors. This is not surprising; matrix notation gives a compact way to express enormous amounts of computation.

Consider two extremes for writing a program that performs 10^{10} multiplies. At one extreme, the programmer writes a few hundred or thousand lines of program statements, many of which are just calls on a library of matrix and vector functions. At the other extreme, the programmer is faced with solving an unstructured problem and has to specify each of the 10^{10} lines individually.

It is quite clear that no one will write the latter code—it takes an extraordinary amount of time to write. At the rate of one arithmetic operation per second, a person working full time would need 30 years to write down all of the arithmetic expressions that describe the workings of the program. A computer that executes at 100 Mflops takes only 100 seconds to execute that program.

Obviously, vector and matrix operations are very important for a high-speed architecture because many very large algorithms are expressed succinctly by such operations. The demonstrated importance of numerical applications for large-scale computations leads us to treat the world of vector and matrix computations in this chapter.

Other notational systems may also be useful. For example, recursively defined functions are succinct descriptions of potentially massive computations. In any case, we are unlikely to generate unstructured large-scale computations simply because the programming effort to write such applications is unreasonable.

5.2.1 Gaussian Elimination

Heller [1978] covers a number of algorithms for solving linear systems of the type

$$\mathbf{Ax} = \mathbf{b}$$

where $\mathbf{A}$ is an $N \times N$ matrix, and $\mathbf{x}$ and $\mathbf{b}$ are $N \times 1$ column vectors. The objective is to find $\mathbf{x}$, given $\mathbf{A}$ and $\mathbf{b}$. The techniques available depend on the specific characteristics of the matrix $\mathbf{A}$.

When $\mathbf{A}$ is dense, that is, when all or nearly all of the components of $\mathbf{A}$ are nonzero, the solution of the linear system of equations can be found by carrying out a succession of row and column operations on $\mathbf{A}$, with corresponding changes made to $\mathbf{b}$ during the course of the computation.

One efficient and effective method of solution, Gaussian elimination, factors **A** into the product of two triangular matrices, **L** and **U** where **L** is lower triangular and **U** is upper triangular. We see this in the previous chapter for the special case in which **A** is tridiagonal, and **L** and **U** are bidiagonal. In both the general and the special case, the factorization must compute the elements of **L** and **U**, and this is possible to do by means of operations on row and column vectors.

Once the factorization produces **L** and **U**, the next steps solve the triangular systems

$$\mathbf{Ly} = \mathbf{b}$$

and

$$\mathbf{Ux} = \mathbf{y}$$

to obtain a value of **x** that satisfies the original equation since

$$\mathbf{Ax} = \mathbf{LUx} = \mathbf{Ly} = \mathbf{b}$$

The solutions to the triangular systems are particularly easy to obtain by means of vector operations on rows of the **L** and **U** matrices.

When **A** is developed from partial differential equations that describe a problem in the continuum, **A** is a sparse, highly regular matrix whose solution can be determined quite efficiently using techniques such as cyclic reduction, which is described in the previous chapter. Although we may view such a matrix **A** as being composed of a collection of row or column vectors, the nonzero components of **A** in problems that arise from continuum formulations tend to lie only along a few diagonals. Many algorithms approach the solutions of this type of sparse-matrix problem by treating the matrix as composed of diagonal vectors, so that vector operations manipulate streams of data fetched from various diagonals of the **A** matrix.

It is worthwhile to examine in detail one example of a parallel algorithm for computing the solution to a linear equation. In this case, we look at classical Gaussian elimination and assume that the basic parallel operation can manipulate a row or column of **A** in equal time. This assumption is not true for all architectures, and its correctness requires some resourcefulness from both the computer architect and the numerical programmer. Nevertheless, let us assume that rows and columns are equally accessible and explore how to create an algorithm from row and column operations.

The core of the algorithm produces a new column of **L** and row of **U** at each of N iterations. The new data for **L** and **U** overwrite corresponding locations of **A** and are unchanged for the remainder of the computation. Before producing the next elements of **L** and **U**, the algorithm updates the entire portion of the **A** matrix that has not yet been overwritten. The diagonal of **L**, which is forced by this algorithm to be all 1s, is not stored explicitly. The diagonal of **A** is eventually overwritten by the diagonal of **U**.

At each iteration, one diagonal element of **A** is overwritten. We call this element the *pivot* for that iteration. In the matrix below the pivot is stored the new column of **L**, and to the right of the pivot is stored the new row of **U**. Figure 5.11 shows the various portions of the data at the start of an iteration. The *L* and *U* denote the columns of **L** and rows of **U** that have been computed up to this point. The *P* designates the pivot. The *L'* and *U'* denote the new data to be computed during this iteration, and the *A* denotes the elements of **A** that will be transformed during this iteration.

For numerical stability, we should choose as the pivot the element with the greatest magnitude in the region that includes *P*, *L'*, *U'*, and *A*. If this element is not *P*, then that element can be brought to position *P* by a swap of rows and columns. Most algorithms, however, do not search such a large area for the new pivot.

The algorithm remains stable, although it has a larger error bound, if the pivot element is the largest element in the area that includes *P* and *L'*. If the largest is not in position *P*, then by exchanging the row containing the element and the pivot row, we can move the large element to position *P*. Row and column exchanges are permitted because they do not change the solution to the original system of equations, although the elements in the solution vector in general will have to be permuted to produce a solution vector whose elements are ordered correctly in regard to the original problem.

Program 5.1 is a simplified version of an algorithm for Gaussian elimination that appears in Forsythe and Moler [1967]. This algorithm is expressed in vector notation, where the notation $A[i,j]$ designates a single element $a_{i,j}$, of **A**,

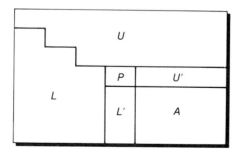

Fig. 5.11 The regions of a matrix revealed during a single cycle of an LU-decomposition algorithm for performing Gaussian elimination.

Program 5.1 Gaussian elimination.

FACTOR is a vector algorithm for factoring matrix **A** into **L** and **U**, where **A** = **LU**, **L** is lower triangular, and **U** is upper triangular. The diagonal elements of all matrices are equal to 1; they are not stored explicitly. **L** overwrites the lower triangular portion of **A**, and **U** overwrites the diagonal and upper triangular portion of **A**.

```
for i := 1 to N do
    begin {* Search Column for a pivot element. *}
            {* Find the index of the element with the largest absolute
            value in the pivot column. *}
    imax := index_of_Max(abs(A[i ... N, i]));
            {* Swap Row imax with Row i. This produces a new row of U. *}
    Swap(A[i, i ... N],A[imax, i ... N]);
            {* Check for singularity, and terminate if so. *}
    if A[i, i] := 0 then singular matrix;
            {* Find the new column of L, and store it in A. *}
    A[i+1 ... N, i] := A[i+1 ... N, i]/A[i, i];
            {* Update the remaining part of the A matrix. *}
    for k := i+1 to N do
        A[k, i+1 ... N] := A[k, i+1 ... N] − A[k, i]×A[i, i+1 ... N];
    end; {* Outer loop *}
```

and $A[1 \ldots j - 1, j]$ designates a column vector of **A**. In this case, the subscript range $1 \ldots j - 1$ designates all subscript values lying between 1 and $j - 1$. The single subscript in the second component designates the jth column. Hence, $A[1 \ldots j - 1, j]$ is the vector that consists of the first $j - 1$ elements of the jth column of **A**. The same notation holds for rows, except that the subscript range is placed in the second subscript position.

The important aspects of this example are that:

1. The algorithm as expressed accesses both rows and columns.
2. The majority of the vector operations have either two vector operands or a scalar and vector operand, and they produce a vector result.
3. The MAX operation on a vector returns the index of the maximum element, not the value of the maximum element.
4. The length of the vector of items accessed decreases by 1 for each successive iteration.

The first point is consistent with our assumption that we need to access both rows and columns in some algorithms. It turns out in this problem that the inner loop can be done either by rows or by columns; the choice is up to the programmer. But the algorithm does require both a column and a row operation elsewhere, so a vector computer should provide easy access to both rows and columns, at least, and possibly other interesting forms of access.

The next point indicates that a vector pipeline should provide a mechanism to have a scalar serve as one of the operands, and in so doing it should produce an answer faster or more efficiently than a similar operation that has both operands as vectors.

The third point suggests that the pipelined arithmetic unit should provide some mechanism for producing results that are scalar, such as results produced by the functions MAX, MIN, and SUM. Note as well that the scalar result might be an index of an important element in the vector and not necessarily the value of a vector element or of a combination of vector elements. In our example, the information required by the algorithm is the index, not the matrix element.

The last point is the most perplexing. The vectors used by this algorithm shrink with each step, and thus the last step uses vectors of length 1. Pipelined arithmetic and vector operations have a certain overhead, and we should attempt to amortize that overhead over many operands by treating long vectors as much as possible. We have an efficient machine if the overhead for starting a vector computation is small compared to the amount of useful work it produces. However, if the useful work produced by a vector operation is very small, the overhead may be painfully expensive and drastically reduce the efficiency of the system. The last point forces us to keep vector overhead as small as possible because we inherently must deal with short vectors for some portions of important computations.

The next section illustrates some techniques for solving the access problem and gives insight into the structure of efficient vector processors.

5.3 Data-Structuring Techniques for Vector Machines

In this section we explore the problem of accessing data in ways that are constrained by an algorithm. If a data structure such as a matrix is to be accessed only by rows, we can store rows so that consecutive elements lie at successive addresses. If only columns of a matrix are required, we could store the matrix in a column-oriented fashion, by putting consecutive elements of each column at consecutive memory addresses. But if both row access and column access were required, there is no obvious way to meet both constraints efficiently.

The problem is illustrated in Fig. 5.12, in which a matrix is stored in a main memory composed of eight independent memory modules. The modules are represented as columns. In Fig. 5.12(a), an 8 × 8 matrix is stored so that its row

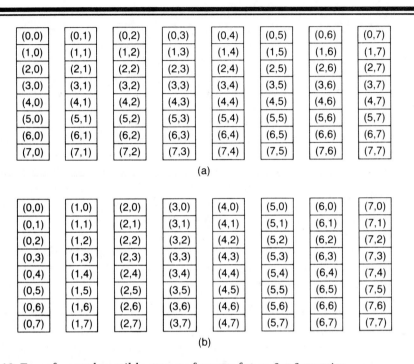

(0,0)	(0,1)	(0,2)	(0,3)	(0,4)	(0,5)	(0,6)	(0,7)
(1,0)	(1,1)	(1,2)	(1,3)	(1,4)	(1,5)	(1,6)	(1,7)
(2,0)	(2,1)	(2,2)	(2,3)	(2,4)	(2,5)	(2,6)	(2,7)
(3,0)	(3,1)	(3,2)	(3,3)	(3,4)	(3,5)	(3,6)	(3,7)
(4,0)	(4,1)	(4,2)	(4,3)	(4,4)	(4,5)	(4,6)	(4,7)
(5,0)	(5,1)	(5,2)	(5,3)	(5,4)	(5,5)	(5,6)	(5,7)
(6,0)	(6,1)	(6,2)	(6,3)	(6,4)	(6,5)	(6,6)	(6,7)
(7,0)	(7,1)	(7,2)	(7,3)	(7,4)	(7,5)	(7,6)	(7,7)

(a)

(0,0)	(1,0)	(2,0)	(3,0)	(4,0)	(5,0)	(6,0)	(7,0)
(0,1)	(1,1)	(2,1)	(3,1)	(4,1)	(5,1)	(6,1)	(7,1)
(0,2)	(1,2)	(2,2)	(3,2)	(4,2)	(5,2)	(6,2)	(7,2)
(0,3)	(1,3)	(2,3)	(3,3)	(4,3)	(5,3)	(6,3)	(7,3)
(0,4)	(1,4)	(2,4)	(3,4)	(4,4)	(5,4)	(6,4)	(7,4)
(0,5)	(1,5)	(2,5)	(3,5)	(4,5)	(5,5)	(6,5)	(7,5)
(0,6)	(1,6)	(2,6)	(3,6)	(4,6)	(5,6)	(6,6)	(7,6)
(0,7)	(1,7)	(2,7)	(3,7)	(4,7)	(5,7)	(6,7)	(7,7)

(b)

Fig. 5.12 Two of several possible storage formats for an 8 × 8 matrix:
(a) Suitable for access to row vectors, but bad for column vector; and
(b) Suitable for access to column vectors, but bad for row vectors.

elements can be accessed in a pipeline fashion. Each successive row element is stored in the next memory module.

If a memory access takes several clock cycles, this memory can still deliver one row element per clock cycle after an initial delay. To fetch the row vector for Row 0, for example, initiate a fetch to the (0,0) element, and before this element is delivered to the memory bus, initiate a fetch to the (0,1) element on the next clock cycle. On Clock i, initiate a fetch to element $(0,i)$.

If the memory access time produces a delay d between the initial access to an item and the time at which it appears at the memory output port, then in our example the element $(0,i)$ can be placed on the memory bus at the end of Clock $i + d$. This is the method of overlapped access described at the beginning of this chapter. If d does not exceed 8, the number of distinct memory modules in the example, the vector can be arbitrarily long. If d is greater than 8, however, attempts to access vectors longer than eight result in collisions at some memory module because the module is asked to initiate a fetch for a new element before its access to an old element has been completed.

Another way to describe the situation is that the memory bandwidth must be great enough to support the memory demand. If the delay d is greater than 8, then the aggregate bandwidth of the eight memories is less than one item per clock period, yet the pipeline demand is for one item per clock period. With delay d, the aggregate bandwidth is one item per clock period only if there are at least d independent memory modules, each capable of accessing one item per d clock periods. If an instruction requires three streams, two for input operands and one for results, then the aggregate bandwidth of memory must be at least three items per clock period, so the number of memory modules must be at least $3d$ to support a pipeline rate of one result per clock time.

Figure 5.12(a) shows that the memory bandwidth available is not the whole story. Consider what happens if you need to access columns of the matrix, for example Column 0. In this figure, Column 0 lies wholly in one memory module. No matter how many other modules are in the system, access to the elements of Column 0 is limited by the maximum bandwidth of the single module. In this case, at most one item can be delivered every d units of time, and it is impossible to support a rate of one column element accessed per clock period unless one module by itself can produce data at this rate—that is, unless d is unity.

In Fig. 5.12(b) we transpose the matrix to give fast access to columns, which are now stored across the memories, but we give up fast access to rows. The Gaussian elimination algorithm, as reproduced in the previous section, requires both row and column access, so neither the storage pattern of Fig. 5.12(a) nor Fig. 5.12(b) is acceptable. One way to circumvent the problem is to rewrite the algorithm to use column or row access exclusively. This happens to be possible for Gaussian elimination, but it is not always possible to revise an algorithm to live within the access constraints of memory.

Another approach is to alter the structure of data in memory. Figure 5.13 shows the same matrix stored so that successive rows are skewed with respect to the previous row. In this case Row 0 starts in Module 0, Row 1 starts in Module 1, . . . , with each row shifted to the right by one column with respect to the immediately preceding row.

In this storage scheme the address of an item in a system address space is $8 \times$ (local address) + module number, where each individual memory has a local address-space, and the module numbers range from 0 to 7. Row elements lie at successive addresses in the system address-space. Successive column elements lie at addresses that differ by nine in system address space. Note that successive column elements lie in different memories in this system, and that they can be accessed in pipeline fashion as efficiently as successive row elements.

Even though the matrix is 8×8, we store the matrix as if it were 8×9 (8 rows by 9 columns), wasting the memory allocated to the ninth column. The extra column provides the cyclical offset of successive rows, so column elements are spread across all memories just as row elements are.

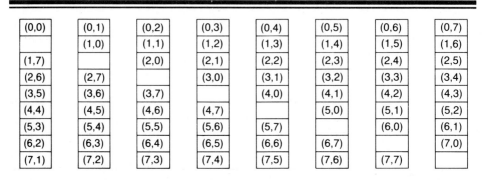

(0,0)	(0,1)	(0,2)	(0,3)	(0,4)	(0,5)	(0,6)	(0,7)
	(1,0)	(1,1)	(1,2)	(1,3)	(1,4)	(1,5)	(1,6)
(1,7)		(2,0)	(2,1)	(2,2)	(2,3)	(2,4)	(2,5)
(2,6)	(2,7)		(3,0)	(3,1)	(3,2)	(3,3)	(3,4)
(3,5)	(3,6)	(3,7)		(4,0)	(4,1)	(4,2)	(4,3)
(4,4)	(4,5)	(4,6)	(4,7)		(5,0)	(5,1)	(5,2)
(5,3)	(5,4)	(5,5)	(5,6)	(5,7)		(6,0)	(6,1)
(6,2)	(6,3)	(6,4)	(6,5)	(6,6)	(6,7)		(7,0)
(7,1)	(7,2)	(7,3)	(7,4)	(7,5)	(7,6)	(7,7)	

Fig. 5.13 A data structure that permits access to both rows and columns. Row access has stride 1. Column access has stride 9. The blank entries in the matrix form a dummy ninth column of the 8 × 8 matrix.

To use this storage structure in a vector processor similar to those shown in Figs. 5.7 and 5.10, the vector operand must be specified by four quantities:

1. Starting address;

2. Number of elements;

3. Precision (number of bits per element); and

4. Stride (offset between successive elements).

The *stride* for a vector expresses the address increment used to move from one element to the next in a vector access. The stride for row access in Fig. 5.13 is 1, and the stride for column access is 9. In general, if the stride is relatively prime to M, the number of memories, then M successive accesses for that stride are directed to M distinct memories. More generally, for any M and stride s, M successive accesses of stride s are directed to $M/\text{GCD}(s, M)$ different memories, where GCD is the greatest common divisor function. GCD is equal to unity, by definition, when its arguments are relatively prime.

Since M is usually a power of 2, this is equivalent to saying that any vector access with an odd stride produces M consecutive accesses to M distinct memories. In Fig. 5.13, one can easily verify that 11 × 11 and 13 × 13 matrices support row and column access as readily as the 9 × 9 matrix. For column accesses, address conflicts arise when a matrix has an even number of columns because even numbers are not relatively prime to M. For example, a 12 × 12 matrix causes problems when d exceeds 2 because column elements 1, 3, 5, . . . , all lie in the same memory module. For a similar reason, 8 × 8 and 24 × 24 matrices lead to the same inefficient access to columns.

Fortunately, for every even number the next number is odd, so for every bad value for a number of columns, the next larger number is good. Hence, we can always add a wasted column to a data structure and provide a storage structure that is ideally suited to pipelined row and column access.

If row and column access were the only requirements, our discussion would end here. But the designer should not limit a design to a small class of problems. If a few changes can greatly increase the number of problems that can run efficiently, we must explore those changes and the consequences of making them.

Kuck's study of parallelism [1976] (*see also* Budnik and Kuck [1971]) suggests that typical access patterns to matrices include access to

- Matrix diagonals in the major and minor directions;
- Square subarrays; and
- Rows and columns.

Note that the stride required to access the major diagonal of a matrix is one greater than the stride required to access a column of a matrix. If M, the number of memory modules, is a power of 2, then column access and major diagonal access cannot both be efficient since one stride or the other is not relatively prime to M.

Budnik and Kuck [1971] make a startling suggestion—use a number of memories that is not a power of 2. For example, if the number of memories is a prime p, then all strides less than p are relatively prime to p. Therefore, we can store arrays in a structure that yields equally efficient access to rows, columns, and diagonals. Budnik and Kuck explore this notion in the context of a parallel computer that is fully parallel in access, rather than pipelined. This notion was developed further by Burroughs in the design of an unusual supercomputer called the BSP (Burroughs' Scientific Processor), whose structure is shown in Fig. 5.14.

The BSP design provided for 17 memories, rather than 16, to solve the problem of supporting all interesting ways to access a matrix. Memory is not pipelined in this architecture. Rather, in one memory cycle the memory system delivers one block of 17 memory lines, each line from a distinct memory. Two networks separate the 17 memories from 16 processors. The input alignment network shrinks a 17-way access to 16 operands by deleting some operand and compressing the remaining 16 operands into a contiguous vector.

This process is shown in Fig. 5.15 in simplified form for compressing a five-way vector read to deliver data to four processors. Figure 5.15(a) shows access to a column of a 4×4 matrix, and Fig. 5.15(b) shows access to a diagonal of the same matrix. The output alignment network reverses this process for data travelling between the arithmetic processors and main memory.

In Fig. 5.15, note that the 4×4 matrix has two dummy columns stored, so

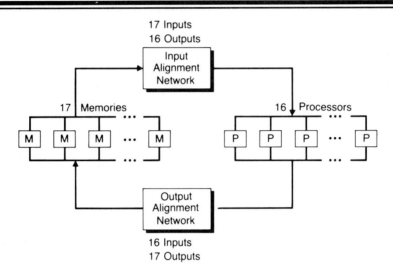

Fig. 5.14 The data flow and processor/memory structure of the Burroughs Scientific Processor.

it is stored as a 4 × 6 matrix. In this form, rows are accessed with a stride of 1, columns with a stride of 6, and diagonals with a stride of 7. Since 1, 6, and 7 are relatively prime to 5, in each case there are no memory conflicts when accessing the particular slice of the array of interest. If the matrix is stored without the dummy columns, then the stride to access diagonals is 5, which is equal to the number of memories and therefore causes a maximum number of conflicts.

The BSP processor was never sold and eventually the project was abandoned. Although the 17-memory structure solves some problems of access, it creates others. Addressing is more complex for this structure than for storage systems in which M is a power of 2. But more important is that the 17-memory system requires that access to the matrix components be made at the memory system, which is quite far from the processor. Obtaining a row of a matrix and then a column of the matrix, perhaps at a later time, forces the matrix to be in main memory and not in a buffer close to the processor. Hence, there is potentially high traffic to and from main memory just for the purpose of reformatting data.

Contrast the 17-memory structure with a Cray-like structure as shown in Fig. 5.10. The striking difference with respect to performance is that the Cray architecture drives the arithmetic units from a high-speed buffer memory (the vector registers), whereas the 17-memory structure drives the arithmetic units

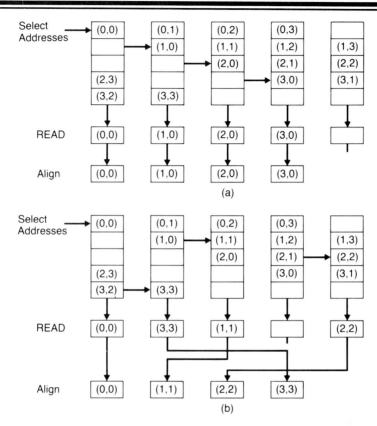

Fig. 5.15 A data structure that supports easy access to rows, columns, and diagonals:
(a) Access to columns with stride 6; and
(b) Access to diagonals with stride 7.

from a more remote main memory with two alignment networks contributing to storage delay. The high-speed buffer of the Cray provides for the possibility of loading data into the buffer just prior to when they are needed.

While data reside in the buffer memory, they can take part in multiple operations before being returned to main memory. Moreover, it is conceivable to provide a sufficiently large buffer memory so that reasonably large portions of matrices can be loaded into the buffer using an access pattern such as row access, that is supported by main memory.

The buffer memory can be structured for access to the various matrix components of interest, so once a matrix is loaded into the buffer, its elements can be accessed in any of several ways. A high-speed buffer can be structured to access the matrix by rows, columns, and diagonals by designing its cycle time to be equal to one clock cycle. For a one-cycle memory, the stride for pipeline access to a vector can be arbitrary.

The type of buffer we describe here is very costly when built in some popular high-speed technologies. A very simple alternative is to reformat matrices when necessary by transferring them between main memory and the high-speed buffer. For example, consider an 8×8 matrix stored by rows in an eight-module memory. If the next phase of the algorithm must access columns, we can reformat the rows from 8×8 to 8×9 by loading each eight-element row into the high-speed buffer and then storing back a nine-element replacement. The destination vector can be written to a different region of main memory to prevent overwriting of the source by destination during the reformatting. Since the row operations are pipelined, reading an entire row of eight elements takes only a little longer than reading a single element. After the matrix is restored to memory, it is in a format in which columns can be accessed with a stride of 9.

The reformatting time is approximately equal to the time required for two to four vector transfers, depending on the overhead per vector initiated and the startup time for a vector load or vector store. The reformatted matrix can be accessed by columns about d times faster than the original matrix, where d, as you recall, is the memory-access cycle time.

Depending on the value of d and the overhead per vector operation, the reformatting of the matrix may be the preferred way of gaining access to the entities needed. The reformatting process might well lead to less performance degradation than do the alignment networks shown in Fig. 5.15 because reformatting degrades performance only when it is needed, whereas the alignment networks tend to increase the latency of every vector fetch and store.

Architectures with high-speed buffers appear to have several advantages over architectures whose memory couples directly to an arithmetic unit. Although this observation is very dependent on existing technology, the trend today seems to be toward vector processors that use high-speed buffers to gain speed, as opposed to architectures that place needed operands far away from the processor that needs them.

The major design problem for the buffer architecture is building a memory that is both large enough to hold an interesting amount of data and fast enough to run at the clock cycle of the arithmetic units. The number of times that a datum in the buffer can be used in a computation before it is returned to main memory tends to decrease as buffer size decreases, so a small buffer may yield little or no savings in the total number of accesses to main memory.

Device technology has a strong influence on how designs will achieve variable-stride access in the future. Current trends suggest that the density of high-speed memory is increasing and that high-speed buffers, although very costly today, will tend to grow larger in the future. Cooling is another problem of importance because large amounts of high-speed memory packed very densely lead to potentially high power density per unit volume. The Cray II, for example, has so high a power density that it is cooled by immersion in liquid.

Technology trends suggest that both the power consumption per bit and the cost per bit are moving downward, which lends support to the evolution of high-speed buffers for variable-stride access as opposed to the BSP approach of handling variable-stride access exclusively in main memory.

5.4 Attached Vector-Processors

An important means for achieving economical high-speed computation is to provide for customization of each processor to the needs of each user. The idea is to partition an architecture into building blocks that can be combined in various ways to achieve different levels of performance with commensurate costs.

Figure 5.16 shows a basic high-speed conventional processor to which is connected a numerical processor that we call an *attached vector-processor*. The basic machine without the attached processor serves a large group of users with conventional workloads, and the machine with the attached processor satisfies the needs of the specialized group of users. This tends to reduce the cost to the specialized user because both the software and hardware of the general-purpose machine enjoy the advantages of the lower cost of high-volume production.

Some manufacturers of attached processors offer a model that can be connected to a variety of different host machines. Attached processors cover a very broad range of costs and performance, from low-cost units that attach to microcomputers to high-performance systems that attach to high-end commercial computers. Many commercial manufacturers offer vector

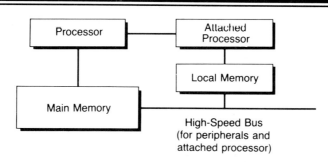

Fig. 5.16 The structure of a typical computer system with an attached processor.

attachments of their own or a compatible model with a superset of instructions for vector operations. These approaches are used by Fujitsu, IBM, Hitachi, and NEC.

Our discussion in this section covers the generic architecture of an attached processor. We also give some specific details regarding the FPS-164 from Floating-Point Systems by way of example to make the details more concrete. Charlesworth and Gustafson [1986] provide interesting background information on this topic.

We know from prior discussions that vector access to rows and columns, and possibly to other matrix components, are essential for efficient numerical computations. This requirement forces the architect to design the memory system to support such access, but places very few constraints on the design of the arithmetic processor. The arithmetic unit should also be structured to support the most common and demanding needs of the users. So let us review a few of the algorithms encountered earlier in the text.

For most numerical applications, the solution of linear equations of various forms is the most central requirement. Linear programming requires related techniques to solve constrained optimization problems. Even for nonlinear problems, linear techniques are very important.

Nonlinear systems of equations are often solved by iterative linear methods. The idea is that some nonlinear systems behave linearly with respect to small perturbations about a solution. Consequently, it is possible to produce a full trajectory for a nonlinear solution from a sequence of solutions to a linear system that describes the small-perturbation behavior of the nonlinear system. Iterative techniques are often employed to produce a solution to the full nonlinear system from the solution obtained by using the linear approximation.

For both linear programming and linear algebra operations, the inner loop of the computation often takes the general form

$$a := a + b \times c \tag{5.1}$$

where a, b, and c are scalar. In a general-purpose structure, the product can be computed and stored in a register and then added to a sum stored in a different register.

Since this operation is so common, we can make it a three-operand operation and provide for both the multiplication and addition to be done in one arithmetic unit, without requiring an intervening store and load of the product to and from a high-speed register. The structure commonly used takes the form shown in Fig. 5.17, in which two operands enter a multiplier whose output is tied directly to an adder, to which a third operand is connected.

Equation (5.1) can be evaluated in several different contexts, depending on the order in which data are presented to the arithmetic unit. The most efficient computation occurs when Eq. (5.1) is used to produce a vector of outputs from

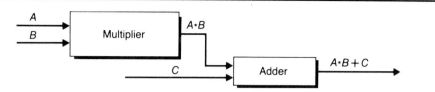

Fig. 5.17 The structure of a multiply-adder.

a vector of inputs. Using our vector notation, Eq. (5.1) in this context becomes

$$a[1 \ldots N] := a[1 \ldots N] + b \times c[1 \ldots N] \qquad (5.2)$$

An efficient pipeline implementation of this equation provides for loading a scalar variable to one input of the multiplier and streaming vectors **A** and **C** through the arithmetic unit. The output vector is the updated **A** vector, which is returned to the buffer storage area reserved for **A**.

Another possible context for Eq. (5.1) is one in which two vectors are reduced to a scalar by an inner-product operation, which produces a single scalar output from two vector inputs. This form of Eq. (5.1) is

$$a := a + b[i] \times c[i] \qquad (5.3)$$

where the products of the form $b[i] \times c[i]$ are accumulated into the scalar variable a. The initial value of a is zero when an ordinary inner product is required. However, some algorithms use Eq. (5.3) in a manner that requires a nonzero initial value for a.

The difficulty with Eq. (5.3) is that there is an interlock required between successive iterations since the output variable a for one iteration is an input variable for the next iteration. If addition is performed in a pipeline with d units of delay, the interlock may require as many as $d - 1$ idle times between successive outputs in order to give the pipeline time to compute a new value for variable a to be used in the next iteration. This is as much as d times longer than the execution time required for Eq. (5.2), and the inefficiency arises only because of the interlock used.

A way around this problem is described in Kogge [1981] and is discussed in Section 3.4.5. The trick is to produce d different sums by computing Eq.(5.3) according to the schedule

$$a_i := a_{i-d} + b_i \times c_i \qquad (5.4)$$

The subscripts in Eq. (5.4) denote the operand that appears at the arithmetic unit input or output at time i. This form of the computation does not require any interlocks because a_{i-d} is available for use at a pipeline input just after it emerges from the output end of the pipeline.

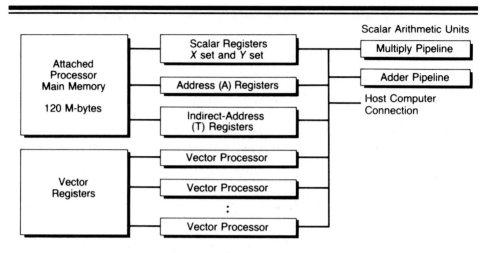

Fig. 5.18 The structure of the FPS-164 attached processor.

Unfortunately, Eq. (5.4) produces d distinct sums, which is not the intended result of Eq. (5.3). So at the completion of the calculation described by Eq. (5.4), it is necessary to sum the d output variables into a final result. The final summation requires a small additional time that degrades performance negligibly when the **B** and **C** vectors are long. The performance degradation cannot be neglected when the **B** and **C** vectors are short, in which case the methodology described by Eq. (5.4) should be avoided in favor of an alternate problem formulation that makes more efficient use of the architecture.

The FPS-164 processor [Charlesworth and Gustafson 1986] is an example of an attached processor. Figure 5.18 shows that the vector processor has its own main memory, high-speed scalar arithmetic, and a variable number of pipelined vector units. The system has a high-speed connection to a host computer. The host function is to provide data and programs for the vector processor and to receive results when they are available. The vector processor is designed specifically for high-speed floating-point operations and has virtually no support for general applications and utility functions. These are supported by the host.

Note that the scalar processor shown in Fig. 5.18 is built for fast scalar operations in that it has a separate multiplier and adder, two sets of operand registers (X and Y registers), one set of address registers (A registers), and a set of indirect-address registers (T registers). The scalar processor broadcasts instructions and data to up to 15 vector processors, one of which is shown in block-diagram form in Fig. 5.19.

The vector processor has two multiply-add units, each capable of producing one output per cycle. There are two sets of vector and scalar registers and

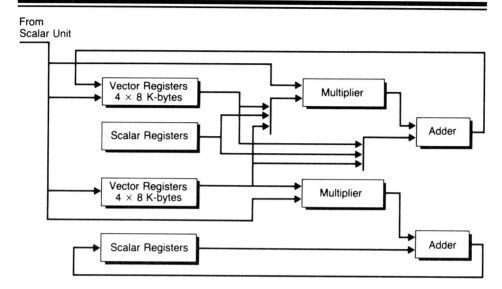

Fig. 5.19 The structure of an FPS-164 vector processor.

an input that receives data broadcast from the scalar processor. To make the best use of the vector processor, this architecture is designed to have sufficient buffer space locally in the vector processor to eliminate some loads and stores of vector data. Consequently, the vector registers are very long, 2K operands long, and there are four vector registers in each of two sets of registers. Thus one processor can hold $2 \times 4 \times 2K = 16K$ elements from vectors.

The scalar registers are far less numerous. Each of two sets holds four operands. The reason for having four scalar operands is that, for any given vector, up to four different scalar multiples of that vector can be computed without the need to obtain new data. This tends to reduce traffic to memory in that each vector can be used up to four times once it is loaded into a vector processor, and therefore it is not necessary to store and reload the operand vector. So there has been a deliberate effort in this design to design the number of scalar registers and the size of the vector registers in such a way as to reduce memory traffic.

The operation of this processor is rather interesting. The vector processors act as slaves to the scalar processor. They receive instructions and data from the scalar processor—individually or in a broadcast mode that transmits data or instructions to all vector processors simultaneously. In this mode the scalar processor can also read selectively from the registers of any selected vector processor.

The normal mode of operation is to load individual vector registers with starting data, with this done selectively rather than in broadcast mode. Thereafter, scalar data and instructions are broadcast, and the processors react synchronously, each performing the same step, but operating on different data.

When the scalar processor transmits in selective mode rather than in broadcast mode, all processors except the receiving processor are idle. Therefore this mode is used as infrequently as possible. Since the vector registers can hold collectively as many as $15 \times 8 \times 2000 = 240{,}000$ operands, two or more matrices of rather substantial size can be stored within the vector processors. This tends to reduce the need to store and reload data selectively to and from the vector registers.

Vector operations can be performed concurrently with scalar operations that take place in the scalar processor. Hence the architecture provides for overlapping the serial computations that constitute loop overhead with the parallel execution of the prior loop. Earlier in this text, this process has been described as an essential aspect of efficient processing.

The machine is heavily oriented to typical computations associated with large-scale numerical processing. The benefit of using this approach is that its users can purchase only what they need, since they can purchase as many or as few vector processors as they can justify. Moreover, they can use an existing on-site processor as a host and need not support the design and development of a distinct host.

We discuss the role of the indirect-address pointers in the next section, which focuses on techniques for handling sparse matrices.

5.5 Sparse-Matrix Techniques

In many matrix problems, relatively few elements of a matrix are nonzero. Such matrices arise in finite-element problems in which a nonzero entry represents the interaction of one element of volume with a neighboring volume element. The number of nonzero elements is related to the number of neighbors per volume element and is generally a very small fraction of the total number of matrix entries.

These matrices are very similar to matrices that describe continuum-model problems, and indeed they should be, because the finite-element model is a continuum model. The difference is the irregularity of the surface or volume that is being modeled. In modeling the stresses on an airframe, for example, near-neighbor descriptions of a cylindrical fuselage produce a sparse matrix whose structure leads to very simple near-neighbor operations. If the model extends beyond the fuselage, however, the problem can become very difficult to solve. If the model includes the wings, for example, then, at the place the wings are joined to the fuselage, we must include some interactions that explain the stresses likely to be found there. These interactions give rise to nonzero elements that lie in the matrix in relatively unpredictable places.

When a sparse matrix is highly structured with no irregularities, it is often possible to deal with the nonzero elements exclusively. In the continuum-model problems investigated earlier, this is precisely what the programs do. In two dimensions, a typical code accesses the four nearest neighbors, and no other accesses are required.

If we move to a finite-element description of an airframe, then near-neighbor accesses suffice for most interactions, but the remaining interactions, such as the ones that describe the stresses where the wing joins the fuselage, require nonlocal accesses. Moreover, the nonlocal accesses need not follow any uniform or predictable pattern. Hence, to process only the nonzero matrix elements may require rather rich and expensive interconnections. Moreover, the interconnections may need to be used selectively rather than in parallel because of the absence of regularity in the distribution of the nonzero elements in the sparse matrix.

Several approaches have been used in architectures to solve sparse-matrix problems. An early attempt in the CDC STAR created what was known as *sparse vectors*. A sparse vector consists of two vectors—one is a short vector that contains just the nonzero elements of a vector, and the other is a bit vector whose 1s indicate where the nonzero elements belong, and whose 0s represent the zeros in the vector. The length of the bit vector is equal to the length of the sparse vector, but there is a 64-to-1 reduction in the number of bits when the vector elements are 64-bit operands.

When accessing or storing sparse vectors, the CDC STAR uses the bit vector to determine whether an access has to be made in a particular index position. The access is skipped if the bit vector has a 0 in the corresponding position. Although the bit vector can reduce the number of memory accesses, the items that are accessed may lie in conflicting memory modules, which leads to delays in the pipeline. This can negate some of the performance gain attributed to the accesses saved by dealing only with the nonzero elements. There is a small additional processing overhead per 0 in the bit vector, but not as large a penalty as a full memory access.

Obviously an architecture of this type can incorporate various other facilities for sparse vectors, such as the ability to translate a vector from sparse format into a full vector format and to translate back again. Also, the pipeline arithmetic units can be organized to accept sparse vectors at their inputs and to produce sparse vectors at their outputs by doing conversions on the fly from sparse to computational and back to sparse.

The major problem with this approach is that there is only a 64-to-1 reduction in the information saved since, at best, it still takes a single bit to represent 64 bits. Large sparse matrices are so sparse in many applications that a 64-to-1 improvement is minuscule compared to what is possible. How this basic approach might be extended is still an open question for research.

An alternative method for representing sparse matrices is to store only the nonzero elements, and with each array of elements store a list of indices in the original matrix. It may be necessary as well to invert this structure by mapping indices to pointers by a hashing scheme that maintains a compact storage representation of the inverted list.

If the hash lookup finds an index, then the corresponding element is nonzero, and the hash table contains the storage address of the corresponding datum. If the hash lookup fails to find an item, the corresponding item has a zero value. Hashing for access to data is very much like a cache lookup. Just as a cache lookup can be pipelined, so can hash access, and therefore this method for dealing with sparse arrays is potentially useful in pipeline computers.

Returning to Fig. 5.18, the T-registers in the scalar processor contain the indices of nonzero elements of a sparse matrix. When operations need to be done for nonzero items only, as each new item is accessed, the scalar processor finds the address of the next nonzero element and fetches that datum instead of fetching the next sequential datum. The program has to deal with the zero elements that have been skipped, but the cost of skipping and the additional performance degradation from memory contention can be very small relative to the large gains in processing speed due to the elimination of processing the 0s in the sparse matrix.

Apart from methods related to the representation of sparse matrices are algorithms that perform computations only on nonzero elements of sparse matrices. The major difficulty is to develop such algorithms when the sparse matrix does not have a simple structure. Hoshino [1989] gives an example of how to treat a sparse problem that is almost tridiagonal, and is an excellent model of a successful methodology that can be used for sparse problems in which the majority of the nonzero elements fall into a particular structure. The problem treated by Hoshino is the solution of a block tridiagonal system of linear equations. The nonzero elements of the **A** matrix lie exclusively in smaller blocks that lie on the diagonal or immediately above or below it. The small blocks are themselves tridiagonal matrices. Standard techniques for tridiagonal matrices can reduce this system to a smaller system of equations, but the reduction cannot be taken to the full solution of the equations when the original equations are block tridiagonal. However, the result of the reduction produces a reduced set of equations that is solvable, in this case by standard tridiagonal techniques. For finite-element codes, in particular, sparse techniques reduce the equations to a much smaller set that may well be dense or have a sparse structure that can be exploited. Consequently, there is hope that sparse problems that arise in actual practice can be solved successfully on a parallel computer with high efficiency, but as yet this problem area has not been deeply explored.

This completes our discussion of sparse-matrix techniques. In the next section we take a quick tour of a very high-performance machine somewhat different from the ones mentioned thus far in the chapter.

5.6 The GF-11—A Very High-Speed Vector Processor

This chapter has assumed that pipelining techniques are the principle techniques for vector processors. The FPS-164 example suggests that pipeline processing may not give enough performance, and that some combination between pipeline and fully parallel implementation may be useful as well.

In this section we describe a machine architecture developed by IBM that is yet another combination of pipelined and parallel design, with a much stronger parallel component than the FPS-164 has. The machine is called the GF-11 [Beetem, Denneau, and Weingarten 1985], which stems from its peak performance of 11 Gflops (1100 Mflops).

The general structure of the GF-11 is very much like a richly connected ILLIAC IV; it appears in Fig. 5.20. The interconnection network is capable of producing any permutation whatsoever among the 576 processors in the system. The interconnection network is a three-stage network with two shuffles between the three stages. However, these shuffles lie between 24 × 24 crossbar switches, as shown in Fig. 5.21, rather than between 2 × 2 switching elements. This network is sometimes called a *Benes* network [Benes 1964], and it is known to be capable of producing an arbitrary permutation.

Since the GF-11 is a vector processor, it issues vector instructions from a control unit, and they are obeyed by the 576 processors. The memory per processor is modest—64 K-bytes of high-speed and 256 K-bytes of slower-speed memory—but the total memory in the processor is very large because of

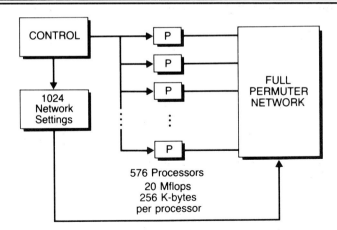

Fig. 5.20 The structure of the GF-11 research machine.

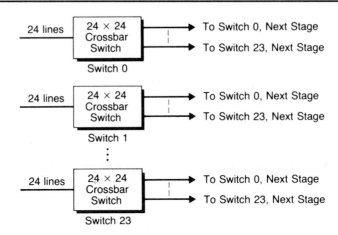

Fig. 5.21 Detailed view of a portion of the GF-11 full permuter switch. The 576 lines pass through three ranks of switches, one rank of which is shown here. Each switch is connected to all 24 switches in the next rank.

the multiplier of 576. The slow memory alone accounts for 144 M-bytes. Slow memory is expandable to 2M per processor as higher density chips become available, which allows expansion to 1.125 G-bytes in the system.

The processor speed is several times faster than the speed of fast local memory. Consequently, each processor has a very high speed register file that serves as the fastest level of the memory hierarchy. The arithmetic processor itself is pipelined to maintain high throughput for floating-point operations. Hence the pipelining occurs mainly within the arithmetic unit, and the high-replication factor of 576 gives the extraordinary throughput for the system.

The primary purpose for the construction of this processor is to solve a problem in quantum chromodynamics whose solution can produce the mass of various elementary particles through lengthy calculations. If the computed mass is equal to the observed measurements of mass, the predictions of the underlying theory will be confirmed, thereby lending some evidence that the theory is correct. If not, the theory needs to be modified or abandoned. Unfortunately, the computation involves the evaluation of very slowly converging multiple integrals. At the rate of 11 Gflops, the computation takes about one calendar year.

The structure of the GF-11 is vector-oriented, with a single broadcast instruction stream. This structure is used because the quantum chromo-dynamics problem calls for repeated summations that must be synchronized across all processors. The communication requirements of the problem stem from reliability considerations. The GF-11 programs are designed for only 512 processors, and the idea is to use the 64 remaining processors as spares. Should any processor fail, it can be quickly mapped out of the array, and a spare processor can be mapped into the array in its place. The machine then needs to be restarted from the last checkpoint, but it should continue to operate at full speed after it is restarted.

The switch permutation is controlled by a collection of bit vectors stored in the memory called *permutation memory* in Fig. 5.20. This memory holds 1024 bit vectors, each selectable by a 10-bit index issued from the control unit. To perform a specific permutation, the controller issues the 10-bit index to the permutation memory. Then the bit vector produced by this read is loaded into the switch, and the settings are made. Then data traverses the switch.

The quantum chromodynamics problem uses only 6 of the 1024 possible settings. In the event of a processor failure, it is relatively straightforward to compute a new bit vector that maps out the failed processor and replaces it with a spare. When that bit vector is stored in the permutation memory, the computation can proceed.

The GF-11 is a research vehicle, not a commercial machine. If it is successful as a research machine for solving the problem posed, that does not mean that this architecture is cost-effective for problems in general. However, its rich interconnection structure enhances the GF-11's ability to execute more problems in general. The major constraint on GF-11 programs is that all processors execute the same instruction stream.

5.7 Final Comments on Vector Computers

It is interesting to contrast and compare the ideas that emerge from the discussion in this chapter to see their strengths and to identify future trends in vector machines. We have explored the pure pipeline structures of the CDC STAR and Cray I, the combination of pipeline and parallel structure of the FPS-164 and the GF-11, and in Chapter 4, the purely parallel structure of the ILLIAC IV. These machines span a rather broad set of design choices. The major trends identified are to:

- Provide vector instructions to take advantage of this approach for numerical applications;
- Provide facilities to extend the range of applicability of the architecture beyond vector processing;
- Use multiple levels of memory, particularly high-speed buffers; and
- Mix pipeline and parallel techniques in various degrees to achieve an acceptable value of price to performance.

On the other hand, the characteristics that differ from processor to processor concern the specific design choices that trade-off speed against cost and flexibility against efficiency. No one design is best. Choices were driven in many cases by available technology, which differed considerably for the designs described in this text. Had all designers been given the same underlying technology, some individual design choices might be common among several architectures, but even then it is unlikely that any two designs would be markedly similar.

The examples we discuss show the final choices of the designers, and our discussion illustrates various aspects of the choices that affect cost and performance. Unfortunately, we are not able to present the interesting choices that were investigated along the way and abandoned for various reasons.

The trends listed here are by no means the only ones that exist, nor can we rule out new trends in the future as technology makes new designs possible. The future architect should use this discussion as a guide, but not as an exhaustive treatment of the subject. Examine any attractive idea and be prepared to develop it into a full-fledged machine design. But be sure to examine it carefully. Rarely is there a case for building a machine that is handicapped by some inherent inefficiency.

The major implementation technique for vector machines appears to be pipelining. We see two basic reasons for this to be true:

1. Pipelining provides a means for coupling a slow memory to a fast arithmetic unit.

2. Pipelining enables arithmetic units to produce a sequence of results at a rate much faster than their inherent latency in forming a single result.

If we view the memory system and the arithmetic system as two distinct bottlenecks in a conventional computer system, then we can see that pipelined architecture attempts to relieve both bottlenecks. For memory systems, the rate at which operands are produced at a memory port is anywhere from 5 to 20 times the rate at which the memory system cycles one memory module. Similarly, the rate at which sums and products are produced at the output of an arithmetic unit is from three to ten times faster for a pipelined structure than for a conventional serial structure. These are significant speed improvements whose individual cost is relatively low compared to the cost of a full computer system. Consequently, we can expect to see the continuation of the trend to build pipelined arithmetic units driven by pipelined memory systems.

In the last chapter we introduced six technology constraints that have to be overcome by a high-performance design. In this section we review those constraints and discuss how a vector architecture deals with them in achieving high performance.

- *Processor bandwidth:* Two major ways of boosting processing bandwidth are discussed here. Pipelined arithmetic is probably the most widely used method because of its high performance at relatively low cost. To deliver speeds beyond those available from pipelined arithmetic alone, replication of arithmetic units into fully parallel systems is the technique of choice.

- *Memory bandwidth:* For main memory, designers build large memory systems from multiple independent memory modules. Bandwidth grows with the number of independent modules. To match the bandwidth of arithmetic units, one or two levels of high-speed memory are used, most frequently in the form of addressable registers. The trend is to make the high-speed buffers very large, offering from 256K to 1M of storage currently and larger storage in the years to come.

- *Input/output bandwidth:* Although we have not discussed input/output in this chapter, it is clear that input/output bandwidth can be increased proportionally to increases in memory bandwidth if we assume that input/output operations require a fixed fraction of memory operations. Most high-performance systems incorporate 10 to 20 direct memory-access channels whose speeds are compatible with main memory speed. They rely heavily on a high-memory bandwidth, usually obtained through the use of multiple-memory modules.

- *Communication bandwidth:* the majority of the vector architectures discussed in this chapter do not require processor-to-processor communication. Information is distributed among operands within the vector operation itself by means, for example, of a scalar product that combines information from all elements in two vectors. Information is also distributed among different vectors through a common memory. The arithmetic unit can obtain operand values that are the results of various computations by accessing those values in main memory. In this case communication bandwidth and memory bandwidth refer to the same quantity.

  The exception in this chapter is the GF-11. It has local memory only, and computations interact through an interconnection network. This bandwidth is made very high by disallowing conflicts in the network. The interconnections are set according to precomputed control data, so they yield a useful processor-to-processor permutation. The communication bandwidth is comparable to memory bandwidth.

- *Synchronization:* for one pipeline, synchronization is accomplished automatically because operations are performed in the order in which they enter the pipeline. For multiple pipelines, the FPS-164 approach is to synchronize by using a single program to control all pipelines. The GF-11 approach is similar in that a single control unit issues a broadcast command to all processors.

  Both the FPS-164 and GF-11 synchronize all processors at each step through the instruction stream. The Cray architecture uses pipeline interlocks to control vector operations so that nonconflicting operations can be done in parallel, and dependent operations are chained to overlap as much as possible, provided that the overlap does not create an incorrect answer.

- *Multiple purpose:* the vector machines discussed in this chapter tend to be useful over a large class of vector problems, mainly because they support a variety of data-access modes and have rich sets of vector instructions. Nevertheless, their utility is biased strongly to numerical applications, and it is not clear that they are efficient for nonnumerical applications.

These characteristics clearly show that the major advantages of a vector architecture are:

- Efficient use of memory bandwidth through pipelined access;
- The excellent cost-performance of pipelined arithmetic; and
- The very simple mechanisms that serve the needs of communication and synchronization.

These three characteristics yield a combination of high performance and high efficiency. Unfortunately, they do not yield a system that is well suited to all purposes. In general, vector processors have a much larger area of applications than do continuum-model processors with near-neighbor connections. The key difference is that vector processors can deal with both local and remote operands by making use of a large random-access main memory to fetch data at arbitrary locations. Processors with only near-neighbor mesh connections have limited ability to reach remote data. With a larger realm of application, vector processors have created an important niche in computing and are far more widely used than continuum-model processors.

Exercises

5.1 The purpose of this exercise is to explore techniques for implementing the individual operations of Program 5.1. The algorithm scans a column for a maximum element, pivots by interchanging rows, then updates a partial row, partial column, and a square subarray. Your objective is to work out a pipelined architecture that can perform each of the processes of scan for maximum, pivot, row update, column update, and subarray update individually in pipelined fashion without requiring overlap between operations. Your goal is to produce one result per machine cycle within each process, but you are allowed to have periods between processes during which no results are produced. (For the MAX operation, try to produce one comparison per cycle.)

For timing, assume the following total delays per operation:

Memory access	four cycles
Add	two cycles
Multiply	two cycles
Divide	eight cycles

You are constrained to use main memory for vector storage since your arithmetic subsystem has insufficient register storage to hold vectors or substantial portions of vectors. In your answer you must show at least:

- The storage format of the array in memory;
- The machine instructions for each of the processes (with a clear description of the action of these instructions);
- A block diagram of the computer system showing the principal elements; and
- A discussion of the way that each of the five processes is handled.

5.2 The object of this exercise is to write programs for a processor designed for vector operations. Carefully study Program 5.1. Assume that it is executed on a processor similar to the one shown in Fig. 5.1. There are 64 independent memories, and the matrix is 32 × 32. Memory operations take 12 machine cycles, and all arithmetic results are delivered by vector instructions at the rate of one per cycle.

a) Consider operations on a matrix stored with entire columns in individual memories and rows stored across memories. For each major portion of the program, what speedup is achieved?

b) Consider the matrix stored in skewed format so that rows and columns are each accessible in a single access. What is the speedup for each major section of the code? Consider the effects of nonunit stride when calculating the speedup.

c) If variable delays are used to align vectors, what is the maximum length of each delay required for any vector allocation, assuming that vector access for both sources and the destination have a stride of 1?

5.3 The purpose of this exercise is to contrast the results obtained for a pipelined architecture in the previous problem with a parallel vector architecture similar to the ILLIAC IV. For this problem assume that the 32 × 32 matrix problem of Exercise 5.2 is to be solved on an ILLIAC IV architecture that contains 64 processors connected as an 8 × 8 array. Each processor is connected to four processors whose indices differ by +1, −1, +8, and −8 modulo 64.

a) Let the matrix be stored with columns in individual memories and rows across memories. For each major portion of the program, what speedup is achieved?

b) If the matrix is stored in skewed format so that rows and columns are each accessible in a single access, what is the speedup for each major section of the code? Assume that deskewing can be done at no cost.

c) If each unit shift requires one cycle, what is the speedup for each major section of code in this version of the program?

d) If you use the interconnections as given to speed up the deskewing, and each single interconnection takes one cycle, what is the speedup for each major section of code in this version of the program?

5.4 The algorithm for Gaussian elimination used in Exercise 5.3 accesses both rows and columns of a matrix. Access in two different dimensions may reduce efficiency, and it is worthwhile to modify the algorithm to work out a variation that uses column access only.

a) Consider how to change the algorithm so that it accesses columns only, yet is faithful to the intent of the original algorithm and has an efficiency that is competitive with (but possibly poorer than) the algorithm implementation of

Exercise 5.3. Describe your new algorithm briefly, then give a detailed discussion of the portions of the algorithm that differ from the implementation in Exercise 5.3.

b) The new portions of the algorithm may require somewhat different architecture than that described in Exercise 5.3. Describe an architectural design that is well suited to implementing those portions of the new version of the algorithm that differ from the corresponding portions of the old version. Give enough information to establish that your implementation is efficient and reasonable.

5.5 The purpose of this exercise is to examine vector pipeline techniques. Consider the recurrence equation, Eq. (4.13), and explore its implementation in a pipelined computer system.

a) To obtain maximum parallelism, Eq. (4.13) should be solved by recursive doubling. Find a recursive doubling solution or use the solution obtained in the answer to Exercise 4.7.

b) Show the block diagram of a specialized pipeline to evaluate one cycle of a recursive doubling version of the recurrence. This diagram can be broken into blocks that are addition, subtraction, multiplication, and division. The blocks are assumed to be multicycle floating-point units, each capable of being pipelined with a rate of completion of one result per cycle.

c) Show how to stream the constant vectors into a processing unit based on your pipelined design so that the recursive doubling solution is fully pipelined. Use delays in place of interlocks and attempt to produce results at the rate of one result per cycle. Use multiple copies of the units designed in b and give the structure of the full processor by showing how to connect each of the copies from b with extra delays to produce the answers to the recurrence.

5.6 The purpose of this exercise is to contrast caches with high-speed storage registers in systems that use vector arithmetic. Reconsider the Gaussian elimination algorithm of Program 5.1, operating on a 64×64 matrix. In this exercise, when we refer to the array-update process, we refer to the innermost loop of that algorithm.

a) Assume that there are 32 independent memories, each capable of a two-cycle access time. Compare the relative timing for accessing a row versus a column when accesses are pipelined.

b) Now consider the effect of a cache. The cache consists of 64 sets, two-way associative, with each line of the cache holding one operand. Assume that a single vector of length 64 is accessed two consecutive times and no intervening access is made. For the second vector access, how many misses will there be if the vector is a row vector? How many if the vector is a column vector? State your assumptions on the storage format and the mapping of addresses to cache lines.

c) In one iteration of the array-update process in the algorithm, how many misses will there be? (To simplify the calculation, you may assume that all vector accesses are of length 64, even though the actual length depends on the specific iteration of the algorithm.) Note that you may completely ignore the other accesses as if they were not present at all. A miss is defined to be an access to an item that is not present because it either was not accessed in the previous iteration of the algorithm or was displaced from the cache because at least two other lines in the same set were accessed more recently.

d) Now assume that there are two vector registers, each 64 items long. Show how to load data into the vector registers to reduce the number of data accesses to memory as much as you can.

e) Use the data you have developed and parameters given to calculate the relative number of accesses to main memory for the cache-based computer and the register-based computer when the array-update process is performed.

5.7 The inner loop of an algorithm performs the following operation:

$$Sum: = Sum + b \times C[i]/d$$

Assume that b, $C[i]$, and d are variables that can be streamed into a pipeline from memory with one cycle delay between accesses to each variable, so that memory is not a bottleneck for computation. The objective is to perform the operation given to produce the final sum in minimum time.

a) Design the block diagram and functional behavior of a three-function pipeline whose operations are multiply, add, and divide. Find the collision vectors for controlling the system and the fastest possible cycle for the sequence of multiplication, division, and addition when operating on independent operands. (This does not account for the interlocking necessary to make sure that the value of Sum used as an input is derived from the most recent value of Sum as an output.)

b) Now consider the maximum speed attainable when the input to the adder is interlocked to the output of the adder. What is this maximum speed in your design?

c) If we want to produce one update of Sum per cycle on the average, how can we structure the computation to come close to achieving this rate?

5.8 Consider an architecture similar to the Burroughs' Scientific Processor (BSP) in which 17 items are read from memory, but only 16 are delivered to the arithmetic unit.

a) For a 16×16 matrix, consider how to select the elements of a column and permute them into column order for delivery to the arithmetic unit. What are the selection and permutation operations required to access Column 0? Column 3? Column 4? Assume that the matrix rows are stored across the memories.

b) What are the selection and permutation operations required to access Row 0? Row 3? Row 4?

c) What basic permutations would you build into this machine to facilitate row access? What permutations would you build in to facilitate column access?

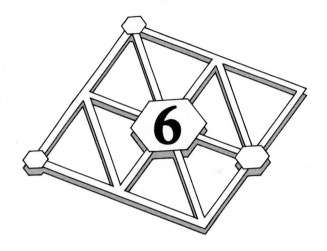

Multiprocessors

6.1 Background
6.2 Multiprocessor Performance
6.3 Multiprocessor Interconnections
6.4 Cache Coherence in Multiprocessors
6.5 Summary

Thus far we have treated methods for speeding up a single instruction stream. Although there is but a single program in execution, the designs discussed earlier exploit concurrency within the instruction stream and within individual instructions. In this chapter we turn to the discussion of *multiprocessors*—computer systems composed of several independent processors. The motivation for moving toward multiple processors is strictly a matter of performance because device technology places an upper bound on the speed of any single processor. To exceed that bound requires multiple processors.

The central themes of this chapter are multiprocessor structures and performance. Our objective is to show several interesting techniques for organizing multiple processors into highly parallel systems and to give insight into the potential performance improvements and bottlenecks of such systems. Chapter 7 treats software strategies for using the available parallelism of these systems.

6.1 Background

Our earlier discussions of high-performance machines study two important classes of parallelism. Pipeline machines produce high performance by placing several stages of a pipeline in operation simultaneously. Machines for continuum calculations have multiple processors, each executing the same program. In both cases, a single program is used to operate on vectors or arrays of data. Flynn [1966] termed this type of parallelism *single-instruction stream, multiple-data stream (SIMD)* parallelism. Recall, for example, an extreme implementation of this idea in the form of the GF-11, in which each of 576 processors executes identical instructions broadcast to them by a single control unit.

Another SIMD machine with massive parallelism is the Connection Machine [Hillis 1986] with 64K 1-bit processors. The architect is truly fortunate when an application can be executed on machines that are built around the lock-step parallelism required for SIMD machines because the architecture efficiently executes programs well suited to SIMD execution.

High performance on such machines requires rewriting conventional algorithms to manipulate many data simultaneously by means of instructions broadcast to all processors. Although programming for these machines can be difficult in principle, in the ideal case, a serial algorithm can be converted to an SIMD algorithm by replacing each inner loop with a single broadcast instruction that implements the complete loop. The fact that an important, but limited, class of problems fits this model extremely well has provided the impetus for the design and construction of these machines.

Clearly, some large problems do not lend themselves to efficient execution in an SIMD architecture. The operations required for such problems cannot easily be organized into repetitive operations on uniformly structured data. They tend to be unstructured and unpredictable. Addressing patterns tend to be data dependent, so the architecture cannot easily preload data by anticipating future accesses.

The architect who must attain high performance for such problems inevitably looks for a solution in a multiprocessor structure. Such an architecture is composed of several independent computers, each capable of executing its own program. Flynn [1966] calls this type of architecture *multiple-instruction stream, multiple-data stream (MIMD)* architecture. The processors of a multiprocessor are interconnected in some fashion to permit programs to exchange data and synchronize activities.

A model of such an architecture is shown in Fig. 6.1. In this figure each processor has registers, arithmetic and logic units, and access to memory and input/output modules. In Fig. 6.1(a) we show the memory and input/output systems as separate subsystems shared among all of the processors. Figure 6.1(b) shows the memory and input/output units attached to individual processors. No sharing of memory and input/output is permitted in Fig. 6.1(b). In both cases, because the system contains multiple processors, each capable of executing an independent program, the system fits Flynn's MIMD model.

In both systems depicted in Fig. 6.1 the processors cooperate by exchanging data through the interconnection system and by synchronizing activities. The shared memory in Fig. 6.1(a) provides a convenient means for information interchange and synchronization since any pair of processors can communicate through a shared location. The structure in Fig. 6.1(b) supports communication through point-to-point exchange of information. Obviously, multiprocessors can have any reasonable combination of shared global mem-

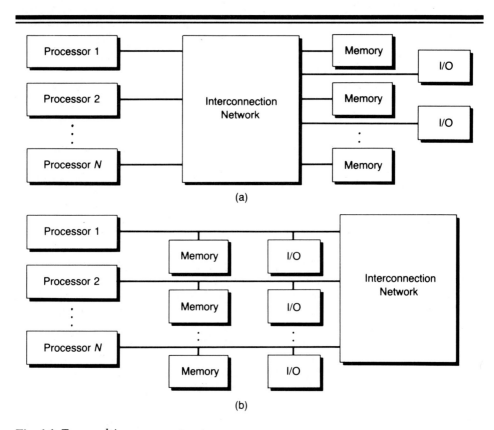

Fig. 6.1 Two multiprocessor structures:
(a) All memory and I/O are remote and shared; and
(b) All memory and I/O are local and private.

ory or private local memory. Figure 6.1 shows the extremes in the design space, and practical designs lie at the extremes or anywhere in between.

The main purpose of a high-speed multiprocessor is to complete a job faster by using several machines concurrently than can be done by using a single copy of the same machine. In some applications, the main purpose for using multiple processors is for reliability rather than high performance. The idea is that if any single processor fails, its workload can be performed by other processors in the system. Since the design principles of such systems are quite different from the principles that guide the design of high-performance systems, we do not address design for reliability in this text, but rather we limit our attention to issues related to performance.

When a multiprocessor is operating at peak performance, all processors are engaged in useful work. No processor is idle, and no processor is executing an instruction that would not be executed if the same algorithm were executing on a single processor. In this state of peak performance, all N processors of a multiprocessor are contributing to effective performance, and the processing rate is increased by a factor of N.

Peak performance is a very special state that is rarely achievable. There are several factors that introduce inefficiency. Among the factors are:

- The delays introduced by interprocessor communications;
- The overhead in synchronizing the work of one processor with another;
- Lost efficiency when one or more processors run out of tasks;
- Lost efficiency due to wasted effort by one or more processors; and
- The processing costs for controlling the system and scheduling operations.

Both scheduling and synchronization are sources of overhead on serial machines. In citing these factors together with the other factors, we are citing how they degrade multiprocessor performance beyond the effects that may already be present on individual processors.

A high-performance vector processor is free from many of the problems, but it does suffer from lost performance because it is unable to keep all of the processing units busy. This latter problem arises particularly when a computation is not easily implemented as a sequence of vector operations performed on highly structured, densely stored data.

The architect who designs and builds a multiprocessor must pay close attention to the sources of inefficiency exposed here. They can lead to serious degradation in performance. For example, if the combined inefficiencies produce an effective processing rate of only 10 percent of the peak rate, then ten processors are required in a multiprocessor system just to do the work of a single processor.

Fortunately, for a small number of processors, careful design can hold the inefficiency to a low figure, but inefficiencies tend to climb as the number of processors increase. There is a point where adding additional processors can lengthen, not shorten, computation time.

The fact that inefficiency tends to grow with the number of processors is the underlying reason why many commercial offerings of multiprocessors have a small number of processors, such as 4, 8, or 16. The fastest machines are built from the fastest devices available and have relatively few processors.

Consider, for example, the Cray XMP, a four-processor version of the Cray I. Another example is the IBM 309X family for which systems with up to six processors are available. Both of these implementations start with very high speed devices and use architectural techniques such as cache and pipelining to produce very high performance single processors for their respective markets.

Users of these machines may have workloads or individual problems whose needs exceed the capacity of a single machine. Additional performance is not readily available from faster versions of the same machine because the machines are already at the limits imposed by architecture and device technology. An effective way to attain small multiples of performance improvement is to group together two or four identical processors.

Some computer architects take note of a cost characteristic mentioned in Chapter 1. The discussion there indicates that high-speed device technology is much more expensive than lower-speed technology.

Moreover, with today's devices the cost of fast devices tends to grow faster than the performance benefit of the increased device speed. Hence, the cost per unit of computing power tends to be greater for high-end machines than for low-end machines, although this trend is technology dependent and could change over time. Nevertheless, when lower-speed technology has a cost advantage, we have an opportunity to create a cost-effective high-performance system by combining hundreds or thousands of slow-speed processors built with low-cost devices.

The cost advantage of using low-cost technology is balanced by the degradation in efficiency that inevitably occurs as the number of processors increases. If the degradation due to the large number of processors exceeds the cost advantage of the low-cost technology, then there is no particular advantage to using hundreds of slow processors over using a few very fast processors.

Moreover, the complexity of programming a machine with hundreds of processors far exceeds the complexity of programming a single processor or a computer system with just a few processors. Consequently, although economics might enhance the attractiveness of a machine with hundreds of low-speed computers, the advantage of this structure disappears if efficiency is not held high.

Thus, there is no particular magic in the parallelism of a multiprocessor. The parallelism yields a useful benefit when it successfully produces higher performance. When the parallelism cannot be tapped effectively, it simply adds to the system cost and complexity. In such a case, the end user is best served by reducing the parallelism to a point where the parallelism available can be used effectively. Whether there are 10, 1000, or 1,000,000 processors, it is bad practice to squander processing power. The argument that "processors are cheap" is irrelevant if, by using fewer processors, performance goes up.

In the next section we address the question of efficiency more carefully, especially considering the ratio of the time spent executing useful instructions compared to the time spent communicating with other processors.

6.2 Multiprocessor Performance

The point of this section is to analyze the performance benefit of multiple processors in the face of overhead incurred to create parallelism. The models studied are variations of models introduced by Indurkhya, Stone, and Xi-Cheng [1986]. This section shows that performance benefits strongly depend on the ratio R/C, where R is the length of a run-time quantum and C is the length of communications overhead produced by that quantum. The ratio expresses how much overhead is incurred per unit of computation. When the ratio is very low, it becomes unprofitable to use parallelism. When the ratio is very high, parallelism is potentially profitable. Note that a large ratio can be obtained by partitioning a computing job into relatively few large pieces, and that the amount of parallelism for such a ratio might be much smaller than the maximum available.

The ratio R/C is a measure of *task granularity*:

- In *coarse-grain* parallelism, R/C is relatively high, so each unit of computation produces a relatively small amount of communication; and
- In *fine-grain* parallelism, R/C is very low, so there is a relatively large amount of communication and other overhead per unit of computation.

Coarse-grain parallelism arises when individual tasks are large and overhead can be amortized over many computational cycles. Fine-grain parallelism usually provides opportunities to perform execution on many more processors than can fruitfully support coarse-grained parallelism. The idea of fine-grain parallelism is to partition a program into increasingly smaller tasks that can run in parallel. At the ultimate limit, each individual task may be as small as a single operation. More commonly, however, a fine-grained task contains a small number of instructions.

The programmer seeking maximum performance is strongly tempted to partition a problem into the finest possible granularity to create the maximum amount of parallelism. But if the maximum parallelism also has the maximum overhead, it is not clear that maximum parallelism leads to the fastest solution.

The main reason for the presentation of the performance models in this section is to show the pervasive role of the R/C ratio on performance. The discussion that follows shows how a fine-grain partition that happens to have a low R/C ratio produces poorer performance than a much coarser partition with a higher R/C ratio. Hence the much higher parallelism of the fine-grain partition need not produce higher net speed.

The purpose of presenting a number of different performance models to make this point is that no one model is truly representative of multiprocessors or of multiprocessor algorithms. We consider a number of different variations of the basic model to cover a variety of program behaviors and multiprocessor architectures. In every case, the role of R/C is the same. Small ratios lead to poor performance because of high overhead. Large ratios usually reflect poor exploitation of parallelism. For maximum performance, it is necessary to balance parallelism against overhead. The only difference from model to model is the point where the two factors become balanced.

Architects have long debated the relative qualities of fine and coarse granularity. For SIMD machines, the GF-11 is a coarse-grained machine whose individual processors can sustain a peak rate as high as 20 Mflops. The Connection Machine is an SIMD machine whose 1-bit processors are better suited to fine-grained tasks and whose performance stems from the massive number of processors rather than from the computational power of an individual processor.

What reasoning led the architects of one machine to seek such a vastly different solution than did the architects of the other machine? The range of applications is the primary motivation for the difference. The Connection Machine is designed to exploit parallelism of tasks such as image analysis, in which a significant portion of the work is characterized by fine-grained tasks. The GF-11, which is designed for much larger-grained tasks, would be burdened by overhead if the tasks carried the additional overhead attributable to fine granularity. Thus the architects of each machine attempted to match granularity to the applications for the machine.

At one end of the multiprocessor scale are the Cray multiprocessors, such as the Cray XMP—a four-processor system in which each processor is a Cray I supercomputer. Under ideal circumstances, communication in this system occurs only at the end of major phases, which might well be every few million or few billion instructions.

Smaller granularity is evident on microprocessor-based multiprocessors such as the Cosmic Cube and a number of commercial versions of this hypercube-based design. These machines typically use 64 to 256 copies of a high-performance 32-bit microprocessor. The different granularity biases the machines somewhat to different application programs.

The remainder of this section is devoted to performance models. In each model, observe how the ratio R/C determines the strategy that achieves the optimum performance. To simplify the models, we have generally ignored the effects of synchronization and contention except as crudely approximated by the models. In practical systems, the effects ignored here tend to lower performance from that predicted by these models. In most instances, the best way to compensate for the unmodeled effects is to increase the granularity of tasks.

6.2.1 The Basic Model—Two Processors with Unoverlapped Communications

For the first model, consider an application program that contains M tasks. Our objective is to execute this program at maximum speed on a system with N processors. For simplicity, we first consider a system with just two processors and then let the number of processors increase. To model performance we need to characterize the combination of execution time and overhead that will be incurred.

Let us make the following assumptions to obtain our initial results. Subsequently we relax the assumptions and see how the performance changes. Specifically, we assume that:

1. Each task executes in R units of time; and

2. Each task communicates with every other task at an overhead cost of C units of time when the communicating tasks are not on the same processor, and at no cost when the communicating tasks are coresident.

We have various choices of how to execute such an application on a two-processor system. We can assign all tasks to one processor and ignore the second processor, which is a solution that minimizes communication overhead but fails to take advantage of available parallelism, or we can partition the tasks to the two processors in any combination. If the tasks are split across the processors, then the total execution time is a combination of the time spent in execution and the time spent engaged in overhead activities. Although we use the notation C as if C were exclusively due to communication, it is convenient to lump overhead from all sources into C.

To some extent, overhead can be overlapped with computation, especially if processors can perform communication through input/output ports while executing concurrently. However, not all sources of overhead can be hidden by overlapping with computation. Processors can contend for shared data or shared communication paths, and they may be idle during synchronization periods. Therefore, we assume that some portion of overhead operations lengthen total processing time because overhead cannot be fully overlapped with computation. In this case the equation that describes total processing time is the following:

$$\text{Execution time} = R \operatorname{Max}(M-k, k) + C(M-k)k \qquad (6.1)$$

Equation (6.1) expresses execution time as the sum of two terms, one attributed to run time and one to communication and other overhead. The run time for two processors is the larger of the run times experienced and is therefore the larger of $R(M - k)$ or Rk when k tasks are assigned to one processor and $M - k$ to the other. The second term models overhead to be proportional to the number of pair-wise communications that must take place as a function of how tasks are partitioned to the two processors. Note that the first term is a linear function of k, and the second term is a quadratic function of k.

What is the minimum execution time for Eq. (6.1) as a function of k? That is, how shall we assign tasks to two processors to produce the minimum execution time? Figure 6.2 shows a graphic way of finding a solution. The answer for this model is to assign all tasks to one processor if R/C is below $M/2$, or split the tasks evenly between two processors if R/C exceeds that threshold. That is, either $k = 0$ or $k = M/2$. (If k is odd, then make k as close to $M/2$ as possible.)

Figure 6.2 shows the two different cases that arise for the different values of the R/C ratio. The first term of Eq. (6.1) is piece-wise linear, and Fig. 6.2(a) shows that this term looks like the letter V because it is symmetric about the point $k = M/2$. In this figure, when the piece-wise linear term is added to the quadratic term, the resulting figure has a minimum at $M/2$.

In Figure 6.2(b), the minimum occurs at $k = 0$. The minimum has to be at an extreme point in the region $0 \leq k \leq M/2$ because the quadratic curve $k(M - k)$ is concave downward, and, after adding a linear term to this curve, the concavity is unchanged. A curve that is concave downward has its minimum at one of its endpoints. The endpoint of the curve at $k = 0$ (or at $k = M$) is the minimum when $R/C < M/2$; otherwise the minimum occurs at $k = M/2$.

6.2.2 Extension to N Processors

Now let's consider what happens when there are N processors. In this case, we assign k_i tasks to the ith processor. The generalization of Eq. (6.1) becomes

$$\text{Execution time} = R \, \text{Max} \, (k_i) + \frac{C}{2} \sum_i k_i \, (M - k_i)$$

$$= R \, \text{Max} \, (k_i) + \left(\frac{C}{2}\right) \left(M^2 - \sum_i k_i^2\right) \tag{6.2}$$

The first term counts the longest running time among the N execution times. To that time is added the overhead from the second term. That term counts the number of distinct pair-wise links between k_i tasks and $M - k_i$ tasks, each of which contributes an amount C to the total time. The second term in Eq. (6.2) is quadratic just as in Eq. (6.1).

If the reasoning used to analyze Eq. (6.1) holds for this equation, then we expect that the minimum value is for an extreme assignment, and indeed this

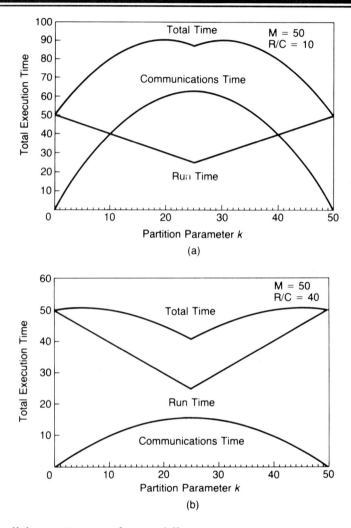

Fig. 6.2 Parallel execution time for two different R/C ratios:
(a) Optimum partition parameter $k = 0$; and
(b) Optimum partition parameter $k = M/2$.

is the case. Either all tasks are assigned to a single processor, or they are distributed "evenly" across all processors. By "evenly," we mean that if M is a multiple of N, then each processor receives M/N tasks. Otherwise, all but one processor receives the integer ceiling of M/N tasks, and one processor receives whatever is left over. This assignment does not necessarily use all N processors.

For example, when there are 19 tasks and six processors, the assignment places 4 tasks on four processors and 3 tasks on a fifth processor, leaving no tasks assigned to the sixth processor.

To show that the even distribution produces a local minimum, assume that k_1 has the maximum number of tasks assigned to it, and show that an assignment in which two processors receive fewer than k_1 tasks can be changed to an assignment with a lower cost, as computed by Eq. (6.2).

For example, assume that both k_2 and k_3 satisfy $k_1 > k_2 \geq k_3 \geq 1$. Consider the assignment that shifts one task from the third processor to the second processor and examine how the cost changes as per Eq. (6.2). The first term does not change because the change does not affect the maximum number of tasks assigned to a processor. The value of the second term is reduced, however, by the amount $C(k_2 - k_3 + 1)$. This assignment produces higher performance, and we can iterate this improvement process until no more than one processor has less than the maximum number of tasks assigned to it.

Equation (6.2) has a threshold for an assignment, just as Eq. (6.1) has, and by a remarkable coincidence the thresholds are identical! We must compare the even assignment of tasks to the assignment that places all tasks on one processor. The latter assignment is preferred when R/C is sufficiently small.

The difference in costs of the "even" distribution to N processors and a 1-processor assignment is given by

$$\text{Time difference} = \frac{RM}{N} + \frac{CM^2}{2} - \frac{CM^2}{2N} - RM \tag{6.3}$$

where the first three terms form the cost of the even distribution of tasks and the last term is the cost of assigning all tasks to one processor.

To simplify the analysis, we have ignored values of M that are not exact multiples of N. To solve for the threshold value of R/C, we set the value of Eq. (6.3) to 0. By removing a factor of M and then grouping terms by coefficients R and C, we can remove another factor of $(1 - 1/N)$. This yields the equation

$$\text{Time difference} = \frac{CM}{2} - R = 0 \tag{6.4}$$

or

$$\frac{R}{C} = \frac{M}{2} \tag{6.5}$$

This model shows that if R/C is greater than the threshold $M/2$, then an even distribution of tasks to as many processors as are available will produce the best time. On the other hand, if R/C is below that threshold, then no matter how many processors are available, no assignment produces a faster time than the assignment that uses only one processor. Here is a situation in which the role of overhead becomes quite clear.

Unless overhead is kept below a certain percentage of execution time, parallel execution cannot be beneficial. If this model holds for a parallel algorithm and architecture, then the control of overhead costs is absolutely essential for parallelism to be successful.

Although this analysis has looked at performance rather than costs, R/C determines the point at which parallelism is cost-effective. Even when R/C is sufficiently high to warrant parallelism, the performance gain is diminished by the second term of Eq. (6.2). The speedup attributable to parallelism is the ratio of the time to run on one processor to the time expressed by Eq. (6.2). This is approximately

$$\text{Speedup} = \frac{RM}{\left(\dfrac{RM}{N} + \dfrac{CM^2}{2} - \dfrac{CM^2}{2N}\right)}$$

$$= \frac{R}{\left(\dfrac{R}{N} + \dfrac{CM(1 - 1/N)}{2}\right)} \tag{6.6}$$

$$= \frac{\dfrac{RN}{C}}{\left(\dfrac{R}{C} + \dfrac{M(N-1)}{2}\right)}$$

If the first term of the denominator is large compared with the second, then the speedup is proportional to N. This requires M and N to be small and for R/C to be large. If parallelism is increased to the extent that the denominator is dominated by its second term because N is very large, the speedup is proportional to R/CM, which does not depend on the number of processors. Hence, as N increases, the speedup approaches a constant asymptote.

At this point each processor added to the system brings extra cost while yielding negligible performance benefit. Even though performance can improve incrementally as processors are added, the diminishing returns in performance are not worth the added cost. The number of processors should not be increased beyond some maximum that is a function of cost and the ratio R/C.

This model is a general picture of how granularity and overhead affect the performance gain of a multiprocessor, and it gives some indication of the importance of minimizing overhead and selecting the right granularity. It is only one model, however, and it cannot encompass the full spectrum of actual applications.

Let us alter the model in various ways and observe how the findings change. In general, we discover that R/C plays a critical role, regardless of the model. In some cases, there is the same type of threshold in which the best solutions are extreme. That is, use all available processors or just one processor, depending on the value of R/C. In some models, the extreme solutions are not the best. The best solutions for these models distribute work among several processors, but do not use all processors because the use of too many leads to performance degradation and extra cost. Moreover, in the general case, work need not be distributed evenly to achieve the optimum performance.

6.2.3 A Stochastic Model

Consider what happens when all tasks are not equal in execution time. The leading term in Eq. (6.2) is smallest when all processors run for equal lengths of time, so the objective is to scatter tasks among processors so that all processors are occupied for equal times. If this is not possible, the maximum running time among the processors should be as short as possible.

The second term in Eq. (6.2) is smallest when tasks are distributed as unevenly as possible. Consequently, among all ways of distributing tasks to processors so that processors have nearly equal running times, find a distribution in which the number of tasks assigned to each processor is as uneven as possible. That is, find schemes that assign as few or as many tasks per processor as possible, subject to the requirement that the total workload on a processor be equal to a given amount.

In this model, the best assignment need not be the most evenly distributed workload. If the workload is slightly uneven, it may become possible to assign tasks to processors in such a way that overhead is greatly diminished. That is, a small increase in the linear first term of Eq.(6.2) can be more than balanced by a large decrease in the quadratic second term.

A stochastic variation of the deterministic model presented here appears in Indurkhya, Stone, and Xi-Cheng [1986]. Instead of having all execution and communication times as fixed constants, the model assumes that the times are independent and identically distributed random variables with a mean R for the running times and a mean C for the communication times. To solve the model, Indurkhya *et al.* appeal to the central limit theorem and the additional assumption that

$$E\left[\text{Max}\left\{\sum_{i=1}^{k} r_i, \sum_{i=k+1}^{M} r_i\right\}\right] = \text{Max}\left\{E\left[\sum_{i=1}^{k} r_i\right], E\left[\sum_{i=k+1}^{M} r_i\right]\right\} \qquad (6.7)$$

The E in Eq. (6.7) denotes the expected value. Equation (6.7) says that the maximum of a set of expected values of sums of independent and identically distributed random variables r_i, the running times of the tasks, is equal to the expected value of the maximum of the sums. With these two assumptions, the model reduces to the deterministic model expressed by Eq.(6.2), and the results are identical.

The assumption underlying Eq. (6.7) is actually false, as is stated by Indurkhya *et al.*, but the point is that when the equation breaks down, it is close enough to being correct that the results produced are reasonably accurate. If one of the summations in Eq. (6.7) has many more summands than any other, then almost surely it has the maximum expected value, and its expected value is the value of both sides of Eq. (6.7). If two or more summations have almost the same number of terms, and this number is maximum among all equations, then it is possible for the left-hand side of Eq. (6.7) to select one summation and the right-hand of Eq. (6.7) to select another summation, but the values of summations will be fairly close, so that Eq. (6.7) is approximately if not exactly correct.

Nicol [1989] explored the model more deeply and discovered that the results reported by Indurkhya *et al.* can be proved to be true in some instances without relying on Eq. (6.7). Indeed, the model appears to be robust in the sense that small perturbations in the underlying assumptions do not alter the gross conclusions from the model, although specific details in the conclusions may change.

6.2.4 A Model with Linear Communication Costs

Let us examine a model that is less drastic with regard to communication costs to show a more optimistic result with regard to parallelism. Our first model assumes that each task communicates with every other task, and, as a consequence, the communications overhead grows quadratically as the number of processors increases. This is the case when each task sends unique information to every other task, but such a program structure is very poorly suited for multiple processors. Some programs may well have this structure, and if so, our results suggest how much speedup one can expect and at what cost. But there are surely many other programs better suited for parallel computation on multiprocessors. We need to know the performance potential for such programs and how to achieve it. What is rather surprising is that the analysis is remarkably similar with a rather similar optimal strategy, although the speedup available is greater.

For this model, assume that the cost of communication is proportional to the number of processors, not to the number of tasks assigned remotely. This model holds if a task has to communicate with all other tasks but sends the same information to all other tasks. Then the information has to be sent only once to each processor, and after it reaches a remote processor it can be sent from task to task within that processor for no charge.

In this model the cost of an assignment on N processors becomes

$$\text{Execution time} = R \, \text{Max} \, (k_i) + CN \qquad (6.8)$$

For each value of N, the first term depends on the assignment but the second does not. This model produces the best time by distributing tasks evenly across all processors to make the first term approximately equal to RM/N. However, as the value N increases, the increase in the second term eventually becomes larger than the decrease in the first term, so there is a maximum value of N for which performance increases, and this is a function of R/C.

Since the best assignment produces a first term of approximately RM/N, the decrease in time in going from N to $N + 1$ processors is approximately

$$\text{Execution time decrease} = RM \left(\frac{1}{N} - \frac{1}{N+1} \right) - C$$

$$= \frac{RM}{N(N+1)} - C \qquad (6.9)$$

This decrease is negative, that is, it becomes a time increase when

$$\frac{R}{C} = \frac{N(N+1)}{M}$$

or equivalently when

$$N = \sqrt{\frac{RM}{C}} \qquad (6.10)$$

The square root function in Eq. (6.10) is a disaster. We expect that M tasks can be done quickly on M independent processors, but this model says that because of communication costs, the effective parallelism is reduced to the square root of what we anticipated. The bad news is mitigated somewhat by a high R/C factor, so coarse granularity is desirable here, but its effect is also diminished by a square root factor.

The news is even more pessimistic if we consider the cost of the extra processors in relation to their benefit. Given that the time no longer decreases when we reach the threshold given in Eq. (6.10), long before N becomes that large, we have reached the point at which the cost of adding an extra processor is not justified by the benefit gained. Thus a problem with 10,000 tasks that fits this model may well run faster with up to 100 processors and might be economical with at most 10 processors.

This model differs from our original model in the second term. In the original model the cost of the second term grows quadratically with the constant M and diminishes inversely with N. The dependence on N is due to the reduction in overhead when N things are grouped together on one processor.

Because both the first and second terms grow smaller with N in the new model, execution time decreases for all N.

In the present model, the second term grows linearly with N, and this accounts for the threshold for N above which performance degrades. The two models tell us that the penalty for overhead exists, and it manifests itself by limiting the effective use of parallelism in some way.

6.2.5 An Optimistic Model—Fully Overlapped Communication

Perhaps the models described thus far are too pessimistic. After all, they all incur an overhead penalty for communication since none provides a means for overlapping overhead with useful and necessary computation. We have argued that in practical systems some overhead cannot be masked because contention, finite communications bandwidth, and synchronization each make their own contributions to elapsed computation time, although in the best circumstances some overhead penalties can be successfully overlapped with useful computation to reduce the overhead penalty.

Let us develop an optimistic model in which overhead potentially can go to zero if overlapped with computation. We simply alter our model in Eq. (6.2) to permit the overhead in the second term to be overlapped as much as possible with the first term. The equation becomes

$$\text{Execution time} = \text{Max} \left\{ \text{Max}\,(k_i), \frac{C}{2} \sum_i k_i\,(M - k_i) \right\} \qquad (6.11)$$

For two processors, the situation described by Eq. (6.11) is depicted in Fig. 6.2. The piece-wise linear line expresses the contribution of the first term, and the quadratic curve expresses the contribution of the second term. Their intersection is the minimum value of the maximum function expressed in Eq. (6.11). At this point the execution time is just long enough to mask completely the overhead that is occurring concurrently.

This model is obviously optimistic because it is rather unlikely that overhead can be fully overlapped with processing. Nevertheless, we can compute where the threshold occurs. For two processors, we seek the point of intersection of the linear and quadratic curves in Fig. 6.2. This occurs at the point

$$R(M - k) = C(M - k)k \qquad (6.12)$$

which occurs at

$$k = \frac{R}{C} \qquad (6.13)$$

with k restricted to the range $1 \le k \le M/2$. If we substitute Eq. (6.13) into Eq. (6.11) the computation time becomes $R(M - R/C)$, and the speedup is $1/[(1 - R/C\,M)]$. Since k is restricted in range for Eq. (6.13), the equivalent restriction on R/C is that $1 \leq R/C \leq M/2$. For R/C in this range, the speedup for two processors lies between 1 and 2 and is maximized when $R/C = M/2$, the same value obtained in the first model.

At the maximum speedup, the tasks are evenly divided among the processors, that is, $k = M/2$. As R/C decreases toward 1, the speedup falls off toward unity, and the optimum task distribution becomes more skewed. Hence, this model also depends on R/C, but it is more optimistic in its performance predictions because all or a substantial portion of overhead can be overlapped with computation if R/C is high enough.

For N processors, the overlapped-overhead model is easy to analyze because of the results reported here. For any given maximum value of k_i that determines the contribution of execution time, the even distribution of tasks to processors as defined earlier produces the minimum communication time. Hence, the best possible execution time for fully overlapped communication occurs when

$$\frac{RM}{N} = \frac{CM^2}{2}\left(1 - \frac{1}{N}\right) \tag{6.14}$$

which for large N occurs roughly when

$$\frac{R}{C} = \frac{NM}{2} \tag{6.15}$$

In this case, for a minimum total time, the number of processors as a function of R/C and M is given by the function

$$N = \frac{2R}{CM} \tag{6.16}$$

and the optimum choice for the number of processors is inversely proportional to the number of tasks available.

As the available parallelism grows, the best policy is to use increasingly fewer processors. For small N, we cannot neglect the $1/N$ term in (6.14), and we obtain slightly different but consistent results. For $N = 2$, Eq. (6.14) produces a minimum-time solution when $M/2 = R/C$, which is consistent with our previous findings.

The fact that the number of processors decreases with the available parallelism in this model is clearly the result of overhead time climbing M times faster than execution time. The effect of overlapping overhead with computation time is actually more pessimistic than we imagined because this model makes elapsed time totally dependent on communication overhead time when run time is smaller than communication time. Hence, it is absolutely essential to keep communication time no greater than execution time if there is to be speedup.

6.2.6 A Model with Multiple Communication Links

A common assumption in all previous models is that parallelism allows run time to be overlapped in several processors, but overhead operations accounted by the term with coefficient C are done sequentially. If the overhead operations are strictly limited to communications costs, then this model holds for systems in which there is a single communications channel common to all processes. This is the case when all processors are connected to a single bus or ring or when all processors access the same shared-memory cell in an exclusive-access manner.

It is perfectly possible to replicate communications links and other architectural features that contribute to the overhead bottleneck of the second term. In so doing, the factor C is not a constant, but itself becomes a function of N. For example, consider a model in which every process has to communicate with every other process. Our original estimate for run time is Eq. (6.2).

If we allow communication links to increase with N so that each processor has a dedicated link to every other processor, then communication operations can be overlapped among themselves. However, even with $O(N^2)$ links installed, we still cannot support more than $O(N)$ concurrent conversations because each processor can talk or listen only to one other processor at a time.

In this case, we can divide the second term of Eq. (6.2) by N, and we obtain

$$\text{Execution time} = R \, \text{Max} \, (k_i) + \frac{C}{2N} \sum_i k_i (M - k_i) \tag{6.17}$$

Equation (6.17) assumes that a processor is either computing, communicating, or idle, and that the total cost of communications decreases inversely with N because up to N conversations can be held concurrently. The idle time in part is due to the fact that early finishers have to wait for late finishers.

The first term of Eq. (6.17) tends to decrease inversely with N, and the second term tends to increase linearly with N, which is a situation studied earlier in this section. The first term is minimized by an even distribution of tasks to processors, but this is offset by an increase in the second term.

We know that for any N, Eq. (6.17) is minimized by assigning tasks as evenly as possible, so that all except possibly one processor are given the maximum number of tasks. Under such an assignment, the execution time for Eq. (6.17) becomes

$$\text{Execution time} = \frac{RM}{N} + \frac{CM^2}{2N} \left(1 - \frac{1}{N} \right) \tag{6.18}$$

Parallelism is useful in this case until execution time fails to decrease as new processors are added. This occurs when the following equation is negative.

$$\text{Execution time decrease} = \frac{RM + \dfrac{CM^2}{2}}{N(N+1)} - \frac{\left(\dfrac{CM^2}{2}\right)(2N+1)}{[N(N+1)]^2} \qquad (6.19)$$

By removing a factor of $M/N(N+1)$ and letting N become very large, Eq. (6.19) reduces to

$$\text{Execution time decrease} = \left[R + \left(\frac{CM}{2}\right)\left(1 - \frac{2}{N}\right)\right]\left(\frac{M}{N(N+1)}\right) \qquad (6.20)$$

which is positive for $N > 2$, and so execution time improves for all N, except possibly for small N.

To discover if N processors yield a better time than does one processor, compare Eq. (6.18) with RM, the time for one processor. These times are equal when

$$RM = \frac{RM}{N} + \left(\frac{CM^2}{2N}\right)\left(1 - \frac{1}{N}\right) \qquad (6.21)$$

The breakeven point occurs when

$$\frac{R}{C} = \frac{M}{2N} \qquad (6.22)$$

In this case the granularity factor R/C and N are inversely related at the breakeven point. Hence, the larger that N is, the smaller the granularity that we can permit at the breakeven point. At breakeven, however, the parallel machine is a gross failure in terms of cost/performance. Its total performance for N processors is identical to that of a single processor, yet its cost is higher by a factor of $O(N)$ for processors and $O(N^2)$ for communication links. We never want to operate a parallel system at breakeven!

The point of this example is that by increasing the bandwidth of the communication links, we can permit smaller granularity than is otherwise possible. However, the smaller granularity comes at an expense that rises faster than the increase in processing cost. Whether or not the speed obtained by the higher bandwidth communications is worth the cost depends very strongly on the technology available for processor-to-processor communications.

To summarize the findings of the models presented in this section, we have discovered:

1. Multiprocessor architecture produces an overhead cost that is an additional burden not present in serial processors and vector (or other single instruction-stream) architectures. The overhead cost includes the cost of scheduling, contention for shared resources, synchronization, and processor-to-processor communications.

2. Although running time for a computational portion of a program tends to diminish as the number of processors working on that program increases, the overhead costs tend to grow with the number of processors. In fact, it is possible for overhead costs to grow faster than linearly in the number of processors.

3. The ratio R/C is a measure of the amount of program execution (running time) per unit overhead (communication time), within a program implementation on a specific architecture. The larger this ratio, the more efficient the computation because a relatively smaller proportion of time is devoted to overhead as this ratio increases. However, if the ratio is made large by partitioning a computation into a few large pieces instead of many small pieces, the parallelism available is greatly reduced, which limits the speedup that can be attained on a multiprocessor.

We clearly have a dilemma. On the one hand, R/C has to be small to create a large number of potentially concurrent tasks, and on the other hand, R/C has to be large to prevent the overhead costs from becoming excessive. Because of the dilemma, we cannot expect to build fast multiprocessors simply by expanding the number of processors as much as technology allows.

There is some maximum number of processors that is cost-effective, and that number depends a great deal on the architecture of the machine, on the underlying technology (especially communications technology), and on the characteristics of each specific application.

6.2.7 Multiprocessor Models

The multiprocessor challenges the computer architect and the algorithm designer somewhat differently. The computer architect must produce a system for which R/C is acceptably high and provide a number of processors that can be used effectively at that ratio. The algorithm designer has a different problem.

Given a fixed system with N processors and a ratio R/C that reflects an achievable ratio of running time per unit overhead, how can an application be partitioned and executed on the multiprocessor architecture to make the most effective use of resources? The algorithm designer has to partition the application across the multiprocessor and must choose a granularity that balances useful parallel computation against communications and other overhead.

For some applications the most effective solution might not use all of the processors available. Fewer processors might complete the job earlier or at lower cost. In essence, we are trying to determine if it is better to plow a field with one ox, four horses, or 1024 chickens. The solution with the maximum parallelism is not always the fastest.

Most people take as an act of faith that one might as well use as many processors as available if there is work to be done. However, some models discussed in this section show that computation speed can eventually decline as processors are added. So maximum parallelism is not synonymous with maximum speed. Moreover, the multiprocessor is somewhat less effective at producing speed at reasonable cost than are several techniques described earlier in the text.

For example, cache memory boosts the effective speed of all of central memory, yet only a relatively small fraction of memory actually needs to run at cache memory speed. Hence, there is a performance leverage in using a cache. You pay for a small fraction of what you obtain.

Similarly, pipeline computers improve performance in proportion to the number of stages in the pipeline. In the best case, an N-stage pipeline achieves an N-fold speedup. But the N-fold speedup does not require an N-fold replication of hardware. Again, there is leverage in this type of architecture because by less than an N-fold increase of hardware, one obtains up to an N-fold improvement in speed.

In both cases the leverage is available because the item replicated is a bottleneck that leaves other system resources idle. By breaking the bottleneck the idle resources become available, and the total gain appears to be greater than the gain that can be attributed to the fixed bottleneck by itself.

For cache, the bottleneck is memory, specifically the frequently referenced areas of memory. For pipelines, it is some computational stage or critical register. Cache replicates memory; pipelines replicate storage cells and arithmetic units. But multiprocessors do not obviously offer the same leverage as do caches and pipelines. The component replicated is the full processor, not some critical portion of the processor. Moreover, we are likely to obtain less than proportionate return as we add processors.

Therefore, the design of multiprocessor architecture is far more challenging than the techniques we describe earlier. One cannot simply lash together 1000 processors and expect to obtain 1000-times improvement. In fact, performance improvements of only 100 to 200 might be all that could be achieved under favorable circumstances, and under less favorable circumstances, improvement might be only around 10 or less.

On the other hand, with a greater understanding of overhead costs, algorithms, and design approaches available, it is possible to construct efficient multiprocessors. Our analyses in this section strongly suggest that efficiency becomes limited as the number of processors increases. Perhaps an architecture with 4 to 16 processors can be viewed as "general purpose," but with 1K or 64K processors, almost surely the architecture is limited to applications for which the inherent parallelism is large and the granularity is in the range for which the architecture runs well.

Hoshino [1989] has performed a granularity study of programs that are operational on the PAX machine. The results of his study are consistent with the predictions of this model. He measured the actual computation time and communication overhead for various applications from timings taken on a 128-processor machine. These timings were then scaled for various numbers of processors, and various amounts of local memory. Because synchronization and communication tend to be unoverlapped in the PAX architecture, the basic model introduced early in this section tends to capture the performance of many of the PAX applications. Hoshino's general conclusion is that the speedup attainable on a 1000-processor machine is quite reasonable, provided that the granularity ratio R/C is high enough to make the overhead a negligible portion of the computation. His data indicate for each application how much local memory is required to attain a satisfactory granularity.

Efficiency is clearly a major concern in the design of multiprocessors. A design that uses $2N$ processors inefficiently cannot compete on a cost basis with a design that uses N identical processors twice as efficiently. The next section treats some of the more promising candidate architectures for multiprocessors.

6.3 Multiprocessor Interconnections

This chapter investigates the following leading candidates for multiprocessor systems:

- Bus-oriented systems;
- Ring networks;
- Crossbar-connected systems;
- Two- and three-dimensional meshes;
- Multilevel switched-network systems; and
- Hypercubes.

This is not an exhaustive, but rather a representative list of the possibilities. As we examine low-cost, low-bandwidth communications through high-cost, high-bandwidth communications, the system issues are fairly constant across the spectrum.

Our major conclusion is that the multiprocessor interconnection structure is felt most strongly by imposing a saturation point for system communications. Consequently, peak throughput is limited by the interconnection structure. For performance below saturation, the interconnection structure affects performance through the ratio of R/C. A good design is one that runs below saturation for typical workloads, and at a typical operating point, it produces high throughput by attaining a large R/C ratio. If for a particular workload, the interconnection network of such a design is modified in some major way without altering throughput, then there is some flexibility in the set of interconnections that can be used for that workload. The architect seeks the least costly set of interconnections that achieves good performance over a large class of applications.

6.3.1 Bus Interconnections

Our discussion of performance stresses the need for efficiency and shows the important role of the ratio R/C. The simplest way to construct a multiprocessor that meets the efficiency goals is to connect the processors on a shared bus, which thereby provides shared global memory to all processors. Figure 6.3 illustrates the block diagram of such a system.

　　Each processor has access to a common bus. To this bus is attached the central memory, which is a global resource for all processors. Each processor, in addition, has a local memory and a cache memory. The local memory and local cache enable the processors to reduce their use of the shared bus and thereby limit the effects of contention on performance when processors have to go to shared memory.

　　If neither cache nor local memory were present, the cost of memory access would be relatively high, and, moreover, since all processes access memory frequently under these conditions, there could be severe contention at the bus, causing arbitration delays that reduce performance. So the long delays due to

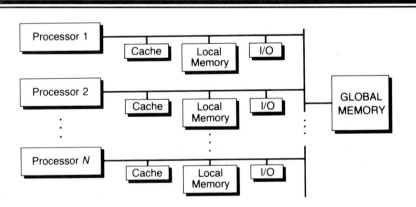

Fig. 6.3 A bus-connected multiprocessor.

remote access coupled with additional delays due to contention effectively increase the value of C in the R/C ratio and thereby reduce speedup and the number of processors for which the scheme is effective.

The objective in using cache and local memory is to shorten the effective memory cycle and reduce the use of the bus so that one processor does not slow down another through bus interference. If together the local memory and cache reduce accesses on the bus by 90 percent (which should be readily achievable), then 10 times as many processors can share a bus at a given level of contention than in the system that has no local memory or cache. If the global accesses are reduced by 95 percent, the factor climbs to 20 times as many processors.

Historically, commercial releases of bus-based multiprocessors supported as many as 32 microprocessors. Above 32 processors, bus contention leads to degraded performance. Unfortunately, the present trends in technology tend to reduce the number of processors that can be attached to a bus rather than increases it. The problem is that the mature interconnection technology available for such systems uses metal conductors, and the maximum clock speed of such buses is somewhere between 200 MHz and 300 MHz. The limiting factor turns out to be stray capacitance at the receivers on the bus, which causes reflections to travel backward toward the transmitters, from where they are again reflected toward the receivers where they are received as false pulses. The cure for this disease is to limit the rise-time of the transmitted signals, and therein lies the bandwidth limitation of the interconnection technology. Another possible cure is to reduce the physical dimensions of all devices and components in order to reduce stray capacitance. Although this is effective and is used successfully in the Cray III computer to support a 1 GHz clock cycle, it is also very costly.

If we restrict attention to low-cost high-volume technology, then the present trend is for individual components and processors to become faster every year while the clock cycle on the bus is fixed at an upper limit because of fundamental limitations. When processor clock rates were in the 5 MHz region, a 200 MHz limitation on bus clock rate did not overly constrain multiprocessor structure. With processor clocks reaching 50 MHz, 100 MHz, and 150 MHz in recent releases, it becomes clear that just a few active processors can saturate a bus. If the trend continues and bus technology remains based on metal interconnections, we are likely to see no increase in the number of processors in bus-based systems, and may even see a reduction as processors become faster relative to the bus

Optical technology provides an alternative implementation of processor-to-processor interconnections. The technology is still developing, and it may be quite reasonable to use this technology for the backbone of a highly parallel bus-based computer system. Consequently, the future exploitation of bus-based architecture is intimately tied in the future success of optical buses.

Apart from the physical realization of a bus-based architecture, there are special issues involved in using caches in this architecture that we examine later in this chapter. The problems stem from the need to maintain consistency of data in all of the caches. If a shared item is changed in one cache and read by another processor, the second processor must be able to locate the new value of the shared variable. This forces the cache controllers to follow a protocol that guarantees that all loads and stores access the correct value of an item, regardless of whether that item is in local cache, remote cache, or global shared memory. The bus-based multiprocessor is a natural structure for building an effective cache-coherence protocol.

Usually such a protocol produces additional operations on the shared bus whose purpose is to guarantee cache consistency. If caches were not present, these operations might not be necessary. Hence, a cache architecture reduces bus accesses when the cache hit ratio is high, but the reduction is partially offset by additional bus transactions caused by the consistency protocol. With cache sizes large enough to reduce miss ratios to 1 percent, the potential impact on bus traffic is to reduce it 100-fold, thereby providing for as much as 100 times as many processors on a bus than could be supported without a cache. This calculation is overly optimistic because of the extra traffic to maintain cache coherence. Most of the traffic is required to communicate WRITEs so that all processors see updated data in case they need to have the most recent values of shared data. WRITEs account for 15 to 25 percent of memory operations, but in a cache-based processor that uses a store-in cache policy rather than a write-through cache policy, the percentage of memory operations that have to be communicated on a bus to other processors may drop to 5 to 10 percent. So cache may provide only a 10 to 20 times reduction in bus traffic rather than a 100-fold reduction, but the improvement from using a cache is a definite advantage in any case.

Technology plays a major role in making a bus-oriented multiprocessor practical, and, in fact, the bus presents an excellent opportunity for technology leverage. An N-processor system requires a bus whose bandwidth is on the order of N times that of a uniprocessor bus. Therefore, the bus bandwidth constrains the number of processors that can be interconnected as N increases.

If exotic technology is used only for the bus and its interfaces, but ordinary technology is used in the processors, then the cost of the exotic technology can be held fairly low, while the gain due to its use is amplified by greatly increasing the number of processors on the bus. Consequently, it may be feasible to use bus interconnections that run perhaps 100 times faster than basic processor technology and are capable of supporting 1000 processors. As we suggested earlier, a possibility for the future is to use optical links and gallium-arsenide transmitters and receivers whose information rate is in the 1 GHz to 10 GHz region.

But exotic technology can also work against the architect. If it can be used in the communication link, then equivalent technology might well be used throughout the system, boosting basic throughput in each processor by perhaps a hundredfold. In this case, perhaps only 10 super-technology processors can do the work of 1000 low-technology processors with a super-technology bus. The 10-processor, all-super-technology system might well be more cost-effective than the 1000-processor system because it is likely to be more efficient and less complex. The computer architect has to evaluate where and how to use exotic technology, carefully considering reasonable alternatives rather than committing arbitrarily to a specific use of the technology in a particular architecture.

Note that the bus is only one potential bottleneck in the bus-oriented multiprocessor. The shared memory is another one. As bus bandwidth increases, performance is eventually limited by the bandwidth of the shared memory. Because processors synchronize their activities by reading and writing shared memory cells, as the number of processors increases, there is a tendency for some shared cells to receive an increasing proportion of the memory references.

For example, consider a single memory cell that controls the execution of N processors by acting as a barrier. Processors wait at the barrier until all processors have reached it. Then they are free to continue. The barrier cell can be initialized to the value N, and, as each processor reaches it, the cell is decremented. When the cell is decremented to 0, all processors are released.

If the shared cell is accessed by one processor at a time, then clearly the time required for the barrier to go from N to 0 is $O(N)$ time. If the processors executing in parallel are performing some function that requires constant time, then for sufficiently large N the barrier itself becomes a bottleneck of the computation and greatly limits the useful work performed by the system.

To overcome the bottleneck in the shared memory, it is necessary to seek creative solutions in technology, architecture, or algorithms:

- *Technology*: use very high-speed devices for shared memory or move to an exotic memory technology that supports multiple simultaneous accesses.
- *Architecture*: design a system with high-bandwidth architectural support for sharing and control.
- *Algorithms*: for specific applications, seek means to distribute control to reduce or eliminate bottlenecks at centralized control variables.

All of the approaches are potentially viable. Any one approach may be sufficient to create a system of the desired performance. Relatively few ideas have been implemented and evaluated, and many opportunities for advances still exist.

Returning to bus-based interconnections, consider what techniques are available for bus implementation. The highest-speed electrical buses must be very short. This limitation is strictly a matter of physics because high speed implies fast changes of voltage and current. Such physical quantities are limited in their switching speed by capacitance and inductance. To hold these quantities small requires small physical distances because capacitance and inductance are proportional to conductor length.

Signal fidelity also diminishes when signals are sent over long distances, and the degradation in fidelity increases the probability of error during transmission. Therefore, if a bus is long or has other characteristics that slow transmission or degrade signal quality, the bandwidth of such a bus is lower than that of a short bus with excellent signal qualities. Yet another problem is crosstalk noise stemming from mutual interference from adjacent signals. This too grows with physical distance.

The problem is that as the number of processors tied to a bus increases, most electrical buses suffer degradation that tends to reduce bandwidth. Hence, not only does each processor have to share the bus bandwidth with $N - 1$ other processors, but as N increases the bandwidth available to share decreases. Bus technology suitable for small N is probably not feasible for large N, and for N somewhere in between lies a region where buses change from being effective to being unacceptable. The exact breakpoint is technology dependent and has to be evaluated for each individual type of bus and interface technology.

One possible way to build a bus with many processors is to build a physically short bus, as shown in Fig. 6.4, and to tie the processors to the bus through a longer connection that attaches to the bus through a special inter-

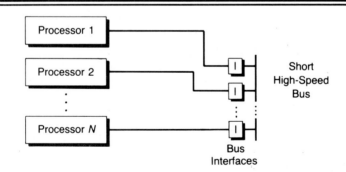

Fig. 6.4 A high-speed bus with a short physical length connecting a collection of processors. The I-unit is an interface that permits processors to be relatively far from the bus when compared to the physical length of the bus itself.

face, as shown in the figure. The objective of the short bus is to provide a medium for the interchange of signals with physically acceptable parameters and good signal quality. It might be only 25 cm long, for example, and provide 100 connection points. The 100 interfaces must be located very close to the physical bus, which is possible for interfaces alone, but may be very difficult to accomplish if all 100 processors have to be physically close to the bus.

The interfaces provide signal buffering that permits the processors to be located at least far enough away to meet the packaging requirements of the processor technology. Although Fig. 6.4 suggests that the electrical bus is external to the modules that hold processors, the structure in the figure also holds to some extent for super-VLSI systems with the bus and multiple processors implemented together, possibly on a whole wafer if not on one chip.

6.3.2 Ring Interconnections

Although a bus interconnection has advantages for a small number of processors, electrical buses are highly constrained by fundamental physical principles. The goal of the architect is to find an interconnection that has the simplicity of the bus for support of computation, but is able to exceed the physical limitations inherent in buses. One possible solution is to build a logical bus that is physically something else.

Figure 6.5 shows a loop arrangement with point-to-point connections between processors and a cyclic interconnection overall. In this system, a transmitting process places a message on the loop, and it is repeated by each receiver until it returns to the transmitter, which stops the message by failing to repeat it.

There are various ways to operate such a loop, but one protocol that turns the loop into a logical bus is the IEEE 802.5 token-ring standard. A transmitting processor is distinguished from all other processors because it holds a token, of which one and only one exists among all processors. When the transmitting processor sends a message through the token ring, the ring acts like a bus, and all other processors listen.

At the end of transmission, the transmitter broadcasts a token, which is a unique combination of signals that cannot exist in an ordinary message. Each receiver sees the token in turn, and if a receiver is waiting to be a transmitter, it accepts the token without retransmitting it, and instead transmits its message on the ring. If no receiver is waiting to transmit, the token circulates on the ring and can subsequently be removed by any processor that needs to transmit.

The advantage of the token ring is that the connections are point to point, not bus connections. Physical parameters can be more readily kept in control. In fact, the token ring is ideally suited to very high bandwidth optical fibers, which are difficult to adapt to bus technology for small numbers of processors and have not yet been adapted to buses for large numbers of processors.

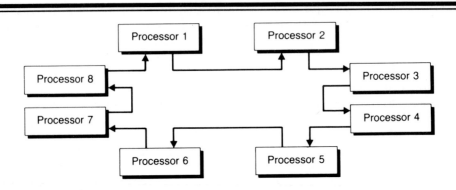

Fig. 6.5 A multiprocessor based on a loop interconnection.

A major disadvantage of the token ring is that each bus interface adds a short delay, usually a 1-bit delay, when it repeats an incoming message. As the number of processors increases, the delay around the ring increases proportionately. The bandwidth, however, does not necessarily decrease as it does for buses when they are heavily loaded.

To take advantage of the token ring, the architect views the token ring as if it were a pipeline with a short cycle time and long delay. The effective bandwidth can be utilized as long as computations keep the pipeline filled. Therefore, each processor should overlap transmissions with local computations.

Moreover, a protocol for a high-speed ring network ought to provide a means for a transmitter to pass its token to a new transmitter without having to wait to receive its own transmission. Such a protocol provides for pipelining messages on long rings, which is necessary to tap the available bandwidth. If a new message can be started only if no other message is on the ring, the net effect is the same as requiring a pipeline to drain between operations, which causes severe bandwidth degradation as the number of processors on the ring increases.

In today's technology, short electrical buses are limited to run at 100 to 200 MHz, depending on their length and maximum loading. Obviously, the longer and more heavily loaded buses run at the low end of the speed spectrum. Buses that are limited to the confines of a single VLSI chip can run in the high end of the range, and it is conceivable to run such systems at clock rates in excess of 200 MHz. However, if a bus leaves a chip, then maximum clock rates fall back to the 100-to-200 MHz area, and only denser packaging with special attention to low capacitance and inductance can increase the speed.

Optical connections for a token ring can run at much higher speeds. Early commercial installations of optical loops had bandwidths of 100 MHz in 1982, and by the beginning of the 1990s links running at a clock speed of 400 MHz were in use commercially. Clock rates exceeding 1 GHz are likely to appear in the early 1990s.

6.3.3 Crossbar Interconnections

The bus interconnection offers the simplest topology but has the highest potential contention. The crossbar is the antithesis of the bus. It offers the least contention, but has the highest complexity. We take a brief look at crossbars here. In the next section we look at interconnections that fall between crossbars and buses.

Figure 6.6 shows a crossbar that connects N processors with N memories. Although the number of memories is equal to the number of processors in the figure, this need not be the case in general. Usually, the number of memories is at least equal to or a small multiple of the number of processors.

The path between a processor and memory has a delay only at the crosspoint, so each processor is a unit (one crosspoint) delay from any memory. The communications network has no contention. Contention exists only at processors and memories—that is, if Processor 1 has to access Memory 1, and Processor 2 has to access Memory 2, then both accesses can occur simultaneously in the crossbar switch. In fact, any number of simultaneous accesses up to N can be done simultaneously, providing that no two accesses involve the same memory or processor.

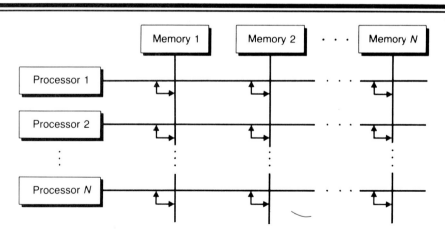

Fig. 6.6 An $N \times N$ crossbar switch in an N-processor multiprocessor. At each crossing in the network is a switch that permits any processor to connect to any memory.

Contention occurs if two or more accesses are made to the same memory. Consequently, if both Processor 1 and 2 attempt to access Memory 1 in the same cycle, one of the processors has to wait for the other to complete.

There are various architectural tricks available to reduce contention. If the contention occurs because processors are attempting to access different data that happen to be stored in the same memory module, then one possible solution is to allocate data so that accesses tend to be more evenly distributed across all memories rather than clustered to a single memory.

An obvious way to achieve this goal is to allocate blocks of data so that successive elements lie in successive modules. Similarly, shared program code should be allocated so that sequentially increasing addresses lie in successive modules. In either case, when shared data or code is accessed by two or more processors simultaneously, contention will delay one processor, and thereafter the later processor will trail the earlier processor without conflict as long as the two processors continue to access memories sequentially. This same addressing technique is used in pipelined processors that access vectors of data with a stride of unity.

If the accesses that cause contention are to a single cell or to a few shared cells, there is a more fundamental problem that requires a different approach. Some of the issues are explained in more detail in Chapter 7, but the discussion here illustrates the problem more clearly.

Consider Program 6.1, which shows the code for a processor that is forming the sum of local data and then adding the local sum to a global sum. Presumably, the local data are placed in a memory that is physically close to a processor and can be accessed without contention. The shared variable *Global_Sum* is to contain the sum of all elements in the data vectors. The objective is to obtain speedup by adding the local data in parallel, then tallying the local sums into *Global_Sum*. This is much like an election process, where each precinct tallies its ballots locally, then reports the results to Election Central, where precinct tallies are summed. The problem is that the tallying at the shared datum can take $O(N)$ time, and thereby it becomes a serious bottleneck that negates the parallelism achievable.

In Program 6.1, the local operation computation tallies data into LOCAL_SUM, and from there LOCAL_SUM is added to *Global_Sum*. The addition into the shared variable has to be done very carefully. Therefore, we must provide a mechanism for that variable to be read and rewritten by a single processor without an intervening operation occurring.

For example, if Processor 1 has to add the value 10 to *Global_Sum*, it must obtain the current value, add 10 to the current value, then write back the new value. If several processors attempt to do the same process concurrently, the results of global tallying can be incorrect. For example, consider the following situation in which the initial value of *Global_Sum* is 0, and Processors 1 and 2 attempt to add 10 and 15, respectively, to the sum.

Program 6.1 The use of locking to assure correct updating of a shared variable.

```
Procedure Add_to_Sum(var Global_Sum: Real, Shared; Local_Table:
  array of Real);
var
  i:              integer;
  Local_Sum: real;
begin
  Local_Sum := 0.0;
  for i := 1 to Max do
    Local_Sum := Local_Sum + Local_Table[i];
  {* The next statement obtains exclusive access to Global_Sum by some mechanism built
  into the architecture. At any given time, only one processor can be executing statements in
  the region between LOCK and UNLOCK. *}
  LOCK(Global_Sum);
  Global_Sum := Global_Sum + Local_Sum;
  UNLOCK(Global_Sum);
end; {* Procedure Add_to_Sum *}
```

1. Processor 1 reads the value 0 from *Global_Sum*.
2. Processor 2 reads the value 0 from *Global_Sum*.
3. Processor 1 computes the updated value of *Global_Sum* to be 15 and writes this back to *Global_Sum*.
4. Processor 2 computes the updated value of *Global_Sum* to be 10 and writes this back to *Global_Sum*.
5. The final value of *Global_Sum* is 10.

The error in this process causes the final outcome to miss the tally of 15 computed by Processor 1. Processor 2 reads the value of *Global_Sum* to be 0, but the instantaneous residence location of *Global_Sum* in shared memory is temporarily incorrect.

The true location of *Global_Sum* has moved to Processor 1, where it is updated and then restored in shared memory. During the time that Processor 1 "owns" *Global_Sum*, access to it in shared memory must be prevented. In essence, Processor 1 should be able to read, modify, and write *Global_Sum* as a single primitive operation without any other processor accessing *Global_Sum* in the meantime. In Program 1, this is indicated by the statements LOCK(*Global_Sum*) and UNLOCK(*Global_Sum*) that surround the READ/MODIFY/WRITE operation on *Global_Sum*.

The Lock statement permits a processor to pass the statement if the variable is currently unlocked. Otherwise it forces the processor to wait until the variable becomes unlocked. It has to be implemented very carefully in both hardware and software because it is prone to error.

One possible failure mode from improper implementation or incorrect use is a situation known as *deadlock*, in which two or more processes mutually block each other from further progress. Neither process can continue until the other unlocks a variable, but since they cannot continue, they cannot reach the unlock point in a program. An erroneous implementation of a Lock primitive can cause deadlock if it inadvertently leaves a variable in a locked state, and no processor can thereafter unlock that variable.

If a LOCK/UNLOCK is embedded in a program, such as Program 1, then no matter how the LOCK/UNLOCK is implemented, we have a potential bottleneck in a parallel processor. In computers with bus interconnections, the bottleneck is more likely to be at the bus rather than the memory. When the bus is replaced by a crossbar, communications bottlenecks disappear, but performance is limited by the next tightest bottleneck, which is likely to be at the shared memory.

The LOCK/UNLOCK code of Program 6.1 demonstrates a realistic way that the shared memory bottleneck can arise. Of course, the major reason to move to a crossbar is to remove a critical bottleneck that causes N simultaneous bus requests to take $O(N)$ time. The crossbar drops this time to $O(1)$ time, but the shared-variable bottleneck is still $O(N)$, so all the crossbar brings us is high performance in some portions of a program, with other portions of code dominating the performance and forcing the system to operate inefficiently.

These are performance-oriented arguments. We must also look at cost. The cost of a crossbar is usually proportional to the number of crosspoints, which grows as N^2, whereas the cost of a bus grows only linearly in N since cost is proportional to the number of bus interfaces. For large N, the crossbar is extremely expensive and may well dominate the entire cost of a multiprocessor. Large crossbars are feasible only if the cost per crosspoint can be held very low. The danger in building a crosspoint switch is that the bandwidth available cannot be used effectively, so the extra cost brings little benefit.

A very interesting example of a crosspoint architecture is the C.mmp computer [Mashburn 1982] built and in operation at Carnegie-Mellon University over a span that ran from the early 1970s to the early 1980s. This architecture tied 16 PDP-11/40's to 16 memories. It was never intended to be a prototype of a commercial system, but rather served as a proving ground for developing parallel applications and parallel operating systems. As such, it stimulated a substantial pool of research results that formed the foundation of the present knowledge of multiprocessor systems.

Our major thrust is high performance, but that was not the major thrust of C.mmp. If all 16 PDP-11s could be put together on one problem to obtain a 16-fold speedup, then the total speed would be much slower than the speed available on high-end uniprocessors, although a 16-way PDP-11 might provide a less expensive way to attain that type of performance than would the purchase of a single 16-times-faster machine.

One benefit that the C.mmp did provide is the access to a memory 16 times larger than was available for a single PDP-11 at that time. Since memory was relatively expensive, the C.mmp provided a way of allocating the expensive resource among several independent processors. This was a cost-effective alternative to configuring each of N machines with a fixed amount of unshared memory. The larger shared memory provided a resource pool that could be allocated dynamically to individual processors.

The C.mmp also provided a pool of processors that could be allocated flexibly and dynamically to programs. In theory, all 16 processors could be used on a single program, or, for example, one program could be assigned five processors, another program three processors, and so on, until all processors are assigned.

In practice, programs often needed fairly large chunks of memory for individual processes, so fewer than 16 processors could easily exhaust the supply of memory. Nevertheless, the C.mmp demonstrated the feasibility of multiprocessors and parallel programming on various types of problems. This demonstration held even though the crossbar interconnection itself may not necessarily be feasible for large numbers of processors.

One can easily substitute any other connection of sufficient bandwidth for the crossbar in C.mmp, and there would be virtually no difference in performance from the crossbar-based C.mmp. The important point is that the replacement interconnection structure should be fast enough to meet the C.mmp demands without introducing a new bottleneck into the system. The new structure does not necessarily have to have a bandwidth equal to a crossbar.

C.mmp illustrates an important principle for the architect of a multiprocessor system. The total system cost and performance is the factor of major importance; the interconnection network is but one component of the system. The lesson is that if the architect expends extra effort to remove a communication bottleneck, that effort may just move the bottleneck to a different part of the system, and the cost may not be justifiable.

In terms of applications, it is most important to determine if an application can run effectively on a multiprocessor even if the communications subsystem has infinite bandwidth and is contention-free. If this can be done, then the next most important consideration is how to provide at reasonable cost a communications network whose finite bandwidth does not reduce performance below a reasonable threshold.

6.3.4 Two- and Three-Dimensional Meshes

Our discussion of architectures for the continuum model in Chapters 4 and 5 indicated that mesh interconnections have excellent characteristics for numerical problems that arise in scientific contexts. The combination of low cost and high speed for near-neighbor interactions makes such connections quite attractive for implementation.

Apart from their advantages, the most serious disadvantage is that they do not support global communication and synchronization directly. The overall speed of a parallel calculation on a mesh-based structure will depend on the proportion of global operations that have to be performed. If a mesh structure is supported by a second interconnection structure for global operations, the two structures together can provide a computer system that is well suited to a broad class of scientific applications.

Hoshino's PAX computer [1989], for example, incorporates a global synchronization bus, a global broadcast bus, and a two-dimensional mesh that connects near neighbors. Even though this architecture does not have the capacity of a crossbar network with respect to simultaneous communications between arbitrary pairs of processors, it supports a sufficiently broad spectrum of the frequently used types of communication to be effective for scientific problems. Even within this class of applications, there are instances that saturate PAX interconnections momentarily. However, the degradation due to saturation of the interconnection bandwidth can be made quite small for many scientific applications. If each processor is assigned a contiguous square region of a mesh of points on a lattice, then the calculations performed tend to grow as the area of the region whereas the communication and overhead tends to grow as the perimeter of the region. So, by assigning a suitably large region of a mesh of data points to each processor, R/C can be made as large as desired, and thereby decrease the relative cost of communications that are not directly supported by near-neighbor mesh connections.

In general, the longest distance travel between two arbitrary nodes in a two-dimensional mesh with N processors is $O(\sqrt{N})$. For 1024 processors, the worst-case delay is 32 if the end connections of the mesh are cyclic as each node is within 16 nodes of every other node on its own row and column. By a combination of row and column moves, a datum can move from any processor to any other processor. The longest path in a shuffle-exchange network grows only as $O(\log N)$, which appears to be much shorter. However, for 1024 processors, the path length is 10 stages. So the difference in path length for a mesh and shuffle-exchange network that connect 1024 processors is only a factor of 3 in the number of nodes. The nodes themselves may change the total factor because the delays at the nodes in the two types of networks may be different. Consequently, for multiprocessors with up to 1024 processors, performance degradation due to long paths will not be much different in a two-dimensional mesh connection as compared to a shuffle-exchange network, especially if long paths are rarely used in an application.

6.3.5 The Shuffle-Exchange Interconnection and the Combining Switch

The shuffle-exchange connection described earlier in this text can be used to interconnect independent multiple processors as well as vector processors, such as those used for cyclic reduction or recursive doubling. In this section we consider the shuffle-exchange as an alternative to the shared bus or the crossbar, since both the bandwidth and cost of the shuffle-exchange lie between those of the bus and the crossbar.

The shuffle-exchange network offers an important additional function known as a *combining switch*, which can reduce contention by performing operations *in parallel* within the network that otherwise must be serialized at the memory. This technique has excellent potential for parallel applications that require processes to have momentary exclusive access to a shared variable.

The exclusive-access requirement limits the performance of most multiprocessor architectures, so when access to a shared variable is saturated, no additional speed improvement is possible no matter how many more processors are added to the system. However, this limitation does not exist in the original designs of the RP3 and Ultracomputer systems, described later in this section, when the exclusive access can be accomplished in part in the communication network and in part in the memory. In effect, the exclusive access is done in parallel, rather than serially, by making use of facilities built into the shuffle-exchange network.

The conditions under which exclusive access can be supported efficiently by the network are rather stringent. For some applications, the combining switch satisfies the needs for serialization, but for others it might not. For those applications for which the combining switch is not suitable, either some other mechanism has to be brought into play or such applications may simply not be candidates for parallel execution except possibly on multiprocessors with a small number of processors.

The shuffle-exchange network depicted in Fig. 6.7 shows processors at one side and memories at the other. Although the memories are quite far from the processors in terms of delay, the processors can have large caches and local memories to reduce the traffic to remote memories.

The important aspect of the architecture shown in the figure is that it supports the same multiprocessor applications as do the bus and crossbar interconnections. Its bandwidth is higher than the bus, but lower than the crossbar. Its cost is $O(N \log N)$ as opposed to $O(N)$ for the bus and $O(N^2)$ for the crossbar. The shuffle-exchange network lies at an intermediate point in the spectrum of possible networks.

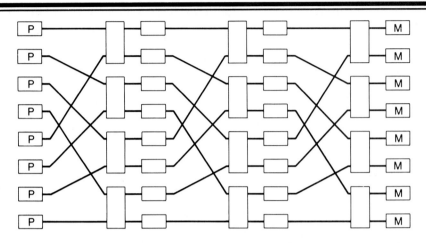

Fig. 6.7 A shuffle-exchange network for connecting eight processors to eight memories. Processors are labeled with P and memories with M.

The bandwidth for shuffle-exchange is very high for operations that do not conflict. Lawrie [1975] has shown that if N processors place simultaneous synchronized requests so that Processor i requests data from Memory $i + c$, for any constant c, the requests can be honored simultaneously without conflict. Moreover, no contention occurs if Processor i requests data from Memory $pi + c$, when p is an odd number and N is a power of 2.

Although we presume that the processors are independent and need not be synchronized precisely, many applications require processors to synchronize at certain points before proceeding. In most multiprocessor implementations of the fast Fourier transform (FFT), for example, each of the $\log N$ iterations is completed by all processors before the next is begun, so there are synchronization points at the end of each iteration.

Once processors are synchronized, they launch their new accesses to memory more or less concurrently. If in a vector architecture a collection of accesses to a vector has little or no contention, the equivalent accesses will tend to have low contention after synchronization in a multiprocessor architecture.

6.3.6 The Butterfly Operation and the Reverse-Binary Transformation

For the FFT there are two types of processor-to-processor communications. One is a butterfly operation, in which pairs of processors exchange data and compute weighted sums and differences of the items exchanged. The other is a reverse-binary transformation that alters the order of the output data from the ordering produced by the computations to one that is lexically ascending in the independent variable.

Cvetanovic [1987] showed that the two operations are incompatible with the shuffle-exchange operation in the sense that if data are stored among processors so that the butterfly operation proceeds without conflict, then the reverse-binary operation results in a maximum conflict in the network. Conversely, if the reverse binary is conflict free, then the butterfly results in maximum conflicts.

At least one of the two types of operations will cause some problems in the network. A typical implementation of the FFT uses $\log N$ butterfly operations on N-vectors, followed by or preceded by one reverse-binary operation. Consequently, it is best to organize data across the memories so that the butterfly is conflict free and then pay the conflict penalty for the reverse binary operation.

How bad can the conflicts be? The worst possible case is that all N items to be accessed reside in a single memory at one node of the shuffle-exchange network. $O(N)$ time is required to obtain the data, as opposed to $O(1)$ time if data are ideally stored across the network. However, the conflicts that arise for the reverse-binary permutation while doing the FFT are not this bad. Since the butterfly operation is assumed to be able to access N distinct items in a single operation, those items must be distributed across all memories.

When these same N items are subsequently accessed for a reverse-binary transformation, contention does not occur at the memories, but rather it occurs within the communications network. According to Cvetanovic's results, the worst-case contention for the reverse-binary permutation actually occupies only $O(N^{1/2})$ time, not $O(N)$ time, which essentially wastes $O(N^{1/2})$ of the $O(N)$ bandwidth available.

For a permutation of data to be free of conflicts as it passes through a shuffle-exchange network, at each switch node the two operands at the inputs must be directed to two distinct outputs. A conflict occurs if the two operands go to the same destination.

The bottleneck of the network for a permutation access is the stage (or pair of stages) in the center of the network. To see why this is true, consider a permutation that has the maximum possible contention. At the first stage, the worst possible situation is for each of the $N/2$ switch nodes to direct both their inputs to only one output. This creates a situation at the second stage in which half of the inputs are empty and half have two operands.

The same contention problem can occur at each successive stage up to the middle of the network, creating $2^{(\log N)/2}$ operands queued on each of $2^{(\log N)/2}$ lines, and with all other lines empty. However, since the operands lie in distinct memories at the far end of the network, the paths followed by the queued operands in reaching the far end of the network must diverge, starting at the bottleneck. Therefore, at each successive stage the queue lengths diminish by a factor of 2, and twice as many lines become active, until at the far end all lines are active and contain one operand. Figure 6.8 shows the reverse-binary transformation for a network with 16 processors and 16 memories. For this permutation, the target of Processor i is Memory i', where i' is the integer obtained by reversing the binary digits of i. Thus Processor 2 targets Memory 4 because the reversal of $(0,0,1,0) = 2$ is $(0,1,0,0) = 4$.

The discussion on contention within the shuffle-exchange network reveals that there exist algorithms for which we must suffer $O(2^{(\log N)/2}) = O(N^{1/2})$ delay because of communication contention, even when there is no contention at the memory at all. In a crossbar network, the FFT has neither communication nor memory contention, and therefore it is potentially faster by a factor of $O(N^{1/2})$. The problem is restricted solely to the reverse-binary transformation applied at the last step, and this step is rarely discussed in the literature in evaluating parallel execution of the FFT. Cvetanovic's work has brought the communication-contention issue directly into focus.

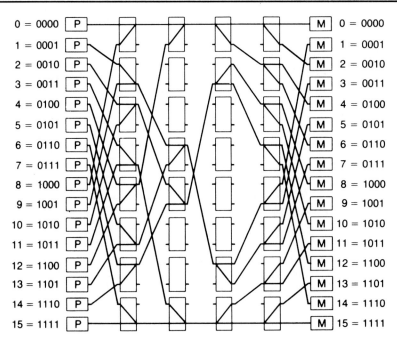

Fig. 6.8 The interconnections used to create a reverse-binary transformation in a shuffle-exchange network. Note that only some of the interconnections are used among the internal paths of the network.

Now that we understand the poor performance of the reverse-binary transformation, we can reduce its effects. For example, in some applications, the processing steps are:

1. Use the FFT to transform from the time domain to the frequency domain.
2. Process in the frequency domain.
3. Use the FFT to transform from the frequency domain back to the time domain.

We need not apply the reverse-binary transformation at the end of the first step if the frequency-domain operations are ordered compatibly. This places the input to the last step in reverse-binary order, rather than lexical order. For such an input, the FFT produces an output that is in lexical order. Hence, no reverse-binary transformation is performed, and the bottleneck is neatly sidestepped.

More generally, it is necessary to locate the contention problems in the communication network and to take steps to remove the problems if this is possible. The FFT is an example in which the bottleneck can be removed in the context given. We cannot promise that this is always possible, but clearly the bottlenecks have to be discovered if they are to be removed.

The discussion thus far illustrates a potential shortcoming of the shuffle-exchange network. This particular defect occurs for accesses that are balanced across the outputs of the network. But accesses do not have to be balanced at the outputs. Algorithms might well bias their accesses to memory, so that on the whole the accesses are uniformly distributed, but some small fraction of accesses is directed to a particular memory module. This might be the case if processors operate on data scattered across all memories, then reference shared control-variables to synchronize activity with other processors. We are interested in the effective bandwidth of the switch under these circumstances.

The calculation of effective bandwidth is difficult even for simpler problems. Consider the least-restrictive set of assumptions, namely that accesses are uniformly distributed and uncorrelated. The reason that this becomes difficult to evaluate is that we do not have a good model of how to deal with internal conflicts in the network. When two operands collide somewhere, for example because they both request the same output of a particular switching node, what happens? The network can

1. Abandon one arbitrarily and pass the other;
2. Queue one request in a local memory and pass the other; and
3. Refuse one request while passing the other, under the assumption that the request refused is buffered by the sender and will be repeated.

This list of options is representative but not exhaustive in the assumptions that have been treated in the literature in papers by Dias and Jump [1981],

Thanawastien and Nelson [1981], Chen *et al.* [1981], Kruskal and Snir [1983], Yew *et al.* [1983], and Padmanabhan and Lawrie [1985].

Kruskal and Snir have a very elegant result based on the solution of a difference equation that describes the number of messages remaining after conflicting messages are discarded. They found that the effective bandwidth is $O(N/\log N)$, so the contention within the network reduces bandwidth by a factor of $O(\log N)$. The other researchers have obtained roughly comparable findings using queueing analyses and simulations.

The analyses in general do not relate the assumed input to the access patterns of real programs. To what extent is the literature realistic? From Cvetanovic's work on the FFT we know that the effect of periodic synchronization could be either beneficial or disastrous. Synchronization tends to cause accesses to the network to come in clumps. This is beneficial if the accesses are nonconflicting, so that a large number of accesses can be honored in a short time. It is disastrous when the accesses are highly conflicting because it causes much higher contention than predicted by statistical methods.

The architect cannot take for granted that average bandwidth will be $O(N)$, $O(N/\log N)$, $O(N^{1/2})$, $O(1)$, or any other function that we have ascribed to the switching network. The architect has to explore the performance of the network on realistic applications, if they are available, or on faithful models of the access patterns of real applications.

This is the problem attacked by Pfister and Norton [1985] in their influential paper on hot-spot contention in shuffle-exchange networks. They sought the effective bandwidth of shuffle-exchange networks when accesses are not entirely uniformly distributed across memory. Their model permits a small number of accesses to be made to a specific memory and all others to be uniformly distributed. Their results show that effective bandwidth falls off dramatically as correlation of accesses increases.

In the Pfister-Norton model, a "hot" memory module is referenced with probability h; otherwise accesses are uniformly distributed. Therefore, when each of N processors produces r references per cycle to the memory system, the hot memory module receives requests at the rate:

$$\text{Requests at hot memory} = r(1 - h) + rhN \qquad (6.23)$$

The first term accounts for the uniform share of the load, and the second term accounts for the hot module receiving more than its share of requests from all processors.

Since a memory cannot honor more than one request per cycle, the request rate on the left-hand side of Eq. (6.23) cannot exceed unity. Therefore the maximum effective rate of generating requests, R, is the rate at which Eq. (6.23) reaches unity and is given by:

$$\text{Maximum generation rate } R = \frac{1}{1 + h(N - 1)} \qquad (6.24)$$

This function falls off dramatically with increasing N. The effective bandwidth of the switching network is N times the generation rate given in Eq. (6.24).

When h is 0, Eq. (6.24) is unity, bandwidth is N, and no degradation due to nonuniform access is present. As h increases just a little bit, for example to 1 percent, then for 1024 processors the denominator of (6.24) increases to 11, and bandwidth is down by a factor of 11 from the ideal. Even when hot-spot probability is tiny, for example 0.1 percent, the impact is an increase in the denominator to a value of 2, which reduces bandwidth by a factor of 2.

Pfister and Norton confirmed their findings by means of simulations, which showed that contention caused the network to saturate in tree-like regions, as shown in Fig. 6.9. This figure assumes that requests are held until they can be honored. The internal queue at a node can be of any integral length, including 0.

The hot memory cannot accept new data, so its predecessors become backed up when those predecessors cannot output their data to the memory. Next, the predecessors of predecessors saturate, and so on. As nodes saturate, they interfere with communication to other nodes in the system, and performance diminishes rapidly. In Fig. 6.9 the saturated nodes are indicated by shading, and they form a tree whose root is the hot memory.

A path from a processor to a different memory that has to use a saturated path becomes blocked, so bandwidth is somewhat lower than predicted by Eq.

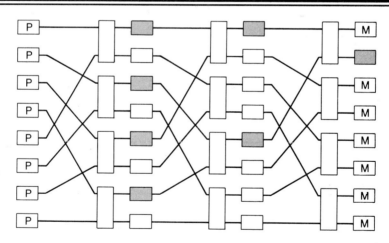

Fig. 6.9 A "hot" spot in a memory module (indicated by shading) and the switching modules that block as a result. The path from Processor 0 (the top processor) to Memory 3 is blocked, although neither Processor 0 nor Memory 3 is very active.

(6.24), depending on the size of the tree of saturated nodes. This in turn depends on the amount of queueing available within each node. If the architect wants to install queues in the network, Fig. 6.9 suggests that to reduce hot-spot contention, the best place to put such queues is in the rank of switches closest to the memory system. The queues might well be placed elsewhere, perhaps uniformly through the switching network to make all switches alike, to alleviate other forms of contention.

6.3.7 The Combining Network and Fetch-and-Add

Whether queues are added at the hot memory or somewhere within the network, they smooth out the effects of peak loads over longer periods. Queues do not alleviate the bottleneck caused by frequent memory accesses. To solve the problem, the request rate to the hot memory has to be decreased.

Gottlieb *et al.* [1983] propose a very unusual solution that involves using logic within the switch nodes to perform computations whose effect is to reduce the rate of requests to a shared-memory cell. In essence, two or more requests for access to the same shared cell can be combined into a single access under certain conditions. This tends to reduce the peak access-rate to a shared cell and thereby reduces contention and the bandwidth reduction due to contention.

The architectural solution is sometimes called a *combining network*, and the functional capability it gives programs is a collection of new instructions, one of which is called the Fetch-and-Add instruction.

To illustrate how the combining switch works, we propose to examine some subtree of the communication network, namely the tree of shaded nodes that appears in Fig. 6.9, and note that its root is a specific memory module that receives more than its share of references. In this example we give a possible case for the contention and show how the Fetch-and-Add instruction solves the problem.

The sample problem is a queueing problem in which each of N requesters attempts to add an item to a queue. In conventional solutions, the queue pointers cannot be updated by two or more processors concurrently because, if this is attempted, a pointer update might be done incorrectly for the same reasons that cause a concurrent summation on a shared variable to fail. Our solution in Program 6.1 forces the updates to be done sequentially, with each process using LOCK and UNLOCK operations to obtain exclusive access to a shared variable while updating that variable.

Our present solution permits all processors or any subset of processors to update the queue pointer simultaneously. To do so, we make use of Fetch-and-

Add as defined here for a single processor.

> *Definition:* Fetch-and-Add(Address,Increment);
>
> Temp := Memory[Address];
> Memory[Address] := Memory [Address] + Increment;
> Return Temp;

When Fetch-and-Add is used concurrently by M processors, we require the following conditions:

1. The cell at Memory[Address] is read only once and written only once, rather than read and written M times, to satisfy the M concurrent requests.

2. The set of M values returned to the M requesters is the same as some set of values that would be returned to the M requesters for some ordering of the requests executed serially with each request having exclusive access to Memory[Address] during the update of the cell.

The definition is not particularly unusual. Fetch-and-Add acts much like an Add-to-Memory instruction. The only difference of note is that Fetch-and-Add returns the prior contents of memory. The first characteristic of concurrent execution is crucial, for it is this characteristic that reduces contention in multiprocessors.

As an example of the basic idea, consider three processors that execute Fetch-and-Add concurrently to the same memory cell, SUM. If the initial value of SUM is 10, the three increments are respectively 2, 5, and 12. Then the network produces the total of the increments, 19, which is the only number added to SUM. SUM is fetched once to obtain the value 10, and the new value $29 = 19 + 10$ is the updated value of SUM. Meanwhile the network computes the values to return to the three requesters. One possible set of values that could be returned is 10, 12, and 17, which are the values that would have been returned had the increments 2, 5, and 12 been used sequentially in that order.

The trick to the implementation is illustrated in Fig. 6.10, where we see how the cells in the shaded subtree produce the necessary behavior. Each cell combines data moving toward memory and does an inverse operation for data moving away from memory. In this case, each cell detects when two Fetch-and-Add operations for the same shared variable reach its inputs simultaneously. The two increments are added internally to produce a sum, which is routed to the memory. Thus, one cell adds 2 and 5 to produce 7, and the second cell adds 7 and 12 to produce 19.

To prepare for the return trip, each cell stores the value of one of the two increments, in this case the left-hand input. Hence the first cell stores the value 2, and the second one stores the value 7. By storing the value of the left-hand input, when data traverse the network from memory to processors, the results

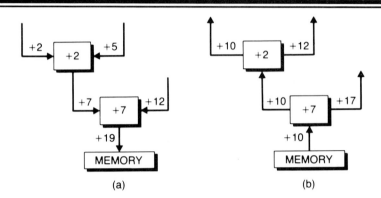

Fig. 6.10 Two phases of a Fetch-and-Add instruction:
(a) The data flow toward memory when increments of 2, 5, and 12 are applied. The numbers in the switch cells show the saved datum; and
(b) The data flow away from memory for the return of information to the requesting processors. The memory returns the value $+10$, and the switching cells modify the returned datum as shown before reporting the datum back to the requester.

returned will be as if the left-hand increment were used before the right-hand increment to update the shared variable. In this case, on the return trip, the number 10 reaches the cell with the stored value. It places the 10 on the left-hand port, and the sum $17 = 10 + 7$ on the right-hand port. The right-hand port now has a value that would be seen if the value of SUM were 17 just before the 12 were added to it.

Meanwhile the value 10 travels to the first cell. There the unmodified value of 10 is reported to the left port, and the sum $12 = 10 + 2$ is reported to the right port. The left port, therefore, has a value of 10, which would be the value before the increment 2 is used to update SUM. The right-hand port has the value 12, which is the value it would see if SUM were updated by 2 just before the 5 from the right-hand port is used to update SUM.

Each cell in the combining switch has at least the following capabilities:

1. Detect a matching address on left and right inputs.

2. Add two increments.

3. Save one increment.

4. Match a returning value for Fetch-and-Add to a saved increment for the instruction.

These capabilities in a combining switch are fairly costly, but the combining switch potentially can increase performance due to hot-spot contention by removing critical sections for some shared variables. An open question is whether the cost of the combining network is justified by its impact on performance.

As a concrete example of an extremely important use of Fetch-and-Add, consider the problem of enqueueing and dequeueing requests in a multiprocessor. An obvious mechanism for controlling a multiprocessor is to place tasks on a queue when no processor is available to execute them. As a processor completes its present work, it inspects the queue and removes a new task for execution if there is one.

The queue itself is a bottleneck when queue pointers must be locked and unlocked for safe updating. If, for example, a queue holds N independent tasks, all ready for immediate execution, and N processors suddenly complete a phase of activity and become available for new task assignments, ideally we would like to hand over the tasks in a single cycle so that all processors can start immediately. However, when pointer updating is serialized, then handing out the tasks takes $O(N)$ time, which could be quite significant for large N. This overhead is intolerable if the tasks are short, for example $O(1)$ time in length.

The basic idea in using the Fetch-and-Add is that each processor attempting to enqueue an item requests a position in the queue. This can be done with a statement of the form:

enqueue_position := Fetch_and_Add(Head,1);

In this case the first argument of Fetch-and-Add is a counter, Head, which gives the present position in the queue at which an item is to be added. The second argument is the increment by which Head is increased when a new item is added to the queue.

When the code is executed serially, the Fetch-and-Add returns the position of the next item. When the code is executed concurrently by two or more processors, all Fetch-and-Adds can be done at the same time, yet each processor will receive a unique, valid index into the queue because the values returned by Fetch-and-Add are the same values that would have been returned for some serialization of the Fetch-and-Adds. Any serialization of the enqueue requests yields correct code for sequencing N requests, and the Fetch-and-Add mimics one such serialization, but it does so with as little as one memory cycle.

We have not treated here the need to make the queue cyclical, nor have we treated the case of the empty or full queue. Chapter 7 studies these programming issues more fully. The example has served our purposes sufficiently well to show the potential use of the Fetch-and-Add instruction. In spite of the potential improvement offered by Fetch-and-Add, it is uncertain whether it is worthwhile incorporating into a multiprocessor, and if so, to determine how many processors must be in the system in order to gain sufficient performance improvement to offset the cost of the implementation.

In the ideal case, the combining network removes a bottleneck, and the next bottleneck is at a much higher level of throughput. The value of the combining network is the gain in speed in being able to operate at a much higher throughput rate than permitted without the combining network. However, it is quite possible to find that the combining network eliminates a bottleneck that is only marginally below the next bottleneck in the system, so its cost is hardly justified in such circumstances.

An essential element of the Fetch-and-Add instruction is that it returns data sufficient to serialize a computation. Sullivan *et al.* [1977] proposed a machine that reduces bandwidth by combining read accesses to a common address in memory. If two or more accesses ask for the same item, the shuffle-exchange network in their architecture has the ability to combine the multiple requests into a single request and route the resulting data from memory to all requestors. Thus, the proposal by Sullivan *et al.* illustrates how to embed a broadcast-like capability into the shuffle-exchange network to combine multiple read accesses, and this capability is retained in the Fetch-and-Add implementation. This design undoubtedly influenced the inventors of the Fetch-and-Add, but it is generally less useful than is the Fetch-and-Add because of Fetch-and-Add's additional ability to perform arithmetic as part of the combining process. It is this additional ability that gives Fetch-and-Add the potential for eliminating hot spots due to synchronization and queueing traffic.

Can Fetch-and-Add eliminate hot-spot contention as actually observed in practical applications? A hot memory can be hot if it receives a disproportionate number of accesses for any reason, but a combining network is effective only if all those accesses are to the same address. Is this case realistic? Yes, it is if the reason for the biased distribution of accesses is due to accesses to shared data such as for synchronization and locking. If the hot-spot contention is for other reasons, then Fetch-and-Add is of minimal benefit. What is the answer?

A research effort that is exploring this question and other related ones is the RP3 project at IBM [Pfister *et al.* 1985]. Its structure is outlined in Fig. 6.11. At the left is a processor, one of 64 in the operational configuration, and at the right is a network of shuffle-exchange stages. The original design of RP3 incorporated two distinct networks between processors and memories—one a conventional shuffle-exchange network designed for low latency and high-bandwidth, and the other a combining network that supports the Fetch-and-Add. The idea of using two networks is that the noncombinable accesses should be directed to the fast, conventional network, and that the combinable accesses produced by Fetch-and-Add should be routed through the combining network. The higher latency of the combining network is charged only to the requests that might be combined, and thus the majority of the requests are not affected by the additional latency.

As RP3's design evolved, the combining network was dropped from the implementation because the development cost was disproportionately high

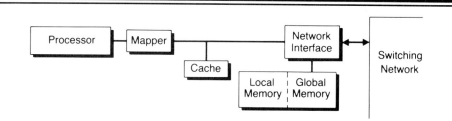

Fig. 6.11 The structure of one of the 512 processors of the full implementation of the IBM RP3. The switching network is a shuffle-exchange network with combining logic.

for the potential performance improvement in a 64-processor system. The Ultracomputer project at NYU also dropped its planned implementation of Fetch-and-Add. Consequently, no implementation is in progress at the time of the writing of this text.

Nevertheless, let us return to the description of the shuffle-exchange network in the RP3, and in particular, to look at an interesting idea embodied in the implementation. The network in Fig. 6.11 is shown with its inputs and outputs on the same side. In effect each processor node of Fig. 6.9 is identical to the corresponding memory node in that figure. The global memory is spread among the processors so that each processor has one independent block of memory, some of which can be used as global memory, and the remainder of which is used for local data. Between the processor and the network is an address mapper, a cache, and an interface for routing requests to local or global memory or to the network, where it can be routed to a remote block of global or local memory.

Addressing in this system is rather novel. To reduce contention, it is extremely advantageous to distribute the global address-space evenly across all memory modules to balance requests across all modules. This is most easily done by using the least-significant bits of a memory address to specify the module that has the data. Then references to items close to each other in the logical address-space are scattered more or less uniformly to all physical modules. Local memory, however, cannot be treated in the same way. Local memory should be physically close to its associated processor. Local memory should use the most-significant, not the least-significant, bits to select a physical memory. Thus, items that lie close to each other in the address space of local memory should lie in the same physical memory module.

RP3's approach to this dilemma is to use a boundary within the address space to separate the subspace that has interleaved addresses from the subspace that has block addressing. If an effective address falls above the boundary, for example, then the least-significant bits determine the physical module, and the most-significant bits are the address within module. If an effective address falls below the boundary, the most-significant bits determine the physical module and the least-significant bits are the address within the module. In the former case, the address subspace is used for shared, global data, and in the latter case, the address subspace is used for local data.

Local data are not private in the sense that it is possible for a processor to produce an address in the local address space of a remote processor, but the main objective is to use the local address space for items that are unshared and frequently accessed and that should be held in close proximity to a processor. The RP3 has an additional degree of freedom in that the boundary between local and global subspaces is software controllable. Thus a control program can select a suitable ratio for the sizes of the subspaces, and this is not fixed in advance by the hardware.

6.3.8 Hypercube Interconnections

In our discussion of interconnections we have covered an extensive range of possibilities that illustrate the variety of trade-offs in cost and performance available in a multiprocessor. The shuffle-exchange network and the two-dimensional mesh network lie somewhere in the middle of the possible trade-offs, where buses represent one extreme and crossbars represent the other. Note that both the shuffle-exchange and the mesh connections have a small permissible fan-in and fan-out per network node. This reduces cost. The network topology determines performance and link bandwidth per wire.

The low fan-in and fan-out of a shuffle-exchange network can be increased, and thereby reduce the number of nodes on the longest paths in a network. Several hypercube computers based on this general principle were introduced in the mid-1980s, the most parallel being the Connection Machine, with 64K 1-bit processors [Hillis 1986], and the most influential being the Cosmic Cube [Seitz 1985], that has been described in Chapter 4 in greater detail. Fox *et al.* [1988] analyze the program implementation and performance of a number of scientific applications on an Intel Hypercube, and bring together a number of important research results that pertain to hypercubes in general.

It is interesting that the Connection Machine implements combining by means of software that exploits the topology of the hypercube connections. Because the hypercube connection pattern is an extension of the shuffle-exchange connection, the notion of a combining switch for the shuffle-exchange network extends to the hypercube network by analogy. The details of the software implementation are in Hillis and Steele [1986].

In all cases, from bus to crossbar and in between, the ratio R/C determines how many processors can fruitfully be put to work on a single problem simultaneously. The bus has the lowest potential value of R/C, and it is the topology most likely to be ineffective as the number of processors increases. Note that the architecture of the RP3 attempts to keep local data and frequently used data within a processor, thereby increasing the R/C ratio as well as the number of processors that can be used effectively.

At this writing the multiprocessor is still in its infancy in the commercial world. One dramatic lesson of the experience obtained thus far is that the major unknown area to explore is software. What are good parallel algorithms for solving various important problems? The key approach is the ability to partition the problem into modules that require relatively little intermodule communication. If the partitioning can be done successfully, then communication requirements are rather small, and the dependency on the interconnection topology is greatly diminished. On the other hand, if communication requirements cannot be made small, then the interconnection topology becomes important, and the major parameter of interest is the R/C ratio.

6.4 Cache Coherence in Multiprocessors

The key to using interconnection networks in processors is to send data over the networks rather rarely. This tends to reduce contention, and, as the use per processor diminishes, the number of processors that can be served increases. Obviously, a cache memory provides an effective means for maintaining local copies of data to reduce the need to traverse a network for remote data.

We point out in the previous section that if a cache misses only 10 percent of the time, and remote fetches occur only on misses, then the number of processors supportable on the interconnection network is ten times greater than for a cacheless processor. The multiplier climbs inversely with the miss ratio, so the potential parallelism is quite dramatic when the miss ratio is near 0.

Caches in multiprocessors must operate in concert with each other. Specifically, any datum that can be updated simultaneously by two or more processors must be treated in a special way so that its value can be updated successfully regardless of the instantaneous location of the most recent version of the datum. The purpose of this section is to explore multiprocessor caches and examine the control algorithms required for these caches to behave correctly.

First, let us examine the nature of how caches might reach inconsistent states. This will give us some insight into mechanisms suitable for correcting the problem.

We have discussed the special requirement for handling shared variables in memory, and a similar requirement holds for shared variables in caches. When a shared variable is resident in memory, we can view the memory cell as being the current residence of the variable.

Earlier in this chapter we find a problem in trying to update the value of a variable shared by two processors. What goes wrong with the update process is that momentarily the current value of the shared variable moves from memory to the first processor, Processor 1. While Processor 1 holds the current value and updates that value, Processor 2 accesses shared memory. But the current value of the variable is no longer there. The variable has moved to Processor 1, but Processor 2's request is not redirected. It erroneously goes to the normal place for storing the shared variable.

Our example presumes that Processor 1 updates the shared variable and immediately returns it to memory, but in a cache-based system, Processor 1 may well hold the variable indefinitely in the cache. The failure exhibited in the example becomes much more likely when caches are present. The failure interval is not limited to a very brief update period, but can happen for any access to the variable in shared memory while that variable is held in Processor 1's cache. Whether the failure probability is low or high, the treatment of shared variables must be handled correctly. There has to be some solution that has truly zero probability of failure. Can you imagine the havoc wreaked in a system in which this were not the case? Programs would almost always work correctly, but would fail randomly when timing conditions caused the shared variables to be misread. The failures would be nonrepeatable and extremely difficult to diagnose. They might well be misdiagnosed as intermittent hardware failures.

There is a related failure mode that also has to be considered. If Processor 1 copies a shared variable to its cache and updates that variable both in cache and in shared memory, then problems can arise if the values in cache and in shared memory do not track each other identically.

Suppose, for example, that Processor 2 updates shared memory. At a later time Processor 1 requests the value of the variable, but takes that value from its copy in the cache and ignores altogether the change in the variable from the update performed by Processor 2. Processor 1's access is to a stale copy of the data held in cache, and it should be the fresh data held in shared memory.

Another form of the stale-data problem occurs when a program's footprint is not flushed completely from cache when that program is moved to a different processor and returns at a later time. Suppose that Processor 1 is running a program that leaves in cache the value 0 for variable X. Then the program shifts to a different processor and writes a new value of 1 for variable X in the cache of that processor. Finally, the program shifts back to Processor 1 and attempts to read the current value of X. It obtains the old, stale value of 0 when it should have obtained the new, fresh value of 1 for X. Note that X does not have to be a shared variable for this type of error to occur.

In all failure modes discussed here, the common problem is for each processor to direct its memory accesses to the current active location of any variable whose true physical location can change. Simple solutions are possible, but they have performance penalties.

For example, each shared datum can be made noncacheable to eliminate the difficulty in finding its current location among N caches and main memory. This can be done, for example, by providing a special range of addresses for noncacheable data, or by using special LOAD and STORE instructions that do not access cache at all.

To eliminate stale-data problems for cacheable, nonshared data, the processor can flush its cache each time a program leaves a processor. This guarantees that main memory becomes the current active location for each variable formerly held in cache.

While these simple solutions have been adopted in some multiprocessors, the solutions have a negative effect on performance because they reduce the effective use of cache. We want to explore other solutions that retain a higher effective use of cache while still guaranteeing that the total system can operate error free.

The general problem is called the *cache-coherence* problem, and it has been studied in the literature by Dubois and Briggs [1982] and Archibald and Baer [1986]. These articles examine the performance impact of protocols for maintaining consistent caches. Goodman [1983] is an early paper that outlines in detail a reasonably efficient cache-coherence mechanism. Sweazey and Smith [1986] explore a variety of cache-coherence protocols and delineate virtually all the possible variations of the Goodman proposal.

Of the many proposals, our discussion picks a single reasonable solution to cache coherence. We examine its characteristics to determine its performance limitations in a multiprocessor. Architects should be familiar with the entire spectrum of protocols and with the relative performance of different solutions as measured on their own workloads on their own machine environments. We specifically do not recommend any one approach because the actual choice of the best protocol is quite dependent on the computer structure and the workload for which it is used.

Here are the basic operations that must take place to maintain cache coherence:

1. If a READ operation for a shared datum misses in cache, then all caches in the system must be interrogated for a copy of the datum.

2. All WRITE operations to a shared datum, whether they are hits or misses, force all caches in the system to be checked for a copy of the datum. A possible exception to this rule is if the datum is tagged as being the only cached copy of the data in the system, in which case no external broadcast is necessary.

Before discussing alternatives, note that there is a severe performance penalty associated with cache-coherence protocols. The first requirement causes a broadcast operation followed by a cache read in every cache in the system, which tends to increase network contention and reduces available cache bandwidth. Since this operation takes place only on misses to shared data, its frequency should be just a few percent of the reads on any single processor.

As the number of processors increases, however, the load on the communications network and cache traffic quickly approaches saturation. For example, a 1 percent miss rate on shared data in each of 100 processors of a multiprocessor generates $100 \times 0.01 = 1$ broadcast request and one cache read per clock cycle. This broadcast will saturate the communications system and the individual caches of all processors.

Potentially greater degradation is caused by the second requirement, which requires a broadcast on every WRITE to a shared datum unless the system is able to tell that the shared datum is not resident in any other cache. The difference between the READ and WRITE penalties is that immediately after a READ miss occurs, the shared item becomes available in a local cache, and subsequent READs can be performed without broadcast. However, if two or more processors attempt to access and modify the same shared variable several times over a brief period of time, and if the requests by each processor are interleaved in some order, then the cache-coherency protocol generally causes heavy traffic due to frequent broadcasts that progressively move the datum from one cache to another as it is read and modified repeatedly. Although this behavior appears to be unlikely, it is extremely likely to occur in multiprocessor systems at barriers in programs and at locks that protect regions requiring exclusive access.

The basic mechanism for broadcast is best suited for a bus interconnection because a bus transaction is automatically assured that all receivers are listening to the bus when the transmitting processor gains access to the bus. Broadcasts can easily be implemented in shuffle-exchange networks and hypercubes, but they suffer from the problem that extra bandwidth available in these networks is lost momentarily when a broadcast saturates the interconnection network.

Similarly, a crossbar network is saturated by a single broadcast message, and that broadcast has to be delayed until all receivers are listening, which causes additional loss of useful bandwidth. Most proposals for cache-coherence protocols are therefore based on bus-connected multiprocessors. The RP3, for example, with its combining-switch network does not have a cache-coherence protocol, but instead caches only nonshareable data. References to shared data are routed directly to memory without interrogating cache.

Given the basic principles of cache coherence, the least complex solution is to broadcast a READ on every read miss of shared data, and to broadcast a

WRITE on every write to shared data. A cache listener responds to a READ by interrogating its own cache and reporting back the data.

If two or more respondents exist, then any respondent can report back data because the data should be identical. Most protocols, however, provide a unique ownership tag that dictates which respondent should deliver the data requested. When a WRITE is received, a listener can respond either by replacing the local value with the broadcast value or by purging the local value. Which of these is preferred depends on such factors as the cache size and the likelihood of accessing a shared variable again in the immediate future.

The basic protocol provides an opportunity to reduce broadcasts on WRITEs if there is a means for tagging an item in cache to indicate that it is the only copy of the item in any cache. If we add such a tag, then WRITE broadcasts need to occur only for cache misses and for cache hits to items that are resident elsewhere as well. But the tag has to be maintained so that its state is an accurate reflection of the state of the caches.

It is clear that if any datum is flagged as exclusive, then at any point that a broadcast for that item is observed, the tag has to be altered. Each of the proposed protocols provides a means for updating that tag. For example, a possible protocol for maintaining the flag is the following:

1. If the item in a cache is exclusive, and a read request for the item is observed on the network, then change the flag to nonexclusive and deliver a copy of the item to the requester. The requester tags the item as nonexclusive as well.

2. Purge any item in the cache when a write to that address is observed on the network.

3. When writing a datum to the cache, mark the datum as exclusive and notify other processors that the datum has been written. Write the new value of the item in shared memory as well.

A modification of the protocol avoids the purge noted in Item 2 and retains the new value of the item. If this is done, then the tags throughout the system must show nonexclusive ownership, so that Item 3 marks an item as exclusive if no other cache has the item, and otherwise marks the item as nonexclusive.

We cannot easily judge if the modification gives better or worse performance overall because much depends on the likelihood of repeated accesses to shared variables. The modified protocol gives better performance for heavy use of shared variables, whereas the basic protocol gives better performance when the right decision is to purge the variable when the vacancy in the cache can be put to immediate use holding other data.

Very little is known today about the likely access patterns to shared data in multiprocessors, so all coherence protocols are worthy of consideration in the immediate future. As multiprocessors become more widely used, performance data that can be used to evaluate the protocols and identify which one or ones are best for specific implementations should become available.

6.5 Summary

This chapter treats multiprocessors from a performance and topological point of view. The fundamental advantage of the multiprocessor architecture is its generality. Algorithms for such systems are much less constrained than are algorithms for vector and continuum-model computations because the individual processes in execution need not be identical or nearly identical.

The disadvantage of a multiprocessor architecture is that performance relies strongly on replication of hardware, but replication introduces serious problems regarding cost and contention. Programming complexity is greatly increased because of matters regarding synchronization and the correct use of shared data.

The negative factors tend to make multiprocessors most attractive for architectures with a small number of processors. The problem size is also important. To keep overhead low compared to useful computation, multiprocessors are best suited for large problems that cannot easily be treated on a single processor. Because of the extra complexity and overhead cost introduced to support parallel execution, multiprocessors become less attractive for dealing with problems that are solvable in reasonable time on a uniprocessor. Breakthroughs in languages and operating systems for multiprocessors could enhance the relative attractiveness of multiprocessors by eliminating the complexity that now falls on the programmer, but, to tap the potential power of the multiprocessor, the breakthroughs must necessarily provide high efficiency as well as complexity reduction.

For the near future, the likelihood of success in multiprocessor systems is assured for systems with a small number of processors. Chances for success diminish rapidly as N approaches 100 to 1000. It will take the efforts of many talented researchers pushing at the frontiers of computing research to make the 1000-processor system a cost-effective reality.

Our comments here suggest that overhead and communications costs have to be held to a minimum to achieve that reality. The hardware and software technology to keep those costs low is just developing. The combining switch is an example of a new technology that could make a substantial difference in the future. We expect other ideas of this type to emerge in the next few years to help shape future architectural developments.

Exercises

6.1 Consider the performance model expressed by Eq. (6.1). Suppose the two processors have unequal speeds and that Processor 1 is α times faster than Processor 2. What is the optimum distribution of tasks to processors?

6.2 The model expressed by Eq. (6.2) is suitable for a system in which transmission time is independent of the number of processors. The cost of communication is a fixed constant C, and the formula multiplies this cost by the number of communication transactions. In a token ring, the time of transmission increases with the number of processors. Develop a model that reflects this characteristic of token rings, and find the optimum task allocation for your model.

6.3 The purpose of this exercise is to find a performance model that fits a realistic program. Consider Program 5.1. The innermost pair of loops updates a rectangular region of a matrix. The outer loop repeats this operation N times. To answer the questions that follow, ignore the cost of synchronization and count only the communications costs for data.

  a) Partition the problem so that each row of the matrix lies totally within one processor. Determine the processor-to-processor communication transactions that have to occur within the algorithm. If there is no broadcast capability, how many communications occur during the algorithm? Compare this to the number of times that the innermost loop is executed on a serial computer and on the multiprocessor you are modeling.

  b) If your architecture supports a one-cycle broadcast transaction in which a transmitting processor can send a common message to all listeners, how does this facility change your answer to a?

  c) Let $N = 10$, and $R/C = 1$. What is the optimum distribution of tasks to processors for your system with a broadcast capability?

6.4 Repeat Exercise 6.3, but this time assign each column of the matrix to lie totally within one processor. Compare your answers for row and column assignments and discuss how the storage format affects the optimum way to distribute tasks among processors.

6.5 The purpose of this exercise is to investigate the effects of synchronization. For the row-oriented data structure of Exercise 6.3, reexamine Program 5.1 and discover where synchronization is required. That is, find where processors have to wait for events in other processors before they can proceed. Alter the performance model of Exercise 6.3 to account for the synchronization operations required.

6.6 Assume that the matrix of Program 5.1 is stored in N processors with one column in each processor of a multiprocessor. Let each column be updated in parallel when the subarray is updated. At the end of the update, assume that synchronization is done by means of a shared semaphore resident in Processor 0. Before an iteration begins, the variable is initialized to a value equal to the number of active processors in the forthcoming iteration. As each processor completes its work, the processor gains exclusive access to the shared variable, decrements the variable, then releases exclusive access. If a processor produces the value zero after a decrement, it initiates the next subarray update. Otherwise, processors become idle after decrementing the shared variable.

a) For $N = 16, 32$, and 128, determine the values of parameters r and h in Eq. (6.23) for a multiprocessor based on a crossbar-interconnection scheme. From these parameters, compute the maximum generation rate for memory requests.

b) Consider the question in a for a multiprocessor based on a bus interconnection. For this system, the point of contention is the shared bus rather than the memory system. Extend the model of a to cover all sources of bus contention to find a maximum rate for generating requests similar in intent to Eq. (6.24).

c) Consider the same problem executed on a machine with a shuffle-exchange network and the capability of performing Fetch-and-Add. Find the maximum rate for generating requests for this architecture for Program 5.1.

6.7 The structure of Program 5.1 requires access to both rows and columns of a matrix. Consider a very simple algorithm that accesses a matrix by two scans of the matrix. In the first scan, the matrix is accessed by rows. In the second scan, the matrix is accessed by columns. The matrix is $N \times N$.

a) For a crossbar-based multiprocessor with N processors and memories, show how to store the matrix to minimize the time for the required forms of access and state how much time is required to complete the two scans.

b) Repeat a for a bus-based multiprocessor.

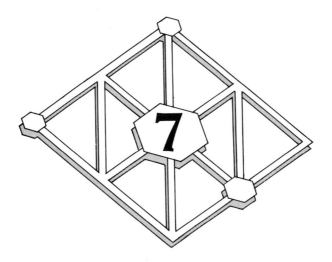

Multiprocessor Algorithms

7.1 Easy Parallelism

7.2 Synchronization Techniques

7.3 Parallel Search—How To Use and Not Use Parallelism

7.4 Transforming Serial Algorithms into Parallel Algorithms

7.5 Final Comments on Multiprocessors

This chapter explores the means for programming multiprocessors for high performance. A major portion of the chapter is dedicated to efficient mechanisms for ensuring the correct execution of programs. Our approach is to look at the easy parallelism first. The obvious ways to execute in parallel produce the bulk of the gains for most applications.

When one attempts to wrest the ultimate performance from a parallel process, it becomes necessary to explore more sophisticated notions. This chapter shows that search algorithms, for example, yield rather poor speedup when the programmer naively assigns dependent tasks to different processors. This is the case, for example, if a search terminates when any processor finds a solution, and the search space is divided among all processors.

We show a different approach that uses parallelism rather efficiently to solve a classic optimization problem, the Traveling Salesman Problem, in a time that on the average grows less than quadratically in the size of the problem. This may appear to be rather astounding, since the Traveling Salesman Problem is one of the so-called *hard* (NP-complete) problems, and therefore there exists no known algorithm that solves this problem in a time that grows less than exponentially in the problem size. But theory covers the worst case and says nothing about the average case. We cover the average case for a random problem in this text, and that has a very low complexity.

Correctness of parallel algorithms requires some mechanism for handling the updates of shared variables. We introduce the performance notion of **SYPS** (SYnchronizations Per Second, pronounced "sips"), which is normally measured in **MSYPS** (MegaSYPS).

In this chapter we show how the **MSYPS** capacity of an architecture affects throughput. Throughput is limited both by its **MIPS** and **MSYPS** capacity and cannot exceed the throughput permitted by the more constraining of the two measures. Thus a high-**MIPS**, low-**MSYPS** machine may be outstanding at numerical operations, but can run rather poorly for applications that require a high volume of synchronizations. The **MIPS** measure alone suggests a high throughput, but the architectural constraint on **MSYPS** can prevent the potential **MIPS** from being realized.

7.1 Easy Parallelism

Parallelism is best used for programs that require a significant number of cycles. We have accomplished something worthwhile when we reduce a ten-day execution to one day, whereas the reduction of a ten-minute program to one minute is an equal but far less interesting speedup. We argue here that long programs almost surely contain some region of code that accounts for the bulk of the execution by being executed repeatedly for a massive number of times.

At a clock rate of 100 ns, there are on the order of 10^{12} clock ticks in a day. Consider any program that takes a full day to execute and examine where it spends the bulk of its time. If there is some subroutine or code sequence that is repeated a large number of times, say a million times, then our thesis is justified. The alternative is that no program instruction is executed more than a few times.

At ten ticks per instruction and as many as ten repetitions of an instruction, we find that the program must contain about 10^{10} distinct instructions to execute for one full day. Such a program would indeed be unusual because of its gigantic size, and the effort to construct such a program would take thousands of man-years at current rates of software productivity. The program is more likely to have only 10^4 to 10^6 instructions, therefore requiring an average repetition factor of roughly 10^5 to 10^7.

With some body of instructions being repeated a million times or more, we have an opportunity for parallelism if we can spread those million executions in some way across N processors. This is a simple recipe to achieve parallelism:

1. Analyze the program for a loop or recursion structure;

2. Find the instructions that account for the most time, usually the regions repeated the greatest number of iterations;

3. Split the instruction execution of these regions across N processors, if this can be done correctly; and

4. Add synchronization and data-transmission statements as required to create a correct parallel implementation.

As an example of the application of this idea, consider Program 7.1, which revisits the Poisson calculation introduced in Chapter 4. Recall from our earlier discussions that the near-neighbor iteration is usually not the most efficient way to solve the Poisson problem. Nevertheless, iteration is what appears in Program 7.1.

Suppose, also, that we know in advance that $10M$ cycles are required for the iteration to converge. Program 7.1 shows three nested loops. The outer loop repeats $10M$ times to obtain the necessary convergence. (The fixed number of outer iterations is just a convenience for this example. Most implementations repeat the outer iteration until some convergence test is satisfied.)

In the two inner loops, each point $P[i, j]$ in a square region is updated once. The innermost loop updates a line in the region, and the next level of iteration treats the collection of lines that cover a rectangle. The outermost iteration forces the rectangle to be updated $10M$ times.

A purely sequential program updates all points in the rectangle one time before any point in the rectangle is updated a second time. To enforce this behavior in a parallel program, we require that the parallelism be limited to a single update of the rectangular region. Therefore, we seek a scheme that uses

---

Program 7.1 Poisson solver, serial version.

```
for k := 1 to 10 × M do
   begin
     for i := 1 to M do
        begin
          for j := 1 to M do
             begin
               P[i, j] :=
                  (P[i, j + 1] + P[i, j − 1] + P[i + 1, j] + P[i − 1, j])/4;
             end; {* j loop *}
        end; {* i loop *}
   end; {* k loop *}
```

Notes:

1. Boundary conditions are held in Rows 0 and $M + 1$ and Columns 0 and $M + 1$ of array P.

---

parallel processors as effectively as possible for a single update of the rectangular region, and we perform $10M$ executions of the parallel update, with the updates occurring one after another, without any overlap among them. Figure 7.1 shows a possible execution diagram, with the number of processors busy as a function of time and the outer iteration that they are performing at any given time.

7.1.1 The do par and do seq Constructions

From a programming point of view, we need the concept of parallel and serial embedded in a language to distinguish between iterations that can be done in parallel across many processors and those that have to be done one after another. A simple way to extend a Pascal- or FORTRAN-like language is to introduce these forms of the **do** construction:

- **do par** to execute loop iterations in parallel; and
- **do seq** to execute loop iterations sequentially.

Then the form

```
for i := 1 to M do seq
    begin
        Iteration A
    end; {* do seq *}
```

produces M serial executions of Iteration A, whereas

```
for i := 1 to M do par
    begin
        Iteration A
    end; {* do par *}
```

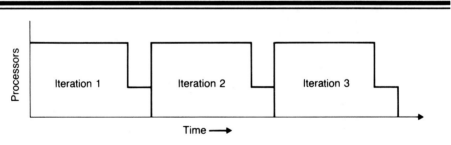

Fig. 7.1 Processors busy as a function of time. All available processors are busy until most of the work for an iteration is done. As an iteration nears completion, some processors become idle and must wait until a new iteration starts before they can resume computation.

causes all M copies of Iteration A to be alive concurrently, and any or all those copies can be executed concurrently, depending on scheduling policies and the resources available. The **do par** construction creates a separate instance of the loop body for each value of i in the range of **do par.**

To describe our findings regarding the parallel and sequential behavior of Program 7.1, consider Program 7.2, in which the two inner loops use the **do par** construction, and the outer loop uses the **do seq** construction. During the course of execution, this program creates M^2 copies of the inner iteration, one for each (i, j) pair, parcels these out among the processors, then awaits their completion. When they have completed, the program performs the same process again and continues repeating it until it is done $10M$ times.

7.1.2 Barrier Synchronization

Notice the synchronization that is implied by the **do seq** construction in Program 7.2. A processor ready to begin a new outer iteration has to be informed when all work for the last outer iteration has been completed.

In essence, the **do seq** construction has placed a barrier after each of its iterations. As many processors as can be used effectively can be allocated to a single iteration of a **do seq,** but those processors must stop at a barrier at the end of the iteration. No processor can cross this barrier until all processors performing the loop iteration have reached the barrier.

In Program 7.2, we can have as many as M^2 processors executing within a single iteration of the outer loop, and these processors have to stop and wait at

---

Program 7.2 Poisson solver, parallel version.

```
for k := 1 to 10 × M do seq
    begin
        for i := 1 to M do par
            begin
                for j := 1 to M do par
                    begin
                        P[i, j] :=
                            (P[i, j + 1] + P[i, j − 1] + P[i + 1, j] + P[i − 1, j])/4;
                    end; {* j loop *}
            end; {* i loop *}
    end; {* k loop *}
```

Notes:

1. Boundary conditions are held in Rows 0 and $M + 1$ and Columns 0 and $M + 1$ of array P.

the implicit barrier for all to finish before any one processor can start a new iteration. We call this type of synchronization *barrier* synchronization. Although it is not used explicitly in Program 7.2, it is implicitly used at the end of each iteration of the **do seq.**

An explicit form of the barrier can be used as shown in Program 7.3 within the body of a **do par** construction. In this case, the body of the loop has three parts, Steps A through C. The **do par** creates M instances of the loop body, one for each value of i, and parcels these tasks to as many processors as are available.

In the absence of barriers, for any single iteration we are guaranteed to execute Step A(i), then B(i), then C(i), in that order. The order in which the steps are performed across iterations is rather arbitrary, and anything could happen. For example, we could see the completion sequence A(1), A(2), B(2), C(2), B(1), C(1). We could not see a sequence in which B(1) completed before C(1) because a loop body for a specific iteration has to be executed serially.

Program 7.3 has a barrier inserted after Step B. The effect of the barrier is to force all iterations to complete Steps A and B before any iteration continues to Step C. With the barrier in place, the sequence A(1), A(2), B(2), C(2), B(1), C(1) cannot occur because C(2) completes (and hence must have been started) before B(1) has been completed. The barrier should be inserted if Step C of each iteration depends on Steps A and B of prior iterations.

The barrier is a rather strong means for synchronizing, and it may be more severe than is actually necessary. It may be possible to use more focused methods of synchronization that can start Step C in various iterations at much earlier times. Such methods necessarily have the ability to sense when specific conditions are satisfied so that Step C can start, which is more flexible than sensing the single condition that all processors have reached a barrier.

Program 7.3 Barrier example.

```
for i := 1 to M do par
    begin
        Step A(i)
        Step B(i)
        Barrier;
        Step C(i)
    end; {* i loop *}
```

Notes:

  1. The Barrier forces all iterations of A and B to complete before any iteration of C is started.

7.1.3 Performance Considerations

Given these basic notions of parallel and sequential execution of loops, let us examine the performance aspects of the parallel code. For the moment, let us ignore the specific details of initiating a parallel task at the beginning of a **do par** and of handling a barrier, if any, associated with the **do par.** Our objective is to determine the R/C ratio for a program so that we can relate the results of Chapter 6 to multiprocessor algorithm development.

In Program 7.2, a single task corresponds to the one statement of the innermost loop. This statement takes roughly six instructions, consisting of a LOAD, three ADDS, a SHIFT or DIVIDE, and a STORE. Address calculations might be required as well, but they might be avoidable if the address computations required can be done totally by means of the effective-address mechanism without requiring additional instructions. We also should include some additional time to charge to the iteration for the calculation of the values of i and j to use for this particular iteration. In total, roughly ten instructions are necessary to perform the iteration. This corresponds to R, the run time.

The overhead and communication encompassed by C includes the work required to generate the task, to enqueue it while waiting for a processor, to dequeue it when a processor becomes available, and to log the completion of the task so that some barrier can be passed when all tasks are completed.

We may be fortunate enough to avoid an ENQUEUE/DEQUEUE pair, but there have to be some instructions to generate and terminate the task. A very low estimate for this overhead is two instructions for each of generation and termination. A more realistic estimate is hundreds, possibly thousands, of instructions.

The ratio R/C might be as high as 2 or 3, and it could be as low as 1/100 or 1/1000. For most of the models mentioned in Chapter 6, these ratios do not support a good deal of parallelism. Depending on the architecture and the ratio, the fastest implementation of Program 7.2 uses only one processor or possibly just a few processors. But this is still rather optimistic because our earlier models ignore the effects of synchronization. Synchronization produces further degradation that biases the best solution towards fewer processors.

To be more specific, consider how synchronization affects a single task in Program 7.2. The task has to be generated, enqueued, dequeued, and terminated. The enqueue, dequeue, and terminate processes are likely to involve shared variables that have to be updated. The task-generation process might introduce its own overhead as well if it, too, updates shared variables.

Let us count the updating of a shared variable as a basic operation that we call a *synch*. Then one task of Program 7.2 requires three synchs (for enqueue/dequeue/terminate), plus roughly ten instructions for task generate, loop body, and task terminate. Most multiprocessor architectures are highly constrained in how synchs are implemented, and the number of synchs that can be performed in parallel is typically rather limited, sometimes as few as one. An exception to this is an architecture with the combining switch described in Chapter 6, such as the IBM RP3 and NYU Ultracomputer architectures.

To understand the synch problem more thoroughly, consider a bus-oriented multiprocessor that uses a READ/MODIFY/WRITE operation on the bus to perform a synch. Then at most one synch per cycle is possible. For a cycle time of 100 ns, this limits performance to at most 10^7 SYPS (synchs per second), or 10 MSYPS.

If in one cycle the multiprocessor can execute one instruction in each of N processors, then the performance of the composite system is $10N$ MIPS for instructions, but only 10 MSYPS for synchs. The MIPS rate is N times greater than the MSYPS rate. Our example program demands roughly two or three instructions per synch, so that for N greater than 3, the system becomes saturated at the synchronization interface; otherwise, the system is saturated at the instruction-execution interface.

A combining switch provides a mechanism for supporting synchs in parallel, and thereby it provides an MSYPS rate more nearly on the order of $10N$ MSYPS for a system with a 100 ns clock. The coefficient need not be 10; it may be considerably less. The point is that the sustainable MSYPS rate grows with N, and it thereby provides a means for breaking the synch bottleneck.

Architectures that do not have a combining switch or an equivalent mechanism for executing synchronizations in parallel are subject to a saturation phenomenon depicted in Fig. 7.2. The assumption in this figure is that there is a fixed maximum MSYPS supportable by the system, independent of the number of processors. As processors are added, the MIPS rate of the system grows linearly with the number of processors, but the MSYPS rate is fixed. Eventually the MSYPS demand reaches the limit, and no additional speedup is possible as new processors are added.

The figure shows linearly increasing speedup until ten processors are in the system; thereafter speedup remains at the saturation limit of ten as new processors are added. Two curves are shown—an idealized piece-wise linear curve that reflects the bounds on speedup, and a curve that falls below this bound, which suggests what might be observed in actual situations. The true curve shows speedup falling off with additional processors because overhead tends to increase and MSYPS capacity remains at the fixed limit as new processors are added.

We have reached an interesting challenge for a computer architect. Suppose that an application such as Program 7.2 is implemented for a multiprocessor, and performance turns out to be sharply restricted because of an MSYPS bottleneck. What avenues are open to the architect to improve performance? Here are three obvious directions to follow:

1. Increase R/C and thereby do more computation per synch.

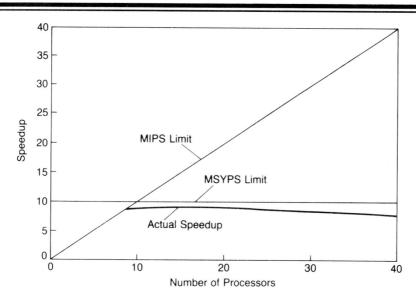

Fig. 7.2 Speedup curves.

2. Balance the system by making architectural changes to increase the MSYPS rate of the architecture.

3. Balance the system by reducing the MIPS rate of the processors.

The first approach is the easiest and most cost-effective. We can substantially improve performance for essentially no cost in hardware or software by increasing granularity. This is the preferred solution that is discussed at some length in this section.

The second approach forces the architect to build into the architecture mechanisms that support a high MSYPS rate. The combining switch is the only approach being implemented today for which the MSYPS rate increases linearly with the number of processors, but other techniques that may raise the MSYPS rate high enough for specific applications are also possible. For example, the architect can incorporate a high-speed specialized processor for synchronizations that does nothing but manage locks and the updating of shared data. In a multiprocessor, the architect might also include a hardware scheduler/dispatcher for task and processor management.

The third approach, reducing the MIPS rate of the processors, corrects system imbalance but reduces overall throughput. The idea here is that if system imbalance results in idle processors, one may be able to obtain nearly equal speed by using less expensive slower processors. This approach attempts to exploit the cost disparity between low-speed and high-speed technology, and can be successful if the change in throughput by reducing the speed or number of processors is sufficiently low compared to the reduction in the cost of the system. The idea is to change from an inefficient system to a much less expensive system of slightly lower capacity by exploiting higher efficiency.

7.1.4 Increasing Granularity

To continue this discussion, let us see how easy it is to increase R/C for Program 7.2. The granularity assumed in the program is that there is one assignment statement per task. To increase granularity we can group several statements together, as suggested by Program 7.4.

Program 7.4 is identical to Program 7.2 except that the innermost loop contains the phrase **chunksize** 50. This phrase instructs the compiler and operating system to group 50 successive index values into each task, instead of assigning one index value to each task. The last task to be assigned receives

---

Program 7.4 Poisson solver, parallel version with chunking.

```
for k := 1 to 10 × M do seq
   begin
      for i := 1 to M do par
         begin
            for j := 1 to M do par chunksize 50;
               begin
                  P[i, j] :=
                     (P[i, j + 1] + P[i, j − 1] + P[i + 1, j] + P[i − 1, j])/4;
               end; {* j loop *}
         end; {* i loop *}
   end; {* k loop *}
```

Notes:

1. Boundary conditions are held in Rows 0 and $M + 1$ and Columns 0 and $M + 1$ of array P.

2. The phrase **chunksize** 50 forces iterations to be parcelled out to processors in chunks of size 50, with each of the iterations in a chunk performed sequentially. Different chunks can be executed concurrently on different processors.

---

whatever index values remain, which may be fewer than 50. With the chunk-size set to 50, R/C is 50 times greater for Program 7.4 than for Program 7.2, and the MSYPS requirement is reduced by a factor of 50. Of course, the parallelism available is also reduced by a factor of 50, but the point is that the reduction in parallelism might be quite tolerable if it were not usable in the first place.

For example, consider the potential for parallelism when M in Programs 7.2 and 7.4 is equal to 100. The two inner loops create 10,000 tasks in Program 7.2. The number of tasks actually created depends on the program, not on the architecture. If the architecture has fewer than 10,000 processors available, as is likely to be the case, then the excess tasks created will probably be enqueued and dequeued or generated on demand, but in any case will result in 10,000 instances of overhead related to their management. Program 7.4 gives the programmer the ability to reduce the overhead by controlling how many independent tasks are created, as well as the R/C ratio for those tasks.

For the example we are considering, Program 7.4 creates 200 tasks, which is appropriate for architectures with 200 or more processors. If the architecture has fewer than 200 processors, the chunksize should be made even larger, and it is realistic for the chunksize to be computable dynamically to be a function of the number of the processors actually available for execution of the loop body.

The purpose of a small granularity, after all, is to increase the available parallelism, but there is no point to increasing parallelism beyond the amount that can be exploited. Granularity should be set no smaller than the size that creates enough tasks to fill available processors, and perhaps even this size is too small if R/C for that granularity is below the break-even point for the processors available. The point in making the chunksize selectable by the programmer is that the programmer can experiment with grain size to find some optimum size for a given application and architecture.

Granularity is only one of several factors that the programmer has to consider. We have not addressed the issues regarding local and global storage and allocation of data to reduce memory contention. When the programmer chooses a granularity by choosing a chunksize, the programmer is actually binding together various iterations and is thereby creating an environment in which some data can possibly be reused several times in a local context before being returned to a global memory. In this environment, the task can be structured as follows:

1. Acquire locks as required for global variables to be updated.
2. Read variables from global memory to local memory.
3. Perform the computation, updating the local variables.
4. Update the global variables from the local copies of the variables.
5. Release the locks on the global variables.

While the computation is being executed, contention with other processes is held to a minimum because all accesses are to local memory. However, locking and the synchronization overhead required to obtain and release locks can degrade performance. Much depends on the likelihood that processors will be left idle while waiting for locks to be released.

In creating a large task by choosing a large chunksize, the programmer actually has more flexibility than is shown in Program 7.4. That program provides only for creating tasks by grouping together iterations that fall on a single row of the square array. The program can be reorganized so that chunks fall instead along columns, or in rectangular or square subarrays.

The structure that forms the best possible chunk has a good granularity and can operate on the data for that chunk with minimum interference with processors that operate on their chunks. The amount of interference expected to occur depends on the architecture and the allocation of data to memory modules within that architecture. The designer of the architecture has to be aware of the control choices available to the programmer and should create an architecture in which one or more of those choices leads to efficient execution across a range of important problems.

The programmer has a rather powerful means for controlling the size of R/C by controlling chunksize and by selecting which statements are grouped together within one chunk. If the chunksize is fixed for an architecture, as several proposals for fine-grained architectures have suggested, the programmer loses the flexibility to adjust the R/C ratio to obtain maximum performance. First- and second-generation multiprocessors should leave the ratio in the hands of programmers until sufficient experience is obtained to build machines with optimal or near-optimal R/C ratios.

The second technique for eliminating an MSYPS bottleneck is to reduce the cost of a synchronization, or equivalently, to increase the MSYPS rate of the architecture. This subject is sufficiently complex to warrant its own section within this chapter. We defer discussion at this point and explore the subject in depth later.

The last technique achieves balance within a system by slowing down the processors relative to the synchronization mechanism. Thus, the MIPS rate of the system is reduced while the MSYPS rate is fixed, and this yields a better balance if MSYPS are not well matched to the initial value of MIPS.

Figure 7.3 shows speedup as a function of the clock period as the clock is slowed. Note how speedup in this system increases as the processors become slower. Recall that speedup is a measure of the speed of an N-processor system as compared to a system that has one processor identical to any one of the N processors. Figure 7.3 is plotted for $N = 100$. Since clock period increases along the x-axis, the processors at the right-hand side of the figure are slower than the processors at the left-hand side of the figure.

The figure shows that the speedup obtained from 100 processors is greater

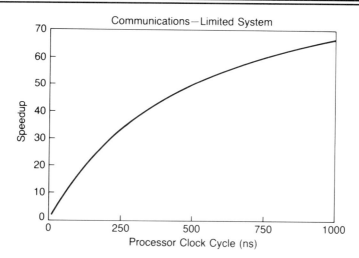

Fig. 7.3 Speedup versus clock period.

for slow processors than for fast processors. However, speedup is not the same as performance. The performance from 100 fast processors is greater than the performance available from 100 slow processors, even though speedup is less for the fast processors. On the left side of the diagram, the fast processors are not well matched to the slow synchronization mechanism, and many are left idle during a computation. Adding new processors to this system does not improve performance very much, so speedup is relatively low.

As we move from the left to the right of the figure, the bottleneck in the system shifts from the synchronization mechanism to the processors themselves. When the processor performance is the chief component of the bottleneck, then by adding new processors, the bottleneck is reduced so that speedup tends to increase. Cvetanovic [1985, 1987] made this observation in regard to her study of an RP3-like architecture, but the phenomenon holds in general for systems that have two or more potential bottlenecks.

The lesson to be learned from Fig. 7.3 is that the architect should select a design point in which bottleneck capacities are close to being in balance. For the multiprocessor architecture, the maximum system MIPS and MSYPS rates should be balanced with respect to each other to match the demands of most workloads. If the system is out of balance by being on the left side of Fig. 7.3, the processors are too expensive for the system performance they give. On the right side of the figure, the processors themselves are the bottleneck, and additional speed can be obtained by faster processors.

7.1.5 Initiating Tasks

One topic of importance that we have overlooked thus far concerns the mechanism for initiating individual tasks. If, in Program 7.2 or Program 7.4, the **do par** construction is implemented by generating the tasks one by one, then the task generation is a serial overhead that must be added to C in the R/C ratio.

Program 7.2 depicts a situation in which the inner loop requires $O(N)$ instructions just to generate the tasks if task generation is done sequentially. Yet the tasks themselves take only ten or so instructions that are supposedly done in parallel.

This situation becomes rather comical if you observe a processor executing the **do par** and spinning off 100 tasks by executing 1000 instructions. After spending all of this time generating the work, within ten more instructions all the work is done. We have simply shifted execution time from doing the main iteration to the overhead in starting up the processors. Obviously, the R/C ratio is far too low to be useful, but more fundamental is the fact that we cannot afford to use sequential execution to spin off the tasks to be executed concurrently.

A good approach is to produce the tasks during compilation, provided that the value of N is known during compilation. Then the tasks are created once for all executions of the program. Presumably, once the tasks are created, they can be loaded in parallel into all processors, and thereby we avoid the serial time for their initiation.

An alternative approach that has somewhat higher overhead is to generate the tasks dynamically in $O(\log N)$ time by means of a binary task-generation tree. To generate the tasks for the innermost **do par** loop of Program 7.1, the root node of the generation tree generates two subtasks. The first is responsible for generating the first half of the tasks, and the second is responsible for generating the second half of the tasks. These in turn split into four subtasks, each responsible for generating a quarter of the tasks. After $O(\log N)$ steps, no additional subtasks are generated, and the tasks themselves can be generated.

The tree-generation scheme or an equivalent is absolutely essential for dynamic task-initiation. Any $O(N)$ process for task generation can create sufficient overhead to severely impair multiprocessor performance.

The task-generation scheme appears to be an obvious requirement. Yet it has been overlooked repeatedly in the literature in serious proposals for multiprocessors. Halstead [1985] describes an interesting multiprocessor architecture called *Concert*, in which the user has explicit control of task generation. This paper describes an example of parallel sorting using the well-known quicksort algorithm, which has an average complexity of $M \log M$ for sorting M items.

The initial phase of the Halstead algorithm is a linear pass over the M items. This phase generates a collection of tasks that can be executed in parallel. Subsequent phases of the algorithm exploit parallelism rather well, but the first phase does the damage. No matter how many processors are used, the algorithm cannot run faster than $O(M)$, thereby dooming speedup to $O(\log M)$. Halstead reports near linear speedup for a small number of processors, but as the number of processors grows close to $\log M$, speedup must level off.

The limitation on speedup in this case is not the fault of the architecture because Concert, like many multiprocessors, supports task-generation trees. The fault lies in the data representation of the problem. The data to be sorted in this problem are presented to the algorithm as a LISP one-way linked list. The only way to inspect the data is to follow the chain of pointers from one item to the next, taking $O(M)$ time to do so.

Here is a situation in which the data representation from a serial programming language is strongly incompatible with high-performance parallel processing. Although Halstead's article articulates the strengths of the Concert architecture, it does not specifically address the weaknesses of a linked-list structure in the context of the algorithm. The data representation in this case imposes an inherent inefficiency on what otherwise appears to be an interesting and effective technique for exploiting parallelism in a multiprocessor.

The key to architectural evaluation is identifying how performance changes as a function of critical parameters such as the number of processors, R/C, and the choice of data structure. We have shown how a few simple notions provide extremely powerful tools for identifying major bottlenecks that are otherwise hidden from view.

In closing our discussion of easy parallelism, note how the example for this discussion shows the advantages of the multiprocessor over a near-neighbor SIMD machine and other various forms of vector machines.

Program 7.2 is ideal for a near-neighbor or a vector machine, as stated, but real applications are seldom as simple as Program 7.2. The boundary calculations are often rather complex, and in the more usual case, the region is irregularly shaped or has internal cavities or other structures that alter the simplicity of the solution.

Each different type of point within the region of computation requires a slightly different program. A purely SIMD machine cannot easily deal with such differences and still retain high efficiency. Each different type of point, in the worst case, requires its own program execution, done with all other processing turned off. Thus, an SIMD machine may have to perform successive computations for the points of Region A, Region B, and so on, and thereby reduce the effective parallelism available in the architecture.

The multiprocessor can produce different programs for each region and perform the computations for all regions concurrently, thus achieving greater parallelism than an SIMD architecture can achieve. We presume that the number of different programs required is a small number, such as 10 to 20, and that the execution time per iteration is equal to the longest time logged by any of the different programs. If there are k different programs to execute, then the gain of the multiprocessor over the SIMD architecture is at most a factor of k.

7.2 Synchronization Techniques

Synchronization is probably the most difficult and error-prone type of programming that exists. Its difficulty arises because it involves the understanding of the potential simultaneous actions of multiple processors. The huge number of possibilities to consider is beyond the capability of most people. Moreover, synchronization also depends on the nature of the interfaces among the multiprocessors. Many schemes have fallen because the programmers have made false assumptions about how the hardware works.

As an example of this problem, consider the landmark work of Dijkstra [1965]. At issue at that time was whether or not processors could be synchronized with just the standard operators of an ordinary programming language such as ALGOL 60. Dijkstra's solution was the first to show that this is possible for a reasonable set of assumptions. He states that this is the most difficult program he has ever written.

The statements in this program make no use of instructions that can perform uninterruptible READ/MODIFY/WRITE operations because ALGOL did not supply this operation in any form as a primitive operation. But the program does assume that a certain observability condition holds. That is, if Processor A performs WRITE X followed by WRITE Y, then all other processors will observe the WRITEs performed in this order. That is, if Processor A executes WRITE X then WRITE Y, no other processor that executes READ Y followed by READ X will see the new value of Y and the old value of X. If it sees the old value of X, it will also see the old value of Y because Y is changed after X is changed. This assumption is totally reasonable, yet it need not be obeyed in multiprocessors unless it is specifically designed into the architecture.

Any processor that uses a multilevel switching network between processors and memory can potentially violate the assumption. The action of WRITE X followed by WRITE Y presumably launches these two activities into the switching network, and they quickly make their respective ways to distinct memory modules.

Suppose that WRITE X hits a hot spot and is buffered, while WRITE Y succeeds in reaching memory and updating Y. Meanwhile the actions READ Y and READ X are issued from a different processor. READ Y readily wends its way to memory, obtains the new value of Y, and reports it back. READ X finds a direct route to memory, avoiding the hot spot that is holding back WRITE X. READ X finds the old value of X and reports it back to the requestor. Now the observability assumption is not satisfied, and the Dijkstra synchronization algorithm fails.

Dijkstra's synchronization solution is not important today because almost all synchronization is done with a READ/MODIFY/WRITE operation of some form, which is far more efficient than solutions that have to do a number of operations to make up for the lack of a READ/MODIFY/WRITE instruction.

The fact that Dijkstra's solution fails when the WRITE/WRITE observability condition does not hold is not significant as far as Dijkstra's algorithm is concerned, but the failure mode itself is rather important because any multiprocessor algorithm can inadvertently depend on the WRITE/WRITE observability condition and will fail when that condition does not hold. Programmers are usually not aware when their codes require WRITE/WRITE observability. The codes may work perfectly when executed serially and in some parallel systems, but may well fail when transported to new environments.

In the remainder of this section we treat a sequence of four methods for synchronizing processes. The progression moves from the least powerful to the most powerful, and the discussion suggests how the additional power can be used to obtain enhanced capabilities. The four methods treated here are

1. *Test-and-Set*: operate on a single bit.
2. *Increment, Decrement*: produce sums and differences.
3. *Compare-and-Swap*: reduce a complex critical section to a single instruction.
4. *Fetch-and-Add*: eliminate critical sections in some cases.

The remainder of this section treats each of the alternatives in order.

7.2.1 Synchronization with Test-and-Set

The first synchronizing method uses an instruction called *Test-and-Set*, which performs the following operation:

```
Definition: Test-and-set (address, bit_position);
    begin
        Temp := Memory[address].bit_position;
        Memory[address].bit_position := 1;
        Condition_code := Temp.bit_position;
    end; {* definition *}
```

The Test-and-Set instruction sets a designated bit of a shared datum to 1, and returns in the condition code the value of that bit prior to setting it to 1. The two parameters of the instruction are the address of the shared datum and the bit-position of the datum at the address that is to be tested. The notation "A.b" denotes bit position *b* of datum *A*.

This instruction has the classic form of READ/MODIFY/WRITE, which is a key characteristic of synchronizing instructions. To ensure that it can be used successfully for synchronizing, the Test-and-Set instruction must be uninterruptible. That is, once it is initiated and the READ access is completed, no other access can be made to the operand until the operand is rewritten during the second step of the Test-and-Set. If an intervening access were permitted, synchronization could fail.

Multiprocessors that have cache memories must treat Test-and-Set as a special type of instruction. Since Test-and-Set is used to update shared data, shared data held in cache must be kept consistent across all caches and with respect to main memory.

One possibility is to force accesses produced by Test-and-Set to go to shared memory and avoid the cache altogether. The companion operation that resets bits of shared operands should be implemented in a similar fashion. Another alternative is to permit shared data to be cached and to build the necessary synchronization behavior into the cache-consistency protocol.

One possibility here is to use an ownership bit in the cache directory to indicate which copy of a shared datum resident in one or more caches is the principal copy. When the READ of the READ/MODIFY/WRITE is performed, the cache that owns the shared datum passes its current value to the requester. All processors, including the current owner, mark the datum as absent. When the datum is rewritten, it can be rewritten to the local cache, with the datum tag showing the datum being owned by the local processor.

Now consider how one might use a Test-and-Set instruction to implement an elementary update of a shared variable. The skeleton for a program is:

> **Lock**(*shared_datum*);
> Update (*shared_datum*);
> **Unlock**(*shared_datum*);

With each shared datum or data structure, we can associate a single bit, called its *semaphore*. The Lock and Unlock statements operate on the semaphore of a datum or data structure rather than on the content of the datum. The semaphore is the traffic director that tells a process whether or not to proceed past the LOCK statement. The semaphore permits at most one process at a time to execute the code in the update region of the program. If Process *A* executes the Lock statement successfully, then all other processes must be halted there until Process *A* executes the UNLOCK statement.

The LOCK statement can be implemented in part with a Test-and-Set instruction. The Test-and-Set forces the semaphore for the shared datum to be set, whether or not it has been set before the Test-and-Set. To pass the lock, the process must see 0 returned in the condition code as the value of the semaphore just prior to the Test-and-Set.

If several processes execute a LOCK on a semaphore concurrently, the requests will be serialized and executed one by one because of the characteristics of the READ/MODIFY/WRITE operations that force this serial behavior. Given serial execution of LOCK, no more than one process of a set of concurrent requesters can observe a zero value of the semaphore and thereby move past the LOCK to the update. When one process passes the LOCK and reaches the UNLOCK, the semaphore can be returned to a 0 state and thereby permit another process to pass the LOCK statement and update a shared variable.

In terms of MSYPS, the LOCK/UNLOCK pair take at least one instruction each. The update code protected by the LOCK/UNLOCK requires two or three instructions and could be 10 to 100 instructions, depending on the nature of the update. This puts anywhere from 5 to 100 or more instructions in the serial section.

The number of serial sections executed sequentially in one second gives the MSYPS rate, which is therefore anywhere from 5 to 100 times slower than the MIPS rate of the processor. The MIPS rate is likely to be the bottleneck if its MSYPS rate is very high, for example, 10 percent or more of the MIPS rate. The bottleneck shifts to the MSYPS rate if MSYPS is relatively low, for example, 1 percent or less of the MIPS rate, depending on the application.

In multiprocessor systems the peak MIPS rate increases proportionally with the number of processors assigned to a problem, but the MSYPS rate in most architectures is a fixed limit for a system regardless of how many processors are actually assigned to a program.

If we focus on the MIPS rate exclusively and ignore the MSYPS limit, we tend to believe that by assigning more processors to a program, we are making available more machine capacity. But this is not strictly true.

Indeed, as more processors are assigned, a program has more MIPS and more memory available, but MSYPS may not be increasing at all. If this is the bottleneck, then additional processors will not result in faster computation. In fact, because of contention among processors, the LOCK/UNLOCK and the update operations on shared data tend to take longer with more processors active, with the result that computation time may increase instead of decrease as more processors are assigned to a computation.

The MSYPS bottleneck is only one of several potential sources of performance degradation. For example, consider what happens when a processor is blocked by a LOCK operation. Perhaps it can be put to use doing other useful work and continue to expend MIPS fruitfully in spite of the MSYPS bottleneck. The Test-and-Set is only half of a lock. The other half is the action taken depending on whether the lock has been granted or not. If the Test-and-Set observes a prior semaphore value of 0, then the lock has been granted, and the processor continues on to the update section. If not, there are at least two different actions that can be taken:

1. *Spin lock*: branch backward and reexecute LOCK, repeating the process until the lock is granted.

2. *Enqueue a task*: suspend the blocked process, and enqueue its status on a queue associated with the semaphore. Reassign the processor to other work currently enqueued and ready for execution.

Neither of these alternatives is particularly attractive. The spin lock wastes computer cycles and causes memory contention at the semaphore. When many processors are waiting at a semaphore, the contention causes additional cycles of delay while a process is attempting to release a lock. This tends to decrease the sustainable MSYPS rate and magnifies the effect of the bottleneck at the semaphore.

Task enqueueing appears to be efficient because it devotes available cycles to useful work. However, the overhead for ENQUEUE/DEQUEUE tends to be very high, which may well be greater in cost than the cost of the cycles lost in a spin lock. Worse yet, to enqueue a task, a processor has to access and update a shared queue pointer. This access itself involves a LOCK/UNLOCK of some kind.

If this lock is not granted, we have come full cycle and face the problem of enqueueing a task at one queue to enqueue it at another queue. This could repeat *ad infinitum*. Obviously, at some level, such as the first or second, we have to break the chain of events by forcing a LOCK to be implemented by means of a spin lock rather than by enqueueing a task at a semaphore.

In terms of performance, the two alternatives of spin lock and task enqueue have opposite effects on MIPS and MSYPS measures. Task enqueueing tends to increase MIPS available by reassigning idle processors to other useful work. Spin locks tend to decrease MIPS by dedicating potentially useful machine cycles to the effort of repeatedly testing a semaphore. The opposite effect occurs with respect to MSYPS. One effect of task enqueueing is to increase the number and length of critical sections protected by locks. By increasing the number of critical sections, the MSYPS demand is increased. Since only one processor at a time can execute a critical section, by increasing the length of critical sections, presumably because of the various actions required during an ENQUEUE and DEQUEUE, the maximum potential MSYPS rate is decreased.

If a parallel process is limited mainly by MSYPS rather than by MIPS, then the effect of changing spin locks into ENQUEUE/DEQUEUEs will tend to lower throughput. Conversely, if the limitation is a MIPS rather than an MSYPS limitation, then a change from spin locks to ENQUEUE/DEQUEUEs may have the opposite effect. It may lead to higher performance, provided that the ENQUEUE/DEQUEUE overhead is sufficiently low that the system with ENQUEUE/DEQUEUE locks is still MIPS limited rather than MSYPS limited.

Before closing this section, we describe briefly the implementation of UNLOCK because it is very different depending on whether the corresponding LOCK is a spin lock or an ENQUEUE lock. To unlock a spin lock, the owner processor does no more than write a 0 in the semaphore. It is not necessary to do a READ/MODIFY/WRITE to unlock the semaphore.

The performance problem that results when N processes are spinning on one semaphore is that the unlocking process is competing with those processes for access to the semaphore and may be delayed an amount of time proportional to N while attempting to let another processor pass through the lock. To avoid this problem, the architect can bias the memory system to give priority to a WRITE request over a READ/MODIFY/WRITE request, provided that other rules of arbitration guarantee that every requester eventually obtains service. A process cannot loop endlessly at a lock while other processes receive more than their fair share of service.

If the LOCK operation enqueues idle tasks, then the UNLOCK operation can dequeue a task waiting for that semaphore. The dequeued task can be started after the LOCK without having to test the semaphore, provided that the unlocking process dequeues a task instead of unlocking the semaphore, since a DEQUEUE is the same as an UNLOCK immediately followed by a LOCK. If the UNLOCK operation does not check the queue of tasks waiting at the semaphore, there must be some other mechanism to restart enqueued tasks, for otherwise tasks could wait indefinitely. The dequeueing form of UNLOCK almost certainly requires a READ/MODIFY/WRITE operation instead of a simple WRITE operation because it inspects shared queue pointers, which have to be protected during concurrent updating.

7.2.2 Synchronization with Increment and Decrement

The architect can implement selected instructions that perform READ/MODIFY/WRITE in a way that permits these instructions to perform the same function as Test-and-Set and possibly yield greater functionality as well. Obvious candidates for this purpose are Increment Memory and Decrement Memory, which respectively increment or decrement a designated memory location.

To use these instructions for synchronization, the architect has to implement them in such a way that each instruction "owns" its designated memory cell for the duration of its execution. Once the designated memory cell is accessed by the READ, no other instruction can access that cell until after the modified contents are rewritten to the cell.

A plain Increment or Decrement instruction simply updates an operand and need not perform an uninterruptible READ/MODIFY/WRITE. Such an instruction can be used freely for updating unshared data without regard for correctness of usage in multiprocessor systems.

Only if the instruction is guaranteed to be uninterruptible can it be used as well to update shared data. If an uninterruptible version of the instruction is incorrectly implemented or if a programmer inadvertently uses an interruptible version of the instruction under the mistaken impression that the instruction is uninterruptible, then the instruction works correctly almost all of the time. However, in improbably rare instances, an access by another processor will occur between the READ and the WRITE of the Increment/Decrement instruction, and in these rare instances, a program failure occurs. When used in this manner, the interruptible Increment instruction might well be called "Increment Almost Always," because that is its behavior.

Extensive debugging and program testing is not likely to reveal the existence of a timing hazard in the Increment, and a programmer may be fooled into believing that the program is correct. But a truly correct program must have a truly zero probability of failure, and this requires synchs to be performed by uninterruptible READ/MODIFY/WRITE instructions.

For architectures in which Increment and Decrement are uninterruptible primitive operations, some synchronization functions require fewer instructions with Increment/Decrement than with Test-and-Set. Test-and-Set returns a single bit of information. Increment and Decrement can return the full contents of a memory cell, and the additional bits available can reduce the number of instructions required for synchronization.

For example, consider a shared buffer of length M. Up to M processes can be adding to that buffer concurrently, provided that they operate on separate cells. If M processes are actively adding to a buffer, and one more process requests concurrent access, the $M + 1st$ process has to wait. In essence, we need a generalization of a semaphore.

A semaphore as implemented with Test-and-Set permits one process to pass and denies access for subsequent processes until the semaphore is unlocked. This is satisfactory for controlling a buffer of length 1. The generalized semaphore permits up to M processes to pass concurrently and denies access to subsequent processes until one or more processes unlock the semaphore. Each UNLOCK allows one additional process to pass the semaphore.

A very simple means for using Increment and Decrement to implement this form of the semaphore is to start the semaphore with an initial value of M and have each requesting process decrement the semaphore. A processor that sees a nonnegative number after decrementing has access to the buffer. A processor that observes a negative number is blocked from access and should increment the semaphore immediately to reflect the fact that it is not actively working on the buffer. Blocked processes can be enqueued or can retest the semaphore, as discussed earlier for Test-and-Set instructions. A processor that has completed access to a buffer increments the semaphore to indicate that there is room for another process at the buffer.

The naive implementation of this form of synchronization exhibits an interesting failure mode known as *livelock*. Program 7.5(a) is a direct implementation of the steps described previously. Buffer access is protected by a decrement of the semaphore. If the result is negative, the semaphore is incremented, and the test repeats to make a spin-lock implementation. If the result is nonnegative, the processor enters the protected section of the program, and exits by incrementing the semaphore.

Program 7.5 Synchronization with and without livelock.

```
while decrement(semaphore) < 0
   do increment(semaphore);
{* Critical Section *}
increment(semaphore);
```

(a) With livelock; and

```
LOOP: while semaphore < 0 do;
   if decrement(semaphore) < 0 then
      begin
         increment(semaphore);
         go to LOOP;
      end;
   {* Critical Section *}
   increment(semaphore);
```

(b) Without livelock.

Notes:

1. Instructions **increment** and **decrement** are uninterruptible READ/ MODIFY/WRITE instructions.

2. The parameter *semaphore* is a semaphore variable that guards the critical section.

The problem is that the system can enter a state in which no useful work is accomplished, yet there are openings available at the buffer—a state of livelock. The "live" in livelock contrasts this state with deadlock, which occurs when a cycle of precedence exists in which A is waiting for B, B is waiting for C, and so forth, with the last item in the cycle waiting for A. Deadlock is "dead" because the state is permanent. The processes within the deadlock cycle cannot end the deadlock unless one or more of them aborts.

Livelock, however, is not inherently persistent. Processors enter a livelock state because of a quirk in timing, and they can leave the livelock state for an active state if timing of events becomes more fortuitous.

To observe livelock in Program 7.5(a), consider what happens if a huge number of processors issue a decrement to the semaphore immediately after the semaphore reaches a value of 0. The semaphore will then reach a value of $-HUGE$. Will it ever become positive? Not necessarily.

If each of the blocked processors performs an Increment, jump to Retest, and Decrement without interruption, and then turns the semaphore over to the next processor, the semaphore will momentarily change value from $-HUGE$ to $-HUGE + 1$ and then return to $-HUGE$. As the M active processors complete, they will increase the semaphore value to $-HUGE + M$, but this is still negative and will not permit other processors to access the buffer. Hence, useful work is blocked just because of the current order of events. A change in the order of events could result in the semaphore becoming nonnegative, at which point useful work is resumed.

Program 7.5(b) shows a mechanism for eliminating the livelock in Program 7.5(a). The trick is to test the semaphore before decrementing. Program 7.5(b) appears to prevent the value of the semaphore from becoming less than -1, but actually it can become very negative.

In the worst possible case a huge number of processors observe a nonnegative value of the semaphore and all proceed to decrement the semaphore, giving it the value of $-HUGE$. Once the processors have decremented the semaphore, incremented it, and are preparing to retest it, no further decrementing is permitted until the value of the semaphore becomes nonnegative.

When the value becomes nonnegative, at least one process is permitted to pass before the value becomes negative again. Hence, useful work continues to be done, although in the worst possible (and highly improbable) case, the average number of active processors is sharply below the available potential.

7.2.3 Synchronization with Compare-and-Swap

The Compare-and-Swap instruction produces the maximum possible MSYPS rate for a conventional processor because it reduces locked regions of a program to a single instruction—the Compare-and-Swap instruction. A shared datum is locked at the beginning of the instruction, updated during the instruction, and unlocked at the end. This is in contrast to the prior examples, which create a critical section of instructions by manipulating a semaphore before and after the update to a shared datum. The Compare-and-Swap is useful in a limited number of very important circumstances, including the queueing and dequeueing of tasks.

The execution of a Compare-and-Swap is very mysterious at first glance, and only after examining its operation in practice does its power become clear. The Compare-and-Swap operates as defined in Program 7.6. The definition shows that Compare-and-Swap requires two machine registers, one to hold an old value of shared datum, and one to hold a new value.

The objective of updating a shared variable with Compare-and-Swap is to use ordinary instructions to compute the new value of the shared datum without locking it. Then, in one uninterruptible operation, Compare-and-Swap refetches the shared datum, tests to see that its value is unchanged, and

Program 7.6 Compare-and-Swap.

```
Definition: Compare-and-Swap(Address, Reg_old_val, Reg_new_val);
temp := Memory[Address];
if temp = Reg_old_val then
   begin
      Memory[Address] := Reg_new_val;
      Condition_Code := 1;
   end
else
   begin
      Reg_old_val := temp;
      Condition_Code := 0;
   end;
end;
```

Notes:

1. Variable *Address* is a memory address.
2. *Reg_old_val* and *Reg_new_val* are machine registers.
3. The instruction is uninterruptible after it is started.
4. The condition code can be tested after execution is completed to determine if the update took place.

if so, performs an update. If the value has changed, the current value is loaded into the register that holds the old value. At this point, the program can recompute a new value and attempt an update with another execution of Compare-and-Swap.

A simple example of the use of Compare-and-Swap is shown in Program 7.7. In this case, the program adds a locally computed increment to a shared variable. Note that the program reads the current value of the variable into *Reg_old_val*, computes the new value in *Reg_new_val*, and attempts to update the variable with the Compare-and-Swap.

If no conflicts occur during the computation of the new value, the update is successful. If not, the program returns to the loop and computes a new updated value of the sum. Recall from Program 7.6 that Compare-and-Swap loads the current value of the shared variable into *Reg_old_val* in this case, so it is not necessary to read the shared variable again when computing its updated value.

Compare Program 7.7 with our original model of how to update a shared variable with a sequence of LOCK, READ, MODIFY, WRITE, UNLOCK

Program 7.7 Updating a shared sum with Compare-and-Swap.

```
              Local_sum := 0;
              for i := 1 to N do
                 Local_sum := Local_sum + X[i];
              Reg_old_val := Memory[Address];
        LOOP: Reg_new_val := Local_sum + Reg_old_val;
              Compare-and-Swap(Address, Reg_old_val, Reg_new_val);
              if Condition_Code = 0 then go to LOOP;
```

Notes:

1. Variable *Address* is the memory address of a gobal sum.

2. *Reg_old_val* and *Reg_new_val* are machine registers.

3. The program adds the values of *N* entries of vector *X*, then adds these to the global sum.

operations. When a LOCK/UNLOCK pair are used, no more than one processor at a time can execute the instructions that perform READ, MODIFY, WRITE.

In Program 7.7 many processors can execute the instructions of this program concurrently, arbitrarily interlacing their access and execution patterns. However, the Compare-and-Swap is uninterruptible. Because many processors can read and write the shared sum, it is possible for the sum to change value between the time a processor reads it at the beginning of Program 7.7 and the time that processor updates it at the Compare-and-Swap. There is no LOCK to prevent such concurrent access.

The key to ensuring correct program behavior is the test made by the Compare-and-Swap. The new value of the shared variable is a function of the old value, and the test ensures that the old value has not changed. If the old value is unchanged, then the new value is correct, and it is stored in the shared variable.

The most valuable application of Compare-and-Swap is for enqueueing and dequeueing without locking. Because queue pointers are shared variables, typical ENQUEUE/DEQUEUE programs lock the queue pointers before changing their values. This creates a multiprocessor bottleneck at the queue routines by limiting the maximum MSYPS rate of a computer system.

Compare-and-Swap provides a means for concurrent updating of queue pointers by limiting the locked segment of code to a single Compare-and-Swap instruction, similar to the way that Program 7.7 limits the locked segment for updating a sum to a single Compare-and-Swap instruction.

　　The computer literature on this particular application of Compare-and-Swap is rather sparse considering the importance of the idea. Sites [1980] describes the ENQUEUE process, but is not complete because the DEQUEUE process is left as an exercise. Hwang and Briggs [1984] give a rather brief discussion that serves only as an introduction to Compare-and-Swap. Treiber [1986] highlights Compare-and-Swap in more detail in a brief research report. The most complete source of information at this writing is the IBM System/370 Principles of Operations [1983], which gives several examples of correct applications and also shows pitfalls of incorrect use of Compare-and-Swap.

　　In spite of the apparent simplicity of Program 7.7, Compare-and-Swap is extremely tricky to use correctly. The problem lies in the potentially large number of ways that concurrent execution can occur. After all, the idea of Compare-and-Swap is to foster concurrency. However, when many processors execute the same code concurrently, a variety of events can occur in sequences unforeseen by the programmer, and synchronization can fail. Compare-and-Swap is both one of the most valuable tools for multiprocessor software and one of the most difficult tools to use for that environment.

　　To show both the power and the danger in the use of Compare-and-Swap, consider the problem of enqueueing data. Figure 7.4 illustrates the data structure for the queue and shows Compare-and-Swap permits queueing to be done with high concurrency. Figure 7.4(a) shows a queue represented as a one-way linked list whose *Head* pointer designates the first item in the queue, the one to be removed next. The *Tail* pointer designates the last item in the queue, the point at which new items are added.

　　Our objective for concurrent enqueueing is to do the equivalent of the following three-line code segment that places the entry at memory address *Item* at the end of the queue:

```
Memory[Item].Link := nil;
Memory[Tail].Link := Item;
Tail := Item;
```

The notation ".*Link*" denotes a link field of an item in memory. The last two statements in this example have to be executed without interruption because *Tail* is a shared variable that is read, modified, and rewritten.

　　When the code is executed correctly, the result of inserting one item is as shown in Fig. 7.4(b). However, if Processor 1 and then Processor 2 read the current value of *Tail* at the second statement, then Processor 1 and 2 in that order modify the value of *Tail* at the third statement, and then one of the items enqueued will be lost. The pointer to this item will be overwritten. If the last statement is executed first by Processor 2 and then by Processor 1, *Tail* will be left pointing at an item not on the queue. All subsequent items enqueued will be unreachable from the *Head* pointer. This situation is shown in Fig. 7.4(c).

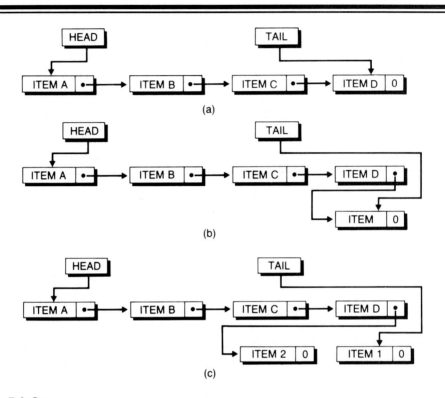

Fig. 7.4 Queues:
(a) A linked-list representation of a queue;
(b) A queue after the insertion of a new item; and
(c) A queue after executing two concurrent insertions without locking. Processor 1 inserts Item 1, and Processor 2 inserts Item 2, with accesses interlaced as described in the text.

Conventional programming techniques lock this set of statements before they are executed and unlock them when they are completed. A solution based on Compare-and-Swap is shown in Program 7.8. This program avoids the pitfall of an interrupted READ/MODIFY/WRITE. Exactly one processor of a group of concurrently executing processors uses the Compare-and-Swap successfully to read a value of *Tail* and write a pointer to *Item*. This leaves *Tail* pointing to the new *Item*. The former value of *Tail*, now in the register *Reg_Tail*, points to the former end of the queue. The queue is extended by linking that entry to *Item*.

Program 7.8 Enqueueing an item with Compare-and-Swap.

```
Memory[Item].Link := nil;
    {* Initialize Item for insertion at end of queue *}
Reg_Tail := Tail; {* Read Tail to a register *}
LOOP:
    {* Perform checks that depend on Tail here. Make no permanent changes to
    items reachable through the Tail pointer *}
    Compare-and-Swap (Tail, Reg_Tail, Item);
    if Condition_Code = 0 then go to LOOP;
        {* Loop back on failure of Compare-and-Swap *}
    {* Link in the item through Head if the queue were empty or through its
    predecessor if the queue were nonempty. *}
    if Reg_Tail = 0 then
        Head := Item
    else
        Memory[Reg_Tail].Link := Item;
```

Notes:

1. The DEQUEUE process sets *Tail* to 0 only after *Head* is 0. Hence, if ENQUEUE discovers a zero value of *Tail*, it is assured that *Head* is 0.

2. This program is correct for concurrent ENQUEUEs.

3. The program as written here may fail if DEQUEUEs and ENQUEUEs can execute concurrently.

4. Dequeueing may require additional tests, depending on the handling of empty lists.

If a Compare-and-Swap fails, the processor repeats with the new value of *Tail* that was loaded into *Reg—Tail* by the Compare-and-Swap. The net effect of Compare-and-Swap is to guarantee that the values stored in *Tail* and in *Memory*[*Tail*].*Link* are consistent.

By various arguments we can show that Program 7.8 is correct for concurrent ENQUEUE operations. However, the program as written does not treat empty lists in full detail, nor is it correct if ENQUEUE operations occur concurrently with DEQUEUE operations. These additional considerations greatly complicate matters. Compare-and-Swap is extremely difficult to use correctly as complexity grows, and its use is prone to very subtle errors that may never be detected.

Consider, for example, Program 7.8 when execution reaches the Compare-and-Swap. This statement relies on the fact that if *Reg—Tail* = *Tail*, then no other concurrent ENQUEUEs have updated *Tail* since it was last read from memory. If we allow concurrent DEQUEUEs as well as concurrent ENQUEUEs, this may not be the case. A DEQUEUE could have removed the item at *Reg_Tail* from the queue, and subsequently, an ENQUEUE could have reached a Compare-and-Swap to restore this item to the queue. This would leave *Tail* at its former value, a value equal to the contents of *Reg_Tail*, and we have reached a condition at which two different processors will attempt to update *Memory[Tail].Link* with different addresses.

This failure mode requires Program 7.8 to be interrupted just prior to Compare-and-Swap, and then requires other processors to execute DEQUEUE and ENQUEUE, and the ENQUEUE to put back the item just dequeued. Although this is highly unlikely to occur, it is possible, and it will be undetected by the Compare-and-Swap.

The failure arises simply because the Compare-and-Swap is not powerful enough to sense a history of changes. The fact that *Tail* equals *Reg_Tail* is treated as if *Tail* has not changed since it was last read. However, this inference is incorrect, and any sequence of events that leaves *Tail* in its original state can potentially lead to the failure of Program 7.8. Since concurrent ENQUEUEs by themselves cannot restore the value of *Tail*, Program 7.8 is safe for concurrent ENQUEUEs.

A practical solution to improving the safety of Compare-and-Swap is outlined in the IBM System/370 Principles of Operations [1983]. The idea is to extend the Compare-and-Swap to deal with two variables rather than one. The two variables must be contiguous so that they can be fetched and rewritten with one READ and WRITE.

Program 7.9 illustrates how this extension improves the code reliability. In this program, *Tail* is concatenated with a variable *Count*. The current value of the *Tail/Count* pair is copied to local registers. Just prior to the Double Compare-and-Swap, the local copy of *Count* is incremented and moved to the register *New_Count*. The Double Compare-and-Swap verifies that the *Tail/Count* pair has not changed, and it updates this pair of values with the pair *Item/New_Count*.

Since each successful execution of Compare-and-Swap updates both *Tail* and *Count*, if *Tail* is changed and restored by concurrent queue operations, then the new value of *Count* would show that other queue operations have taken place or are in progress concurrently. This forces an unsuccessful Compare-and-Swap, which in turn causes a loop to occur and prevents an erroneous update. An update takes place only if both *Tail* and *Count* have not changed.

The sustained value of *Count* is intended to signify that no other concurrent operations are in the process of manipulating *Tail*. In the System/370 architecture, *Count* returns to its former value after no sooner than 4 billion operations. Consequently, Program 7.9 has a highly improbable failure mode

Program 7.9 Enqueueing an item with double Compare-and-Swap.

```
    Memory[Item].Link := nil;
      {* Initialize Item for insertion at end of queue *}
    Reg_Tail&Reg_Count := Tail&Count;
      {* Read double-variable Tail and Count to two registers *}
LOOP: New_Count := Reg_Count + 1;
      {* Prepare to update Count *}
    Double Compare-and-Swap (Tail&Count, Reg_Tail&Reg_Count,
    Item&New_Count);
    if Condition_Code = 0 then go to LOOP;
    {* Link in the item through Head if the queue were empty or through its
    predecessor if the queue were nonempty. *}
    if Reg_Tail = 0 then
      Head := Item
    else
      begin {* Attempt to set the link in memory. Make sure the link is still 0. *}
        Reg_Tail := 0;
        Compare-and-Swap (Memory[Reg_Tail].Link, Reg_Tail, Item);
        if Condition_Code = 0 then
          {* Concurrent ENQUEUE/DEQUEUE is treated here. *}
      end;
```

Notes:

1. The notation *Tail&Count* designates two variables stored contiguously or two contiguous registers that are accessed by a single double-length operation.

2. Double Compare-and-Swap reads a double-length operand from *Memory[Tail]*, compares this to the double-length operand *Reg_Tail* and *Reg_Count*, and updates *Tail* with the double-length operand *Item* and *New_Count* if the equality comparison is satisfied. *Reg_Tail* and *Reg_Count* are updated if the equality comparison fails.

3. To assure correct operation when EQUEUEs and DEQUEUEs occur concurrently, the DEQUEUE process must detect that when it is attempting to remove the last item in the queue (the link field in that item is 0) and *Tail* is nonzero, to indicate that the ENQUEUE process has entered a new item but has not yet changed the link. The DEQUEUE should use Compare-and-Swap to store a special nonzero flag in the link field to indicate to the ENQUEUE process that special actions are required.

4. The program as written here may fail if *Count* is incremented a sufficient number of times to overflow back to its original value, and *Tail* is left in its original state.

in which a failure occurs if a process is suspended at a Double Compare-and-Swap while other processors increment *Count* 4 billion times and leave *Tail* in its original state.

Program 7.9 also gives a hint on the proper treatment of concurrent ENQUEUEs and DEQUEUEs. After a successful update of *Tail*, the ENQUEUE process must update the link field of the predecessor of the new item. In Program 7.8, this is done by a simple assignment statement. In Program 7.9, where we permit concurrent DEQUEUEs, the update is done by using a Compare-and-Swap to discover if the prior link were 0, which is the correct condition for the last item in the queue prior to an insert. If the DEQUEUE process removes the item before the link has been set, then the ENQUEUE process must be notified. For purposes this example, we assume that the DEQUEUE process detects this condition, and stores a special nonzero flag in the link field to indicate special handling is required. Note that ENQUEUE uses a Compare-and-Swap rather than a simple assignment to update the link in Program 7.9 because a DEQUEUE process may be conditionally storing a special flag concurrently. The precise details of the correct ENQUEUE and DEQUEUE process provide an interesting challenge to the reader, and is the subject one of the exercises in this chapter.

To summarize the characteristics of Compare-and-Swap synchronization, it is extremely efficient, and highly desirable to use. However, it is very dangerous and subject to subtle failure modes. It has to be used carefully and by experienced programmers.

7.2.4 Synchronization with Fetch-and-Add

The three synchronization methods discussed thus far have in common the property that they are serial methods. No more than one processor at a time can execute the READ/MODIFY/WRITE operation embedded in them.

The Fetch-and-Add operation is different—it is truly parallel. Conceivably, all N processors in a multiprocessor can execute a Fetch-and-Add instruction simultaneously, provided that all processors update the same variable. Fetch-and-Add operations executed on different variables may have to be done sequentially if those variables reside in the same memory or share access circuitry of some other form.

The instruction Fetch-and-Add(*Sum, Increment*) provides for adding an increment to a shared sum, and the addition is done in parallel as explained earlier. No locking and unlocking is required, nor is a retry test and loop required as with Compare-and-Swap.

In terms of performance, the Compare-and-Swap is as efficient or more efficient than the Fetch-and-Add if on the average only one processor at a time requests an update of *Sum*. This is because Compare-and-Swap is not burdened by delays by network access introduced by the hardware implementation of Fetch-and-Add. However, when the update becomes a bottleneck to the extent that 10 or 100 requests for access are active concurrently, Fetch-and-Add is far faster than Compare-and-Swap because it can honor all the requests simultaneously.

For systems with relatively few processors, Compare-and-Swap is the better approach. As the processors increase, Fetch-and-Add provides potential performance improvement not available with Compare-and-Swap. Fetch-and-Add becomes more attractive as the number of processors increases, but whether or not Fetch-and-Add is cost-effective is still a matter of research interest. Its implementation cost is high, and its potential is limited to simultaneous access of the same shared variable by all contending processors. It provides no help for contention produced by concurrent accesses to different variables in the same memory.

For large values of N, for example 1000 to 10,000, Fetch-and-Add or an equivalent mechanism for parallel synchronization is a practical necessity. Without such a mechanism the MSYPS limit will severely impair performance in a 1000-processor system. In 10,000-processor systems, other system bottlenecks may be so severe that Fetch-and-Add by itself may not be sufficient to produce acceptable performance.

To show Fetch-and-Add at its best, let us reconsider the problem of enqueueing and dequeueing items on a shared queue. The Compare-and-Swap approach is pointer oriented, that is, the links are treated as addresses, and the algorithm builds linked lists.

Fetch-and-Add, however, is best used for counters rather than pointers, where counters are variables that are manipulated by addition and subtraction. The result of a sequence of counting operations is not sensitive to the order in which increments and decrements are applied, which is desirable for Fetch-and-Add because concurrent executions receive a set of results that represent some arbitrary ordering of the individual summations. We want to create algorithms for which all of the arbitrary orderings are consistent with correct execution of the algorithm. Consequently, the most appropriate implementation of ENQUEUE with Fetch-and-Add is to use a counter-based implementation.

The basic idea is to use a counter, *Tail*, that is incremented by ENQUEUE. The value of *Tail* is the offset in the queue of the next insertion point. A simple and incomplete implementation of ENQUEUE with Fetch-and-Add is

```
Procedure Enqueue(Item, Queue);
   begin Place := Fetch-and-Add(Tail,1);
      Queue[Place] := Item;
   end; {* Enqueue *}
```

The Fetch-and-Add increases *Tail* and returns the value of *Tail* before the increment. This value is used as the offset in the queue for inserting an item. If the Fetch-and-Add is executed simultaneously by several processors, *Tail* receives the sum of the increments, and each processor receives a different value for *Place*, so each processor has a unique position for queue insertion.

This is the basic idea of enqueueing with Fetch-and-Add, but the full implementation becomes very complex because of a variety of conditions that have to be satisfied. Among the conditions are:

1. The queue should be circular, so *Tail* should be set to a base value of 0 when it exceeds the length of the *Queue* vector.

2. The total number of active entries in the queue cannot exceed the length of the queue vector.

3. The DEQUEUE operation should permit parallel removal entries from the queue.

4. The DEQUEUE operation should not permit a dequeue to succeed on an empty queue.

5. Both ENQUEUE and DEQUEUE should be safe from livelock.

Two implementations of ENQUEUE/DEQUEUE with Fetch-and-Add appear in Gottlieb *et al.* [1983] and Stone [1984]. Both solutions are too complex to reproduce in this text. However, the implementations illustrate general principles worth discussing here.

If we use variables *Tail* and *Head*, respectively, to control the insertion and deletion points in a queue, then the number of items in a queue is the difference between *Tail* and *Head*. However, because both *Tail* and *Head* are reset to 0 when they exceed the length of the queue, the difference in their values is the number of active elements modulo the length of the queue, so finding the number of active elements from the values of *Head* and *Tail* is rather tricky. It is much easier instead to maintain a separate variable *Count* that gives the current number of active elements. ENQUEUE and DEQUEUE operate on this variable with Fetch-and-Add with increments of $+1$ and -1, respectively. The value returned by Fetch-and-Add can be used to control actions on queue overflow and underflow.

To prevent livelock, ENQUEUE should first test *Count* before incrementing it, and DEQUEUE should test *Count* before decrementing it. The queue full and queue empty conditions that cause processors to loop back to retry their operations should loop back to the test of *Count* in a manner similar to the way that livelock is treated with the Increment and Decrement instructions. In this way processors remain at the outermost test and are prevented from further incrementing or decrementing until *Count* reaches a safe value.

To handle the queue circularity, when a Fetch-and-Add increments *Head* beyond the end of the queue, the set of processors making concurrent access to *Head* will discover its value to be less, equal to, or greater than the queue length. The processors that receive legal values for *Head* simply continue. The processors that discover values beyond the end of the queue abort their activity by decrementing *Head* and return to a place earlier in the program to request a spot in the queue again. Eventually *Head* will return to the least illegal value.

The processor that decrements *Head* to this value decrements *Head* again by the length of the queue and thereby resets *Head* to start at the beginning of the *Queue* vector. Livelock prevention tests have to protect *Head* from livelock during the incrementing and decrementing that occur in this process.

The full algorithm for ENQUEUE/DEQUEUE

- Manipulates *Count, Head,* and *Tail*;
- Handles queue circularity, queue empty, queue full; and
- Protects from processing livelock.

Working out the details of the algorithm is very instructive and shows the complexity of synchronization with Fetch-and-Add.

We stated that Compare-and-Swap is difficult to use correctly, but Fetch-and-Add is far more difficult to use. Compare-and-Swap is subject to subtle failures from concurrency before and after it is executed. Because it forces serial behavior when it is executed, some simplification is achieved when verifying the correctness of Compare-and-Swap algorithms. But Fetch-and-Add supports all of the concurrency of Compare-and-Swap and more.

The fact that many processors can perform Fetch-and-Add concurrently on the same datum greatly increases the number of possible outcomes to consider and makes verification extremely difficult. Obviously, Fetch-and-Add has to be used very carefully by experienced programmers. Fetch-and-Add synchronization will probably be used mostly through library calls rather than individually programmed statements because most programmers are not likely to be able to create correct, efficient programs based on Fetch-and-Add.

Although Fetch-and-Add points the way to break the MSYPS bottleneck, the implementation of Fetch-and-Add in a multilevel interconnection is expensive and its use in programs is difficult and error-prone. Is there are effective alternative? Indeed, there are several less powerful, but far less expensive techniques to implement the most useful feature of Fetch-and-Add—the ability to parallelize synchs. These are treated in the next section.

7.2.5 Other Architectural Support for Parallel Synchronization

This section discusses low-cost implementations of a collection of alternatives to Fetch-and-Add, none of which has the full power and generality of Fetch-and-Add. The reason for considering alternatives is that Fetch-and-Add does not make efficient use of the hardware required for its realization. The total number of nodes in a switching network that can accept N concurrent requests is at least $O(N)$ if the network is a simple tree, and is $O(N \log N)$ if the network is a full shuffle-exchange network as proposed by Gottlieb *et al.* [1983]. However, in actual practice the majority of the combining is performed at the nodes at the root of the tree centered on a hot spot, and very little combining is performed at the leaves. Consequently, the cost of the network in components grows at least linearly in the number of processors, and the delay experienced grows as the depth of the network times a large constant to reflect the delay per combining node in the network. Yet, on the average, only very few nodes in the network actually do useful work in practical cases.

When a combining network is working at peak capacity, all of its leaves receive combinable requests simultaneously, and these all combine stage-by-stage to produce a single request at the hot-spot root. If this behavior were typical of every machine cycle, then a combining network would produce a performance commensurate with its cost. What happens in actual practice is that the combinable requests are received over a period of time. If two combinable requests enter a node on different inputs in the same cycle, they are combined into a single request. If they enter on different cycles, they are forwarded sequentially toward the root of the tree on the same path. Thus, there is a window of time during which two requests can combine at a node, and if they miss that window they will not combine there. Each node can include some buffering to enlarge the window of combination to greater than a single cycle, but the effect of buffering is to add delay and cost in each node.

In the exercises for this chapter is one that reveals that each request is most likely to combine with a request at the root of the tree because half of the possible requests join with it there. Half as many requests join with a request at the second level in the tree, and half as many in the next level, and so on. When requests arrive at a combining network over a period of time, with high probability they pass through the first few levels of the tree without combining, and eventually combine near or at the root if the arrival rate is high enough to produce one or more requests per cycle at the network inputs. If k out of N requests arrive on the average per cycle, the requests will tend to saturate the $\log k$ levels of the combining network at the root, and relatively few requests will be combined at other levels.

Consequently, the peak rate of combining supportable by a combining network is far greater than the actual rate that the network has to support. An effective compromise for the computer architect is to put full combining only in a few levels of a combining network, and to make the remainder of the nodes the same as transmission nodes in a conventional multilevel interconnection network.

Given that a combining network may be more powerful than what is actually required, what less powerful functions can be implemented to produce the capability that we actually need? A good candidate is to implement the synchronization functions on a global bus that visits all processors. The reason that this is attractive is that synchronization by itself does not demand high bandwidth. A synchronization message can be as short as one bit. The bit of a synchronization changes rather slowly in time, possibly once every 10,000 to 100,000 instructions. We can afford to deliver the bit a few cycles late because of low bandwidth on the delivery system, provided that the lateness is a constant delay or grows very slowly with the number of processors in the system.

We propose a sequence of bus-based synchronization techniques, each more powerful than its predecessor. They are:

1. Barrier synchronization.
2. Multiple barriers.
3. Find the maximum.
4. Fetch-and-increment.

The first of these, barrier synchronization, has been implemented successfully on the PAX computers by Hoshino [1989]. Each processor sets a single bit to indicate when it has arrived at a barrier. The collection of bits is brought to an AND gate and an OR gate, each of which has one input per processor. The outputs of both gates are bused to all processors. Thus every processor can determine when all processors have reached the barrier, when none have reached it, or when some but not all have reached it. The number of synchs per cycle in this machine grows almost linearly with N. (The growth would be linear if a change in a bit could be propagated in a single cycle regardless of N. In practice, the propagation time grows slowly as N grows, and is $O(\log N)$ with a very small constant coefficient.) The delay in performance caused by a barrier is measured by the number of cycles after the last processor arrives at the barrier before the collection of processors can begin new tasks. This is a few machine cycles at most, even in a multiprocessor with 1000 processors.

A practical implementation of a fast barrier was patented by Thompson [1985] and is shown in Fig. 7.5. Thompson proposed to use an adder with fast-carry lookahead to implement a barrier. In this case, the adder is capable of adding two 4-bit numbers and an incoming carry to produce a sum output and a carry output. The sum output is ignored for the barrier function, and the carry output is fed back to the four inputs of one 4-bit operand. This configuration can synchronize five different processors. Each processor is assigned one of the five available inputs, either one of the four inputs for the 4-bit operand or the input for the carry in.

We assume that we start in a state in which no processors are at the barrier. All processors place a 0 on their respective inputs, and the carry out produced by the device is 0. The carry out remains at 0 until all processors reach the barrier. At this point it becomes 1, and stays at 1 until all processors signify that they have observed the synchronization by removing their 1 bits. When all processors have left the barrier, the carry out drops to 0. If each processor uses

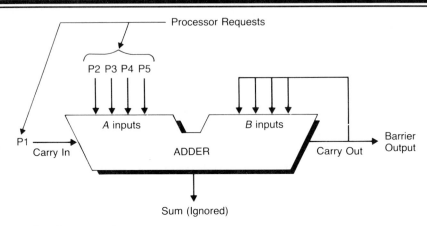

Fig. 7.5 The Thompson barrier.

a rule that it places a 1 on the barrier only if the present barrier value is 0, then the barrier can be safely reused in a program. Thus, Thompson's barrier supports both the reuse of the barrier and the fast implementation.

In a 1000-processor multiprocessor, a single barrier is inadequate for synchronization. But since many processors use an active barrier, in actual circumstances perhaps only 32 or 64 distinct barriers are sufficient to support 1000 processors. The technology to build 32 or 64 Thompson barriers with 1000 inputs each is much less demanding than the technology required to put 1000 processors and memories together, so that we can conceive of a multiprocessor supported by a collection of addressable barriers. However, the interconnections to these barriers present an interesting challenge to the architect.

The scheme illustrated in Fig. 7.6 indicates how one might take advantage of the low bandwidth on the barriers to reduce the interconnection complexity. It is based on work by Heidelberger, Rathi, and Stone [1988]. The device shown in Fig. 7.6 contains all of the addressable barriers for some subset of processors, and it produces summary data on a few output lines that are forwarded to a similar chip whose function is to synchronize a different subset of processors. Each processor is attached to one chip through one input line and to the output bus, and possibly to one dedicated output line per processor. A processor signals its intentions to a chip sequentially by giving the address of a barrier and the value of the bit to set at the barrier. The chip also recognizes special codes for initialization of a barrier, and for masking in or out the processors that are not participating at a barrier. Since one barrier chip may

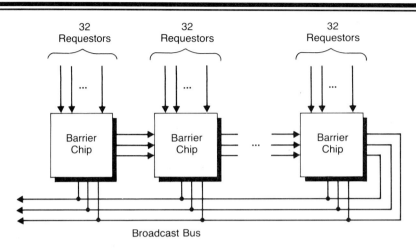

Fig. 7.6 A VLSI implementation of a set of barriers.

be limited by input/output pins to handling requests from some fixed number of processors, the barrier chip outputs have to be combined together to produce a single global bus output that is observed by all processors and by all chips. In general, each chip output and the global bus output is an indication of the states of the various barriers. The output bus may have many lines, one for each barrier, if technology provides this capability at reasonable cost. If this is not feasible, the output bus can signal when any barrier changes state by signaling the address of the barrier and its new state. Since state changes of barriers are quite rare, a bus with a single conductor or a few conductors may have sufficient bandwidth to satisfy the requirements for a large multiprocessor, and a few conductors should provide ample bandwidth to meet peak requirements.

Given that metal interconnections are limited in bandwidth, and are bulky and costly, an all optical barrier may one day be practical and be preferred to a device based on the Thompson barrier. An optical barrier can be constructed by using two wavelengths, λ_{busy} and λ_{done}, to signify, respectively, that a processor is busy before reaching a barrier or has reached the barrier [Green and Stone 1989]. We presume that every processor can produce illumination on one wavelength or the other, and that the illumination can be amplified and bused to all other processors. Each processor operates two receivers, one sensitive to λ_{busy} and the other sensitive to λ_{done}. The illumination from all processors is combined at or before it reaches a receiver, so that each receiver sees a composite signal. If a receiver detects energy at its tuned wavelength, it concludes that some processor is in the state associated with that wavelength, either *busy* or *done*. The barrier is unused when no processor is busy and no processor is done. It is an active barrier when at least one processor is busy. Processors can move past the barrier when no processor is busy. Before a barrier can be reused, each processor must verify that no processor is signaling "done." Only when all processors have left the barrier, can any processor safely signal reuse the barrier for a new cycle by signaling "busy." This implementation is an optical analog of the AND and OR gates used by Hoshino in PAX.

The optical system can support multiple barriers on a common interconnection system by using pairs of wavelengths for each distinct barrier. Because each individual barrier requires so little of the available bandwidth, there is substantial available bandwidth to multiplex many barriers together on one optical interconnection system.

Since optical technology for the barrier application is still in its infancy, we cannot claim that the implementation described here is feasible today or will be the preferred embodiment when and if optical technology can support barriers. Nevertheless, the discussion indicates how new technology may alter the approaches that we take to solve specific problems.

The next function of interest is the ability to find the maximum value of a set of values held in distinct processors. A classic method to find the maximum is for each processor to gain exclusive access to a single global shared variable, and to update the variable if the local value is greater than the global value. Each processor then proceeds to a barrier where it waits until all updates have been done. Then the global value is known to be the maximum of all values.

This process is rather inefficient to perform in a highly parallel multiprocessor because of the serial bottleneck it creates at the global variable. A FETCH-and-MAX operation is an effective, but costly solution. Recursive doubling as described in Chapter 4 is also effective, but the delay in the process requires the latest participating processor to make $O(\log N)$ remote comparisons before reaching the barrier. This determines how soon the processors can be released from the barrier as a function of the time when the latest processor initiates its computation of the maximum. We may be able to reduce this number, or reduce the cost of a comparison.

An efficient solution lies in the use of a broadcast bus of low bandwidth that visits all processors. Each processor attempts to gain access to the broadcast bus, compare its local value to a global value, update the global value if necessary, and broadcast the new value of the global variable. If, while a processor's request for the bus is pending, the processor observes a higher global value, it removes its request and moves to the barrier. If all processors are vying for the bus when the latest participating processor requests a bus transaction, approximately $O(\log N)$ bus transactions on the average will take place before all processors reach the barrier. If only k processors are vying for the bus at this point, then only $O(\log k)$ bus transactions are necessary. This is a small reduction if all processors tend to initiate the computation of the maximum in a short interval of time. But the reduction is quite useful and worthwhile when a few stragglers tend to arrive very late, in which case, k may be only 1 or 2 in such situations.

What is interesting about this form of solution is the fact that the solution is compatible with the barrier chip solution of Fig. 7.6. The device in that figure needs to be only slightly more versatile to support both barriers and the maximum operation, but the interconnections shown are sufficient to implement both functions.

The last function of interest is Fetch-and-Increment. This is the same as Fetch-and-Add except that the value added has to be $+1$. We can also support a Fetch-and-Decrement with a minor embellishment of the basic idea. Thus, a processor can add or subtract 1 from a global counter, and perform this in parallel with all other processors. This function is sufficient for performing enqueueing and dequeueing operations without enforcing a strict serialization.

The basic implementation of this idea was discovered independently by Heidelberger, Rathi, and Stone [1989] and Sohi, Goodman, and J. E. Smith [1989]. It uses a bus much like the bus described above for computing the global maximum. All processors that wish to perform Fetch-and-Increment request access to a global bus. When any one processor is granted access, all other processors observe the address that is to be incremented. Then all requestors for that address respond together with the original requestor in a portion of the same bus cycle reserved for responses. For N responders, the bus should have N distinct data conductors. Each responder places a 1 on a conductor dedicated to that responder. If a processor is not an active responder because it does not have a Fetch-and-Increment pending, then its corresponding conductor carries the logic value 0. Since all processors see all data wires, each processor can tell the total increment applied to the global variable and each can tell its priority with respect to all other processors. For example, if Processor 5 sees that Processor 2 and 3 have responded, then Processor 5's request is third in line. If the request is for a queue entry, then Processor 5 can immediately access the third entry of a queue.

The scheme has to provide a means to update the global variable with the sum of the increments of the requestors. A suitable protocol is to assign the update task to the processor with highest or lowest priority. Also, all requestors should see the current value of the global variable in order to compute their local variant of the global value. The current value can be transmitted on the same bus on a different part of the same cycle. This scheme is also compatible with the implementation described in Fig. 7.6, provided that the bus has a number of wires equal to the number of processors. By multiplexing and coding responses, it is possible to reduce the number of physical conductors. In order to achieve the best performance at reasonable cost, the number of distinct conductors should be roughly equal to the expected number of active requestors on any cycle.

This brings us to the end of the discussion of synchronization techniques. The next section revisits cache coherence and describes why cache coherence and synchronization are alternative solutions to the same problem.

7.2.6 Cache Coherence Versus Synchronization

The cache-coherence protocols described in Chapter 6 assure that multi-processor programs can synchronize correctly. Consider, for example, the software implementation of a barrier. A simple scheme is to use a counter initialized to N, and to have each of N processors decrement the counter as they reach the barrier. If the decrement operation is an uninterruptible READ/ MODIFY/WRITE operation, then each processor need do nothing more than decrement the barrier and test it continually until the barrier reaches zero. No lock, Fetch-and-Add, or other specialized technique is required to implement the barrier. The cache-coherence protocol assures that each processor will eventually see the zero value of the barrier variable, and the barrier variable will become zero if and only if all N processors have reached the barrier.

If this is the case, then why is there a special requirement for synchronization hardware such as the combining network or the Thompson barrier? The issue is the implementation of the cache-coherence protocol. Bus-based protocols are limited to one bus transaction per cycle. If at most one synchronization can be done per bus transaction, then an MSYPS bottleneck exists. For multiprocessors with hundreds or thousands of processors, a cache-coherence protocol is not likely to be bus based, and its implementation is an interesting question in itself.

The point of this section is to illustrate that the synchronization techniques explored thus far may provide a substantial part of the cache-coherence function, and conversely, a cache-coherence protocol can provide a reasonable means for implementing synchronization primitives. For large numbers of processors, a dedicated synchronization subsystem may be preferred, and for a small number of processors, a bus-based cache coherence protocol may be preferred. These comments are illustrative of possible choices, and actual decisions must account for the characteristics of the applications.

We proceed by illustrating how a cache-coherence protocol can assure the correctness and efficiency of a barrier synchronization. For the barrier, we will decrement a counter as described above. The cache-coherence protocol is bus-based, and assumes that all processors observe all bus transactions. In Chapter 6, we indicated that we have some choice of protocol. To conserve the use of the bus, recall that it is not necessary to broadcast the update of a cached variable if that variable is held exclusively. To obtain a variable exclusively, it is sufficient to broadcast a cache-invalidate command to all other processors when a processor with permission to update the variable actually performs the update. Let's call this protocol the Write-Invalidate Protocol.

An alternative protocol is to broadcast the updated value of the variable at the time of its update. Any other processor that holds that variable in cache, can overwrite the local value with the updated value. Of course, when this occurs, the variable is not held exclusively by any processor, and subsequent updates have to be broadcast. We call this protocol the Write-Update protocol.

Yet another possibility is for each processor to load into its cache the value of a broadcast update, regardless of whether or not it currently has a copy of that variable. This is contrary to what seems to be reasonable, but it is worthwhile to include it for comparison purposes. We call this protocol the Write-Load protocol.

In terms of efficiency, our expectations are that the three protocols fall in the order below from most efficient to least efficient:

1. Write Invalidate,
2. Write Update,
3. Write Load.

The reasoning behind this ordering is that the Write Invalidate may eliminate future bus transactions when a local update occurs, but both Write Update and Write Load must broadcast that a change has occurred whenever it occurs. Moreover, the Write Load can lower performance by displacing some item from a remote cache that would be more useful in the near future than the item just broadcast to the remote cache.

The ordering of efficiency is correct for many kinds of accesses, but it is undoubtedly in the wrong order for a barrier synchronization. Observe what happens when N processors attempt to synchronize at a barrier under the Write Invalidate protocol. As each processor obtains the barrier variable for updating, the processor places the barrier variable in its local cache. Shortly thereafter another processor reaches the barrier, requests the current value of the barrier variable, and invalidates the value in all other caches. Hence, the variable is invalidated in the cache where it had formerly just been updated, and the processor that just held that variable is forced to refetch it.

When the Nth processor attempts to update the barrier variable, it has to contend for the bus with $N - 2$ other processors that are trying to refetch the variable. In the worst possible case, the number of bus transactions can grow quadratically in N, but the growth reduces to only linear in N if all active requests for a variable are satisfied by one broadcast. Because each update of a variable invalidates all caches, at least N bus transactions have to take place to satisfy the barrier. The fact that a processor can determine when it has the exclusive copy of a variable is not important in this instance because each processor only updates a barrier variable once. The Write-Invalidate protocol is most useful when a processor updates a variable several times during one period of cache residence. Hence, the effectiveness of the Write-Invalidate protocol is wasted on barrier synchronizations. In fact the Write-Invalidate causes a problem because it forces all processors to rerequest the shared variable at the same time, and this tends to saturate the bus.

The second protocol, Write Update, is better in the sense that it does not remove an active variable from remote caches. In fact, it automatically delivers a new value for the remote processors to examine. When the barrier is finally satisfied, the update operation delivers the final value to active processors without requiring them to request the value individually. Hence, Write Update is distinctly better than Write Invalidate for implementing barrier synchronization.

The last protocol is actually slightly better than Write Update because it sends the current value of the barrier variable to remote caches prior to actual need. As each processor first comes to a barrier, it normally experiences a cache miss. If the first access is a read access, the Write Load protocol turns that access into a cache hit, and saves the cost of the miss and the cycle required on the bus. If the first access of a process is a decrement, then Write Load will be essentially the same as Write Update because under both protocols, the processor attempting to update the barrier variable must request a bus cycle to obtain write permission before updating the variable.

Because synchronizations, in general, require close cooperation among several processors, the Write Load and Write Update protocols will tend to yield better performance than Write Invalidate when used on synchronization variables. Eggers and Katz [1989] confirmed the findings in this discussion in a study that evaluated several different protocols by means of trace-driven simulations. They found that a protocol closely related to Write Load gave better hit ratios than Write Update, and attributed this to its use for synchronization purposes.

This short example illustrates that synchronization functions require close cooperation among many processors, and this can be sustained only with the right kind of information transferred at the right time. For multiprocessors with very few processors, it is possible to use a bus-based cache-coherence protocol for synchronization, but that protocol might not be the same one used for other shared variables. For example, one may choose to use Write Load for barrier variables and Write Invalidate for other kinds of variables. Because shared variables can be used in different ways, it is essential to match the cache-coherence protocol to the particular use of a shared variable.

For large-scale multiprocessing with 100 or 1000 processors, cache coherence may not be feasible to implement if it has to satisfy the needs of both synchronization and normal sharing. Consider the cache-coherence traffic in a 1000-processor system in which the interconnection network between processors has infinite bandwidth and no delay. If a broadcast invalidate or update is issued by a processor once every 100 clock cycles, then each processor receives 10 broadcasts per cycle on the average, and could receive up to 999 on any single cycle. Clearly, the broadcast has to be avoided in such a multi-processor, yet the broadcast is the preferred mechanism for synchronization. The protocol has to be more selective and should not broadcast information to processors that do not need it. Even this type of protocol produces so many messages that the caches are kept busier by the cache-coherence protocol than by doing useful work in support of their local processor.

Because the bulk of the load on a cache-coherence mechanism may well be caused by synchronization operations, a practical way to build such a multi-processor is to provide a low-cost subsystem dedicated to synchronization. If this successfully removes the bulk of the operations that otherwise would be performed by a cache-coherence network and protocol, then the operations that remain may be relatively easy to satisfy at reasonable cost. To satisfy a 1000-processor barrier by means of conventional cache-coherence techniques overburdens the cache-coherence network, and thereby severely degrades system performance. Yet a very simple low-cost dedicated network can implement the 1000-processor barrier with high efficiency. Clearly, specialized techniques for synchronization are quite attractive in highly parallel multi-processors and they may open the way to practical implementations of cache-coherence protocols in such systems.

This completes the discussion of synchronization and cache coherence. The following sections return to techniques for writing efficient multi-processor algorithms.

7.3 Parallel Search—How to Use and Not Use Parallelism

One of the most obvious ways to use parallel processors is for searching. Many researchers report excellent computation speeds in search applications, mainly based on the number of processors that are busy during the search process. Unfortunately, there is quite a difference between the number of processors busy and the true speedup in a multiprocessor since processors need not be doing useful work.

In this section we describe two different search algorithms. One is a search for a maximum of a function. For this problem it is rather surprising that the optimal search strategy yields only an $O(\log N)$ speedup. Even more surprising is the fact that all processors are busy during every step of the algorithm, so the magnitude of the wasted computing effort is not obvious. The second algorithm is a more sophisticated search algorithm. It is reproduced here to illustrate where one might look for useful parallelism.

7.3.1 Searching for the Maximum of a Unimodal Function

Karp and Miranker [1968] investigated the problem of finding the maximum of a unimodal function with N processors. A typical function to explore is shown in Fig. 7.7. By definition a unimodal function has a single mode or maximum located between its endpoints. Our objective is to find that maximum to within a unit interval on the x-axis. The search is to be conducted on a multiprocessor whose processors can evaluate $f(x)$ at any given x between the endpoints of the interval. We assume that the evaluation takes a fixed constant time so that all processors start and finish simultaneously. After evaluating the function, the processors can exchange information and determine the next point to evaluate. This too takes a fixed constant time.

The full search algorithm consists of a repetition of the processes that respectively evaluate and exchange information. The repetition continues until the maximum is pinned to within a unit interval. Karp and Miranker show that the optimum strategy depends on the parity of the number of processors, but whether that parity is odd or even, the optimum strategy produces an $O(\log N)$ speedup with respect to a single processor.

What is deceptive about this problem is that every processor is busy at every step, and we intuitively do not expect the final computation time to be so poor as to yield only an $O(\log N)$ improvement. In fact, with a sufficiently large number of processors we can pin the maximum to a unit interval in a single step—the ultimate in high speed. But since a single processor can find the

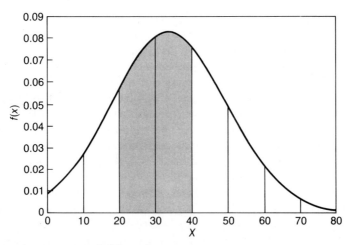

Fig. 7.7 Searching a unimodal function.

maximum with a binary search in O(log N) steps, it becomes clear that O(log N) is all the speedup possible.

Figure 7.7 shows a typical situation during the execution of the algorithm. The vertical lines show where seven simultaneous probes are executed. The lines are uniformly spaced in this example. Karp and Miranker describe where the probes should be made for the optimum strategy, but the details of the optimum strategy are not important for this discussion.

What is important is the nature of the information returned. From the given set of probes, we can conclude that the maximum must lie somewhere in the shaded region. The reason is that we can compute the derivative of the function by examining two neighboring values of the function. At the maximum of the function the derivative goes to zero. Only in the shaded regions can the derivative of a unimodal function become zero. Therefore, the next step is to assign the seven processors to evaluate the function in the shaded region and repeat the process.

A little reflection shows where the wasted effort is going. The only information actually used to guide the search is where the derivative changes sign. The outlying processors work as hard as the middle processors in evaluating the function, but the results produced by the outlying processors are of no value.

The only information extracted is the derivative of the function, and because the function is unimodal we know that if the derivative is negative at x, it is negative at all $y > x$. Consequently, if we find some x with a negative derivative, then the processors to the right of this point are wasting their effort. Similarly, if the derivative is positive at some x, it is positive at all $y < x$. Processors operating to the left of a point with a positive derivative are wasting their effort as well.

Let's examine the problem from the point of the view of the information available and the information actually used. Each of N processors returns essentially one bit of information, namely the sign of the derivative of the function. Thus in one step of the parallel algorithm we compute N bits of information. The bits, however, are not independent. In fact, the N processors create $N + 1$ intervals on the x-axis, producing exactly N possible choices for an adjacent pair of intervals to search on the next step. The amount of information in N choices is only log N bits, not N bits. Hence we expend the effort to produce N bits of information and obtain only log N useful bits. In essence, the algorithm throws away $N -$ log N bits per iteration, which accounts for the wasted effort in this algorithm.

Is there a way to speed up this search? No, not if the constraints are obeyed. But there could be a way if other options are available. For example, the processors are constrained to evaluate $f(x)$. This is not satisfactory because it almost surely forces some evaluations to be useless. If the processors are given a different representation of $f(x)$ so that each evaluation gives independent information, the speedup might be greater. It might be possible, for example, for each processor to work with a Fourier transform of $f(x)$, which is helpful because each point in the transform contains information about all points of the function.

The fact that the function is unimodal forces the derivative information to be redundant. If the function were multimodal, and we had to find a global maximum, the work per processor would no longer be redundant because information produced about one region of the function sheds no light about the function in a different region.

The unimodal function is very important, however, because this is the function encountered in database searches for using lookups by sorted key. When the search key is compared to a probe key, the difference is computed. The next point in the search depends on the sign of the difference. The absolute value of the difference function is unimodal, in this case having a single minimum instead of a single maximum.

Karp and Miranker's results show that multiple processors will not be very efficient if they are used to perform a search by making multiple probes to a file ordered by a single search key. Instead, multiple processors should be used to conduct independent searches. Therefore we cannot expect a multiprocessor to perform any single-key search much faster than a single processor can, but we can expect a multiprocessor to do many different searches in parallel with high efficiency.

Does the analysis suggest that multiprocessors are not useful for conducting parallel search for a single key? In some, but not all, cases, parallel search is indeed doomed to be inefficient and is reasonable for only small numbers of processors.

When a database is sorted by some key, the distance between the search key and a probe key is a unimodal function, so this problem definitely fits the Karp-Miranker model. When database keys are unsorted, we have the equivalent of a multimodal function, and the Karp-Miranker assumptions do not hold. A serial search might have to examine the entire database. In this case, a multiprocessor search has a potential for excellent speedup.

Therefore, we are tempted to take advantage of multiprocessors for search by using them on unsorted databases and claiming excellent performance. In this case, however, the savings from parallelism is not truly the speedup observed; it is the savings in the overhead used to sort the database and maintain that sorted order. If this overhead is small, then the effectiveness of the parallelism is small. If this overhead is large, then the parallelism is potentially beneficial. The actual choices available to the user thus are:

1. Use a serial computer, and use sorting or a database index to facilitate fast searching; or

2. Use a multiprocessor, and avoid the additional cost to sort the database or to produce an index.

We must compare the cost and performance of these two alternatives in order to evaluate parallel searching. We should not compare parallel search to ordinary serial search unless serial search is truly the only other alternative.

In many business applications the cost of sorting or building an index can be amortized over hundreds or thousands of searches. Rarely in such instances does it pay to perform parallel search. On the other hand, some problems in cryptography are essentially enormous searches that are only performed once per database. The equivalent of building an index (or sorting the database) is far more costly than searching the database in parallel by using a multi-processor.

A comparison of parallel and serial search in the recent literature was stimulated by an article by Stanfill and Kahle [1986] regarding a highly parallel search of a large data base. The solution proposed by Stanfill and Kahle involved the use of a Connection Machine with 64,000 1-bit processors to search a multigigabyte database, but their solution required the entire database to be read from disk while doing the search. Because disk operations are very slow compared to operations done at the clock speed of a processor, the enormous cost of reading an entire data base from disk almost certainly cannot be offset by the speed gain due to parallel search. Boral and DeWitt [1983] brought this fact to light, and questioned the practicality of a parallel database machine until technology can provide a much faster auxiliary storage.

Nevertheless, Stanfill and Kahle implemented a parallel search of the type that Boral and DeWitt indicated would not be efficient. The weakness of the Stanfill-Kahle approach was observed independently by Stone [1987] and Salton and Buckley [1988]. Stone's analysis suggested that just one of the 64,000 processors working with the same total memory of the Connection Machine could perform the same task somewhat faster if it used an index in order to reduce the total traffic from disk. Salton and Buckley's analysis demonstrated that a low-cost workstation had roughly comparable performance as the Connection Machine when the workstation used an index. In both studies the gain in performance is strictly to due to the much smaller volume of data actually read from disk. An algorithm that succeeds in keeping 64,000 processors busy is not necessarily a fast algorithm—the processors have to be performing useful work.

The important observation here is that parallelism is only one of many possible techniques for solving a problem. It may fare badly with respect to good serial techniques. Performance evaluation is crucial in judging the effectiveness of parallel programs. The comparison must always be done by seeking good serial algorithms against which to compare the parallel algorithms.

The ultimate quality measure of a parallel algorithm is performance per unit cost, not just performance alone. All algorithms for all processors can be reduced to this common measure. While it may be interesting to learn that a

1024-processor search is faster than a serial search, it becomes far less interesting when we discover that the speedup over a serial search is a factor 10, and that we can obtain a factor of 5 speedup by using only 32 processors.

7.3.2 Parallel Branch-and-Bound—The Traveling-Salesman Problem

A remarkable algorithm for solving the Traveling-Salesman Problem provides an excellent example of where and where not to exploit parallelism. The Traveling-Salesman Problem is rather deceptive because it is easily described and simple in concept, but extremely difficult to solve. The problem is to find a minimum-distance tour of N cities that visits each city exactly once and returns to the first city on the tour at the end. The problem input is a list of the distances between each pair of cities.

It is well known that this problem belongs to the class of hard problems known as *NP-complete*, for which the best available algorithms exhibit a worst-case computation time that grows faster than any polynomial function of the size of the input [*see* Aho, Hopcroft, and Ullman 1974]. Many researchers believe that the computation time for NP-complete problems actually grows at least exponentially with the size of the input, but this question is unanswered at this writing.

The algorithm we describe is remarkable because its average complexity is only $O(N^3 \log N)$ on a class of randomly selected input problems which is less than quadratic in the size of the problem since the problem size is $O(N^2)$. This appears to contradict the findings that the problem is NP-hard, but there is no contradiction.

The algorithm has a low complexity on the average, but its worst case may require exponential time, even though this event is extremely unlikely. The algorithm is from D. R. Smith [1984], who proved the results on average time and demonstrated that these results are consistent with actual running times on randomly generated sets of problems. The analysis might not hold for a class of problem instances whose characteristics are rather skewed and are not adequately represented by the more uniform distributions assumed in Smith's analysis.

The branch-and-bound technique executed on a serial processor is illustrated in Fig. 7.8. The algorithm depends on a subroutine that can compute the least-cost permutation for visiting N cities. We use the notation (1 2 3) to describe a route that visits City 1, then City 2, then City 3, and then returns to City 1. We call such a visit a *cycle* because its starting point is the same as its finishing point. We call a *permutation* of the cities to be a set of cycles such as (1 2 3)(4 5 6 7), such that every city appears in exactly one cycle.

A permutation is not necessarily a tour because in this case if you start at City 1, you return to City 1 after visiting Cities 2 and 3, and without having visited any of the other cities. A tour has to visit all of the cities exactly once.

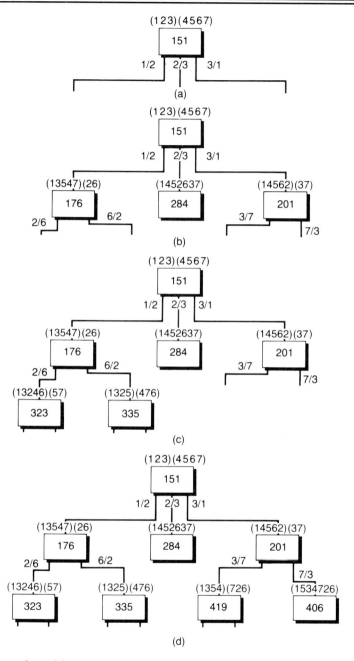

Fig. 7.8 Branch-and-bound search for the Traveling Salesman Problem:
(a) Initial solution of the problem (three subproblems open);
(b) After examining the three subproblems;
(c) After expanding the two leftmost solutions; and
(d) The search after expanding the node for permutation (1 4 5 6 2) (3 7).

Obviously, a tour is a permutation that has but a single cycle, such as the permutation (1 2 3 4 5 6 7) for seven cities.

The subroutine that finds the least-cost permutation finds a permutation whose sum of city-to-city distances is the minimum among all permutations of the cities. The reason for finding the least-cost permutation is that it gives a lower bound on the shortest tour. Since a tour is a special kind of permutation, the shortest tour for a given problem cannot be shorter than the least-cost permutation.

Finding the shortest tour is extremely difficult, but finding the least-cost permutation is relatively easy [*see* Lawler 1976]. This takes only $O(N^3)$ time the first time we execute the subroutine. On subsequent executions, the input data will be only marginally different. Only $O(N^2)$ additional work is required to obtain the solutions for these subroutine calls. Lawler shows that the discovery of the least-cost permutation, which in his terminology is the *assignment problem*, reduces to a minimum-cost, network-flow problem [Ford and Fulkerson 1956], which is solved by repeated applications of Dijkstra's shortest-path algorithm [1959].

Figure 7.8 illustrates how the lower bound information is used. In Fig. 7.8(a), we show a single node of the search tree labeled by the permutation (1 2 3)(4 5 6 7), with a total distance of 151 shown inside the node. The algorithm produces this number by running a least-cost permutation algorithm on the original algorithm. (To prevent solutions with one-city cycles, the original problem has an infinite cost of going from any city to itself). Since (1 2 3)(4 5 6 7) is not a tour, the best tour has an equal or higher cost. The least-cost tour must differ from this permutation on at least one branch of each cycle, so without loss of generality, we examine the shortest cycle, which in this case is (1 2 3).

The least-cost tour differs from this cycle in at least one way, and possibly in more ways. That is, either the tour does not go from City 1 to City 2, from City 2 to City 3, or from City 3 to City 1. These three possibilities are shown in Fig. 7.8(a) as three labeled arcs leaving the original node.

Since at least one of these three roads is not on the least-cost tour, we can create three new subproblems to investigate. In each of three subproblems we eliminate the possibility that one of the three roads of interest is in the least-cost permutation. Figure 7.8(b) shows the result of this step.

The leftmost node at the second level shows what happens when the distance from City 1 to City 2 is made infinite. When we call the least-cost permutation subroutine with this new condition, it reports back that the least-cost permutation is (1 3 5 4 7)(2 6), with a cost of 176. Note that the road from City 1 to City 2 is not on this permutation because that road happens to be infinitely long.

When the road from City 2 to City 3 is infinite, the least-cost permutation happens to be a tour with a cost of 284. Although a tour has been produced by the algorithm, the tour is not necessarily the least-cost tour for the original problem. Additional work is required to show that this tour is optimal or to find a lower-cost tour.

When the road from City 3 to City 1 is infinite, the least-cost permutation is (1 4 5 6 2)(3 7), with a cost of 201. Although we have now discovered a tour that has a low cost, it might not be the least-cost tour. Both of the other subproblems are open to the possibility that further exploration of these candidates could yield tours of cost lower than 284, although we know now that no tour can have a cost lower than 176.

To investigate the leftmost node, note that the permutation can be broken at its shortest cycle by opening the road from City 2 to City 6 or by opening the road from City 6 to City 2. (These roads do not have to be the same road.)

Similarly, the rightmost node can break the cycle that contains City 3 and City 7 by opening the road either from City 3 to City 7 or City 7 to City 3. Thus there are four search paths that warrant further exploration. The two best candidates are the descendants of the leftmost node in the figure because this node has the least bound of any node on the perimeter of the search tree.

Figures 7.8(c) and (d) show what happens when we follow the four open subproblems. Searching beneath the node with the lowest bound obtains two new permutations, whose costs are 323 and 335, respectively. Note, for example, that the leftmost permutation is (1 3 2 4 6)(5 7), which is the least-cost permutation for the case in which City 2 does not follow City 1 and City 6 does not follow City 2.

At this point, the rightmost node has the lowest bound, and the search branches to that node for further exploration. Examining the two subproblems of this node produces two new permutations, whose costs are 419 and 406. The latter permutation happens to be a tour. None of the subproblems yields either a tour or permutation whose cost is lower than the cost 284 for the least-cost tour discovered in Fig. 7.8(b). Hence, the tour (1 4 5 2 6 3 7) is optimal and the problem has been solved.

Although this highly contrived example is not necessarily typical of real problems, the power of the branch-and-bound algorithm is quite clear. By expending $O(N^2)$ time at a node, we can find out how expensive a tour might be if we examined the descendants of that node in the search for a tour. If a bound is very high, the search path is not promising, and we can abandon the search from that node.

In Fig. 7.8, there are 6! = 720 distinct tours of the 7 cities, and the bounding operation eliminates 718 of them from consideration. We do not claim that the algorithm behaves this efficiently in general. But D. R. Smith [1984] does claim that the average number of times that a least-cost permutation is generated is $O(N \log N)$ although the proof is not in this article. With a cost of $O(N^2)$ time to generate a least-cost permutation, the total time for the algorithm on the average is $O(N^3 \log N)$.

Since Smith's results assume an unbiased distribution of problems, his results may not hold for problem distributions with strong statistical biases. Nevertheless, let us assume that Smith's results hold for a particular set of problems and consider how parallelism can be put to effective use.

The search tree in Fig. 7.8 in general has $(N - 1)!$ leaf nodes, one for each possible tour, assuming that each tour starts at City 1. Therefore its depth is $O(N)$ if the average branching factor is proportional to N, and its depth is $O[\log (N!)] = O(N \log N)$ if the average branching factor is not larger than a constant that does not depend on N. If the depth is $O(N)$, then we can say that on the average we examine $O(\log N)$ parallel paths while visiting $O(N \log N)$ nodes. This suggests that as many as $O(\log N)$ paths can be usefully examined concurrently in a multiprocessor. If we expend $O(N)$ processors to examine the open subproblems, we would obtain a useful speedup of only $O(\log N)$, and the speedup is similar to the Karp-Miranker problem.

Note in Fig. 7.8(b) that we can commit two processors simultaneously to the open subproblems for the leftmost node. We can also commit two processors to the rightmost node. However, if the leftmost node returns tours whose cost is lower than 201, which is the cost of the rightmost node, then any additional computation expended on the rightmost node is wasted effort. This situation is analogous to the wasted effort in the Karp-Miranker search.

If the depth of the search tree turns out to be of $O(N \log N)$, then the possibility of using parallelism effectively to explore multiple paths is rather unpromising. On the average only one path is actively pursued by a serial search in this case, and if multiple paths are pursued concurrently, all path computations but one are almost surely wasted.

The obvious way to apply parallelism is to apply all processors to the computation at one node to perform the evaluation of the least-cost permutation. An efficient approach is to examine only the nodes that a purely serial algorithm examines. This ensures that no effort is wasted examining other nodes.

In the process of examining a node, apply as many processors as can be applied efficiently to find the least-cost permutation. That number may vary with the architecture, depending on communications and access to shared variables.

Dijkstra's shortest-path algorithm can be executed with a speedup of $O(N/\log N)$ on some N-processor parallel architectures, assuming that contention for shared resources does not produce excessive performance degradation. The speedup, however, is architecture dependent. If an architecture can produce a speedup of $O(N/\log N)$ or better for Dijkstra's shortest-path algorithm, then this architecture will produce a very fast, efficient parallel solution of the Traveling-Salesman Problem, provided that the statistical distributions of the problems to be solved are similar to those assumed by Smith.

In this example, the key observation is that searches along parallel paths are not independent and can produce wasted effort, whereas there is an opportunity for parallelism in performing the work along one path. Pick a promising candidate and focus the computing power on this candidate, rather than spread the computation across several candidates.

7.3.3 Speed-Up and Parallel Complexity

We have stressed efficiency in parallel computation, and have used speedup as a means to express efficiency. While it is an excellent single measure, speedup measures when used improperly can be misleading.

For example, consider an FFT algorithm whose serial complexity is $O(N \log N)$ for N data points. Using a technique such as described by Pease [1968] we can construct an N-processor computer that computes an N-point FFT in a time proportional to $\log N$. Thus, the parallel computer achieves a speedup of N, and the efficiency is excellent.

Now consider a different problem and perform a similar analysis. Let this problem be Problem X for which there exists some very efficient serial algorithm that solves any instance of Problem X of size N in time $O(N^3)$ in the worst case. We say that the complexity of the algorithm is $O(N^3)$. Assume that we are very fortunate, and are able to demonstrate that no algorithm exists that has a lower complexity. Consequently, we have a serial algorithm against which can compare parallel algorithms.

After some careful study, assume that we produce a novel parallel computer and a suitable algorithm for that machine that work extremely well together to solve Problem X. The match is so good that an N-processor version of the computer system can solve any instance of Problem X of size N in a time $O(N^2)$ in the worse-case. In other words, the parallel complexity of the algorithm on the computer system is $O(N^2)$. The research community quickly endorses this as an efficient scheme, and heralds it as having an $O(N)$ speedup.

But some surprises lie ahead. We build a 100-processor version of the machine, implement the algorithm, and confirm that it is working correctly. Then we enter real data of size 100. We run the parallel algorithm on the 100-processor machine and run the same problem on a serial machine that implements the efficient serial algorithm. The serial and parallel machine use the same level of device technology. Our expectation is that we achieve a large speed-up, not necessarily a 100-to-1 because we have not accounted for constant factors, but nevertheless we expect to see the parallel algorithm running much faster than the serial algorithm. But we do not achieve any speedup at all. The parallel implementation seems to run somewhat slower. Where is the N-fold speedup? Perhaps the constant factors are working against us in this instance.

We explore further. We run many problems and we let the problems grow and shrink in size. We also vary the number of processors. As the performance picture becomes clearer we discover that the speedup is not $O(N)$ but only $O(\log N)$. How can this be true?

We have been misled because the problems that we have been using to test the algorithm are not the same problems that determine the complexity of either the serial or parallel algorithms. When we say that an algorithm has a complexity of $O(N^3)$, we are only saying that the most difficult possible input configuration of size N can be solved in a time that grows as N^3. We have presented no information on other input configurations. These may or may not be as difficult to solve. Similarly, to say that the parallel complexity is $O(N^2)$ is the same as saying that the most difficult problem to solve in parallel can be solved in a time proportional to $O(N^2)$. The most difficult problem to solve in serial need not even be related to the most difficult problem to solve in parallel.

When we attempted to test the parallel program, we happened to select problems in a way that produces an average serial complexity of $O(N^2 \log N)$. For this selection of problems, the parallel algorithm happens to produce only $O(\log N)$ speedup, and runs in a time proportional to $O(N^2)$, which does not violate the claim that the parallel complexity is $O(N^2)$. The constant coefficients are just different enough to cause the first parallel test to run slower than the serial algorithm, and the full battery of tests confirmed that true speedup is $O(\log N)$.

Although this example sounds hypothetical, it is illustrative of actual research results reported in the literature. In the case of parallel algorithms for the FFT, the speedup measure is accurate because all input configurations run in the same amount of time. That is, the worst case, the best case, and the average case are all the same.

In the case of Problem X, the worst case and the average case are far different. A measure of complexity based on the worst case misleads us when we produce instances of the average case. Even if we had produced instances of the worst-case parallel input, we may still be in trouble because the worst-case parallel input is not necessarily the worst-case serial input. Hence, the worst-case parallel input need not produce the speedup of $O(N)$. The only sure way to see N-fold speedup is to select instances of the worst-case serial input. Though we are promised N-fold speedup for these inputs, the speedup for all other inputs is totally unknown from the information at hand. The algorithm we treated originally as a breakthrough may be only a useless curiosity, or alternatively may eventually be shown to meet our original expectations. We cannot tell until we investigate the behavior of the parallel algorithm on a realistic set of data inputs.

The important lesson is to understand the limitations of the speedup measure. Does the speedup reported for a parallel algorithm hold for all input data, typical input data, or for some small subset of input data? Unless the measure holds for all input data, the measure gives an incomplete picture of the efficiency of an algorithm. To be a useful measure, the measure should report on typical input data, whereas the tendency in the literature is to report on worst-case input data. We must be able to define and analyze the typical case, but rarely can we find the characteristics of the typical case. This is the difficulty that has led to worst-case studies, and in turn has produced speedup measures whose true significance is still unknown.

7.4 Transforming Serial Algorithms into Parallel Algorithms

In putting multiprocessors to use, a major hurdle is writing programs for such architectures. In the worst case, every problem has to be studied anew and solved by an algorithm implementation tuned to a particular architecture. This technique will certainly be used for the very largest problems, which consume days or weeks of computation time, because the human effort expended to optimize the algorithm is paid back by a large reduction in computer time. But for more moderate problems, those that take a fraction of an hour, for example, the human effort to optimize the algorithm might save only a few minutes of computation, which may not be worthwhile. Therefore, a major objective is to use programmed transformations to produce reasonably good parallel programs from serial programs.

One way to automate the production of parallel programs is to construct a compiler for a standard high-level language to produce output for a multiprocessor. With such a compiler, existing software libraries can be mapped to a multiprocessor with a minimum of effort. Some fraction of the library undoubtedly will exhibit negligible parallelism and will produce rather inefficient parallel implementations. These programs can be run serially.

The interesting programs are those that yield efficient parallel codes. The codes need not be as efficient as hand-coded versions of the programs, provided they come within a factor of 2 to 5 of a hand-coded translation. If the inefficiency is as high as a factor of 10, the compiler is still useful as a stopgap tool that provides a fast way of producing programs for a parallel architecture. The inefficient translations it produces eventually have to be reprogrammed by hand or by a better compiler to create versions that are satisfactory for production use.

Creating a high-quality optimizing compiler for a multiprocessor is a formidable task. An early attempt by Kuck *et al.* [1972] showed that there is easily exploitable parallelism on the order of 10 to 100 in many ordinary FORTRAN programs. The next decade produced far more sophisticated developments that have been used extensively for real applications.

For vector architectures, leading work by Miura [1986], a student of Kuck's, for Fujitsu vector processors and by F. Allen for the IBM 3090 vector processor produce code that is nearly as efficient as the best programmers can produce and is much more efficient than can be produced by inexperienced programmers.

Compilers for multiprocessors have lagged behind compilers for vector processors because the translation problem is far more complex for multiprocessors. Vector compilers find a way to do one operation simultaneously across many processors; multiprocessor compilers find a way to do many operations across many processors at unpredictable times. The thread common to the two types of compilers is that they need to identify dependences from statement to statement to determine the order in which events can be scheduled.

For vectorizing compilers, published work by Kuck *et al.* [1984], J. R. Allen *et al.* [1983], J. R. Allen [1983], and Padua and Wolfe [1986] illustrate the underlying theory and the directions taken by compiler writers. The actual art of vectorizing compilers is more advanced than the literature indicates, but the literature captures the most important and useful transformations. Cytron [1984] and Padua and Wolfe [1986] address the problem of optimizing code for multiprocessors.

7.4.1 Dependence Analysis

The most fruitful way to obtain parallelism in serial programs is by executing loop iterations across several processors. We illustrate this technique earlier in this chapter, and we also introduce the notion of *chunksize* in Program 7.4 to show that one processor can execute a group of iterations instead of a single iteration. Although other forms of parallelism exist and are potentially detectable by an optimizing compiler, in typical applications the bulk of the speedup obtained from parallelism is through the parallel execution of loop iterations. Therefore, we focus on ways to perform loop iterations in parallel in this text.

An optimizing multiprocessor compiler has the task of detecting parallelism, but the task name is misleading. The compiler actually detects serial behavior, and, by default, everything left is potentially executable in parallel. To produce parallel code for a loop iteration, the compiler has to detect when successive iterations have to be executed serially. As an example of dependence analysis, consider the loop:

```
For i := 1 to N do
    A[i] := A[i − 1] / B[i];
    end; {* do loop *}
```

As written, each iteration depends directly on the prior iteration because a variable written in the prior iteration is read by this iteration. This is WRITE/READ dependence. Other dependences possible are READ/WRITE and

WRITE/WRITE. The READ/WRITE dependence requires the variable to be read by a prior iteration before it is written by this one, and the WRITE/WRITE dependence forces the value of the variable to be written last by the present iteration rather than by a prior iteration.

The dependence in the example is very easy for a compiler to detect because it is forced by a single variable. Other examples lead to more complex cases, such as an iteration with the following statement:

$$A[i] := A[C[i]];$$

In this case, the dependence is READ/WRITE if $C[i]$ is less than i and WRITE/READ if $C[i]$ is greater than i. Moreover, if the values in C are computed during execution, the compiler cannot determine which dependence exists and therefore cannot optimize the code. Therefore, the compiler can detect loop-to-loop dependences only when all subscript expressions in an iteration and the loop increment have values known to the compiler. Optimizing compilers are forced to assume that the dependences are present if index variables depend on execution-time program behavior. Otherwise, the optimization process is likely to produce a translated program that runs incorrectly.

A general procedure for detecting dependences is to list the names of the variables read and written in a loop iteration. If a name appears on both lists, it potentially leads to a READ/WRITE or WRITE/READ dependence. All variables that are written are potentially WRITE/WRITE dependences. The compiler has to examine each case further to determine if an actual dependence exists.

For the WRITE/WRITE dependence to exist, one variable has to be written by two different loop iterations. This situation usually has two distinct statements in the loop, such as

$$A[i] := B[i]/10;$$
$$A[i - 1] := C[i] + B[i];$$

With both statements present in one iteration, it becomes clear that the prior iteration, using the value $i - 1$ as an index value, writes $A[i - 1]$ and $A[i - 2]$, leading to the WRITE/WRITE dependence for variable $A[i - 1]$. Note that we assume that the loop index is increased by 1 during each iteration. If the loop index is increased by 2, then there is no dependence caused by writing two successive values into A. READ/WRITE and WRITE/READ dependences are equally easy to detect as WRITE/READ dependences.

7.4.2 Exploiting Parallelism Across Iterations

In this section we show how to use dependence information to guide the translation of serial programs into multiprocessor programs. There are just a few techniques given here, but they are widely useful and produce the bulk of the speedup obtainable in typical programs. However, there are many other techniques not discussed in this section that are also of value, especially techniques designed for specific classes of programs. Interested readers will find J. R. Allen [1983], Cytron [1984], and Padua and Wolfe [1986] useful in-depth treatments of the topic.

Our objective for a multiprocessor is to split apart iterations that are independent. This boosts speedup, provided that independent iterations have a sufficiently high R/C ratio. We also want to chunk iterations together into larger tasks to boost efficiency by improving the R/C ratio when this also boosts performance, even if it reduces parallelism. The ideal situation is to chunk dependent iterations together into large tasks in a way that creates a collection of independent large tasks.

As an example of this idea, consider Program 7.10. The program is shown as it would probably be found in a program for a conventional serial machine. We assume that the program uses neither **do seq** nor **do par** phrases, described earlier in this chapter, because it is written specifically for serial execution.

A straightforward dependence analysis shows that Column 0 of matrix A is the cause of the dependences. There is a WRITE/READ dependence from iteration (i, j) to iteration $(i, j+1)$ because $A[i, 0]$ is both read and written for these iterations. This suggests that successive iterations in the serial program have to be executed serially.

A sophisticated compiler should detect that there are no dependences due to the i index, so the i and j loops can be interchanged, as shown in Program 7.11. The inner loop satisfies the READ/WRITE dependence on the index i. To ensure that Column 0 is properly initialized, it is initialized separately in an earlier loop. Note that successive serial executions of the inner loop can be chunked together into a single task that does all N iterations for one value of i. Each of these large tasks is independent and can be executed concurrently.

Program 7.10 Computing row sums of a matrix.

```
for i := 1 to N do
  begin
    A[i, 0] := 0.0;
    for j := 1 to N do
      A[i, 0] := A[i, 0] + A[i, j];
  end; {* i loop *}
```

Notes:

1. Matrix A is $N \times N$, with indices running from 1 to N.
2. The sum of Row i is computed and stored in $A[i, 0]$.

Program 7.11 Computing row sums of a matrix, transformed version.

```
for i := 1 to N do
    A[i, 0] := 0.0;
for j := 1 to N do
    begin
        for i := 1 to N do
            A[i, 0] := A[i, 0] + A[i, j];
    end; {* j loop *}
```

Notes:

1. Matrix A is $N \times N$, with indices running from 1 to N.

2. The sum of Row i is computed and stored in $A[i, 0]$.

3. For a multiprocessor, the loop on i can be chunked together to make larger tasks which improves R/C.

It is also possible to obtain greater parallelism by observing that the inner loop can be chunked into several medium-size tasks, for example, k of them, that each form the sum of N/k row elements. For a particular value of i, the variable $A[i, 0]$ is a variable shared across k tasks, which forces serialization of the tasks because of a READ/WRITE conflict.

A clever compiler can detect that the summation into the row sum can be done in any order and can change strictly serial execution of the k tasks into parallel execution, with each task computing a local sum that is added to the shared variable at the end of the chunk. The addition at the end is controlled by a LOCK/UNLOCK, Compare-and-Swap, Fetch-and-Add, or other similar means. The value of k should be selected to reflect the available parallelism and the best choice for the R/C ratio.

The key idea illustrated by this example is to observe the essential dependences exhibited by the algorithm. The order of execution is free to be changed, provided that the dependences are satisfied. In the example, the order of indexing of the loops is changed, which is a common situation among algorithms. By changing the order, the transformed program structure has N parallel tasks (or kN if chunking is used), instead of N^2 serial iterations. Not only is the transformed program more parallel, but its R/C ratio can be adjusted to minimize synchronization inefficiency.

As a second example, let us return to the familiar example of the inner loop of a Poisson solver. In Program 7.1, the item updated depends on its north, east, south, and west neighbor. No matter how we choose the iterations, by row or by column, ascending or descending, we will have READ/WRITE and WRITE/

READ conflicts. Therefore interchanging the iterations is not particularly helpful for this program.

There is, however, a parallel structure that can be exploited here. If the cells of the matrix are laid out on a checkerboard, then the iteration in Program 7.1 shows how to update a black square by averaging the values in its neighboring red squares, and similarly, how to update a red square by updating the values in its neighboring black squares. The red and black squares form two independent sets of variables, since no red square depends directly on a red square, no black square depends directly on a black square.

Therefore, a possible approach is to create a task that updates red squares from black ones, and another task that updates black squares from red ones. The two tasks can be divided into smaller tasks by chunking indices, and the chunksize should be chosen to reflect available parallelism and R/C. The iteration of Program 7.1 can be done by updating the black squares, then updating the red squares, with each update done across the available processors. Barrier synchronization is required at the end of an update of each color.

The parallel computation using red and black squares produces an iteration that is not quite identical to the iteration given in Program 7.1. Note that as each point is updated, two of its four neighbors have already been updated. For example, at Row i, Row $i - 1$ has new data already, but Row $i + 1$ has not been updated. So the north and west neighbors of each point are new, and the south and east neighbors are old. This iteration is called the *Gauss-Seidel* iteration [*see* Varga 1962].

Another possible technique is to compute the updated data for the entire matrix before making any update. Such a scheme, called the *Jacobi* iteration, uses old data for all neighbors. The red-black scheme is equivalent to selecting new data for all neighbors. In typical situations, all three schemes converge to the same solution at different rates. The red-black scheme converges the fastest because it uses new data more quickly than do the other two schemes. The slowest convergence occurs for the Jacobi iteration.

In general, iterative calculations such as the one illustrated in Program 7.1 may converge or diverge, or they may oscillate while neither converging nor diverging. If the numerical conditions are such that convergence occurs, then in general, the more new data used in an iteration, the faster the convergence will be. Thus, the transformation of Program 7.1 to one that uses a red-black ordering and executes in parallel on a multiprocessor is likely to be an effective transformation. If this is done automatically, the program should produce a warning that the iterative method has been altered in the transformation.

The red-black scheme for Program 7.1 is ideal for multiprocessor use. Because half of the points in a mesh can be executed in parallel, the program can be split across any reasonable number of processors, and the chunksize can be set large enough to keep synchronization overhead small. In a multiprocessor, irregular boundaries and special regions within the mesh are treated easily and far more efficiently than in a vector architecture that broadcasts one instruction to all processors.

Is it reasonable to assume that an optimizing compiler is clever enough to change an iteration from one form to another? If the optimizing compiler is used for general-purpose computation, the answer is no. There are literally hundreds of useful transformations that could be applied, which is far too many to incorporate in a compiler.

However, if the compiler is dedicated to a specific class of computations, such as partial differential equations, it is quite reasonable to incorporate within the compiler the most useful transformations that occur in practical problems. In this case, the transformation of the Gauss-Seidel iteration in Program 7.1 to a red-black iteration is frequently done by hand.

Optimizing compilers may be viewed as programs that have a repertoire of tricks to apply, and they do their work by searching through their bag of tricks for the most appropriate ones to apply. A clever researcher might discover a new trick, such as the red-black transformation, which no compiler can discover on its own. Once the trick is known and published widely, the compiler writer can add the new trick to the compiler's repertoire. The compiler might not be very good when it is first completed, but as the bag of tricks grows, the compiler may be able to produce better parallel code than can most programmers.

Nevertheless, we may insist that any program transformation must leave the iteration unchanged. If this is the case for Program 7.1, we need a parallel program that does the Gauss-Seidel iteration. Lamport [1974] observes that a diagonal scheme, as shown in Fig. 7.9, is equivalent to the Gauss-Seidel iteration. In Lamport's scheme, the matrix is not scanned by rows or columns, but by diagonals. Along any diagonal, all the points depend on the previous and next diagonals. The previous diagonal holds the north and west neighbors; the next diagonal holds the south and east neighbors. Since each diagonal sees new data from the prior diagonal and old data on the next diagonal, the iteration that marches from diagonal to diagonal is a Gauss-Seidel iteration. Lamport shows that the transformation of a program written in the form of Program 7.1 into a diagonal scan can be incorporated into a compiler and fully automated.

The diagonal scheme has a serious disadvantage because some diagonals are very short and severely limit parallel execution. Recall that there has to be Barrier synchronization along a diagonal to ensure that one diagonal is completely updated before the next diagonal is started. Lamport, however, shows that it is possible to combine two diagonals N apart, to obtain a total of N points to update, lying on two different diagonals that can be updated simultaneously. In the first pass across the diagonals, this algorithm updates Diagonals 1 through N, one at a time. When Diagonal $N + 1$ (of length $N - 1$) is

1	2	3	4	5	6	7	8
2	3	4	5	6	7	8	1
3	4	5	6	7	8	1	2
4	5	6	7	8	1	2	3
5	6	7	8	1	2	3	4
6	7	8	1	2	3	4	5
7	8	1	2	3	4	5	6
8	1	2	3	4	5	6	7

Fig. 7.9 Lamport's diagonal sweep for the Poisson problem on a square. The number within each cell identifies the iteration in which the cell is updated. This algorithm is equivalent to the Gauss-Seidel iteration because the north and west neighbors have new data, and the south and east neighbors have old data. By scanning two diagonals concurrently, the number of data treated in each operation is constant.

reached, it is paired with the second iteration of Diagonal 1, to produce work for N points. Next, Diagonal $N + 2$ is paired with Diagonal 2 to produce another set of N points for updating. This continues through the last iteration, during which it is not necessary to update the first N diagonals. Although all N points along the two diagonals can be updated independently on N processors, they can be chunked together arbitrarily to match the parallelism to the architecture and raise the R/C ratio, if necessary. If the number of processors available exceeds N, it is possible to update odd-numbered and then even-numbered diagonals in parallel and obtain greater use of parallelism.

7.4.3 The Effects of Scheduling on Parallelism

The last topic we consider in this section is from Cytron [1984], who considered the effects of scheduling on parallelism. The idea is to schedule dependent tasks so that dependences are satisfied, and yet tasks are executed at least partially in parallel.

As an example of the use of scheduling, consider any loop body in which there is a WRITE/READ dependence from one iteration to a later iteration. A typical loop of this type has statements of the form

$$A[i] := B[i - 1]$$
$$B[i] := C[i];$$

In this example, Iteration i cannot begin until the prior iteration has written the value of $B[i - 1]$. If these two statements form the entire iteration, then Iteration i cannot start until Iteration $i - 1$ has ended. This is how we expect iterations to execute when dependences are discovered. But Cytron points out that lengthy iterations can be partially overlapped.

In our example, the 2 statements could be the first of 20 statements, rather than the only statements in the iteration. If so, and if no other dependences exist from iteration to iteration, then Iteration i can begin while Iteration $i - 1$ is executing, provided that Iteration i waits until $B[i - 1]$ has been computed.

The overlapping of iterations is analogous to pipelined execution of vector operations, except that the operations within one iteration can be arbitrarily complex, and the delay between initiations of successive iterations has to be long enough to satisfy the dependence constraint.

A compiler that exploits this form of parallelism has to be able to control execution-time scheduling in some way. In the compiled code it can produce an interrupt, message, or other form of control information at the point that a dependence is satisfied. The control information should be transmitted to a scheduler or equivalent task to force the release of a task waiting for the update to complete. The added overhead of the control information has to be low enough to make concurrent execution worthwhile. There is no point in seeking concurrent operation if the control required is extensive enough to create its own bottleneck.

7.5 Final Comments on Multiprocessors

This brings us to the close of this chapter. We have only presented a small portion of the current state of multiprocessor architecture, but we believe that the highlights discussed in this chapter give an accurate picture of the potential and pitfalls of multiprocessors.

Problems of overhead and effective parallelism are serious problems, and they are likely to limit multiprocessors to relatively few processors in practical systems. The 1000-processor system can become a reality in years to come, but much research is necessary in the interim to solve problems related to efficiency. Exploitation of multiprocessors depends strongly on finding ways to:

- Eliminate the MSYPS bottleneck;
- Reduce overhead for scheduling tasks;
- Solve the cache-coherency problem or to find an alternate means of providing fast local memory;
- Map serial programs to parallel programs; and
- Identify useful parallelism, as opposed to parallelism that leads to wasted effort.

As progress is made on these fronts, the multiprocessor becomes more attractive and eventually could be the architecture of choice for high-performance systems.

In earlier chapters we discuss six technology constraints that have to be overcome in an architecture. Some of the constraints are included in the problems preceding list. Overall, the comparison is as follows:

1. *Processor bandwidth*: processor bandwidth is extremely satisfactory for the multiprocessor because each distinct processor in the architecture has the potential to supply the full processor bandwidth to a problem. This facet of the architecture is one of its strengths.

2. *Memory bandwidth*: available memory bandwidth depends strongly on the mechanism for multiple accesses to memory. If no memory is shared, gross bandwidth is very high since it is N times the bandwidth of a single processor. But effective bandwidth is lower because access to remote memories requires passing messages between one or more intermediate nodes.

   If shared memory is available, the bandwidth depends strongly on the implementation of shared access. A variety of implementations, ranging from a shared bus to a full crossbar, provide a spectrum of performance and cost for the architect to consider. The bus is best suited to systems with few processors, and the shuffle-exchange network, or other similar multilayer interconnection, is an attractive mechanism to use for larger systems because it offers increased performance over the shared bus at a cost that is likely to be commensurate with the performance improvement.

   Cache is potentially useful for multiprocessors with a small number of processors. As the number grows to 8, 16, 32, and larger, the cache-coherence problem becomes difficult to solve at reasonable cost. Consequently, caches are likely to be limited in their use to local variables and instructions or in other ways that eliminate the problem of maintaining consistency. Accesses to uncacheable items tend to occupy a disproportionate fraction of memory bandwidth of shared memory and are one of the limiting factors in performance.

   Bandwidth is also limited by "hot spots," regions of memory that receive more than their share of accesses. A combining switch reduces the effect of hot spots by reducing the physical data traffic required for concurrent accesses to shared data. Whether or not the combining switch is a cost-effective means for dealing with hot spots is still a matter of intense research, and the outcome of that study may have a profound impact on the future of multiprocessors with hundreds of processors.

3. *Input/output bandwidth*: the multiprocessor provides input/output bandwidth that grows proportionally to the number of processors. To tap the full bandwidth potential, it may be necessary to store data externally in

unusual ways. One individual file should be partitioned into multiple segments that can be accessed concurrently by multiple processors, one processor per segment. In general, the multiprocessor offers excellent input/output bandwidth, provided that each processor has independent input/output capability.

4. *Communication bandwidth*: communication bandwidth available within a multiprocessor is strictly a function of the interconnection structure. Bandwidth available through ring and bus interconnections is low in cost, but suitable for systems with up to only 8 or 16 processors. As the number of processors increases above this amount, contention at the communications network tends to degrade performance. To support hundreds or thousands of processors requires a more sophisticated interconnection structure to tie processors to the memory system and to each other.

5. *Synchronization*: multiprocessors without combining networks or the equivalent have a maximum MSYPS rate that is independent of the number of processors, and therefore the maximum sustainable MSYPS rate becomes a serious bottleneck for systems with a moderate to large number of processors.

   The combining switch or the synchronization bus may provide a means for the maximum sustainable MSYPS rate to increase proportionally with the number of processors in a system. The synchronization bus is more attractive because of its lower cost. However, research is still in progress to determine if either or both solutions are cost-effective and practical to implement.

6. *Multiple purpose*: the most versatile parallel processors are multiprocessors because each processor can operate independently of all other processors if this behavior is desirable and all constraints can be satisfied.

This list shows the strengths and weaknesses of multiprocessors. The strengths for multiprocessors are high processing and input/output bandwidths and great flexibility. The weaknesses are synchronization limitations, memory bandwidth, and communication bandwidth. These three areas provide a great challenge for the computer architect because, in an era of fast technological change, new approaches become feasible almost overnight, and old approaches become obsolete as quickly.

Multiprocessors are not as well understood as are vector processors, mainly because their development lagged behind the development of vector processors by more than a decade. In speculating about the future of multiprocessors, we expect to see many systems with a small number of processors. Whether or not the 1000-processor system becomes widely used is only conjectural today and depends strongly on how well new technology can be adapted to the needs of multiprocessors.

Exercises

7.1   The inner loop of an iteration has the following form:

$$A[i] := B[i];$$
$$C[i] := A[i] + B[i - 1];$$
$$D[i] := A[i + 1];$$

  a) Find the precedence constraints among three successive iterations of this loop. Which statements depend directly on which statements? Are the individual iterations executable in parallel?

  b) Let the middle equation be changed so that $B[i - 1]$ becomes $B[i]$. Repeat a.

  c) Let the middle equation be changed so that $B[i - 1]$ becomes $B[i + 1]$. Repeat a.

7.2   The inner loop of a program is the following:

$$A[i, j] := A[i + 1, j - 1];$$

  a) Let this statement be nested within two loops, the outer loop on i and the inner loop on j. Give an example of loop-control statements that permit the iterations on j to be chunked together and the iterations on i to be independent processes that can be executed in parallel.

  b) Give an example of loop-control statements that do not permit independent execution of iterations on j that are chunked together.

7.3   The purpose of this exercise is to explore architectural support for the **do par** phrase. Consider a **do par** loop that is to be repeated N times.

  a) Assume a multiprocessor that has access to shared and local memory. Before the **do par** is reached, all program instructions and data are resident in shared memory. Assume that the iterations are truly independent in that there are no READ/WRITE, WRITE/WRITE, or WRITE/READ conflicts. Show a scheme for initializing the iterations so that each iteration can execute concurrently with other iterations, and one copy of the program in shared memory is used for all iterations. Let the index variable for the loop be i and assume that the loop references vector elements $A[i]$ and $B[i]$. To achieve maximum performance, how do you decide whether a datum should be moved to local memory or left in global memory during a loop iteration?

  b) The process of initializing and initiating loop iterations can be done sequentially in $O(N)$ time or in parallel in $O(\log N)$ time. Write a brief program suitable for execution in a multiprocessor computer that is capable of initiating 128 iterations of a **do par** loop and has a complexity of $O(\log N)$. Assume the shared and local memory structure used in a, and assume that the processes can be initiated immediately and need not be queued while waiting for a processor to become available.

  c) Devise some architectural support for the process of b to simplify its programming. The support should consist of one or more machine instructions specific to this process. Describe each instruction and the operands that it requires.

Describe any other facilities in a multiprocessor architecture required by these instructions to facilitate the initiation process.

7.4 Exercise 7.3 ignores the problem of queueing tasks if processors are unavailable. Assume an $O(\log N)$ task-generation process and consider how to implement task queueing if no processors are available.

a) Assume that the multiprocessor shared memory is accessed via a crossbar switch and that pending tasks are queued on a single-task queue. Develop a performance model that estimates the cost of task queueing and dequeueing under the condition that the number of iterations to run concurrently is twice the number of available processors. How does this change when the number of iterations to run is 1024 times the number of available processors?

b) What specialized instructions for task queueing can assist the process in *a*? Describe what each such instruction does and the operands that it requires. To demonstrate their use, show a program fragment for task queueing that uses these instructions. Include a mechanism for determining whether or not a task has to be queued.

c) Consider an architecture that supports Fetch-and-Add. Repeat *a*.

7.5 The purpose of this exercise is to consider the implementation of the **Barrier** operation. Assume a multiprocessor with shared memory accessed by means of a crossbar switch.

a) Show a sequence of machine instructions that implements the **Barrier** operation. Estimate the machine performance of your code when N processors attempt to execute the code concurrently. Describe why your code works correctly in a concurrent-execution environment.

b) Repeat *a* for a multiprocessor based on a bus interconnection.

c) Repeat *a* for a multiprocessor based on an interconnection network that supports Fetch-and-Add.

7.6 The purpose of this exercise is to compare different synchronization techniques. The objective of the exercise is to create a circular buffer of length N. There are two subroutines, *Put* and *Get*, that control input and output to the buffer. The implementation has to be free of deadlock and livelock.

a) Show an implementation of *Put* and *Get* that uses Test-and-Set for synchronization. Use a high-level language plus Test-and-Set to describe your implementation.

b) Repeat *a* using Increment and Decrement instead of Test-and-Set.

c) Repeat *a* using Compare-and-Swap instead of Test-and-Set.

d) Repeat *a* using Fetch-and-Add instead of Test-and-Set.

7.7 The purpose of this exercise is to explore the use of Compare-and-Swap on linked-list implementations of queues.

a) Consider a queue implemented as a linked list with *Head* and *Tail* pointers as described in the body of the chapter. Assume that DEQUEUEs cannot run concurrently with ENQUEUEs and that as many as N ENQUEUEs can run concurrently. Give an implementation of ENQUEUE with Compare-and-

    Swap that works correctly under these conditions, including the ability to add an item to an empty queue.

   b) Construct an implementation of DEQUEUE with Compare-and-Swap. How does your implementation handle the special case in which DEQUEUE produces an empty queue? Does your implementation work correctly if run concurrently with ENQUEUE from the first part?

7.8   The purpose of this exercise is to take the reader through the details of a complete and correct implementation of Compare-and-Swap.

   a) Examine the skeleton of ENQUEUE as shown in Program 7.9. Note that part of the program is missing. The program does not specify what happens when it tries to place a new value in a link field and discovers that the link field has changed to nonzero. Study this carefully and write a corresponding DE-QUEUE program. In your DEQUEUE program you should remove an item from the queue by copying the item in its link field to the *Head* pointer. Note that the instant the *Head* pointer is updated with a 0 value marks an instant in which the ENQUEUE must alter the outcome of its test on the value of *Head*. Your program should install a new link value in a link field of the item deleted that takes on a special value that signifies "Deleted." You should consider writing the DEQUEUE program in either of two ways—one way that modifies the *Head* pointer and then modifies the link field with the "Deleted" value, and the other way that reverses the order.

   b) In your DEQUEUE program insert the code that tests for an empty queue, and attempt to set *Tail* to 0 to indicate this condition. Before *Tail* is set to 0, what is the value that should be in this variable if no ENQUEUEs are active? If any ENQUEUES are active, what should be the action of DEQUEUE?

   c) Now consider the missing code from Program 7.9 for ENQUEUE. When EN-QUEUE discovers that a link with a nonzero value that expects to have the value 0, under what condition can this happen? In that case, what code should be executed for ENQUEUE to exit correctly?

   d) In either your ENQUEUE or DEQUEUE programs, you may have written a loop that repeatedly tests some variable waiting for another program to alter it. Although this is correct in a technical sense, it is not necessarily a preferred solution. Examine any such loop you have written and determine what function has to be performed after the loop that cannot be performed until the second program takes some action. If the looping program were to exit immediately, the function could be performed instead by the program whose unfinished execution caused the loop to occur. Find a means to eliminate the loop by moving the function to be performed after the loop from one program to another.

   e) Reexamine the Compare-and-Swaps in your program. Some or all of them may have to be double Compare-and-Swaps in which one of two items is a counter, as shown in Program 7.9, in order to detect the occurrence of a sequence of events that leaves *Head* or *Tail* or some other variable in a final state that is the same as the initial state. Determine which Compare-and-Swaps must be double (shared variable and a counter variable) and which can be single (no counter variable).

7.9   The purpose of this exercise is to investigate the performance of Dijkstra's shortest path algorithm [1959] on various multiprocessors. The objective is to find the length of the shortest path from Node 1 to Node x for an arbitrarily specified node x in a graph. Dijktra's algorithm accepts as input N^2 point-to-point distances among N nodes. Let the distances be given in the matrix $D[i, j]$. The matrix is symmetric and all entries are nonnegative. The algorithm is a node-labeling algorithm in which nodes are initially given temporary labels that give an upper bound on the shortest path to each node. At the end of each major iteration, some temporary label becomes permanent and never changes again in the course of the algorithm. Eventually all labels are made permanent, at which point the algorithm has found the length of the shortest path from Node 1 to any other node in the graph. Labels are held in the array L.

Write a parallel code for the following algorithm and find its complexity.

a) Give Node 1 the permanent label 0, that is, set $L[1]$ to 0.

b) Label Nodes 2 through N with temporary labels such that $L[i]$, the label for Node i, receives the value $D[1, i]$. (The distance to Node i is not greater than $D[1, i]$.)

c) Among the temporary labels, find the node with the smallest label, breaking ties arbitrarily. Let this be Node j. Make this label permanent.

d) For each node with a temporary label, such as Node k, change its label to $L[j] + D[j, k]$ if that is less than its current label. (The shortest path to Node j, followed by the direct path from Node j to Node k, is shorter than the best path to Node k found thus far.)

7.10 *QuickSort* is a very fast sorting algorithm that can be described succinctly by the following Pascal-like program.

```
Procedure QuickSort(Low: integer,High: integer,var A array of real);
{* Sort the array A for the range starting at Low and ending at High *}
begin
    var Pivot: integer;
    procedure Partition(Low,High,A,Pivot);
    {* Partition guesses the median of the numbers in the array between Low
       and High, then moves data around in the array so that A[Pivot]
       contains its guess for the median, and the indices between Low and
       Pivot – 1 contain smaller values than A[Pivot], and the indices be-
       tween Pivot + 1 and High contain larger values than A[Pivot]. *}
    begin
        . . .
    end; {* of Partition *}
    if Pivot – Low > 1 then QuickSort(Low,Pivot – 1,A);
    if High – Pivot > 1 then QuickSort(Pivot + 1,High,A);
end;
```

We wish to run this program on a multiprocessor.

a) Modify the algorithm in some fashion to exploit multiprocessing. Use a high-level language to describe your multiprocessing version of the algorithm, and explain in English how your algorithm functions.

b) Describe the architecture of a multiprocessor that executes your algorithm. If your architecture passes messages among processors when a parallel procedure is invoked, indicate how much information is passed for a call on *QuickSort*. If your processor has a shared memory, describe how many references occur to shared memory at the point of calling a parallel procedure, and count these references for the case of a call to *QuickSort*.

c) Hand simulate the execution of *QuickSort* on your architecture for a small example. In this example, what are the bottlenecks for a multiprocessor implementation?

d) Assume that *Partition* fortuitously always finds the median in its assigned region of an array, and that it does so in time proportional to the size of that portion of the array. Then what is the asymptotic complexity of the *QuickSort* problem on your architecture. Show your derivation.

7.11 The intent of this question is to explore the effectiveness of parallel search in an AND/OR search tree.

a) Consider a very simple OR search tree that consists of M alternatives, any one of which might lead to a satisfactory solution for a search. Assume that each alternative has a probability p of being satisfactory, and q for being unsatisfactory, and the alternatives are independent. A serial search of this tree completes the exploration of one alternative during a single step, and halts when the first success is discovered or when all alternatives are exhausted.

If N processors are used to search the tree in parallel, they take a single step to search N of the possible alternatives, assuming that $N \le M$. What is the speedup for $p = 0.1$? For $p = 0.9$? Why is the speedup dependent on p? Give an intuitive explanation for your answer.

b) Repeat the first part for a similar tree whose root node is an AND node instead of an OR node. That is, the tree search is successful only if all alternatives succeed, otherwise it is unsuccessful. A serial search terminates when the first unsuccessful alternative is found, or if the entire tree is searched and all alternatives are successful.

c) Consider a two-level tree whose root node is a two-alternative AND node and whose nodes at the next level are two-alternative OR nodes. Let p be the probability of success of an OR-node alternative. For small values of p, what is the potential speedup of a parallel search and how do you schedule processors to achieve this speedup? For large values of p, what is the potential speedup, and how do you schedule processors to achieve this speedup?

d) Finally, consider multilevel trees, with all nodes having two successors, and with nodes at successive levels alternating between OR nodes and AND nodes. (The top node is an AND node; its offspring are OR nodes; their offspring are AND nodes, ...). If the tree has M levels, each node with two offspring, then the number of leaf nodes is 2^M. The potential parallelism thus is 2^M. If p is the probability of success of a leaf node, show that the best possible parallelism is $O(\sqrt{M})$ for large and small p. What happens for p that near the center of the range?

References

Agarwal, A., J. Hennessy, and M. Horowitz. "An analytical cache model." *ACM Transactions on Computer Systems*, **7**, no. 2, 184–215, May 1989.

Agerwala, T., and J. Cocke. "High performance reduced instruction set processors." IBM Research Division Report RC 12434, March 31, 1987.

Aho, A. V, J. E. Hopcroft, and J. D. Ullman. *The Design and Analysis of Computer Algorithms*. Reading, Mass.: Addison-Wesley, 1974.

Allen, J. R. *Dependence Analysis for Subscripted Variables and its Application to Program Transformation*. Ph.D. thesis, Rice University, 1983.

Allen, J. R., K. Kennedy, C. Porterfield, and J. Warren. "Conversion of control dependence to data dependence." *Conference Record of the Tenth Annual ACM Symposium on Principles of Programming Languages*, Austin, Tex., January 1983.

Amdahl, G. M., G. A. Blaauw, and F. P. Brooks, Jr. "Architecture of the IBM System/360." *IBM Journal of Research and Development*, **8**, no. 2, 87–101, April 1964.

Archibald, J., and J.-L. Baer. "Cache coherence protocols: Evaluation using a multiprocessor simulation model." *ACM Transaction on Computers*, **4**, no. 4, 273–298, November 1986.

Baer, J.-L. *Computer Systems Architecture*. Potomac, Md.: Computer Science Press, 1980.

Batcher, K. E. "Sorting networks and their applications." *AFIPS Conference Proceedings, 1968 SJCC*, **32**, Washington, D.C.: Thompson Books, 307–314, 1968.

Beetem, J., M. Denneau, and D. Weingarten. "The GF-11 supercomputer." *Proceedings of the 1985 International Conference on Parallel Processing*. IEEE Cat. No. 85CH2140-2, 108–115, August 1985.

Belady, L. "A study of replacement algorithms for a virtual-store computer." *IBM Systems Journal*, **5**, no. 2, 78–101, 1966.

Bell, C. G., and A. Newell. *Computer Structures: Readings and Examples*, New York: McGraw-Hill, 1971.

Benes, V. "Optimal rearrangeable multistage connecting networks." *Bell System Technical Journal*, **43**, no. 4, 1641–1656, July 1964.

Booth, A. D. "A signed binary multiplication technique." *Quarterly Journal of Mech. Appl. Math.*, **4**, part 2, 1951.

Boral, H., and D. J. DeWitt. "Database machines: An idea whose time has passed? A critique of the future of database machines." In *Database Machines*, edited by H. O. Leilich and M. Missikoff, Berlin: Springer Verlag, 166–187, 1983.

Brunk, H. D. *An Introduction to Mathematical Statistics*, Boston: Ginn and Co., 1960.

Budnik, P. P., and D. J. Kuck. "The organization and use of parallel memories." *IEEE Transactions on Computers*, **C-20**, no. 12, 1566–1569, 1971.

Burks, A. W., H. H. Goldstine, and J. von Neumann. "Preliminary discussion of the logical design of an electronic computing instrument." *U. S. Army Ordnance Department Report*, 1946. Reprinted in Bell and Newell [1971], 92–119.

Buzbee, B. L., G. H. Golub, and C. W. Nielson. "On direct methods for solving Poisson's equation." *SIAM Journal of Numerical Analysis*, **7**, 627–656, 1970.

Charlesworth, A. E., and J. L. Gustafson. "Introducing replicated VLSI to supercomputing: the FPS-164/MAX scientific computer." *Computer*, **19**, no. 3, 10–23, March 1986.

Chen, P. Y., D. H. Lawrie, P. C. Yew, and D. A. Padua. "Interconnection networks using shuffles." *Computer*, **14**, no. 12, 55–64, December 1981.

Chen, T. C. "Overlap and pipeline processing." Chapter 9 of *Introduction to Computer Architecture*, edited by H. Stone, Chicago: Science Research Assoc., 427–486, 1980.

Chu, W. W., and H. Opderbeck. "Program behavior and the page-fault-frequency replacement algorithm." *Computer*, **9**, no. 11, 29–38, November 1976.

Clark, D. W, and J. S. Emer. "Performance of the VAX-11/780 translation buffer: simulation and measurement." *ACM Transactions on Computer Systems*, **3**, no. 1, 31–62, February 1985.

Coffman, E. G., Jr. and P. J. Denning. *Operating Systems Theory*. Englewood Cliffs, N.J.: Prentice-Hall, 1973.

Colwell, R. P., *et al.* "Computers, complexity, and controversy." *Computer*, **18**, no. 9, 8–19, September 1985.

Cooley, J. W., and J. W. Tukey. "An algorithm for the machine calculation of complex Fourier series." *Mathematics of Computation*, **19**, 297–301, April 1965.

Coonen, J. T. "An implementation guide to a proposed standard for floating-point arithmetic." *Computer*, **13**, no. 1., 68–79, January 1980.

Crowther, W., *et al.* "Performance measurements on a 128-node butterfly parallel processor." *Proceedings of the 1985 International Conference on Parallel Processing*. IEEE Cat. No. 85CH2140-2, 531–540, August 1985.

Cvetanovic, Z. *Performance Analysis of Multiple-Processor Systems.* Ph.D. thesis, ECE Department, University of Massachusetts, 1985.

Cvetanovic, Z. "Performance analysis of the FFT algorithm on a shared-memory parallel architecture." *IBM Journal of Research and Development,* **31,** no. 4, 435–451, July 1987.

Cytron, R. G. *Compile-Time Scheduling and Optimization for Asynchronous Machines.* Ph.D thesis, Univ. of Illinois, 1984.

Davidson, E. S. "The design and control of pipelined function generators." *Proceedings of the 1971 International Conference on Systems, Networks, and Computers.* Oaxtepec, Mexico, 19–21, January 1971.

Denning, P. J. [1968a]. "Thrashing: Its causes and prevention." *AFIPS Conference Proceedings, 1968 FJCC,* **33,** Washington, D.C.: Thompson Books, 915–922, 1968.

Denning, P. J. [1968b]. "The working-set model for program behavior." *Communications of the ACM,* **11,** no. 5, 323–333, May 1968.

Denning, P. J., J. E. Savage, and J. R. Spirn. "Models for locality in program behavior." Department of Electrical Engineering, Princeton Univ., Princeton, New Jersey Computer Science Report TR-107, April 1972.

Dias, D. M., and J. R. Jump. "Packet switching interconnection networks for modular systems." *Computer,* **14,** no. 12, 43–54, December 1981.

Dijkstra, E. W. "A note on two problems in connexion with graphs." *Numerishce Mathematik,* **1,** 269–271, 1959.

Dijkstra, E. W. "Solution of a problem in concurrent programming." *Communications of the ACM,* **8,** 569–570, September 1965.

Ditzel, D. R., and H. R. McLellan, "Branch folding in the CRISP microprocessor: Reducing branch delay to zero." *Proceedings of the 14th International Symposium on Computer Architecture.* IEEE Cat No. 87CH2420-8, Pittsburgh, Pa., 2–9, June 1987.

Dubois, M., and F. A. Briggs. "Effects of cache coherency in multiprocessor systems." *IEEE Transactions on Computers,* **C-31,** no. 11, 1083–99, November 1982.

Eckhouse, R. H., Jr., and H. M. Levy. *Computer Programming and Architecture: The VAX-11,* Bedford, Mass.: Digital Press, 1980.

Eggers, S. J., and R. H. Katz. "Evaluating the performance of four snooping cache coherency protocols." *Proceedings of the 16th International Symposium on Computer Architecture.* IEEE Catalog Number 89CH2705-2, 2–15, June 1989.

Flynn, M. J. "Very high-speed computers." *Proceedings of the IEEE,* **54,** 1901–1909, December 1966.

Ford, L. R., Jr., and D. R. Fulkerson. "Maximal flow through a network." *Canadian Journal of Mathematics,* **8,** 399–404, 1956.

Forsythe, G., and C. B. Moler. *Computer Solution of Linear Algebraic Systems.* Englewood Cliffs, N.J.: Prentice-Hall, 1967.

Fox, G., *et al. Solving Problems on Concurrent Processors, Vol. 1, General Techniques and Regular Problems.* Englewood Cliffs, N.J.: Prentice-Hall, 1988.

Goodman, J. "Using cache memory to reduce processor-memory traffic." *Proceedings of the 10th International Symposium on Computer Architecture*. Stockholm, Sweden, 124–131, June 1983.

Gottlieb, A., *et al.* "The NYU Ultracomputer–Designing an MIMD shared-memory parallel computer." *IEEE Transactions on Computers*, **C-32**, no. 2, 175–189, February 1983.

Green, P. E., Jr., and H. S. Stone. "The implementation of a barrier for multiprocessors by means of an optical bus." IBM Research, Technical Disclosure YO888-00018, 9 January 1989, to appear in *IBM Technical Disclosure Bulletin*.

Halstead, R. "Multilisp: An overview and working example." *ACM Transactions on Programming Languages and Systems*, **7**, no. 4, 501–538, October 1985.

Hayes, J. P. *Computer Architecture and Organization*. New York: McGraw-Hill, 1978.

Heidelberger, P., B. D. Rathi, and H. S. Stone. "A low-cost device for contention-free barrier synchronization." IBM Research, Technical Disclosure YO888-0218, 16 March 1988, to appear in *IBM Technical Disclosure Bulletin*.

Heidelberger, P., B. D. Rathi, and H. S. Stone. "A device for performing efficient task-distribution with a bus connection." IBM Research, Technical Disclosure YO889-0053, 20 January 1989, to appear in *IBM Technical Disclosure Bulletin*.

Heller, D. E. "Some aspects of the cyclic reduction algorithm for block tridiagonal linear systems." *SIAM Journal of Numerical Analysis*, **13**, 484–496, 1976.

Heller, D. E. "A survey of parallel algorithms in numerical linear algebra." *SIAM Review*, **20**, no. 4, 740–777, 1978.

Hill, M., *et al.* "Design decisions in SPUR." *Computer*, **19**, no. 11, 8–22, November 1986.

Hill, M., and A. Smith, "Evaluating associativity in CPU Caches." Tech. Rpt. #823, Computer Science Dept., Univ. of Wisconsin, February 1989.

Hillis, W. D. *The Connection Machine*. Cambridge, Mass.: MIT Press, 1986.

Hillis, W. D., and G. L. Steele, Jr. "Data parallel algorithms." *Communications of the ACM*, **29**, no. 12, 1170–1184, December 1986.

Hoshino, T. "Invitation to the world of 'Pax'." *Computer*, **19**, no. 5, 68–79, May 1986.

Hoshino, T. *PAX Computer: High-Speed Parallel Processing and Scientific Computing*. Reading, Mass.: Addison-Wesley, 1989.

Hwang, K., *Computer Arithmetic: Principles, Architecture and Design*. New York: Wiley, 1978.

Hwang, K., and F. A. Briggs. *Computer Architecture and Parallel Processing*. New York: McGraw-Hill, 1984.

IBM System/370 Principles of Operation, GA22-7000-9, File No. S370-01, Tenth Edition, 1983.

IEEE. *IEEE Standard 754–1985 for Binary Floating-Point Arithmetic*. Order No. CN953, 1985.

Indurkhya, B., H. S. Stone, and L. Xi-Cheng. "Optimal partitioning of randomly generated distributed programs." *IEEE Transactions on Software Engineering*, **SE-12**, no. 3, 483–495, March 1986.

Karp, R. M., and W. L. Miranker. "Parallel minimax search for a maximum." *Journal of Combinatorial Theory*, **4**, no. 1, 19–39, 1968.

Kilburn, T. D., R. B. Payne, and D. J. Howarth. "One-level storage system." *IRE Transactions on Electronic Computers*, **EC-11**, no. 2, 223–235, April 1962.

Kobayashi, M., and M. H. MacDougall. "The stack growth function: cache line reference models." *IEEE Transactions on Computers*, **C-38**, no. 6, 798–804, June, 1989.

Kogge, P. M. *The Architecture of Pipelined Computers*. New York: McGraw-Hill, 1981.

Kogge, P. M., and H. S. Stone. "A parallel algorithm for the efficient solution of a general class of recurrence equations." *IEEE Transactions on Computers*, **C-22**, 786–93, 1973.

Kruskal, C. P., and M. Snir. "The performance of multistage interconnection networks for multiprocessors." *IEEE Transactions on Computers*, **C-32**, 1091–1098, December 1983.

Kuck, D. J. "Parallel processing in ordinary programs." In *Advances in Computers*, **15**, edited by Rubinoff and Yovits, New York: Academic Press, 119–179, 1976.

Kuck, D. J., R. H. Kuhn, B. Leasure, and M. Wolf. "The structure of an advanced vectorizer for pipelined programs." In *Tutorial on Supercomputers: Designs and Applications*, edited by K. Hwang, New York: IEEE Press EH0219-6, 163–178, 1984.

Kuck, D. J., Y. Muraoka, and S.-C. Chen. "On the number of operations simultaneously executable in FORTRAN-like programs and their resulting speedup." *IEEE Transactions on Computers*, **C-21**, no. 12, 1293–1310, December 1972.

Kung, H. T., and C. E. Leiserson. "Systolic arrays (for VLSI)." In *1978 Symposium on Sparse Matrix Computations and Their Applications*, edited by I. S. Duff and G. W. Stewart, 48–53, 1978.

Laha, S., J. H. Patel, and R. K. Iyer. "Accurate low-cost methods for performance evaluation of cache memory systems." *IEEE Transactions on Computers*, **C-37**, no. 11, 1325–1336, November 1988.

Lamport, L. "The parallel execution of DO loops." *Communications of the ACM*, **17**, no. 2, 83–93, February 1974.

Lawler, E. L. *Combinatorial Optimization: Networks and Matroids*. New York: Holt, Rinehart, and Winston, 1976.

Lawrie, D. H. "Access and alignment of data in an array processor." *IEEE Transactions on Computers*, **C-24**, 496–503, December 1975.

Losq, J. J., G. S. Rao, and H. E. Sachar. "Decode history table for conditional branch instructions." U. S. Patent No. 4,477,872, October 1984.

Mashburn, H. H. "The C.mmp/Hydra project: an architectural overview." Chapter 22 of *Computer Structures: Principles and Examples*. D. P. Siewiorek, C. G. Bell, and A. Newell, New York: McGraw-Hill, 350–370, 1982.

Mattson, R. L., J. Gecsei, D. R. Slutz, and I. L. Traiger. "Evaluation techniques for storage hierarchies." *IBM Systems Journal*, **9**, 78–117, 1970.

Mead C., and L. Conway. *Introduction to VLSI Systems*. Reading, Mass.: Addison-Wesley, 1980.

Miura, K. "Vectorization of phase space Monte Carlo code in FACOM vector processor VP-200." *Proceedings of the 1985 Conference on Computing in High Energy Physics*, edited by L. O. Hertzberger and W. Hoogland, Amsterdam: North-Holland, Elsevier, 401–408, 1986.

Nicol, D. M. "Optimum partitioning of random-programs across two processors." *IEEE Transactions on Software Engineering*, **SE-15**, no. 2, 134–141, February 1989.

Organick, E. I. *The Multics System: An Examination of Its Structure*. Cambridge, Mass.: MIT Press, 1972.

Organick, E. I. *Computer System Organization: the B5700/B6700 Series*. New York: Academic Press, 1973.

Padmanabhan, K., and D. H. Lawrie. "Performance analysis of redundant-path networks for multiprocessor systems." *ACM Transactions on Computer Systems*, **3**, no. 2, 117–144, May 1985.

Padua, D. A., and M. J. Wolfe. "Advanced compiler optimizations for supercomputers." *Communications of the ACM*, **29**, no. 12, 1184–1201, December 1986.

Patel, J. H., and E. S. Davidson. "Improving the throughput of a pipeline by insertion of delays." *Proceedings of the Third Annual Computer Architecture Symposium*. IEEE No. 76CH 0143-5C, 159–163, 1976.

Patterson, D. A., and C. H. Sequin, "A VLSI RISC." *Computer*, **15** no. 9, 8–21, September 1982.

Pease, M. C. "An adaptation of the fast Fourier transform for parallel processing." *Journal of the ACM*, **15**, 252–264, 1968.

Pfister, G., *et al.* "The IBM Research Parallel Prototype (RP3): Introduction and architecture." *Proceedings of the 1985 International Conference on Parallel Processing*. IEEE Cat. No. 85CH2140-2, 764–771, August 1985.

Pfister, G., and V. A. Norton. "'Hot Spot' contention and combining in multistage interconnection networks." *Proceedings of the 1985 International Conference on Parallel Processing*. IEEE Cat. No. 85CH2140-2, 790–795, August 1985.

Pomerene, J., T. R. Puzak, R. Rechtschaffen, and F. Sparacio. "Prefetching mechanism for a high-speed buffer store." Patent Pending, 1984.

Preparata, F., and J. Vuillemin. "The cube-connected cycles: A versatile network for parallel computation." *Communications of the ACM*, **25**, 300–309, 1981.

Puzak, T. R. *Cache-Memory Design*. Ph.D. thesis, ECE Department, University of Massachusetts, 1985.

Radin, G. "The 801 minicomputer." *Proceedings of the Symposium for Programming Languages and Operating Systems Support*, 39–47, 1982.

Salton, G., and C. Buckley. "Parallel text search methods." *Communications of the ACM*, **31**, no. 2, 202–215, February 1988.

Seitz, C. L. "The Cosmic Cube." *Communications of the ACM*, **28**, no. 1, 22–33, January 1985.

Shar, L. E., and E. S. Davidson. "A multiminiprocessor system implemented through pipelining." *Computer*, **7**, no. 2, 42–51, February 1974.

Shemer, J. E., and S. C. Gupta. "On the design of Bayesian storage allocation algorithms for paging and segmentation." *IEEE Transactions on Computers*, **C-18**, no. 7, 644–651, July 1969.

Shemer, J. E., and B. Shippey. "Statistical analysis of paged and segmented computer systems." *IEEE Transactions on Electronic Computers*, **EC-15**, no. 6, 855–863, December 1966.

Siewiorek, D. P., C. G. Bell, and A. Newell. *Computer Structures: Principles and Examples.* New York: McGraw-Hill, 1982.

Singh, J. P., H. S. Stone, and D. F. Thiebaut, "An analytical model for fully associative cache memories." IBM Research Division Report RC-14232, 30 November 1988.

Singleton, R. C. "On computing the fast Fourier transform." *Communications of the ACM*, **10**, 647–654, 1967.

Sites, R. "Operating systems and computer architecture." Chapter 12 of *Introduction to Computer Architecture*, 2nd ed., edited by H. S. Stone, Chicago: Science Research Associates, 1980.

Slotnick, D. L., W. C. Borck, and R. C. McReynolds. "The SOLOMON computer." *AFIPS 1962 Fall Joint Computer Conference*, **22**, Washington, D.C.: Spartan books, 97–107, 1962.

Smith, A. "Cache memories." *ACM Computing Surveys*, **14**, no. 3, 473–530, September 1982.

Smith, A. "Cache evaluation and the impact of workload choice." *Proceedings of the 12th Annual Computer Architecture Symposium*, IEEE No. 85CH2 144–4, 64–75, June 1985.

Smith, A. "Line (block) size choice for CPU cache memories." *IEEE Transactions on Computers*, **C-36**, no. 9, 1063–1075, September 1987.

Smith, D. R. "Random trees and the analysis of branch and bound procedures." *Journal of the ACM*, **31**, no. 1, 163–188, January 1984.

Smith, J. E., and J. R. Goodman. "Instruction cache replacement policies and organizations." *IEEE Transactions on Computers*, **C-34**, no. 3, 234–241, March 1985.

Sohi, G. S., J. E. Smith, and J. R. Goodman. "Restricted Fetch & Φ Operations for parallel processing." *Proceedings of the 3rd International Conference on Supercomputing*, Crete, Greece, 410–416, June, 1989.

Sterbenz, P. H. *Floating-Point Computation.* Englewood Cliffs, N.J.: Prentice-Hall, 1974.

Stanfill, C., and B. Kahle. "Parallel free-text search on the Connection Machine system." *Communications of the ACM*, **29**, no. 12, 1229–1239, December 1986.

Stone, H. S. "Parallel processing with the perfect shuffle." *IEEE Transactions on Computers*, **C-20**, 153–161, 1971.

Stone, H. S. "An efficient parallel algorithm for the solution of a tridiagonal linear system of equations." *Journal of the ACM*, **20**, 27–38, January 1973.

Stone, H. S. "Database applications of the Fetch-and-Add instruction." *IEEE Transactions on Computers*, **C-33**, no. 7, 604–612, July 1984.

Stone, H. S. "Parallel querying of large databases: A case study." *Computer,* **20,** no. 10, 11–21, October 1987.

Stone, H. S., ed. *Introduction to Computer Architecture* Chicago, Ill.: Science Research Associates, 1974.

Stone, H. S., ed. *Introduction to Computer Architecture.* Second ed. Chicago, Ill.: Science Research Associates, 1980.

Strecker, W. D. "Transient behavior of cache memories." *ACM Transactions on Computer Systems,* **1,** no. 4, 281–293, November 1983.

Sullivan, H., T. Bashkow, and D. Klappholtz. "A large-scale homogeneous fully distributed parallel machine." *Proceedings of the Fourth Annual Symposium on Computer Architecture,* 105–124, 1977.

Sussenguth, E. "Instruction sequence control." U. S. Patent No. 3,559,183, January 26, 1971.

Sweazey, P., and A. J. Smith. "A class of compatible cache-consistency protocols and their support by the IEEE Futurebus." *Proceedings of the 13th International Symposium on Computer Architecture.* Tokyo, Japan, 414–423, June 1986.

Tanenbaum, A. S. *Structured Computer Organization.* Englewood Cliffs, N.J.: Prentice Hall, 1976.

Thanawastien, S., and V. P. Nelson. "Interference analysis of shuffle/exchange networks." *IEEE Transactions on Computers.* **C-30,** 545–556, August 1981.

Thiebaut, D., and H. S. Stone. "Footprints in the cache." *ACM Transactions on Computer Systems,* **5,** no. 4, 305–329, November 1987.

Thiebaut, D. F. "On the fractal dimension of computer programs and its application to the prediction of the cache miss ratio." *IEEE Transactions on Computers,* **C-38,** no. 7, 1012–1026, July 1989.

Thompson, D. "Multi-device apparatus synchronized to the slowest device." U. S. Patent No. 4,493,053, January 8, 1985.

Thompson, J. G., and A. J. Smith. "Efficient (stack) algorithms for analysis of write-back and sector memories." *ACM Transactions on Computer Systems,* **7,** no. 1, 78–116, February 1989.

Thornton, J. E. *Design of a Computer: The Control Data 6600.* Glenview, Ill: Scott, Foresman, 1970.

Tomasulo, R. M. "An efficient algorithm for exploiting multiple arithmetic units." *IBM Journal of Research and Development.* **11,** no. 1, 25–33, January 1967.

Treiber, R. K. "Systems programming: Coping with parallelism." IBM Research Report RJ 5118, IBM T. J. Watson Research Center, April 1986.

Trivedi, K. S. *Probability and Statistics with Reliability, Queueing, and Computer Science Applications.* Englewood Cliffs, N.J.: Prentice-Hall, 1982.

Varga, R. S. *Matrix Iterative Analysis.* Englewood Cliffs, N.J.: Prentice-Hall, 1962.

Voldman, J., and L. W. Hoevel. "The software-cache connection." *IBM Journal of Research and Development,* **25,** no. 6, 877–893, November 1981.

Voldman, J., *et al.* "Fractal nature of software-cache interaction." *IBM Journal of Research and Development,* **27,** no. 2, 164–170, March 1983.

Wallace, C. C. "A suggestion for a fast multiplier." *IEEE Transactions on Electronic Computers,* **EC-13,** 14–17, 1964.

Wang, W.-H., and J.-L. Baer. "Efficient trace-driven simulation methods for cache performance analysis," TR-89-09-02, Dept. of Computer Science, University of Washington, September 1989.

Waser, S., and M. J. Flynn. *Introduction to Arithmetic for Digital Systems Designers.* New York: CBS College Publishing, 1982.

Wilkes, M. V. "Slave memories and dynamic storage allocation." *IEEE Transactions on Electronic Computers.* **EC-14,** no. 2, 270–271, 1965.

Yew, P.-C., D. A. Padua, and D. H. Lawrie. "Stochastic properties of a multiple-layer single-stage shuffle-exchange network in a message-switching environment." *Journal of Digital Systems,* **VI,** no. 4, 387–410, 1983.

Index and Glossary

Access A memory operation that is either a READ or a WRITE; 23

Access patterns The statistical behavior of a sequence of memory operations; 274–279

Access sequence The sequence of memory addresses produced during the execution of a program; 26–29

Action at a distance A physical force exerted at a point due to the influence of a remote source of the force; 222

Adder, 397–398

Address generation During the execution of an instruction, the cycle in which an effective address is calculated by means of indexing or indirect addressing; 125–127, 129

Address mapper The device that transforms a virtual address to a physical (real) address; 87–88, 91–99, 185–187
See also Virtual memory, mapping

Address-reference stream The sequence of memory addresses accessed during the execution of a program; 40–41
See also Address trace

Address trace A recorded sequence of the memory addresses visited during the execution of a program; 39–65, 114–116, 118

Agarwal, A., 48–49

Agerwala, T., 188

Aho, A. E., 410

ALGOL 60, 376

Algorithm (interaction with architecture), 17–19

Alignment network A network that selects a subset of items read simultaneously from memory and permutes them to permit them to be manipulated in parallel; 283–286

Allen, F., 418

Allen, J. R., 418, 420

ALU (Arithmetic-logic unit) The portion of a processor that performs arithmetic and logic operations on data; 189–190

Amdahl Corporation, 39, 187

Amdahl, G. M., 19–20

AND A boolean operation; 229, 397, 400, 432

Archibald, J., 355

Architecture. *See* Computer architecture

Arithmetic pipeline A multistage arithmetic unit that is capable of starting a new operation while one or more operations are currently in execution, with the time interval between successive outputs less than the total time required to produce a single output; 262–267

Array processor A parallel computer, usually with near-neighbor connections between processors and capable of executing a single stream of instructions broadcast simultaneously to all processors; 137–141

Artificial Intelligence The study of computational techniques for solving difficult

Artificial Intelligence (*continued*)
   problems for which human-like approaches are required in their solutions;
   12
Assignment problem   A combinatorial problem whose solution assigns N tasks to N
   workers such that each worker is
   assigned a single task and such that the
   sum of the values of the worker-task
   assignments is maximized; 412
Associative access   A memory access in
   which the access is made to an item
   whose key matches an access key as
   distinct from an access to an item at a
   specific address in memory; 32
   See also Set associative
Associative memory   A memory whose contents are accessed by key rather than by
   address; 32
Atlas computer, 25–26, 88
Attached vector-processor   A processor specialized for vector computations that is
   designed to be connected to a general-
   purpose host processor, which supplies
   input/output functions, a file system,
   and other aspects of a computing system
   environment, 287–292
Auxiliary memory   A bulk memory that is
   usually large, slow, and inexpensive, often a rotating magnetic or optical memory, whose main function is to store
   large volumes of data and programs that
   are not currently being accessed by a
   processor; 89–91, 103, 107–112

Baer, J. L., 20, 355
Balance (of a computer system's components)   A state in which the processor
   bandwidth matches closely the bandwidths of the memory, interconnection
   network, and input/output system so
   that no specific component strongly
   limits the system throughput; 369
Bandwidth   The number of bits per second
   that can be processed by a memory,
   arithmetic unit, input/output processor
   or communication system; 135–136, 183
   of combining switch, 397
   of communication system, 210, 216, 299,
      326–327, 341–342, 427
   of input/output system, 210, 216, 299,
      426–427
   of memory, 21–22, 201, 209–210, 270,
      216, 261, 281, 299, 426–427
   of processor, 201, 210, 216, 261, 298–299,
      426
   of synchronizer, 397, 399

Bank (of memory)   A module of memory
   that can sustain a single access to one
   physical cell of memory per memory
   cycle; 136
Barrier synchronization   A means for synchronizing a set of processors in a multiprocessor system by halting processors
   in that set at a specified barrier point in
   a program until every processor in the
   set reaches the barrier; 329, 338,
   365–366, 397–405, 423
Base address (of a page)   The physical address of the start of a page; 92–97
Batcher, K. E., 239, 249
BBN Butterfly, 251–252
Beetem, J., 295
Belady, L., 59, 102
Bell, C. G., 20
Benes, V., 295
Benes network   A switching network proposed by V. Benes that is capable of producing an arbitrary permutation of its
   inputs at its outputs; 295
Berkeley RISC, 192, 194
Bernoulli bound (on trace length), 45–47
Bernoulli process   A random process in
   which a random variable is selected
   with a probability of success p and a
   probability of failure $q = 1 - p$. Successive selections are independent of each
   other; 45–46, 69
Bidiagonal system of equations   A linear
   system in which the only nonzero coefficients lie on the major diagonal and on
   one diagonal immediately below or
   above the major diagonal; 232–233
Binary search   A search algorithm in which
   the region to be searched shrinks by half
   at each step; 407
Binomial distribution   The probability distribution that describes independent
   tosses of a fair coin; 69, 71
   See also Bernoulli process
Bitonic sequence   A sequence of numbers
   that is the concatenation of an ascending
   and a descending sequence, or is a cyclic
   shift of such a sequence; 249–251, 258
Bitonic sorter   A sorting network whose
   subnetworks sort bitonic subsequences
   into fully sorted subsequences; 249–251,
   258
Block (of a cache), 32
   See also Line
Bolt, Beranek, and Newman. *See* BBN
Booth, A. D., 196
Booth's algorithm   An efficient algorithm
   for integer multiplication; 196

Boral, H., 409

Bottleneck, 21, 122, 324, 329, 336, 341–346, 368–369, 372–373, 386, 393, 425

Branch-and-bound search A search technique in which the search eliminates large numbers of cases by determining that the solutions eliminated fall above a computed bound; 410–415

Branch-history table A hardware device that saves the recent history of conditional branches in order to use this information for branch prediction; 170, 173–175

Branch prediction The use of history, statistical methods, or heuristic rules to predict the outcome of conditional branches; 172–175, 191

Breakeven point The number of processors in a multiprocessor system whose combined throughput is equal to that of a single processor of the same power; 322

Briggs, F. A., 355, 387

Broadcast A form of communication in which one transmitter sends one message simultaneously to many receivers; 225–226, 355–356

Buckley, C., 409

Budnik, P., 283

Buffer effects (in virtual memory) A phenomenon that causes a fraction of real memory to serve as a buffer for pages flowing to and from auxiliary memory; 107–112

Buneman, O., 232

Burks, A. W., 123

Burroughs' B5700, 197

Burroughs' B6700, 197

Burroughs' Scientific Processor (BSP), 283–285, 303

Bus (interconnection) An interconnection in which all transmitters and receivers are directly connected to a common set of interconnection lines that comprise the bus; 325–330, 336, 352, 360, 426

Butterfly operation The core operation of a Fast Fourier Transform that consists of forming the weighted sum and difference of two operands; 340–342

Buzbee, B. L., 232

C.mmp multiprocessor, 336–337

Cable density, 252

Cache A small capacity, high-speed buffer memory; 22, 29–87, 135, 184–190, 271, 273, 324, 328, 351

for bus-based multiprocessors, 328, 402–405

coherence, 353–358, 403–404, 425–426

for data, 136

design of, 112–115, 117–121

for instructions, 136

miss ratio, 98

performance model, 79–85

replacement policy, 51, 59–65

set of data in, 32–35

simulation of, 41–49

structure of, 29–39

tag (in directory), 30, 35, 42–43, 54–55, 65

techniques for analysis of, 39–59

two-level, 39

vector operands stored in, 302–303

writing to, 73–76

Cache coherence The state that exists in a multiprocessor system when any shared variable is held by two more or caches, and no two caches hold different values of such a shared variable simultaneously; 353–358

Cache directory The collection of tags in a cache that are used for associative access to cached data; 32, 74–76

Cache hit A cache access that successfully finds a datum requested in the cache; 31, 61–65

Cache miss A cache access that fails to find a datum requested in the cache; 30, 36–37, 52–59, 61–73, 112–115, 121, 136, 191

Cache-reload transient The cache misses that occur when a program formerly in execution is restarted after other programs have used the cache; 65–73

Carnegie-Mellon University, 336

Carry-lookahead adder An adder in which special logic propagates carries with a delay that grows logarithmically in the number adder stages rather than linearly in the number of adder stages; 397–398

CDC 6600, 123, 130–132, 134–135, 181–184, 197

CDC STAR, 144, 267–270, 293, 297

Central Limit Theorem The theorem that states that the distribution of the sum of identical and independently distributed random variables asymptotically approaches a normal distribution; 316

Chaining (of computations) The technique in which an output stream of vector results is directed to the input of another vector operation without being returned to intermediate storage between operations; 145

Charlesworth, A. E., 288, 290

Checkerboard ordering (for a mesh calculation) An ordering of operations in
which an iterative calculation is performed first on the "red" nodes and then
on the "black" nodes in the mesh;
422–424

Chen, P. Y., 344

Chen, T. C., 137, 142

Chickens, 323

Chu, W. W., 105–106

Chunksize The number of iterations to be
grouped together as a single task in
order to increase task granularity;
370–373, 418, 421–424

CISC (Complex Instruction-Set Computer) A computer with an instruction
set that includes complex (multicycle)
instructions; 192–196

Clark, D. W., 98

Coarse-grain parallelism Parallel execution
in which the amount of computation per
task is several times larger than the
overhead and communication expended
per task; 309–323

Cocke, John, 188

Coffman, E. G., Jr., 41, 104, 107

Coherence (of cache). *See* Cache coherence

Collision An event in which two or more
different operations require the use of
the same pipeline stage at the same
clock cycle; 154

Collision vector A binary control-vector
whose bits indicate when an operation
can be initiated safely in a pipeline computer; 154–161, 198–199

Column access A concurrent memory access to all elements of a column of a
matrix; 277–287, 300–302, 359

Colwell, R. P., 195

Combining switch A switching element of
an interconnection network that has the
ability to combine certain types of requests into one request, and to produce
a response that mimics serial execution
of the requests; 339–340, 346–352, 368,
396, 426–426

Common data-bus A hardware mechanism
for transmitting results produced by a
collection of arithmetic units to machine
registers and reservation stations;
182–183

Communication cost, 309–325

Compare-and-Swap An instruction that is
used for processor synchronization; 377,
384–392, 421, 429–430

Compatibility, 19–20

Compiler optimization, 417–425

Complex instruction-set computer. *See* CISC

Computer architecture The study of computer structures, their applications, and
their performance; 1–2, 13
cost of, 7–9
evaluation of, 7–9, 18–19
performance of, 7–9
special purpose vs. all purpose, 13
and technology, 1–3
textbooks, 20

Computer vision, 12

Concert multiprocessor, 374

Conditional branch A computer instruction
that alters the sequence of execution if a
condition is true, and otherwise falls
through to the next instruction in sequence; 126, 133, 191, 201, 257
in a pipeline, 170–175, 191

Confidence interval An interval based on
statistical sampling that shows where a
population of random variables lies to
within a specified level of confidence;
45–47, 57

Conflict A situation in which two or more
operations require the same resource,
forcing one operation to wait for the
other to complete; 133–135, 162–168,
175, 340–346, 386
in a network, 340–346
in a pipeline, 133–135, 162–168, 175
See also Contention, READ/WRITE conflict, WRITE/READ conflict, WRITE/
WRITE conflict

Connection Machine, 305, 310, 352, 409

Contention Interference among tasks
caused by tasks competing for shared
resources, thereby forcing one or more
tasks to become idle momentarily while
waiting for resources to become available; 333–334, 339–345, 370–373,
426–427

Context switch The process of saving the
state of one task and restoring the state
of a second task to enable a computer
system to change execution from one
program to another; 99

Continuum model A model of physical systems in which continuous quantities are
modeled at discrete points and physical
interactions are modeled as interactions
among neighboring mesh points;
205–207, 211–236, 253–255, 259, 300

Cooley, J. W., 254

Coonen, J. T., 196

Cosmic Cube, 219–220, 228, 236, 254–255,
257, 352

Cost, 4–15
of development, 5
per-unit, 5
Cost-performance ratio, 10–11, 15–16, 261, 322
Cray I, 145, 270–274, 284–285, 297, 308, 310
Cray II, 145–146, 287
Cray XMP, 308, 310
Critical section A section of a program that can be executed by at most one process at a time; 334–337, 339, 346, 348–349, 376–405
Crossbar (interconnection) An interconnection network in which each input is connected to each output through a path that contains a single switching node; 333–337, 341, 352, 360
Crosspoint A switching node in a crossbar that connects a single input to a single output; 333
Crowther, W., 251
Cvetanovic, Z., 341–342, 344, 373
Cycle (of computer clock) An electronic signal that counts a single unit of time within a computer; 16, 170, 188, 191, 262–267, 280, 372–373, 396–397, 404–405
Cycle (of a permutation), 410
Cycle (in reduced state-diagram) A path in a reduced state-diagram that specifies a steady-state schedule for introducing operations to a pipeline; 160–161, 198
Cycle time The length of a single cycle of a computer function such as a memory cycle or processor cycle; 23–24, 30–31, 38
effective, 31, 38, 188
Cyclic reduction An algorithm used to solve linear systems that have a particular structure; 232, 234–235, 256–257
Cytron, R. G., 418, 420, 424–425

Data cache A cache that holds data, but does not hold instructions; 136, 188–191
Data flow (analysis of requirements) The sequence of processes and data transmissions that are performed on a collection of data during a computation; 221–226
Database system, 12, 408–409
Davidson, E. S., 147, 155, 160
Dead line A line of a cache that will be discarded from cache before it will be the target of a cache access; 62
Deadlock The state in which two or more processes are deferred indefinitely because each process is awaiting another

process to make progress, and no process is able to make progress; 336, 383, 429
DEC PDP-11, 20, 336–337
DEC VAX, 20, 95–99, 101–102, 192, 196
Decode-history table A small cache-like memory that saves the recent history of decoding information for conditional-branch instructions so that this information can be used by a branch prediction mechanism; 173–175
Decrement (for synchronization), 381–384, 429
de Kooning, W., 3
Delay (in pipeline) A logic device used to store and synchronize data in a pipeline; 162–168, 268–270
Delayed branch A branch instruction that defers altering the flow of control until one or more instructions that follow it have completed execution; 171–172
Denneau, M., 295
Denning, P. J., 41, 103–104, 107
Dependence analysis An analysis that reveals which portions of a program depend on the prior completion of other portions of the program; 418–424, 428–429
DEQUEUE A high-level function that removes an item from a queue; 380–381, 384, 386, 389–395, 429–430
Development cost, 5
DeWitt, D. J., 409
Dias, D. M., 343
Digital Equipment Corporation. *See* DEC
Dijkstra, E. M., 376, 412, 414, 431
Direct mapping A cache that has a set associativity of one so that each item has a unique place in the cache at which it can be stored; 34, 43–44
Directory (of a cache) The portion of a cache that holds the access keys that support associative access; 32, 63
See also Cache, tag
Disk buffer A high-speed buffer memory resident within a disk controller that is used as a private cache for the disk system; 110–111, 117
Disk cache. *See* Disk buffer
Disk memory, 107–112
See also Auxiliary memory
Ditzel, D. R., 191
Division, 193, 199–200
do par A program statement that permits the iterations of a loop to be executed in parallel; 364–367, 374, 428
do seq A program statement that forces the

do seq (*continued*)
    iterations of a loop to be executed sequentially, 364–366
Dubois, M., 355

ECL (Emitter-coupled logic), 14
Efficiency
    of array computer, 137–141
    of multiprocessor computer, 307–325, 336, 367–370
    of pipeline computer, 142–143
Eggers, S. J., 404
Emer, J. S., 98
ENQUEUE   A high-level function that adds an item to a queue; 380–381, 384, 386–395, 429–430
Exchange. *See* Pair-wise exchange, Shuffle-exchange
Exclusive access   A state in which some single process is granted the right to read, modify, and write a shared datum, and no other processor can access the datum while the first program has exclusive access to the shared datum; 334–335, 339, 346, 348–349, 376–405
    See also Critical section
Execute stage   The stage in a pipelined processor at which an instruction is executed; 131–132, 176–177, 181–182
Exponent, 147–150

Fan-in   The number of logic signals that directly drive a given logic gate; 224
Fan-out   The number of logic gates driven by a specific logic gate; 224
Feedback path   A path from the output of a functional unit to an input of the same unit; 149
Fetch-and-Add   A computer instruction that updates a memory operand, returns the value of the operand before the update, and if executed concurrently by several processors simultaneously, produces a set of results as if the processors executed in some serial order; 346–352, 377, 392–395, 421, 429
    Fetch-and-Decrement form, 401
    Fetch-and-Increment form, 401
Finite-cache effect   The performance decrease measured in cycles per instruction due to the use of a finite cache in place of an ideal infinite cache; 191
FFT (Fast Fourier Transform). *See* Fourier transform
Fine-grain parallelism   A form of parallel execution in which the amount of work per task is small compared to the

amount of work per task required for communication and overhead; 309–323
Finite-element method   A numerical technique in which physical systems are analyzed mathematically by modeling the system at the nodes of a mesh of data points; 12, 293
Floating-point arithmetic, 147–157, 193–195, 202–203
    addition, 149–155
    multiplication, 147–149, 152–154
Fluid flow, 12
Flynn, M. J., 197, 305–306
Footprint   The distinct lines of a process held in an infinite cache that are touched during the execution of the process; 67–73, 80–83, 103, 118
Footprint size   The number of lines of a process footprint held in a cache; 67
Forbidden cell   A cell of a reservation table for one operation that cannot be used by another operation because of a timing conflict; 162–168
Ford, L. R., Jr., 412
Forsythe, G., 197, 277
FORTRAN, 205, 417
Forwarding register   A register that is temporarily assigned the role of a different register; 176
    See also Internal forwarding
Fourier transform, 223, 239, 254–255, 340–343, 408
FPS-164, 288–292, 297
Free pool   A collection of registers available for use as forwarding registers; 177–180
Freeable   The state of a forwarding register after its contents have been used and the register can be returned to the free pool; 179–180
Fujitsu Corporation, 187, 288, 418
Fulkerson, D. R., 412
Full-information function   A multi-output function each of whose outputs depends on every input; 221–223
Fully associative   A cache structure in which every tag in the cache is compared to the tag of the datum being accessed; 34, 80

Gauss-Seidel iteration   An iterative scheme for solving linear equations in which each interior point is updated with two neighboring values from the present iteration and two neighboring values from the prior iteration; 422–424
Gaussian elimination   A method for solving

linear systems of equations; 275–279, 281, 300–302, 359–360

GCD (Greatest Common Divisor), 282

GF-11. *See* IBM GF-11

Gflops (Gigaflops) A computation rate of one billion floating-point operations per second; 295

Gigaflops. *See* Gflops

Global memory A memory directly accessible by every processor in a multiprocessor; 326, 371–372
See also Shared memory

Golub, G. H., 232

Goodman, J., 43, 47, 355, 401

Gottlieb, A., 346, 394, 396

Granularity A measure of the size of an individual task to be executed on a parallel processor; 309–323, 325–327, 367–370

Gravitation, 207

Greatest common divisor (GCD), 282

Greedy strategy A strategy that initiates a new pipeline operation at the earliest opportunity; 158–160

Green, P. E., Jr., 399

Grosch's Law An empirical rule that says that the cost of computer systems increases as the square root of the computational power of the systems; 13

Gupta, S. C., 41

Gustafson, J. L., 288, 290

Halstead, R., 374–375

Hash lookup A search technique in which the search key is transformed to an address at which the search begins; 294

Hayes, J. P., 20

Heidelberger, P., 398, 401

Heller, D. E., 235, 275

Hennessy, J., 48–49

Hierarchy (of memory system) A multilevel memory structure in which successive levels are progressively larger, slower, and less costly; 22, 26–27, 119–120

High-speed buffer memory A memory that holds data en route between a large main memory and the registers of a high-speed processor; 285
See also Intermediate memory

Hill, M., 195

Hillis, W. D., 305, 352

Hit. *See* Cache hit

Hit ratio The ratio of the number of cache hits to the total number of cache accesses; 31, 38–39

Hitachi Corporation, 39, 288

Hoevel, L. W., 65

Hopcroft, J. E., 410

Horowitz, M., 48–49

Hoshino, T., 203, 205, 220, 255, 325, 338, 397, 400

Hot-spot contention An interference phenomenon observed in multiprocessors due to memory access statistics being slightly skewed from a uniform distribution to favor a specific memory module; 344–345, 350–351, 396, 426

HP Spectrum, 192

Hwang, K., 196, 387

Hypercube A parallel processor whose interconnection structure treats individual processors as the nodes of a multidimensional cube and interconnects two processors if the corresponding nodes of the cube are neighbors; 257, 352–353
See also Cosmic Cube

IBM Corporation, 188, 288

IBM GF-11, 295–297, 305, 310

IBM RP3, 251, 339, 350–352, 368, 373

IBM STRETCH, 123

IBM 801, 188

IBM System 360/91, 181–184

IBM System 360-370, 19–20, 80, 192, 387

IBM 3090, 175, 308, 418

IEEE 802.5 Token-Ring Standard, 331

IEEE Standard for Floating-Point Arithmetic, 196

ILLIAC IV, 143–144, 204, 214–218, 225–226, 255, 257, 295, 297, 301

Image processing A computation performed on a digitized representation of an image whose purpose is to enhance the image or to extract information about the image; 12

Increment (for synchronization), 381–384, 429

Indurkhya, B., 309, 316–317

Inferencing system A programming system that produces results by following a logical chain of inferences; 12

Initialization (of cache simulation), 41–49

Inner product The sum of the component-by-component products of the elements of two vectors; 169, 289

Input/output overlap The act of performing input/output processing concurrently with other processing; 123

Input/output processor A processor whose function is specialized to input/output processing; 74–76

Instruction buffer A small high-speed memory that holds instructions recently executed or about to be executed; 271

Instruction cache A cache memory dedicated to the storage of instructions; 136,
188–191

Instruction decode The machine cycle during which an instruction is examined
and the control signals required for the
execution of the instruction are produced; 125–127, 129, 176–177

Instruction fetch The machine cycle dedicated to the access and retrieval of the
next instruction to execute; 125–127,
129, 136, 176–177, 192–193

Instruction set The repertoire of instructions executable by a computer; 2
See also CISC, RISC

Intel 8080, 79–80

Intel 8086, 70–80, 123, 219

Intel 8087, 219

Intel 808X, 19

Intel 80X86, 79–80

Intel i860, 193–194

Interconnection network The system of
logic and conductors that connects together the processors in a parallel computer system; 225, 236–252, 305–306
See also Bus, Crossbar, Hypercube, Mesh,
Near-neighbor interconnection, Perfect
shuffle, Ring, Shuffle-exchange

Interlock A control device or signal that defers the execution of one function until a
conflicting function has completed execution; 134, 175–176, 181, 289
elimination of, 168–170

Intermediate memory, 270–274
See also High-speed buffer memory

Internal forwarding An execution technique
in which special registers are temporarily assigned the function of physical
machine registers to hold operands
while awaiting execution in order to reduce conflicts for machine resources that
otherwise would occur; 175–184, 198

Interprocessor communication The data
and control information that passes
among the processors of a parallel computer during the execution of a parallel
program; 307

Interrupt A temporary suspension of the
normal sequence of program execution
to perform a function that has been initiated by an external event or by an internal trap or monitor function; 66,
386–388

Interrupt-driven A means of initiating execution of a program in response to an
interrupt caused by an external event;
66, 72

Invalidate The process that removes a
cache entry by changing its directory entry into an empty entry; 75

Inverse mapper A device that computes a
virtual address from a physical (real)
address; 186

Inverse perfect shuffle. *See* Perfect shuffle,
inverse of

Iyer, R. K., 43, 48, 66

Jacobi iteration An iterative method for
solving linear equations that updates
each point in a new iteration only after
all points have been updated for the
prior iteration; 422

Jump, J. R., 343

Kahle, B., 409

Karp, R. M., 406–408, 414

Katz, R. H., 404

Kilburn, T., 25–26

Knowledge base A collection of rules and
data used by inferencing programs during computations; 12

Kobayashi, M., 80, 82, 86

Kogge, P. M., 147, 160, 169, 230, 269, 289

Kruskal, C. P., 344

Kuck, D. J., 283, 417

Kung, H. T., 252

Laha, S., 43, 48, 66

Lamport, L., 423–424

Latch A one-bit storage device that saves
the contents of its input at the instant a
clock signal changes state; 132

Latency The delay between the request for
information and the time the information is supplied to the requester; 89–90,
108–109

Lawler, E. L., 412

Lawrie, D. H., 340, 344

Leading-edge effect (of a cache) The performance degradation due to the delay between the occurrence of a cache miss
and the arrival of the first portion of
that cache line; 78
See also Trailing-edge effect

Least-recently used. *See* LRU

Leiserson, C. E., 252

Length (of a trace). *See* Trace length

Line (of a cache) A collection of contiguous
data that are treated as a single entity of
cache storage; 32

Line size The number of bytes in a cache
line; 34, 53–59

Linear equation An equation that depends on its variables only through the addition of a multiple of each variable; 288

Linear-equation solver An algorithm for solving linear equations; 197–198

Linear programming An optimization technique for solving constrained problems in which behavior equations and constraint equations are linear functions of the variables; 288

Linear recurrence A recurrence relation in which each successive result is a linear function of past results; 229–231

LISP, 375

Livelock A state in which actions taken by concurrently executing processes prevent computation from proceeding, but computation can proceed if some processes alter their execution behavior; 382–384, 394–395, 429

Local memory The private memory directly connected to a processor in a parallel computer; 326, 351–352, 371–372

Locality (of memory references) The characteristic tendency for programs to access regions in the near future that were accessed in the recent past; 26–29, 99–102
    See also Spatial locality, Temporal locality

Lock A primitive operation that grants a process the exclusive right to continue execution only if no other processor currently holds that exclusive right; 335–336, 346, 369, 371, 378–382, 385–386, 421
    See also Unlock

Loop interconnection. *See* Ring

Losq, J. J., 173

LRU (Least-Recently Used) replacement policy A memory management strategy that purges the least recently used candidate from memory, while retaining candidates used more recently; 51–52, 59–65, 69–70, 102–103, 274

LU decomposition A method for solving linear equations based on Gaussian elimination; 197–198, 232–234, 275–278, 359–360

MacDougall, M. H., 80, 82, 86

McLellan, H. R., 191

Mantissa The significant-bit field of a floating-point operand; 147–150

Mapper. *See* Address mapper

Mashburn, H. H., 336

Mattson, R. L., 51–53, 60, 77

MAX, 229

Maximum (computation of), 397, 400

Maximum compatible set A set of integers, no two of which are incompatible and to which no other compatible integer can appended; 167–168

Megaflops. *See* Mflops

Memory, 21–121
    access patterns, 26–29
    bandwidth, 22
    bottleneck, 21, 122, 336, 372–373
    cycle time, 23–24, 30–31
    hierarchy, 22, 26–27. *See also* Hierarchy, 119–120
    random access, 23–24, 32, 35
    sequential access, 24
    structure for a pipeline computer, 135–136
    See also Virtual memory

Memory access, 26–29, 274–279
    See also Access

Memory address The unique location for each item in a memory by which that item is accessed; 23–24

Memory hierarchy, 22, 26, 119–120
    See also Hierarchy

Memory management The process of controlling the flow of data among the levels of memory hierarchy; 87–91, 102–107, 109–112

Mesh calculation, 143, 204, 212–217, 255–257
    See also Continuum model, Finite-element method

Mesh interconnection, 338

Mflops (Megaflops) An execution rate of millions of floating-point instructions per second; 260, 275

MIMD (Multiple Instruction-stream, Multiple Data-stream) parallel computer structure composed of multiple independent processors; 305–306
    See also Multiprocessor, SIMD

MIN, 229

MIPS (Millions of Instructions per Second) A measure of the computation rate of a computer; 14–16, 362, 373, 379–380

Miranker, W. L., 406–408, 414

Miss ratio The ratio of cache misses to total cache accesses; 42–49, 65, 85, 98, 353
    steady-state, 66
    See also Cache miss, Hit ratio

MIT Multics, 197

Miura, K., 418

Model (of cache behavior), 41, 48–49, 79–85

Model (of multiprocessor performance), 311–325, 359, 367–370
See also Performance model
Moler, C. B., 197, 277
Monte Carlo simulation A computational method in which physical calculations are performed by simulating the statistical behavior of elementary components of a physical system; 12, 204
MOS (Metal-Oxide Semiconductor), 14
Motorola 680XX, 19, 192, 196
MSYPS (Millions of SYnchronizations Per Second) A measure of the rate at which a multiprocessor performs synchronizations among its processors; 362, 368–369, 373, 379–380, 393, 427
Multics, 197
Multiple instruction-stream, multiple data-stream. *See* MIMD
Multiple-purpose architecture A computer structure that can perform a broad variety of computations; 210–211, 217, 300, 427
Multiplier tree, 196
Multiprocessor A parallel computer composed of multiple independent processors and facilities for controlling their interaction and cooperation; 304–358
cache coherence in, 353–358, 425–426
compiler optimization for, 417–425
efficiency of, 307–325, 336, 367–370, 405–417
interconnections, 325–353, 368–370
parallel execution of, 362–376, 405–417
parallel search in, 405–410
performance of, 309–325, 367–370, 405–417
synchronization of, 367–370, 376–405
task initiation, 374–376, 429
See also MIMD
Multiprogramming A technique for executing more than one program at a time in a single processor by periodically changing the program currently being executed by the processor; 89–91

Near-neighbor interconnection An interconnection structure for a parallel processor in which each processor is connected directly to its near neighbors; 208–209, 224, 226, 252–255, 259, 300
NEC (Nippon Electric Corporation), 288
Nelson, V. P., 344
Newell, A., 20
Nicol, D. M., 317
Nielson, C. W., 232

NMOS Negatively doped MOS (Metal-oxide semiconductor); 14
Nonlinear systems of equations A system of equations in which the variables are linked by one or more nonlinear relations; 288
Normal distribution The statistical distribution whose probability density follows a bell-shaped curve; 72
Normalization The process that transforms a floating-point number into a representation such that the leading digit of a nonzero mantissa is nonzero; 147–150
Norton, V. A., 344–345
NP-complete A class of problems for which there exists no current algorithm that can solve any problem in the class in a time guaranteed to be less than exponential in the size of the problem; 361–362, 410
NYU Ultracomputer, 339, 368

Offset A small integer whose value is the relative displacement from a base address to the address at which an access is to be made; 92–97
One-level store A multilevel memory hierarchy that functions as if there were a single level in the memory hierarchy; 26
Opderbeck, H., 105–106
Operand fetch The machine cycle dedicated to the access and retrieval of an operand; 125–127, 129, 136, 176–177
OPT A nonrealizable optimum replacement policy for cache and virtual memory; 60–64
Optical transmission, 252, 327–328, 332–333, 399–400
OR A boolean operation; 229, 397, 400, 432
Organick, E. I., 197
Overflow The state in which a numerical value exceeds the maximum representable numerical value; 147–150,196
Overlap The ability to perform two or more functions concurrently; 143–146, 309–325
Overlay, 25

Padmanabhan, K., 344
Padua, D. A., 418, 420
Page A contiguous region of memory that is treated as the smallest allocatable unit by a virtual-memory manager; 26
Page fault An access to a page that is not resident in main memory; 27, 30, 89–91, 93, 96, 102–109

Page-fault frequency replacement (PFF) An algorithm for managing a virtual memory that increases the number of pages assigned to a process when page faults occur at a rate above a fixed threshold; 105–107, 116

Page number The field of a virtual address that identifies the page to be accessed; 94–99

Page replacement The process that determines which page to move from main memory to auxiliary memory to make room for a new page in main memory; 102–107, 116–117

Page size The number of bytes in a page; 28

Page table A table used by a page mapper in a virtual memory system that contains the physical (real) address for each page, and is accessed by page number; 94–97

Pair-wise exchange An interconnection switch that swaps data between adjacent processors; 245, 248

Parallel architecture, 18–19

Parallel computation, 12, 143–144, 204, 214–218, 225–226, 228–235, 254–258, 361–366, 428–432

Parallel time The elapsed execution time for a parallel computation; 143, 415–417

Partial differential equation An equation that expresses the relations among variables and their partial derivatives; 206

Particle model A computational process in which physical behavior is modeled through the simulation of discrete particles acted upon by physical forces produced remotely; 205–209, 259
See also Monte Carlo simulation

Partitioning (of programs to pages or segments) The process of grouping related portions of programs together to force them to reside in contiguous regions of memory so that they tend to be transferred together among the levels of a memory hierarchy; 91

Patel, J. H., 44, 48, 66, 127, 160

Patterson, D. A., 192, 194

PAX Computer, 217, 220, 255, 325, 338, 397, 400

PDP-11. *See* DEC PDP-11

Pease, M. C., 239, 243

Per-unit cost The manufacturing cost of one additional item; 5

Perfect-shuffle interconnection An interconnection structure that connects processors according to a permutation that corresponds to a perfect shuffle of a deck of cards; 236–252, 254–255, 258, 295–300, 339–352, 396
inverse of, 244–245

Performance model An idealized mathematical model that is useful for predicting the performance of a computer system
cache behavior, 41, 48–49, 79–85
fully overlapped communication, 319–320
linear communication costs, 317–319
multiple communication links, 321–323
N processors with overlapped communication, 312–316
stochastic, 316–317
two processors with overlapped communication, 311–312

Permutation A one-to-one mapping from a set of objects onto the same set of objects; 410–413

Permutation memory (in the GF-11) A memory that stores the control settings for a collection of permutations, each of which is to be used for routing information among processors and memories; 297

PFF. *See* Page-fault frequency

Pfister, G., 251, 344–345, 350

Physical address The address of an item in physical (real) memory; 88, 92, 94–96, 98–99, 184–188

Pipeline (in a computer system) A structure that consists of a sequence of stages through which a computation flows with the property that new operations can be initiated at the start of the pipeline while other operations are in progress through the pipeline; 122–197, 260–270, 289–292
adding delays to, 160–168
arithmetic units, 289–291
conditional branches in, 170–175
conflicts in, 133–135
control of, 147–157, 198–200
design of, 123–135
maximum performance of, 158–168
performance of, 137–146, 324
in RISC computer, 188–192
streaming operation of, 262–274, 302–303
in vector computer, 260–261

Pivot (in Gaussian elimination) The largest element in a region of an array, which is chosen to serve as the element around which a transformation of a subarray is performed; 277–278, 300–302

Poisson's equation   An equation that describes physical potential as a function of charge density; 212–217, 223, 232, 255–257, 363–365, 422–424

Polynomial, 258

Pomerene, J., 63

Port (of a memory)   An interface to a memory system that supplies up to one operand per memory cycle; 190, 268–269

Power law, 80, 85

Preparata, F., 251

Primed set (in a cache memory)   A set of lines of a set associative cache that has received a sufficient number of references during a cache simulation to initialize all entries of the set; 44

Process tag (in a cache memory)   A field that gives the identity of the specific process that created a particular line in the cache; 99

Program partitioning, 25
See also Partitioning

Propagation effects   Physical effects that tend to degrade signal quality and to increase propagation delays; 252

Protocol   A set of rules or conventions that govern how processors communicate, synchronize, or maintain coherent information in caches or in local memories; 355–357, 403–404

Purge (of cache and TLB)   The process that removes all entries in a cache or cache-like memory that are associated with a process that has relinquished its use of a processor; 99

Puzak, T. R., 52–59, 62

Quantum chromodynamics   A branch of theoretical physics concerned with the behavior and properties of elementary particles; 296

Queue (for shared access), 346–349, 367–369, 379–381, 384–392, 429

R/C **ratio**   The ratio of a task's running time to its overhead and communications time; a measure of task granularity; 309–323, 325–327, 352, 367–368, 420–422, 424

Radin, G., 188

RAM. *See* Random-Access Memory

Random-access memory (RAM)   A memory in which the time required to access an item is independent of the past history of accesses; 23–24, 89–90, 119

Rao, G. S., 173

Rathi, B. D., 398, 401

Ray tracing   An algorithm used to render life-like graphic images by tracing the path of rays of light from a source to an illuminated object; 12

READ/MODIFY/WRITE   A noninterruptible sequence of operations required for operations that synchronize access to shared variables; 335, 368, 376–382, 385–386

READ/WRITE conflict, 133–135, 181, 418–422, 428
See also Conflict

Real address. *See* Physical address

Real time, 12

Rechtschaffen, R., 438

Recurrence relation   A relation that expresses the next item of a sequence as a function of the earlier items in the sequence; 200, 226–231, 257

Recursive doubling   A technique for parallel execution that at each stage doubles the number of variables that influence the partial results at that stage of the computation; 232–233, 235, 255, 257–258, 302, 400

Red-black ordering (for a mesh calculation), 422–424
See also Checkerboard ordering

Reduced instruction-set computer. *See* RISC

Reduced state-diagram   A diagram that describes the possible sequences of initiation of operations in a pipelined processing unit; 158–160, 199

Reformatting (of data structures)   The process of transforming a data structure from one storage representation to another to facilitate parallel access to substructures of the data structure; 286
See also Column access, Row access

Register windows   A processor mechanism in which sets of registers automatically change their function when procedures are entered and exited; 194–195

Remote effects   Physical effects caused by interactions that are not near-neighbor interactions; 207–208
See also Action at a distance

Replacement policy   A policy that governs which items are to be removed from one level of a memory hierarchy when new items are put there; 51–53, 59–65, 91, 102–107, 110
See also LRU, OPT

Reservation station   A collection of hardware registers that hold data or reservations for data to be used in a future operation; 178–180, 182

Reservation table   A table that describes

which resources are needed at each step of a pipelined computation; 151–154, 161, 198–199

Reverse-binary operation A permutation that maps Item i to the item whose is index is obtained by reversing the bits in the binary representation of i; 340–343

Ring (interconnection) An interconnection structure in which nodes are connected in a loop structure; 330–332, 359, 427

RISC (Reduced instruction-set computer) A computer in which all instructions are simple instructions that take one cycle to execute, except for instructions that require conditional execution and for delays to access memory; 79, 171–172, 188–196

Routing register In ILLIAC IV, a register used for exchanging data among neighboring processors; 215–216

Row access A concurrent memory access to all elements of a row of a matrix; 277–287, 300–302, 359

RP3. *See* IBM RP3

Sachar, H. E., 173

Salton, G., 409

Savage, J. E., 41

Scalar arithmetic Arithmetic operations that manipulate individual data as opposed to arithmetic operations in which one operation manipulates an entire vector or matrix; 290–292

Scalar operation Any operation performed on individual data; 203, 270

Scalar processor A processor whose basic operations manipulate individual data elements rather than vectors or matrices; 291–292

Scalar register A register whose function is to hold scalar operands; 270–271

Scheduling, 307, 425

Scoreboard A hardware device that maintains the state of machine resources to enable instructions to execute without conflict at the earliest opportunity to do so; 134–135, 181–182

Search techniques, 405–415

Segment A method for partitioning data into variable-length blocks of memory so that items grouped together are logically related; 94–102

Segment number The field of a virtual address that specifies which segment of a program is to be accessed; 94–98

Segment table The table in a virtual-memory system that is used to translate segment references in a virtual address to physical (real) addresses in main memory; 94–97

Segmented memory A virtual memory system whose address space is partitioned into a disjoint collection of regions known as segments; 99–102

Seitz, C. L., 219

Semaphore A variable that is used to control access to shared data; 378–384

Sequential-access memory A memory system such as a magnetic tape memory in which items must be accessed sequentially, and in which the access time to a random item depends on which item in memory was accessed immediately prior to the given access; 24

Sequin, C. H., 192, 194

Serial access. *See* Sequential access

Serial correlation The statistical correlation among the addresses in a sequence of addresses in an address trace from which it is possible to predict future accesses; 27–29
See also Locality

Serial time The time it takes to execute an efficient version of an algorithm on a serial computer; 143, 415–417

Serialization The process that forces a collection of complex tasks to take place one at a time rather than in parallel; 347, 349

Set. *See* Cache, set

Set associative A cache structure in which all tags in a particular set are compared with an access key in order to access an item in cache. The set may have as few as one element or as many elements as there are lines in the full cache; 32–35, 38, 44, 51–59, 77–78, 85

Shadow directory A cache directory that contains cache tags only, and no data; 63–65

Shadow miss A cache miss for which an entry exists in a shadow directory; 64

Shar, L. E., 147

Shared memory, 325–328, 353–358, 367–370, 376–405
See also Global memory

Shared page A page of a virtual memory system that is shared by two or more programs; 97–98

Shared segment A segment of a virtual memory system that is shared by two or more programs; 101–102

Shemer, J. E., 41

Shift-register analogy A method for predicting the trajectory of an item in a perfect-shuffle network by observing the successive states of a cyclic shift register; 241–242, 248

Shift-register controller (for a pipeline), 155–160
See also Collision vector

Shippey, B., 41

Shortest-path problem A problem that requires the discovery of the shortest path between two nodes of a graph; 412, 414, 431

Shuffle-exchange (interconnection) An interconnection network that consists of a perfect shuffles and pair-wise exchanges; 329–352, 396

Siewiorek, D. P., 20

SIMD (Single Instruction-stream, Multiple Data-stream) A processor structure in which a single instruction manipulates an entire data structure; 305, 375–376
See also Array processor, Connection Machine, Vector Processor

Singh, J. P., 41, 83–84, 86

Single instruction-stream, multiple data-stream. *See* SIMD

Singleton, R. C., 239, 243

Sites, R., 387

Skewed storage A technique for storing matrices to facilitate parallel access to rows and columns; 281–286

Slave memory Cache memory; 29

Slotnick, D. L., 214, 220

Smith, A. J., 37, 77–78, 86, 355

Smith, D. R., 410, 413–414

Smith, J. E., 43, 47, 401

Snir, M., 344

Sohi, G. S., 401

SOLOMON Computer, 218

Sorting, 222, 224, 239, 249–251, 258, 431–432

SPARC processor, 194

Sparse matrix A matrix whose elements are mostly zeros; 12, 276, 292–294

Sparse vector A technique used in the CDC STAR for representing vectors whose elements are mostly zeros; 293

Spatial locality The tendency for references to a particular item in memory to be clustered together with references to nearby items; 85
See also Locality, Spatial locality

Speech recognition, 12

Speedup The ratio of the time to execute an efficient serial program for a calculation to the time to execute a parallel program for the same calculation on N processors identical to the serial processor; 128, 141, 218, 231, 315, 320, 324–325, 361, 368–369, 372–373, 407–408, 414–417

Spin lock A implementation of the LOCK primitive that causes a processor to re-test a semaphore continuously until the semaphore changes value; 379

Spirn, J. R., 41

Stable (numerically) An algorithm that produces small changes in the numerical answers in response to small changes in input data; 277

Stack-replacement policy A memory-replacement policy for which items that are retained in a small memory are a subset of the items retained if the memory size is increased; 52

Stage (of a pipeline), 126, 130–132

Stale data Data that remain in a cache when a process is moved to a different processor; 355

Standard deviation A measure of the likely deviation from the mean of a random variable; 45–46
See also Variance

Stanfill, C., 409

Startup transient The period immediately after the initiation of a vector instruction during which a pipeline produces no results or produces results at a low rate; 136

Statistical sampling A trace-reduction technique that predicts full cache performance by sampling the performance on a small number of cache sets; 57, 114
See also Trace reduction

Steele, G. L., Jr., 352

Sterbenz, P. H., 196

Stone, H. S., 20, 41, 66, 83–84, 230, 232, 240–241, 309, 316, 394, 398, 401, 409

Stream (of data) A set of successive data presented to a pipeline arithmetic unit, 264–270, 302

Strecker, W. D., 66

Stride The constant difference between successive addresses in a stream of data generated by a vector access; 282

Sullivan, H. T., 350

Sussenguth, E., 173

Sweazey, P., 355

Synch An elementary synchronization operation; 367–368

Synchronization An operation in which two or more processors exchange information to coordinate their activity; 210,

216–217, 220–221, 299, 307, 329, 362–370, 376–405, 427

Synonym (in a cache) A situation in which two different items have the same virtual address but reside at a different physical address; 186–187

Synthetic workload, 91

SYPS (SYnchronizations Per Second) A processing rate of one synchronization per second; 362, 368
See also MSYPS

Systolic array A parallel computer with a highly structured, iterative interconnection pattern; 252

Tag. *See* Cache, tag

Tanenbaum, A. S., 20

Tapped delay-line A device whose taps produce delayed versions of the input data with each tap associated with a different delay, 268

Temporal locality The tendency for references to a particular item in memory to be clustered together in time; 85
See also Locality, Spatial locality

Test-and-Set A primitive instruction that performs a READ/MODIFY/WRITE operation for synchronization of processors; 377–382, 429

Thanawastien, S., 344

Thiebaut, D., 41, 66, 80–84

Thirty-percent rule, 37–38, 48–49, 82

Thompson, D., 397–398

Thompson, J. G., 77–78

Thornton, J. E., 132, 181, 197

Thrashing A state in which multiple programs compete for real memory and no program is able to obtain enough memory to reduce its fault rate to a low value; 103

Three-address instruction format An instruction format with two fields for input operands and one field for a result operand; 134, 183

Threshold (for page-fault frequency), 105–106

Threshold phenomenon For some physical systems, the situation in which behavior changes dramatically when a parameter crosses a threshold; 72

TLB. *See* Translation-lookaside buffer

Token A unique data symbol used to control transmission for a parallel computer system connected as a ring; 331–332

Token ring. *See* Ring interconnection

Tomasulo, R. M., 181–182

Tour A path on a graph that visits every node exactly once and terminates at the starting node; 410–414

Trace-driven analysis A performance analysis technique based on simulating the behavior of a computer system responding to stimuli obtained from a program trace; 39–52, 80, 98, 114–115

Trace length, 41–49, 57–58

Trace reduction A technique for reducing the number of address references on an address trace while retaining the ability to use the trace to analyze cache performance; 52–59, 114–115

Trace stripping. *See* Trace reduction

Trailing-edge effect (of a cache) The performance degradation due to the delay between the arrival of the first portion of a cache line and and the arrival of subsequent portions of that line when the line is reloaded in response to a cache miss; 78–79
See also Leading-edge effect

Transaction system, 12

Transient (of cache simulation) The misses that occur during the beginning of a cache simulation due to incorrect initialization of the cache; 40–44, 47–49, 57–58

Transient miss A cache miss caused by a reference to an item that has long intervals between periods of brief use; 64

Translation-lookaside buffer (TLB) A cache-like memory that holds recently used mappings of virtual addresses to physical (real) addresses; 93–94, 98

Traveling Salesman Problem A problem whose solution is the shortest path among N cities such that the path begins and ends at City 1 and no city is visited twice; 361–362, 410–415

Treiber, R. K., 387

Triangular matrix A matrix whose nonzero elements lie on the major diagonal and in a triangular region that lies either above or below the major diagonal; 275–278

Tridiagonal system of equations A linear system whose defining matrix is a triangular matrix; 232–235, 256–257, 275–278

Trivedi, K., 41

Tukey, J. W., 254

Two-address instruction format An instruction format in which one field specifies an operand and a second field specifies an operand that also receives the result of the operation; 183, 198

Two-level mapping A mapping from virtual addresses to physical (real) addresses that requires two successive table accesses; 93–97

Two-port memory A memory system that supports a simultaneous READ and WRITE; 269

Ullman, J. D., 410

Ultracomputer. *See* NYU Ultracomputer

Underflow A state in which a nonzero number becomes too small to be represented in a number system; 196

Unimodal Having a single mode (maximum or minimum); 406

University of Manchester, 25

Unlock A primitive operation that performs the inverse of a Lock by granting processors access to a critical section; 335, 346, 371–372, 378–382, 385–386, 421

Variance The square of the standard deviation of a probability distribution; 45–46

Varga, R. S., 214, 422

Vector A data structure that consists of an ordered set of elements; 137

Vector arithmetic Arithmetic operations whose operands are vectors of data; 260–262

Vector computer A computer whose instructions include instructions for vector arithmetic; 259–300
generic, 260–274

Vector instruction An instruction whose operands are vectors; 29, 203, 260–261, 300–303

Vector processor A computing device, not necessarily a full computer, capable of operating on vectors as basic data structures; 290–292, 307
attached to host computer, 287–292
data-structuring techniques for, 279–287

Vector register A high-speed register in a vector processor that holds a vector operand; 270–271

Very large-scale integration. *See* VLSI

Virtual address The address of an item as produced by a program before the address is mapped into physical (real) memory; 88, 92–99, 185–188

Virtual memory A memory system in which addresses produced by programs lie in an address space that is not the address space of physical (real) memory so that all such addresses must be translated to physical addresses prior to access. In such a system, portions of programs and data can be freely moved among the levels of a hierarchical memory, and brought into physical memory only when actually needed; 22, 26, 28, 87–113, 115–119, 184–188
buffering effects, 107–112
evaluation of, 91
locality, 99–102
management of, 88–91, 99
mapping, 91–99
replacement policy, 102–107

VLSI (Very Large-Scale Integration) A manufacturing process that uses a fixed number of manufacturing steps to produce all components and interconnections for hundreds of devices each with millions of transistors; 3, 6, 13–14, 20, 79, 183, 192, 194, 251–252, 255, 330, 332

Voldman, J., 46, 65

von Neumann, 21, 123

von Neumann bottleneck The notion that the data path between the processor and memory of a von Neumann computer is the facet that most constrains performance of such a computer; 21

Vuillemin, J., 251

Wallace, C. C., 196

Waser, S., 197

Weather modeling, 12

Weingarten, D., 295

Wilkes, M. V., 29

Window (of working set) The time period during which accesses made by a program determine the contents of its working set; 104, 107

Wolfe, M. J., 418, 420

Working set A model of program behavior that says that the future references made by a program with high probability belong to a set of addresses recently referenced; 85, 103–104, 106–107, 116–117

Workload, 37, 40–41, 80, 82, 85–86, 91, 205

Write-back cache. *See* Write-in cache

Write-in cache A cache in which WRITEs to memory are stored in cache and written to memory only when a rewritten item is removed from cache; 75–76

Write Invalidate A cache-coherence protocol in which information in remote caches is invalidated by a writer; 355–357, 403–404
See also Cache, coherence

Write Load A cache-coherence protocol in which information is forced into remote caches whether or not a remote cache

holds an earlier version of the information; 403–404
See also Cache, coherence
WRITE/READ conflict, 133–135, 181, 418–419, 421–422, 424, 428
See also Conflict
Write-through cache A cache in which WRITEs to memory are recorded concurrently both in cache and in main memory; 75–76
Write Update A cache-coherence protocol in which information in remote caches is updated by a writer; 355–357, 403–404
See also Cache, coherence
WRITE/WRITE conflict, 133–135, 181, 418–419, 428
See also Conflict

Xi-Cheng, L., 309, 316
XOR The Exclusive OR boolean operation; 229

Yew, P.C., 344